Rick Steves®

BEST OF
ENGLAND

Including EDINBURGH

Contents

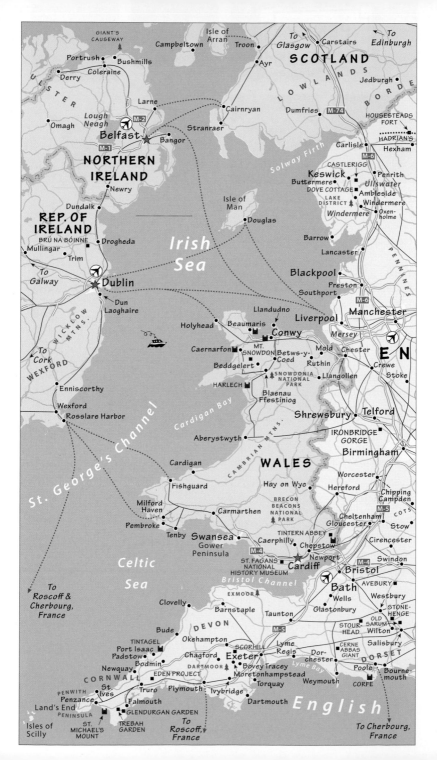

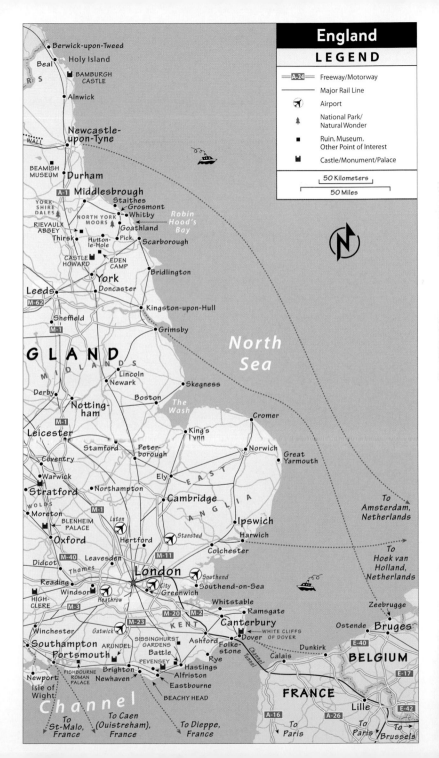

Introduction

Climb the dome of St. Paul's Cathedral and marvel at the pageantry of the guards at Buckingham Palace. Strike up a conversation just to hear the Queen's English. Ponder an ancient stone circle and wander the windswept hills that inspired Wordsworth. See a Shakespeare play or the latest splashy West End musical. Bite into a scone smothered with clotted cream, sip a cup of tea, and wave your pinky as if it's a Union Jack. From appealing towns to the grandeur of London, England delights.

England is the cultural heart of the United Kingdom and a touchstone for the almost one billion people who speak English. This ever-popular tourist destination has a strange influence and power over us. Regardless of the revolution we had a couple of centuries back, many American travelers feel that they "go home" when they visit England.

The English people have a worldwide reputation for being cheery, courteous, and well-mannered. When times get tough, they maintain a stiff upper lip ("Keep calm and carry on" is a now-famous English motto from pre–World War II).

Even as England races forward as a leading global player, it preserves its rich past. This means stone circles, ruined abbeys, cathedrals, castles, and palaces are still yours to explore.

Britannia rules—enjoy it royally.

THE BEST OF ENGLAND

In this selective book, I recommend England's top destinations, offering a mix of exciting cities and irresistible villages. London is one of the grandest cities in the world. The town of Bath has attracted visitors for centuries—back to the time of ancient Rome. Quaint Cotswolds towns offer an endearing contrast to the modern-day world. The serene Lake District—crisscrossed with trails, ridges, and lakes—has enough pubs to keep hikers watered and fed. York, with its colorful old town and ghost walks, is a popular haunt for travelers. Across the northern border, Edinburgh is too convenient to pass up—adding a wee bit of Scotland and the trill of bagpipes to your trip.

When there are interesting sights or towns near my top destinations, I cover these briefly (as "Near" sights), to help you fill out a free day or a longer stay.

Beyond the major destinations, I'll cover the Best of the Rest—great destinations that don't quite make my top cut, but are worth seeing if you have more time or specific interests: the historic college town of Oxford, majestic Blenheim Palace, Shakespeare's hometown of Stratford-upon-Avon, rejuvenated Liverpool, small Durham with its big cathedral, and ancient Hadrian's Wall.

To help you link the top sights, I've designed a two-week itinerary (see page 26) with tips to help you tailor it to your interests and time.

THE BEST OF LONDON

This thriving, teeming metropolis packs in all things British with a cosmopolitan flair: royal palaces, soaring churches, world-class museums, captivating theater, and people-friendly parks. Come prepared to celebrate the tradition and fanfare of yesterday while catching the buzz of a trend-setting city forging its future.

❶ *London's many grand parks provide a peaceful respite from the big city.*

❷ *Plays at **Shakespeare's Globe** attract modern-day Juliets and Romeos.*

❸ *Spanning the Thames, the pedestrian-only **Millennium Bridge** connects St. Paul's Cathedral and Tate Modern.*

❹ *The pomp and pageantry of the **Changing of the Guard** entertains onlookers.*

❺ *It's easy to eat well and affordably in cosmopolitan London.*

❻ *A statue of Churchill overlooks historic **Parliament Square.***

❼ *The **London Eye** Ferris wheel, a fun addition to the cityscape, offers stunning views to riders.*

❽ *Street performers give London a lively vibe.*

THE BEST OF BATH

This genteel Georgian showcase city, built around the remains of an ancient Roman bath, hosts an abbey, museums, a spa, walking tours, and graceful architecture that was part of Jane Austen's world.

Proud locals remind visitors that the town is routinely banned from the "Britain in Bloom" contest to give other towns a chance to win.

❶ *Bath's glorious **abbey** takes center stage in town.*

❷ ***Jane Austen** lived—and set two of her novels—in Bath.*

❸ *The **baths** that gave the town its unusual name date to Roman times.*

❹ *The **Pump Room** has tea, goodies, and samples of "curative" spa water to drink.*

❺ *The fanciful **Parade Gardens,** worth a stroll, are near the shop-lined Pulteney Bridge.*

❻ *The **Bizarre Bath walking tour** makes any evening enjoyable.*

❼ *The **Thermae Bath Spa** taps the thermal springs burbling under Bath.*

❽ *The lawn in front of the **Royal Crescent** offers a royal place to relax.*

THE BEST OF THE COTSWOLDS

Scattered over this hilly countryside are fragrant fields, peaceful sheep, and dear villages. My favorites are cozy Chipping Campden and engaging Stow-on-the- Wold—each with pubs, hikes, and charm to spare. All the Cotswold towns run on slow clocks and yellowed calendars. If the 21st century has come, they don't care.

❶ *Lovely little* **Chipping Campden** *invites and rewards exploration.*

❷ **Sheep** *are as much a part of the Cotswolds as the people.*

❸ *Visitors cool off at* **Bourton-on-the-Water.**

❹ *The lodgings in* **Stow-on-the-Wold** *can be as quaint as the village itself.*

❺ *In* **Broadway,** *the buildings—made of local limestone—give off a warm glow.*

❻ *At* **Cotswold Farm Park,** *it's easy to make new friends.*

❼ **Pubs** *throughout the Cotswolds provide an atmospheric destination for hikers, bikers, and drivers.*

THE BEST OF THE LAKE DISTRICT

The Lake District, about 30 miles long and 30 miles wide, is nature's lush, green playground. This idyllic region of rugged ridges and tranquil lakes offers scenic hikes, cruises, joyrides, timeless vistas, and William Wordsworth and Beatrix Potter sights, plus an ancient stone circle perfect for pondering it all.

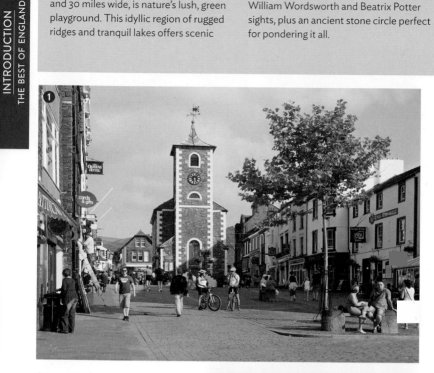

❶ *Keswick,* the best home base, has an appealing main square, fine eateries, and a lovely lake.

❷ *Ullswater* is one of the many lakes that give the district its name.

❸ At *Dove Cottage,* William Wordsworth wrote his finest poetry, inspired by the wonders of nature.

❹ *Old-time* **signs** *mark old-time pubs.*

❺ *Castlerigg Stone Circle,* just outside Keswick, is 5,000 years old— as old as Stonehenge.

❻ *B&Bs* provide a welcome home away from home.

❼ *An easy loop trail around* **Buttermere Lake** *rewards hikers with serene views.*

THE BEST OF YORK

Encircled by medieval walls, compact York has a glorious Gothic cathedral, a ruined abbey, modern museums (on Vikings and more), and an atmospheric old center called The Shambles. York, founded in ancient Roman times, still knows how to draw a crowd.

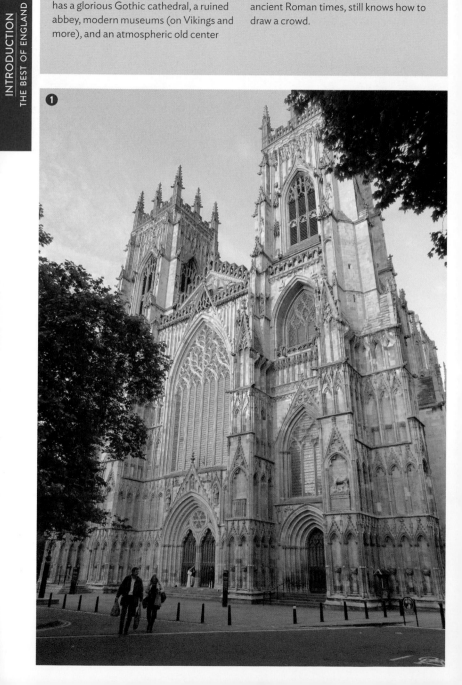

❶ *York's massive* **Minster** *offers up a divine evensong and magnificent, medieval stained glass.*

❷ *The* **National Railway Museum**'s *models range from early "stagecoaches on rails" to the sleek Eurostar.*

❸ *Gurkha soldiers in the* **British Army** *march past the Minster.*

❹ *A Viking amusement ride or a museum?* **Jorvik Viking Centre** *is a bit of both.*

❺ *Breaking from the pope, Henry VIII closed all monasteries, leaving many—like* **St. Mary's Abbey**—*in ruins.*

❻ *Along the* **Shambles** *street, shops hang old-fashioned signs from old, tilting buildings.*

❼ *At* **Bettys Café Tea Rooms,** *window seats offer the best people-watching.*

THE BEST OF EDINBURGH

Just north of England's border is Scotland's showpiece city. Nestled by craggy bluffs, photogenic Edinburgh is studded with a prickly skyline of spires, towers, and domes. Its Royal Mile, lined with medieval buildings, connects the castle and palace in a wonderful way. Edinburgh's proximity and exuberance (nonstop during August's festivals) bring a Scottish flair to an England trip.

❶ Edinburgh's famous street, the **Royal Mile,** offers a pleasing array of attractions, pubs, shops, and historic churches.

❷ **Highland dancers** stepping over crossed swords practice the Sword Dance.

❸ Some shops make **custom kilts** using woven (not cheaply printed) tartan material.

❹ A **bagpiper** in full regalia plays Scotland's national instrument.

❺ **Shops and pubs,** fueled by Scotland's many whisky distilleries, sell the national drink.

❻ Try a few drams of **whisky** at a tasting.

❼ Edinburgh's **formidable castle** repelled foes long ago and attracts visitors today.

THE BEST OF THE REST

With extra time, splice any of these destinations into your trip. **Oxford** has revered colleges and illustrious alumni, plus nearby **Blenheim Palace**—good enough for Churchill. All the world's a stage, but if you want Shakespeare, **Stratford-upon-Avon** is the top venue. The lively port of **Liverpool** launched the Beatles. **Durham,** with a cavernous cathedral, makes a good stop before or after **Hadrian's Wall,** near the Scottish border.

❶ *Durham's cathedral has Europe's tallest bell tower and memorials for saints, scholars, and coal miners.*

❷ *In Oxford, rental **punts** await unsuspecting novices who think punting looks easy.*

❸ *The dining hall at **Oxford**'s Christ Church College puts most college cafeterias to shame.*

❹ *Near Oxford, **Blenheim Palace** attracts historians and garden lovers.*

❺ *In Liverpool, **John Lennon** hangs out at the Cavern Club, named after the original club (now gone) where the Beatles played.*

❻ *Through his work, Stratford-born **Shakespeare** explored the sweet sorrow of the human condition.*

❼ *Built by Romans, the now-ruined **Hadrian's Wall** blocked out invaders from what is Scotland today.*

❽ *Liverpool's **Albert Dock** is awash with attractions—museums, restaurants, and nighttime fun.*

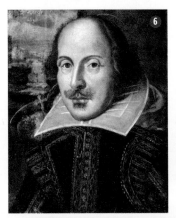

TRAVEL SMART

Approach England like a veteran traveler, even if it's your first trip. Design your itinerary, get a handle on your budget, make advance arrangements, and follow my travel strategies on the road.

For my best advice on sightseeing, accommodations, restaurants, and transportation, see the Practicalities chapter.

Designing Your Itinerary

Decide when to go. July and August are peak season in England, with long days, the best weather, and a busy schedule of tourist fun. May and June can be lovely anywhere. Spring and fall offer smaller crowds and decent weather.

Winter travelers encounter few crowds and soft room prices (except in London), but sightseeing hours are shorter and the weather is reliably bad. In the countryside, some attractions open only on weekends or close entirely (Nov-Feb). While rural charm falls with the leaves, city sightseeing is fine in winter.

Choose your top destinations. My itinerary (on page 26) gives you an idea of how much you can reasonably see in 14 days, but you can adapt it to fit your own interests and timeframe.

London offers an amazing variety of sights, food, markets, and the most entertainment. Many travelers could spend a week here (and make easy day trips, if desired). Edinburgh offers similar big-city excitement, especially during its festivals in August. If you prefer midsize towns, Bath and York have much to offer.

Historians can choose among sights prehistoric (Stonehenge), Roman (Bath and Hadrian's Wall), medieval (York and Warwick), royal (Tower of London, Windsor, and Blenheim), and many more.

Nature lovers linger in the Lake District (offering a range of easy-to-challenging hikes in a lakes-and-hills setting) and the Cotswolds (with easier hikes through villages, meadows, and rolling hills).

Literary fans make a pilgrimage to Stratford (Shakespeare), Oxford (Tolkien, Lewis, Woolf, Wilde, and more), Bath (Austen), the Lake District (Wordsworth and Potter), and Edinburgh (Burns, Stevenson, Scott, and more). Beatles fans from here, there, and everywhere head to Liverpool.

Draft a rough itinerary. Figure out how many destinations you can comfortably fit

in the time you have. Don't overdo it—few travelers wish they'd hurried more. Allow enough days per stop: Figure on at least two days for most destinations and four or more for London. Staying in a home base—like London or Bath—and making day trips can be more time-efficient than changing locations and hotels. Minimize one-night stands, especially consecutive ones; it can be worth taking a late-afternoon train ride or drive to get settled into a town for two nights.

Connect the dots. Link your destinations into a logical route. If your plans extend beyond England, determine which cities in Europe you'll fly into and out of. Begin your search for transatlantic flights at Kayak.com.

Instead of spending the first few days of your trip in busy London, I'd recommend a gentler small-town start in Bath and saving London for the grand finale. Going from Heathrow Airport to Bath takes just two hours by train. You'll be more rested and ready to tackle England's greatest city at the end of your trip.

Decide if you'll travel by car or public transportation or a combination. A car is helpful for exploring the Cotswolds and

Shakespeare fans visit Stratford-upon-Avon.

the Lake District (where public transportation can be time-consuming), but is useless in big cities. Some travelers rent a car on site for a day or two, and use public transportation for the rest of their trip.

Trains are faster and more expensive than buses (which run less frequently on Sundays), though buses get you to some places that trains don't. If relying on public transportation, you'll likely use a mix of trains and buses. Also, for efficient regional sightseeing, consider minibus tours (offered from London, Bath, the Lake District, York, and Edinburgh). With more time, everything is workable without a car.

To determine approximate transportation times between your destinations, study the driving chart (see the Practicalities chapter), train schedules (www.nationalrail.co.uk or www.bahn.com), or this route-planning site that includes train and bus options: www.traveline.info.

If traveling beyond England, consider taking the Eurostar train (to the Continent) or a flight; check Skyscanner.com for budget flights within Europe.

Plan your days. Finetune your trip; write out a day-by-day plan of where you'll be and what you want to see. To help you make the most of your time, I've suggested day plans for destinations. But check the opening hours of sights; avoid visiting a town on the one day a week that your must-see sight is closed. Research whether any holidays or festivals will fall during your trip—these attract crowds and can close sights (for the latest, visit England's website, www.visitbritain.com).

Give yourself some slack. Nonstop sightseeing can turn a vacation into a blur. Every trip, and every traveler, needs downtime for doing laundry, picnic shopping, relaxing, people-watching, and so on. Pace yourself. Assume you will return.

Ready, set. . . You've designed the perfect itinerary for the trip of a lifetime.

BEST OF ENGLAND IN 2 WEEKS

This unforgettable trip will show you the very best that England has to offer, with a little help from Scotland. You can use public transit, rent a car, or use a combination. Renting a car for just a day or two is most fun in the Cotswolds and the Lake District.

DAY	PLAN	SLEEP IN
	Arrive in London, head to Bath (2 hours by train from Heathrow, transfer at London's Paddington Station)	Bath
1	Bath	Bath
2	Bath (could add day for Stonehenge, Wells, and/or Glastonburg)	Bath
3	To Cotswolds (2 hours by train to Moreton-in-Marsh, then 45-minute bus ride)	Chipping Campden
4	Cotswolds	Chipping Campden
5	To Lake District (a minimum of 6 hours by bus, with transfers in Stratford-upon-Avon and Penrith)	Keswick
6	Lake District (hikers could add another day here)	Keswick
7	To Edinburgh, Scotland (allow 3 hours: bus to Penrith, then train to Edinburgh)	Edinburgh
8	Edinburgh	Edinburgh
9	To York later in day (2.5 hours by train)	York
10	York	York
11	To London (2 hours by train)	London
12	London	London
13	London	London
14	London	London
	Fly home	

Adding Best of the Rest Destinations: Visit Oxford and Blenheim Palace after Bath and before the Cotswolds. Stratford and/or Liverpool fall logically between the Cotswolds and the Lake District. Hadrian's Wall (easier for drivers) and Durham (on the main train line) can be added between Edinburgh and York.

Average Daily Expenses per Person: $160 in England ($200 in London)

Cost	Category	Notes
$75	Lodging	Based on two people splitting the cost of a $150 double room that includes breakfast
$45	Meals	$15 for lunch and $30 for dinner
$30	Sights and Entertainment	This daily average works for most people.
$10	City Transit	Tube or buses
$160	**Total**	Figure on $200 for London

Trip Costs

Run a reality check on your dream trip. You'll have major transportation costs in addition to daily expenses.

Flight: A round-trip flight from the US to London costs about $1,000-2,000.

Car Rental: Figure on a minimum of $250 per week, not including tolls, gas, parking, and insurance. Rentals and leases (an economical way to go if you need a car for at least three weeks) are cheaper if arranged from the US.

Public Transportation: For a two-week trip, you'd spend about $600 to cover second-class train and bus fares, including Tube fare in London. To reduce your train costs, you'll likely save money by getting a Britrail pass that matches your train travel days ("standard" class is cheaper than first class, buy in US before you go); for specifics, see page 407.

By purchasing individual train tickets online, you can get advance-purchase discounts, though you'll be locked into the travel time you choose; a rail pass gives you more flexibility if your plans change.

Budget Tips: Cut your daily expenses by taking advantage of the deals you'll find throughout England and mentioned in this book.

City transit passes (for multiple rides or all-day usage) decrease your cost per ride. For example, it's smart to get an Oyster card in London to cover your Tube and bus travel affordably.

Avid sightseers buy combo-tickets or passes that cover multiple museums. (For country-wide passes, see page 393.) If a town doesn't offer deals, see only the sights you most want to see, and seek out free experiences and sights (offered even in London—see page 54).

Some businesses—especially hotels and walking-tour companies—offer discounts to my readers (look for the RS% symbol in the listings in this book).

Book your rooms directly with the hotel. Some hotels offer a discount if you pay in cash and/or stay three or more nights (check online or ask). Rooms can cost less outside of peak-season July and August. And even seniors can sleep cheap in hostels (some have double rooms) for as little as $30 per person. Or check Airbnb-type sites for deals.

It's no hardship to eat cheap in England. You can get tasty, inexpensive meals at pubs, cafeterias, chain restaurants, ethnic eateries, and fish-and-chips joints. Some upscale restaurants offer early-bird dinner specials. Groceries sell ready-made sandwiches; cultivate the art of picnicking in atmospheric settings.

When you splurge, choose an experience you'll always remember, such as an elegant high tea or a splashy London musical. Minimize souvenir shopping—how will you get it all home? Focus instead on collecting vivid memories, wonderful stories, and new friends.

Before You Go

You'll have a smoother trip if you tackle a few things ahead of time. For more information on these topics, see the Practicalities chapter, and check www.ricksteves.com for book updates, more travel tips, and travel talks.

Make sure your passport is valid. If it's due to expire within six months of your ticketed date of return, you need to renew it. Allow up to six weeks to renew or get a passport (www.travel.state.gov).

Arrange your transportation. Book your international flights early. Figure out your main form of transportation within England: It's worth thinking about buying train tickets online in advance, getting a rail pass, renting a car, or booking cheap British flights. (You can wing it once you're there, but it may cost more.)

Book rooms well in advance, especially if your trip falls during peak season or any major holidays or festivals.

Reserve or buy tickets ahead for must-see plays and special tours. If there's a particular play or musical you're set on seeing, you can buy tickets before you go; otherwise get tickets on site. At Stonehenge, most visitors are happy to view the stones from a distance, but to go inside the circle, you'll need reservations. To tour the interior of Lennon and McCartney homes in Liverpool, reserve ahead.

Edinburgh's festivals in August are popular; book ahead for any events you must see (theater, dance, and the Military Tattoo). You can also book online for Edinburgh Castle.

Specifics on booking tickets and reservations are in the individual chapters.

Consider travel insurance. Compare the cost of the insurance to the cost of your potential loss. Check whether your existing insurance (health, homeowners, or renters) covers you and your possessions overseas.

Call your bank. Alert your bank that you'll be using your debit and credit cards in Europe. Ask about transaction fees, and get the PIN number for your credit card. You don't need to bring pounds for your trip; you can withdraw pounds from cash machines in England and Scotland.

Use your smartphone smartly. Sign up for an international service plan to reduce your costs, or rely on Wi-Fi in Europe instead. Download any apps you'll want on the road, such as maps, transit schedules, and Rick Steves Audio Europe (see sidebar).

Pack light. You'll walk with your luggage more than you think. Bring a single carry-on bag and a daypack. Use the packing checklist in Practicalities as a guide.

∩ Stick This Guidebook in Your Ear!

My free Rick Steves Audio Europe app makes it easy for you to download my audio tours of many of Europe's top attractions and listen to them offline during your travels. For England, these include major museums and neighborhoods in London, and for Edinburgh, the Royal Mile. Sights covered by audio tours are marked in this book with this symbol: ∩. The app also offers insightful travel interviews from my public radio show with experts from England and around the globe. It's all free! You can download the app via Apple's App Store, Google Play, or Amazon's Appstore. For more info, see www.ricksteves.com/audioeurope.

Travel Strategies on the Road

If you have a positive attitude, equip yourself with good information (this book), and expect to travel smart, you will.

Read—and reread—this book. To have an "A" trip, be an "A" student. Note opening hours of sights, closed days, crowd-beating tips, and whether reservations are required or advisable. Check the latest at www.ricksteves.com/update.

Be your own tour guide. As you travel, get up-to-date info on sights, reserve tickets and tours, reconfirm hotels and travel arrangements, and check transit connections. Find out the latest from tourist-information offices (TIs), your hoteliers, checking online, or phoning ahead. Upon arrival in a new town, lay the groundwork for a smooth departure; confirm the train, bus, or road you'll take when you leave.

Give local tours a spin. Your appreciation of a city or region and its history can increase dramatically if you take a walking tour in any big city (try London Walks) or at a museum (some offer live or audio tours), or even hire a private guide (some will drive you around). If you want to learn more about any aspect of England, you're in the right place with experts happy to teach you in a language you understand.

Plan for rain. No matter when you go, the weather can change several times in a day, but rarely is it extreme. Bring a jacket and dress in layers. Just keep traveling and enjoy the "bright spells." A bout of rain is the perfect excuse to go into a pub and make a new friend.

Outsmart thieves. Particularly in London, pickpockets abound in crowded places where tourists congregate. Treat commotions as smokescreens for theft. Keep your cash, credit cards, and passport secure in a money belt tucked under your clothes; carry only a day's spending money in your front pocket. Don't set valuable items down on counters or café tabletops, where they can be quickly stolen or easily forgotten.

To minimize potential loss, keep your expensive gear to a minimum. Bring photocopies or take photos of important documents (passport and cards) to aid in replacement if they're lost or stolen.

Guard your time and energy. Taking a taxi can be a good value if you're too tired to tackle public transit. To avoid long lines,

Welcome to Rick Steves' Europe

Travel is intensified living—maximum thrills per minute and one of the last great sources of legal adventure. Travel is freedom. It's recess, and we need it.

I discovered a passion for European travel as a teen and have been sharing it ever since—through my tours, public television and radio shows, and travel guidebooks. Over the years, I've taught thousands of travelers how to best enjoy Europe's blockbuster sights—and experience "Back Door" discoveries that most tourists miss.

This book offers you a balanced mix of England's biggies (such as Big Ben and Stonehenge) and more intimate locales (windswept Roman lookouts and nearly edible Cotswold villages). It's selective: There are dozens of hikes in the Lake District; I recommend only the best ones. It's in-depth: My self-guided museum tours and city walks give insight into the country's vibrant history and today's living, breathing culture. And for a Scottish fling, I've added Edinburgh, because it's close and refreshing.

I advocate traveling simply and smartly. Take advantage of my money- and time-saving tips on sightseeing, transportation, and more. Try local, character-istic alternatives to expensive hotels and restaurants. In many ways, spending more money only builds a thicker wall between you and what you traveled so far to see.

We visit England to experience it—to become temporary locals. Thoughtful travel engages us with the world, as we learn to appreciate other cultures and new ways to measure quality of life.

Judging from the positive feedback I receive from readers, this book will help you enjoy a fun, affordable, and rewarding vacation—whether it's your first trip or your tenth.

Have a brilliant holiday! Happy travels!

Rick Steves

follow my crowd-beating tips, such as making advance reservations, or sightseeing early or late. In London, you can buy Fast Track tickets for some popular sights in advance, saving you time in line.

Be flexible. Even if you have a well-planned itinerary, expect changes, closures, sore feet, drizzly days, and so on. Your Plan B could turn out to be even better. And when problems arise (a bad meal or a noisy hotel room), keep things in perspective. You're on vacation in a beautiful country.

Connect with the culture. Interacting with locals carbonates your experience. Enjoy the friendliness of the English people; most interactions come with an ample side-helping of fun banter. Ask questions—many locals are as interested in you as you are in them. Slow down, step out of your comfort zone, and be open to unexpected experiences. When an interesting opportunity pops up, make it a habit to say "yes."

Ready for a spot of tea and a freshly baked scone? Hear the friendly buzz from the corner pub?

Your next stop...England!

London

A longtime tourist destination, London seems perpetually at your service, with an impressive slate of sights and entertainment. Blow through this urban jungle on the open deck of a double-decker bus and take a pinch-me-I'm-here walk through the West End. Hear the chimes of Big Ben and ogle the crown jewels at the Tower of London. Cruise the Thames River and take a spin on the London Eye. Hobnob with poets' tombstones in Westminster Abbey and rummage through civilization's attic at the British Museum.

London is also more than its museums and landmarks, it's a living, breathing, thriving organism...a coral reef of humanity. The city has changed dramatically in recent years: Many visitors are surprised to find how diverse and cosmopolitan it is. Chinese takeouts outnumber fish-and-chips shops. Eastern Europeans pull pints in British pubs, and Italians express your espresso. Outlying suburbs are home to huge communities of Indians and Pakistanis. This city of eight million separate dreams is learning—sometimes fitfully—to live as a microcosm of its formerly vast empire.

LONDON IN 4 DAYS

Day 1: Get oriented by taking my Westminster Walk from Big Ben to Trafalgar Square (stop in Westminster Abbey and the Churchill War Rooms on the way). Grab lunch near Trafalgar Square (maybe at the café at St. Martin-in-the-Fields Church), then visit the nearby National Gallery or National Portrait Gallery.

On any evening: Have an early-bird dinner and take in a play in the West End or at Shakespeare's Globe. Choose from a concert, walking tour, or nighttime bus tour. Extend your sightseeing into the evening hours; some attractions stay open late. Settle in at a pub, or do some shopping at any of London's elegant department stores (generally open until 21:00). Stroll any of the main squares, fine parks, or the Jubilee Walkway for people-watching. Ride the London Eye Ferris wheel for grand city views.

Day 2: Early in the morning, take a double-decker hop-on, hop-off sightseeing bus tour from Victoria Station, and hop off for the Changing of the Guard at Buckingham Palace. After lunch, tour the British Museum and/or the nearby British Library.

Day 3: At the Tower of London, see the crown jewels and take the Beefeater tour. Then grab a picnic, catch a boat at Tower Pier, and have lunch on the Thames while cruising to Blackfriars Pier.

Tour St. Paul's Cathedral and climb

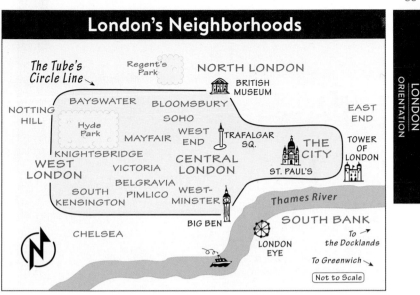

London's Neighborhoods

The Tube's Circle Line

Regent's Park

NORTH LONDON

BRITISH MUSEUM

BAYSWATER

BLOOMSBURY

NOTTING HILL

Hyde Park

SOHO

EAST END

MAYFAIR

WEST END

TRAFALGAR SQ.

THE CITY

TOWER OF LONDON

KNIGHTSBRIDGE

CENTRAL LONDON

ST. PAUL'S

WEST LONDON

VICTORIA

BELGRAVIA

SOUTH KENSINGTON

PIMLICO

WEST-MINSTER

Thames River

BIG BEN

SOUTH BANK

CHELSEA

LONDON EYE

To the Docklands

To Greenwich

Not to Scale

its dome for views, then walk across Millennium Bridge to the South Bank to visit the Tate Modern, tour Shakespeare's Globe, or stroll the Jubilee Walkway.

Day 4: Take your pick of the Victoria and Albert Museum, Tate Britain, Imperial War Museum, or Houses of Parliament. Hit one of London's many lively open-air markets. Or cruise to Greenwich or Kew Gardens.

THE CROWN JEWELS

ORIENTATION

To grasp London more comfortably, see it as the old town in the city center without the modern, congested sprawl.

The River Thames (pronounced "tems") runs roughly west to east through the city, with most of the visitor's sights on the North Bank. Mentally, maybe even physically, trim down your map to include only the area between the Tower of London (to the east), Hyde Park (west), Regent's Park (north), and the South Bank (south). This is roughly the area bordered by the Tube's Circle Line. This four-mile stretch between the Tower and Hyde Park (about a 1.5-hour walk) looks like a milk bottle on its side (see map), and holds most of the sights mentioned in this chapter.

The sprawling city becomes much more manageable if you think of it as a collection of neighborhoods.

Central London contains **Westminster,** the location of Big Ben, Parliament, Westminster Abbey, Buckingham Palace, and Trafalgar Square, with its many major museums. It also includes the **West End,** the center of London's cultural life, where

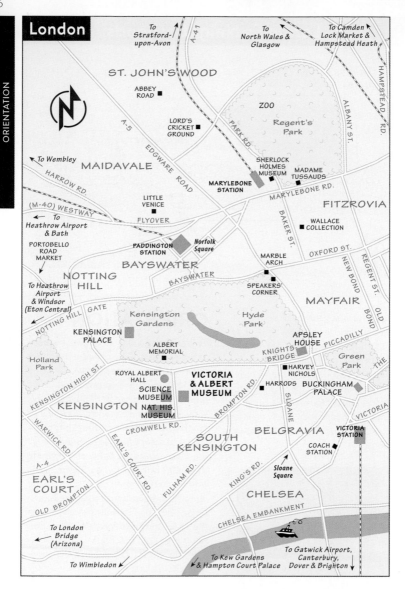

London

To Stratford-/upon-Avon

To North Wales & Glasgow

To Camden Lock Market & Hampstead Heath

A-41

HAMPSTEAD RD.

ST. JOHN'S WOOD

ABBEY ROAD ■

ZOO

Regent's Park

ALBANY ST.

A-5

LORD'S CRICKET GROUND ■

EDGWARE ROAD

PARK RD.

To Wembley

MAIDAVALE

HARROW RD.

SHERLOCK HOLMES MUSEUM ■

MADAME TUSSAUDS

MARYLEBONE STATION

MARYLEBONE RD.

FITZROVIA

LITTLE VENICE

(M-40) WESTWAY

BAKER ST.

WALLACE COLLECTION ■

To Heathrow Airport & Bath

FLYOVER

OXFORD ST.

REGENT ST.

PORTOBELLO ROAD MARKET

PADDINGTON STATION

Norfolk Square

NEW BOND ST.

BAYSWATER

MARBLE ARCH ■

NOTTING HILL

BAYSWATER

SPEAKERS' CORNER

OLD BOND ST.

To Heathrow Airport & Windsor (Eton Central)

NOTTING HILL GATE

Kensington Gardens

Hyde Park

MAYFAIR

KENSINGTON PALACE ■

ALBERT MEMORIAL ■

APSLEY HOUSE ■

KNIGHTS BRIDGE

PICCADILLY

Green Park

THE

Holland Park

ROYAL ALBERT HALL

SCIENCE MUSEUM

VICTORIA & ALBERT MUSEUM

HARVEY NICHOLS ■

HARRODS ■

BUCKINGHAM PALACE ◆

KENSINGTON HIGH ST.

KENSINGTON

NAT. HIS. MUSEUM

CROMWELL RD.

BROMPTON RD.

SLOANE ST.

VICTORIA

WARWICK RD.

EARL'S COURT RD.

SOUTH KENSINGTON

BELGRAVIA

VICTORIA STATION

A-4

FULHAM RD.

KING'S RD.

COACH STATION

EARL'S COURT

OLD BROMPTON

Sloane Square

CHELSEA

To London Bridge (Arizona)

CHELSEA EMBANKMENT

To Wimbledon

To Kew Gardens & Hampton Court Palace

To Gatwick Airport, Canterbury, Dover & Brighton

---

bustling Piccadilly Circus and Leicester Square host cinemas, tourist traps, and nighttime glitz. Soho and Covent Garden are thriving people zones with theaters, restaurants, pubs, and boutiques. And Regent and Oxford streets are the city's main shopping zones.

North London and its neighborhoods—including Bloomsbury, Fitzrovia, and Marylebone—contain such major sights as the British Museum and the overhyped Madame Tussauds Waxworks. Nearby, along busy Euston Road, is the British Library.

"The City," which is today's modern financial district, was a walled town in

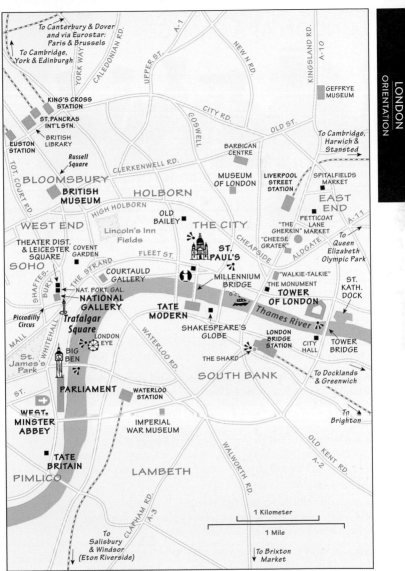

Roman times. Gleaming skyscrapers are interspersed with historical landmarks such as St. Paul's Cathedral and the Museum of London. The Tower of London and Tower Bridge lie at The City's eastern border.

The East End is the increasingly gentrified former stomping ground of Cockney ragamuffins and Jack the Ripper.

The South Bank of the Thames River offers major sights—Tate Modern, Shakespeare's Globe, and the London Eye—linked by a riverside walkway. Within this area, Southwark (SUTH-uck) stretches from the Tate Modern to London Bridge. Pedestrian bridges connect the South Bank with The City and Trafalgar Square.

LONDON AT A GLANCE

▲▲▲**Westminster Abbey** Britain's finest church and the site of royal coronations and burials since 1066. **Hours:** Mon-Fri 9:30-16:30, Wed until 19:00, Sat until 14:30, closed Sun to sightseers except for worship. See page 47.

▲▲▲**Churchill War Rooms** Underground WWII headquarters of Churchill's war effort. **Hours:** Daily 9:30-18:00. See page 55.

▲▲▲**National Gallery** Remarkable collection of European paintings (1250-1900), including Leonardo, Botticelli, Velázquez, Rembrandt, Turner, Van Gogh, and the Impressionists. **Hours:** Daily 10:00-18:00, Fri until 21:00. See page 56.

▲▲▲**British Museum** The world's greatest collection of artifacts of Western civilization, including the Rosetta Stone and the Parthenon's Elgin Marbles. **Hours:** Daily 10:00-17:30, Fri until 20:30 (selected galleries only). See page 67.

▲▲▲**British Library** Fascinating collection of important literary treasures of the Western world. **Hours:** Mon-Fri 9:30-18:00, Tue-Thu until 20:00, Sat until 17:00, Sun 11:00-17:00. See page 72.

▲▲▲**St. Paul's Cathedral** The main cathedral of the Anglican Church, designed by Christopher Wren, with a climbable dome and daily evensong services. **Hours:** Mon-Sat 8:30-16:30, closed Sun except for worship. See page 76.

▲▲▲**Tower of London** Historic castle, palace, and prison housing the crown jewels and a witty band of Beefeaters. **Hours:** Tue-Sat 9:00-17:30, Sun-Mon from 10:00; Nov-Feb closes one hour earlier. See page 82.

▲▲▲**Victoria and Albert Museum** The best collection of decorative arts anywhere. **Hours:** Daily 10:00-17:45, Fri until 22:00 (selected galleries only). See page 95.

▲▲**Houses of Parliament** London landmark famous for Big Ben and occupied by the Houses of Lords and Commons. **Hours:** When Parliament is in session, generally open Oct-late July Mon-Thu, closed Fri-Sun and during recess late July-Sept. Guided tours offered year-round on Sat and most weekdays during recess. See page 51.

▲▲**Trafalgar Square** The heart of London, where Westminster, The City, and the West End meet. See page 56.

▲▲**National Portrait Gallery** A *Who's Who* of British history, featuring portraits of this nation's most important historical figures. **Hours:** Daily 10:00-18:00, Fri until 21:00, first and second floors open Mon at 11:00. See page 61.

▲▲**Covent Garden** Vibrant people-watching zone with shops, cafés, street musicians, and an iron-and-glass arcade that once hosted a produce market. See page 64.

▲▲**Changing of the Guard at Buckingham Palace** Hour-long spectacle at Britain's royal residence. **Hours:** May-July daily at 11:00, Aug-April on Sun, Mon, Wed, and Fri. See page 64.

▲▲**London Eye** Enormous observation wheel, dominating—and offering commanding views over—London's skyline. **Hours:** Daily June-Aug 10:00-20:30 or later, Sept-May 11:00-18:00. See page 87.

▲▲**Imperial War Museum** Exhibits examining military conflicts from the early 20th century to today. **Hours:** Daily 10:00-18:00. See page 88.

▲▲**Tate Modern** Works by Monet, Matisse, Dalí, Picasso, and Warhol displayed in a converted powerhouse complex. **Hours:** Daily 10:00-18:00, Fri-Sat until 22:00. See page 90.

▲▲**Shakespeare's Globe** Timbered, thatched-roof reconstruction of the Bard's original "wooden O." **Hours:** Theater complex, museum, and actor-led tours generally daily 9:00-17:30; April-Oct generally morning theater tours only. Plays are also staged here. See page 91.

▲▲**Tate Britain** Collection of British painting from the 16th century through modern times, including works by William Blake, the Pre-Raphaelites, and J. M. W. Turner. **Hours:** Daily 10:00-18:00. See page 92.

West London contains neighborhoods such as Mayfair, Belgravia, Pimlico, Chelsea, South Kensington, and Notting Hill. It's home to London's wealthy and has many trendy shops and enticing restaurants. Here you'll find the Victoria and Albert Museum, Tate Britain, and more museums, lively Victoria Station, and the vast green expanses of Hyde Park and Kensington Gardens.

Rick's Tip: *Through an initiative called Legible London, the city has erected pedestrian-focused maps around town—especially handy when exiting Tube stations. In this sprawling city—where predictable grid-planned streets are relatively rare—it's also smart to buy and use a good map.*

Tourist Information

It's hard to find unbiased sightseeing information and advice in London. You'll see "Tourist Information" offices advertised everywhere, but most are private agencies that make a big profit selling tours and advance sightseeing and/or theater tickets.

The **City of London Information Centre** next to St. Paul's Cathedral (just outside the church entrance) is the city's only publicly funded—and impartial—"real" TI. It sells Oyster cards, London Passes, and advance "Fast Track" sightseeing tickets. It also stocks various free publications: *London Planner* (a free monthly that lists all the sights, events, and hours), some walking-tour brochures, the *Official London Theatre Guide,* a free Tube and bus map (also see Tube map in "Transportation," later), and the *Guide to River Thames Boat Services.* The TI gives out a free map of The City and sells several city-wide maps; ask if they have yet another free map with various coupons for discounts on sights (Mon-Sat 9:30-17:30, Sun 10:00-16:00; Tube: St. Paul's, tel. 020/7332-1456, www.visitthecity.co.uk).

Visit London, which serves the greater London area, doesn't have an office you can visit in person—but does have an info-packed website (www.visitlondon.com).

Sightseeing Passes and Advance Tickets

To skip the ticket-buying queues at certain London sights, you can buy **Fast Track tickets** (sometimes called "priority pass" tickets) in advance—and they can be cheaper than tickets sold right at the sight. They're smart for the Tower of London, the London Eye, and Madame Tussauds Waxworks, which get busy in high season. They're available through various sales outlets (including the City of London TI, souvenir stands, and faux-TIs scattered throughout touristy areas).

The **London Pass** covers many big sights and lets you skip some lines. It's expensive but potentially worth the investment for extremely busy sightseers (£62/1 day, multi-day options available; sold at City of London TI, major train stations, and airports, www.londonpass.com).

Rick's Tip: *The Artful Dodger is alive and well in London.* **Beware of pickpockets,** *particularly on public transportation, among tourist crowds, and at street markets.*

Tours

To sightsee on your own, download my free Rick Steves Audio Europe app with **audio tours** of London's top sights and neighborhoods (see page 29 for details).

▲▲▲HOP-ON, HOP-OFF DOUBLE-DECKER BUS TOURS

London is full of hop-on, hop-off bus companies competing for your tourist pound. I've focused on the two companies I like the most: **Original** and **Big Bus.** Both offer essentially the same two tours of the city's sightseeing highlights.

Rick's Tip: *For an efficient intro to London, catch an 8:30 departure of a* **hop-on, hop-off overview bus tour,** *riding most of the loop (which takes about 1.5 hours, depending on traffic—lightest on Sunday morning). Hop off just before 10:00 at Trafalgar Square (Cockspur Street, stop "S"), then walk briskly to Buckingham Palace to find a spot to watch the* **Changing of the Guard ceremony** *at 11:00.*

Each company offers at least one route with live guides, and a second (sometimes slightly different route) with recorded narration. Buses run daily about every 10-15 minutes in summer and every 10-20 minutes in winter, starting at about 8:30. The last full loop usually leaves Victoria Station at about 20:00 in summer, and at about 17:00 in winter.

You can buy tickets online in advance, or from drivers or from staff at street kiosks (credit cards accepted at kiosks at major stops such as Victoria Station, ticket valid 24 hours in summer, 48 hours in winter).

Original: £32, £6 less with this book, limit four discounts per book, they'll rip off the corner of this page—raise bloody hell if the staff or driver won't honor this discount; also online deals, info center at 17 Cockspur Street; tel. 020/7389-5040, www.theoriginaltour.com.

Big Bus: £35, discount available online; tel. 020/7808-6753, www.bigbustours. com.

NIGHT BUS TOURS

Various companies offer a lower-priced, after-hours sightseeing circuit (1-2 hours). **Golden Tours** buses depart at 19:00 and 20:00 from their offices on Buckingham Palace Road (tel. 020/7630-2028; www.goldentours.com). **See London By Night** buses offer live English guides and frequent evening departures—starting from at 19:30—from Green Park (next to the Ritz Hotel); October-March at 19:30 and 21:20 only (tel. 020/7183-4744, www. seelondonbynight.com).

Rick's Tip: *If you're taking a bus tour mainly to get oriented,* **save time and money by taking a night tour.** *You can munch a memorable picnic dinner while riding on the top deck.*

▲▲WALKING TOURS

Top-notch local guides lead (sometimes big) groups on walking tours through specific slices of London's past. London Walks lists its daily schedule online, as well as in a beefy brochure available at hotels and in racks all over town. Their two-hour walks are led by top-quality professional guides (£10 cash only, private tours for groups-£140, tel. 020/7624-3978 for a live person, tel. 020/7624-9255 for a recording of today's or tomorrow's walks and the Tube station they depart from, www.walks.com).

London Walks also offers day trips into the countryside (£18 plus £36-64 for transportation and admission costs, cash only: Stonehenge/Salisbury, Oxford/Cotswolds, Bath, and so on).

PRIVATE GUIDES AND DRIVERS

Rates for London's registered Blue Badge guides are standard (about £160-200 for four hours; £260 or more for nine hours). I know and like five fine local guides: **Sean Kelleher** (tel. 020/8673-1624, mobile 07764-612-770, sean@seanlondonguide.com); **Britt Lonsdale** (£250/half-day, £350/day, tel. 020/7386-9907, mobile 07813-278-077, brittl@btinternet.com); **Joel Reid** (mobile 07887-955-720, joelyreid@gmail.com); and two others who work in London when they're not on the road leading my Britain tours: **Tom Hooper** (mobile 07986-048-047, tomh@ricksteves.net), and **Gillian Chadwick** (mobile 07889-976-598, gillychad@hotmail.co.uk). If you have a particular interest, London Walks (listed earlier) can book a guide for your exact focus (£180/half-day).

These guides have cars or a minibus for day trips, and also do walking-only tours: **Janine Barton** (£390/half-day, £560/day, tel. 020/7402-4600, http://seeitinstyle.synthasite.com, jbsiis@aol.com); cousins **Hugh Dickson** and **Mike Dickson** (£345/half-day, £535/day; Hugh's mobile 07771/602-069, hughdickson@hotmail.com; Mike's mobile 07769/905-811, michael.dickson5@btinternet.

com); and **David Stubbs** (£225/half-day, £330/day, about £50 more for groups of 4-6 people, mobile 07775-888-534, www.londoncountrytours.co.uk, info@londoncountrytours.co.uk).

▲▲CRUISE BOAT TOURS

London offers many made-for-tourist cruises, most on slow-moving, open-top boats accompanied by entertaining commentary. Take a **short city center cruise** by riding a boat 30 minutes from Westminster Pier to Tower Pier (particularly handy if you're interested in visiting the Tower of London anyway), or choose a **longer cruise** that includes a peek at the East End, riding from Westminster all the way to Greenwich (save time by taking the Tube back).

Each company runs cruises daily, about twice hourly, from morning until dark; many reduce frequency off-season. Boats come and go from various docks in the city center (see sidebar). The most popular places to embark are Westminster Pier (at the base of Westminster Bridge across the street from Big Ben) and London Eye Pier (also known as Waterloo Pier, across the river on the South Bank).

A one-way trip within the city center costs about £10. A transit card (Travelcard

Thames Boat Piers

While Westminster Pier is the most popular, it's not the only dock in town. Consider all the options (listed from west to east, as the Thames flows).

Millbank Pier (North Bank): At the Tate Britain Museum, used primarily by the Tate Boat ferry service (express connection to Tate Modern at Bankside Pier).

Westminster Pier (North Bank): Near the base of Big Ben, offers round-trip sightseeing cruises and lots of departures in both directions (though the Thames Clippers boats don't stop here). Nearby sights include Parliament and Westminster Abbey.

London Eye Pier (a.k.a. **Waterloo Pier,** South Bank): At the base of the London Eye; good, less-crowded alternative to Westminster, with many of the same cruise options (Waterloo Station is nearby).

Embankment Pier (North Bank): Near Covent Garden, Trafalgar Square, and Cleopatra's Needle (the obelisk on the Thames). This pier is used mostly for special boat trips, such as some RIB (rigid inflatable boats) and lunch and dinner cruises.

Festival Pier (South Bank): Next to the Royal Festival Hall, just downstream from the London Eye.

Blackfriars Pier (North Bank): In The City, not far from St. Paul's.

Bankside Pier (South Bank): Directly in front of the Tate Modern and Shakespeare's Globe.

London Bridge Pier (a.k.a. **London Bridge City Pier,** South Bank): Near the HMS *Belfast*.

Tower Pier (North Bank): At the Tower of London, at the east edge of The City and near the East End.

St. Katharine's Pier (North Bank): Just downstream from the Tower of London.

---

or Oyster card) can snare you a discount on some cruises (see page 121).

The three dominant companies are **City Cruises** (handy 45-minute cruise from Westminster Pier to Tower Pier; www.citycruises.com), **Thames River Services** (fewer stops, classic boats, friendlier and more old-fashioned feel; www.thamesriverservices.co.uk), and **Circular Cruise** (full cruise takes about an hour, operated by Crown River Services, www.circularcruise.london).

Cruising Downstream, to Greenwich: Both **City Cruises** and **Thames River Services** head from Westminster Pier to Greenwich. To maximize both efficiency and sightseeing, take a narrated cruise to Greenwich one way, and go the other way on the DLR (Docklands Light Railway).

Cruising Upstream, to Kew Gardens: **Thames River Boats** leave for Kew Gardens from Westminster Pier (£13 one-way, £20 round-trip, cash only, discounts with Travelcard, 2-4/day depending on season, 1.5 hours, boats sail April-Oct, about half the trip is narrated, www.wpsa.co.uk).

Rick's Tip: *Zipping through London every 20-30 minutes, the* **Thames Clippers are designed for commuters.** *With no open deck and no commentary, they're* **not the best option for sightseeing.**

Helpful Hints

Wi-Fi: Besides your hotel, many major museums, sights, and even entire neighborhoods offer free Wi-Fi. For easy access everywhere, sign up for a free account with **The Cloud,** a Wi-Fi service found in many convenient spots around London (www.skywifi.cloud, you'll be asked to enter a street address and postal code—use your hotel's, or the Queen's: Buckingham Palace, SW1A 1AA).

Useful Apps: Mapway's free **Tube Map London Underground** and **Bus Times London** (www.mapway.com) apps show the easiest way to connect Tube stations and provide bus stops and route information. The handy **Citymapper** app for London covers every mode of public transit in the city. **City Maps 2Go** lets you download searchable offline maps; their London version is quite good. And **Time Out London**'s free app has reviews and listings for theater, museums, and movies (download the "Make Your City Amazing" version—it's updated weekly—not the boilerplate "Travel Guide" version).

Baggage Storage: Train stations have replaced lockers with more secure left-luggage counters. Each bag must go

through a scanner (just like at the airport). Expect long waits in the morning to check in (up to 45 minutes) and in the afternoon to pick up (most stations daily 7:00-23:00). You can also store bags at the airports (www.left-baggage.co.uk).

WESTMINSTER WALK

Just about every visitor to London strolls along historic Whitehall from Big Ben to Trafalgar Square. This walk gives you a whirlwind tour as well as a practical orientation to London. Most of the sights you'll see are described in more detail later in this chapter. ∩ You can download a free, extended audio version of this walk; see page 29.

Rick's Tip: Cars drive on the left side of the road—*confusing for foreign pedestrians and for foreign drivers. Always look right, look left, then look right again just to be sure.* **Jaywalking is treacherous** *when you're disoriented about which direction traffic is coming from.*

❍ Self-Guided Walk

Start halfway across ❶ **Westminster Bridge** for that "Wow, I'm really in London!" feeling. Get a close-up view of the **Houses of Parliament** and **Big Ben.** Downstream you'll see the **London Eye,** the city's giant Ferris wheel. Down the stairs to Westminster Pier are boats to the Tower of London and Greenwich (downstream) or Kew Gardens (upstream).

En route to Parliament Square, you'll pass a ❷ **statue of Boadicea,** the Celtic queen who unsuccessfully resisted Roman invaders in A.D. 60. Julius Caesar was the first Roman general to cross the Channel, but even he was weirded out by the island's strange inhabitants, who worshipped trees, sacrificed virgins, and went to war painted blue. Later, Romans subdued and civilized them, building

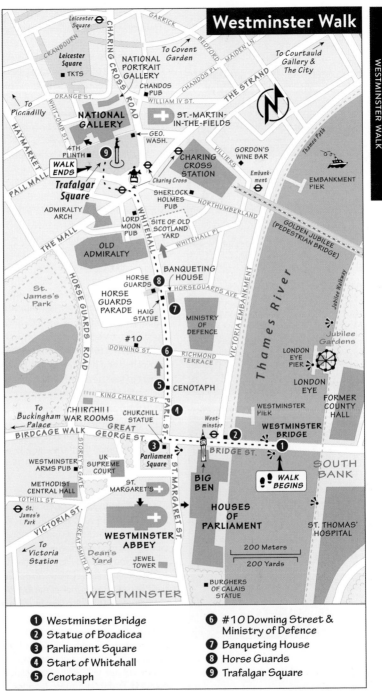

Westminster Walk

1 Westminster Bridge
2 Statue of Boadicea
3 Parliament Square
4 Start of Whitehall
5 Cenotaph
6 #10 Downing Street & Ministry of Defence
7 Banqueting House
8 Horse Guards
9 Trafalgar Square

A Boadicea statue

B Churchill statue in Parliament Square

C Horse Guards

roads and making this spot on the Thames—"Londinium"—a major urban center.

You'll find four red phone booths lining the north side of ❸ **Parliament Square** along Great George Street—great for a phone-box-and-Big-Ben photo op.

Wave hello to Winston Churchill and Nelson Mandela in Parliament Square. To Churchill's right is the historic **Westminster Abbey,** with its two stubby, elegant towers. The white building (flying the Union Jack) at the far end of the square houses Britain's **Supreme Court.**

Head north up Parliament Street, which turns into ❹ **Whitehall,** and walk toward Trafalgar Square. You'll see the thought-provoking ❺ **Cenotaph** in the middle of the boulevard, reminding passersby of the many Brits who died in the last century's world wars. To visit the **Churchill War Rooms,** take a left before the Cenotaph, on King Charles Street.

Continuing on Whitehall, stop at the barricaded and guarded ❻ #**10 Downing Street** to see the British "White House," the traditional home of the prime minister since the position was created in the early 18th century. Break the bobby's boredom and ask him a question. The huge building across Whitehall from Downing Street is the **Ministry of Defence** (MOD), the "British Pentagon."

Nearing Trafalgar Square, look for the 17th-century ❼ **Banqueting House** across the street, which is just about all that remains of what was once the biggest palace in Europe—Whitehall Palace. If you visit, you can enjoy its ceiling paintings by Peter Paul Rubens, and the exquisite hall itself. Also take a look at the ❽ **Horse Guards** behind the gated fence. For 200 years, soldiers in cavalry uniforms have guarded this arched entrance that leads to Buckingham Palace. These elite troops constitute the Queen's personal bodyguard.

The column topped by Lord Nelson marks ❾ **Trafalgar Square,** London's

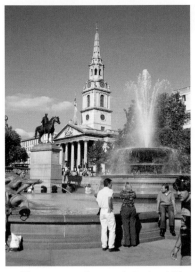

Trafalgar Square and St. Martin-in-the-Fields

central meeting point. The stately domed building on the far side of the square is the **National Gallery,** which is filled with the national collection of European paintings, and has a classy café in the Sainsbury wing. To the right of the National Gallery is the 1722 **St. Martin-in-the-Fields Church** and its Café in the Crypt.

• *Our Westminster walk is over. But if you want to keep going, walk up Cockspur Street to Haymarket, then take a short left on Coventry Street to colorful Piccadilly Circus. Near here, you'll find several theaters and Leicester Square, with its half-price "TKTS" booth for plays (see page 103) Walk through trendy Soho (north of Shaftesbury Avenue) for its fun pubs.*

SIGHTS

Central London
Westminster
These sights are listed in roughly geographical order from Westminster Abbey to Trafalgar Square, and are linked in my self-guided Westminster Walk, earlier, and the ∩ free Westminster Walk audio tour (see page 29 for details).

▲▲▲WESTMINSTER ABBEY

The greatest church in the English-speaking world, Westminster Abbey is where the nation's royalty has been wedded, crowned, and buried since 1066. Indeed, the histories of Westminster Abbey and England are almost the same. A thousand years of English history—3,000 tombs, the remains of 29 kings and queens, and hundreds of memorials to poets, politicians, scientists, and warriors—lie within its stained-glass splendor and under its stone slabs.

Cost and Hours: £22, £44 family ticket (covers 2 adults and 1 child), includes cloister and audioguide; Mon-Fri 9:30-16:30, Wed until 19:00 (main church only), Sat until 14:30, last entry one hour before closing, closed Sun to sightseers but open for services, guided tours available; cloister—daily 8:00-18:00; Tube: Westminster or St. James's Park, tel. 020/7222-5152, www.westminster-abbey.org.

Rick's Tip: Westminster Abbey *is most crowded at midmorning and all day Saturdays and Mondays.* **Visit early, during lunch, or late.** *Weekdays after 14:30—especially Wednesday—are less congested; come late and stay for the 17:00 evensong. Skip the line by booking tickets in advance via the Abbey's website at www.westminster-abbey.org.*

Church Services and Music: Mon-Fri at 7:30 (prayer), 8:00 (communion), 12:30 (communion), 17:00 evensong (except on Wed, when the evening service is generally spoken—not sung); **Sat** at 8:00 (communion), 9:00 (prayer), 15:00 (evensong; May-Aug it's at 17:00); **Sun** services generally come with more music: at 8:00 (communion), 10:00 (sung Matins), 11:15 (sung Eucharist), 15:00 (evensong), 18:30 (evening service). Services are free to anyone, though visitors who haven't paid church admission aren't allowed to linger afterward. Free **organ recitals** are usually held Sun at 17:45 (30 minutes).

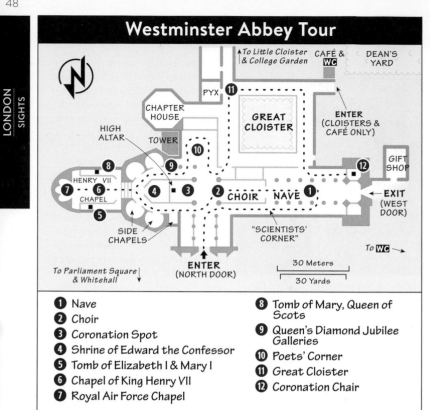

Westminster Abbey Tour

To Little Cloister & College Garden
CAFÉ & WC
DEAN'S YARD
PYX
CHAPTER HOUSE
GREAT CLOISTER
ENTER (CLOISTERS & CAFÉ ONLY)
HIGH ALTAR
TOWER
GIFT SHOP
HENRY VII
CHAPEL
CHOIR
NAVE
EXIT (WEST DOOR)
SIDE CHAPELS
"SCIENTISTS' CORNER"
To WC
To Parliament Square & Whitehall
ENTER (NORTH DOOR)
30 Meters
30 Yards

1 Nave
2 Choir
3 Coronation Spot
4 Shrine of Edward the Confessor
5 Tomb of Elizabeth I & Mary I
6 Chapel of King Henry VII
7 Royal Air Force Chapel
8 Tomb of Mary, Queen of Scots
9 Queen's Diamond Jubilee Galleries
10 Poets' Corner
11 Great Cloister
12 Coronation Chair

The west facade of Westminster Abbey

Tours: The included **audioguide** is excellent. The Westminster Abbey Official Tour **app** includes an audio tour narrated by Jeremy Irons. To add to the experience, you can take an entertaining **guided tour** from a verger—the church equivalent of a museum docent (£5, schedule posted both outside and inside entry, up to 6/day in summer, 2-4/day in winter, 1.5 hours).

❯ SELF-GUIDED TOUR

You'll have no choice but to follow the steady flow of tourists through the church, along the route laid out for the audioguide. My tour covers the Abbey's top stops.

• *Walk straight through the north transept. Follow the crowd flow to the right and enter the spacious...*

❶ **Nave:** The Abbey's 10-story nave is the tallest in England. With saints in stained glass, heroes in carved stone, and the bodies of England's greatest citizens under the floor stones, Westminster Abbey is the religious heart of England.

The king who built the Abbey was Edward the Confessor. Find him in the stained-glass windows on the left side of the nave (as you face the altar). He's in the third bay from the end (marked *S: Edwardus rex...*), with his crown, scepter, and ring.

On the floor near the west entrance of the Abbey is the flower-lined Grave of the Unknown Warrior, one ordinary WWI soldier buried in soil from France with lettering made from melted-down weapons from that war. Contemplate the million-man army from the British Empire and all those who gave their lives. Their memory is so revered that when Kate Middleton walked up the aisle on her wedding day, by tradition she had to step around the tomb (and her wedding bouquet was later placed atop this tomb, also in accordance with tradition).

• *Walk up the nave toward the altar. This is the same route every future monarch walks on the way to being crowned. Midway up the nave, you pass through the colorful screen of an enclosure known as the...*

❷ **Choir:** These elaborately carved wood and gilded seats are where monks once chanted their services in the "quire"—as it's known in British churchspeak. Today, it's where the Abbey boys' choir sings the evensong. You're approaching the center of a cross-shaped church. The "high" (main) altar (which usually has a cross and candlesticks atop it) sits on the platform up the five stairs in front of you.

• *It's on this platform that the monarch is crowned.*

❸ **Coronation Spot:** The area immediately before the high altar is where every English coronation since 1066 has taken place. Royalty are also given funerals here. Princess Diana's coffin was carried to this spot for her funeral service in 1997. The "Queen Mum" (mother of Elizabeth II) had her funeral here in 2002. This is also where most of the last century's royal weddings have taken place, including the unions of Queen Elizabeth II and Prince Philip (1947), Prince Andrew and Sarah Ferguson (1986), and Prince William and Kate Middleton (2011).

• *Veer left and follow the crowd. Pause at the wooden staircase on your right.*

❹ **Shrine of Edward the Confessor:** Step back and peek over the dark coffin of Edward I to see the tippy-top of the green-and-gold wedding-cake tomb of King Edward the Confessor—the man who built Westminster Abbey.

God had told pious Edward to visit St. Peter's Basilica in Rome. But with the Normans thinking conquest, it was too dangerous for him to leave England. Instead, he built this grand church and dedicated it to St. Peter. It was finished just in time to bury Edward and to crown his foreign successor, William the Conqueror, in 1066. After Edward's death, people prayed at his tomb, and, after getting good results, Pope Alexander III canonized him. This elevated, central tomb—which lost some of its luster when Henry VIII melted down the gold coffin-case—is surrounded by the tombs of eight kings and queens.

• *At the top of the stone staircase, veer left into the private burial chapel of Queen Elizabeth I.*

❺ **Tomb of Queens Elizabeth I and Mary I:** Although only one effigy is on the tomb (Elizabeth's), there are actually two queens buried beneath it, both daughters of Henry VIII (by different mothers). Bloody Mary—meek, pious, sickly, and Catholic—enforced Catholicism during her short reign (1553-1558) by burning "heretics" at the stake.

Elizabeth—strong, clever, and Protestant—steered England on an Anglican course. She holds a royal orb symbolizing that she's queen of the whole globe. When 26-year-old Elizabeth was crowned in the Abbey, her right to rule was questioned (especially by her Catholic subjects) because she was considered the bastard seed of Henry

VIII's unsanctioned marriage to Anne Boleyn. But Elizabeth's long reign (1559-1603) was one of the greatest in English history, a time when England ruled the seas and Shakespeare explored human emotions. When she died, thousands turned out for her funeral in the Abbey. Elizabeth's face on the tomb, modeled after her death mask, is considered a very accurate take on this hook-nosed, imperious "Virgin Queen" (she never married).

• *Continue into the ornate, flag-draped room up a few more stairs, directly behind the main altar.*

❻ **Chapel of King Henry VII (The Lady Chapel):** The light from the stained-glass windows; the colorful banners overhead; and the elaborate tracery in stone, wood, and glass give this room the festive air of a medieval tournament. The prestigious Knights of the Bath meet here, under the magnificent ceiling studded with gold pendants. The ceiling—of carved stone, not plaster (1519)—is the finest English Perpendicular Gothic and fan vaulting you'll see (unless you're going to King's College Chapel in Cambridge). The ceiling was sculpted on the floor in pieces, then jigsaw-puzzled into place. It capped the Gothic period and signaled the vitality of the coming Renaissance.

• *Go to the far end of the chapel and stand at the banister in front of the modern set of stained-glass windows.*

❼ **Royal Air Force Chapel:** Saints in robes and halos mingle with pilots in parachutes and bomber jackets. This tribute to WWII flyers is for those who earned their angel wings in the Battle of Britain (July-Oct 1940). A bit of bomb damage has been preserved—look for the little glassed-over hole in the wall below the windows in the lower left-hand corner.

• *Exit the Chapel of Henry VII. Turn left into a side chapel with the tomb (the central one of three in the chapel).*

❽ **Tomb of Mary, Queen of Scots:** The beautiful, French-educated queen

Tomb of Elizabeth I (and Mary I)

(1542-1587) was held under house arrest for 19 years by Queen Elizabeth I, who considered her a threat to her sovereignty. Elizabeth got wind of an assassination plot, suspected Mary was behind it, and had her first cousin (once removed) beheaded. When Elizabeth died childless, Mary's son—James VI, King of Scots—also became King James I of England and Ireland. James buried his mum here (with her head sewn back on) in the Abbey's most sumptuous tomb.

• *Exit Mary's chapel. Continue on, until you emerge in the south transept. Look for the doorway that leads to a stairway and elevator to the...*

❾ Queen's Diamond Jubilee Galleries: In the summer of 2018, the Abbey will open a space that has been closed off for 700 years—an internal gallery 70 feet above the main floor known as the triforium. This balcony will house the new Queen's Diamond Jubilee Galleries, a small museum where you'll see exhibits covering royal coronations, funerals, and much more from the Abbey's 1,000-year history. There will also be stunning views of the nave straight down to the Great West Door. Because of limited access to the galleries, it's likely visitors will need a timed-entry ticket (see the Abbey website for details).

• *After touring the Queen's Galleries, return to the main floor. You're in...*

❿ Poets' Corner: England's greatest artistic contributions are in the written word. Here the masters of arguably the world's most complex and expressive language are remembered: Geoffrey Chaucer *(Canterbury Tales),* Lord Byron, Dylan Thomas, W. H. Auden, Lewis Carroll *(Alice's Adventures in Wonderland),* T. S. Eliot *(The Waste Land),* Alfred Tennyson, Robert Browning, and Charles Dickens. Many writers are honored with plaques and monuments; relatively few are actually buried here. Shakespeare is commemorated by a fine statue that stands near the end of the transept,

Poets' Corner

overlooking the others.

• *Exit the church (temporarily) at the south door, which leads to the...*

⓫ Great Cloister: The buildings that adjoin the church housed the monks. Cloistered courtyards gave them a place to meditate on God's creations.

• *Go back into the church for the last stop.*

⓬ Coronation Chair: A gold-painted oak chair waits here under a regal canopy for the next coronation. For every English coronation since 1308 (except two), it's been moved to its spot before the high altar to receive the royal buttocks. The chair's legs rest on lions, England's symbol.

▲▲HOUSES OF PARLIAMENT (PALACE OF WESTMINSTER)

This Neo-Gothic icon of London, the site of the royal residence from 1042 to 1547, is now the meeting place of the legislative branch of government. Like the US Capitol in Washington, DC, the complex is open to visitors. You can view parliamentary sessions in either the bickering House of Commons or the sleepy House of Lords. Or you can simply wander on your own (through a few closely monitored rooms) to appreciate the historic building itself.

The Palace of Westminster has been the center of political power in England for nearly a thousand years. In 1834, a horrendous fire gutted the Palace. It was rebuilt in a retro, Neo-Gothic style that recalled England's medieval Christian roots—pointed arches, stained-glass

Houses of Parliament

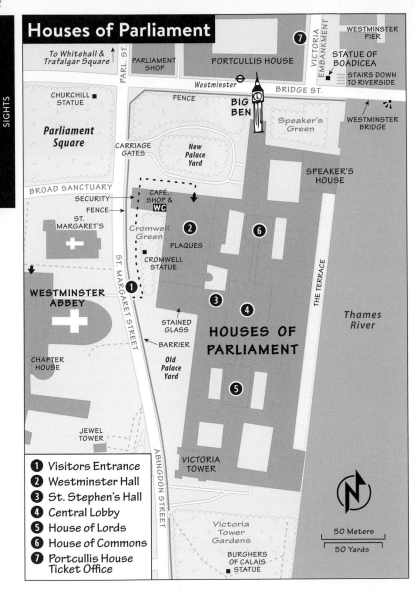

To Whitehall & Trafalgar Square

PARL. ST.

PARLIAMENT SHOP

PORTCULLIS HOUSE

7

VICTORIA EMBANKMENT

WESTMINSTER PIER

STATUE OF BOADICEA

STAIRS DOWN TO RIVERSIDE

Westminster

BRIDGE ST.

CHURCHILL STATUE

FENCE

BIG BEN

Speaker's Green

WESTMINSTER BRIDGE

Parliament Square

CARRIAGE GATES

New Palace Yard

SPEAKER'S HOUSE

BROAD SANCTUARY

SECURITY

FENCE

CAFÉ, SHOP & WC

ST. MARGARET'S

Cromwell Green

2

6

PLAQUES

CROMWELL STATUE

THE TERRACE

Thames River

WESTMINSTER ABBEY

1

3

4

STAINED GLASS

HOUSES OF PARLIAMENT

BARRIER

CHAPTER HOUSE

Old Palace Yard

5

JEWEL TOWER

ABINGDON STREET

VICTORIA TOWER

N

1 Visitors Entrance
2 Westminster Hall
3 St. Stephen's Hall
4 Central Lobby
5 House of Lords
6 House of Commons
7 Portcullis House Ticket Office

Victoria Tower Gardens

BURGHERS OF CALAIS STATUE

50 Meters

50 Yards

windows, spires, and saint-like statues. At the same time, Britain was also retooling its government. Democracy was on the rise, the queen became a constitutional monarch, and Parliament emerged as the nation's ruling body. The Palace of Westminster became a kind of cathedral of democracy.

Cost and Hours: Free when Parliament is in session, otherwise must visit with a paid tour (see next); hours for nonticketed entry to House of Commons—Oct-late July Mon 14:30-22:30, Tue-Wed 11:30-19:30, Thu 9:30-17:30; for House of Lords—Oct-late July Mon-Tue 14:30-22:00, Wed 15:00-22:00, Thu 11:00-19:30;

last entry depends on debates; exact schedule at www.parliament.uk.

Tours: Audioguide-£18.50, guided tour-£25.50, Sat year-round 9:00-16:30 and most weekdays during recess (late July-Sept), 1.5 hours. Confirm the tour schedule and book ahead at www.parliament.uk or by calling 020/7219-4114 The ticket office also sells tour tickets, but there's no guarantee same-day spaces will be available (ticket office open Mon-Fri 10:00-16:00, Sat 9:00-16:30, closed Sun, located in Portcullis House next to Westminster Tube Station, entrance on Victoria Embankment).

Choosing a House: The House of Lords is less important politically, but they meet in a more ornate room, and the wait time is shorter (likely less than 30 minutes). The House of Commons is where major policy is made, but the room is sparse, and wait times are longer (30-60 minutes or more).

The history of the Houses of Parliament spans more than 900 years.

Rick's Tip: *For the **public galleries** in either House, **lines are longest** at the start of each session, particularly on Wednesdays. For the shortest wait, try to show up **later in the afternoon** (but don't push it, as things sometimes close down early).*

● SELF-GUIDED TOUR

Enter midway along the west side of the building (across the street from Westminster Abbey), where a tourist ramp leads to the ❶ **visitors entrance.** Line up for the airport-style security check. You'll be given a visitor badge. If you have questions, the attendants are extremely helpful.

• *First, take in the cavernous...*

❷ **Westminster Hall:** This vast hall—covering 16,000 square feet—survived the 1834 fire, and is one of the oldest and most important buildings in England. England's vaunted legal system was invented in this hall, as this was the major court of the land for 700 years. King Charles I was tried and sentenced to death here. Guy Fawkes

The history of the Houses of Parliament spans more than 900 years.

Affording London's Sights

London is one of Europe's most expensive cities, with the dubious distinction of having some of the world's steepest admission prices. But with its many free museums and affordable plays, this cosmopolitan, cultured city offers days of sightseeing thrills without requiring you to pinch your pennies (or your pounds).

Free Museums: Free sights include the British Museum, British Library, National Gallery, National Portrait Gallery, Tate Britain, Tate Modern, Imperial War Museum, Victoria and Albert Museum, Natural History Museum, and the Museum of London. Some museums request a donation of a few pounds, but whether you contribute is up to you.

Free Churches: Smaller churches let worshippers (and tourists) in free, although they may ask for a donation. The big sightseeing churches—Westminster Abbey and St. Paul's—charge higher admission fees, but offer free evensong services nearly daily (though you can't stick around afterward to sightsee). Westminster Abbey also offers free organ recitals most Sundays.

Other Freebies: London has plenty of free performances, such as lunch concerts at St. Martin-in-the-Fields. For other freebies, check out www.whatsfreeinlondon.co.uk. There's no charge to enjoy the pageantry of the Changing of the Guard, rants at Speakers' Corner in Hyde Park (on Sun afternoon), displays at Harrods, the people-watching scene at Covent Garden, and the colorful streets of the East End. It's free to view the legislature at work in the Houses of Parliament. You can get into the chapel at the Tower of London by attending Sunday services. And Greenwich is an inexpensive outing.

Good-Value Tours: The London Walks tours with professional guides (£10) are one of the best deals going. Hop-on, hop-off big-bus tours, while expensive (around £30), provide a great overview and include free boat tours as well as city walks. (Or, for the price of a transit ticket, you could get similar views from the top of a double-decker public bus.) A one-hour Thames ride to Greenwich costs about £12 one-way, but most boats come with entertaining commentary.

Theater: Compared with Broadway's prices, London's theater can be a bargain. Seek out the freestanding TKTS booth at Leicester Square to get discounts from 25 to 50 percent on good seats. And a £5 "groundling" ticket for a play at Shakespeare's Globe is the best theater deal in town.

was condemned for plotting to blow up the Halls of Parliament in 1605.

• *Continue up the stairs, and enter...*

❸ St. Stephen's Hall: This long, beautifully lit room was the original House of Commons. Members of Parliament (MPs) sat in church pews on either side of the hall—the ruling faction on one side, the opposition on the other

• *Next you reach the...*

❹ Central Lobby: This ornate, octagonal, high-vaulted room is often called the "heart of British government," because it sits midway between the House of Commons (to the left) and the House of Lords (right). Video monitors list the schedule of meetings and events in this 1,100-room governmental hive. This is the best place to admire the Palace's carved wood, chandeliers, statues, and floor tiles.

• *This lobby marks the end of the public space where you can wander freely. To see the House of Lords or House of Commons, you must wait in line and check your belongings.*

❺ **House of Lords:** When you're called, you'll walk to the Lords Chamber by way of the long Peers' Corridor—referring to the House's 800 unelected members, called "Peers." Paintings on the corridor walls depict the antiauthoritarian spirit brewing under the reign of Charles I. When you reach the House of Lords Chamber, you'll watch the proceedings from the upper-level visitors gallery. Debate may occur among the few Lords who show up at any given time, but these days, the Peers' role is largely advisory—they have no real power to pass laws on their own.

The Lords Chamber is church-like and impressive, with stained glass and intricately carved walls. At the far end is the Queen's gilded throne, where she sits once a year to give a speech to open Parliament. In front of the throne sits the woolsack—a cushion stuffed with wool. Here the Lord Speaker presides, with a ceremonial mace behind the backrest. To the Lord Speaker's right are the members of the ruling party (a.k.a. "government") and to his left are the members of the opposition (the Labour Party). Unaffiliated Crossbenchers sit in between

❻ **House of Commons:** The Commons Chamber may be much less grandiose than the Lords', but this is where the sausage gets made. The House of Commons is as powerful as the Lords, prime minister, and Queen combined.

When the prime minister visits, her ministers (or cabinet) join her on the front bench, while lesser MPs (the "backbenchers") sit behind. It's often a fiery spectacle, as the prime minister defends her policies, while the opposition grumbles and harrumphs in displeasure. It's not unheard-of for MPs to get out of line and be escorted out by the Serjeant at Arms.

Big Ben

Nearby: Across the street from the Parliament building's St. Stephen's Gate, the **Jewel Tower** is a rare remnant of the old Palace of Westminster, used by kings until Henry VIII. The crude stone tower (1365-1366) was a guard tower in the palace wall, overlooking a moat. It contains a fine exhibit on the medieval Westminster Palace and the tower (£5.20, daily 10:00-18:00, Oct until 17:00; Nov-March Sat-Sun until 16:00, closed Mon-Fri; tel. 020/7222-2219). Next to the tower (and free) is a quiet courtyard with picnic-friendly benches.

Big Ben, the 315-foot-high clock tower at the north end of the Palace of Westminster, is named for its 13-ton bell, Ben. The light above the clock is lit when Parliament is in session. The face of the clock is huge—you can actually see the minute hand moving. For a good view of it, walk halfway over Westminster Bridge.

▲▲▲ CHURCHILL WAR ROOMS

Take a fascinating walk through the underground headquarters of the British government's WWII fight against the Nazis. It has two parts: the war rooms themselves, and a top-notch museum dedicated to Winston Churchill, who steered the war from here. Pick up the excellent audioguide at the entry, and dive in. The museum's gift shop is great for anyone nostalgic for the 1940s.

Cost and Hours: £19, includes audioguide, daily 9:30-18:00, last entry one hour before closing; café on site; on King Charles Street, 200 yards off Whitehall—follow signs, Tube: Westminster; tel. 020/7930-6961, www.iwm.org.uk/churchill-war-rooms.

Visiting the War Rooms and Museum: The 27 **War Rooms,** the heavily fortified nerve center of the British war effort, was used from 1939 to 1945. Churchill's room, the map room, and other rooms are just as they were in 1945. As you follow the one-way route, take advantage of the audioguide, which explains each room and offers first-person accounts of wartime happenings here. Be patient—it's well worth it. While the rooms are spartan, you'll see how British gentility survived even as the city was bombarded—posted signs informed those working underground what the weather was like outside, and a cheery notice reminded them to turn off the light switch to conserve electricity.

The **Churchill Museum,** which occupies a large hall amid the war rooms, dissects every aspect of the man behind the famous cigar, bowler hat, and V-for-victory sign. Artifacts, quotes, political cartoons, clear explanations, and interactive

Churchill War Rooms

exhibits to bring the colorful statesman to life. Many of the items on display—such as a European map divvied up in permanent marker, which Churchill brought to England from the postwar Potsdam Conference—drive home the remarkable span of history this man influenced.

Rick's Tip: *Some sights automatically add a* **"voluntary donation" of about 10 percent** *to their admission fees (those are the prices I quote), and some free museums request donations. All such contributions are completely optional.*

On Trafalgar Square

Trafalgar Square, London's central square (worth ▲▲), is at the intersection of Westminster, The City, and the West End. It's the climax of most marches and demonstrations, and is a thrilling place to simply hang out. At the top of Trafalgar Square (north) sits the domed National Gallery with its grand staircase, and to the right, the steeple of St. Martin-in-the-Fields, built in 1722. In the center of the square, Lord Nelson stands atop his 185-foot-tall fluted granite column, gazing out toward Trafalgar, where he lost his life but defeated the French fleet. Part of this 1842 memorial is made from his victims' melted-down cannons. He's surrounded by spraying fountains, giant lions, and hordes of people (Tube: Charing Cross).

▲▲▲NATIONAL GALLERY

Displaying an unsurpassed collection of European paintings from 1250 to 1900—including works by Leonardo, Botticelli, Velázquez, Rembrandt, Turner, Van Gogh, and the Impressionists—this is one of Europe's great galleries.

Cost and Hours: Free, £5 suggested donation, special exhibits extra, daily 10:00-18:00, Fri until 21:00, last entry to special exhibits 45 minutes before closing, on Trafalgar Square, Tube: Charing Cross or Leicester Square.

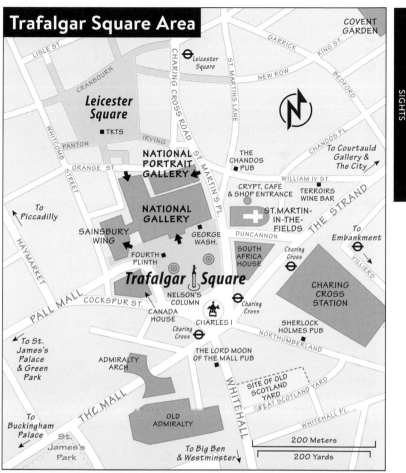

Trafalgar Square Area

COVENT GARDEN

LISLE ST.

CRANBOURN

GARRICK

KING ST.

NEW ROW

BEDFORD

Leicester Square

CHARING CROSS ROAD

Leicester Square

ST. MARTINS LANE

Leicester Square

WHITCOMB

PANTON

■ TKTS

IRVING

ORANGE ST.

CHANDOS PL.

To Courtauld Gallery & The City

NATIONAL PORTRAIT GALLERY

STREET

ST. MARTIN'S PL.

THE CHANDOS PUB

WILLIAM IV ST.

CRYPT, CAFÉ & SHOP ENTRANCE

TERROIRS WINE BAR

THE STRAND

To Piccadilly

NATIONAL GALLERY

ST.MARTIN-IN-THE-FIELDS

To Embankment

SAINSBURY WING

GEORGE WASH.

DUNCANNON

HAYMARKET

FOURTH PLINTH

SOUTH AFRICA HOUSE

Charing Cross

VILLIERS

Trafalgar **Square**

Charing Cross

CHARING CROSS STATION

PALL MALL

COCKSPUR ST.

NELSON'S COLUMN

CANADA HOUSE

CHARLES I

Charing Cross

SHERLOCK HOLMES PUB

To St. James's Palace & Green Park

Charing Cross

NORTHUMBERLAND

THE LORD MOON OF THE MALL PUB

ADMIRALTY ARCH

WHITEHALL

SITE OF OLD SCOTLAND YARD

GREAT SCOTLAND YARD

To Buckingham Palace

THE MALL

St. James's Park

OLD ADMIRALTY

WHITEHALL PL.

To Big Ben & Westminster

200 Meters

200 Yards

The massive National Gallery is one of the world's great art museums.

MEDIEVAL & EARLY RENAISSANCE
1 ANONYMOUS – The Wilton Diptych
2 UCCELLO – Battle of San Romano
3 VAN EYCK – The Arnolfini Portrait

ITALIAN RENAISSANCE
4 LEONARDO – The Virgin of the Rocks
5 BOTTICELLI – Venus and Mars
6 CRIVELLI – The Annunciation,
with Saint Emidius

HIGH RENAISSANCE & MANNERISM
7 LEONARDO – Virgin and Child with
St. Anne and St. John the Baptist
8 MICHELANGELO – The Entombment
9 RAPHAEL – Pope Julius II
10 BRONZINO – An Allegory with
Venus and Cupid
11 TINTORETTO – The Origin of the
Milky Way

NORTHERN PROTESTANT ART
12 VERMEER – A Young Woman
Standing at a Virginal
13 VAN HOOGSTRATEN – A Peepshow with
Views of the Interior of a Dutch House
14 REMBRANDT – Belshazzar's Feast
15 REMBRANDT – Self-Portrait at the
Age of 63

BAROQUE & FRENCH ROCOCO
16 RUBENS – The Judgment of Paris
17 VELÁZQUEZ – The Rokeby Venus
18 VAN DYCK – Equestrian Portrait
of Charles I
19 CARAVAGGIO –The Supper at
Emmaus
20 BOUCHER – Pan and Syrinx

BRITISH ROMANTIC ART
21 CONSTABLE – The Hay Wain
22 TURNER – The Fighting
Téméraire

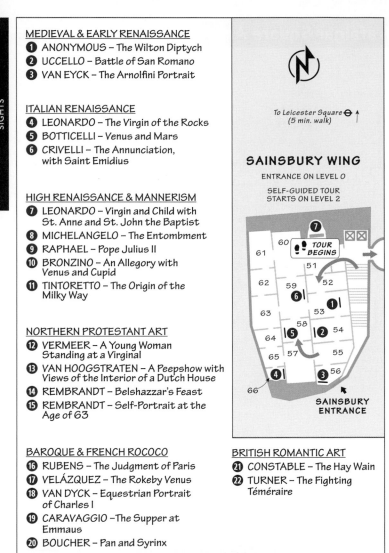

To Leicester Square ⊖
(5 min. walk)

SAINSBURY WING

ENTRANCE ON LEVEL 0

SELF-GUIDED TOUR
STARTS ON LEVEL 2

TOUR
BEGINS

SAINSBURY
ENTRANCE

Information: Helpful £1 floor plan available from information desk; free one-hour overview tours leave from Sainsbury Wing info desk daily at 11:30 and 14:30, plus Fri at 19:00; excellent £4 audioguides—choose from one-hour highlights tour, several theme tours, or an option that lets you dial up info on any painting in the museum; tel. 020/7747-2885, www.nationalgallery.org.uk.

Eating: Consider splitting afternoon tea at the excellent-but-pricey National Dining Rooms, on the first floor of the Sainsbury Wing. The National Café, located near the Getty Entrance, has a table-service restaurant and a café. Seek out the Espresso Bar, near the Portico and Getty entrances, for sandwiches, pastries, and soft couches.

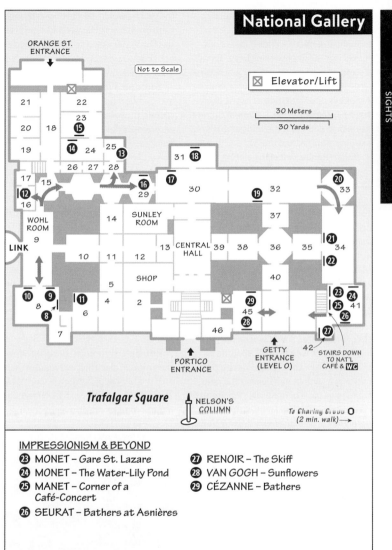

National Gallery

ORANGE ST.
ENTRANCE

Not to Scale

⊠ Elevator/Lift

30 Meters

30 Yards

LINK

WOHL
ROOM

SUNLEY
ROOM

CENTRAL
HALL

SHOP

GETTY
ENTRANCE
(LEVEL 0)

PORTICO
ENTRANCE

STAIRS DOWN
TO NAT'L
CAFÉ & WC

Trafalgar Square   NELSON'S
COLUMN

To Charing Cross O
(2 min. walk)→

IMPRESSIONISM & BEYOND

㉓ MONET – *Gare St. Lazare*
㉔ MONET – *The Water-Lily Pond*
㉕ MANET – *Corner of a
Café-Concert*
㉖ SEURAT – *Bathers at Asnières*

㉗ RENOIR – *The Skiff*
㉘ VAN GOGH – *Sunflowers*
㉙ CÉZANNE – *Bathers*

Visiting the Museum: Enter through the Sainsbury Entrance (in the smaller building to the left of the main entrance), and approach the collection chronologically.

Medieval and Early Renaissance: In the first rooms, you see shiny paintings of saints, angels, Madonnas, and crucifixions floating in an ethereal gold never-never land. Art in the Middle Ages was religious, dominated

by the Church. The illiterate faithful could meditate on an altarpiece and visualize heaven. It's as though they couldn't imagine saints and angels inhabiting the dreary world of rocks, trees, and sky they lived in.

After leaving this gold-leaf peace, you'll stumble into Uccello's *Battle of San Romano* and Van Eyck's *The Arnolfini Portrait,* called by some "The Shotgun

Wedding." This painting—a masterpiece of down-to-earth details—was once thought to depict a wedding ceremony forced by the lady's swelling belly. Today it's understood as a portrait of a solemn, well-dressed, well-heeled couple, the Arnolfinis of Bruges, Belgium (she likely was not pregnant—the fashion of the day was to gather up the folds of one's extremely full-skirted dress).

Italian Renaissance: In painting, the Renaissance meant realism. Artists rediscovered the beauty of nature and the human body, expressing the optimism and confidence of this new age. Look for Botticelli's *Venus and Mars,* Michelangelo's *The Entombment,* and Raphael's *Pope Julius II.*

In Leonardo's *The Virgin of the Rocks,* Mary plays with her son Jesus and little Johnny the Baptist (with cross, at left) while an androgynous angel looks on. Leonardo brings this holy scene right down to earth by setting it among rocks, stalactites, water, and flowering plants. But looking closer, we see that Leonardo has deliberately posed his people into a pyramid shape, with Mary's head at the peak, creating an oasis of maternal stability and serenity amid the hard rock of the earth.

In *The Origin of the Milky Way* by Venetian Renaissance painter Tintoretto, the god Jupiter places his illegitimate son, baby Hercules, at his wife's breast. Juno says, "Wait a minute. That's not my baby!" Her milk spurts upward, becoming the Milky Way.

Northern Protestant: While Italy had wealthy aristocrats and the powerful Catholic Church to purchase art, the North's patrons were middle-class, hardworking, Protestant merchants. They wanted simple, cheap, no-nonsense pictures to decorate their homes and offices. Greek gods and Virgin Marys are out, and hometown folks and hometown places are in.

Highlights include Vermeer's *A Young Woman Standing at a Virginal* and Rembrandt's *Belshazzar's Feast.* Rembrandt painted his *Self-Portrait at the Age of 63* in the year he would die. He throws the light of truth on...himself. He was bankrupt, his mistress had just passed away, and he had also buried several of his children. We see a disillusioned, well-worn, but proud old genius.

Baroque: While artists in Protestant and democratic Europe painted simple scenes, those in Catholic and aristocratic countries turned to the style called Baroque—taking what was flashy in Venetian art and making it flashier, what was gaudy and making it gaudier, what was dramatic and making it shocking.

The museum's outstanding Baroque collection includes Van Dyck's *Equestrian Portrait of Charles I* and Caravaggio's *The Supper at Emmaus.* In Velázquez's *The Rokeby Venus,* Venus lounges diagonally across the canvas, admiring herself, with flaring red, white, and gray fabrics to highlight her rosy white skin and inflame our passion. This work by the king's personal court painter is a rare Spanish nude from that ultra-Catholic country.

British: The reserved British were more comfortable cavorting with nature than with the lofty gods, as seen in Constable's *The Hay Wain.* But Constable's landscape was about to be paved over by the Indus-

Van Eyck, The Arnolfini Portrait

trial Revolution, as Turner's *The Fighting Téméraire* shows. Machines began to replace humans, factories belched smoke over Constable's hay cart, and cloud-gazers had to punch the clock. But alas, here a modern steamboat symbolically drags a famous but obsolete sailing battleship off into the sunset to be destroyed. Turner's messy, colorful style influenced the Impressionists and gives us our first glimpse into the modern art world.

Impressionism: At the end of the 19th century, a new breed of artists burst out of the stuffy confines of the studio. They donned scarves and berets and set up their canvases in farmers' fields or carried their notebooks into crowded cafés, dashing off quick sketches in order to catch a momentary...impression. Check out Impressionist and Post-Impressionist masterpieces such as Monet's *Gare St. Lazare* and *The Water-Lily Pond,* Renoir's *The Skiff,* Seurat's *Bathers at Asnières,* and Van Gogh's *Sunflowers.*

Cézanne's *Bathers* are arranged in strict triangles. Cézanne uses the Impressionist technique of building a figure with dabs of paint (though his "dabs" are often larger-sized "cube" shapes) to make solid,

3-D geometrical figures in the style of the Renaissance. In the process, his cube shapes helped inspire a radical new style—Cubism—bringing art into the 20th century.

▲▲NATIONAL PORTRAIT GALLERY

Put off by halls of 19th-century characters who meant nothing to me, I used to call this museum "as interesting as someone else's yearbook." But a selective walk through this 500-year-long *Who's Who* of British history is quick and free, and puts faces on the story of England. The collection is well-described, not huge, and in historical sequence, from the 16th century on the second floor to today's royal family, usually housed on the ground floor. Highlights include Henry VIII and wives; portraits of the "Virgin Queen" Elizabeth I, Sir Francis Drake, and Sir Walter Raleigh; the only real-life portrait of William Shakespeare; Oliver Cromwell and Charles I with his head on; portraits by Gainsborough and Reynolds; the Romantics (William Blake, Lord Byron, William Wordsworth, and company); Queen Victoria and her era; and the present royal family, including the late Princess Diana and the current Duchess of Cambridge—Kate.

Cost and Hours: Free, £5 suggested donation, special exhibits extra; daily 10:00-18:00, Fri until 21:00, first and second floors open Mon at 11:00, last entry to special exhibits one hour before closing; excellent audioguide-£3, floor plan-£1; entry 100 yards off Trafalgar Square (around the corner from National Gallery, opposite Church of St. Martin-in-the-Fields), Tube: Charing Cross or Leicester Square, tel. 020/7306-0055, recorded info tel. 020/7312-2463, www.npg.org.uk.

▲ST. MARTIN-IN-THE-FIELDS

The church, built in the 1720s with a Gothic spire atop a Greek-type temple, is an oasis of peace on wild and noisy Trafalgar Square. St. Martin cared for the poor. "In the fields" was where the first church stood on this spot (in the 13th century), between Westminster and The City. Stepping inside, you

Princess Diana's portrait at the National Portrait Gallery

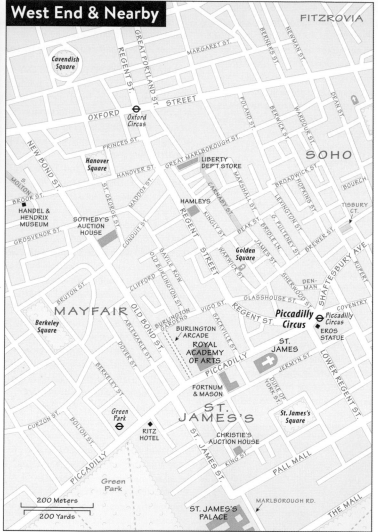

West End & Nearby

FITZROVIA

Cavendish Square

SOHO

LIBERTY DEP'T STORE

HAMLEYS

Hanover Square

Handel & Hendrix Museum

SOTHEBY'S AUCTION HOUSE

Golden Square

MAYFAIR

Berkeley Square

BURLINGTON ARCADE

ROYAL ACADEMY OF ARTS

Piccadilly Circus

EROS STATUE

ST. JAMES

FORTNUM & MASON

Green Park

RITZ HOTEL

ST. JAMES'S

St. James's Square

CHRISTIE'S AUCTION HOUSE

Green Park

ST. JAMES'S PALACE

MARLBOROUGH RD.

THE MALL

200 Meters

200 Yards

still feel a compassion for the needs of the people in this neighborhood—the church serves the homeless and houses a Chinese community center. The modern east window—with grillwork bent into the shape of a warped cross—was installed in 2008 to replace one damaged in World War II.

A freestanding glass pavilion to the left of the church serves as the entrance to the church's underground areas. There you'll find the concert ticket office, a gift shop, brass-rubbing center, and the recommended support-the-church Café in the Crypt.

Cost and Hours: Free, donations welcome; hours vary but generally Mon-Fri 8:30-13:00 & 14:00-18:00, Sat 9:30-18:00, Sun 15:30-17:00; services listed at entrance; Tube: Charing Cross, tel. 020/7766-1100, www.stmartin-in-the-fields.org.

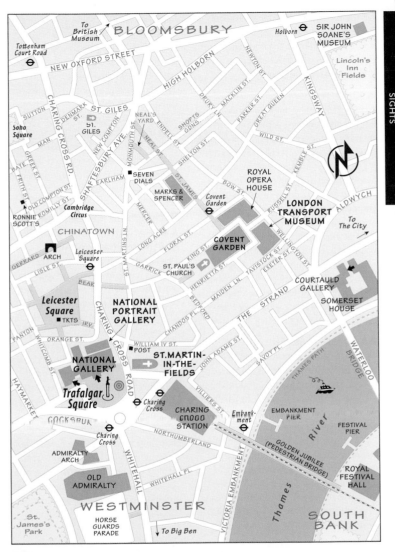

Rick's Tip: St. Martin-in-the-Fields *is famous for its* **concerts.** *Consider a free lunchtime concert (£3.50 suggested donation; Mon, Tue, and Fri at 13:00), an evening concert (£9-28, several nights a week at 19:30), or* **Wednesday night jazz** *(£8-15, at 20:00). See www.stmartin-in-the-fields.org for the schedule.*

The West End and Nearby

▲PICCADILLY CIRCUS

Although this square is slathered with neon billboards and tacky attractions (think of it as the Times Square of London), the surrounding streets are packed with great shopping opportunities. Nearby Shaftesbury Avenue and Leicester Square teem with fun-seekers, theaters, Chinese restaurants, and street singers. To the northeast is London's Chinatown and, beyond that, the funky Soho neighborhood. And curling to the northwest from Piccadilly Circus is genteel Regent Street, lined with exclusive shops.

▲SOHO

North of Piccadilly, once-seedy Soho has become trendy—with many recommended restaurants—and is well worth a gawk. It's the epicenter of London's thriving, colorful youth scene, a fun and funky *Sesame Street* of urban diversity.

Soho is also London's red light district (especially near Brewer and Berwick Streets), where "friendly models" wait in tiny rooms up dreary stairways, voluptuous con artists sell strip shows, and eager male tourists are frequently ripped off. But it's easy to avoid trouble if you're not looking for it. In fact, the sleazy joints share the block with respectable pubs and restaurants.

▲▲COVENT GARDEN

This large square teems with people and street performers—jugglers, sword swallowers, and guitar players. London's buskers (including those in the Tube) are auditioned, licensed, and assigned times and places where they are allowed to perform.

The square's centerpiece is a covered marketplace. A market has been here since medieval times, when it was the "convent" garden owned by Westminster Abbey. In the 1600s, it became a housing development with this courtyard as its center, done in the Palladian style by

Inigo Jones. Today's fine iron-and-glass structure was built in 1830 to house the stalls of what became London's chief produce market. In 1973, its venerable arcades were converted to boutiques, cafés, and antique shops. A tourist market thrives here today.

Browse trendy crafts, market stalls, and food that's good for you (but not your wallet). For better Covent Garden lunch deals, walk a block or two to check out the places north of the Tube station, along Endell and Neal Streets.

Buckingham Palace Area
▲▲CHANGING OF THE GUARD AT BUCKINGHAM PALACE

This is the spectacle every visitor to London has to see at least once: stone-faced, red-coated (or in winter, gray-coated), bearskin-hatted guards changing posts with much fanfare, in an hour-long ceremony accompanied by a brass band.

Most tourists just show up and get lost in the crowds, but those who anticipate the action and know where to perch will enjoy the event more. The most famous part takes place right in front of Buckingham Palace at 11:00. But there actually are several different guard-changing ceremonies and parades going on simultaneously, at different locations within a few hundred yards of the palace. To plan your sightseeing strategy (and understand what's going on), see the "Changing of the Guard Timeline."

Piccadilly Circus

Covent Garden

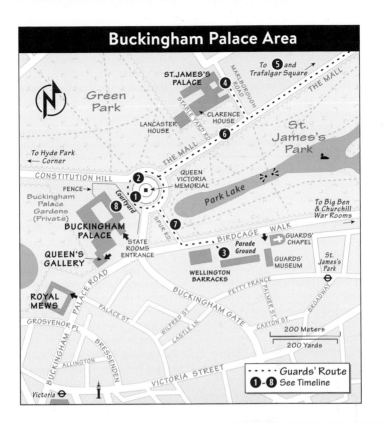

Buckingham Palace Area

Changing of the Guard Timeline

10:00	Arrive now for a spot front and center by the ❶ fence outside Buckingham Palace.
10:30-10:45	❷ Victoria Memorial gets crowded. "New Guard" gathers for inspection at ❸ Wellington Barracks. "Old Guard" gathers at ❹ St. James's Palace.
10:30 (9:30 Sun)	Changing of the Horse Guard at ❺, farther away, along Whitehall.
10:43-11:00	Tired St. James's Palace guards march down ❻ the Mall toward Buckingham Palace. Replacement troops head from Wellington Barracks down ❼ Spur Road to the palace. All guards gradually converge around the Victoria Memorial.
11:00-11:30	Changing of the Guard ceremony takes place inside ❽ the palace courtyard.

Rick's Tip: *Want to go inside* **Buckingham Palace?** *It's* **open to the public only in August and September,** *when the Queen is out of town (£23 for State Rooms; Aug-Sept daily from 9:30, last admission 17:15 in Aug and 16:15 in Sept; book timed-entry ticket in advance by phone, tel. 0303/123-7300, or online, www.royalcollection.org.uk).*

Cost and Hours: Free, May-July daily at 11:00, Aug-April Sun, Mon, Wed, and Fri; no ceremony in very wet weather; exact schedule can change—call 020/7766-7300 for the day's plan, or check www.householddivision.org.uk (search "Changing the Guard"); Buckingham Palace, Tube: Victoria, St. James's Park, or Green Park.

Sightseeing Strategies: The action takes place in stages over the course of an hour, at multiple locations; see the map. Here are a few options to consider:

Watch near the Palace: The main event is in the forecourt right in front of Buckingham Palace (between the palace and the fence) from 11:00 to 11:30. Arrive as close to 10:00 as possible to get a place front and center, next to the fence or on some raised surface to stand or sit on—a balustrade or a curb—so you can see over people's heads.

Watch near the Victoria Memorial: The high ground on the circular Victoria Memorial provides good (if more distant) views of the palace as well as the arriving and departing parades along The Mall and Spur Road. Come before 10:30 to get a place.

Watch near St. James's Palace: If you don't feel like jostling for a view, stroll down to St. James's Palace and wait near the corner for a great photo-op. At about 11:45, the parade marches up The Mall to the palace and performs a smaller changing ceremony—with almost no crowds.

Follow the Procession: You won't get the closest views, but you'll get something even better—the thrill of participating in the action. Start with the "Old Guard" mobilizing in the courtyard of St. James's Palace (10:30). Arrive early, and grab a spot just across the road (otherwise you'll be asked to move when the inspection begins). Just before they prepare to leave

The Changing of the Guard is all about pomp and ceremony.

(at 10:43), march ahead of them down Marlborough Street to The Mall. Pause here to watch them parade past, band and all, on their way to the Buckingham Palace, then cut through the park and head to the Wellington Barracks—where the "New Guard" is getting ready to leave for Buckingham (10:57). March along with full military band and fresh guards from the barracks to the palace. At 11:00 the two guard groups meet in the courtyard, the band plays a few songs, and soldiers parade and finally exchange compliments before returning to Wellington Barracks and St. James's Palace (11:40). Use this time to snap a few photos of the guards—and the crowds—before making your way across the Mall to Clarence House (on Stable Yard Road), where you'll see the "New Guard" pass one last time on their way to St. James's Palace. On their way, the final piece of ceremony takes place—one member of the "Old Guard" and one member of the first-relief "New Guard" change places here.

Join a Tour: Local tour companies such as **Fun London Tours** more or less follow the self-guided route above but add in history and facts about the guards, bands, and royal family to their already entertaining march (£17, Changing of the Guard tour starts at Piccadilly Circus at 9:40, must book online in advance, www. funlondontours.com).

North London

▲▲▲BRITISH MUSEUM

Simply put, this is the greatest chronicle of civilization...anywhere. A visit here is like taking a long hike through *Encyclopedia Britannica* National Park. The vast British Museum wraps around its Great Court (the huge entrance hall), with the most popular sections filling the ground floor: Egyptian, Assyrian, and ancient Greek, with the famous frieze sculptures from the Parthenon in Athens. The museum's stately Reading Room sometimes hosts special exhibits.

Cost and Hours: Free, £5 donation requested, special exhibits usually extra (and with timed ticket); daily 10:00-17:30, Fri until 20:30 (selected galleries only),

British Museum

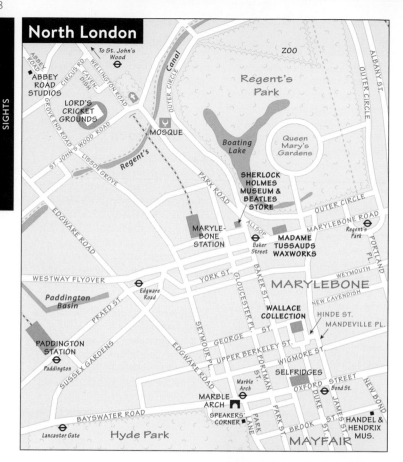

North London

To St. John's Wood

ABBEY ROAD STUDIOS

ABBEY ROAD

CIRCUS RD.

CAVEN-DISH

WELLINGTON ROAD

LORD'S CRICKET GROUNDS

GROVE END ROAD

ST. JOHN'S WOOD ROAD

LISSON GROVE

MOSQUE

Regent's

Canal

OUTER CIRCLE

ZOO

Regent's Park

Boating Lake

Queen Mary's Gardens

OUTER CIRCLE

ALBANY ST.

OUTER CIRCLE

EDGWARE ROAD

PARK ROAD

SHERLOCK HOLMES MUSEUM & BEATLES STORE

MARYLE-BONE STATION

ALLSOP

MADAME TUSSAUDS WAXWORKS

Baker Street

OUTER CIRCLE

MARYLEBONE ROAD

Regent's Park

PORTLAND PL.

WESTWAY FLYOVER

Edgware Road

YORK ST.

GLOUCESTER PL.

BAKER ST.

MARYLEBONE

WEYMOUTH

NEW CAVENDISH

Paddington Basin

PRAED ST.

SEYMOUR PL.

WALLACE COLLECTION

HINDE ST.

MANDEVILLE PL.

PADDINGTON STATION

Paddington

SUSSEX GARDENS

EDGWARE ROAD

GEORGE ST.

UPPER BERKELEY ST.

SEYMOUR ST.

PORTMAN ST.

ST.

WIGMORE ST.

SELFRIDGES

OXFORD STREET

Bond St.

DUKE ST.

JAMES ST.

NEW BOND

MARBLE ARCH

Marble Arch

BAYSWATER ROAD

Lancaster Gate

SPEAKERS' CORNER

PARK LANE

PARK ST.

BROOK ST.

ST.

HANDEL & HENDRIX MUS.

Hyde Park

MAYFAIR

least crowded late on weekday afternoons, especially Fri; Great Russell Street, Tube: Tottenham Court Road, ticket desk tel. 020/7323-8181, www.britishmuseum. org.

Tours: Free 30- to 40-minute **Eye-Opener tours** are led by volunteers, who focus on select rooms (daily 11:00-15:45, generally every 15 minutes). Free 45-minute **gallery talks** on specific subjects are offered Tue-Sat at 13:15; a free 20-minute **spotlight** tour runs on Friday evenings. The £6 **multimedia guide** offers dial-up audio commentary and video on 200 objects, as well as several theme tours (must leave photo ID). There's also a fun family multimedia guide (£5). Or 🎧 download my free audio tour.

A mummy case

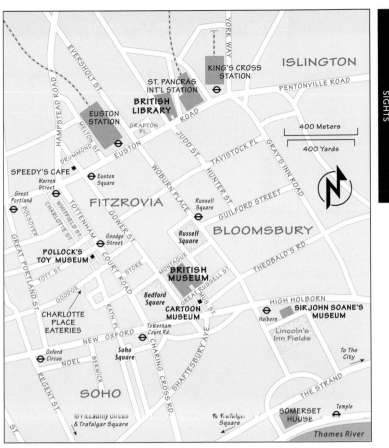

⊙ SELF-GUIDED TOUR

From the Great Court, doorways lead to all wings. To the left are the exhibits on Egypt, Assyria, and Greece—the highlights of your visit.

EGYPT

Egypt was one of the world's first civilizations. The Egypt we think of—pyramids, mummies, pharaohs, and guys who walk funny—lasted from 3000 to 1000 B.C. with hardly any change in the government, religion, or arts.

The first thing you'll see in the Egypt section is the **Rosetta Stone.** When this rock was unearthed in the Egyptian desert in 1799, it was a sensation in Europe. This black slab, dating from 196 B.C., caused a quantum leap in the study of ancient history. Finally, Egyptian writing could be decoded.

Next, wander past the many **statues,** including a seven-ton Ramesses, with the traditional features of a pharaoh (goatee, cloth headdress, and cobra diadem on his forehead). When Moses told the king of Egypt, "Let my people go!" this was the stony-faced look he got. You'll also see the Egyptian gods as animals—these include Amun, king of the gods, as a ram, and Horus, the god of the living, as a falcon.

At the end of the hall, climb the stairs or take the elevator to **mummy** land. To mummify a body is much like following a recipe. First, disembowel it (but leave the heart inside), then pack the cavities

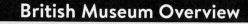

British Museum Overview

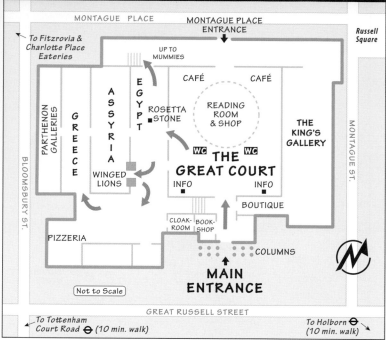

MONTAGUE PLACE

MONTAGUE PLACE ENTRANCE

Russell Square

To Fitzrovia & Charlotte Place Eateries

UP TO MUMMIES

CAFÉ   CAFÉ

PARTHENON GALLERIES

GREECE

ASSYRIA

EGYPT

ROSETTA STONE

READING ROOM & SHOP

THE KING'S GALLERY

MONTAGUE ST.

BLOOMSBURY ST.

WINGED LIONS

WC **THE GREAT COURT** WC

INFO   INFO

BOUTIQUE

PIZZERIA

CLOAK-ROOM BOOK-SHOP

COLUMNS

Not to Scale

↑ **MAIN ENTRANCE**

GREAT RUSSELL STREET

To Tottenham Court Road ⊖ (10 min. walk)

To Holborn ⊖ (10 min. walk)

with pitch, and dry it with natron, a natural form of sodium carbonate (and, I believe, the active ingredient in Twinkies). Then carefully bandage it head to toe with hundreds of yards of linen strips. Let it sit 2,000 years, and...*voilà!* The mummy was placed in a wooden coffin, which was put in a stone coffin, which was placed in a tomb. The result is that we now have Egyptian bodies that are as well preserved as Larry King. Many of the mummies here are from the time of the Roman occupation, when fine memorial portraits painted in wax became popular. X-ray photos in the display cases tell us more about these people. Don't miss the animal mummies. Cats were popular pets. They were also considered incarnations of the cat-headed goddess Bastet. Worshipped in life as the sun god's allies, preserved in death, and memorialized with statues, cats were given the adulation they've come to expect ever since.

ASSYRIA

The British Museum's valuable collection of Assyrian artifacts has become even more priceless since the recent destruction of ancient sites in the Middle East by ISIS terrorists. Long before Saddam Hussein, Iraq was home to other palace-building, iron-fisted rulers—the Assyrians, who conquered their southern neighbors and dominated the Middle East for 300 years (c. 900-600 B.C.). Their strength came from a superb army (chariots, mounted cavalry, and siege engines), a policy of terrorism against enemies ("I tied their heads to tree trunks all around the city," reads a royal inscription), ethnic cleansing and mass deportations of the vanquished, and efficient administration (roads and express postal service).

Standing guard over the Assyrian exhibit halls are two human-headed **winged lions.** These stone lions guarded

Assyrian human-headed lions

A reconstructed Greek temple

an Assyrian palace (11th-8th century B.C.). With the strength of a lion, the wings of an eagle, the brain of a man, and the beard of ZZ Top, they protected the king from evil spirits and scared the heck out of foreign ambassadors and left-wing newspaper reporters. (What has five legs and flies? Take a close look. These winged quintupeds, which appear complete from both the front and the side, could guard both directions at once.)

Carved into the stone between the bearded lions' loins, you can see one of civilization's most impressive achievements—writing. This wedge-shaped **(cuneiform)** script is the world's first written language, invented 5,000 years ago by the Sumerians (of southern Iraq) and passed down to their less-civilized descendants, the Assyrians.

The **Nimrud Gallery** is a mini version of the throne room and royal apartments of King Ashurnasirpal II's Northwest Palace at Nimrud (9th century B.C.). It's filled with royal propaganda reliefs, 30-ton marble bulls, and panels depicting wounded lions (lion-hunting was Assyria's sport of kings).

GREECE

During their civilization's Golden Age (500-430 B.C.), the ancient Greeks set the tone for all of Western civilization to follow. Democracy, theater, literature, mathematics, philosophy, science, gyros, art, and architecture as we know them, were virtually all invented by a single generation of Greeks in a small town of maybe 80,000 citizens.

Your walk through Greek art history starts with pottery, usually painted red and black, and a popular export product for the sea-trading Greeks. The earliest featured geometric patterns (eighth century B.C.), then a painted black silhouette on the natural orange clay, then a red figure on a black background. Later, painted vases show a culture really into partying.

The highlight is the **Parthenon Sculptures**—taken from the temple dedicated to Athena—the crowning glory of an enormous urban-renewal plan during Greece's Golden Age. While the building itself remains in Athens, many of the Parthenon's best sculptures are right here in the British Museum. The sculptures are also called the Elgin Marbles, named for the shrewd British ambassador who had his men hammer, chisel, and saw them off the Parthenon in the early 1800s. Though the Greek government complains about losing its marbles, the Brits feel they rescued and preserved the sculptures. These much-wrangled-over bits of the Parthenon (from about 450 B.C.) are indeed impressive. The marble panels you see lining the walls of this large hall are part of the frieze that originally ran around the exterior of the Parthenon, under the eaves. The statues at either end of the hall once filled the Parthenon's triangular-shaped pediments and showed the birth of Athena. The relief panels known as metopes tell the story of the struggle between the forces of human civilization and animal-like barbarism.

THE REST OF THE MUSEUM

Venture upstairs to see artifacts from **Roman Britain** that surpass anything at Hadrian's Wall or elsewhere in the country. Also look for the Sutton Hoo Ship Burial artifacts from a seventh-century royal burial on the east coast of England (Room 41). A rare Michelangelo cartoon (preliminary sketch) is in Room 90 (level 4).

▲▲▲BRITISH LIBRARY

Here, in just two rooms, are the literary treasures of Western civilization, from early Bibles to Shakespeare's *Hamlet* to Lewis Carroll's *Alice's Adventures in Wonderland* to the *Magna Carta*. You'll see the Lindisfarne Gospels transcribed on an illuminated manuscript, Beatles lyrics scrawled on the back of a greeting card, and Leonardo da Vinci's genius sketched into his notebooks. The British Empire built its greatest monuments out of paper.

Cost and Hours: Free, £5 suggested donation, admission charged for special exhibits; Mon-Fri 9:30-18:00, Tue-Thu until 20:00, Sat until 17:00, Sun 11:00-17:00; 96 Euston Road, Tube: King's Cross St. Pancras or Euston, tel. 019/3754-6060 or 020/7412-7676, www.bl.uk.

The British Library is filled with treasures ranging from the Magna Carta to Beatles song sheets.

Tours: There are no guided tours or audioguides for the permanent collection, but you can 🎧 download my free British Library **audio tour.** Touch-screen computers in the permanent collection let you page virtually through some of the rare books.

❯ SELF-GUIDED TOUR

Everything that matters for your visit is in a tiny but exciting area variously called "The Sir John Ritblat Gallery," "Treasures of the British Library," or just "The Treasures." We'll concentrate on a handful of documents—literary and historical—that changed the course of history. Note that exhibits change often, and many of the museum's old, fragile manuscripts need to "rest" periodically in order to stay well-preserved.

Upon entering the Ritblat Gallery, start at the far side of the room with the display case of historic ❶ **maps** showing how humans' perspective of the world expanded over the centuries. Next, move into the area dedicated to ❷ **sacred texts and early Bibles** from several cultures, including the Codex Sinaiticus. This early bound book from around A.D. 350 is one of the oldest complete Bibles in existence. In the display cases called ❸ **Art of the Book,** you'll find beautifully illustrated, or "illuminated," Bibles from the early medieval period, including the Lindisfarne Gospels (A.D. 698). Look out for some Early English Bibles—the King James Version, the Wycliffe Bible, or others—dating from the 15th, 16th, and 17th centuries.

In the glass cases featuring early ❹ **printing,** you'll see the Gutenberg Bible, the first book printed in Europe using movable type (c. 1455)—a revolutionary document. Suddenly, the Bible was available for anyone to read, fueling the Protestant Reformation.

Through a nearby doorway is a small room that holds versions of the ❺ **Magna Carta,** assuming they're not "resting" when you visit (though historians talk about *the* Magna Carta, several different versions of the document exist). The basis for England's constitutional system of Government, this "Great Charter" listing rules about mundane administrative issues was radical because of the simple fact that the king had agreed to abide by them as law.

Return to the main room to find display cases featuring trailblazing ❻ **art and science** documents by early scientists such as Galileo, Isaac Newton, and many more. Pages from Leonardo da Vinci's notebook show his powerful curiosity, his genius for invention, and his famous backward and inside-out handwriting. Nearby are many more ❼ **historical documents.** The displays change frequently, but you may see letters by Henry VIII, Queen Elizabeth I, Darwin, Freud, Gandhi, and others.

Next, trace the evolution of ❽ **English literature.** Check out the A.D. 1000 manuscript of *Beowulf,* the first English literary masterpiece, and *The Canterbury Tales* (c. 1410), Geoffrey Chaucer's bawdy collection of stories.

The only known manuscript of the epic saga Beowulf

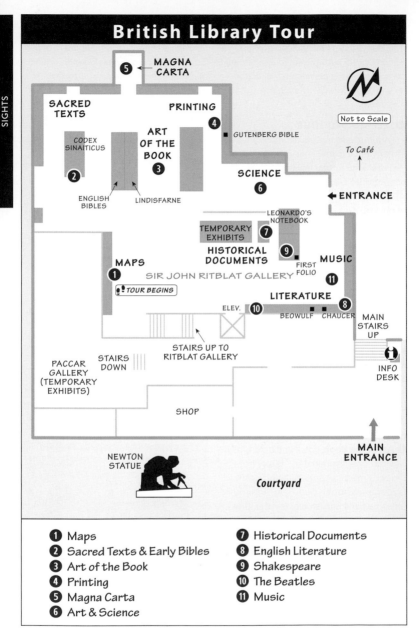

British Library Tour

MAGNA CARTA

SACRED TEXTS

PRINTING

CODEX SINAITICUS

ART OF THE BOOK

GUTENBERG BIBLE

To Café

SCIENCE

ENGLISH BIBLES   LINDISFARNE

ENTRANCE

LEONARDO'S NOTEBOOK

TEMPORARY EXHIBITS

HISTORICAL DOCUMENTS

MUSIC

MAPS

SIR JOHN RITBLAT GALLERY

FIRST FOLIO

LITERATURE

TOUR BEGINS

ELEV.

BEOWULF   CHAUCER

MAIN STAIRS UP

STAIRS UP TO RITBLAT GALLERY

INFO DESK

PACCAR GALLERY (TEMPORARY EXHIBITS)

STAIRS DOWN

SHOP

MAIN ENTRANCE

NEWTON STATUE

Courtyard

Not to Scale

① Maps
② Sacred Texts & Early Bibles
③ Art of the Book
④ Printing
⑤ Magna Carta
⑥ Art & Science

⑦ Historical Documents
⑧ English Literature
⑨ Shakespeare
⑩ The Beatles
⑪ Music

Lewis Carroll's manuscript for Alice's Adventures in Wonderland

The Literature wall is often a greatest-hits sampling of literature in English, from Brontë to Kipling to Woolf to Joyce to Dickens. The original *Alice's Adventures in Wonderland* by Lewis Carroll created a fantasy world, where grown-up rules and logic were turned upside down. The most famous of England's writers—❾ Shakespeare—generally gets his own display case. Look for the First Folio—one of the 750 copies of the first complete collection of his plays, published in 1623.

Now fast-forward a few centuries to ❿ The Beatles. Look for photos of John Lennon, Paul McCartney, George Harrison, and Ringo Starr before and after their fame, as well as manuscripts of song lyrics written by Lennon and McCartney. In the ⓫ music section, there are manuscripts by Mozart, Beethoven, Schubert, and others (kind of an anticlimax after the Fab Four, I know). George Frideric Handel's famous oratorio, the *Messiah* (1741), is often on display and marks the end of our tour. Hallelujah.

▲MADAME TUSSAUDS WAXWORKS

This waxtravaganza is gimmicky, crass, and crazily expensive, but dang fun...a hit with the kind of tourists who skip the British Museum. The original Madame Tussaud did wax casts of heads lopped off during the French Revolution (such as Marie-Antoinette's). She took her show on the road and ended up in London in 1835. Now it's all about singing with Lady Gaga, partying with Benedict Cumberbatch, and hanging with the Beatles. In addition to posing with all the eerily realistic wax dummies—from the Queen and Will and Kate to the Beckhams—you'll have the chance to learn how they created this waxy army; hop on a people-mover and cruise through a kid-pleasing "Spirit of London" time trip; and visit with Spider-Man, the Hulk, and other Marvel superheroes. A nine-minute "4-D" show features a 3-D movie heightened by wind, "back ticklers," and other special effects.

Rick's Tip: *To* skip Madame Tussauds' ticket-buying line *(which can be an hour or more), purchase a Fast Track ticket in advance (available from souvenir shops or at the TI), or consider getting the pricey* Priority Entrance *ticket and reserving a time slot at least a day in advance. The place is less crowded if you arrive after 15:00.*

Cost: £35, kids-£30 (free for kids under 5), up to 25 percent discount and shorter lines if you buy tickets in advance on their website; combo-deal with the London Eye.

Hours: Roughly July-Aug and school holidays daily 8:30-18:00, Sept-June Mon-Fri 10:00-16:00, Sat-Sun 9:00-17:00, these are last entry times—it stays open roughly two hours later; check website for the latest times as hours vary widely depending on season, Marylebone Road, Tube: Baker Street, tel. 0871-894-3000, www.madametussauds.com.

The Beatles at Madame Tussauds

The City

When Londoners say "The City," they mean the one-square-mile business center in East London that 2,000 years ago was Roman Londinium. The outline of the Roman city walls can still be seen in the arc of roads from Blackfriars Bridge to Tower Bridge. It's a fascinating district to wander on weekdays, but since almost nobody actually lives there, it's dull in the evening and on Saturday and Sunday.

You can 🎧 download my free audio tour of The City, which peels back the many layers of history in this oldest part of London.

▲▲▲ST. PAUL'S CATHEDRAL

Sir Christopher Wren's most famous church is the great St. Paul's, its elaborate interior capped by a 365-foot dome. There's been a church on this spot since 604. After the Great Fire of 1666 destroyed the old cathedral, Wren created this Baroque masterpiece. And since World War II, St. Paul's has been Britain's symbol of resilience. Despite 57 nights of bombing, the Nazis failed to destroy the cathedral, thanks to St. Paul's volunteer fire watchmen, who stayed on the dome.

Even now, as skyscrapers encroach, the 365-foot-high dome of St. Paul's rises majestically above the rooftops of the neighborhood. The tall dome is set on classical columns, capped with a lantern, topped by a six-foot ball, and iced with a cross. As the first Anglican cathedral built in London after the Reformation, it is Baroque: St. Peter's in Rome filtered through clear-eyed English reason. Though often the site of historic funerals (Queen Victoria and Winston Churchill), St. Paul's most famous ceremony was a wedding—when Prince Charles married Lady Diana Spencer in 1981.

Cost and Hours: £18, £16 in advance online, includes church entry, dome climb, crypt, tour, and audio/videoguide; Mon-Sat 8:30-16:30 (dome opens at 9:30), closed Sun except for worship; book ahead online to skip the line, 15-30-minute wait at busy times; Tube: St. Paul's; recorded info tel. 020/7246-8348, reception tel. 020/7246-8350, www.stpauls.co.uk.

Music and Church Services: Worship times are available on the church's website. Communion is generally Mon-Sat

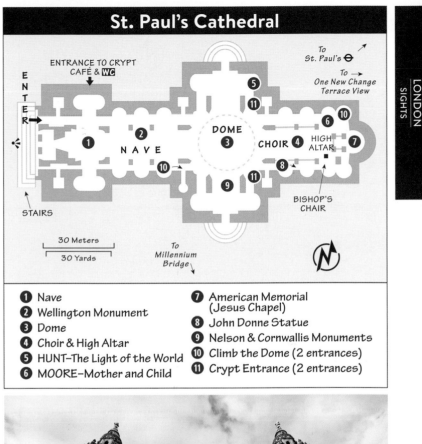

St. Paul's Cathedral

ENTRANCE TO CRYPT
CAFÉ & **WC**

ENTER

To
St. Paul's Ⓔ

To →
One New Change
Terrace View

DOME ③

NAVE

CHOIR ④ HIGH
ALTAR

STAIRS

BISHOP'S
CHAIR

30 Meters
30 Yards

To
Millennium
Bridge ↓

Ⓝ

① Nave
② Wellington Monument
③ Dome
④ Choir & High Altar
⑤ HUNT–The Light of the World
⑥ MOORE–Mother and Child

⑦ American Memorial
(Jesus Chapel)
⑧ John Donne Statue
⑨ Nelson & Cornwallis Monuments
⑩ Climb the Dome (2 entrances)
⑪ Crypt Entrance (2 entrances)

Majestic St. Paul's Cathedral is one of London's most iconic buildings.

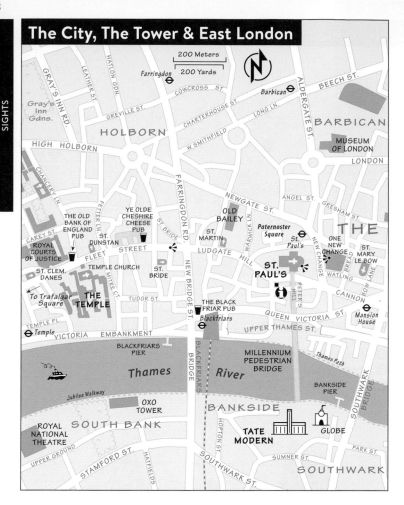

The City, The Tower & East London

at 8:00 and 12:30. On Sunday, services are held at 8:00, 10:15 (Matins), 11:30 (sung Eucharist), 15:15 (evensong), and 18:00. The rest of the week, evensong is at 17:00 (Mon is spoken—not sung). For more on evensong, see page 104. On some Sundays, there's a free organ recital at 16:45.

Rick's Tip: *If you come to St. Paul's 20 minutes* **early for evensong worship** *(under the dome), you may be able to grab a big wooden stall in the choir, next to the singers.*

Tours: Admission includes an **audio-guide** (with video clips), as well as a 1.5-hour guided **tour** (Mon-Sat at 10:00, 11:00, 13:00, and 14:00; call 020/7246-8357 to confirm or ask at church). Free 20-minute **introductory talks** are offered throughout the day. You can also 🎧 download my free St. Paul's Cathedral **audio tour**.

⊙ SELF-GUIDED TOUR

Enter, buy your ticket, pick up the free visitor's map, and stand at the far back of the ➊ **nave,** behind the font. This big church feels big. At 515 feet long and 250 feet wide, it's Europe's fourth largest, after

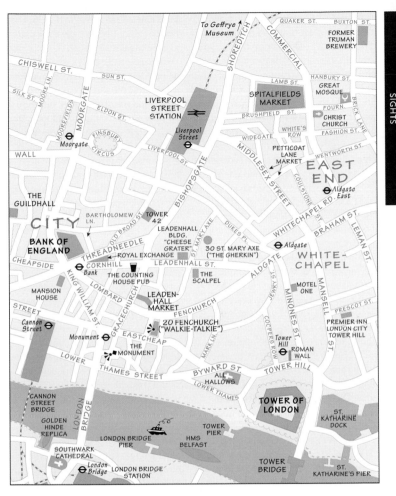

those in Rome (St. Peter's), Sevilla, and Milan. The spaciousness is accentuated by the relative lack of decoration. The simple, cream-colored ceiling and the clear glass in the windows light everything evenly. Wren wanted this: a simple, open church with nothing to hide. Unfortunately, only this entrance area keeps his original vision—the rest was encrusted with 19th-century Victorian ornamentation.

Ahead and on the left is the towering, black-and-white ❷ **Wellington Monument.** Wren would have been appalled, but his church has become

so central to England's soul that many national heroes are buried here (in the basement crypt).

The ❸ **dome** you see from here, painted with scenes from the life of St. Paul, is only the innermost of three. From the painted interior of the first dome, look up through the opening to see the light-filled lantern of the second dome. Finally, the whole thing is covered on the outside by the third and final dome, the shell of lead-covered wood that you see from the street. Wren's ingenious three-in-one design was psychological as well as functional—he wanted a low, shallow inner dome so worshippers wouldn't feel diminished. The ❹ **choir** area blocks your way, but you can see the altar at the far end under a golden canopy.

Do a quick clockwise spin around the church. In the north transept (to your left as you face the altar), find the big painting ❺ *The Light of the World* (1904), by the Pre-Raphaelite William Holman Hunt. Inspired by Hunt's own experience of finding Christ during a moment of spiritual crisis, the crowd-pleasing work was criticized by art highbrows for being "syrupy" and "simple"—even as it became the most famous painting in Victorian England.

Along the left side of the choir is the modern statue ❻ *Mother and Child,* by the great modern sculptor Henry Moore. Typical of Moore's work, this Mary and Baby Jesus—inspired by the sight of British moms nursing babies in WWII bomb shelters—renders a traditional subject in an abstract, minimalist way.

The area behind the altar, with three bright and modern stained-glass windows, is the ❼ **American Memorial Chapel**— honoring the Americans who sacrificed their lives to save Britain in World War II. In colored panes that arch around the big windows, spot the American eagle (center window, to the left of Christ), George Washington (right window, upper-right corner), and symbols of all 50 states (find your state seal). In the carved wood beneath the windows, you'll see

birds and foliage native to the US. The Roll of Honor (a 500-page book under glass immediately behind the altar) lists the names of 28,000 US servicemen and women based in Britain who gave their lives during the war.

Around the other side of the choir is a shrouded statue honoring ❽ **John Donne** (1621–1631), a passionate preacher in old St. Paul's, as well as a great poet ("never wonder for whom the bell tolls—it tolls for thee"). In the south transept are monuments to military greats ❾ **Horatio Nelson,** who fought Napoleon, and **Charles Cornwallis,** who was finished off by George Washington at Yorktown.

❿ **Climbing the Dome:** You can climb 528 steps to reach the dome and great city views. Along the way, have some fun in the **Whispering Gallery** (257 steps up). Whisper sweet nothings into the wall, and your partner (and anyone else) standing far away can hear you. For best effects, try whispering (not talking) with your mouth close to the wall, while your partner stands a few dozen yards away with his or her ear to the wall.

⓫ **Visiting the Crypt:** The crypt is a world of historic bones and interesting cathedral models. Many legends are buried here—Horatio Nelson, who wore down Napoleon; the Duke of Wellington, who finished Napoleon off; and even Wren himself. Wren's actual tomb is marked by a simple black slab with no statue, though he considered this church

The cathedral's interior is dazzling.

Views from St. Paul's dome are worth the climb.

London's Best Views

For some viewpoints, you need to pay admission. At the bars or restaurants, you'll need to buy a drink. The only truly free spots are Primrose Hill, One New Change Rooftop Terrace, and the Sky Garden at 20 Fenchurch.

London Eye: Ride the giant Ferris wheel for stunning London views. See page 87.

St. Paul's Dome: You'll earn a striking, unobstructed view by climbing hundreds of steps to the cramped balcony of the church's cupola.

One New Change Rooftop Terrace: Get fine, free views of St. Paul's Cathedral and surroundings—nearly as good as those from St. Paul's Dome—from the rooftop terrace of the One New Change shopping mall just behind and east of the church.

Tate Modern: Take in a classic vista across the Thames from the restaurant/bar on the museum's sixth level and from the new Blavatnik Building (a.k.a. the Switch House). See page 90.

20 Fenchurch (a.k.a. "The Walkie-Talkie"): Get 360-degree views of London from the mostly enclosed Sky Garden. It's free, but you'll need to make reservations in advance and bring photo ID (Mon-Fri 10:00-18:00, Sat-Sun 11:00-21:00, 20 Fenchurch Street, Tube: Monument, www.skygarden.london).

National Portrait Gallery: A mod top-floor restaurant peers over Trafalgar Square and the Westminster neighborhood.

Waterstones Bookstore: Its hip, low-key, top-floor café/bar has reasonable prices and sweeping views of the London Eye, Big Ben, and the Houses of Parliament (Mon-Sat 9:00-22:00, Sun 12:00-18:30, café closes hour earlier on Sun, 203 Piccadilly, www.5thview.co.uk).

The Shard: The observation decks that cap this 1,020-foot-tall skyscraper offer London's most commanding views in clear weather, but at a steep price (£31, less if booked online at least a day in advance; daily 10:00-22:00, shorter hours Oct-March; Tube: London Bridge—use London Bridge exit and follow signs, www.theviewfromtheshard.com).

to be his legacy. Back up in the nave, on the floor directly under the dome, is Christopher Wren's name and epitaph (written in Latin): "Reader, if you seek his monument, look around you."

▲MUSEUM OF LONDON

This museum tells the fascinating story of London, taking you on a walk from its pre-Roman beginnings to the present. It features London's distinguished citizens through history—from Neanderthals, to Romans, to Elizabethans, to Victorians, to Mods, to today. The displays are chronological, spacious, and informative without being overwhelming. Scale models and costumes help you visualize everyday life in the city at different periods. There are enough whiz-bang multimedia displays (including the Plague and the Great Fire) to spice up otherwise humdrum artifacts. This regular stop for the local school kids gives the best overview of London history in town.

Cost and Hours: Free, daily 10:00-18:00, last entry one hour before closing, see the day's events board for special talks and tours, café, baggage lockers, 150 London Wall at Aldersgate Street, Tube: Barbican or St. Paul's plus a 5-minute walk, tel. 020/7001-9844, www.museumoflondon.org.uk.

THE MONUMENT

Wren's recently restored 202-foot-tall tribute to London's 1666 Great Fire is at the junction of Monument Street and Fish Street Hill. Climb the 311 steps inside the column for a monumental view of The City (£4.50, £11 combo-ticket with Tower Bridge, cash only, daily 9:30-18:00, until 17:30 Oct-March, Tube: Monument).

▲▲▲TOWER OF LONDON

The Tower has served as a castle in wartime, a king's residence in peacetime, and, most notoriously, as the prison and execution site of rebels. You can see the crown jewels, take a witty Beefeater tour, and ponder the executioner's block

Tower of London

that dispensed with Anne Boleyn, Sir Thomas More, and troublesome heirs to the throne.

Cost and Hours: £28, family-£70, entry fee includes Beefeater tour (described later), Tue-Sat 9:00-17:30, Sun-Mon from 10:00, Nov-Feb until 16:30, skippable audioguide-£4; Tube: Tower Hill, tel. 0844-482-7788, www.hrp.org.uk.

Advance Tickets: To avoid the long ticket-buying lines, and save a few pounds off the gate price, buy a **voucher** in advance. You can purchase vouchers at the Trader's Gate gift shop, located down the steps from the Tower Hill Tube stop (pick it up on your way to the Tower; vouchers here can be used any day), or on the Tower website (£24, family-£59, vouchers purchased online are valid any day up to 7 days after the date you select). All vouchers, regardless of where purchased, must be exchanged for tickets at the Tower's group ticket office (see map). You can also try buying tickets, with credit card only, at the Tower Welcome Centre to the left of the normal ticket lines—though on busy days they may turn you away. Tickets are also sold by phone (tel. 0844-482-7788 within UK or tel. 011-44-20-3166-6000 from the US; £2 fee, pick up your tickets at the Tower's group ticket office).

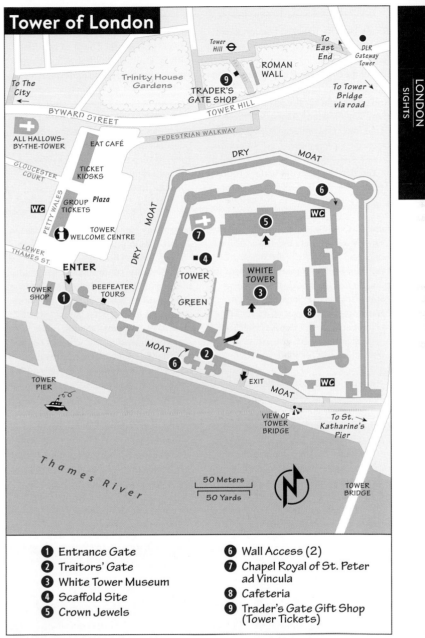

Tower of London

To The City ←

BYWARD STREET

Tower Hill ⊖

To East End →

● DLR Gateway Tower

ROMAN WALL

⑨ TRADER'S GATE SHOP

TOWER HILL

To Tower Bridge via road →

Trinity House Gardens

PEDESTRIAN WALKWAY

ALL HALLOWS-BY-THE-TOWER

EAT CAFÉ

GLOUCESTER COURT

TICKET KIOSKS

DRY   MOAT

WC

PETTY WALES

GROUP TICKETS

Plaza

⑥

DRY

⑤

WC

TOWER WELCOME CENTRE

⑦

LOWER THAMES ST.

ENTER

⑦

④

WHITE TOWER

③

TOWER SHOP ①

BEEFEATER TOURS

TOWER GREEN

⑧

MOAT

⑥ ②

EXIT

MOAT

WC

TOWER PIER

VIEW OF TOWER BRIDGE

To St. Katharine's Pier →

Thames River

50 Meters

50 Yards

Ⓝ

TOWER BRIDGE

① Entrance Gate
② Traitors' Gate
③ White Tower Museum
④ Scaffold Site
⑤ Crown Jewels

⑥ Wall Access (2)
⑦ Chapel Royal of St. Peter ad Vincula
⑧ Cafeteria
⑨ Trader's Gate Gift Shop (Tower Tickets)

Rick's Tip: *The* **Tower of London** *is most crowded in summer, on weekends (especially Sundays), and during school holidays. The line for the crown jewels can be just as long as the line for tickets.* **Arrive before 10:00 and go straight for the jewels.** *Alternatively, arrive in the afternoon, tour the rest of the Tower first, and see the jewels an hour before closing time, when crowds die down.*

Yeoman Warder (Beefeater) Tours:

Today, while the Tower's military purpose is history, it's still home to the Beefeaters—the 35 Yeoman Warders and their families. (The original duty of the Yeoman Warders was to guard the Tower, its prisoners, and the jewels.) Free, worthwhile, one-hour Beefeater tours leave every 30 minutes from just inside the entrance gate (first tour Tue-Sat at 10:00, Sun-Mon at 10:30, last one at 15:30—or 14:30 in Nov-Feb). The boisterous Beefeaters are great entertainers, whose historical talks include lots of bloody anecdotes and corny jokes.

Sunday Worship: For a refreshingly different Tower experience, come on Sunday morning, when visitors are welcome on the grounds for free to worship in the Chapel Royal of St. Peter ad Vincula. You get in without the lines, but you can only see the chapel—no sightseeing (9:15 Communion or 11:00 service with fine choral music, meet at west gate 30 minutes early, dress for church, may be closed for ceremonies—call ahead).

Rick's Tip: *To scenically—though circuitously—connect the* **Tower of London with St. Paul's Cathedral,** *detour through Southwark on the South Bank (and stop by Borough Market for the fun food scene).*

Visiting the Tower: William the Conqueror, still getting used to his new title, built the stone "White Tower" (1077-1097) to keep the Londoners in line, a gleaming reminder of the monarch's absolute power. You could be feasting on roast boar in the banqueting hall one night and chained to the walls of the prison the next. The Tower also served as an effective lookout for seeing invaders coming up the Thames.

This square, 90-foot-tall tower was the original structure that gave this castle complex of 20 towers its name. William's successors enlarged the complex to its present 18-acre size. Because of the security it provided, the Tower of London served over the centuries as a royal residence, the Royal Mint, the Royal Jewel House, and, most famously, as a prison and execution site.

You'll find more bloody history per square inch in this original tower of power than anywhere else in Britain. Inside the White Tower is a **museum** with exhibits re-creating medieval life and chronicling the torture and executions that took place here. In the Royal Armory, you'll see some suits of armor of Henry VIII—slender in his youth (c. 1515), heavyset by

A Beefeater on duty

Execution ax and block

Henry VIII (1491-1547)

The notorious king who single-handedly transformed England was a true Renaissance Man—six feet tall, handsome, charismatic, well-educated, and brilliant. He spoke English, Latin, French, and Spanish. A legendary athlete, he hunted, played tennis, and jousted with knights and kings. When 17-year-old Henry, the second monarch of the House of Tudor, was crowned king in Westminster Abbey, all of England rejoiced.

Henry left affairs of state to others, and filled his days with sports, war, dice, women, and the arts. But in 1529, Henry changed the course of history. He wanted a divorce: His wife had become too old to bear him a son, and he'd fallen in love with Anne Boleyn. Henry begged the pope for an annulment, but—for political reasons—the pope refused. Henry divorced his wife anyway, and he was excommunicated.

Henry's rejection of papal authority sparked the English Reformation. He forced monasteries to close, sold off some church land, and confiscated everything else for himself and the Crown. Within a decade, monastic institutions that had operated for centuries were left empty and gutted. Meanwhile, the Catholic Church was reorganized into the (Anglican) Church of England, with Henry as its head. Though Henry himself basically adhered to Catholic doctrine, he discouraged the veneration of saints and relics, and commissioned an English translation of the Bible.

Henry famously had six wives. The issue was not his love life (which could have been satisfied by his numerous mistresses), but the politics of royal succession. To guarantee the Tudor family's dominance, he needed a male heir born by a recognized queen. Henry's first marriage, to Catherine of Aragon, had been arranged to cement an alliance with her parents, Ferdinand and Isabel of Spain. Catherine bore Henry a daughter, but no sons. Next came Anne Boleyn, who also gave birth to a daughter. After a turbulent few years with Anne and several miscarriages, a frustrated Henry had her beheaded. His next wife, Jane Seymour, finally had a son (but Jane died soon after giving birth). A blind-marriage with Anne of Cleves ended quickly when she proved to be both politically useless and ugly. Next, teen bride Catherine Howard ended up cheating on Henry, so she was executed. Henry finally found comfort—but no children—in his later years with his final wife, Catherine Parr.

Henry's last years were marked by paranoia, sudden rages, and despotism. He gave his perceived enemies the pink slip in his signature way—charged with treason and beheaded. Once-wealthy England was becoming depleted, thanks to Henry's expensive habits, which included making war on France, building and acquiring 50 palaces, and collecting fine tapestries and archery bows.

Henry forged a large legacy. He expanded the power of the monarchy, making himself the focus of a rising, modern nation-state. Simultaneously, he strengthened Parliament—largely because it agreed with his policies. He annexed Wales, and imposed English rule on Ireland (provoking centuries of resentment). He expanded the navy, paving the way for Britannia to soon rule the waves. And—thanks to Henry's marital woes—England would forever be a Protestant nation.

1540—with his bigger-is-better codpiece. On the top floor, see the Tower's actual execution ax and chopping block. The **scaffold site,** however, in the middle of Tower Green, looks pleasant enough today. Henry VIII axed a couple of his ex-wives here, including Anne Boleyn and Catherine Howard.

Across from the White Tower is the entrance to the **crown jewels.** The Sovereign's Scepter is encrusted with the world's largest cut diamond—the 530-carat Star of Africa, beefy as a quarter-pounder. The Crown of the Queen Mother (Elizabeth II's famous mum, who died in 2002) has the 106-carat Koh-I-Noor diamond glittering on the front (considered unlucky for male rulers, it only adorns the crown of the king's wife). The Imperial State Crown is what the Queen wears for official functions such as the State Opening of Parliament. Among its 3,733 jewels are Queen Elizabeth I's former earrings (the hanging pearls, top center), a stunning 13th-century ruby look-alike in the center, and Edward the Confessor's ring (the blue sapphire on top, in the center of the Maltese cross of diamonds).

At the far end of the Tower Green is the **Bloody Tower,** and beyond that, the **Medieval Palace.** From the medieval palace's throne room you can continue up the stairs to **walk the walls.** The Tower was defended by state-of-the-art walls and fortifications in the 13th century. Walking along them offers a good look at the walls, along with a fine view of the famous Tower Bridge, with its twin towers and blue spans.

TOWER BRIDGE

The iconic Tower Bridge (often mistakenly called London Bridge) was built in 1894 to accommodate the growing East End. While fully modern and hydraulically powered, the drawbridge was designed with a retro Neo-Gothic look. The bridge is most interesting when the drawbridge lifts to let ships pass, as it does a thousand times a year (best viewed from the Tower side of the Thames). For the bridge-lifting schedule, check the website or call.

You can tour the bridge at the **Tower Bridge Exhibition,** with a history display

The Tower Bridge has spanned the Thames since 1894.

and a peek at the Victorian-era engine room that lifts the span. Included in your entrance is the chance to cross the bridge—138 feet above the road along a partially see-through glass walkway. As an exhibit, it's overpriced, though the adrenaline rush and spectacular city views from the walkway may help justify the cost.

Cost and Hours: £9, £11 combo-ticket with The Monument, daily 10:00-18:00 in summer, 9:30-17:30 in winter, enter at northwest tower, Tube: Tower Hill, tel. 020/7403-3761, www.towerbridge.org.uk.

On the South Bank

The South Bank of the Thames is a thriving arts and cultural center, tied together by the riverfront Jubilee Walkway. For fun lunch options in this area, consider one of the nearby street food markets.

▲JUBILEE WALKWAY

This riverside path is a popular pub-crawling pedestrian promenade that stretches all along the South Bank, offering grand views of the Houses of Parliament and St. Paul's. On a sunny day, this is the place to see Londoners out strolling. The Walkway hugs the river except just east of London Bridge, where it cuts inland for a couple of blocks. It has been expanded into a 60-mile "Greenway" circling the city, including the 2012 Olympics site.

Rick's Tip: *If you're visiting London in summer,* **visit the South Bank after hours.** *Take a trip around the* **London Eye at sunset** *(the wheel spins until late—last ascent at 20:30, later in July-Aug). Then cap your night with a stroll along the* **Jubilee Walkway.**

▲▲LONDON EYE

This giant Ferris wheel, towering above London opposite Big Ben, is one of the world's highest observational wheels and London's answer to the Eiffel Tower. Riding it is a memorable experience, even though London doesn't have much of a skyline, and the price is borderline outrageous. Whether you ride or not, the wheel is a sight to behold.

Twenty-eight people ride in each of its

The London Eye adds whimsical fun to London's stately skyline.

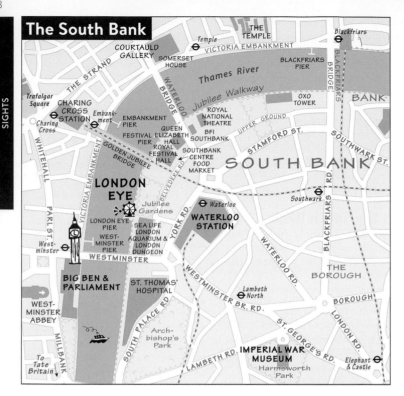

The South Bank

THE
TEMPLE

Temple
VICTORIA EMBANKMENT

Blackfriars

COURTAULD
GALLERY

SOMERSET
HOUSE

BLACKFRIARS
PIER

BLACKFRIARS PIER

BLACKFRIARS
BRIDGE

THE STRAND

WATERLOO BRIDGE

Thames River

Jubilee Walkway

Trafalgar
Square

CHARING
CROSS
STATION

Embankment

EMBANKMENT
PIER

OXO
TOWER

BANK

Charing
Cross

Embankment

QUEEN
FESTIVAL
PIER

ROYAL
NATIONAL
THEATRE

UPPER GROUND

VICTORIA EMBANKMENT

ELIZABETH
HALL

BFI
SOUTHBANK

STAMFORD ST.

SOUTHWARK ST.

ROYAL
FESTIVAL
HALL

SOUTHBANK
CENTRE
FOOD
MARKET

SOUTH BANK

GOLDEN JUBILEE
BRIDGE

LONDON
EYE

Jubilee
Gardens

BELVEDERE RD.

Waterloo

Southwark

BLACKFRIARS RD.

WHITEHALL

PARL ST.

LONDON EYE
PIER

SEA LIFE
LONDON
AQUARIUM &
LONDON
DUNGEON

YORK RD.

WATERLOO
STATION

WEST-
MINSTER
PIER

West-
minster

WESTMINSTER

WATERLOO RD.

WESTMINSTER BR. RD.

THE
BOROUGH

BIG BEN &
PARLIAMENT

ST. THOMAS'
HOSPITAL

Lambeth
North

BOROUGH

WEST-
MINSTER
ABBEY

LONDON RD.

ST. GEORGE'S RD.

Elephant
& Castle

MILLBANK

SOUTH PALACE RD.

Arch-
bishop's
Park

LAMBETH RD.

IMPERIAL WAR
MUSEUM

Harmsworth
Park

To
Tate
Britain

32 air-conditioned capsules (representing the boroughs of London) for the 30-minute rotation (you go around only once). From the top of this 443-foot-high wheel—the second-highest public viewpoint in the city—even Big Ben looks small.

Cost: £24.95, about 10 percent cheaper if bought online. Combo-tickets save money if you plan on visiting Madame Tussauds. Buy tickets in advance at www.londoneye.com or try in person at the box office (in the corner of the County Hall building nearest the Eye), though day-of tickets are often sold out.

Hours: Daily June-Aug 10:00-20:30 or later, Sept-May generally 11:00-18:00, check website for latest schedule, these are last-ascent times, closed Dec 25 and a few days in Jan for maintenance, Tube: Waterloo or Westminster. Thames boats come and go from London Eye Pier at the foot of the wheel.

Rick's Tip: *The* **London Eye** *is busiest between 11:00 and 17:00, especially on weekends year-round and every day in July and August.* **Go online to book your ticket,** *then print it at home, retrieve it from an onsite ticket machine (bring your payment card and confirmation code), or stand in the "Ticket Collection" line. Even if you buy in advance, you may wait a bit to board the wheel (but it's not worth paying extra for a Fast Track ticket).*

▲▲IMPERIAL WAR MUSEUM

This impressive museum covers the wars of the 20th and 21st centuries—from World War I biplanes, to the rise of fascism, the Cold War, the Cuban Missile Crisis, the Troubles in Northern Ireland, the wars in Iraq and Afghanistan, and terrorism. Rather than glorify war, the

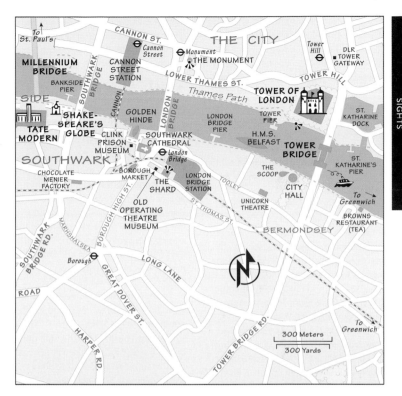

museum encourages an understanding of the history of modern warfare and the wartime experience, including the effect it has on the everyday lives of people back home. The museum's coverage never neglects the human side of one of civilization's more uncivilized, persistent traits.

Allow plenty of time, as this powerful museum—with lots of artifacts and video clips—can be engrossing. War wonks love the place, as do general history buffs who enjoy patiently reading displays. For the rest, there are enough interactive experiences and multimedia exhibits and submarines for the kids to climb in to keep it interesting.

Cost and Hours: Free, £5 suggested donation, special exhibits extra, daily 10:00-18:00, last entry one hour before closing, Tube: Lambeth North or Elephant and Castle; buses #3, #12, and #159 from Westminster area; tel. 020/7416-5000, www.iwm.org.uk.

◆ SELF-GUIDED TOUR

Start with the atrium to grasp the massive scale of warfare as you wander among and under notable battle machines, then head directly for the museum's recently renovated **WWI galleries.** Here firsthand accounts connect the blunt reality of a brutal war with the contributions, heartache, and efforts of a nation.

Imperial War Museum

How different this museum would be if the war to end all wars had lived up to its name. Instead, the museum, much like history, builds on itself. Ascending to the first floor, you'll find the permanent **Turning Points** galleries progressing up to and through World War II, including sections explaining the Blitzkrieg and its effects (see an actual Nazi parachute bomb like the ones that devastated London). The **Family in Wartime** exhibit shows London through the eyes of an ordinary family.

The second floor houses the **Secret War** exhibit, which peeks into the intrigues of espionage in World Wars I and II through present-day security. You'll learn about MI5 (Britain's domestic spy corps), MI6 (their international spies—like the CIA), and the Special Operations Executive (SOE), who led espionage efforts during World War II.

The third floor houses various (and often rotating) temporary art and film exhibits speckled with military-themed works including (when not on its own tour of duty) **John Singer Sargent**'s *Gassed* (1919), showing besieged troops in World War I.

The fourth-floor section on the **Holocaust,** one of the best on the subject anywhere, tells the story with powerful videos, artifacts, and fine explanations.

Crowning the museum on the fifth floor is the Lord Ashcroft Gallery and the **Extraordinary Heroes** display. Here, more than 250 stories celebrate Britain's highest military award for bravery with the world's largest collection of Victoria Cross medals. Civilians who earned the George Cross medal for bravery are also honored.

▲▲TATE MODERN

Dedicated in the spring of 2000, the striking museum fills a derelict old power station across the river from St. Paul's—it opened the new century with art from the previous one. Its powerhouse collection includes Dalí, Picasso, Warhol, and much more.

Cost and Hours: Free, £4 donation appreciated, fee for special exhibits; open daily 10:00-18:00, Fri-Sat until 22:00, last entry to special exhibits 45 minutes before closing, especially crowded on weekend days (crowds thin out Fri and Sat evenings); view restaurant on top floor; tel. 020/7887-8888, www.tate.org.uk.

Tours: Multimedia guide-£4.75, free 45-minute guided tours at 11:00, 12:00, 14:00, and 15:00.

Getting There: Cross the Millennium Bridge from St. Paul's; take the Tube to Southwark, London Bridge, St. Paul's, Mansion House, or Blackfriars and walk 10-15 minutes; or catch Thames Clippers' Tate Boat ferry from the Tate Britain (Millbank Pier) for a 15-minute crossing (£8 one-way, every 40 minutes Mon-Fri 10:00-16:00, Sat-Sun 9:15-18:40, www.tate.org.uk/visit/tate-boat).

Visiting the Museum: The permanent collection is generally arranged according to theme—such as "Poetry and Dream"—not chronologically or by artist. Paintings by Picasso, for example, are scattered all

Imperial War Museum atrium

Tate Modern

over the building. Don't just come to see the Old Masters of modernism. Push your mental envelope with more recent works by Miró, Bacon, Picabia, Beuys, Twombly, and others.

Temporary exhibits are cutting-edge. Each year, the main hall features a different monumental installation by a prominent artist. The Tate recently opened a new wing to the south: This new Blavatnik Building (Switch House) gave the Tate an extra quarter-million square feet of display space. Besides showing off more of the Tate's impressive collection, the space hosts changing themed exhibitions, performance art, experimental film, and interactive sculpture incorporating light and sound.

▲MILLENNIUM BRIDGE

The pedestrian bridge links St. Paul's Cathedral and the Tate Modern across the Thames. This is London's first new bridge in a century, nicknamed the "blade of light" for its sleek minimalist design (370 yards long, four yards wide, stainless steel with teak planks). Its clever aerodynamic handrails deflect wind over the heads of pedestrians.

▲▲SHAKESPEARE'S GLOBE

This replica of the original Globe Theatre was built as it was in Shakespeare's time, half-timbered and thatched (in fact, with the first thatched roof constructed in London since they were outlawed after the Great Fire of 1666.) The original Globe opened in 1599, with its debut play, Shakespeare's *Julius Caesar*.) It accommodated 2,200 seated and another 1,000 standing. Today's Globe, leaving space for reasonable aisles, is slightly smaller, holding 800 seated and 600 groundlings. The working theater hosts authentic performances of Shakespeare's plays with actors in period costumes, modern interpretations of his works, and some works by other playwrights. For details on attending a play, see page 102.

The Globe complex has four parts: the Globe theater itself, the box office, a museum (called the Exhibition), and the Sam Wanamaker Playhouse (an indoor Jacobean theater around back). The Playhouse, which hosts performances through the winter, is horseshoe-shaped, intimate (seating fewer than 350), and sometimes uses authentic candle-lighting for period performances. The repertoire focuses less on Shakespeare and more on the work of his contemporaries (Jonson, Marlow, Fletcher), as well as concerts.

Cost: £16 for adults, £9 for kids 5-15, free for kids 5 and under, family ticket available; ticket includes Exhibition, audioguide, and 40-minute tour of the Globe; when theater is in use, you can tour the Exhibition only for £6.

Hours: The complex is open daily 9:00-17:30. Tours start every 30 minutes; during Globe theater season (late April-mid-Oct), last tour Mon at 17:00, Tue-Sat at 12:30, Sun at 11:30—it's safest to arrive for a tour before noon. Located on the South Bank over the Millennium Bridge

Millennium Bridge

Shakespeare's Globe

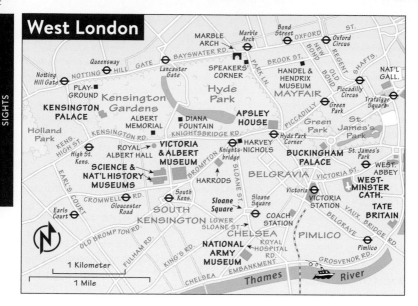

West London

from St. Paul's, Tube: Mansion House or London Bridge plus a 10-minute walk; tel. 020/7902-1400, box office tel. 020/7401-9919, www.shakespearesglobe.com.

Visiting the Globe: You browse on your own in the **Exhibition** (with the included audioguide) through displays of Elizabethan-era costumes and makeup, music, script-printing, and special effects (the displays change). There are early folios and objects that were dug up on site. Videos and scale models help put Shakespearean theater within the context of the times. You'll also learn how they built the replica in modern times, using Elizabethan materials and techniques.

You must **tour the theater** at the time stamped on your ticket, but you can come back to the Exhibition museum afterward. A guide (usually an actor) leads you into the theater to see the stage and the various seating areas for the different classes of people. Learn how the new Globe is similar to the old Globe (open-air performances, standing-room by the stage, no curtain) and how it's different (female actors today, lights for night performances, concrete floor). It's not a

backstage tour, but the guides bring the Elizabethan period to life.

Eating: The **$$$$ Swan at the Globe** café offers a sit-down restaurant (for lunch and dinner, reservations recommended, tel. 020/7928-9444), a drinks-and-plates bar, and a sandwich-and-coffee cart (Mon-Fri 8:00-closing, depends on performance times, Sat-Sun from 10:00).

West London
▲▲TATE BRITAIN

One of Europe's great art houses, the Tate Britain specializes in British painting from the 16th century through modern times. This is people's art, with realistic paintings rooted in the individuals, landscape, and stories of the British Isles. The Tate shows off Hogarth's stage sets, Gainsborough's ladies, Blake's angels, Constable's clouds, Turner's tempests, the naturalistic realism of the Pre-Raphaelites, and the camera-eye portraits of Hockney and Freud.

Cost and Hours: Free, £4 donation suggested, admission fee for special exhibits; daily 10:00-18:00, last entry 45 minutes before closing, map-£1 suggested donation; free tours generally daily at

11:00, 12:00, 14:00, and 15:00, or download the Tate's handy app for a room-by-room guide; café and restaurant, tel. 020/7887-8888, www.tate.org.uk.

Getting There: It's on the River Thames, south of Big Ben and north of Vauxhall Bridge. Tube to Pimlico, then walk seven minutes. Or hop on the Tate Boat museum ferry from Tate Modern.

❯ SELF-GUIDED TOUR

Works from the early centuries are located in the west half of the building, 20th-century art is in the east half, the works of J. M. W. Turner and John Constable are in an adjacent wing (the Clore Gallery), and William Blake's work is upstairs. The Tate's great strength is championing contemporary British art in special exhibitions. There are generally two exhibition spaces: one in the east half of the main floor (often free), and another downstairs (usually requiring separate admission).

• *From the main Millbank entrance, walk through the bright, white rotunda and down the long central hall. Near the far end, enter the rooms on the left, labeled Walk Through British Art, where you'll find the beginnings of British painting (as you enter each room, you'll see the year etched into the floor).*

1700s—Art Blossoms: With peace at home (under three King Georges), a strong overseas economy, and a growing urban center in London, England's artistic life began to bloom. As the English grew more sophisticated, so did their portraits. Painters branched out into other subjects, capturing slices of everyday life (find William Hogarth, with his unflinchingly honest portraits, and Thomas Gainsborough's elegant, educated women).

1800-1850—The Industrial Revolution: Newfangled inventions were everywhere. Many artists rebelled against "progress" and the modern world. They escaped the dirty cities to commune with nature (Constable and the Romantics). Or they found a new spirituality in intense human emotions (dramatic scenes from history or literature). Or

they left the modern world altogether. William Blake, whose work hangs in a darkened room upstairs to protect his watercolors from deterioration, painted angels, not the dull material world. He turned his gaze inward, illustrating the glorious visions of the soul. His pen and watercolor sketches glow with an unearthly aura. In visions of the Christian heaven or Dante's hell, his figures have superhero musculature. The colors are almost translucent.

1837-1901—The Victorian Era: In the world's wealthiest nation, the prosperous middle class dictated taste in art. They admired paintings that were realistic (showcasing the artist's talent and work ethic), depicting Norman Rockwell-style slices of everyday life. Some paintings tug at the heartstrings, with scenes of parting couples, the grief of death, or the joy of families reuniting.

Overdosed with the gushy sentimentality of their day, a band of 20-year-old artists—including Sir John Everett Millais, Dante Gabriel Rossetti, and William Holman Hunt—said "Enough!" and dedicated themselves to creating less saccharine art (the Pre-Raphaelites). Like the Impressionists who followed them, they donned their scarves, barged out of the stuffy studio, and set up outdoors, painting trees, streams, and people, like scientists on a field trip. Still, they often captured nature with such a close-up clarity that it's downright unnatural.

Victorian-era Lady of Shalott

British Impressionism: Realistic British art stood apart from the modernist trends in France, but some influences drifted across the Channel (Rooms 1890 and 1900). John Singer Sargent (American-born) studied with Parisian Impressionists, learning the thick, messy brushwork and play of light at twilight. James Tissot used Degas' snapshot technique to capture a crowded scene from an odd angle. And James McNeill Whistler (born in America, trained in Paris, lived in London) composed his paintings like music—see some of his paintings' titles.

1900-1950—World Wars: As two world wars whittled down the powerful British Empire, it still remained a major cultural force. British art mirrored many of the trends and "-isms" pioneered in Paris (room marked 1930). You'll see Cubism like Picasso's, abstract art like Mondrian's, and so on. But British artists also continued the British tradition of realistic paintings of people and landscapes. Henry Moore's statues—mostly female, mostly reclining—catch the primitive power of carved stone. He captured the human body in a few simple curves, with minimal changes to the rock itself.

With a stiff upper lip, Britain survived the Blitz, World War II, and the loss of hundreds of thousands of men—but at war's end, the bottled-up horror came rushing out. Francis Bacon's deformed half-humans/half-animals express the existential human predicament of being caught in a world not of your making, isolated and helpless to change it.

1950-2000—Modern World: No longer a world power, Britain in the Swinging '60s became a major exporter of pop culture. British art's traditional strengths—realism, portraits, landscapes, and slice-of-life scenes—were redone in the modern style. Look for works by David Hockney, Lucian Freud, Bridget Riley, and Gilbert and George.

The Turner Collection: Walking through J. M. W. Turner's life's work, you can trace his progression from a painter of realistic historical scenes, through his wandering years, to Impressionist paintings of color-and-light patterns. You'll also see how Turner dabbled in different subjects: landscapes, seascapes, Roman ruins, snapshots of Venice, and so on. The corner room of the Clore Gallery is dedicated to Turner's great rival and contemporary, John Constable, who brought painting back into the real world. He painted the English landscape as it was—realistically, without idealizing it.

▲HYDE PARK AND SPEAKERS' CORNER

London's "Central Park," originally Henry VIII's hunting grounds, has more than 600 acres of lush greenery, Santander Cycles rental stations, the huge man-made Serpentine Lake (with rental boats and a lakeside swimming pool), the royal Kensington Palace (described next), and the ornate Neo-Gothic Albert Memorial across from the Royal Albert Hall. The western half of the park is known as Kensington Gardens. The park is huge—study a Tube map to choose the stop nearest to your destination (for more about the park, see www.royalparks.org.uk/parks/hyde-park).

On Sundays, from just after noon until early evening, **Speakers' Corner** offers soapbox oratory at its best (northeast corner of the park, Tube: Marble Arch). Characters climb their stepladders, wave their flags, pound emphatically on their sandwich boards, and share what they are

Hyde Park

convinced is their wisdom. Regulars have resident hecklers who know their lines and are always ready with a verbal jab or barb. "The grass roots of democracy" is actually a holdover from when the gallows stood here and the criminal was allowed to say just about anything he wanted to before he swung. I dare you to raise your voice and gather a crowd—it's easy to do.

The **Princess Diana Memorial Fountain** honors the "People's Princess," who once lived in nearby Kensington Palace. The low-key circular stream, great for cooling off your feet on a hot day, is in the south-central part of the park, near the Albert Memorial and Serpentine Gallery (Tube: Knightsbridge). A similarly named but different sight, the Diana, Princess of Wales Memorial Playground, in the park's northwest corner, is loads of fun for kids (Tube: Queensway).

KENSINGTON PALACE

For nearly 150 years (1689-1837), Kensington was the royal residence, before Buckingham Palace became the official home of the monarch. Sitting primly on its pleasant parkside grounds, the palace gives a barren yet regal glimpse into royal life—particularly that of Queen Victoria, who was born and raised here.

After Queen Victoria moved the monarchy to Buckingham Palace, lesser royals bedded down at Kensington. Princess Diana lived here both during and after her marriage to Prince Charles (1981-1997). More recently, Will and Kate moved here. However—as many disappointed visitors

discover—none of these more recent apartments are open to the public. To see what's on during your visit, check online.

Cost and Hours: £19, daily 10:00-18:00, Nov-Feb until 16:00; a long 10-minute stroll through Kensington Gardens from either High Street Kensington or Queensway Tube stations, tel. 0844-482-7788, www.hrp.org.uk.

Nearby: Garden enthusiasts enjoy popping into the secluded Sunken Garden, 50 yards from the exit. Consider afternoon tea at the nearby, recommended Orangery, built as a greenhouse for Queen Anne in 1704 (may be closed for renovation).

▲▲▲VICTORIA AND ALBERT MUSEUM

You could spend days wandering "the V&A," which encompasses 2,000 years of art and design (ceramics, stained glass, fine furniture, clothing, jewelry, carpets, and more). There's much to see, including Raphael's tapestry cartoons, a cast of Trajan's Column that depicts the emperor's conquests, one of Leonardo da Vinci's notebooks, ladies' underwear through the ages, a life-size *David* with detachable fig leaf, and Mick Jagger's sequined jumpsuit.

Cost and Hours: Free, £5 donation requested, extra for some special exhibits, daily 10:00-17:45, some galleries open Fri until 22:00, £1 suggested donation for much-needed museum map, free tours daily, on Cromwell Road in South Kensington, Tube: South Kensington, from the Tube station a long tunnel leads directly to museum, tel. 020/7942-2000, www.vam.ac.uk.

Rick's Tip: *The Victoria and Albert Museum is huge and tricky to navigate. Spend £1 for the* **museum map** *available from the info desk. It tells you how to find the museum's must-see objects.*

Visiting the Museum: In the Grand Entrance lobby, look up to see the colorful **chandelier/sculpture** by American glass artist Dale Chihuly. This elaborate

Kensington Palace

Victoria and Albert Museum

Greenwich

piece epitomizes the spirit of the V&A's collection—beautiful manufactured objects that demonstrate technical skill and innovation, wedding the old with the new, and blurring the line between arts and crafts.

The V&A has (arguably) the best collection of **Italian Renaissance sculpture** outside Italy. One prime example is *Samson Slaying a Philistine,* by Giambologna (c. 1562), carved from a single block of marble, which shows the testy Israelite warrior preparing to decapitate a man who'd insulted him. The statue's spiral-shaped pose is reminiscent of works by Michelangelo.

The museum's **Islamic art** reflects both religious influences and sophisticated secular culture. Notice floral patterns (twining vines, flowers, arabesques) and geometric designs (stars, diamonds). But the most common pattern is calligraphy—elaborate lettering of an inscription in Arabic, the language of the Quran. The **British Galleries** sweep chronologically through 400 years of British high-class living (1500-1900). Look for rare miniature portraits—a popular item of Queen Elizabeth I's day—including Hilliard's oft-reproduced *Young Man Among Roses* miniature. A room dedicated to Henry VIII has a portrait of him, his writing box (with quill pens, ink, and sealing wax), and a whole roomful of the fancy furniture, tapestries, jewelry, and dinnerware.

Greater London
▲▲Greenwich

This borough of London—an easy boat trip or DLR (light rail) journey from downtown—combines majestic, picnic-perfect parks; the stately trappings of Britain's proud nautical heritage; and the Royal Observatory Greenwich, with a fine museum on the evolution of seafaring and a chance to straddle the eastern and western hemispheres at the prime meridian.

Getting There: Ride a boat to Greenwich for the scenery and commentary, and take the Docklands Light Rail (DLR) back. Various **tour boats** with commentary and open-deck seating (2/hour, 30-75 minutes), as well as faster Thames Clippers (departs every 20-30 minutes, 20-45 minutes, though these lack open decks) leave from several piers in central London.

By DLR, ride from Bank-Monument Station in central London to Cutty Sark Station in central Greenwich; it's one stop before the main—but less central—Greenwich Station (departs at least every 10 minutes, 20 minutes, all in Zone 2). Alternately, catch bus #188 from Russell Square near the British Museum (about 45 minutes to Greenwich).

Eating in Greenwich: Greenwich's parks are picnic-friendly, especially around the National Maritime Museum and Royal Observatory. Greenwich has almost 100 pubs, with some boasting that they're mere milliseconds from the prime

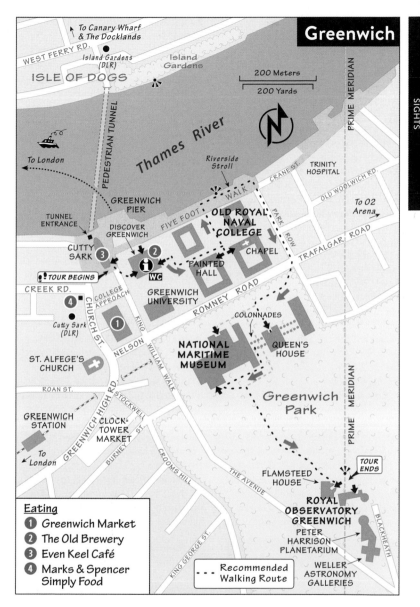

Greenwich

To Canary Wharf & The Docklands

WEST FERRY RD.

Island Gardens (DLR)

Island Gardens

ISLE OF DOGS

200 Meters

200 Yards

N

Thames River

To London

PEDESTRIAN TUNNEL

Riverside Stroll

CRANE ST.

TRINITY HOSPITAL

OLD WOOLWICH RD.

To O2 Arena

GREENWICH PIER

WALK

FIVE FOOT

OLD ROYAL NAVAL COLLEGE

PARK ROW

TRAFALGAR ROAD

TUNNEL ENTRANCE

DISCOVER GREENWICH

CHAPEL

CUTTY SARK 3

TOUR BEGINS

i

WC

PAINTED HALL

CREEK RD.

GREENWICH UNIVERSITY

ROMNEY ROAD

COLLEGE APPROACH

4

KING WILLIAM WALK

1

Cutty Sark (DLR)

CHURCH ST.

NELSON RD.

COLONNADES

QUEEN'S HOUSE

ST. ALFEGE'S CHURCH

ROAN ST.

NATIONAL MARITIME MUSEUM

Greenwich Park

GREENWICH STATION

STOCKWELL ST.

CLOCK-TOWER MARKET

BURNEY ST.

GREENWICH HIGH RD.

To London

CROOMS HILL

THE AVENUE

PRIME MERIDIAN

TOUR ENDS

FLAMSTEED HOUSE

ROYAL OBSERVATORY GREENWICH

PETER HARRISON PLANETARIUM

BLACKHEATH

KING GEORGE ST.

WELLER ASTRONOMY GALLERIES

- - - Recommended Walking Route

Eating
1. Greenwich Market
2. The Old Brewery
3. Even Keel Café
4. Marks & Spencer Simply Food

PRIME MERIDIAN

meridian. **$$$ The Old Brewery,** in the Discover Greenwich center, is a gastropub decorated with all things beer. From Yorkshire pudding to paella to Thai cuisine, food stalls at the Greenwich Market (described next) offer an international variety of tasty options.

Markets: Thanks to its markets, Greenwich throbs with browsing Londoners on weekends. The **Greenwich Market** is an entertaining mini Covent Garden, located in the middle of the block between the Cutty Sark DLR station and the Old Royal Naval College (farmers market, arts and crafts, and food stands; daily 10:00-17:30; antiques Mon, Tue, Thu, and Fri, www. greenwichmarketlondon.com).

▲▲CUTTY SARK

When first launched in 1869, the Scottish-built *Cutty Sark* was the last of the great China tea clippers and the queen of the seas. She was among the fastest clippers ever built, the culmination of centuries of ship design. With 32,000 square feet of sail—and favorable winds—she could travel 300 miles in a day. But as a new century dawned, steamers began to outmatch sailing ships for speed, and by the mid-1920s the *Cutty Sark* was the world's last operating clipper ship.

In 2012, the ship was restored and reopened with a spectacular new glass-walled display space (though one critic groused that the ship now "looks like it has run aground in a giant greenhouse"). Displays explore the *Cutty Sark*'s 140-year history and the cargo she carried—everything from tea to wool to gunpowder—as she raced between London and ports all around the world.

Cost and Hours: £13.50, £7 for kids 5-15, free for kids under age 5, family tickets available, combo-ticket with Royal Observatory-£18.50, kids combo-ticket-£8.50; daily 10:00-17:00; reserve ahead online or by phone for school holidays and weekends, or just try showing up around 13:00; good Even Keel café open to the public; unnecessary £5 guidebook, reservation tel. 020/8312-6608, www.rmg.co.uk.

▲OLD ROYAL NAVAL COLLEGE— PAINTED HALL AND CHAPEL

These grand structures were built (1692) as a veterans' hospital to house disabled and retired sailors who'd served their country. King William III and Queen Mary II spared no expense. They donated land from the former royal palace and hired the great Christopher Wren to design the complex (though other architects completed it). Wren created a virtual temple to seamen. The honored pensioners ate in the Painted Hall and prayed in the Chapel of Sts. Peter and Paul.

In 1873, the hospital was transformed into one of the world's most prestigious universities for training naval officers.

Cost and Hours: Both the Painted Hall and Chapel are free (£3 suggested donation), daily 10:00-17:00, sometimes closed for private events, service Sun at 11:00 in chapel—all are welcome, www.ornc.org.

▲NATIONAL MARITIME MUSEUM

A big glass roof tops three levels of slick, modern, kid-friendly exhibits about all things seafaring. Great for anyone interested in the sea, this museum holds everything from a giant working paddlewheel to the uniform Admiral Horatio Nelson wore when he was killed at Trafalgar (look for the bullet hole, in the left shoulder).

Cost and Hours: Free, daily 10:00-17:00, tel. 020/8858-4422, www.rmg.co.uk. The museum hosts frequent family-oriented events; ask at the desk.

Cutty Sark

Old Royal Naval College

▲▲ROYAL OBSERVATORY GREENWICH

Located on the prime meridian (0° longitude), this observatory is famous as the point from which all time and distances on earth are measured. A visit here gives you a taste of the sciences of astronomy, timekeeping, and seafaring—and how they all meld together—along with great views over Greenwich and the distant London skyline. Outside, you can snap a selfie straddling the famous prime meridian line in the pavement. Within, there's the original 1600s-era **observatory,** the **Weller Astronomy Galleries,** and the state-of-the-art **Peter Harrison Planetarium.**

Cost and Hours: Observatory—£9.50, includes audioguide, combo-ticket with *Cutty Sark*-£18.50, combo-ticket with planetarium-£12.50, daily 10:00-17:00, until later in summer; astronomy galleries—free, daily 10:00-17:00; planetarium—£7.50; 30-minute shows generally run every hour (Mon-Fri 13:00-16:00, Sat-Sun 11:00-16:00, fewer in winter, confirm times in advance and consider calling ahead to order tickets; tel. 020/8858-4422, reservations tel. 020/8312-6608, www.rmg.co.uk).

▲▲KEW GARDENS

This fine riverside park and a palatial greenhouse are every botanist's favorite escape. Wander among 33,000 different types of plants, spread across 300 acres. For a quick visit, spend a fragrant hour wandering through three buildings: the Palm House, a humid Victorian world of iron, glass, and tropical plants that was built in 1844; a Waterlily House that Monet would swim for; and the Princess of Wales Conservatory, a meandering modern greenhouse with many different climate zones. With extra time, check out the Xstrata Treetop Walkway, a 200-yard-long scenic steel walkway that puts you high in the canopy 60 feet above the ground. Young kids will love the Climbers and Creepers indoor/outdoor playground and little zip line, and a slow and easy ride on the hop-on, hop-off Kew Explorer tram.

Cost and Hours: £16.50, June-Aug £11 after 16:00, £3.50 for kids 4-16, free for kids under 4; April-Aug Mon-Thu 10:00-18:30, Fri-Sun 10:00-19:30, closes earlier Sept-March—check schedule online, glasshouses close at 17:30 in high season—earlier off-season, free one-hour walking tours daily at 11:00 and 13:30, tel. 020/8332-5000, recorded info tel. 020/8332-5655, www.kew.org.

Getting There: If taking the Tube, ride to Kew Gardens; from the Tube station, cross the footbridge over the tracks, which drops you in a little community of plant-and-herb shops, a two-block walk from Victoria Gate (the main garden entrance). Another option is to take a boat, which runs April-Oct between Kew Gardens and Westminster Pier.

Eating: For a sun-dappled lunch or snack, walk 10 minutes from the Palm House to the **$$** Orangery Cafeteria

Royal Observatory

Kew Gardens

(Mon-Thu 10:00-17:30, Fri-Sun until 18:30, daily until 15:15 in winter, closes early for events).

EXPERIENCES

Shopping

Most stores are open Monday through Saturday from roughly 9:00 or 10:00 until 17:00 or 18:00, with a late night on Wednesday or Thursday (usually until 19:00 or 20:00). Many close on Sundays. Large department stores stay open later during the week (until about 21:00 Mon-Sat) with shorter hours on Sundays. If you're looking for bargains, visit one of the city's many street markets.

Shopping Streets

London is famous for its shopping. The best and most convenient shopping streets are in the West End and West London (roughly between Soho and Hyde Park). You'll find midrange shops along **Oxford Street** (running east from

Tube: Marble Arch), and fancier shops along **Regent Street** (stretching south from Tube: Oxford Circus to Piccadilly Circus) and **Knightsbridge** (where you'll find Harrods and Harvey Nichols; Tube: Knightsbridge). Other streets are more specialized, such as **Jermyn Street** for old-fashioned men's clothing (just south of Piccadilly Street) and **Charing Cross Road** for books. **Floral Street,** connecting Leicester Square to Covent Garden, is lined with fashion boutiques.

Department Stores

Harrods is London's most famous and touristy department store, with more than four acres of retail space covering seven floors (Mon-Sat 10:00-21:00, Sun 11:30-18:00; Brompton Road, Tube: Knightsbridge, tel. 020/7730-1234, www.harrods.com).

   Harvey Nichols, once Princess Diana's favorite, remains the department store *du jour* (Mon-Sat 10:00-20:00, Sun 11:30-18:00, near Harrods, 109 Knightsbridge, Tube: Knightsbridge, tel. 020/7235-5000, www.harveynichols.com).

Rick's Tip: *The fifth floor at* **Harvey Nichols** *is a* **veritable food fest,** *with a gourmet grocery store, a fancy restaurant, a sushi bar, and a café. Get takeaway food for a* **picnic in the Hyde Park rose garden,** *two blocks away.*

   Fortnum & Mason, the official department store of the Queen, embodies old-fashioned, British upper-class taste, with a storybook atmosphere (Mon-Sat 10:00-21:00, Sun 11:30-18:00, 181 Piccadilly, Tube: Green Park, tel. 020/7734-8040, www.fortnumandmason.com). Elegant tea is served in their Diamond Jubilee Tea Salon.

   Liberty is a still-thriving 19th-century institution known for its artful displays and castle-like interior (Mon-Sat 10:00-20:00, Sun 12:00-18:00, Great Marlborough Street, Tube: Oxford Circus, tel. 020/7734-1234, www.liberty.co.uk).

Street Markets

Antique buffs and people-watchers love London's street markets. The best markets—which combine lively stalls and a colorful neighborhood with cute and characteristic shops of their own—are Portobello Road and Camden Lock Market. Hagglers will enjoy the no-holds-barred bargaining encouraged in London's street markets.

IN NOTTING HILL

Portobello Road stretches for several blocks through the delightful, colorful, funky-yet-quaint Notting Hill neighborhood. Already-charming streets lined with pastel-painted houses and offbeat antique shops are enlivened on Fridays and Saturdays with 2,000 additional stalls (9:00-19:00), plus food, live music, and more (Tube: Notting Hill Gate, near recommended accommodations, tel. 020/7727-7684, www.portobelloroad. co.uk).

Rick's Tip: *Browse* **Portabello Road on Friday.** *Most stalls are open, with half the crowds of Saturday.*

IN CAMDEN TOWN

Camden Lock Market is a huge, trendy arts-and-crafts festival divided into three areas, each with its own vibe. The main market, set alongside the picturesque canal, features a mix of shops and stalls selling boutique crafts and artisanal foods. The market on the opposite side of Chalk Farm Road has ethnic food stalls, lots of canalside seating, and punk crafts. The Stables, a sprawling, incense-scented complex, is squeezed into tunnels under the old rail bridge just behind the main market (daily 10:00-19:00, busiest on weekends, tel. 020/3763-9999, www. camdenmarket.com).

IN THE EAST END

Spitalfields Market combines old brick buildings and sleek modern ones, all covered by a giant glass roof. The shops, stalls, and a rainbow of restaurants are open every day (Mon-Fri 10:00-17:00, Sat from 11:00, Sun from 9:00, Tube: Liverpool Street; from the Tube stop, take Bishopsgate East exit, turn left, walk to Brushfield Street, and turn right; www.spitalfields.co.uk).

Petticoat Lane Market, just a block from Spitalfields Market, sits on the otherwise dull Middlesex Street; adjoining Wentworth Street is grungier and more characteristic (Sun 9:00-14:00, sometimes later; smaller market Mon-Fri on Wentworth Street only; Middlesex Street and Wentworth Street, Tube: Liverpool Street).

The **Truman Markets,** housed in the former Truman Brewery on Brick Lane, are gritty and avant-garde, selling handmade clothes, home decor and ethnic street food in the heart of the "Banglatown" Bangladeshi community. The markets are in full swing on Sundays (roughly 10:00-17:00), though you'll see some action on Saturdays (11:00-18:00). Surrounding shops and eateries are open all week (Tube: Liverpool Street or Aldgate East, tel. 020/7770-6028, www. bricklanemarket.com).

Brick Lane is lined with Sunday market stalls all the way up to Bethnal Green

Road, about a 10-minute walk (leading north out of the Truman Markets). Continuing straight (north) about five more minutes takes you to Columbia Road, a colorful shopping street made even more so on Sunday by the **Columbia Road Flower Market** (Sun 8:00-15:00, http://columbiaroad.info). Halfway up Columbia Road, be sure to loop left up little Ezra Street, with characteristic eateries, boutiques, and antique vendors.

IN THE WEST END

The iron-and-glass **Covent Garden Market,** originally the garden for Westminster Abbey, is a mix of fun shops, eateries, and markets. Mondays are for antiques, while arts and crafts dominate the rest of the week. Produce stalls are open daily (10:30-18:00), and on Thursdays, a food market brightens up the square (Tube: Covent Garden, tel. 020/7395-1350, www.coventgardenlondonuk.com).

Jubilee Hall Market, on the south side of Covent Garden, features antiques on Mondays (5:00-17:00); a general market Tuesday through Friday (10:30-19:00); and arts and crafts on Saturdays and Sundays (10:00-18:00). It's located on the south side of Covent Garden (tel. 020/7379-4242, www.jubileemarket.co.uk).

IN SOUTH LONDON

Borough Market has been serving the Southwark community for more than 800 years. These days there are as many people taking photos as buying fruit, cheese, and beautiful breads, but it's still a fun carnival atmosphere with fantastic stall food. For maximum market and minimum crowds, join the locals on Thursdays (full market open Wed-Sat 10:00-17:00, Fri until 18:00, surrounding food stalls open daily; south of London Bridge, where Southwark Street meets Borough High Street; Tube: London Bridge, tel. 020/7407-1002, www.boroughmarket.org.uk).

Theater (a.k.a. Theatre)

London's theater scene rivals Broadway's in quality and sometimes beats it in price. Choose from 200 offerings—Shakespeare, musicals, comedies, thrillers, sex farces, cutting-edge fringe, revivals starring movie celebs, and more. London does it all well.

Rick's Tip: *For the best list of what's happening and a look at the* **latest London scene,** *check www.timeout.com/london.*

West End Shows

Nearly all big-name shows are hosted in the theaters of the West End, clustering around Soho (especially along Shaftesbury Avenue) between Piccadilly and Covent Garden. With a centuries-old tradition of pleasing the masses, they present London theater at its grandest.

I prefer big, glitzy musicals over serious fare because London can deliver the multimedia spectacle I rarely get back home. If that's not to your taste, you might prefer revivals of classics to cutting-edge works by the hottest young playwrights. London is a magnet for movie stars who want to stretch their acting chops.

The free *Official London Theatre Guide,* updated weekly, is a handy tool (find it at hotels, box offices, the City of London TI, and online at www.officiallondontheatre.co.uk).

Most performances are nightly except Sunday, usually with two or three matinees a week. The few shows that run on Sundays are mostly family fare (such as *The Lion King*). Tickets range from about £25 to £120 for the best seats at big shows. Matinees are generally cheaper and rarely sell out.

Rick's Tip: *Just like at home, London's theaters* **sell seats in a range of levels**—*but the Brits use different terms: stalls (ground floor), dress circle (first balcony), upper circle (second balcony), balcony (sky-high third balcony), and slips (cheap seats on the fringes). Discounted tickets are called "concessions" (abbreviated as "conc" or "s").*

TICKETS

Most shows have tickets available on short notice—likely at a discount. If your time in London is limited or you have your heart set on a particular show that's likely to sell out, you can buy peace of mind by booking your tickets from home. For floor plans of the various theaters, see www.theatremonkey.com.

Advance Tickets: Buy your tickets directly from the theater, either through its website or by calling the theater box office. Often, a theater will reroute you to a third-party ticket vendor such as Ticketmaster. You'll pay with a credit card, and generally be charged a per-ticket booking fee (around £3). You can have your tickets

emailed to you or pick them up before show time at the theater's Will Call window. Many third-party websites sell London theater tickets, but these generally charge higher prices and fees.

Discount Tickets: The **TKTS Booth** at Leicester Square sells discounted tickets (25-50 percent off) for many shows, though they may not have the hottest shows in town. You must buy in person at the kiosk, and the best deals are same-day only (£3/ticket service charge included, open Mon-Sat 10:00-19:00, Sun 11:00-16:30).

The list of shows and prices is posted outside the booth and on their constantly refreshed website (www.tkts.co.uk). Come early in the day—the line starts forming even before the booth opens, but moves quickly. Have a second-choice show in mind, in case your first choice is sold out. If TKTS runs out of its ticket allotment for a certain show, it doesn't necessarily mean the show is sold out—you can still try the theater's box office.

Rick's Tip: *The* **real TKTS booth** *(with its prominent sign) is a freestanding kiosk at the south edge of Leicester Square. Several dishonest outfits nearby advertise "official half-price tickets"—avoid these, where you'll pay closer to full price.*

Theater Box Office: Even if a show is "sold out," there's usually a way to get a seat. Many theaters offer various discounts or "concessions": same-day tickets, cheap returned tickets, standing-room, matinee, senior or student standby deals, and more. Start by checking the show's website, call the box office, or simply drop by (many theaters are right in the tourist zone).

Same-day tickets (called "day seats") are generally available only in person at the box office starting at 10:00 (people start lining up well before then). These tickets (£20 or less) tend to be either in the nosebleed rows or have a restricted

Evensong

One of my favorite experiences in Britain is to attend evensong at a great church. Evensong is an evening worship service that is typically sung rather than said (though some parts—including scripture readings, a few prayers, and a homily—are spoken). It follows the traditional Anglican service in the Book of Common Prayer, including prayers, scripture readings, canticles (sung responses), and hymns that are appropriate for the early evening—traditionally the end of the working day and before the evening meal. In major churches with resident choirs, a singing or chanting priest leads the service, and a choir—usually made up of both men's and boys—sings the responses. The choir usually sings a cappella, or is accompanied by an organ. Visitors are welcome and are given an order of service or a prayer book to help them follow along. (If you're not familiar with the order of service, watch the congregation to know when to stand, sit, and kneel.)

Impressive places for evensong in London include Westminster Abbey and St. Paul's. Evensong typically takes place in the small choir area, which is far more intimate than the main nave. It generally occurs daily between 17:00 and 18:00 (often two hours earlier on Sundays); check with individual churches for specifics. At smaller churches, evensong is sometimes spoken, not sung.

Note that evensong is not a performance—it's a worship service. If you enjoy worshipping in different churches, attending evensong can be a highlight. But if church services aren't your thing, consider an organ or choral concerts—look for posted schedules or ask at the information desk or gift shop.

view (behind a pillar or extremely far to one side).

Another strategy is to show up at the box office shortly before show time (best on weekdays) and—before paying full price—ask about any cheaper options. Last-minute return tickets are often sold at great prices as curtain time approaches.

For a helpful guide to "day seats," consult www.theatremonkey.com/dayseatfinder.htm; for tips on getting cheap and last-minute tickets, visit www.londontheatretickets.org and www.timeout.com/london/theatre.

Other Agencies: Although booking through a middleman such as your hotel or a ticket agency is quick and easy, prices are greatly inflated. Ticket agencies and third-party websites are often just scalpers with an address. If you do buy from an agency, choose one who is a member of the Society of Ticket Agents and Retailers (look for the STAR logo—short for "secure tickets from authorized retailers"). These legitimate resellers normally add a maximum 25 percent booking fee to tickets.

Scalpers (or "Touts"): As at any event, you'll find scalpers hawking tickets outside theaters. And, just like at home, those people may either be honest folk whose date just happened to cancel at the last minute...or they may be unscrupulous thieves selling forgeries. London has many of the latter.

Beyond the West End

Tickets for lesser-known shows tend to be cheaper (figure £15-30), in part because most of the smaller theaters are government-subsidized. Remember that plays don't need a familiar title or famous actor to be a worthwhile experience—read up on the latest offerings online; Time Out's website is a great place to start.

MAJOR THEATERS

One particularly good venue is the **National Theatre,** which has a range of impressive options, often starring recognizable names. While the building is ugly on the outside, the acts that play out upon its stage are beautiful—as are the deeply discounted tickets it commonly offers (looming on the South Bank by Waterloo Bridge, Tube: Waterloo, www. nationaltheatre.org.uk).

The **Barbican Centre** puts on high-quality, often experimental work (right by the Museum of London, just north of The City, Tube: Barbican, www. barbican.org.uk), as does the **Royal Court Theatre,** which has £12 tickets for its Monday shows (west of the West End in Sloane Square, Tube: Sloane Square, www.royalcourttheatre.com).

Menier Chocolate Factory is a small theater in Southwark popular for its impressive productions and intimate setting. Check their website to see what's on—they tend to have a mix of plays, musicals, and even an occasional comedian (behind the Tate Modern at 53 Southwark Street, Tube: Southwark, www. menierchocolatefactory.com).

Royal Shakespeare Company performs at various theaters around London and in Stratford-upon-Avon year-round. To get a schedule, contact the RSC (Royal Shakespeare Theatre, Stratford-upon-Avon, tel. 0844-800-1110, box office tel. 01789/403-493, www.rsc.org.uk).

SHAKESPEARE'S GLOBE

To see Shakespeare in a replica of the theater for which he wrote his plays, attend a play at the Globe. In this round, thatched-roof, open-air theater, the plays are performed much as Shakespeare intended—under the sky, with no amplification. I've never enjoyed Shakespeare as much as here, performed as it was meant to be in the "wooden O." If you can't get a ticket, take a guided tour of the theater and museum by day (see page 91).

The play's the thing from late April

A performance at Shakespeare's Globe

through early October (usually Tue-Sat 14:00 and 19:30, Sun either 13:00 and/ or 18:30, tickets can be sold out months in advance). You'll pay £5 to stand and £20-45 to sit, usually on a backless bench. Because only a few rows and the pricier Gentlemen's Rooms have seats with backs, £1 cushions and £3 add-on backrests are considered a good investment by many. Dress for the weather.

The £5 "groundling" tickets—which are open to rain—are most fun. Scurry in early to stake out a spot on the stage's edge, where the most interaction with the actors occurs. You're a crude peasant. You can lean your elbows on the stage, munch a picnic dinner (yes, you can bring in food), or walk around.

The indoor Sam Wanamaker Playhouse allows Shakespearean-era plays and early-music concerts to be performed through the winter. Many of the productions in this intimate venue are one-offs and can be quite pricey.

To reserve tickets for plays at the Globe or Sam Wanamaker, call or drop by the box office (Mon-Sat 10:00-18:00, Sun until 17:00, open one hour later on performance days, New Globe Walk entrance, no extra charge to book by phone, tel. 020/7401-9919). You can also reserve online (www. shakespearesglobe.com, £2.50 booking fee). If the tickets are sold out, don't despair; a few often free up at the last minute. Try calling around noon the day of the performance to see if the box office expects any returned tickets. If so, they'll advise you to show up a little more than an hour before the show, when these tickets are sold (first-come, first-served).

The theater is on the South Bank, directly across the Thames over the Millennium Bridge from St. Paul's Cathedral (Tube: Mansion House or London Bridge).

EATING

Eating out has become an essential part of the London experience. The sheer variety of foods—from every corner of Britain's former empire and beyond—is astonishing. But the thought of a £50 meal in Britain generally ruins my appetite, so my London dining is limited mostly to easygoing, fun, moderately priced alternatives. Pub grub and ethnic restaurants (especially Indian and Chinese) are good low-cost options.

Popular chain restaurants are a good bet, offering tasty food, reasonable prices, and branches throughout London and the UK (see page 395).

Of course, picnicking is the fastest and cheapest way to go. Good grocery stores and sandwich shops, fine park benches, and polite pigeons abound.

Central London
Soho

Foodies who want to eat well head to Soho. These restaurants are scattered throughout a chic, creative, and once-seedy zone that teems with hipsters, theatergoers, and London's gay community. Even if you plan to have dinner elsewhere, it's a treat just to wander around Soho.

On and near Wardour Street

$$ Princi is a vast, bright, efficient, wildly popular Italian deli/bakery with Milanese flair. Along one wall is a long counter with display cases offering a tempting array of *pizza rustica, panini* sandwiches, focaccia, pasta dishes, and desserts. Order your food at the counter, then find a space to share at a long table; or get it to go. They also have a classy restaurant section with reasonable prices if you'd rather have table service (daily 8:00-24:00, 135 Wardour Street, tel. 020/7478-8888).

$$$ The Gay Hussar, dressy and tight, squeezes several elegant tables into what the owners say is the only Hungarian restaurant in England. It's traditional Hungarian fare: cabbage, sauerkraut, sausage, paprika, and pork, as well as duck and chicken and, of course, Hungarian wine (Mon-Sat 12:15-14:30 & 17:30-22:45, closed Sun, 2 Greek Street, tel. 020/7437-0973).

$$$ Bocca di Lupo, a stylish and popular option, serves half and full portions of classic regional Italian food. Dressy but with a fun energy, it's a place where you're glad you made a reservation. The counter seating, on cushy stools with a view into the lively open kitchen, is particularly memorable, or you can take a table in the snug, casual back end (daily 12:30-15:00 & 17:15-23:00, 12 Archer Street, tel. 020/7734-2223, www.boccadilupo.com).

$$ Yalla Yalla is a bohemian-chic hole-in-the-wall serving up high-quality Beirut street food—hummus, baba ghanoush, tabbouleh, and *shawarmas.* It's tucked down a seedy alley across from a sex shop. Eat in the cramped and cozy interior or at one of the few outdoor tables (£4 sandwiches and *meze,* £8 mezes platter available until 17:00, daily 10:00-24:00, 1 Green's Court—just north of Brewer Street, tel. 020/7287-7663).

Gelato: Across the street from Bocca di Lupo (listed earlier) is its sister *gelateria,* **Gelupo,** with a wide array of ever-changing but always creative and delicious dessert favorites. Take away or enjoy their homey interior (daily 11:00-23:00, 7 Archer Street, tel. 020/7287-5555).

ON LEXINGTON STREET
$$$ Andrew Edmunds Restaurant is a tiny candlelit space where you'll want to hide your guidebook and not act like a tourist. This little place—with a jealous and loyal clientele—is the closest I've

found to Parisian quality in a cozy restaurant in London. The extensive wine list, modern European cooking, and creative seasonal menu are worth the splurge (daily 12:30-15:30 & 17:30-22:45, these are last-order times, come early or call ahead, request ground floor rather than basement, 46 Lexington Street, tel. 020/7437-5708, www.andrewedmunds.com).

$$ Mildred's Vegetarian Restaurant, across from Andrew Edmunds, has a creative, fun menu and a tight, high-energy interior filled with happy herbivores (Mon-Sat 12:00-23:00, closed Sun, vegan options, 45 Lexington Street, tel. 020/7494-1634).

Near Piccadilly

$$$$ The Wolseley is the grand 1920s showroom of a long-defunct British car. The last Wolseley drove out with the Great Depression, but today this old-time bistro bustles with formal waiters serving traditional Austrian and French dishes in an elegant black-marble-and-chandeliers setting fit for its location next to the Ritz. Although the food can be unexceptional, prices are reasonable considering the grand presentation and setting. Reservations are a must (cheaper soup, salad, and sandwich "café menu" available in all areas of restaurant, daily 7:00-24:00, 160 Piccadilly, tel. 020/7499-6996, www.thewolseley.com). They're popular for their fancy cream tea and afternoon tea.

$$$$ The Savini at the Criterion is a palatial dining hall offering an Italian menu in a dreamy neo-Byzantine setting from the 1870s. It's right on Piccadilly Circus but a world away from the punk junk, with fairly normal food served in an unforgettable Great Gatsby space. It's a deal for the visual experience during lunch or early (before 19:00) or late (after 22:00)—and if you order the £29-36 fixed-price meal or £16 cream tea (daily 12:00-23:30, 224 Piccadilly, tel. 020/7930-1459, www.saviniatcriterion.co.uk).

Covent Garden

$$$ Dishoom is London's hotspot for upscale Indian cuisine, with top-quality ingredients and carefully executed recipes. The dishes seem familiar, but the flavors are a revelation. People line up early (starting around 17:30) for a seat, either on the bright, rollicking, brasserie-like ground floor or in the less appealing basement. Reservations are possible only until 17:45 (daily 8:00-23:00, 12 Upper St. Martin's Lane, tel. 020/7420-9320). They also have locations near King's Cross Station, Carnaby Street, and in Shoreditch.

$$ Lamb and Flag Pub is a survivor—a spit-and-sawdust pub serving traditional grub (like meat pies) two blocks off Covent Garden, yet seemingly a world away. Here since 1772, this pub was a favorite of Charles Dickens and is now a hit with local workers. At lunch, it's all food. In the evening, the ground floor is for drinking and the food service is upstairs (long hours daily, 33 Rose Street, across from Stanfords bookstore entrance on Floral Street, tel. 020/7497-9504).

Near Trafalgar Square

$$ St. Martin-in-the-Fields Café in the Crypt is just right for a tasty meal on a monk's budget—maybe even on a monk's tomb. You'll dine sitting on somebody's gravestone in an ancient crypt. Their enticing buffet line is kept stocked all day, serving breakfast, lunch, and dinner (hearty traditional desserts, free jugs

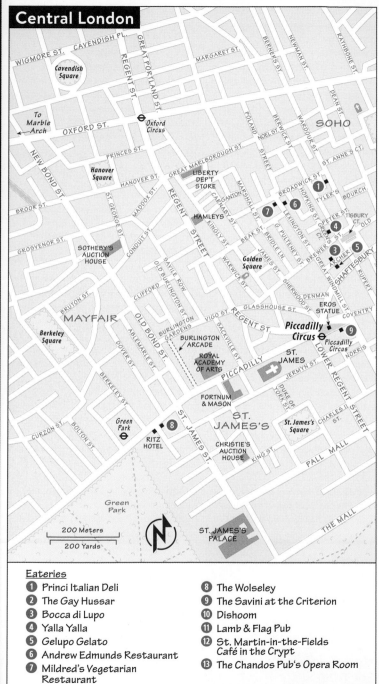

Central London

Eateries

1. Princi Italian Deli
2. The Gay Hussar
3. Bocca di Lupo
4. Yalla Yalla
5. Gelupo Gelato
6. Andrew Edmunds Restaurant
7. Mildred's Vegetarian Restaurant
8. The Wolseley
9. The Savini at the Criterion
10. Dishoom
11. Lamb & Flag Pub
12. St. Martin-in-the-Fields Café in the Crypt
13. The Chandos Pub's Opera Room

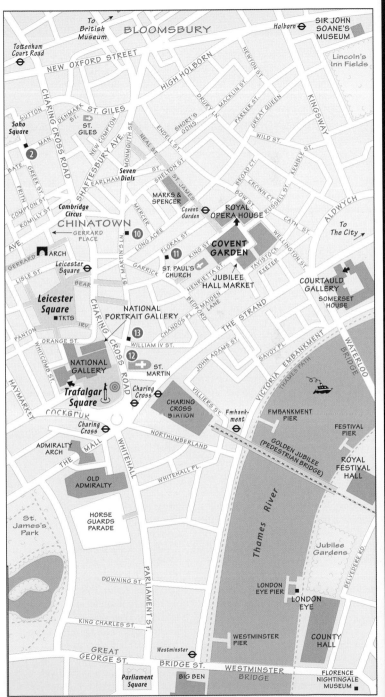

Taking Tea

Many London visitors partake in this most British of traditions. While some tearooms—such as the finicky Fortnum & Mason—still require a jacket and tie, most others happily welcome tourists in jeans and sneakers. Most tearooms are usually open for lunch and close about 17:00.

Popular choices are a "cream tea," which consists of tea and a scone or two, or the pricier "afternoon tea," which comes with pastries and finger foods such as small, crust-less sandwiches (for more tea options, see page 396). Even at the fancier places, two people can order one afternoon tea and one cream tea and share the afternoon tea's goodies.

Many museum cafés offer a fine, inexpensive tea service; try the **$$ Victoria and Albert Museum** café.

$$$ The Wolseley serves a good afternoon tea between their meal service (£13 cream tea, £30 afternoon tea, £40 champagne tea, generally served 15:00-18:30 daily).

$$$$ The Orangery at Kensington Palace serves a £28 "Orangery tea" and a £35 champagne tea in its bright white hall near William and Kate's residence. You can also order treats à la carte. The portions aren't huge, but who can argue with eating at a royal orangery or on the terrace? (tea served 12:00-18:00; a 10-minute walk through Kensington Gardens from either Queensway or High Street Kensington Tube stations to orange brick building, about 100 yards from Kensington Palace—see map on page 116; tel. 020/3166-6113, www.hrp.org.uk).

$$$$ Fortnum & Mason department store offers tea at several different restaurants within its walls. You can "Take Tea in the Parlour" for £22 (including ice cream and scones; Mon-Sat 10:00-19:30, Sun 11:30-17:00). The pièce de resistance is their Diamond Jubilee Tea Salon, named in honor of the Queen's 60th year on the throne (and, no doubt, to remind visitors of Her Majesty's visit for tea here in 2012 with Camilla and Kate). At these royal prices, consider it dinner (£48, Mon-Sat 12:00-19:00, Sun until 18:00, dress up a bit—no shorts, "children must be behaved," 181 Piccadilly, smart to reserve at least a week in advance, tel. 020/7734-8040, www.fortnumandmason.com).

of water). They also serve a restful £10 afternoon tea (daily 12:00-18:00). You'll find the café directly under St. Martin-in-the-Fields, facing Trafalgar Square—enter through the glass pavilion next to the church (generally about 8:00-20:00 daily, profits go to the church, Tube: Charing Cross, tel. 020/7766-1158). On Wednesday evenings you can dine to the music of a live jazz band at 20:00 (£8-15 tickets). While here, check out the concert schedule for the busy church upstairs (or visit www.stmartin-in-the-fields.org).

$$ The Chandos Pub's Opera Room floats amazingly apart from the tacky crush of tourism around Trafalgar Square. Look for it opposite the National Portrait Gallery (corner of William IV Street and St. Martin's Lane) and climb the stairs—to the left or right of the pub entrance—to the Opera Room. This is a fine Trafalgar rendezvous point and a wonderfully local pub. They serve £7 sandwiches and a better-than-average range of traditional pub meals for £10—meat pies and fish-and-chips are their specialty. The ground-floor pub is stuffed with regulars and offers snugs (private booths) and more serious beer drinking. To eat on that level, you have to order upstairs and carry it down (kitchen open daily 11:30-21:00, Fri until 18:00, order and pay at the bar, 29 St. Martin's Lane, Tube: Leicester Square, tel. 020/7836-1401).

Near the British Museum and British Library

To avoid the touristy crush right around the British Museum, head a few blocks west to the Fitzrovia area. Here, tiny Charlotte Place is lined with small eateries (including the first two listed below); nearby, the much bigger Charlotte Street has several more good options. This area is a short walk from the Goodge Street Tube station.

$ Salumeria Dino serves up hearty £5 sandwiches, pasta, and Italian coffee. Dino, a native of Naples, has run his little shop for more than 30 years and has managed to create a classic-feeling Italian deli (cheap takeaway cappuccinos, Mon-Fri 9:00-18:00, closed Sat-Sun, 15 Charlotte Place, tel. 020/7580-3938).

$ Lantana OUT, next door to Salumeria Dino, is an Australian coffee shop that sells modern soups, sandwiches, and salads at their takeaway window (£8 daily hot dish). **Lantana IN** is an adjacent sit-down café that serves pricier meals (both open long hours daily, 13 Charlotte Place, tel. 020/7637-3347).

$$ Indian Food near the British Library: Drummond Street (running just west of Euston Station) is famous for cheap and good Indian vegetarian food. For a good, moderately priced *thali* (combo platter) consider **Chutneys** (124 Drummond, tel. 020/7388-0604) and **Ravi Shankar** (135 Drummond, tel. 020/7388-6458, both open long hours daily).

West London
Victoria Station Area

$$$ Grumbles brags it's been serving "good food and wine at non-scary prices since 1964." Offering a delicious mix of "modern eclectic French and traditional English," this unpretentious little place with cozy booths inside (on two levels) and a few nice sidewalk tables is the best spot to eat well in this otherwise workaday neighborhood. Their traditional dishes are their forte (early-bird specials, open daily 12:00-14:30 & 18:00-23.00, reservations wise, half a block north of Belgrave Road at 35 Churton Street, tel. 020/7834-0149, www.grumblesrestaurant.co.uk).

$$ Pimlico Fresh's breakfasts and lunches feature fresh, organic ingredients, served up with good coffee and/or fresh-squeezed juices. Choose from the dishes listed on the wall-sized chalkboard that lines the small eating area, then order at the counter. This place is heaven if you need a break from your hotel's bacon-eggs-beans routine (takeout lunches, plenty of vegetarian options; Mon-Fri 7:30-18:30, breakfast served until 15:00; Sat-Sun 9:00-18:00; 86 Wilton Road, tel. 020/7932-0030).

$$ Seafresh Fish Restaurant is the neighborhood place for plaice—and classic and creative fish-and-chips cuisine. You can either take out on the cheap or eat in, enjoying a white-fish ambience. Though Mario's father started this place in 1965, it feels like the chippy of the 21st century (Mon-Sat 12:00-15:00 & 17:00-22:30, closed Sun, 80 Wilton Road, tel. 020/7828-0747).

$$ The Jugged Hare, a 10-minute walk from Victoria Station, fills a lavish old bank building, with vaults replaced by kegs of beer and a kitchen. They have a traditional menu and a plush, vivid pub scene good for a meal or just a drink (food served Mon-Fri 11:00-21:00, Sat-Sun until 20:00, 172 Vauxhall Bridge Road, tel. 020/7828-1543).

$$ St. George's Tavern is the neighborhood's best pub for a full meal. They serve dinner from the same menu in three zones: on the sidewalk to catch the sun and enjoy some people-watching, in the ground-floor pub, and in a classier downstairs dining room with full table service.

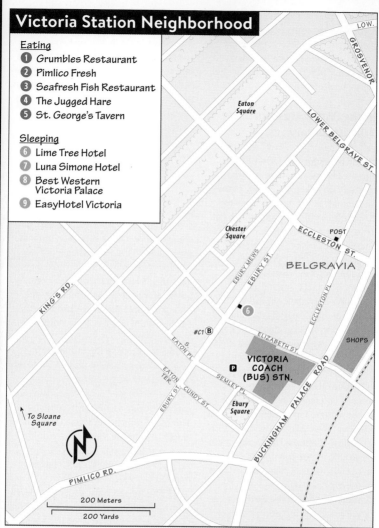

Victoria Station Neighborhood

Eating
1. Grumbles Restaurant
2. Pimlico Fresh
3. Seafresh Fish Restaurant
4. The Jugged Hare
5. St. George's Tavern

Sleeping
6. Lime Tree Hotel
7. Luna Simone Hotel
8. Best Western Victoria Palace
9. EasyHotel Victoria

Map labels: LOW. · GROSVENOR · Eaton Square · LOWER BELGRAVE ST. · Chester Square · POST · ECCLESTON ST. · EBURY MEWS · EBURY ST. · BELGRAVIA · ECCLESTON PL. · KING'S RD. · #C1 B · ELIZABETH ST. · SHOPS · EATON PL. · EATON TER. · EBURY ST. · CUNDY ST. · P VICTORIA COACH (BUS) STN. · SEMLEY PL. · BUCKINGHAM PALACE ROAD · To Sloane Square · Ebury Square · N · PIMLICO RD. · 200 Meters · 200 Yards

The scene is inviting for just a beer, too (food served daily 12:00-22:00, corner of Hugh Street and Belgrave Road, tel. 020/7630-1116).

Bayswater and Notting Hill

$$$ Geales, which opened its doors in 1939 as a fish-and-chips shop, has been serving Notting Hill ever since. Today, while the menu is more varied, the emphasis is still on fish. The interior is casual, but the food is upscale. The crispy battered cod that put them on the map is still the best around (£10 two-course express lunch menu; Tue-Sun 12:00-15:00 & 18:00-22:00, closed Mon, reservations smart, 2 Farmer Street, just south of Notting Hill Gate Tube stop, tel. 020/7727-7528, www.geales.com).

$$ The Churchill Arms Pub and Thai Kitchen is a combo establishment that's a hit in the neighborhood. It offers good

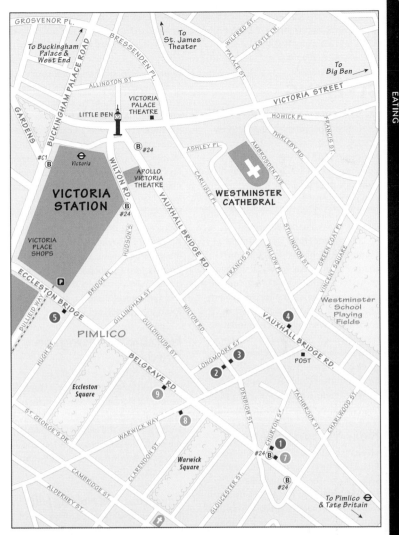

beer and a thriving old-English ambience in front and hearty £9 Thai plates in an enclosed patio in the back. Arrive by 18:00 or after 21:00 to avoid a line (food served daily 12:00-22:00, 119 Kensington Church Street, tel. 020/7727-4242 for the pub or 020/7792-1246 for restaurant, www. churchillarmskensington.co.uk).

$$$ Hereford Road is a cozy, mod eatery tucked away on Leinster Square. It's stylish but not pretentious, serv-

ing heavy, meaty English cuisine made with modern panache. Cozy two-person booths face the open kitchen up top; the main dining room is down below. There are also a few sidewalk tables (daily 12:00-15:00 & 18:00-22:00, reservations smart, 3 Hereford Road, tel. 020/7727-1144, www. herefordroad.org).

$$ The Prince Edward serves good grub in a comfy, family-friendly, upscale-pub setting and at its sidewalk tables (daily 10:30-22:30, 2 blocks north of Bayswater Road at the corner of Dawson Place and Hereford Road, 73 Prince's Square, tel. 020/7727-2221).

SLEEPING

London is an expensive city for lodging. Expect cheaper rooms to be relatively dumpy. I rank accommodations from **$** budget to **$$$$** splurge. To get the best deal, contact my family-run hotels directly by phone or email. Book your accommodations well in advance if you'll be traveling during peak season or if your trip coincides with a major holiday or festival.

Looking for Hotel Deals Online: Given London's high hotel prices, it's worth searching for a deal. For some travelers, short-term, Airbnb-type rentals can be a good alternative; search for places in my recommended hotel neighborhoods. You can also browse these accommodation discount sites: www.londontown.com (an informative site with a discount booking service), athomeinlondon.co.uk and www.londonbb.com (both list central B&Bs), www.lastminute.com, www.visitlondon.com, and www.eurocheapo.com.

Near Victoria Station

The safe, surprisingly tidy streets behind Victoria Station teem with little, moderately-priced-for-London B&Bs.

$$$$ Lime Tree Hotel, enthusiastically run by Charlotte and Matt, is a gem, with 28 spacious, stylish, comfortable, thoughtfully decorated rooms, a helpful staff, and a fun-loving breakfast room (small lounge opens onto quiet garden, 135 Ebury Street, tel. 020/7730-8191, www.limetreehotel.co.uk, info@limetreehotel.co.uk, Laura manages the office).

$$$ Luna Simone Hotel rents 36 fresh, spacious, remodeled rooms with modern bathrooms. It's a smartly managed place, run for more than 40 years by twins Peter and Bernard—and Bernard's son Mark—and they still seem to enjoy their work (RS%, family rooms, 47 Belgrave Road near the corner of Charlwood Street, handy bus #24 stops out front, tel. 020/7834-5897, www.lunasimonehotel.com, stay@lunasimonehotel.com).

$$ Best Western Victoria Palace offers modern business-class comfort compared with some of the other creaky old hotels listed here. Choose from the 43 rooms in the main building (elevator, at 60 Warwick Way), or pay about 20 percent less by booking a nearly identical room in one of the annexes, each a half-block away—an excellent value for this neighborhood if you skip breakfast (breakfast extra, air-con, no elevator, 17 Belgrave Road and 1 Warwick Way, reception at main building, tel. 020/7821-7113, www.bestwesternvictoriapalace.co.uk, info@bestwesternvictoriapalace.co.uk).

$ EasyHotel Victoria, at 34 Belgrave Road, is part of a budget chain.

North of Kensington Gardens

From the core of the tourist's London, the vast Hyde Park spreads west, eventually becoming Kensington Gardens. Bayswater anchors the area; it's bordered by Notting Hill to the west and Paddington to the east. This area has quick bus and Tube access to downtown and, for London, is very cozy.

Bayswater and Notting Hill

$$$ Vancouver Studios offers one of the best values in this neighborhood. Its 45 modern, tastefully furnished rooms come with fully equipped kitchenettes (utensils, stove, microwave, and fridge) rather than breakfast. It's nestled between Kensington Gardens Square and Prince's Square and has its own tranquil garden patio out back (30 Prince's Square, tel. 020/7243-1270, www.vancouverstudios.co.uk, info@vancouverstudios.co.uk).

$$$ Garden Court Hotel is understated, with 40 simple, homey-but-tasteful rooms (family rooms, includes continental breakfast, elevator, 30 Kensington Gardens Square, tel. 020/7229-2553, www.gardencourthotel.co.uk, info@ gardencourthotel.co.uk).

$$$ Princes Square Guest Accommodation is a crisp (if impersonal) place renting 50 businesslike rooms with pleasant, modern decor. It's well located, practical, and a very good value, especially if you can score a good rate (elevator, 23 Prince's Square, tel. 020/7229-9876, www.princessquarehotel.co.uk, info@ princessquarehotel.co.uk).

$$ London House Hotel has 103 spiffy, modern, cookie-cutter rooms on Kensington Gardens Square. Its rates are great considering the quality and fine location (family rooms, breakfast extra, elevator, 81 Kensington Gardens Square, tel. 020/7243-1810, www.londonhousehotels. com, reservations@londonhousehotels. com).

$$$$ Portobello Hotel is on a quiet residential street in the heart of Notting Hill. Its 21 rooms are funky yet elegant—both the style and location give it an urban-fresh feeling (elevator, 22 Stanley Gardens, tel. 020/7727-2777, www.portobellohotel.com, stay@ portobellohotel.com).

Near Paddington Station

$$ Stylotel feels like the stylish, super-modern, aluminum-clad big sister of the EasyHotel chain. Their tidy 39 rooms come with hard surfaces—hardwood floors, prefab plastic bathrooms, and metallic walls. While rooms can be cramped, the beds have space for luggage underneath. You may feel like an astronaut in a retro science-fiction film, but if you don't need ye olde doilies, this place offers a good value (family rooms, elevator, 160 Sussex Gardens, tel. 020/7723-1026, www.stylotel.com, info@stylotel. com, well-run by Andreas). They have eight fancier, pricier, air-conditioned suites across the street with kitchenettes and no breakfast.

$$ Olympic House Hotel has clean public spaces and a no-nonsense welcome, but its 38 business-class rooms offer predictable comfort and fewer old-timey quirks than many hotels in this price range (air-con extra, elevator, pay Wi-Fi, 138 Sussex Gardens, tel. 020/7723-5935, www.olympichousehotel.co.uk, olympichousehotel@btinternet.com).

$ EasyHotel, a budget chain, has a branch at 10 Norfolk Place.

North London

$$$$ The Sumner Hotel rents 19 rooms in a 19th-century Georgian townhouse sporting large contemporary rooms and a lounge with fancy modern Italian furniture. This swanky place packs in all the amenities and is conveniently located north of Hyde Park and near Oxford Street, a busy shopping destination—close to Selfridges and a Marks & Spencer (RS%, air-con, elevator, 54 Upper Berkeley Street, a block and a half off Edgware Road, Tube: Marble Arch, tel. 020/7723-2244, www.thesumner.com, reservations@thesumner.com).

$$$ The 22 York Street B&B offers a casual alternative in the city center, with an inviting lounge and 10 traditional, hardwood, comfortable rooms, each named for a notable London landmark (near Marylebone/Baker Street: From Baker Street Tube station, walk 2 blocks down Baker Street and take a right to 22 York Street—no sign, just look for #22; tel. 020/7224-2990, www.22yorkstreet.co.uk, mc@22yorkstreet.co.uk, energetically run by Liz and Michael Callis).

Other Sleeping Options
Big, Good-Value, Modern Hotels

If you can score a double for £90-100 (or less—often possible with promotional rates) and don't mind a modern, impersonal, American-style hotel, one of these can be a decent value in pricey London (for details on chain hotels, see page 398).

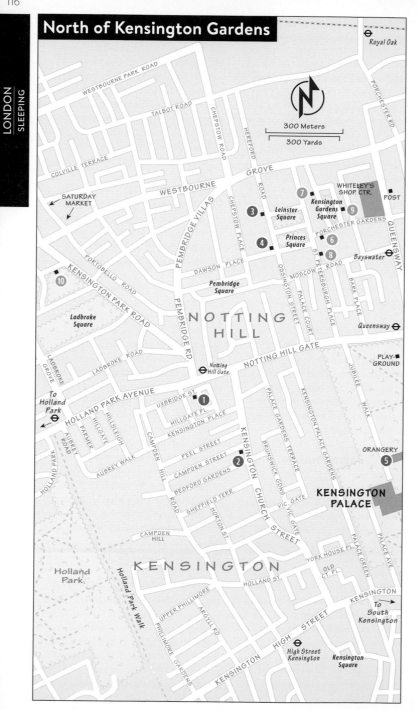

North of Kensington Gardens

Royal Oak

300 Meters

300 Yards

WESTBOURNE PARK ROAD

TALBOT ROAD

CHEPSTOW ROAD

HEREFORD ROAD

GROVE

PORCHESTER RD.

COLVILLE TERRACE

SATURDAY MARKET

WESTBOURNE

PEMBRIDGE VILLAS

CHEPSTOW PLACE

7

WHITELEY'S SHOP. CTR.

Kensington Gardens Square

9

POST

3 Leinster Square

4

Princes Square

6

PORCHESTER GARDENS

QUEENSWAY

DAWSON PLACE

Pembridge Square

MOSCOW RD.

ST PETERSBURGH PLACE

8

Bayswater

OSSINGTON STREET

PALACE COURT

BARK PLACE

PORTOBELLO ROAD

KENSINGTON PARK ROAD

PEMBRIDGE RD.

N O T T I N G HILL

Queensway

Ladbroke Square

10

PLAY-GROUND

LADBROKE GROVE

LADBROKE ROAD

Notting Hill Gate

NOTTING HILL GATE

PALACE GARDENS TERRACE

KENSINGTON PALACE GARDENS

JUBILEE WALK

To Holland Park

HOLLAND PARK AVENUE

UXBRIDGE ST.

1

HILLGATE PL.

KENSINGTON PLACE

PEEL STREET

2

BRUNSWICK GDNS.

ORANGERY

5

HILLGATE

HILLSLEIGH

AUBREY FARMER ROAD

CAMPDEN HILL ROAD

CAMPDEN STREET

BEDFORD GARDENS

KENSINGTON CHURCH STREET

VIC. GATE

AUBREY WALK

HOLLAND PARK

SHEFFIELD TERR.

HORTON ST.

VIC. GATE

KENSINGTON PALACE

CAMPDEN HILL

K E N S I N G T O N

YORK HOUSE PLACE

OLD CT. PL.

PALACE GREEN

PALACE AVE.

KENSINGTON

Holland Park

Holland Park Walk

HOLLAND ST.

To South Kensington

UPPER PHILLIMORE

ARGYLL RD.

PHILLIMORE GARDENS

KENSINGTON HIGH STREET

High Street Kensington

Kensington Square

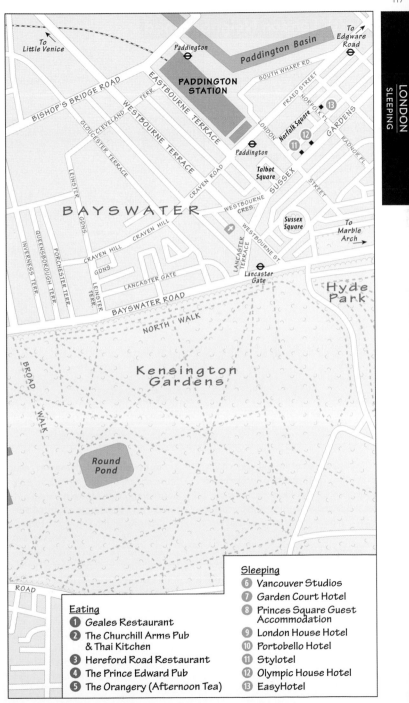

Eating
1. Geales Restaurant
2. The Churchill Arms Pub & Thai Kitchen
3. Hereford Road Restaurant
4. The Prince Edward Pub
5. The Orangery (Afternoon Tea)

Sleeping
6. Vancouver Studios
7. Garden Court Hotel
8. Princes Square Guest Accommodation
9. London House Hotel
10. Portobello Hotel
11. Stylotel
12. Olympic House Hotel
13. EasyHotel

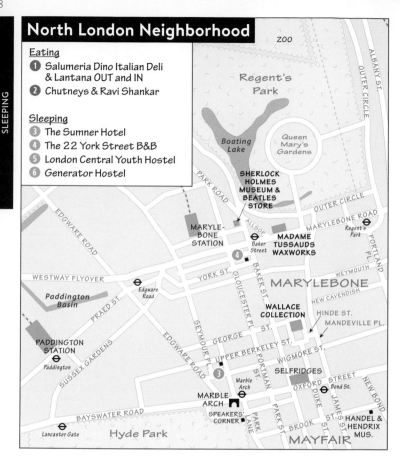

North London Neighborhood

Eating
1. Salumeria Dino Italian Deli & Lantana OUT and IN
2. Chutneys & Ravi Shankar

Sleeping
3. The Sumner Hotel
4. The 22 York Street B&B
5. London Central Youth Hostel
6. Generator Hostel

ZOO

Regent's Park

ALBANY ST.
OUTER CIRCLE

Boating Lake

Queen Mary's Gardens

PARK ROAD

SHERLOCK HOLMES MUSEUM & BEATLES STORE

OUTER CIRCLE

ALLSOP

MARYLEBONE ROAD

Regent's Park

PORTLAND PL.

MARYLE-BONE STATION

Baker Street

MADAME TUSSAUDS WAXWORKS

EDGWARE ROAD

WESTWAY FLYOVER

Edgware Road

YORK ST.

GLOUCESTER PL.

BAKER ST.

WEYMOUTH

MARYLEBONE

NEW CAVENDISH

Paddington Basin

Paddington

PRAED ST.

SEYMOUR PL.

EDGWARE ROAD

GEORGE ST.

UPPER BERKELEY ST.

PORTMAN ST.

WALLACE COLLECTION

HINDE ST.

MANDEVILLE PL.

WIGMORE ST.

PADDINGTON STATION

SUSSEX GARDENS

SELFRIDGES

OXFORD STREET

Bond St.

NEW BOND ST.

MARBLE ARCH

Marble Arch

DUKE ST.

JAMES ST.

BAYSWATER ROAD

SPEAKERS' CORNER

PARK LANE

PARK ST.

BROOK ST.

HANDEL & HENDRIX MUS.

Lancaster Gate

Hyde Park

MAYFAIR

I've listed a few of the dominant chains, along with a quick rundown on their more convenient London locations. Some of these branches sit on busy streets in dreary train-station neighborhoods, so use common sense after dark and wear a money belt.

$$ Motel One, the German chain that specializes in affordable style, has a branch at Tower Hill, a 10-minute walk north of the Tower of London (24 Minories, tel. 020/7481-6427, www.motel-one.com, london-towerhill@motel-one.com).

$$ Premier Inn has more than 70 hotels in greater London. Convenient locations include a branch inside **London County Hall** (next to the London Eye),

at **Southwark/Borough Market** (near Shakespeare's Globe, 34 Park Street), **Southwark/Tate Modern** (Great Suffolk Street), **Kensington/Earl's Court** (11 Knaresborough Place), **Victoria** (82 Eccleston Square), and **Leicester Square** (1 Leicester Place). In North London, the following branches cluster between King's Cross St. Pancras and the British Museum: **King's Cross St. Pancras, St. Pancras, Euston,** and **Brook House.** Avoid the **Tower Bridge** location, south of the bridge and a long walk from the Tube—but London City Tower Hill, north of the bridge on Prescot Street, works fine (www.premierinn.com, tel.

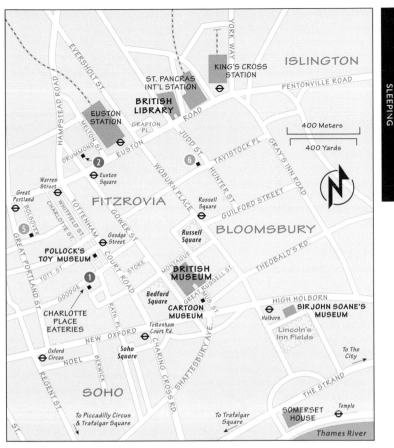

Map labels: EVERSHOLT ST, YORK WAY, KING'S CROSS STATION, ISLINGTON, ST. PANCRAS INT'L STATION, PENTONVILLE ROAD, BRITISH LIBRARY, HAMPSTEAD ROAD, EUSTON STATION, GRAFTON PL., MELTON ST, ROAD, JUDD ST, 400 Meters, 400 Yards, DRUMMOND ST, EUSTON, TAVISTOCK PL, GRAY'S INN ROAD, Euston Square, Warren Street, WOBURN PLACE, HUNTER ST, Great Portland, BOLSOVER, WHITFIELD ST, CHARLOTTE ST, TOTTENHAM, GOWER ST, Russell Square, GUILFORD STREET, FITZROVIA, BLOOMSBURY, GREAT PORTLAND ST, Goodge Street, COURT ROAD, STORE ST, Russell Square, MONTAGUE, THEOBALD'S RD, POLLOCK'S TOY MUSEUM, TOTT. ST, GOODGE, RATH PL, BRITISH MUSEUM, GREAT RUSSELL ST, HIGH HOLBORN, SIR JOHN SOANE'S MUSEUM, Bedford Square, CHARLOTTE PLACE EATERIES, NEW OXFORD, Tottenham Court Rd., CARTOON MUSEUM, Holborn, Lincoln's Inn Fields, Oxford Circus, NOEL, BERWICK, Soho Square, CHARING CROSS RD, SHAFTESBURY AVE, To The City, REGENT ST, SOHO, To Piccadilly Circus & Trafalgar Square, To Trafalgar Square, THE STRAND, SOMERSET HOUSE, Temple, Thames River

0871-527-9222; from North America, dial 011-44-1582-567-890).

$$ Travelodge has close to 70 locations in London, including at **King's Cross** (200 yards in front of King's Cross Station, Gray's Inn Road) and **Euston** (1 Grafton Place). Other handy locations include **King's Cross Royal Scot, Marylebone, Covent Garden, Liverpool Street, Southwark,** and **Farringdon;** www.travelodge.co.uk.

$$ Ibis, the budget branch of the AccorHotels group, has a few dozen options across the city, with a handful of locations convenient to London's center, including **Euston St. Pancras** (on a quiet street a block west of Euston Station, 3 Cardington Street), **London City Shoreditch** (5 Commercial Street), and the more design-focused **Ibis Styles** branches at **Kensington** (15 Hogarth Road) and **Southwark,** with a theater theme (43 Southwark Bridge Road); www.ibishotel.com.

$ EasyHotel, with several branches in good neighborhoods, has a unique business model inspired by its parent company, the easyJet budget airline. The generally tiny, super-efficient, no-frills rooms feel popped out of a plastic mold, down to the prefab ship's head-type "bathroom pod." Rates can be surprisingly low (with doubles as cheap as £30 if you book early enough)—but you'll pay à la carte for expensive add-ons, such as TV use, Wi-Fi, luggage storage, fresh towels, and daily cleaning (breakfast, if available, comes from a vending machine). If you go with the base rate, it's like hosteling with privacy—a hard-to-beat value. But you get what you pay for (thin walls, flimsy construction, noisy fellow guests, and so on). They're only a good deal if you book far enough ahead to get a good price and skip the many extras. Locations include **Victoria** (34 Belgrave Road—see map on page 112), **South Kensington** (14 Lexham Gardens), **Earl's Court** (44 West Cromwell Road), and **Paddington** (10 Norfolk Place); www.easyhotel.com.

Hostels

¢ **London Central Youth Hostel** is the flagship of London's hostels, with all the latest in security and comfortable efficiency. Families and travelers of any age will feel welcome in this wonderful facility. You'll pay the same price for any bed—so try to grab one with a bathroom (families welcome to book an entire room, book long in advance, between Oxford Circus and Great Portland Street Tube stations at 104 Bolsover Street, tel. 0845-371-9154, www. yha.org.uk, londoncentral@yha.org.uk).

¢ **Generator Hostel** is a brightly colored, hip hostel with a café and a DJ spinning the hits. It's in a renovated building tucked behind a busy street halfway between King's Cross and the British Museum (37 Tavistock Place, Tube: Russell Square, tel. 020/7388-7666, www.generatorhostels.com, london@ generatorhostels.com).

TRANSPORTATION

Getting Around London

To travel smart in a city this size, you must get comfortable with public transportation. London's excellent taxis, buses, and subway (Tube) system can take you anywhere you need to go—a blessing for

travelers' precious vacation time, not to mention their feet.

For more information about public transit (bus and Tube), the best single source is the helpful *Hello London* brochure, which includes both a Tube map and a handy schematic map of the best bus routes (available free at TIs, museums, hotels, and at www.tfl.gov.uk). For specific directions on how to get from point A to point B on London's transit, detailed bus maps, updated prices, and general information, check www.tfl.gov.uk or call the automated info line at 0843-222-1234.

Public Transit Tickets and Passes

While the transit system has six zones, almost all tourist sights are within Zones 1 and 2, so those are the prices I've listed. For more information, visit www.tfl.gov. uk/tickets. A few odd special passes are available, but for nearly every tourist, the answer is simple: Get the Oyster card and use it.

INDIVIDUAL TICKETS

Individual paper tickets for the Tube are ridiculously expensive (£5 per Tube ride). Tickets are sold at any Tube station, either at a rare ticket window or at easy-to-use self-service machines (hit "Adult Single" and enter your destination). Tickets are valid only on the day of purchase. But unless you're literally taking only one Tube ride your entire visit, you'll save money (and time) with an Oyster card.

TRANSIT CARDS

Oyster Card: A pay-as-you-go Oyster card (a plastic card embedded with a

microchip) allows you to ride the Tube, buses, Docklands Light Railway (DLR), and Overground (mostly suburban trains) for about half the rate of individual tickets. To use it, simply touch the card against the yellow card reader at the turnstile or entrance. It flashes green and the fare is automatically deducted. (You must also tap your card again to "touch out" as you exit.)

Buy the card at any Tube station ticket window, or look for nearby shops displaying the Oyster logo, where you can purchase a card or add credit without the wait. You'll pay a £5 refundable deposit up front, then load it with as much credit as you'll need. One ride in Zones 1 and 2 during peak time costs £2.90; off peak is a little cheaper (£2.40/ride). The system comes with an automatic price cap that guarantees you'll never pay more than £6.80 in one day for rides within Zones 1 and 2. If you think you'll take more than two rides in a day, £6.80 of credit will cover you, but it's smart to add a little more if you expect to travel outside the city center. If you're staying five or more days, consider adding a 7-Day Travelcard to your Oyster card (details below).

Oyster cards are not shareable among companions taking the same ride; each traveler will need his or her own. If your balance gets low, simply add credit—or "top up"—at a ticket window, machine, or shop. You can always see how much credit remains on your card (along with a list of where you've traveled) by touching it to the pad at any ticket machine. Remember to turn in your Oyster card after your last ride (you'll get back the £5 deposit and unused balance up to £10) at a ticket window or by selecting "Pay as you go refund" on any ticket machine that gives change. This will deactivate your card. For balances of more than £10, you must go to a ticket window for your refund. If you don't deactivate your card, the credit never expires—you can use it again on your next trip.

PASSES AND DISCOUNTS

7-Day Travelcard: Various Tube passes and deals are available. Of these, the only option of note is the 7-Day Travelcard. This is the best choice if you're staying five or more days and plan to use public transit a lot (£34.10 for Zones 1-2; £62.30 for Zones 1-6). For most travelers, the Zone 1-2 pass works best. Heathrow Airport is in Zone 6, but there's no need to buy the Zones 1-6 version if that's the only ride outside the city center you plan to take—instead you can pay a small supplement to cover the difference. You can add the 7-Day Travelcard to your Oyster card or purchase the paper version at any National Rail train station.

Families: A paying adult can take up to four kids (10 and under) for free on the Tube, Docklands Light Railway (DLR), Overground, and buses. Kids 11-15 get a discount. Explore other child and student discounts at www.tfl.gov.uk/tickets or ask a clerk at a Tube ticket window which deal is best.

River Cruises: A Travelcard gives you a 33 percent discount on most Thames cruises. The Oyster card gives you roughly a 10 percent discount on Thames Clippers (including the Tate Boat museum ferry).

THE BOTTOM LINE

On a short visit (three days or fewer), I'd get an Oyster card and add £20-25 of credit (£6.60 daily cap times three days, plus a little extra for any rides outside Zones 1-2). If you'll be taking fewer rides, £15 will be enough (£2.90 per ride during peak time gets you 5 rides); if not, you can always top up. For a visit of five days or more, the 7-Day Travelcard—either the paper version or on an Oyster card—will likely pay for itself.

By Tube

London's subway system is called the Tube or Underground (but never "subway," which, in Britain, refers to a pedestrian underpass). The Tube is one of this

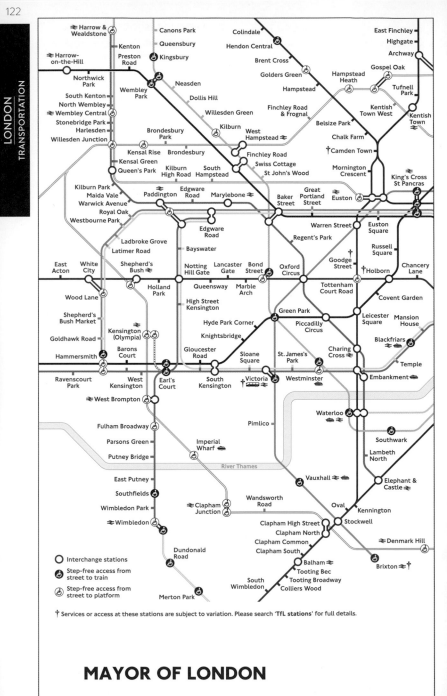

O Interchange stations
Step-free access from street to train
Step-free access from street to platform

† Services or access at these stations are subject to variation. Please search 'TfL stations' for full details.

MAYOR OF LONDON

Correct at time of going to print

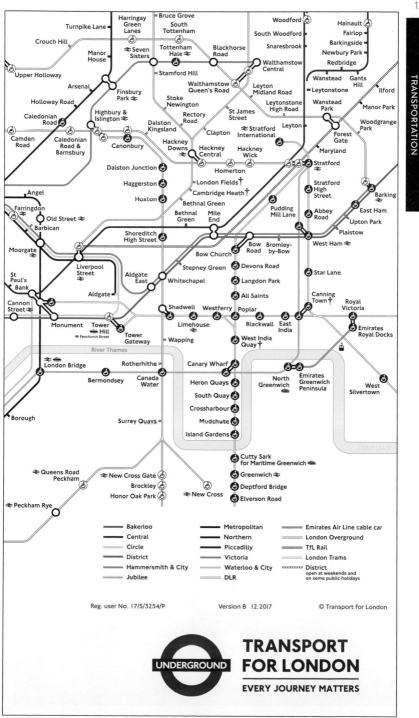

Bakerloo
Central
Circle
District
Hammersmith & City
Jubilee
Metropolitan
Northern
Piccadilly
Victoria
Waterloo & City
DLR
Emirates Air Line cable car
London Overground
TfL Rail
London Trams
District
open at weekends and
on some public holidays

Reg. user No. 17/S/3254/P   Version B 12.2017   © Transport for London

UNDERGROUND

TRANSPORT
FOR LONDON

EVERY JOURNEY MATTERS

planet's great people-movers and usually the fastest long-distance transport in town (runs Mon-Sat about 5:00-24:00, Sun about 7:00-23:00; Central, Jubilee, Northern, Piccadilly, and Victoria lines also run Fri-Sat 24 hours). Two other commuter rail lines are tied into the network and use the same tickets: the Docklands Light Railway (called DLR) and the Overground.

Each line has a name (such as Circle, Northern, or Bakerloo) and two directions (indicated by the end-of-the-line stops). Find the line that will take you to your destination, and figure out roughly which direction (north, south, east, or west) you'll need to go to get there.

At the Tube station, there are two ways to pass through the turnstile. With an Oyster card, touch it flat against the turnstile's yellow card reader, both when you enter and exit the station. With a paper ticket or paper Travelcard, feed it into the turnstile, reclaim it, and hang on to it— you'll need it later.

Find your train by following signs to your line and the (general) direction it's headed (such as Central Line: east). Since some tracks are shared by several lines, double-check before boarding: Make sure your destination is one of the stops listed on the sign at the platform. Also, check the electronic signboards that announce which train is next, and make sure the destination (the end-of-the-line stop) is the direction you want. Some trains, particularly on the Circle and District lines, split off for other directions, but each train has its final destination marked above its windshield.

Trains run about every 3-10 minutes. A general rule of thumb is that it takes 30 minutes to travel six Tube stops (including walking time within stations), or roughly five minutes per stop.

When you leave the system, "touch out" with your Oyster card at the electronic reader on the turnstile, or feed your paper ticket into the turnstile (it will eat your now-expired ticket). With a paper Travelcard, it will spit out your still-valid card. Check maps and signs for the most convenient exit.

The system can be fraught with construction delays and breakdowns. Pay attention to signs and announcements

explaining necessary detours. Rush hours (8:00-10:00 and 16:00-19:00) can be packed and sweaty. If one train is stuffed—and another is coming in three minutes—it may be worth a wait to avoid the sardine routine. If you get confused, ask for advice from a local, a blue-vested staffer, or at the information window located before the turnstile entry. Online, get help from the "Plan a Journey" feature at www.tfl.gov.uk, which is accessible (via free Wi-Fi) on any mobile device within most Tube stations before you go underground.

TUBE ETIQUETTE

- When your train arrives, stand off to the side and let riders exit before you board.
- When the car is jam-packed, avoid using the hinged seats near the doors of some trains—they take up valuable standing space.
- If you're blocking the door when the train stops, step out of the car and off to the side, let others off, then get back on.
- Talk softly in the cars. Listen to how quietly Londoners communicate and follow their lead.
- On escalators, stand on the right and pass on the left. But note that in some passageways or stairways, you might be directed to walk on the left (the direction Brits go when behind the wheel).
- Discreet eating and drinking are fine (nothing smelly); drinking alcohol and smoking are banned.
- Be zipped up to thwart thieves.
- Carefully check exit options before surfacing to street level. Signs point clearly to nearby sights—you'll save lots of walking by choosing the right exit.

By Bus

If you figure out the bus system, you'll swing like Tarzan through the urban jungle of London. Get in the habit of hopping buses for quick little straight shots, even just to get to a Tube stop. However, during bump-and-grind rush hours (8:00-10:00

and 16:00-19:00), you'll usually go faster by Tube.

You can't buy single-trip tickets for buses, and you can't use cash to pay when boarding. Instead, you must have an Oyster card, a paper Travelcard, or a one-day Bus & Tram Pass (£5, can buy on day of travel only—not beforehand, from ticket machine in any Tube station). If you're using your Oyster card, any bus ride in downtown London costs £1.50 (capped at £4.50/day).

When your bus approaches, it's wise to hold your arm out to let the driver know you want to get on. Hop on and confirm your destination with the driver (often friendly and helpful).

As you board, touch your Oyster card to the card reader, or show your paper Travelcard or Bus & Tram Pass to the driver. Unlike on the Tube, there's no need to show or tap your card when you hop off. On the older heritage "Routemaster" buses without card-readers (used on the #15 route), you simply take a seat, and the conductor comes around to check cards and passes.

To alert the driver that you want to get off, press one of the red buttons (on the poles between the seats) before your stop.

By Taxi

London is the best taxi town in Europe. Big, black, carefully regulated cabs are everywhere—there are about 25,000 of them.

Handy Bus Routes

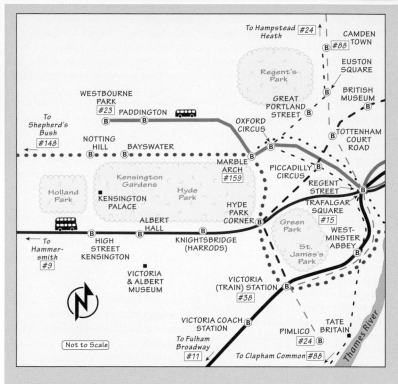

Here are some of the most useful routes:

Route #9: High Street Kensington to Knightsbridge (Harrods) to Hyde Park Corner to Trafalgar Square to Somerset House.

Route #11: Victoria Station to Westminster Abbey to Trafalgar Square to St. Paul's and Liverpool Street Station and the East End.

Route #15: Trafalgar Square to St. Paul's to Tower of London (sometimes with heritage "Routemaster" old-style double-decker buses).

Routes #23 and #159: Paddington Station (#159 begins at Marble Arch) to Oxford Circus to Piccadilly Circus to Trafalgar Square; from there, #23 heads east to St. Paul's and Liverpool Street Station, while #159 heads to Westminster and the Imperial War Museum. In addition, several buses (including #6, #12, and #139) also make the corridor run between Marble Arch, Oxford Circus, Piccadilly Circus, and Trafalgar Square.

Route #24: Pimlico to Victoria Station to Westminster Abbey to Trafalgar Square to Euston Square, then all the way north to Camden Town (Camden Lock Market).

Route #38: Victoria Station to Hyde Park Corner to Piccadilly Circus to British Museum.

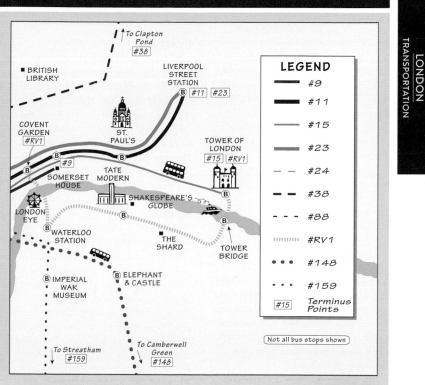

LEGEND

▬▬▬	#9
▬▬▬	#11
▬▬▬	#15
▬▬▬	#23
– – –	#24
▬ ▬ ▬	#38
- - -	#88
⊔⊔⊔⊔⊔	#RV1
● ● ●	#148
· · ·	#159
#15	Terminus Points

Not all bus stops shown

Route #88: Tate Britain to Westminster Abbey to Trafalgar Square to Piccadilly Circus to Oxford Circus to Great Portland Street Station (Regent's Park), then north to Camden Town.

Route #148: Westminster Abbey to Victoria Station to Notting Hill and Bayswater (by way of the east end of Hyde Park and Marble Arch).

Route #RV1 (a scenic South Bank joyride): Tower of London to Tower Bridge to Southwark Street (five-minute walk behind Tate Modern/Shakespeare's Globe) to London Eye/Waterloo Station, then over Waterloo Bridge to Somerset House and Covent Garden.

I've never met a crabby cabbie in London. They love to talk, and they know every nook and cranny in town. I ride in a taxi each day just to get my London questions answered. Drivers must pass a rigorous test on "The Knowledge" of London geography to earn their license.

If a cab's top light is on, just wave it down. Drivers flash lights when they see you wave. They have a tight turning radius, so you can hail cabs going in either direction. If waving doesn't work, ask someone where you can find a taxi stand. Telephoning a cab will get you one in a few minutes, but costs a little more (tel. 0871-871-8710).

Rates: Rides start at £2.60. The regular tariff #1 covers most of the day (Mon-Fri 5:00-20:00), tariff #2 is during "unsociable hours" (Mon-Fri 20:00-22:00 and Sat-Sun 5:00-22:00), and tariff #3 is for nighttime (22:00-5:00) and holidays. Rates go up about 40 percent with each higher tariff. Extra charges are explained in writing on the cab wall. All cabs accept credit and debit cards, including American cards. Tip a cabbie by rounding up (maximum 10 percent).

Connecting downtown sights is quick and easy, and will cost you about £8-10 (for example, St. Paul's to the Tower of London, or between the two Tate museums). For a short ride, three adults in a cab generally travel at close to Tube prices—and groups of four or five adults should taxi everywhere. All cabs can carry five passengers, and some take six, for the same cost as a single traveler.

Don't worry about meter cheating. Licensed British cab meters come with a sealed computer chip and clock that ensures you'll get the correct tariff. The only way a cabbie can cheat you is by taking a needlessly long route. One serious pitfall, however, is taking a cab when traffic is bad to a destination efficiently served by the Tube.

If you overdrink and ride in a taxi, be warned: Taxis charge £40 for "soiling" (a.k.a., pub puke). If you forget this book in a taxi, call the Lost Property office and hope for the best (tel. 0845-330-9882).

By Uber

Uber faces legal challenges in London and may not be operating when you visit. If Uber is running, it can be much cheaper than a taxi and is a handy alternative if there's a long line for a taxi or if no cabs are available. Uber drivers generally don't know the city as well as regular cabbies, and they don't have the access to some fast lanes that taxis do. Still, if you like using Uber, it can work great here.

By Boat

The sleek, 220-seat catamarans used by **Thames Clippers** are designed for commuters rather than sightseers. Think of the boats as express buses on the river—they zip through London every 20-30 minutes, stopping at most of the major docks en route. They're fast: roughly 20 minutes from Embankment to Tower, 10 more minutes to Docklands, and 15 more minutes to Greenwich. However, the only outside access is on a crowded deck at the exhaust-choked back of the boat, where you're jostling for space to take photos. Any one-way ride in Central London (roughly London Eye to Tower Pier) costs £8; a one-way ride to East London (Canary Wharf and Greenwich) is £8.70, and a River Roamer all-day ticket costs £18.50 (discounts with Travelcard and Oyster card, www.thamesclippers.com).

Thames Clippers also offers two express trips. The **Tate Boat** ferry service, which directly connects the Tate Britain (Millbank Pier) and the Tate Modern (Bankside Pier), is made for art lovers (£8 one-way, covered by River Roamer day ticket; buy ticket at kiosks or self-service machines before boarding or use Oyster Card; for frequency and times, see www.tate.org.uk/visit/tate-boat). The **O2 Express** runs only on nights when there are events at the O2 arena (departs from London Eye Pier).

By Bike

London operates a citywide bike-rental program similar to ones in other major European cities, and new bike lanes are still cropping up around town.

Still, London isn't (yet) ideal for biking. Its network of designated bike lanes is far from complete, and the city's many one-way streets (not to mention the need to bike on the "wrong" side) can make biking here a bit more challenging than it sounds.

Santander Cycles, intended for quick point-to-point trips, are fairly easy to rent. Approximately 700 bike-rental stations are scattered throughout the city (£2/day access fee; first 30 minutes free; £2 for every additional 30-minute period). When you're ready to ride, press "Hire a Cycle" and insert your credit card when prompted. You'll then get a ticket with a five-digit code. Take the ticket to any bike that doesn't have a red light (those are "taken") and punch in the number. After the yellow light blinks, a green light will appear: Now you can (firmly) pull the bike out of the slot. When your ride is over, find a station with an empty slot, then push your bike in until it locks and the green light flashes.

You can hire bikes as often as you like (which will start your free 30-minute period over again), as long as you wait five minutes between each use. Pick up a map of the docking stations at any major Tube station. The same map is also available online at www.tfl.gov.uk (click on "Santander Cycles") and as a free app (http://cyclehireapp.com).

By Car

If you have a car, stow it—you don't want to drive in London. An £11.50 **congestion charge** is levied on any private car entering the city center during peak hours (Mon-Fri 7:00-18:00, no charge Sat-Sun and holidays). You can pay the fee either online or by phone (www.cclondon.com, from within the UK call 0343/222-2222, from outside the UK call 011-44-20/7649-9122, phones answered Mon-Fri 8:00-22:00, Sat 9:00-15:00, be ready to give the vehicle registration number and country of registration). There are painfully stiff penalties for late payments.

Arriving and Departing
By Plane

London has six airports; I've focused my coverage on the two most widely used—Heathrow and Gatwick—with a few tips for using the others (Stansted, Luton, London City, and Southend).

HEATHROW AIRPORT

For Heathrow's airport, flight, and transfer information, call the switchboard at 0844-335-1801, or visit the helpful website www.heathrow.com (airport code: LHR).

Heathrow's terminals are numbered T-1 through T-5. Though T-1 is now closed for arrivals and departures, it still supports other terminals with baggage, and the newly renovated T-2 ("Queen's Terminal") will likely expand into the old T-1 digs eventually. Each terminal is served by different airlines and alliances; for example, T-5 is exclusively for British Air and Iberia Air flights, while T-2 serves mostly Star Alliance flights, such as United and Lufthansa. Screens posted throughout the airport identify which terminal each airline uses; this information should also be printed on your ticket or boarding pass.

You can walk between T-2 and T-3. From this central hub (called "Heathrow Central"), T-4 and T-5 split off in opposite directions (and are not walkable). The easiest way to travel between the T-2/T-3 cluster and either T-4 or T-5 is by Heathrow Express train (free to transfer between terminals, departs every 15-20 minutes). You can also take a shuttle bus (free, serves all terminals), or the Tube (requires a ticket, serves all terminals).

London's Airports

Luton

Luton

Stansted

#751 & A1

Not to Scale

ST. PANCRAS

Reading

Windsor
#71 & 77

PADDINGTON

LIVERPOOL STREET

Southend

Southend

Rail Air Link

Tube

D.L.R.

To Bath

Heathrow

VICTORIA

London City

Thames

VICTORIA COACH STN.

London

EUROSTAR

Guildford

Gatwick

Ashford

	Rail
	Eurostar Rail
	Tube & D.L.R.
	Bus

ALL BUSES ARE NATIONAL EXPRESS
UNLESS NOTED

To Brighton

To Paris

English Channel

If you're flying out of Heathrow, it's critical to confirm which terminal your flight will use (look at your ticket/boarding pass, check online, or call your airline in advance)—if it's T-4 or T-5, allow extra time. Taxi drivers generally know which terminal you'll need based on the airline, but bus drivers may not.

Services: Each terminal has an airport information desk (open long hours daily), car-rental agencies, exchange bureaus, ATMs, a pharmacy, a VAT refund desk (tel. 0845-872-7627, you must present the VAT claim form from the retailer here to get your tax rebate on purchased items), and baggage storage (£6/item up to 2 hours, £11/item for 2-24 hours, long hours daily, www.left-baggage.co.uk). Heathrow offers both free Wi-Fi and pay Internet access points (in each terminal, check map for locations). You'll find a post office on the first floor of T-3 (departures area). Each terminal also has cheap eateries.

Heathrow's small **"TI"** (tourist info shop), even though it's a for-profit business, is worth a visit if you're nearby and want to pick up free information, including the *London Planner* visitors guide (long hours daily, 5-minute walk from T-3 in Tube station, follow signs to Underground; bypass queue for transit info to reach window for London questions).

Getting Between Heathrow and Downtown London: You have several options for traveling the 14 miles between Heathrow Airport and downtown London: Tube, bus, express train (with connecting Tube or taxi), or taxi. The one that works best for you will depend on your arrival terminal, your destination in central London, and your budget.

By Tube (Subway): The Tube takes you from any Heathrow terminal to downtown London in 50-60 minutes on the Piccadilly Line (6/hour, buy ticket at Tube station ticket window or self-service machine). If you plan to use the Tube for transport in London, it makes sense to buy a pay-as-you-go Oyster card (possibly adding a 7-Day Travelcard) at the airport's Tube station ticket window. If you add a Travelcard that covers only Zones 1-2, you'll need to pay a small supplement for the initial trip from Heathrow (Zone 6) to downtown.

If you're taking the Tube from downtown London to the airport, note that Piccadilly Line trains don't stop at every terminal. Trains either stop at T-4, then T-2/T-3 (also called Heathrow Central), in that order; or T-2/T-3, then T-5. When leaving central London on the Tube, allow extra time if going to T-4 or T-5, and check the reader board in the station to make sure that the train goes to the right terminal.

By Bus: Most buses depart from the outdoor common area called the Central Bus Station, a five-minute walk from the T-2/T-3 complex. To connect between T-4 or T-5 and the Central Bus Station, ride the free Heathrow Express train or the shuttle buses.

National Express has regular service from Heathrow's Central Bus Station to Victoria Coach Station in downtown London, near several of my recommended hotels. While slow, the bus is affordable and convenient for those staying near Victoria Station (£8-10, 1-2/hour, less frequent from Victoria Station to Heathrow, 45-75 minutes depending on time of day, tel. 0871-781-8181, www.nationalexpress.com). A less-frequent National Express bus goes from T-5 directly to Victoria Coach Station.

By Train: Two different trains run between Heathrow Airport and London's Paddington Station. At Paddington Station, you're in the thick of the Tube system, with easy access to any of my recommended neighborhoods. The **Heathrow Connect** train is the slightly slower, much cheaper option, serving T-2/T-3 at a single station called Heathrow Central; use free transfers to get from either T-4 or T-5 to Heathrow Central (£10.30 one-way, £20.70 round-trip, 2/hour Mon-Sat, 1-2/hour Sun, 40 minutes, tel. 0345-604-1515, www.heathrowconnect.com). By the time you visit, the new **Crossrail Elizabeth line** may be operational, connecting Heathrow Central and T-4 to Paddington (and most likely replacing the Heathrow Connect train service).

The **Heathrow Express** train is fast and runs more frequently, but it's pricey

(£22-25 one-way, price depends on time of day, £37 round-trip, £5 more if you buy your ticket on board, covered by BritRail pass; 4/hour, daily 5:00-24:00, 15 minutes to downtown from Heathrow Central Station serving T-2/T-3, 21 minutes from T-5; for T-4 take free transfer to Heathrow Central, tel. 0345-600-1515, www.heathrowexpress.co.uk).

By Taxi: Taxis from the airport cost £45-75 to west and central London (one hour). For four people traveling together, this can be a reasonable option. Hotels can often line up a cab back to the airport for about £50. If running, Uber also offers London airport pickup and drop-off.

GATWICK AIRPORT

More and more flights land at Gatwick Airport, which is halfway between London and the south coast (airport code: LGW, tel. 0844-892-0322, www.gatwickairport.com). Gatwick has two terminals, North and South, which are easily connected by a free, two-minute monorail ride. Boarding passes say "Gatwick N" or "Gatwick S" to indicate your terminal. British Airways flights generally use Gatwick South. The Gatwick Express trains (described next) stop only at Gatwick South.

Getting Between Gatwick and Downtown London: The best way into London from this airport, Gatwick Express trains shuttle conveniently between Gatwick South and London's Victoria Station (£20 one-way, £35 round-trip, cheaper if purchased online, Oyster cards accepted, 4/hour, 30 minutes, runs 5:00-24:00 daily, a few trains as early as 3:30, tel. 0845-850-1530, www.gatwickexpress.com). When going to the airport, at Victoria Station note that Gatwick Express has its own ticket windows right by the platform (tracks 13 and 14).

A train also runs between Gatwick South and St. Pancras International Station (£10.40, 3-5/hour, 45-60 minutes, www.thetrainline.com)—useful for travelers taking the Eurostar train (to Paris, Brussels, or Amsterdam) or staying in the St. Pancras/King's Cross neighborhood.

While even slower, the **bus** is a cheap and handy option to the Victoria Station neighborhood. National Express runs a bus from Gatwick direct to Victoria Station (£9, at least hourly, 1.5 hours, tel. 0871-781-8181, www.nationalexpress.com).

LONDON'S OTHER AIRPORTS

Stansted Airport: Airport code: STN, tel. 0844-335-1803, www.stanstedairport.com. **Buses** run by National Express (£9-12, www.nationalexpress.com) and Terravision (£4-10) connect the airport and London's Victoria Station neighborhood in about 1.5-2 hours. Or you can take the faster Stansted Express **train** (£19, www.stanstedexpress.com). Stansted is expensive by **cab;** figure £100-120 one-way from central London.

Luton Airport: Airport code: LTN, airport tel. 01582/405-100, www.london-luton.co.uk. The fastest way to go into London is by **train** to St. Pancras International Station (£10-14 one-way, 35-45 minutes, www.eastmidlandstrains.co.uk); catch the 10-minute shuttle bus from outside the terminal to the Luton Airport Parkway Station. The National Express **bus** A1 runs from Luton to Victoria Coach Station (£7-11 one-way, 1-1.5 hours, www.nationalexpress.com). The Green Line express **bus** #757 runs to Buckingham Palace Road, just south of Victoria Station, and stops en route near the Baker Street Tube station (£10 one-way, 1-1.5 hours, www.greenline.co.uk).

London City and Southend Airports: To get into the city center from London City Airport (airport code: LCY, tel. 020/7646-0088, www.londoncityairport.com). Take the Docklands Light Railway (DLR) to the Bank Tube station, which is one stop east of St. Paul's on the Central Line (£6, covered by Travelcard, a bit cheaper with an Oyster card, 20 minutes, www.tfl.gov.uk/dlr). Some easyJet flights land farther out, at Southend Airport (airport code: SEN, tel. 01702/538-500, www.southendairport.com). Trains connect this airport to London's Liverpool Street Station (£16.20, 55 minutes, www. abelliogreateranglia.co.uk).

By Train

London, the country's major transportation hub, has a different train station for each region. There are nine main stations:

- **Euston:** Serves northwest England, North Wales, and Scotland.
- **St. Pancras International:** Serves north and south England, plus the Eurostar to Paris, Brussels, or Amsterdam.
- **King's Cross:** Serves northeast England and Scotland, including York and Edinburgh.
- **Liverpool Street:** Serves east England, including Essex and Harwich.
- **London Bridge:** Serves south England, including Brighton.
- **Waterloo:** Serves south England, including Salisbury and Southampton.
- **Victoria:** Serves Gatwick Airport, Canterbury, Dover, and Brighton.
- **Paddington:** Serves south and southwest England, including Heathrow Airport, Windsor, Bath, Oxford, South Wales, and the Cotswolds.

- **Marylebone:** Serves southwest and central England, including Stratford-upon-Avon.

Any train station has schedule information, can make reservations, and can sell tickets for any destination. Most stations offer a baggage-storage service; because of long security lines, it can take a while to check or pick up your bag (www.left-baggage.co.uk). For more details on the services available at each station, see www.nationalrail.co.uk/stations.

UK **train and bus info** is available at www.traveline.org.uk. For information on tickets and rail passes, see page 407.

TRAIN CONNECTIONS FROM LONDON

From Paddington Station to Points West: Windsor (Windsor & Eton Central Station, 2/hour, 35 minutes, easy change at Slough), **Bath** (2/hour, 1.5 hours), **Oxford** (4/hour direct, 1 hour, more with transfer), **Moreton-in-Marsh** (hourly, 1.5 hours).

From King's Cross Station to Points North: York (hourly, 2 hours), **Durham** (hourly, 3 hours), and **Edinburgh** (4.5 hours).

From Euston Station to Points North: Liverpool (at least hourly, 3 hours, more with transfer), **Keswick** (hourly, 4 hours, transfer to bus at Penrith).

London's Major Train Stations

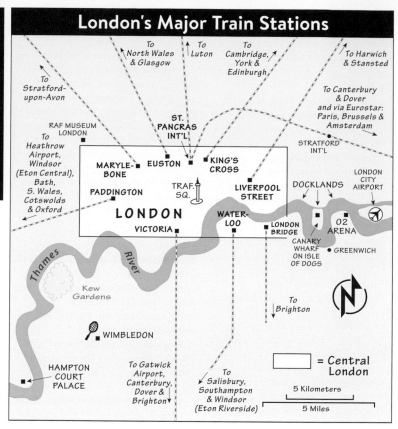

To North Wales & Glasgow

To Luton

To Cambridge, York & Edinburgh

To Harwich & Stansted

To Stratford-upon-Avon

To Canterbury & Dover and via Eurostar: Paris, Brussels & Amsterdam

RAF MUSEUM LONDON

To Heathrow Airport, Windsor (Eton Central), Bath, S. Wales, Cotswolds & Oxford

ST. PANCRAS INT'L

STRATFORD INT'L

MARYLE-BONE EUSTON KING'S CROSS

PADDINGTON

TRAF. SQ.

LIVERPOOL STREET

DOCKLANDS

LONDON CITY AIRPORT

LONDON

VICTORIA

WATER-LOO

LONDON BRIDGE

O2 ARENA

CANARY WHARF ON ISLE OF DOGS

GREENWICH

Thames River

Kew Gardens

To Brighton

WIMBLEDON

HAMPTON COURT PALACE

To Gatwick Airport, Canterbury, Dover & Brighton

To Salisbury, Southampton & Windsor (Eton Riverside)

= Central London

5 Kilometers

5 Miles

From London's Other Stations to: **Stratford-upon-Avon** from Marylebone Station (1-2/hour with transfers, 2.5 hours hours), **Greenwich** from Bank or Monument Tube stop on the DLR—Docklands Light Railway (6/hour, 20 minutes).

By Bus

Buses are slower but considerably cheaper than trains for reaching destinations around Britain and beyond. Most depart from **Victoria Coach Station,** which is one long block south of Victoria Station (Tube: Victoria). Inside the station, you'll find basic eateries, kiosks, and a helpful information desk.

Ideally you'll buy your tickets online (for tips on buying tickets and taking

buses, see page 409). But if you must buy one at the station, try to arrive an hour before the bus departs, or drop by the day before. Ticketing machines are scattered around the station (separate machines for National Express/Eurolines and Megabus; you can buy either for today or for tomorrow); there's also a ticket counter near gate 21. For UK train and bus info, check www.traveline.org.uk.

National Express buses go to: **Bath** (nearly hourly, 3 hours), **Oxford** (2/hour, 2.5 hours), **Stratford-upon-Avon** (3/day, 3.5 hours), **Liverpool** (8/day direct, 5.5 hours, overnight available), **York** (4/day direct, 5 hours), **Durham** (3/day direct, 7 hours, train is better), **Edinburgh,** Scotland (2/day direct, 10 hours, go by train instead).

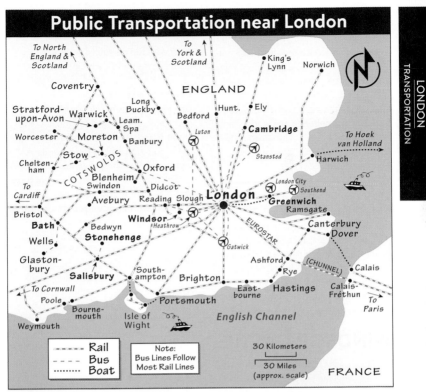

NEAR LONDON

Windsor and Stonehenge are two great day-trip possibilities near London. **Windsor Castle,** the primary residence of Her Majesty the Queen, is regally lived-in yet open to the public (23 miles west of London). **Stonehenge,** the world's most famous rock group, sits lonesome and adored in a mysterious field 90 miles southwest of the city.

Rick's Tip: *Take advantage of* **British Rail's "off-peak day return" ticket.** *This round-trip fare costs virtually the same as one-way, provided you depart London outside rush hour (usually after 9:30 on weekdays and anytime Sat-Sun). Ask for the "day return" ticket (round-trip within a single day) rather than the more expensive standard "return."*

WINDSOR CASTLE

Windsor Castle, rated ▲▲, the official home of England's royal family for 900 years, claims to be the largest and oldest occupied castle in the world. (The current Queen considers Windsor her primary residence, and generally hangs her crown here on weekends.) Thankfully, touring it is simple. You'll see sprawling grounds, lavish staterooms, a crowd-pleasing dollhouse, a gallery of Michelangelo and Leonardo da Vinci drawings, and an exquisite Perpendicular Gothic chapel.

Orientation

Day Plan: Follow my self-guided tour or the included audioguide through the grounds and castle. You could also take the free guided walk of the grounds. A typical castle visit lasts two to three hours.

Getting There: Windsor has two **train stations**—London's Paddington Station connects with Windsor & Eton Central (2-3/hour, 35 minutes, easy change at Slough, www.gwr.com). London's Waterloo Station connects with Windsor & Eton Riverside (2/hour, no changes but slower—55 minutes, www.nationalrail.co.uk).

Green Line **buses** #701 and #702 run from London's Victoria Colonnades to the Parish Church stop on Windsor's High Street (1-2/hour, 1.5 hours, £6-10 one-way, www.firstgroup.com).

Windsor is well-signposted from the **M-4 motorway.** Follow signs from the motorway for pay-and-display parking in the center.

Cost: £20.50, includes entry to castle grounds and all exhibits.

Hours: Grounds and most interiors open daily 9:30-17:15, Nov-Feb 9:45-16:15, except St. George's Chapel, which is

Windsor Castle

Changing of the Guard at Windsor

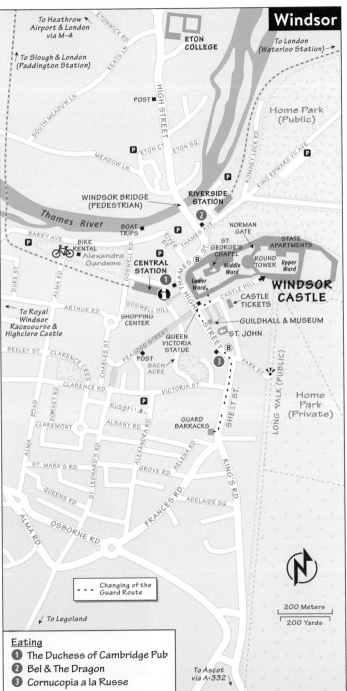

Windsor

To Heathrow Airport & London via M-4

To Slough & London (Paddington Station)

ETONWICK RD.

KEATS LN.

ETON COLLEGE

To London (Waterloo Station)

HIGH STREET

POST ■

SOUTH MEADOW LN.

MEADOW LN.

P ETON CT.

ETON SQ.

P

Home Park (Public)

ROMNEY LOCK RD.

KING EDWARD VII AVE.

P

WINDSOR BRIDGE (PEDESTRIAN)

RIVERSIDE STATION

2

NORMAN GATE

Thames River

BOAT TRIPS ■

P

ST. GEORGE'S CHAPEL

STATE APARTMENTS

BARRY AVE.

BIKE RENTAL

■ Alexandra Gardens

RIVER ST.

THAMES AVE.

THAMES ST.

P

B

Middle Ward

ROUND TOWER

Upper Ward

CENTRAL STATION

1

Lower Ward

DUKE ST.

ALMA RD.

GOSWELL RD.

HIGH STREET

CASTLE HILL

WINDSOR CASTLE

GOSWELL HILL

CASTLE TICKETS

To Royal Windsor Racecourse & Highclere Castle

ARTHUR RD.

SHOPPING CENTER

GUILDHALL & MUSEUM

ST. JOHN

CHARLES ST.

PEASCOD STREET

QUEEN VICTORIA STATUE

B

3

PARK ST.

BEXLEY ST.

CLARENCE CRES.

POST ◆

BACH-ACRE

SHEET ST.

LONG WALK (PUBLIC)

Home Park (Private)

CLARENCE RD.

VICTORIA ST.

ROAD

DORSET RD.

RUSSELL

P

ALBANY RD.

ALEXANDRA RD.

GUARD BARRACKS

CLAREMONT

ST. MARK'S RD.

ST. LEONARD'S RD.

GROVE RD.

HELENA RD.

KING'S RD.

ALMA

QUEENS RD.

FRANCES RD.

ADELAIDE SQ.

OSBORNE RD.

ALMA RD.

To Legoland

Changing of the Guard Route

200 Meters

200 Yards

To Ascot via A-332

Eating
1 The Duchess of Cambridge Pub
2 Bel & The Dragon
3 Cornucopia a la Russe

closed Sun (but open to worshippers; wait at the exit gate to be escorted in).

Information: Tel. 020/7766-7324, www.royalcollection.org.uk. The TI is in the Windsor Royal Shopping Centre's Old Booking Hall, immediately adjacent to Windsor & Eton Central Station.

Crowd Control: In summer, it's smart to buy tickets in advance online at www.royalcollection.org.uk (collect them at the prepaid ticket window), or in person at the Buckingham Palace ticket office in London.

Possible Closures: On rare occasions when the Queen is entertaining guests, the State Apartments close. Check the website (especially in mid-June) to make sure everything is open when you want to go.

Tours: An included **audioguide** covers both the grounds and interiors. Consider the free 30-minute **guided walk** around the grounds (usually 2/hour, schedule posted next to audioguide desk).

Changing of the Guard: The Changing of the Guard takes place Monday through Saturday at 11:00 (April-July; arrive by 10:30) and on alternating days the rest of the year (confirm schedule on website). The fresh guards, led by a marching band, leave their barracks on Sheet Street and march up High Street, hanging a right at Victoria, then a left into the castle's Lower Ward, arriving at about 11:00. After about a half-hour, the tired guards march back the way the new ones came. To watch the actual ceremony inside the castle, you'll need to have already bought your ticket, entered the grounds, and staked out a spot. Alternatively, you could wait for them to march by on High Street or on the lower half of Castle Hill.

Evensong: An evensong takes place in the chapel nightly at 17:15 (free for worshippers, line up at exit gate to be admitted).

Eating: There are no real eateries inside (other than shops selling gifty boxes of chocolates and bottled water), but **The Duchess of Cambridge** serves up pub grub right across from the castle walls (3 Thames Street). Also consider the charming **Bel & The Dragon** (on Thames Street, near the bridge) or the cozy **Cornucopia a la Russe** (closed Sun, 6 High Street).

❍ *Visiting the Castle*

The Grounds: Head up the hill, enjoying the first of many fine castle views you'll see today. The tower-topped conical hill represents the historical core of the castle. William the Conqueror built this motte (artificial mound) and bailey (fortified stockade around it) in 1080—his first castle in England. Among the later monarchs who spiffed up Windsor were Edward III (flush with French war booty, he made it a palace fit for a 14th-century king), Charles II (determined to restore the monarchy properly in the 1660s), and George IV (Britain's "Bling King," who financed many such vanity projects in the 1820s).

The castle has three "baileys" (castle yards), which today make up Windsor's Upper Ward (where the Queen lives), Middle Ward (with St. George's Chapel),

Round Tower

and Lower Ward (residences for castle workers). The Upper Ward's **Quadrangle** is surrounded by the State Apartments and the Queen's private apartments. The **Round Tower** sits atop the original motte. The red, yellow, and blue royal standard flies here when the Queen is in residence.

Queen Mary's Dolls' House: This palace in miniature (1:12 scale, from 1924) is "the most famous dollhouse in the world." It was a gift for the adult Queen Mary (the current Queen's grandmother), who greatly enjoyed miniatures. It's basically one big, dimly lit room with the large dollhouse in the middle, executed with an astonishing level of detail. Each fork, knife, and spoon on the expertly set banquet table is perfect and made of real silver—and the tiny pipes of its plumbing system actually have running water.

Drawings Gallery and China Museum: This gallery displays a changing array of pieces from the Queen's collection—usually including some big names, such as Michelangelo and Leonardo. The China Museum features items from the Queen's many exquisite settings for royal shindigs.

State Apartments: Dripping with chandeliers, finely furnished, and strewn with history and the art of a long line of kings and queens, they're the best I've seen in Britain. This is where Henry VIII and Charles I once lived, and where the current Queen wows visiting dignitaries.

You'll climb the Grand Staircase up to the **Grand Vestibule,** decorated with exotic items seized by British troops during their missions to colonize various corners of the world. (Ask a docent to help you find the bullet that killed Lord Nelson at Trafalgar.) The magnificent wood-ceilinged **Waterloo Chamber** is wallpapered with portraits of figures from the pan-European alliance that defeated Napoleon.

Many rooms are decorated with some of the finest works from the royal collection, including by Rubens, Van Dyck, and Holbein. **St. George's Hall** is decorated with emblems representing the knights of the prestigious Order of the Garter, established by Edward III in 1834. This hall is the site of elaborate royal banquets—imagine one long table stretching from one end of the hall to the other and seating 160 VIPs. The **Garter Throne Room** is where new members of the Order of the Garter are invested (ceremonially granted their titles).

St. George's Chapel: This church is an exquisite example of the Perpendicular Gothic style (dating from about 1500). Pick up a free map and circle the interior to find the highlights, including burial spots of the current Queen's parents, **King George VI and "Queen Mum" Elizabeth,** and **King Henry VIII** and Jane Seymour, Henry's favorite wife (perhaps because she was the only one who died before he could behead her). The body of **King Charles I,** who was beheaded by Oliver Cromwell's forces, was also discovered here...with its head sewn back on.

On your way out, pause at the door of the sumptuous 13th-century **Albert Memorial Chapel** (#28), redecorated in 1861 after the death of Queen Victoria's husband, Prince Albert, and dedicated to his memory.

Lower Ward: This area is a living town where some 160 people who work for the Queen reside.

STONEHENGE

As old as the pyramids, and far older than the Acropolis and the Colosseum, this iconic stone circle amazed medieval Europeans, who figured it was built by a race of giants. And it still impresses visitors today. As one of Europe's most famous sights, Stonehenge, worth ▲▲▲, does a valiant job of retaining an air of mystery and majesty (partly because cordons, which keep hordes of tourists from trampling all over it, foster the illusion that it stands alone in a field). Most of its almost one million annual visitors agree that it's well worth the trip.

Orientation

Day Plan: Tour the visitors center, then head to Stonehenge by shuttle bus or on foot. Allow at least two hours to see everything.

Getting There: Several companies offer **big-bus day trips** to Stonehenge from London. These generally cost about £45-85 (including Stonehenge admission), last 8-12 hours, and pack a 45-seat bus. Well-known companies are **Evan Evans** (www.evanevanstours.co.uk) and **Golden Tours** (www.goldentours.com). **International Friends** runs pricier but smaller 16-person tours that include Windsor and Bath (www.internationalfriends.co.uk).

London Walks offers a guided "Stonehenge and Salisbury Tour" from London by train and bus on Tuesdays from May through October (£78, cash only, www.walks.com).

To go on your own on **public transport,** catch a train (2/hour, 1.5 hours) from London's Waterloo Station to Salisbury (www.southwesttrains.co.uk or www.nationalrail.co.uk). From Salisbury, you can get to Stonehenge by taxi (£40-50) or take the **Stonehenge Tour bus** (£15, £29 with Stonehenge admission; daily June-Aug 10:00-18:00, 2/hour, 30 minutes, fewer departures off-season, timetable at www.thestonehengetour.info).

Cost: £17.50, includes shuttle-bus ride to stone circle, best to buy in advance online, covered by English Heritage Pass (see page 393).

Hours: Daily June-Aug 9:00-20:00, April-May and Sept-mid-Oct 9:30-19:00, mid-Oct-March 9:30-17:00. Note that the last ticket is sold two hours before closing. Expect shorter hours and possible closures June 20-22 due to huge, raucous solstice crowds.

Stonehenge is the most famous of Britain's stone circles.

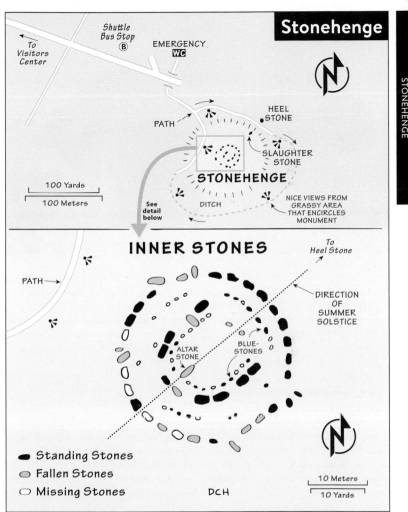

Stonehenge

Shuttle Bus Stop B

EMERGENCY WC

To Visitors Center

PATH

HEEL STONE

SLAUGHTER STONE

STONEHENGE

100 Yards
100 Meters

See detail below

DITCH

NICE VIEWS FROM GRASSY AREA THAT ENCIRCLES MONUMENT

INNER STONES

To Heel Stone

PATH →

DIRECTION OF SUMMER SOLSTICE

ALTAR STONE

BLUE-STONES

● Standing Stones
○ Fallen Stones
○ Missing Stones

DCH

10 Meters
10 Yards

Advance Tickets and Crowd-Beating Tips: You can avoid the long ticket-buying line by prebooking at least 24 hours in advance at www.english-heritage.org.uk/stonehenge. Either print out an e-ticket or bring the booking number from your confirmation email to the designated window at the entrance.

Information: Tel. 0370-333-1181, www.english-heritage.org.uk/stonehenge.

Tours: Worthwhile audioguides are available behind the ticket counter (included with Heritage Pass, otherwise £3). Or you can use the visitors center's free Wi-Fi to download the free "Stonehenge Audio Tour" app.

Visiting the Inner Stones: Special one-hour access to the stones' inner circle is available early in the morning or after closing to the general public. Only 30 people are allowed at a time, so reserve well in advance (£35, for details see the English

Reconstructed Neolithic hut

Heritage website).

Services: The visitors center has WCs, a large gift shop, and free Wi-Fi. Services at the circle itself are limited to emergency WCs.

Eating: There's a large **$ café** within the visitors center.

Rick's Tip: *For a less crowded, more mystical experience,* **come to Stonehenge early or late.** *Things are pretty quiet before 10:30 (head out to the stones first, then circle back to the exhibits); at the end of the day, aim to arrive just before the "last ticket" time (two hours before closing).*

● Self-Guided Tour

Start by touring the visitors center, then take a shuttle (or walk) to the stone circle.
• *As you enter the complex, on the right is the...*

PERMANENT EXHIBIT

This excellent, state-of-the-art exhibit uses an artful combination of multimedia displays and actual artifacts to provide context for the stones. Prehistoric bones, tools, and pottery shards tell the story of the people who built Stonehenge, how

they lived, and why they might have built the stone circle. Then step outside and explore a village of reconstructed **Neolithic huts** modeled after the traces of a village discovered just northeast of Stonehenge.
• *Shuttle buses to the stone circle depart every 5-10 minutes from the platform behind the gift shop. Or you can walk 1.25 miles through the fields to the site.*

Rick's Tip: *If you want to see a large* **Bronze Age burial mound,** *get off the shuttle bus at the Fargo Plantation. From there, you can walk the rest of the way to the stone circle in about 20 minutes. Some visitors prefer this more authentic approach.*

STONE CIRCLE

As you approach the massive structure, walk right up to the knee-high cordon and let your fellow 21st-century tourists melt away. It's just you and the druids...

England has hundreds of stone circles, but Stonehenge—which literally means "hanging stones"—is unique. It's the only one that has horizontal crosspieces (called lintels) spanning the vertical monoliths, and the only one with stones that have been made smooth and uniform. What you see here is a bit more than half the original structure—the rest was quarried centuries ago for other buildings.

Now do a slow **clockwise spin** around the monument. As you walk, mentally flesh out the missing pieces and re-erect the rubble.

It's now believed that Stonehenge, which was built in phases between 3000 and 1500 B.C., was originally used as a cremation **cemetery.** This was a hugely significant location to prehistoric peoples. There are several hundred burial mounds within a three-mile radius of Stonehenge—some likely belonging to kings or chieftains. Some of the human remains are of people from far away, and others show signs of injuries—evidence that Stonehenge may have been used as a place of medicine or healing.

Whatever its original purpose, Stonehenge still functions as a celestial calendar. As the sun rises on the summer solstice (June 21), the **"heel stone"**— the one set apart from the rest, near the road—lines up with the sun and the altar at the center of the stone circle. A study of more than 300 similar circles in Britain found that each was designed to calculate the movement of the sun, moon, and stars, and to predict eclipses in order to help early societies know when to plant, harvest, and party. Even in modern times, as the summer solstice sun sets in just the right slot at Stonehenge, pagans boogie.

Stonehenge's builders used two different types of stone. The tall, stout monoliths and lintels are sandstone blocks called **sarsen stones.** Most of the monoliths weigh about 25 tons (the largest is 45 tons), and the lintels are about 7 tons apiece. These sarsen stones were brought from "only" 20 miles away. The shorter stones in the middle—called **bluestones**— came from the south coast of Wales...240 miles away. Imagine the logistical puzzle of floating six-ton stones across Wales' Severn Estuary and up the River Avon, then rolling them on logs about 20 miles to this position...an impressive feat.

Why didn't the builders of Stonehenge use what seem like perfectly adequate stones nearby? This, like many other questions about Stonehenge, remains shrouded in mystery. Imagine congregations gathering here 5,000 years ago, raising thought levels, creating a powerful life force. Maybe a particular kind of stone was essential for maximum energy transmission. Maybe the stones were levitated here. Maybe psychics really do create powerful vibes. Maybe not. It's as unbelievable as electricity used to be.

Bath

Bath is within easy striking distance of London—just a 1.5-hour train ride away. Two hundred years ago, this city of 90,000 was the trendsetting Tinseltown of Britain. If ever a city enjoyed looking in the mirror, Bath's the one. Built of the creamy warm-tone limestone called "Bath stone," it beams in its cover-girl complexion. It's a triumph of the Neoclassical style of the Georgian era (1714-1830), and—even with its mobs of tourists and high prices—is a joy to visit.

Long before the Romans arrived in the first century, Bath was known for its healing hot springs. In 1687, Queen Mary, fighting infertility, bathed here. Within 10 months, she gave birth to a son...and Bath boomed as a spa resort, which was rebuilt in the 18th century as a "new Rome" in the Neoclassical style. It became a city of balls, gaming, and concerts—the place to see and be seen.

Today, tourism has stoked its economy, as has the fast morning train to London. Renewed access to Bath's soothing hot springs at the Thermae Bath Spa also attracts visitors in need of a cure or a soak.

BATH IN 2 DAYS

Day 1: Take the City Sightseeing bus tour (the city tour—rather than the Skyline tour—offers the better city overview). Visit the abbey. Take the city walking tour at 14:00. Have afternoon tea and cakes in the Pump Room (or a cheaper tearoom). Stroll to Pulteney Bridge (visiting the Guildhall Market en route) and enjoy the gardens.

On any evening: Take a walking tour—the fun Bizarre Bath comedy walk (best choice), a ghost walk, or the free city walking tour. Visit the Roman Baths (open until 22:00 in July-Aug) or soak in the Thermae Bath Spa (both are also open during the day). Linger over dinner, enjoy a pub, or see a play in the classy theater. Just strolling in the evening is a pleasure, given Bath's elegant architecture.

Rick's Tip: *Consider* **starting your trip in Bath** *(using it as your jet-lag recovery pillow), and then* **visit London at the end of your trip.** *You can get from Heathrow Airport to Bath by train, bus, a bus/train combination, or a taxi service (offered by Celtic Horizons, page 152; for train and bus info, see page 169).*

Day 2: Tour the Roman Baths (buying a ticket at the TI saves you time in line). Then visit any of these sights, clustered in the neighborhood that features the architectural splendor of the Royal Crescent and the Circus: the No. 1 Royal Crescent Georgian house, Fashion Museum, or the Museum of Bath at Work.

With extra time: If you have another day, explore nearby sights—such as Stonehenge, Wells, and Glastonbury by car, bus, or minibus tour.

ORIENTATION

Bath's town square, three blocks in front of the bus and train station, is a cluster of tourist landmarks, including the abbey, Roman Baths, and the Pump Room. Bath is hilly. In general, you'll gain elevation as you head north from the town center.

Tourist Information

The TI is in the abbey churchyard (Mon-Sat 9:30-17:30, Sun 10:00-16:00, tel. 0844-847-5256, www.visitbath.co.uk). It sells tickets for the Roman Baths, allowing you to skip the (often long) line.

Helpful Hints

Festivals: In late May, the 10-day **Bath Festival** celebrates art, music, and literature (bathfestivals.org.uk/the-bath-festival/), overlapped by the eclectic **Bath Fringe Festival** (theater, walks, talks, bus trips; www.bathfringe.co.uk). The **Jane Austen Festival** unfolds genteelly in late September (www.janeausten.co.uk/festival). And for three weeks in December, the squares around the abbey are filled with a **Christmas market.**

Event Tickets and Listings: Bath's festival **box office** sells tickets for most events (but not for those at the Theatre Royal), and can tell you exactly what's on tonight (housed inside the TI, tel. 01225/463-362, www.bathfestivals.org.uk). The city's weekly paper, the *Bath Chronicle,* publishes a "What's On" events listing each Thursday (www.thisisbath.com).

Laundry: Try **Spruce Goose Launderette,** between the Circus and the Royal Crescent (self-service—bring £1 and £0.20 coins, daily 8:00-20:00, last load at 19:00), or **Speedy Wash,** which picks up your laundry on weekdays before 9:30 for same-day service (Mon-Fri 8:00-17:30, Sat until 13:00 but no pickup, closed Sun, no self-service, 4 Mile End, London Road, tel. 01225/427-616).

Tours

▲▲▲FREE CITY WALKING TOURS

Free two-hour tours are led by **The Mayor's Corps of Honorary Guides,** volunteers who want to share their love of Bath with its many visitors (as the city's mayor first did when he took a group on a guided walk back in the 1930s). These chatty, historical, and gossip-filled walks are essential for your understanding of this town's amazing Georgian social scene. How else would you learn that the old "chair ho" call for your sedan chair evolved into today's "cheerio" farewell? Tours leave from outside the Pump Room in the abbey churchyard (free, no tips, year-round Sun-Fri at 10:30 and 14:00, Sat at 10:30 only; additional evening walks May-Sept Tue and Thu at 19:00; www.bathguides.org.uk).

▲▲CITY BUS TOURS

City Sightseeing's hop-on, hop-off bus tours zip through Bath. Jump on a bus anytime at one of 17 signposted pickup points, pay the driver, climb upstairs, and hear recorded commentary about Bath. City Sightseeing has two 45-minute routes: a city tour and a "Skyline" route outside town. Try to get one with a live guide (June-Sept city tour usually at :24 and :48 past the hour, Skyline route on the hour—confirm with driver; £15, ticket valid for 24 hours and both tour routes, generally 4/hour daily in summer 9:30-17:30, in winter 10:00-15:30, tel. 01225/330-444, www.city-sightseeing.com).

Rick's Tip: *Local taxis, driven by good talkers, go where big buses can't. A group of up to four can rent a cab for an hour (about £40; try to negotiate) and enjoy a fine, informative, and—with the right cabbie—entertaining private joyride.*

BATH AT A GLANCE

▲▲▲**Free City Walking Tours** Top-notch tours helping you make the most of your visit, led by The Mayor's Corps of Honorary Guides. **Hours:** Sun-Fri at 10:30 and 14:00, Sat at 10:30 only; additional evening walks offered May-Sept Tue and Thu at 19:00. See page 147.

▲▲▲**Roman Baths** Ancient baths that gave the city its name, tourable with good audioguide. **Hours:** Daily 9:00-18:00, July-Aug until 22:00, Nov-Feb 9:30-17:00. See page 152.

▲▲**Bath Abbey** 500-year-old Perpendicular Gothic church, graced with beautiful fan vaulting and stained glass. **Hours:** Mon-Sat 9:00-17:30, Sun 13:00-14:30 & 16:30-17:30. See page 156.

▲▲**The Circus and the Royal Crescent** Stately Georgian (Neoclassical) buildings from Bath's 18th-century glory days. See page 157.

▲▲**No. 1 Royal Crescent** Your best look at the interior of one of Bath's high-rent Georgian beauties. **Hours:** Mon 12:00-17:30, Tue-Sun 10:30-17:30. See page 158.

▲**Pump Room** Swanky Georgian hall, ideal for a spot of tea or a taste of unforgettably "healthy" spa water. **Hours:** Daily 9:30-17:00 for breakfast, lunch, and afternoon tea (open 18:00-21:00 for dinner July-Aug and Christmas holidays only). See page 155.

▲**Pulteney Bridge and Parade Gardens** Shop-strewn bridge and relaxing riverside gardens. **Hours:** Bridge—always open; gardens—daily 10:00-18:00, shorter hours Oct-Easter. See 157.

▲**Fashion Museum** 400 years of clothing under one roof, plus the opulent Assembly Rooms. **Hours:** Daily 10:30-18:00, Nov-Feb until 17:00. See page 159.

▲**Museum of Bath at Work** Gadget-ridden circa-1900 engineer's shop, foundry, factory, and office. **Hours:** Daily 10:30-17:00, Nov and Jan-March weekends only, closed in Dec. See page 159.

▲**Thermae Bath Spa** Relaxation center that put the bath back in Bath. **Hours:** Daily 9:00-21:30. See page 160.

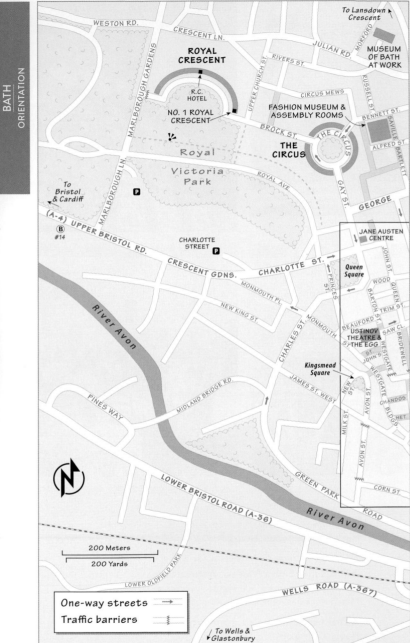

WESTON RD.

CRESCENT LN.

To Lansdown
Cresent

JULIAN RD.

MORFORD

MUSEUM
OF BATH
AT WORK

**ROYAL
CRESCENT**

RIVERS ST.

UPPER CHURCH ST.

CIRCUS MEWS

RUSSELL ST.

MARLBOROUGH GARDENS

R.C.
HOTEL

NO. 1 ROYAL
CRESCENT

FASHION MUSEUM &
ASSEMBLY ROOMS

BENNETT ST.

SAVILLE ST.

BROCK ST.

**THE
CIRCUS**

THE CIRCUS

ALFRED ST.

BARTLETT

Royal

*Victoria
Park*

ROYAL AVE.

GAY ST.

To
Bristol
& Cardiff

MARLBOROUGH LN.

P

GEORGE

(A-4) UPPER BRISTOL RD.

B
#14

CHARLOTTE
STREET

P

JANE AUSTEN
CENTRE

CRESCENT GDNS.

CHARLOTTE ST.

*Queen
Square*

JOHN ST.

MONMOUTH PL.

PRINCES
ST.

WOOD

QUEEN
ST.

NEW KING ST.

BARTON
TRIM ST.

River Avon

CHARLES ST.

MONMOUTH ST.

BEAUFORD
SQ.

USTINOV
THEATRE &
THE EGG

SAW CL.

BRIDEWELL

ST.

JOHN ST.

WESTGATE

PINES WAY

MIDLAND BRIDGE RD.

JAMES ST. WEST

*Kingsmead
Square*

NEW ST.

AVON ST.

WESTGATE
ST.

CHANDOS
BLDGS.

HET

MILK ST.

AVON ST.

CORN ST.

N

GREEN PARK

LOWER BRISTOL ROAD (A-36)

River Avon

ROAD

200 Meters

200 Yards

LOWER OLDFIELD PARK

WELLS ROAD (A-367)

One-way streets ⟶

Traffic barriers

To Wells &
Glastonbury

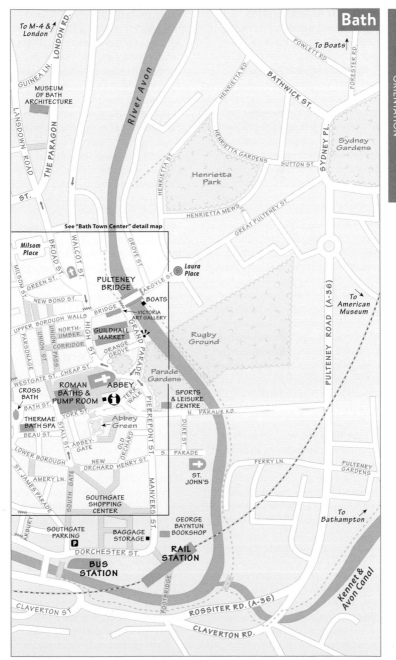

Bath

TOURS TO NEARBY SIGHTS

Bath is a good launchpad for visiting nearby Glastonbury, Wells, Avebury, Stonehenge, and more.

Mad Max Minibus Tours offers thoughtfully organized, informative tours run with entertaining guides and limited to 16 people per group. Check their website for the latest offerings and book ahead—as far ahead as possible in summer. The **Stonehenge, Avebury, and Villages** full-day tour, by far their most popular, covers 110 miles and visits Stonehenge; the Avebury Stone Circles; photogenic Lacock (LAY-cock); and Castle Combe, the southernmost Cotswold village (£42 plus Stonehenge entry fee, tours depart daily at 8:30 and return at 17:30). All tours depart from outside the Abbey Hotel on Terrace Walk in Bath, a one-minute walk from the abbey. Arrive 15 minutes before your departure time and bring cash (or book online with a credit card at least 48 hours in advance, Rick Steves readers get £10 rebate with online purchase of two separate tour itineraries, request by email at time of booking; mobile 07990-505-970, phone answered daily 8:00-18:00, www.madmaxtours.co.uk, maddy@madmaxtours.co.uk).

Lion Tours gets you to Stonehenge on their half-day **Stonehenge and Lacock** tour (£39 including Stonehenge entry fee; leaves daily at 12:15 and returns at 17:30, in summer this tour also leaves at 8:30 and returns at 12:00). They also run full-day tours of Cotswold Villages and King Arthur's Realm. If you ask in advance, you can bring your luggage along and use this tour to get to Stow. Or, for £10 extra per person or group, you can hop off in Moreton-in-Marsh for easy train connections to Oxford and bus connections to Chipping Campden. Lion's tours depart from the same stop as Mad Max Tours—see earlier (mobile 07769-668-668, book online at www.liontours.co.uk).

Scarper Tours runs four-hour narrated minibus tours to Stonehenge—giving you two hours at the site (£20 transportation only, £35 including Stonehenge entry fee, departs from behind the abbey on Terrace Walk; daily mid-March-mid-Oct at 9:30 and 14:00; mid-Oct-mid-March at 13:00; www.scarpertours.com, sally@scarpertours.com).

Celtic Horizons offers tours from Bath to destinations such as Stonehenge, Avebury, and Wells. They can provide a convenient transfer service (to or from London, Heathrow, Bristol Airport, the Cotswolds, and so on), with or without a tour itinerary en route. Allow about £35/hour for a group (comfortable mini-vans seat 4, 6, or 8 people) and £140 for Heathrow-Bath transfers (1-4 persons). Make arrangements and get pricing by email at info@celtichorizons.com (tel. 01373/800-500, US tel. 855-895-0165, www.celtichorizons.com).

SIGHTS

In the Town Center

▲▲▲ROMAN BATHS

In ancient Roman times, high society enjoyed the mineral springs at Bath. From Londinium, Romans traveled so often to Aquae Sulis, as the city was called, to "take a bath" that finally it became known simply as Bath. Today, a fine museum surrounds the ancient bath. With the help of a great audioguide, you'll wander past well-documented displays, Roman artifacts, a temple pediment with an evocative bearded face, a bronze head of the goddess Sulis Minerva, excavated ancient foundations, and the actual mouth of the health-giving spring. At the end, you'll have a chance to walk around the big pool itself, where Romans once lounged, splished, splashed, and thanked the gods for the gift of therapeutic hot water.

Cost and Hours: £15.50, includes audioguide, £21.50 combo-ticket includes Fashion Museum and Victoria Art Gallery temporary exhibits, family ticket available,

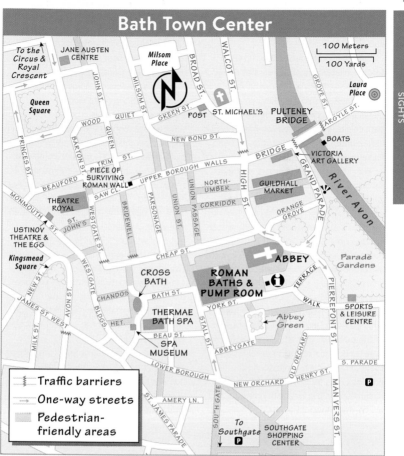

Bath Town Center

daily 9:00-18:00, July-Aug until 22:00, Nov-Feb 9:30-17:00, last entry one hour before closing, tel. 01225/477-784, www.romanbaths.co.uk.

Rick's Tip: *To* avoid long lines at the Roman Baths, buy a ticket at the nearby TI. *With voucher or combo-ticket in hand, enter through the* "fast track" lane, *to the left of the general admission line.* Visit early or late; *peak time is between 13:00 and 15:00.*

Tours: Take advantage of the included essential **audioguide,** which makes your visit easy and informative. In addition to

the basic commentary, look for posted numbers to key into your audioguide for specialty topics—including a kid-friendly tour and musings from American expat writer Bill Bryson. For those with a big appetite for Roman history, in-depth guided tours leave from the end of the museum at the edge of the actual bath (included with ticket, on the hour, a poolside clock is set for the next departure time, 20-40 minutes depending on the guide). You can revisit the museum after the tour.

⊘ **Self-Guided Tour:** Follow the one-way route through the bath and museum complex. This self-guided tour offers a basic overview; for more in-depth commentary, make ample use of the audioguide.

Begin by walking around the upper **terrace,** overlooking the Great Bath. This terrace—lined with sculptures of VIRs (Very Important Romans)—evokes ancient times but was built in the 1890s. The ruins of the bath complex sat undisturbed for centuries before finally being excavated and turned into a museum in the late 19th century.

Peer down into the **spring,** where little air bubbles remind you that 240,000 gallons of water a day emerge from the earth—magically, it must have seemed to Romans—at a constant 115°F. The water you see now, heated more than a mile below the earth's surface, first fell to earth as rain onto nearby hills about 10,000 years ago...making the Romans seem relatively recent.

Now you'll head down to the museum, where exhibits explain the dual purpose of the buildings that stood here in Roman times: a bath complex, for relaxation and for healing; and a temple dedicated to the goddess Sulis Minerva, who was believed to be responsible for the mysterious and much-appreciated thermal springs. Cut-

away diagrams and models resurrect both parts of this complex and help establish your bearings among the remaining fragments and foundations—including the original entrance (just off the main suspended walkway, on your right, as you pass through the temple courtyard and Minerva section).

The fragments of the **temple pediment**—carved by indigenous Celtic craftsmen but with Roman themes—represent a remarkable cultural synthesis. Sit and watch for a while as a slide projection fills in historians' best guesses as to what once occupied the missing bits. The identity of the circular face in the middle puzzles researchers. (God? Santa Claus?) It could be the head of the Gorgon monster after it was slain by Perseus—are those snakes peeking through its hair and beard? And yet, the Gorgon was traditionally depicted as female. Perhaps instead it's Neptune, the god of the sea—appropriate for this aquatic site.

The next exhibits examine living, dying, and worshipping in Aquae Sulis (the settlement here) in antiquity. Much like the pilgrimage sites of the Middle Ages, this spot exerted a powerful pull on people

The ancient Roman baths are surrounded by an excellent museum.

from all over the realm, who were eager to partake in its healing waters and to worship at the religious site. A display of the **Beau Street Hoard**—over 17,500 Roman coins dating from 32 B.C. to A.D. 274 that were found near the Baths—emphasizes just how well-visited this area was.

You'll also see some of the small but extremely heavy carved-stone tables that pilgrims hauled here as an offering to the gods. Take time to read some of the requests (inscribed on sheets of pewter or iron) that visitors made of the goddess—many are comically spiteful and petty, offering a warts-and-all glimpse into day-to-day Roman culture.

As you walk through the temple's original foundations, keep an eye out for the sacrificial altar. The gilded-bronze head of the goddess **Sulis Minerva** (in the display case) once overlooked a flaming cauldron inside the temple, where only priests were allowed to enter. Similar to the Greek goddess Athena, Sulis Minerva was considered to be a life-giving mother goddess.

Engineers enjoy a close-up look at the spring overflow and the original **drain system**—built two millennia ago—that still carries excess water to the River Avon. Marvel at the cleverness and durability of Roman engineering, created in (what we usually imagine to be) a "primitive" time. A nearby exhibit on pulleys and fasteners lets you play with these inventions.

Head outside to the **Great Bath** itself (where you can join one of the included guided tours for a much more extensive visit—look for the clock with the next start time). Take a slow lap (by foot) around the perimeter, imagining the frolicking Romans who once immersed themselves up to their necks in this five-foot-deep pool. The water is greenish because of algae—don't drink it. The best views are from the west end, looking back toward the abbey. Nearby is a giant chunk of roof span, from a time when this was a cavernous covered swimming hall. At the corner, you'll step over a small canal where hot water still trickles into the main pool. Nearby, find a length of original lead pipe, remarkably well preserved since antiquity.

Symmetrical bath complexes branch off at opposite ends of the Great Bath (perhaps dating from a conservative period when the Romans maintained separate facilities for men and women). The **East Baths** show off changing rooms and various bathing rooms, each one designed for a special therapy or recreational purpose (immersion therapy tub, sauna-like heated floor, and so on), as described in detail by the audioguide.

When you're ready to leave, head for the **West Baths** (including a sweat bath and a *frigidarium*, or "cold plunge" pool) and take another look at the spring and more foundations. After returning your audioguide, pop over to the fountain for a free taste of the spa water. Then pass through the gift shop, past the convenient public WCs (which use plain old tap water), and exit through the **Pump Room**—or stay for a spot of tea.

▲PUMP ROOM

For centuries, Bath was forgotten as a spa. Then, in 1687, the previously barren Queen Mary bathed here, became pregnant, and bore a male heir to the throne. A few years later, Queen Anne found the water eased her painful gout. Word of its miraculously curative waters spread, and Bath earned its way back on the aristocratic map. High society soon turned the

Sulis Minerva

place into one big pleasure palace. The Pump Room, an elegant Georgian hall just above the Roman Baths, offers visitors their best chance to raise a pinky in Neoclassical grandeur. Above the clock, a statue of Beau Nash himself sniffles down at you. Come for a light meal, or to try a famous (but forgettable) "Bath bun" with your spa water (the same water that's in the fountain at the end of the baths tour; also free in the Pump Room if you present your ticket). The spa water is served by an appropriately attired waiter, who will tell you the water is pumped up from nearly 100 yards deep and marinated in 43 wonderful minerals. Or, for just the price of a coffee, drop in anytime—except during lunch—to enjoy live music (string trio or piano; times vary) and the atmosphere. Even if you don't eat here, you're welcome to enter the foyer for a view of the baths and dining room.

The **$$$ Pump Room** is open daily 9:30-17:00 for breakfast, lunch, and afternoon tea (tea service starts at 14:30; last orders at 16:00), tea/coffee and pastries also available in the afternoons;

open 18:00-21:00 for dinner July-Aug and Christmas holidays only; tel. 01225/444-477.

▲▲BATH ABBEY

The town of Bath wasn't much in the Middle Ages, but an important church has stood on this spot since Anglo-Saxon times. King Edgar I was crowned here in 973, when the church was much bigger (before the bishop packed up and moved to Wells). Dominating the town center, today's abbey—the last great church built in medieval England—is 500 years old and a fine example of the Late Perpendicular Gothic style, with breezy fan vaulting and enough stained glass to earn it the nickname "Lantern of the West."

Cost and Hours: £4 suggested donation, Mon-Sat 9:00-17:30, Sun 13:00-14:30 & 16:30-17:30, handy flier narrates a self-guided tour, ask about schedule of events—including concerts, services, and evensong—also posted on the door and online, tel. 01225/422-462, www.bathabbey.org.

Evensong: Though the evensong service is spoken, not sung, on Monday through Saturday, it's still a beautiful 20 minutes of worship (nightly at 17:30, choral evensong 15:30 on Sun only).

Visiting the Abbey: Take a moment to appreciate the abbey's architecture from the square. The facade (c. 1500, but mostly restored) is interesting for some of its carvings. Look for the angels going down the ladder. The statue of Peter (to the left of the door) lost its head to mean-spirited iconoclasts; it was recarved out of Peter's once supersized beard.

Going inside is worth the small suggested contribution. The glass, red-iron lamps and the heating grates on the floor are all remnants of the 19th century. (In a sustainable, 21st-century touch, the heat now comes from the baths' hot run-off water.) The window behind the altar shows 52 scenes from the life of Christ. A window to the left of the altar shows Edgar's coronation. Note that a WWII

Bath Abbey

Pulteney Bridge

bomb blast destroyed the medieval glass; what you see today is from the 1950s.

Climbing the Tower: You can reach the top of the tower only with a worthwhile 50-minute guided tour. You'll hike up 212 steps for views across the rooftops of Bath and a peek down into the Roman Baths (£6, generally at the top of each hour when abbey is open, more often during busy times; Mon-Sat 10:00-17:00, Nov-March 11:00-15:00, these are last tour-departure times; today's tour times usually posted outside abbey entrance, no tours Sun, buy tickets in abbey gift shop).

▲PULTENEY BRIDGE AND PARADE GARDENS

Bath is inclined to compare its shop-lined Pulteney Bridge with Florence's Ponte Vecchio. That's pushing it. But to best enjoy a sunny day, pack a picnic lunch and pay £1.50 to enter the Parade Gardens below the bridge (daily 10:00-18:00, shorter hours Oct-Easter, includes deck chairs, ask about concerts held some Sun at 14:00 in summer, entrance a block south of bridge). Relaxing peacefully at the riverside provides a wonderful break (and memory). Across the bridge at Pulteney Weir, tour boat companies run cruises.

Note that one of the free city walking tours covers Pulteney Bridge, Pulteney Street, and Sydney Gardens (see "Tours," earlier).

Northwest of the Town Center

Several worthwhile public spaces and museums can be found a slightly uphill 10-minute walk away.

▲▲THE CIRCUS AND THE ROYAL CRESCENT

If Bath is an architectural cancan, these are its knickers. These first Georgian "condos"—built in the mid-18th century by the father-and-son John Woods (the Circus by the Elder, the Royal Crescent by the Younger)—are well explained by the city walking tours. "Georgian" is British for "Neoclassical." These two building complexes, conveniently located a block apart from each other, are quintessential Georgian and quintessential Bath.

Circus: True to its name, this is a circular housing complex. Picture it as a coliseum turned inside out. Its Doric, Ionic, and Corinthian capital decorations pay homage to its Greco-Roman origin, and are a reminder that Bath (with its seven hills) aspired to be "the Rome of England." The frieze above the first row of columns has hundreds of different panels representing the arts, sciences, and crafts. The ground-floor entrances were made large enough that aristocrats could be carried right through the door in their sedan chairs, and women could enter without disturbing their sky-high hairdos. The tiny round windows on the top floors were the servants' quarters. While the building fronts are uniform, the backs are higgledy-piggledy, infamous for their "hanging loos" (bathrooms added years later).

Royal Crescent: A long, graceful arc of buildings—impossible to see in one glance unless you step way back to the edge of the big park in front—evokes the wealth and gentility of Bath's glory days. As you cruise the Crescent, strut like an aristocrat.

Now imagine you're poor: Notice the "ha ha fence," a drop-off in the front yard that acted as a barrier, invisible from the windows, for keeping out sheep and peasants. The refined and stylish **Royal Crescent Hotel** sits virtually unmarked in the center of the Crescent (with the giant rhododendron growing over the door). You're welcome to (politely) drop in to explore its fine ground-floor public spaces and back garden, where a gracious and traditional tea is served (£16.50 cream tea, £35 afternoon tea, daily 13:30-16:30, sharing is OK, reserve a day ahead—a week ahead for Sat-Sun, tel. 01225/823-333, www.royalcrescent.co.uk).

▲▲NO. 1 ROYAL CRESCENT

This museum (corner of Brock Street and Royal Crescent) takes visitors behind one of those classy Georgian facades, offering your best look into a period house—and how the wealthy lived in 18th-century Bath. Docents in each room hand out placards, but take the time to talk

with them to learn many more fascinating details of Georgian life...such as how high-class women shaved their eyebrows and pasted on carefully trimmed strips of mouse fur in their place.

Cost and Hours: £10, £12.50 combo-ticket with Museum of Bath Architecture, Mon 12:00-17:30, Tue-Sun 10:30-17:30, last entry at 16:30, tel. 01225/428-126, http://no1royalcrescent.org.uk/.

Visiting the Museum: Start with the **parlor,** the main room of the house used for breakfast in the mornings, business affairs in the afternoon, and various other everyday activities throughout the evening. The bookcase was a status symbol of knowledge and literacy. In the **gentleman's retreat,** find a machine with a hand crank. This "modern" device was thought to cure ailments by shocking them out of you—give it a spin and feel for yourself. Shops in town charged for these electrifying cures; only the wealthiest had in-home shock machines. Upstairs in the **lady's bedroom** are trinkets befitting a Georgian socialite; look for a framed love letter, wig scratcher, and hidden doorway (next to the bed) providing direct access to the

Bath's curved Royal Crescent is England's greatest example of Georgian architecture.

servants' staircase. The gentleman's bedroom upstairs is the masculine equivalent of the lady's room—rich colors, scenes of Bath, and manly decor. The back staircase leads directly to the servants' hall. Look up to find Fido, who spent his days on the treadmill powering the rotisserie.

Finally, you'll end in the **kitchen**. Notice the wooden rack hanging from the ceiling—it kept the bread, herbs, and ham away from the mice. The scattered tools here helped servants create the upper-crust lifestyle overhead.

▲FASHION MUSEUM

Housed underneath Bath's Assembly Rooms, this museum displays four centuries of fashion on one floor. It's small, but the fact-filled, included audioguide can stretch a visit to an informative and enjoyable hour. Like fashion itself, the exhibits change all the time. A major feature is the "Dress of the Year" display, for which a fashion expert anoints a new frock each year. Ongoing since 1963, it's a chance to view more than a half-century of fashion trends in one sweep of the head. (The menswear version—awarded sporadically—shows a bit less variation, but has flashes of creativity.) Many of the exhibits are organized by theme (bags, shoes, underwear, wedding dresses). You'll see how fashion evolved—just like architecture and other arts—from one historical period to the next: Georgian, Regency, Victorian, the Swinging '60s, and so on. If you're intrigued by all those historic garments, go ahead and lace up your own trainer corset (which looks more like a life jacket) and try on a hoop underdress.

Cost and Hours: £9, includes audioguide; £21.50 combo-ticket includes Roman Baths and Victoria Art Gallery temporary exhibits, family ticket available; daily 10:30-18:00, Nov-Feb until 17:00, last entry one hour before closing; free 30-minute guided tour in summer at 12:00 and 16:00, in winter at 12:00 and 13:00; self-service café, Bennett Street, tel. 01225/477-789, www.fashionmuseum.co.uk.

Rick's Tip: *Notice the* **proximity of the Fashion Museum and the Museum of Bath at Work.** *While some folks appreciate both places, museum attendants tell me it's standard for husbands to visit the Museum of Bath at Work while their wives tour the Fashion Museum. Maybe it's time to divide and conquer?*

▲MUSEUM OF BATH AT WORK

This modest but informative museum explains the industrial history of Bath. If you want to learn about the unglamorous workaday side to the spa town, this is the place.

Cost and Hours: £6, includes audioguide, daily 10:30-17:00, Nov and Jan-March weekends only, closed Dec, last entry one hour before closing, Julian Road, 2 steep blocks up Russell Street from Assembly Rooms, tel. 01225/318-348, www.bath-at-work.org.uk.

Visiting the Museum: The core of the museum is the well-preserved, circa-1900 fizzy-drink business of one Mr. Bowler. It includes a Dickensian office, engineer's shop, brass foundry, essence room lined with bottled scents, and factory floor. It's

Museum of Bath at Work

just a pile of meaningless old gadgets—until the included audioguide resurrects Mr. Bowler's creative genius. Each item has its own story to tell.

Upstairs are display cases featuring other Bath creations through the years, including a 1914 Horstmann car, wheeled sedan chairs (this *is* Bath, after all), and versatile plasticine (colorful proto-Play-Doh—still the preferred medium of Aardman Studios, creators of the stop-motion animated Wallace & Gromit movies). At the snack bar, ask about buying your own historic fizzy drink (a descendant of the ones once made here). On your way out, don't miss the intriguing collection of small exhibits on the ground floor, featuring cabinetmaking, the traditional methods for cutting the local "Bath stone," a locally produced six-stroke engine, and more.

JANE AUSTEN CENTRE

This exhibition focuses on Jane Austen's tumultuous, sometimes-troubled five years in Bath (circa 1800, during which time her father died) and the influence the city had on her writing. There's little

Jane Austen Centre

of historic substance here. You'll walk through a Georgian townhouse that she didn't live in (one of her real addresses in Bath was a few houses up the road, at 25 Gay Street), and you'll see mostly enlarged reproductions of things associated with her writing as well as her overhyped waxwork likeness, but none of that seems to bother the steady stream of happy Austen fans touring the house.

The exhibit does describe various places from two novels set in Bath (*Persuasion and Northanger Abbey*). Costumed guides give an intro talk (on the first floor, 15 minutes, 3/hour, on the hour and at :20 and :40 past the hour) about the romantic but down-to-earth Austen, who skewered the silly, shallow, and arrogant aristocrats' world, where "the doing of nothing all day prevents one from doing anything." They also show a 15-minute video; after that, you're free to wander through the rest of the exhibit.

Cost and Hours: £11; April-Oct daily 9:45-17:30, July-Aug until 18:00; Nov-March Sun-Fri 11:00-16:30, Sat from 10:00; last entry one hour before closing, between Queen's Square and the Circus at 40 Gay Street, tel. 01225/443-000, www.janeausten.co.uk.

Tea: Upstairs, the award-winning **$ Regency Tea Rooms** (free entrance) hits the spot for Austen-ites with costumed waitstaff and themed teas (£8-10), including the all-out "Tea with Mr. Darcy" for £18 (also £6 sandwiches, opens at 11:00, closes same time as the center, last order taken one hour before closing).

EXPERIENCES

Thermal Baths

▲ THERMAE BATH SPA

After simmering unused for a quarter-century, Bath's natural thermal springs once again offer R&R for the masses. The state-of-the-art spa is housed in a complex of three buildings that combine historic structures with new glass-and-steel architecture.

Is the Thermae Bath Spa worth the time and money? The experience is pretty pricey and humble compared to similar German and Hungarian spas. The tall, modern building in the city center lacks a certain old-time elegance. Jets in the pools are very limited, and the only water toys are big foam noodles. There's no cold plunge—the only way to cool off between steam rooms is to step onto a small, unglamorous balcony. The Royal Bath's two pools are essentially the same, and the water isn't particularly hot in either—in fact, the main attraction is the rooftop view from the top one (best with a partner or as a social experience).

All that said, this is the only natural thermal spa in the UK and your one chance to actually bathe in Bath. Bring your swimsuit and come for a couple of hours (Fri night and all day Sat-Sun are most crowded). Consider an evening visit, when—on a chilly day—Bath's twilight glows through the steam from the rooftop pool.

Cost: The cheapest spa pass is £35 for two hours (£38 on weekends), which includes towel, robe, and slippers and gains you access to the Royal Bath's large, ground-floor "Minerva Bath"; four steam rooms and a waterfall shower; and the view-filled, open-air, rooftop thermal pool. Longer stays are £10 for each additional hour. If you arrived in Bath by train, your used rail ticket will score you a four-hour session for the price of two hours (Mon-Fri only).

Thermae has all the "pamper thyself" extras: massages, mud wraps, and various healing-type treatments, including "watsu"—water shiatsu (£45-98 extra). Book treatments in advance by phone.

Hours: Daily 9.00-21:30, last entry at 19:00, pools close at 21:00. No kids under 16.

Information: It's 100 yards from the Roman Baths, on Beau Street (tel. 01225/331-234, www.thermaebathspa.com). There's a salad-and-smoothies café for guests.

The Cross Bath: Operated by Thermae Bath Spa, this renovated circular Georgian structure across the street from the main spa provides a simpler and less-expensive bathing option. It has a hot-water fountain that taps directly into the spring, making its water hotter than the spa's (£18-20/1.5 hours, daily 10:00-19:30, last entry at 18:00, check in at Thermae Bath Spa's main entrance across the street and you'll be escorted to the Cross Bath, changing rooms, no access to Royal Bath, no kids under 12).

Spa Visitor Center: Also across the street, in the Hetling Pump Room, this free one-room exhibit explains the story of the spa (Mon-Sat 10:00-17:00, Sun 11:00-16:00, audioguide-£2).

Boating

The Bath Boating Station, in an old Victorian boathouse, rents rowboats, canoes, and punts (£7/person for first hour, then £4/hour; all day for £18; Wed-Sun 10:00-18:00, closed Mon-Tue and Oct-Easter, intersection of Forester and Rockcliffe roads, one mile northeast of center, tel. 01225/312-900, www.bathboating.co.uk).

Evening Walks

For an entertaining walking-tour comedy act "with absolutely no history or culture," follow Toby or Noel on their creative and lively **Bizarre Bath** walk. This 1.5-hour "tour," which combines stand-up comedy

Thermae Bath Spa

with cleverly executed magic tricks, plays off unsuspecting passersby as well as tour members. Promising to insult all nationalities and sensitivities, it's sometimes racy but still good family fun (£10, £8 if you show this book, April-Oct nightly at 20:00, smaller groups Mon-Thu, leaves from The Huntsman Inn near the abbey; confirm at TI or see www.bizarrebath.co.uk.

Ghost Walks are a popular way to pass the after-dark hours—although you might save the supernatural for the city of York, which is said to be more haunted (£8, cash only, 1.5 hours, year-round Thu-Sat at 20:00, leave from The Garrick's Head pub—to the left and behind Theatre Royal as you face it, tel. 01225/350-512, www.ghostwalksofbath.co.uk).

Rick's Tip: *In* **July and August,** *the* **Roman Baths are open nightly until 22:00** *(last entry 21:00). The gas lamps flame and the baths are romantic—and less crowded. To take a dip yourself, pop over to the Thermae Bath Spa (last entry at 19:00).*

Theater

The restored 18th-century, 800-seat Theatre Royal, one of England's loveliest, offers a busy schedule of London West End-type plays, including many "pre-London" dress-rehearsal runs.

Cost and Hours: £20-40 plus small booking fee; shows generally start at 19:30 or 20:00, matinees at 14:30, box office open Mon-Sat 10:00-20:00, Sun from

12:00 if there's a show; book in person, online, or by phone; on Saw Close, tel. 01225/448-844, www.theatreroyal.org.uk.

Ticket Deals: Same-day "standby" seats (actually 40 nosebleed spots on a bench) are sold daily except Sunday, starting at noon, for that day's evening performance (£7.50, 2 tickets maximum). Or you can snatch up any "last minute" seats for £15-20 a half-hour before "curtain up" (cash only).

EATING

Bath has something for every appetite and budget—just stroll around the center of town. A picnic dinner of deli food or takeout fish-and-chips in the Royal Crescent Park or down by the river is ideal for aristocratic hoboes. The restaurants I recommend are mostly small and popular—reserve a table for dinner—especially on Friday and Saturday. Most pricey little bistros offer big savings with their two- and three-course lunches and "pre-theatre" specials. Look for early-bird specials: As long as you order within the time window, you're in for a less-expensive meal.

Romantic and Upscale

$$$$ Clayton's Kitchen is fine for a modern English splurge in a woody, romantic, candlelit atmosphere, where Michelin-star chef Rob Clayton aims to offer affordable British cuisine without pretense. The food is artfully prepared and presented—and they love their scallops

Take a fun walking tour in Bath.

Theatre Royal

(daily from noon and from 18:00, a few outside tables, live jazz on Sundays, 15 George Street, tel. 01225/585-100, www.claytonskitchen.com).

$$$$ The Circus Restaurant is a relaxing little eatery serving well-executed English cuisine with European flair. Choose between the modern interior—with seating on the main floor or in the less-charming cellar—and the four tables on the peaceful street connecting the Circus and the Royal Crescent (Mon-Sat 10:00-24:00, closed Sun, 34 Brock Street, tel. 01225/466-020, www.thecircusrestaurant.co.uk).

Pubs

Bath is not a great pub-grub town, and with so many other tempting options, pub dining isn't as appealing as it is elsewhere.

$$$ The Garrick's Head is an elegantly simple gastropub around the corner from the Theatre Royal, with a pricey restaurant on one side, a bar serving affordable pub classics on the other, and some tables outside great for people-watching. They serve traditional English dishes with a few Mediterranean options (lunch and pre-theater specials, daily 12:00-14:30 & 17:30-21:00, 8 St. John's Place, tel. 01225/318-368).

$$$ Crystal Palace, a casual and inviting standby just a block from the abbey, faces the delightful little Abbey Green. With a focus on food rather than drink, they serve "pub grub with a Continental flair" in three different spaces, including an airy back patio (food served Mon-Fri

11:00-21:00, Sat until 20:00, Sun from 12:00, last drink orders at 22:45, 10 Abbey Green, tel. 01225/482-666).

$$ The Raven attracts a boisterous local crowd. It emphasizes beer—with an impressive selection of real ales—but serves some delicious pies for your non-liquid nourishment (food served Mon-Fri 12:00-15:00 & 17:00-21:00, Sat-Sun 12:30-20:30, open longer for drinks; no kids under 14, 6 Queen Street, tel. 01225/425-045, www.theravenofbath.co.uk).

Casual Alternatives

$$$ Hall & Wood House Restaurant is a big, slick, high-energy place with a ground-floor pub (check out the copper bar) and a spiral staircase leading around a palm tree to a woody restaurant and a roof terrace. With lots of beers on tap, traditional English dishes, hamburgers, and salads, it's a hit with local students (daily, 1 Old King Street, tel. 01225/469-259).

$$ The Scallop Shell is the top choice for fish-and-chips in Bath. They also have a modern restaurant—with fancier fish dishes and more people drinking wine than beer—and a takeout counter (Mon-Sat 12:00-21:30, closed Sun, 27 Monmouth Place, tel. 01225/420-928).

$$$ Loch Fyne Fish Restaurant is an inviting outpost of this small chain, serving fresh fish at reasonable prices in what was once a lavish bank building (two-course special until 18:00, daily 12:00-22:00, 24 Milsom Street, tel. 01225/750-120).

Italian

$$$$ Martini Restaurant, a hopping, purely Italian place with jovial waiters, has class (open daily 12:00-14:30 & 18:00-22:30, veggie options, daily fish specials, extensive wine list, 9 George Street, tel. 01225/460-818; Nunzio, Franco, and chef Luigi).

$$ Olé bounces to a flamenco beat, turning out tasty tapas from their minuscule kitchen. If you're hungry for a trip to Spain, arrive early or make a

Eating

1. Clayton's Kitchen
2. The Circus Restaurant
3. The Garrick's Head
4. Crystal Palace
5. The Raven
6. Hall & Wood House Restaurant
7. The Scallop Shell
8. Loch Fyne Fish Restaurant
9. Martini Restaurant
10. Olé
11. Acorn Vegetarian Kitchen
12. Eastern Eye
13. Thai Balcony Restaurant
14. Yak Yeti Yak
15. Yen Sushi
16. Market Café in Guildhall Market
17. Hands Georgian Tearooms
18. Boston Tea Party
19. Chandos Deli
20. The Cornish Bakehouse (2)
21. Milsom Place Eateries
22. Supermarket (3)

Sleeping

23. Marlborough House
24. Brocks Guest House
25. Brooks Guesthouse
26. Parkside Guest House
27. Cornerways B&B
28. The Kennard
29. Henrietta House
30. Apple Tree Guesthouse
31. Three Abbey Green Guest House
32. Harington's Hotel
33. Abbey House Apartments
34. The Henry Guest House
35. YMCA

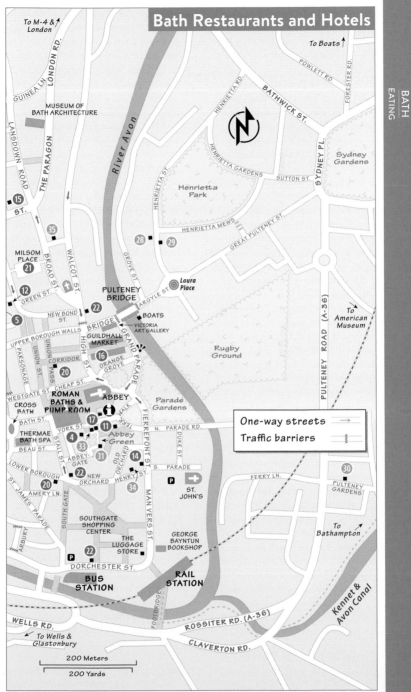

Bath Restaurants and Hotels

One-way streets →

Traffic barriers ⫘

200 Meters
200 Yards

reservation, as there are only a handful of tables (Sun-Thu 12:00-22:00, Fri-Sat until 23:00, up the stairs at 1 John Street, tel. 01225/466-440).

Vegetarian and Asian

$$$$ Acorn Vegetarian Kitchen is pricey but highly rated and ideal for the well-heeled vegetarian. Its tight interior has an understated vibe (daily 12:00-15:00 & 17:30-21:30, 2 North Parade Passage, tel. 01225/446-059).

$$$ Eastern Eye entices with large portions of Indian and Bangladeshi dishes served in an impressive, triple-domed Georgian hall. Service is uneven but the food doesn't disappoint (Mon-Fri 12:00-14:30 & 18:00-23:30, Sat-Sun 12:00-23:30, 8A Quiet Street, tel. 01225/422-323).

$$ Thai Balcony Restaurant's open, spacious interior is so plush, it'll have you wondering, "Where's the Thai wedding?" While residents debate which of Bath's handful of Thai restaurants serves the best food or offers the lowest prices, there's no doubt that Thai Balcony's fun and elegant atmosphere makes for a memorable and enjoyable dinner (daily 12:00-14:30 & 18:00-22:00, Saw Close, tel. 01225/444-450).

$$ Yak Yeti Yak is a fun Nepalese restaurant with both Western and sit-on-the-floor seating. Sera and his wife, Sarah, along with their cheerful, hardworking Nepali team, cook up great traditional food (including plenty of vegetarian plates) at prices that would delight a Sherpa (daily 12:00-14:00 & 18:00-22:00, downstairs at 12 Pierrepont Street, tel. 01225/442-299).

$$ Yen Sushi is your basic little Japanese sushi bar—plain and sterile, with stools facing a conveyor belt that constantly tempts you with a variety of freshly made delights on color-coded plates (daily 12:00-15:00 & 17:30-22:30, 11 Bartlett Street, tel. 01225/333-313).

Simple Lunch Options

$ Market Café, in the Guildhall Market across from Pulteney Bridge, is where you can munch really cheaply on a homemade meat pie or sip tea while surrounded by stacks of used books and honest-to-goodness old-time locals (traditional English meals including fried breakfasts all day, Mon-Sat 8:00-17:00, closed Sun, tel. 01225/461-593 a block north of the abbey, on High Street).

$ Hands Georgian Tearooms is an understated, family-run place a stone's throw from the Abbey and the Baths. It's a good option for breakfast, lunch, or afternoon tea right in the center of the tourist bustle (daily 10:00-17:00, 1 Abbey Street, tel. 01225/463-928).

$ Boston Tea Party is what Starbucks aspires to be—the neighborhood coffee-house and hangout. Its extensive breakfasts, light lunches, and salads are fresh and healthy. The outdoor seating overlooks a busy square. Their walls are decorated with works by local artists (Mon-Sat 7:00-19:30, Sun 9:00-19:00, 19 Kingsmead Square, tel. 01225/314-826).

$ Chandos Deli has good coffee, breakfast pastries, and tasty £3-5 sandwiches made on artisan breads—plus meats, cheese, baguettes, and wine for assembling a gourmet picnic. Upscale yet casual, this place satisfies dedicated foodies who don't want to pay too much (Mon-Fri 8:00-17:30, Sat from 9:00, Sun 10:00-17:00, 12 George Street, tel. 01225/314-418).

$ The Cornish Bakehouse has freshly baked £3 takeaway pasties (Mon-Sat 8:30-17:30, Sun 10:00-17:00, kitty-corner from Marks & Spencer at 1 Lower Borough Walls, second location off High Street at 11A The Corridor, tel. 01225/426-635).

Chain Eateries at Milsom Place: A pleasant hidden courtyard holds several dependable chain eateries.

Supermarkets: With a good salad bar, **Waitrose** is great for picnics (Mon-Sat 7:30-21:00, Sun 11:00-17:00, just west of Pulteney Bridge and across from post office on High Street). **Marks & Spencer,** near the bottom end of town, has a grocery at the back of its department store and two eateries: **M&S Kitchen** on the ground floor and the pleasant, inexpensive **Café Revive** on the top floor (Mon-Sat 8:00-19:00, Sun 11:00-17:00, 16 Stall Street). **Sainsbury's Local,** across the street from the bus station, has the longest hours (daily 7:00-23:00, 2 Dorchester Street).

SLEEPING

Bath is a busy tourist town. Reserve in advance. B&Bs favor those lingering longer; it's worth asking for a weekday, three-nights-in-a-row, or off-season deal. Friday and Saturday nights are tightest, especially if you're staying only one night (rates may go up 25 percent). If you're driving to Bath, stowing your car near the center will cost you—see "Parking" on page 169, or ask your hotelier.

Near the Royal Crescent

These listings are all a 5- to 10-minute walk from the town center, and an easy 15-minute walk from the train station. With bags in tow you may want to either catch a taxi (£5-7) or (except for Brocks Guest House) hop on bus #4 (direction: Weston, catch bus inside bus station, pay driver £2.20, get off at the Comfortable Place stop—just after the park starts on the right, cross the street and backtrack 100 yards).

Marlborough, Brooks, and Cornerways all face a busy arterial street; light sleepers should request a rear- or side-facing room.

$$$ Marlborough House, exuberantly run by hands-on owner Peter, mixes modern style with antique furnishings and features a welcoming breakfast room with an open kitchen. Each of the six rooms comes with a sip of sherry (RS%, air-con, minifridges, free parking, 1 Marlborough Lane, tel. 01225/318-175, www.marlborough-house.net, mars@manque.dircon.co.uk).

$$$ Brocks Guest House rents six rooms in a Georgian townhouse built by John Wood in 1765. Located between the prestigious Royal Crescent and the courtly Circus, it's been redone in a way that would make the great architect proud. Each room has its own Bath-related theme (little top-floor library, 32 Brock Street, tel. 01225/338-374, www.brocksguesthouse.co.uk, brocks@brocksguesthouse.co.uk, Marta and Rafal).

$$ Brooks Guesthouse is the biggest and most polished of the bunch, albeit the least personal, with 22 modern rooms and classy public spaces, including an exceptionally pleasant breakfast room (limited pay parking, 1 Crescent Gardens, Upper Bristol Road, tel. 01225/425-543, www.brooksguesthouse.com, info@brooksguesthouse.com).

$$ Parkside Guest House rents five large, thoughtfully appointed Edwardian rooms. It's tidy, clean, homey, and well-priced—and has a spacious back garden (RS%, limited free parking, 11 Marlborough Lane, tel. 01225/429-444, www.parksidebandb.co.uk, post@parksidebandb.co.uk, kind Inge Lynall).

$$ Cornerways B&B is centrally located, simple, and pleasant, with three rooms and old-fashioned homey touches (RS%, DVD library, free parking, 47 Crescent Gardens, tel. 01225/422-382, www.cornerwaysbath.co.uk, info@cornerwaysbath.co.uk, Sue Black).

East of the River

These listings are a 5- to 10-minute walk from the city center. From the train station, it's best to take a taxi, as there are no good bus connections.

$$$ The Kennard is a short walk from the Pulteney Bridge. Each of the 12 rooms is colorfully and elaborately decorated (free street parking permits, peaceful little Georgian garden out back, 11 Henrietta Street, tel. 01225/310-472, www.kennard.co.uk, reception@kennard.co.uk, Priya and Ajay).

$$$ Henrietta House, with large rooms, hardwood floors, and daily homemade biscuits and jam, is cloak-and-cravat cozy. Even the name reflects English aristocracy, honoring the daughter of the mansion's former owner, Lord Pulteney. Now it's smartly run by Peter and another Henrietta (family-size suites, pay parking available, 33 Henrietta Street, tel. 01225/632-632, www.henriettahouse.co.uk, reception@ henriettahouse.co.uk).

$$ At **Apple Tree Guesthouse,** near a shady canal, hostess Ling rents five comfortable rooms sprinkled with Asian decor (family rooms, 2-night minimum Fri-Sat nights, free parking, 7 Pulteney Gardens, tel. 01225/337-642, www.appletreebath. com, enquiries@appletreebath.com).

In the Town Center

You'll pay a premium to sleep right in the center. While Bath is so manageable by foot that a downtown location isn't essential, these options are particularly well-located.

$$$ **Three Abbey Green Guest House,** renting 10 spacious rooms, is located in a quiet, traffic-free courtyard only 50 yards from the abbey and the Roman Baths. Some of the bright, cheery rooms overlook the trees in the courtyard (family rooms, 2-night minimum on weekends, limited free parking, 2 ground-floor rooms work well for those with limited mobility, tel. 01225/428-558, www.threeabbeygreen.com, stay@ threeabbeygreen.com, Sue, Derek, daughter Nicola, and son-in-law Alan). They also rent a self-catering apartment (2-night minimum).

$$$ **Harington's Hotel** rents 13 fresh, modern rooms on a quiet street. This stylish place feels like a boutique hotel, but with a friendlier, laid-back vibe (RS%, pay parking, 8 Queen Street, tel. 01225/461-728, www.haringtonshotel.co.uk, post@ haringtonshotel.co.uk, manager Eve). Owners Melissa and Peter also rent several self-catering apartments down the street (2-night minimum on weekdays).

$$$ At **Abbey House Apartments,**

Laura rents five flats on Abbey Green and many others scattered around town. The apartments called Abbey Green (which comes with a washer and dryer), Abbey View, and Abbey Flat have views of the abbey from their nicely equipped kitchens. Laura provides a simple breakfast (2-night minimum, rooms can sleep four with Murphy and sofa beds, Abbey Green, tel. 01225/464-238, www. laurastownhouseapartments.co.uk, bookings@laurastownhouseapartments. co.uk).

$$ **The Henry Guest House** is a simple, vertical place, renting seven clean rooms. It's friendly, well-run, and just two blocks from the train station (family rooms, 2-night minimum on weekends, 6 Henry Street, tel. 01225/424-052, www.thehenry.com, stay@thehenry.com, Colin).

Bargain Accommodations

¢ The **YMCA,** centrally located on a leafy square, has 210 beds in industrial-strength rooms—all with sinks and basic furnishings. Although it smells a little like a gym, this place is a godsend for budget travelers—safe, secure, quiet, and efficiently run. With lots of twin rooms and a few double beds, this is the only easily accessible budget option in downtown Bath (family rooms, includes continental breakfast, free linens, rental towels, lockers, laundry facilities, down a tiny alley off Broad Street on Broad Street Place, tel. 01225/325-900, www.bathymca.co.uk, stay@bathymca.co.uk).

TRANSPORTATION

Arriving and Departing
By Train

Bath's train station, called Bath Spa, has a staffed ticket desk and ticket machines (tel. 0345-748-4959). To get to the TI, exit straight ahead and continue up Manvers Street for about five minutes, then turn left at the triangular "square" overlooking the riverfront park, following the small TI arrow on a signpost.

Directly in front of the train station is the SouthGate Bath **shopping center.** You can store bags at **The Luggage Store,** a half block in front of the train station (£2.50/bag/day, daily 8:00-22:00, 13 Manvers Street, tel. 01225/312-685).

Train Connections to: Salisbury (hourly direct, 1 hour), **Moreton-in-Marsh** (hourly, 2.5 hours, 1 transfer, more with additional transfers), **York** (hourly with transfer in Bristol, 4.5 hours, more with additional transfers), **Oxford** (hourly, 1.5 hours, transfer in Didcot).

To/From London: You can catch a **train** to London's Paddington Station (2/hour, 1.5 hours, best deals for travel after 9:30 and when purchased in advance, www.gwr.com),

To/From Heathrow Airport: It's fastest and most pleasant to take the **train via London;** with a Britrail pass, it's also the cheapest option, as the whole trip is covered. Without a rail pass, it's the most expensive way to go (£60 total for off-peak travel without rail pass, £10-20 cheaper bought in advance, up to £60 more for full-fare peak-time ticket; 2/hour, 2.25 hours depending on airport terminal, easy change between First Great Western train and Heathrow Express at London's Paddington Station).

If you don't have a rail pass, doing a **train-and-bus combination** via the town of Reading can make sense, as it's more frequent, can take less time than the direct bus—allow 2.5 hours total—and can be much cheaper (RailAir Link shuttle bus from Heathrow to Reading: 2-3/hour, 45 minutes; train from Reading to Bath: 2/hour, 1 hour; £31-41 for off-peak, nonrefundable travel booked in advance—but up to double for peak-time trains; tel. 0118-957-9425, buy bus ticket from www.railair.com, train ticket from www.gwr.com).

By Bus

The National Express **bus station** is just west of the train station (bus info tel. 0871-781-8181, www.nationalexpress.com). For all public bus services in southwestern England, see www.travelinesw.com.

Bus Connections to: Salisbury (hourly, 3 hours; or National Express #300 at 17:05, 1.5 hours), **Stratford-upon-Avon** (1/day, 4 hours, transfer in Bristol), and **Oxford** (1/day direct, 2 hours, more with transfer).

To/From London: You can save money—but not time—by taking the National Express bus to Victoria Coach Station (direct buses nearly hourly, 3.5 hours, avoid those with layover in Bristol, one-way-£5-12, round-trip-£10-18, cheapest to purchase online several days in advance).

To/From Heathrow Airport: The National Express bus is direct and often much cheaper for those without a rail pass, but it's relatively infrequent and can take nearly twice as long as the train (nearly hourly, 3-3.5 hours, £24-40 one-way depending on time of day, tel. 0871-781-8181, www.nationalexpress.com).

By Plane

Bristol Airport, located about 20 miles west of Bath, is closer to Bath than Heathrow and has good connections by bus (Bristol Air Decker bus #A4, £14, 2/hour, 1.25 hours, www.airdecker.com). Otherwise, you can take a taxi (£40).

By Car

Parking: As Bath becomes increasingly pedestrian-friendly, city-center street parking is disappearing. Park & Ride service is a stress-free, no-hassle option to save time and money. Shuttles from Newbridge, Lansdown, and Odd Down (all just outside of Bath) offer free parking and 10-minute shuttle buses into town (daily every 15 minutes, £3.30 round-trip). If you drive into town, try the SouthGate Bath shopping center lot, a five-minute walk from the abbey (£5/up to 3 hours, £14/24 hours, cash or credit card, open 24/7, on the corner of Southgate and Dorchester streets). For more info on parking (including Park & Ride service), see the "Travel and Maps" section of http://visitbath.co.uk.

Rick's Tip: *Take the* **train or bus to Bath** *from London, and* **rent a car when you leave Bath.**

Renting a Car: Enterprise provides a pickup service for customers to and from their hotels (extra fee for one-way rentals, at Lower Bristol Road outside Bath, tel. 01225/443-311, www.enterprise.

com). Others include **Thrifty** (pickup service and one-way rentals available, in the Burnett Business Park in Keynsham—between Bath and Bristol, tel. 01179/867-997, www.thrifty.co.uk), **Hertz** (one-way rentals possible, at Windsor Bridge, tel. 0843-309-3004, www.hertz.co.uk), and **National/Europcar** (one-way rentals available, about £7 by taxi from the train station, at Brassmill Lane—go west on Upper Bristol Road, tel. 0871-384-9985, www.europcar.co.uk). Most offices close Saturday afternoon and all day Sunday, which complicates weekend pickups.

NEAR BATH

The countryside surrounding Bath holds two particularly fine cathedral towns. Glastonbury is the ancient resting place of King Arthur, and home (maybe) to the Holy Grail. Nearby, medieval Wells gathers around its grand cathedral. Drivers can tour the towns easily in a same-day loop trip from Bath; visit Wells last to attend the afternoon evensong service (Sept-June only).

Glastonbury and Wells are each about 20-25 miles from Bath and 140 miles from London. The nearest train station is in Bath, served by regular trains from London's Paddington Station (2/hour, 1.5 hours).

Day Trip from Bath: Both towns are easily accessible by bus from Bath. Bus #173 goes direct from Bath to Wells (nearly hourly, less frequent on Sun, 1.5

Glastonbury

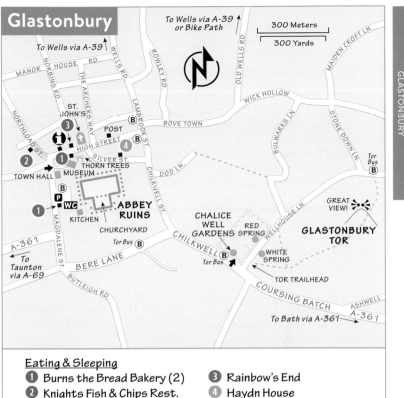

To Wells via A-39
or Bike Path

300 Meters
300 Yards

Glastonbury

To Wells via A-39

MANOR HOUSE RD.
NORBINS RD.
WELLS RD.
ROWLEY RD.
OLD WELLS RD.
MAIDEN CROFT LN.
THE ARCHERS WAY
WICK HOLLOW
ST. JOHN'S
POST
LAMBROOK ST.
BOVE TOWN
BULWARKS LN.
STONE DOWN LN.
Tor Bus
HIGH STREET
SILVER ST.
THORN TREES
NORTHLOAD ST.
TOWN HALL
MUSEUM
DOD LN.
CHILKWELL ST.
GREAT VIEW!
P WC
KITCHEN
ABBEY RUINS
CHURCHYARD
CHALICE WELL GARDENS
RED SPRING
WELLHOUSE LN.
GLASTONBURY TOR
Tor Bus
CHILKWELL ST.
A-361
To Taunton via A-69
BERE LANE
Tor Bus
WHITE SPRING
BUTLEIGH RD.
TOR TRAILHEAD
COURSING BATCH
ASHWELL
A-361
To Bath via A-361

Eating & Sleeping
1 Burns the Bread Bakery (2)
2 Knights Fish & Chips Rest.
3 Rainbow's End
4 Haydn House

---

hours), where you can continue on to Glastonbury by catching bus #376 (2/hour, 25 minutes, drops off directly in front of abbey entrance on Magdalene Street). Note that there are no direct buses between Bath and Glastonbury (but you can backtrack by bus to Wells, then Bath). First Bus Company's £7.50 day pass is a good deal if you plan on connecting Glastonbury and Wells from your Bath home base.

GLASTONBURY

Marked by its hill, or "tor," and located on England's most powerful line of prehistoric sites, the town of Glastonbury gurgles with history and mystery. The extensive Glastonbury Abbey, laid waste by Henry VIII, is among England's oldest religious centers. It's the legendary resting place of the fifth-century King Arthur and his Queen Guinevere. Lore has it that the Holy Grail, the cup used by Christ at the Last Supper, is buried here, inducing a healing spring to flow (now known as the Chalice Well, located near Glastonbury Tor).

Today, Glastonbury and its tor are a center for "searchers"—just right for those looking for a place to recharge their crystals. Glastonbury is also synonymous with its summer music-and-arts festival, a long-hair-and-mud Woodstock re-creation.

Orientation
Day Plan: Tour the abbey when you arrive in town, then ride the shuttle out to the base of the tor. Enjoy the views as you climb to the top of the tor, then stroll back

to town (on the way, drop by the Chalice Well Gardens). You can picnic at the abbey or on the tor—pick something up from the shops on High Street. Note that Tuesday is market day (local produce, arts, and crafts).

Getting There: The nearest train station is in Bath. Buses run from Wells (2/hour, 25 minutes) and Bath (nearly hourly, 2 hours with transfer, www.firstgroup.com).

Arrival in Glastonbury: The bus leaves you right in the town center, in sight of the abbey. Parking is immediately adjacent to the abbey.

Tourist Information: The TI is on High Street in the 15th-century Tribunal townhouse (Mon-Sat 10:00-15:00, closed Sun, 9 High Street, tel. 01458/832-954, www.glastonburytic.co.uk).

Rick's Tip: *Nearly every summer around the June solstice, music fans and London's beautiful people make the trek to the* **Glastonbury Festival** *to see the hottest British and American bands (www.glastonburyfestivals.co.uk). Expect increased traffic and crowds.*

Sights

▲▲GLASTONBURY ABBEY

The massive and evocative ruins of the first Christian sanctuary in the British Isles stand mysteriously alive in a lush 36-acre park. Because it comes with a small museum, a dramatic history, and enthusiastic guides dressed in period costumes, this is one of the most engaging to visit of England's many ruined abbeys.

The space that these ruins occupy has been sacred ground for centuries. The druids used it as a pagan holy site. In the 12th century—because of its legendary connection to King Arthur and the Holy Grail—Glastonbury was the leading Christian pilgrimage site in all of Britain. The popular abbey grew powerful and very wealthy, employing a thousand people to serve the needs of the pilgrims.

Then, in 1539, King Henry VIII ordered the abbey's destruction (as head of the new Church of England, he wanted to remove any reminders of the power of the Catholic Church).

Cost and Hours: £8.25, daily 9:00-20:00, Sept-Nov and March-May until 18:00, Dec-Feb until 16:00.

Information: Tel. 01458/832-267, www.glastonburyabbey.com.

Tours and Demonstrations: Costumed guides offer 30-minute tours (generally daily March-Oct on the hour from 10:00).

⊙ **Self-Guided Tour:** Start by touring the informative **museum** at the entrance building. A model shows the abbey in its pre-Henry VIII splendor, and exhibits tell the story of a place "grandly constructed to entice the dullest minds to prayer."

Next, head out to explore the green park, dotted with bits of the **ruined abbey.** Before poking around the ruins, circle to the left behind the entrance building to find the two **thorn trees.** According to legend, when Joseph of Arimathea came here, he climbed nearby Wearyall Hill and stuck his staff into the soil. A thorn tree sprouted, and its descendant

The ruined Glastonbury Abbey

still stands there today; the trees here in the abbey are its offspring. If the story seems far-fetched to you, don't tell the Queen—a blossom from the abbey's trees sits proudly on her breakfast table every Christmas morning.

Ahead and to the left of the trees, inside what was the north wall, look for two trap doors in the ground. Lift up the doors to see surviving fragments of the abbey's original tiled floor.

Now hike through the remains of the ruined complex to the far end of the abbey. From here, you can envision the longest church nave in England. In this area, you'll find the tombstone (formerly in the floor of the church's choir) marking the spot where the supposed relics of **Arthur and Guinevere** were interred.

Continue around the far side of the abbey ruins, and head for, the only surviving intact building on the grounds—the abbot's conical **kitchen,** with a simple exhibit about life in the abbey.

CHALICE WELL GARDENS

When Joseph of Arimathea brought the Holy Grail to Glastonbury, it supposedly ended up in the bottom of a well, which is now the centerpiece of the peaceful and inviting Chalice Well Gardens. Have a drink or take some of the precious water home—they sell empty bottles to fill.

Cost and Hours: £4.30, daily 10:00-18:00, Nov-March until 16:30, on Chilkwell Street/A-361, tel. 01458/831-154, www.chalicewell.org.uk.

▲GLASTONBURY TOR

Seen by many as a Mother Goddess symbol, the Glastonbury Tor—a natural plug of sandstone on clay—has an undeniable geological charisma. A fine Somerset view rewards those who hike to its 520-foot summit.

As you climb, survey the surrounding land—a former swamp. The ribbon-like man-made drainage canals that glisten as they slice through the farmland are the work of Dutch engineers—Huguenot refugees imported centuries ago to turn the marsh into arable land.

The tor-top tower is the remnant of a chapel dedicated to St. Michael, the warrior angel employed to combat pagan gods.

Getting There: The base of the tor is a 20-minute **walk** from the town center, and the top is another 15-20 brisk uphill

Glastonbury Tor

Wells

minutes from there. While you can hike up the tor from either end, the less-steep approach starts next to the Chalice Well. You can also take the **Tor Bus** shuttle (£3 round-trip, 2/hour, departs from St. Dunstan's parking lot next to the abbey, doesn't run Oct-March) or a **taxi** to the tor trailhead (about £5).

Eating and Sleeping

Burns the Bread makes hearty meat pies—great for a picnic (two branches—14 High Street and in the parking lot next to the abbey). The town's top chippy is **Knights Fish and Chips Restaurant** (closed Sun off-season, 5 Northload Street). For a vegetarian lunch, head to **Rainbow's End** (17 High Street).

$ **Haydn House** rents three rooms in a centrally located 19th-century red-brick house (13a Silver Street, www. haydnhouseglastonbury.com).

WELLS

This well-preserved little town (pop. just under 12,000) has one of the country's most interesting cathedrals and a wonderful afternoon evensong service (Sept-June only). You can still spot a number of the wells, water, and springs that helped give the town its name. Market day fills the town square on Wednesday (farmers' market) and Saturday (general goods).

Orientation

Day Plan: Little Wells is easy to handle in a half-day. You're here to see the cathedral (try to take in the evensong service). Save time to explore the quaint town, especially the medieval, picturesque street called the Vicars' Close.

Getting There: There is no train station in Wells, but nearly hourly buses connect with **Bath** (1.5 hours, www.firstgroup.com) and frequent buses link **Glastonbury** (3-4/hour, 25 minutes). There's one direct bus daily from **London's** Victoria Coach Station (4 hours, www.nationalexpress.com).

Arrival in Wells: If you're coming by **bus,** get off in the city center at the Sadler Street stop, around the corner from the cathedral. **Drivers** will find it simplest to park at the Princes Road lot next to the bus station (enter on Priory Road) and walk five minutes to the cathedral.

Tourist Information: The TI is in the Wells Museum, across the green from the cathedral (Mon-Sat 10:00-17:00, Nov-March until 16:00, closed Sun year-round, 8 Cathedral Green, tel. 01749/673-477, www.wellssomerset.com).

Sights

▲▲WELLS CATHEDRAL

The city's highlight is England's first completely Gothic cathedral (dating from about 1200). Locals claim this church has the largest collection of medieval statuary north of the Alps. It certainly has one of the widest and most elaborate facades I've seen, and unique figure-eight "scissor arches" that are unforgettable.

Cost and Hours: Free but £6 donation requested, daily 7:00-19:00, Oct-Easter until 18:00, daily evensong service (except July-Aug)—described later. Tel. 01749/674-483, www.wellscathedral.org.uk.

Tours: Free one-hour tours run 4-5 times per day April-Oct Mon-Sat; fewer Nov-March.

❷ **Self-Guided Tour:** Begin on the large, inviting **green** in front of the cathedral. In the Middle Ages, the cathedral was enclosed within "The Liberty," an area free from civil jurisdiction until the 1800s. The Liberty included the green on the west side of the cathedral, which, from the 13th to the 17th century, was a burial place for common folk, including 17th-century plague victims. The green became a cricket pitch, then a field for grazing animals and picnicking people.

Today, it's the perfect spot to marvel at an impressive cathedral and its magnificent facade. The west front displays almost 300 original 13th-century carvings of kings and the Last Judgment.

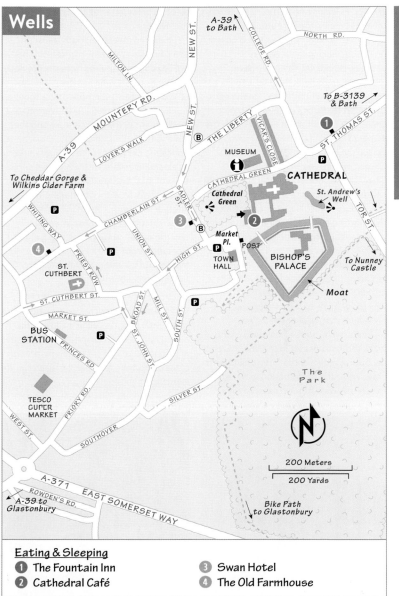

Wells

A-39
to Bath

NORTH RD.

NEW ST.

COLLEGE RD.

To B-3139
& Bath

MOUNTERY RD.

A-39

ST. THOMAS ST.

THE LIBERTY

VICAR'S CLOSE

LOVER'S WALK

NEW ST.

THE LIBERTY

MUSEUM

CATHEDRAL GREEN

CATHEDRAL

To Cheddar Gorge &
Wilkins Cider Farm

SADLER ST.

CHAMBERLAIN ST.

Cathedral
Green

St. Andrew's
Well

TOR ST.

WHITING WAY

UNION ST.

Market
Pl.

BISHOP'S
PALACE

To Nunney
Castle

PRIEST ROW

HIGH ST.

TOWN
HALL

POST

ST.
CUTHBERT

Moat

ST. CUTHBERT ST.

BROAD ST.

MILL ST.

SOUTH ST.

MARKET ST.

BUS
STATION

PRINCES RD.

ST. JOHN ST.

The
Park

TESCO
SUPER
MARKET

PRIORY RD.

SILVER ST.

WEST ST.

SOUTHOVER

200 Meters

200 Yards

A-371

EAST SOMERSET WAY

ROWDEN'S RD.

A-39 to
Glastonbury

Bike Path
to Glastonbury

Eating & Sleeping
1. The Fountain Inn
2. Cathedral Café
3. Swan Hotel
4. The Old Farmhouse

Now head through the cloister and into the cathedral. At your first glance down the **nave,** you're immediately struck by the general sense of light and the unique "scissors" or hourglass-shaped **double arch** (added in 1338 to transfer weight away from where the foundations were sinking). Until Henry VIII and the Reformation, the interior was opulently painted in golds, reds, and greens. Later it was whitewashed. Then, in the 1840s, the church experienced the Victorian "great scrape," as locals peeled moldy whitewash off and revealed the bare stone we see today. The floral ceiling painting is based on the original medieval design.

Small, ornate, 15th-century pavilion-like chapels flank the altar, carved in lacy Gothic for church VIPs. On the right, the **pulpit** features a post-Reformation, circa-1540 English script—rather than the standard Latin (see where the stonemason ran out of space when carving the inscription—we've all been there). Since this was not a monastery church, it escaped destruction in the Reformation.

In the apse you'll find the **Lady Chapel.** Examine the medieval stained-glass windows. Do they look jumbled? In the 17th century, Puritan troops trashed the precious original glass. Much was repaired, but many of the broken panes were like a puzzle that was never figured out. That's why today many of the windows are simply kaleidoscopes of colored glass.

As you walk, notice that many of the black **tombstones** set in the floor have decorative recesses that aren't filled with brass. After the Reformation in the 1530s, the church was short on cash, so they sold the brass lettering to raise money for roof repairs.

Once you reach the south transept, you'll find several items of interest. The **old Saxon font** survives from the previous church (A.D. 705) and has been the site of Wells baptisms for more than a thousand years. (Its carved arches were added by Normans in the 12th century, and the cover is from the 17th century.) Nearby, notice the **carvings** in the capitals of the freestanding pillars, with whimsical depictions of medieval life. On the first pillar, notice the man with a toothache and another man with a thorn in his foot.

Also in the south transept, you'll find the entrance to the cathedral **Reading Room** (free). Housing a few old manuscripts, it offers a peek into a real 15th-century library.

Rick's Tip: *Lined with perfectly pickled 14th-century houses,* **Vicar's Close** *is the oldest continuously occupied complete street in Europe (since 1348). It's just a block north of the cathedral—go under the big arch and look left.*

Wells Cathedral

The nave culminates at the ingenious scissor arch.

▲▲CATHEDRAL EVENSONG SERVICE

The cathedral choir takes full advantage of heavenly acoustics with a nightly 45-minute evensong service. You'll sit right in the old "quire" as you listen to a great pipe organ and the world-famous Wells Cathedral choir.

Cost and Hours: Free, Mon-Sat at 17:15, Sun at 15:00, but usually not offered July-Aug—confirm times beforehand, tel. 01749/674-483, www.wellscathedral.org.uk.

Rick's Tip: *If you attend evensong and* **miss the last bus back to Bath,** *here's what to do: Catch the bus to Bristol instead (hourly, one-hour trip), then take a 15-minute train ride to Bath.*

Eating and Sleeping

For good pub grub, head to **The Fountain Inn** (no lunch on Mon, St. Thomas Street). The **café** in the cathedral welcome center offers a handy if not heavenly lunch.

The comfortable **$$ Swan Hotel** faces the cathedral; you can get a pub lunch in their garden with views over the green and cathedral (Sadler Street, www.swanhotelwells.co.uk). For a B&B, try **$$ The Old Farmhouse** (62 Chamberlain Street).

The
Cotswolds

The Cotswold Hills, a 25-by-90-mile chunk of Gloucestershire, are dotted with enchanting villages. Enjoy a harmonious blend of man and nature—the most pristine of English countrysides decorated with time-passed villages, rich wool churches, tell-me-a-story stone fences, and "kissing gates" you wouldn't want to experience alone.

As with many fairy-tale regions of Europe, the present-day beauty of the Cotswolds was the result of an economic disaster. Wool was a huge industry in medieval England and Cotswold sheep grew the best wool. Wool money built fine towns and houses. With the rise of cotton and the Industrial Revolution, the woolen industry collapsed. Ba-a-a-ad news. The wealthy Cotswold towns fell into depressions; the homes of impoverished nobility became gracefully dilapidated. Preserved as if by a time warp, the Cotswolds are appreciated by 21st-century Romantics.

Two of the region's coziest towns and best home bases are Chipping Campden and Stow-on-the-Wold.

Chipping Campden is prettier (with more thatched roofs), though Stow offers a wider range of restaurants and accommodations. The plain town of Moreton-in-Marsh, the nearest Cotswold town with a train station, is the simplest home base for nondrivers (though basing in Chipping Campden or Stow is possible—either town can be reached by bus from Moreton, except on Sunday, when bus service essentially stops).

Exploring the thatch-happiest of Cotswold villages and countryside is an absolute delight by car and, with a well-organized plan—and patience—are enjoyable even without one. Do your homework in advance; read this chapter carefully, though don't fret over the details. Then decide if you want to rent a car, rely on public transportation (budgeting for an inevitable taxi ride), or reserve a day with a tour company or private driver.

THE COTSWOLDS IN 2 DAYS

Whether exploring by car or public transit, you can visit Chipping Campden (and nearby sights) on one day, and Stow-on-the-Wold (and nearby sights) on the other. If you love open air markets and it's Tuesday, drop by the market in Moreton-in-Marsh.

Distances are short in the Cotswolds; you could visit Chipping Campden and Stow in a half-day (they're 10 miles apart, and respectively 8 and 4 miles away from Moreton-in-Marsh). But rushing the Cotswolds isn't experiencing them. Their charm has a softening effect on many uptight itineraries.

Keep in mind that you can rent a car for just a day or two; for rental agencies near Moreton-in-Marsh, see page 214 (and call in advance to reserve).

With more time: Several worthwhile sights are nearby, which you could visit on your way into or out of the Cotswolds.

To the south lies Oxford, a historic university town, plus Blenheim, England's top countryside palace. Allow a day if you visit both.

To the north are Stratford-upon-Avon and Warwick Castle. Shakespeare fans could easily spend a day in Stratford, and castle lovers storm Warwick in a half-day's time.

By Car

Use a good map and reshuffle this plan to fit your home base.

Day 1: Focus on Chipping Campden and the surrounding area. Browse through the town, following my self-guided walk. Heading south, you can take a loop drive, joyriding through Snowshill (lavender farm nearby), Stanway (Stanway House open Tue and Thu afternoon), and Stanton. If you're a garden lover, sniff out Hidcote Manor Garden.

On any evening, you could have dinner at a pub; take a seat at the bar if you want to talk with locals. The long hours of sunlight in summer make an after-dinner stroll an appealing option.

Day 2: Focus on Stow-on-the-Wold and the surrounding area. Explore Stow and take my self-guided walk. Drive to the Slaughters, Bourton-on-the-Water, and Bibury. If you're up for a hike instead of a drive, walk from Stow to the Slaughters to Bourton-on-the-Water (about 3 hours at a relaxed pace), then catch the bus back to Stow.

Rick's Tip: If you want to sample a bit of **Shakespeare,** *note that* **Stratford is only a 30-minute drive** *from Stow, Chipping Campden, and Moreton-in-Marsh. On the afternoon of your last day in the Cotswolds, you could drive to Stratford, set up in a hotel, and see a play that evening.*

By Public Transportation

This plan is best for any day except Sunday—when virtually no buses run—and assumes you're home-basing in Moreton-in-Marsh.

Day 1: Take the morning bus to Chipping Campden (to explore that town and take my self-guided walk). Hike up Dover's Hill and back (about one-hour round-trip). Eat lunch in Chipping Campden, then squeeze in either Broad Campden or Broadway before returning directly from either town to Moreton by bus #1 or #2. In the evening, have dinner at a pub and a stroll afterwards.

THE COTSWOLDS AT A GLANCE

Chipping Campden and Nearby

▲▲**Chipping Campden** Picturesque market town with finest High Street in England, accented by a 17th-century Market Hall, wool-tycoon manors, and a characteristic Gothic church. See page 185.

▲▲**Stanway House** Grand, aristocratic home of the Earl of Wemyss, with the tallest fountain in Britain and a 14th-century tithe barn. **Hours:** June-Aug Tue and Thu only 14:00-17:00, closed Sept-May. See page 194.

▲**Stanton** Classic Cotswold village with flower-filled exteriors and 15th-century church. See page 196.

▲**Snowshill Manor** Eerie mansion packed to the rafters with eclectic curiosities collected over a lifetime. **Hours:** July-Aug Wed-Mon 11:30-16:30, closed Tue; April-June and Sept-Oct Wed-Sun 12:00-17:00, closed Mon-Tue; closed Nov-March. See page 196.

▲**Hidcote Manor Garden** Fragrant garden organized into color-themed "outdoor rooms" that set a trend in 20th-century garden design. **Hours:** March-Sept daily 10:00-18:00; Oct daily until 17:00; Nov-Dec Sat-Sun 11:00-16:00, closed Mon-Fri; closed Jan-Feb. See page 197.

▲**Broad Campden, Blockley, and Bourton-on-the-Hill** Trio of villages with sweeping views and quaint homes, far from the madding crowds. See page 198.

Stow-on-the-Wold and Nearby

▲▲**Stow-on-the-Wold** Convenient Cotswold home base with charming shops and pubs clustered around town square, plus popular day hikes. See page 198.

▲**Lower and Upper Slaughter** Inaptly named historic villages—home to a working waterwheel, peaceful churches, and a folksy museum. See page 206.

▲**Bourton-on-the-Water** The "Venice of the Cotswolds," touristy yet undeniably striking, with petite canals and impressive Cotswold Motoring Museum. See page 206.

▲**Cotswold Farm Park** Kid-friendly park with endangered breeds of native British animals, farm demonstrations, and tractor rides. **Hours:** Daily 10:30-17:00, Nov-Dec until 16:00, closed Jan. See page 207.

▲**Mechanical Music Museum** Tiny museum brimming with self-playing musical instruments, demonstrations, and Victorian music boxes. **Hours:** Daily 10:00-17:00. See page 208.

▲**Bibury** Village of antique weavers' cottages, ideal for outdoor activities like fishing and picnicking. See page 208.

▲**Cirencester** Ancient 2,000-year-old city noteworthy for its crafts center and museum, showcasing artifacts from Roman and Saxon times. See page 208.

Moreton-in-Marsh

▲**Moreton-in-Marsh** Relatively flat and functional home base with the best transportation links in the Cotswolds and a bustling Tuesday market. See page 209.

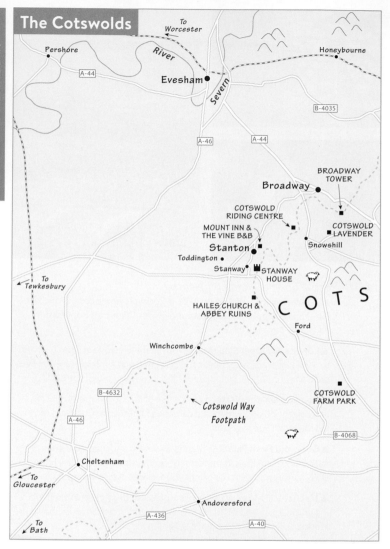

The Cotswolds

To Worcester

Pershore

River Severn

A-44

Evesham

To Tewkesbury

Honeybourne

B-4035

A-46   A-44

BROADWAY TOWER

Broadway

COTSWOLD RIDING CENTRE

MOUNT INN & THE VINE B&B

COTSWOLD LAVENDER

Stanton

Snowshill

Toddington

Stanway   STANWAY HOUSE

HAILES CHURCH & ABBEY RUINS

C O T S

Ford

Winchcombe

Cotswold Way Footpath

COTSWOLD FARM PARK

B-4632

A-46

B-4068

Cheltenham

To Gloucester

Andoversford

A-436   A-40

To Bath

Day 2: Take a morning bus to Stow. After following my self-guided walk and poking around the town, hike from Stow through the Slaughters to Bourton-on-the-Water (a leisurely 3 hours), then return by bus or taxi to Moreton for dinner.

Tourist Information

Local TIs stock a wide array of helpful resources and can tell you about any local events during your stay. Ask for the *Cotswold Lion,* the biannual newspaper, which includes suggestions for walks and hikes (spring/summer); bus schedules for the routes you'll be using; and the *Attractions and Events Guide* (with updated prices and hours for Cotswold sights).

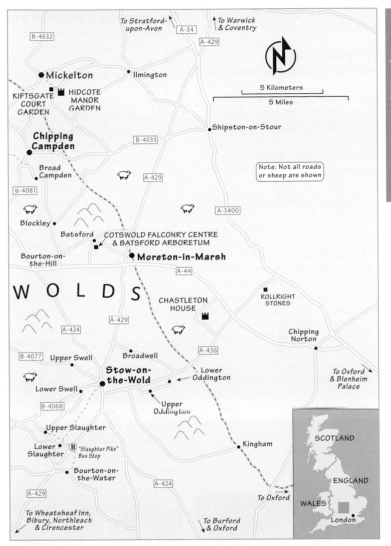

CHIPPING CAMPDEN

Just touristy enough to be convenient, the north Cotswold town of Chipping Campden (CAM-den) is a ▲▲ sight. This market town, once the home of the richest Cotswold wool merchants, has some incredibly beautiful thatched roofs. Both the great British historian G. M. Trevelyan and I call Chipping Campden's High Street the finest in England.

Orientation

Tourist Information: Chipping Campden's TI is tucked away in the old police station on High Street. Get the £1.50 town guide with map, or the local Footpath Guide for £2.50 (April-Oct daily 9:30-17:00; Nov-March Mon-Thu 9:30-13:00,

Fri-Sun until 16:00; tel. 01386/841-206, www.chippingcampdenonline.org).

Helpful Hints

Festivals: The **Cotswold Olimpicks** are a series of tongue-in-cheek countryside games (such as competitive shin-kicking) held atop Dover's Hill, just above town (generally in late spring; check www.olimpickgames.co.uk). Chipping Campden also has a **music festival** in May and an **open gardens festival** the third weekend in June.

Bike Rental: It's **Cycle Cotswolds,** at the Volunteer Inn pub on Lower High Street (£12/day, daily 7:00-dusk, mobile 07549-620-597, www.cyclecotswolds.co.uk).

Parking: Find a spot anywhere along High Street and park for free with no time limit. There's also a pay-and-display lot on High Street, across from the TI (2-hour maximum). On weekends, you can also park for free at the school (see map).

Tours: The **Cotswold Voluntary Wardens** are happy to show you around town for a small donation to the Cotswold Conservation Fund (suggested donation-£4/person, 1.5-hour walks run June-Sept Tue at 14:00 and Thu at 10:00, meet at Market Hall; tel. 0776/156-5661, Vin Kelly).

⊙ Chipping Campden Walk

This self-guided stroll through "Campden" (as locals call their town) takes you from the Market Hall west to the old silk mill, and then back east the length of High Street to the church. It takes about an hour.

Market Hall: Begin at Campden's most famous monument—the Market Hall. It stands in front of the TI, marking the town center. The Market Hall was built in 1627 by the 17th-century Lord of the Manor, Sir Baptist Hicks. (Look for the Hicks family coat of arms on the east end of the building's facade.) Back then, it was an elegant—even over-the-top—shopping hall for the townsfolk who'd come here to buy their produce.

The timbers inside are true to the original. Study the classic Cotswold stone roof, still held together with wooden pegs nailed in from underneath. (Tiles were cut and sold with peg holes, and stacked like waterproof scales.) Buildings all over the region still use these stone shingles. Today, the hall, which is rarely used, stands as a testimony to the importance of trade to medieval Campden.

Adjacent to the Market Hall is the sober WWI monument—a reminder of the huge price paid by nearly every little town. Walk around it, noticing how 1918 brought the greatest losses.

Quaint and cute Cotswolds

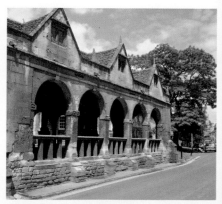

Chipping Campden Market Hall

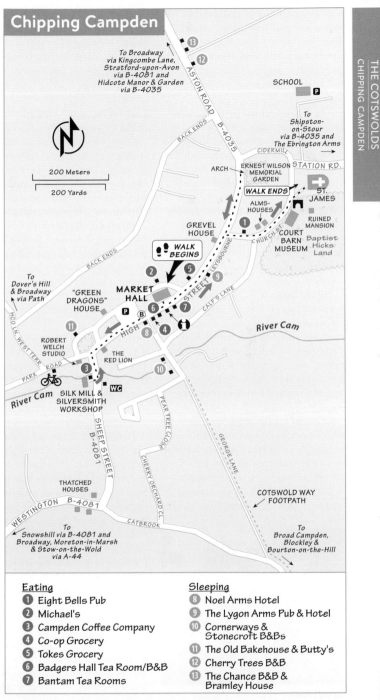

Chipping Campden

To Broadway
via Kingcombe Lane,
Stratford-upon-Avon
via B-4081 and
Hidcote Manor & Garden
via B-4035

SCHOOL

To
Shipston-
on-Stour
via B-4035 and
The Ebrington Arms

ASTON ROAD

BACK ENDS

B-4035

CIDERMILL

STATION RD.

ARCH

ERNEST WILSON
MEMORIAL
GARDEN

WALK ENDS

ST.
JAMES

GREVEL
HOUSE

ALMS-
HOUSES

RUINED
MANSION

200 Meters

200 Yards

WALK BEGINS

COURT
BARN
MUSEUM

Baptist
Hicks
Land

BACK ENDS

To
Dover's Hill
& Broadway
via Path

"GREEN
DRAGONS"
HOUSE

MARKET
HALL

LEYSBOURNE

CALF'S LANE

River Cam

HIGH

STREET

HOO LN WEST TERR.

ROBERT
WELCH
STUDIO

PARK ROAD

THE
RED LION

River Cam

WC

SILK MILL &
SILVERSMITH
WORKSHOP

SHEEP STREET
B-4081

PEAR TREE CLOSE

GEORGE LANE

CHERRY ORCHARD CL.

COTSWOLD WAY
FOOTPATH

THATCHED
HOUSES

WESTINGTON B-4081

CATBROOK

To
Snowshill via B-4081 and
Broadway, Moreton-in-Marsh
& Stow-on-the-Wold
via A-44

To
Broad Campden,
Blockley &
Bourton-on-the-Hill

Eating

1 Eight Bells Pub
2 Michael's
3 Campden Coffee Company
4 Co-op Grocery
5 Tokes Grocery
6 Badgers Hall Tea Room/B&B
7 Bantam Tea Rooms

Sleeping

8 Noel Arms Hotel
9 The Lygon Arms Pub & Hotel
10 Cornerways &
Stonecroft B&Bs
11 The Old Bakehouse & Butty's
12 Cherry Trees B&B
13 The Chance B&B &
Bramley House

Between the Market Hall and the WWI monument you'll find a limestone disc embedded in the ground marking the ceremonial start of the Cotswold Way (you'll find its partner in front of the abbey in Bath—100 miles away—marking the southern end).

The TI is just across the street, in the old police courthouse. If it's open, you're welcome to climb the stairs and peek into the **Magistrate's Court** (free, same hours as TI, ask at TI to go up). Under the open-beamed courtroom, you'll find a humble little exhibit on the town's history.

• *Walk west, passing the Town Hall and the parking lot that was originally the sheep market, until you reach the Red Lion Inn. Across High Street (and a bit to the right), look for the house with a sundial and sign over the door reading...*

"Green Dragons": The house's decorative black cast-iron fixtures (originally in the stables) once held hay and functioned much like salad bowls for horses. Fine-cut stones define the door, but "rubble stones" make up the rest of the wall. The pink stones are the same limestone but have been heated, and likely were scavenged from a house that burned down.

• *At the Red Lion, leave High Street and walk a block down Sheep Street. At the little creek just past the public WC, a 30-yard-long lane on the right leads to an old Industrial-Age silk mill (and the Hart silversmith shop).*

Silk Mill: The tiny River Cam powered a mill here since about 1790. Today it

houses the handicraft workers guild and some interesting history. In 1902, Charles Robert Ashbee (1863-1942) revitalized this sleepy hamlet of 2,500 by bringing a troupe of London artisans and their families (160 people in all) to town. Ashbee was a leader in the romantic Arts and Crafts movement—craftspeople repulsed by the Industrial Revolution who idealized the handmade crafts and preindustrial ways. Ashbee's idealistic craftsmen's guild lasted only until 1908, when most of his men grew bored with their small-town, back-to-nature ideals. Today, the only shop surviving from the originals is that of **silversmith David Hart.** His grandfather came to town with Ashbee, and the workshop (upstairs in the mill building) is an amazing time warp—little has changed since 1902 (Mon-Fri 9:00-17:00, Sat until 12:00, closed Sun, tel. 01386/841-100).

• *While you could continue 200 yards farther to see some fine thatched houses, this walk instead returns to High Street. On the corner is the studio shop of Robert Welch, a local industrial designer who worked in the spirit of the Arts and Crafts movement. His son and daughter carry on his legacy in the fine shop (with a little museum case in the back). Turn right, and walk through town.*

High Street: Chipping Campden's High Street has changed little architecturally since 1840. (The town's street plan and property lines survive from the 12th century.) As you now walk the length of England's finest historic High Street, study the skyline, see the dates on the buildings, and count the sundials. Notice the harmony of the long rows of buildings. While the street comprises different styles through the centuries, everything you see was made of the same Cotswold stone—the only stone allowed today.

To remain level, High Street arcs with the contour of the hillside. Because it's so wide, you know this was a market town. In past centuries, livestock and packhorses laden with piles of freshly shorn fleece would fill the streets. Campden was a sales

On High Street

and distribution center for the wool industry, and merchants from as far away as Italy would come here for the prized raw wool.

High Street has no house numbers: Locals know the houses by their names. In the distance, you'll see the town church (where this walk ends). Notice that the power lines are buried underground, making the scene delightfully uncluttered.

As you stroll High Street, you'll find the finest houses on the uphill side—which gets more sun. Decorative features (like the Ionic capitals near the TI) are added for nonstructural touches of class. Most High Street buildings are half-timbered, but with cosmetic stone facades. You may see some exposed half-timbered walls. Study the crudely beautiful framing, made of hand-hewn oak (you can see the adze marks) and held together by wooden pegs.

Peeking down alleys, you'll notice how the lots are narrow but very deep. Called "burgage plots," this platting goes back to 1170. In medieval times, rooms were lined up long and skinny like train cars: Each building had a small storefront, followed by a workshop, living quarters, staff quarters, stables, and a garden at the very back.

Now the private alleys that still define many of these old lots lead to comfy gardens. While some of today's buildings are wider, virtually all the widths are exact multiples of that basic first unit.

• *Hike the length of High Street toward the church, to just before the first intersection. In front of the door of the old schoolhouse on the left side of the street, notice the rude gargoyle carved by the town's former stonemason. There are more gargoyles hanging out above you a few houses down at the...*

Grevel House: In 1367, William Grevel built what's considered Campden's first stone house. Sheep tycoons had big homes. Imagine back then, when this fine building was surrounded by humble wattle-and-daub huts. It had newfangled chimneys, rather than a crude hole in the roof. (No more rain inside!) Originally a "hall house" with just one big, tall room, it got its upper floor in the 16th century. The finely carved central bay window is a good early example of the Perpendicular Gothic style. The gargoyles scared away bad spirits—and served as rain spouts. The boot scrapers outside each door were fixtures in that muddy age—especially in market towns, where the

Grevel House

streets were filled with animal dung.

• *Continue up High Street for about 100 yards. Go past Church Street (which we'll walk up later). On the right, at a big tree behind a low stone wall, you'll find a small Gothic arch leading into a garden.*

Ernest Wilson Memorial Garden: Once the church's vegetable patch, this small and secluded garden is a botanist's delight today. Pop inside if it's open. The garden is filled with well-labeled plants that the Victorian botanist Ernest Wilson brought back to England from his extensive travels in Asia. There's a complete history of the garden on the board to the left of the entry.

• *Backtrack to Church Street. Turn left, walk past the recommended Eight Bells pub, and hook left with the street. Along your right-hand side stretches...*

Baptist Hicks Land: Sprawling adjacent to the town church, the area known as Baptist Hicks Land held Hicks' huge estate and manor house. This influential Lord of the Manor was from "a family of substance," who were merchants of silk and fine clothing as well as moneylenders. Beyond the ornate gate (which you'll see ahead, near the church), only a few outbuildings and the charred corner of his **mansion** survive. The mansion was burned by royalists in 1645 during the Civil War—notice how Cotswold stone turns red when burned. Hicks housed the poor, making a show of his generosity, adding a long row of almshouses (with his family coat of arms) for neighbors to see as they walked to church. These almshouses (lining Church Street on the left) house pensioners today, as they have since the 17th century. Across the street is a ditch built as a "cart wash"—it was filled with water to soak old cart wheels so they'd swell up and stop rattling.

On the right, filling the old **Court Barn,** is a small, fussy museum about crafts and designs from the Arts and Crafts movement, with works by Ashbee and his craftsmen (£5, Tue-Sun 10:00-17:00, Oct-March until 16:00, closed Mon year-round, tel. 01386/841-951, www.courtbarn.org.uk).

• *Next to the Hicks gate, a scenic, tree-lined lane leads to the front door of the church. On the way, notice the 11 lime trees: Planted in about 1760, there used to be one for each of the apostles, until a tree died recently (sorry, no limes).*

St. James Church: One of the finest churches in the Cotswolds, St. James Church graces one of its leading towns. Both the town and the church were built by wool wealth. Go inside. The church is Perpendicular Gothic, with lots of light and strong verticality. Notice the fine vestments and altar hangings (intricate c. 1460 embroidery) behind protective blue curtains (near the back of the church). Tombstones pave the floor in the chancel (often under protective red carpeting)—memorializing great wool merchants through the ages.

At the altar is a brass relief of William Grevel, the first owner of the Grevel

Baptist Hicks Land

Tomb of Sir Baptist Hicks and his wife

Cotswold Appreciation 101

In the Cotswolds, a town's main street (called High Street) needed to be wide to accommodate the sheep and cattle being marched to market (and today, to park tour buses). Some of the most picturesque cottages were once humble row houses of weavers' cottages, usually located along a stream for their waterwheels (good examples in Bibury and Lower Slaughter). Walls and roofs are made of the local limestone. The limestone roof tiles hang by pegs. To make the weight more bearable, smaller and lighter tiles are higher up. An extremely strict building code keeps towns looking what many locals call "overly quaint."

While you'll still see lots of sheep, the commercial wool industry is essentially dead. It costs more to shear a sheep than the 50 pence the wool will fetch. In the old days, sheep lived long lives, producing lots of wool. When they were finally slaughtered, the meat was tough and eaten as "mutton." Today, you don't find mutton much because the sheep are raised primarily for their meat, and slaughtered younger. When it comes to Cotswold sheep these days, it's lamb (not mutton) for dinner (not sweaters).

Towns are small, and everyone seems to know everyone. In contrast to the village ambience are the giant manors and mansions whose private gated driveways you'll drive past. Many of these now belong to A-list celebrities, who have country homes here. If you live in the Cotswolds, you can call Madonna, Elizabeth Hurley, and Kate Moss your neighbors.

This is walking country. The English love their walks and vigorously defend their age-old right to free passage. Once a year the Ramblers, Britain's largest walking club, organizes a "Mass Trespass," when each of the country's 50,000 miles of public footpaths are walked. By assuring that each path is used at least once a year, they stop landlords from putting up fences. Any paths found blocked are unceremoniously unblocked.

House (described earlier), and his wife. But it is Sir Baptist Hicks who dominates the church. His huge canopied tomb is the ornate final resting place for Hicks and his wife, Elizabeth. Study their faces, framed by fancy lace ruffs (trendy in the 1620s). Adjacent—as if in a closet—is a statue of their daughter, Lady Juliana, and her husband, Lutheran Yokels. Juliana commissioned the statue in 1642, when her husband died, but had it closed up until she died in 1680. Then, the doors were opened, revealing these two people holding hands and living happily ever after—at least in marble. The hinges were likely used only once.

Just outside as you leave the church, look immediately around the corner to the right of the door. A small tombstone reads "Thank you Lord for Simon, a dearly loved cat who greeted everyone who entered this church. RIP 1980."

Hiking

Since this is a particularly hilly area, long-distance hikes are challenging. The easiest and most rewarding stroll is to the thatch-happy hobbit village of **Broad Campden** (about a mile, mostly level). From there, you can walk or take the bus (#2) back to Chipping Campden.

Or, if you have more energy, continue from Broad Campden up over the ridge and into picturesque **Blockley**—and, if your stamina holds out, all the way to **Bourton-on-the-Hill** (Blockley and

Bourton-on-the-Hill are also connected by buses #1 and #2 to Chipping Campden and Moreton).

Alternatively, you can hike up to **Dover's Hill,** just north of the village. Ask locally about this easy circular one-hour walk that takes you on the first mile of the 100-mile-long Cotswold Way (which goes from here to Bath).

For more about hiking, see "Getting Around the Cotswolds—By Foot."

Eating

This town—filled with wealthy residents and tourists—comes with many choices.

$$$ Eight Bells pub is a charming 14th-century inn on Leysbourne with a classy and woody restaurant and a more rustic pub. Neil and Julie keep their seasonal menu as locally sourced as possible. As this is the best deal going in town for top-end pub dining, reservations are smart (daily 12:00-14:00 & 18:30-21:00, tel. 01386/840-371, www.eightbellsinn.co.uk).

$$ The Lygon Arms pub is cozy and inviting, with a good, basic bar menu. You can order from the same menu in the colorful pub or the more elegant dining room across the passage (daily 11:30-14:30 & 18:00-22:00, tel. 01386/840-318).

$$$ Michael's, a fun Mediterranean restaurant on High Street, serves hearty portions and breaks plates at closing every Saturday night. The forte here is Greek, with plenty of mezes—small dishes (Tue-Sun 11:00-14:30 & 19:00-22:00, closed Mon, tel. 01386/840-826).

Light Meals

If you want a quick takeaway sandwich, consider these options. Munch your lunch on the benches on the little green near the Market Hall.

$ Butty's offers tasty sandwiches and wraps made to order (Mon-Sat 7:30-14:00, closed Sun, Lower High Street, tel. 01386/840-401).

$ Campden Coffee Company is a cozy little café with local goodies including sal-ads, sandwiches, and homemade sweets (Sat-Mon 10:00-16:15, Tue-Fri from 9:00, on the ground floor of the Silk Mill, tel. 01386/849-251).

Picnic: The **Co-op** grocery is the town's small "supermarket" (daily, next to TI on High Street). **Tokes,** on the opposite end of High Street, has a tempting selection of cheeses, meats, and wine for a make-your-own ploughman's lunch (daily, just past the Market Hall, tel. 01386/849-345.)

Afternoon Tea: To visit a cute tea-room, try the good-value **$ Bantam Tea Rooms,** near the Market Hall (daily 10:00-16:00, High Street, tel. 01386/840-386). On Fridays and Saturdays **$$ Badgers Hall** opens their lunch and afternoon tea service to visitors not staying at their B&B.

Sleeping

In Chipping Campden—as in any town in the Cotswolds—B&Bs offer a better value than hotels. Try to book well in advance, as rooms are snapped up early in the spring and summer by happy hikers heading for the nearby Cotswold Way.

On or near High Street

$$$ Noel Arms Hotel, the characteristic old hotel on the main square, has welcomed guests for 600 years. Its lobby was remodeled in a medieval-meets-modern style, and its 27 rooms are well-furnished with antiques (some ground-floor doubles, attached restaurant/bar and café, free parking, High Street, tel. 01386/840-317, www.noelarmshotel.com, reception@noelarmshotel.com).

$$$ The Lygon Arms Hotel (pronounced "lig-un"), attached to the popular pub of the same name, has small public areas and 10 cheery, open-beamed rooms (free parking, High Street, go through archway and look for hotel reception on the left, tel. 01386/840-318, www.lygonarms.co.uk, sandra@lygonarms.co.uk, Sandra Davenport).

$$ Cornerways B&B is a fresh, bright, and comfy home (not "oldie worldie") a block off High Street. It's run by the delightful Carole Proctor, who can "look out the window and see the church where we were married." The two huge, light, airy loft rooms are great for families. If you're happy to exchange breakfast for more space, ask about the cottage across the street (2-night minimum, cash only, off-street parking, George Lane, just walk through the arch beside Noel Arms Hotel, tel. 01386/841-307, www.cornerways.info, carole@cornerways.info). For a fee, Les can pick you up from the train station, or take you on village tours.

$$ Stonecroft B&B, next to Corner-ways, has three polished, well-maintained rooms (one with low, slanted ceilings—unfriendly to tall people). The lovely garden with a patio and small stream is a tranquil place for meals or an early-evening drink (family rooms but no kids under 12, George Lane, tel. 01386/840-486, www.stonecroft-chippingcampden.co.uk, info@stonecroft-chippingcampden.co.uk, Roger and Lesley Yates).

$$ The Old Bakehouse, run by energetic young mom Zoe, rents two small but pleasant rooms in a 600-year-old home with exposed beams and cottage charm (cash only, Lower High Street, near intersection with Sheep Street, tel. 01386/840-979, mobile 07717-330-838, www.theoldbakehouse.org.uk, zoegabb@yahoo.co.uk).

A Short Walk from Town on Aston Road

The B&Bs below are a 10-minute walk from Market Hall. They are listed in the order you would find them when strolling from town (if arriving by bus, ask to be dropped off at Aston Road).

$$ Cherry Trees B&B, set well off the road, is bubbly Angie's spacious, modern home, with three king rooms and one superior king room with balcony (free parking, Aston Road, tel. 01386/840-873, www.cherrytreescampden.com, sclrksn7@tiscali.co.uk).

$$ The Chance B&B—a modern home with Cotswold charm—has two tastefully decorated rooms with king beds (which can also be twins if requested) and a breakfast room that opens onto a patio. They also offer two self-catering cottages in town, next to the silk mill (cash only, free parking, 1 Aston Road, tel. 01386/849-079, www.the-chance.co.uk, enquiries@the-chance.co.uk, Sally and Paul).

$$ Bramley House, which backs up to a farm, has a spacious garden suite with a private outdoor patio and lounge area (bathroom downstairs from bedroom) and a superior king double. Crisp white linens and simple country decor give the place a light and airy feel (2-night minimum, homemade cake with tea or coffee on arrival, locally sourced/organic breakfast, 6 Aston Road, tel. 01386/840-066, www.bramleyhouse.co.uk, dppovey@btinternet.com, Jane and David Povey).

NEAR CHIPPING CAMPDEN

Because the countryside around Chipping Campden is particularly hilly, it's also especially scenic. This is a very rewarding area to poke around and discover little thatched villages.

Due west of Chipping Campden lies the famous and touristy town of Broadway. Just south of that, you'll find my nominations for the cutest Cotswold villages. Like marshmallows in hot chocolate, Stanway, Stanton, and Snowshill nestle side by side, awaiting your arrival. (Note the Stanway House's limited hours when planning your visit.)

Hidcote Manor Garden is just northeast of Chipping Campden, while Broad Campden, Blockley, and Bourton-on-the-Hill lie roughly between Chipping Campden and Stow (or Moreton)—handy if you're connecting those towns.

The countryside around Chipping Campden is dotted with charming villages.

Broadway

This postcard-pretty town, a couple of miles west of Chipping Campden, is filled with inviting shops and fancy teahouses. With a "broad way" indeed running through its middle, it's one of the bigger towns in the area. This means you'll likely pass through at some point if you're driving—but, since all the big bus tours seem to stop here, I usually give Broadway a miss. However, with a new road that allows traffic to skirt the town, Broadway has gotten cuter than ever. Broadway has good bus connections with Chipping Campden.

Just outside Broadway, on the road to Chipping Campden, you might spot signs for the **Broadway Tower,** which looks like a turreted castle fortification stranded in the countryside without a castle in sight. This 55-foot-tall observation tower is a "folly"—a uniquely English term for a quirky, outlandish novelty erected as a giant lawn ornament by some aristocrat with more money than taste. If you're also weighted down with too many pounds, you can relieve yourself of £5 to climb to its top for a view over the pastures. But the view from the tower's park-like perch

is free, and almost as impressive (daily 10:00-17:00).

Stanway

More of a humble crossroads community than a true village, sleepy Stanway is worth a visit mostly for its manor house, which offers an intriguing insight into the English aristocracy today. If you're in the area when it's open, it's well worth visiting.

▲▲STANWAY HOUSE

The Earl of Wemyss (pronounced "Weemz"), whose family tree charts relatives back to 1202, opens his melancholy home and grounds to visitors just two days a week in the summer. Walking through his house offers a unique glimpse into the lifestyles of England's eccentric and fading nobility.

Cost and Hours: £9 ticket covers house and fountain, £3 to visit the watermill; ticket includes a wonderful and intimate audioguide, narrated by the lordship himself; June-Aug Tue and Thu only 14:00-17:00, closed Sept-May, tel. 01386/584-469, www.stanwayfountain.co.uk.

Getting There: By car, leave the B-4077 at a statue of (the Christian) George slaying the dragon (of pagan superstition); you'll round the corner and see the manor's fine 17th-century Jacobean gatehouse. Park in the lot across the street. There's no public transportation to Stanway.

Visiting the Manor: The **Tithe Barn** (near where you enter the grounds) dates to the 14th century, and predates the manor. It was originally where monks—in the days before money—would accept one-tenth of whatever the peasants produced. Peek inside: This is a great hall for village hoedowns. While the Tithe Barn is no longer used to greet motley peasants and collect their feudal "rents," the lord still gets rent from his vast landholdings, and hosts community fêtes in his barn.

You're free to wander around the **manor** pretty much as you like, but keep in mind that a family does live here. His lordship is often roaming about as well. The place feels like a time warp. Ask a staff member to demonstrate the spinning rent-collection table. In the great hall, marvel at the one-piece oak shuffleboard table and the 1780 Chippendale exercise chair (half an hour of bouncing on this was considered good for the liver).

The manor dogs have their own cutely painted "family tree," but the Earl admits that his last dog, C. J., was "all character and no breeding." Poke into the office. You can psychoanalyze the lord by the books that fill his library, the DVDs stacked in front of his bed (with the mink bedspread), and whatever's next to his toilet.

The place has a story to tell. And so do the docents stationed in each room—modern-day peasants who, even without family trees, probably have relatives going back just as far in this village. Talk to these people. Learn what you can about this side of England.

Wandering through the expansive back yard you'll see the earl's pet project: restoring "the tallest **fountain** in Britain"—300 feet tall, gravity-powered, and

running for 30 minutes twice a day (at 14:45 and 16:00).

Signs lead to a working **watermill,** which produces flour from wheat grown on the estate (about 100 yards from the house, requires separate ticket to enter).

From Stanway to Stanton

These towns are separated by a row of oak trees and grazing land, with parallel waves echoing the furrows plowed by medieval farmers. Centuries ago, farmers were allotted long strips of land called "furlongs." The idea was to dole out good and bad land equitably. (One square furlong equals 10 acres.) Over centuries of plowing these, furrows were formed. Let someone else drive, so you can hang out the window under a canopy of oaks, passing stone walls and sheep. Leaving Stanway on the road to Stanton, the first building you'll see (on the left, just outside Stanway) is a thatched cricket pavilion overlooking the village cricket green. Originally built for Peter Pan author J. M. Barrie, it dates from 1930 and is raised up (as medieval

Stanway House

buildings were) on rodent-resistant staddle stones. Stanton is just ahead; follow the signs.

Stanton

Pristine Cotswold charm cheers you as you head up the main street of the village of Stanton (rated ▲). Go on a photo safari for flower-bedecked doorways and windows. (A scant few buses serve Stanton.)

Stanton's **Church of St. Michael** (with the pointy spire) betrays a pagan past. It's safe to assume any church dedicated to St. Michael (the archangel who fought the devil) sits upon a sacred pagan site. Stanton is actually at the intersection of two ley lines (a line connecting prehistoric or ancient sights). You'll see St. Michael's well-worn figure (and, above that, a sundial) over the door as you enter. Inside, above the capitals in the nave, find the pagan symbols for the sun and the moon. While the church probably dates back to the 9th century, today's building is mostly from the 15th century, with 13th-century transepts. On the north transept (far side from entry), medieval frescoes show faintly through the 17th-century whitewash. (Once upon a time, these frescoes were considered too "papist.") Imagine the church interior colorfully decorated throughout. Original medieval glass is behind the altar. The list of rectors (at the very back of the church, under the organ loft) goes back to 1269. Finger the grooves in the back pews, worn away by sheepdog

leashes. (A man's sheepdog accompanied him everywhere.)

Horse Riding: Jill Carenza's **Cotswolds Riding Centre,** set just outside Stanton village, is in the most scenic corner of the region. The facility's horses can take anyone from rank beginners to more experienced riders on a scenic "hack" through the village and into the high country (per-hour prices: £32/person on a group hack, £42/person semiprivate hack, £52 private one-person hack; lessons, longer/expert rides, and pub tours available; tel. 01386/584-250, www.cotswoldsriding.co.uk, info@cotswoldsriding.co.uk). From Stanton, head toward Broadway and watch for the riding center on your right after about a third of a mile.

Eating: High on a hill at the far end of Stanton's main drag, nearest to Broadway, the aptly named **$$$ Mount Inn** serves up pricey, upscale meals on its big, inviting terrace with grand views (food served daily 12:00-14:00 & 18:00-21:00, may be closed Mon off-season, Old Snowshill Road, tel. 01386/584-316).

Sleeping: $$ The Vine B&B has five rooms in a characteristic old Cotswold house near the center of town, next to the cricket pitch (most rooms with four-poster beds, some stairs; for contact info, see listing for riding center, above).

Snowshill

Another nearly edible little bundle of cuteness, the village of Snowshill (SNOWS-hill) has a photogenic triangular square with a characteristic pub at its base.

▲SNOWSHILL MANOR

Dark and mysterious, this old palace is filled with the lifetime collection of Charles Paget Wade. It's one big, musty celebration of craftsmanship, from finely carved spinning wheels to frightening samurai armor to tiny elaborate figurines carved by prisoners from the bones of meat served at dinner. Taking seriously his

Pagan symbol in the Church of St. Michael

family motto, "Let Nothing Perish," Wade dedicated his life and fortune to preserving things finely crafted. The house (whose management made me promise not to promote it as an eccentric collector's pile of curiosities) really shows off Wade's ability to recognize and acquire fine examples of craftsmanship.

Cost and Hours: £12; manor house open July-Aug Wed-Mon 11:30-16:30, closed Tue; April-June and Sept-Oct Wed-Sun 12:00-17:00, closed Mon-Tue; closed Nov-March; gardens and ticket window open at 11:00, last entry one hour before closing, restaurant, tel. 01386/852-410, www.nationaltrust.org.uk/snowshillmanor.

Getting There: The manor overlooks the town square, but there's no direct access from the square; instead, the entrance and parking lot are about a half-mile up the road toward Broadway. Park there and follow the long walkway through the garden to get to the house. A golf-cart-type shuttle to the house is available for those who need assistance.

Getting In: This popular sight strictly limits the number of entering visitors by doling out entry times. No reservations are possible; to get a slot, you must report to the ticket desk. It can be up to an hour's wait—even more on busy days, especially weekends (when they can sell out for the day as early as 14:00). Tickets go on sale and the gardens open at 11:00. A good strategy is to arrive close to the opening time, and if there's a wait, enjoy the gardens (it's a 10-minute walk to the manor).

Snowshill Manor

Cotswold Lavender

In 2000, farmer Charlie Byrd realized that tourists love lavender. He planted his farm with 250,000 plants, and now visitors come to wander among his 53 acres, which burst with gorgeous lavender blossoms from mid-June through late August. His fragrant fantasy peaks late each July. Lavender—so famous in France's Provence—is not indigenous to this region, but it fits the climate and soil just fine. A free flier in the shop explains the variations of blooming flowers. Farmer Byrd produces lavender oil (an herbal product valued since ancient times for its healing, calming, and fragrant qualities) and sells it in a delightful shop, along with many other lavender-themed items. In the café, enjoy a pot of lavender-flavored tea with a lavender scone.

Cost and Hours: Free to enter shop and café, £3.50 to walk through the fields and the distillery; generally open June-Aug daily 10:00-17:00, closed Sept-May, schedule changes annually depending on when the lavender blooms—call ahead or check their website; tel. 01386/854-821, www.cotswoldlavender.co.uk.

Getting There: It's a half-mile out of Snowshill on the road toward Chipping Campden (easy parking). Entering Snowshill from the road to the manor (described earlier), take the left fork, then turn left again at the end of the village.

Hidcote Manor Garden

This is less "on the way" between towns than the other sights in this section—but the grounds around this manor house are well worth a detour if you like gardens. Rated ▲, Hidcote is where garden designers pioneered the notion of creating a series of outdoor "rooms," each with a unique theme (such as maple room, red room, and so on) and separated by a yew-tree hedge. The garden's design, inspired by the Arts and Crafts movement, is most formal near the house and becomes more pastoral as it approaches the countryside.

Cotswold lavender

A "garden room" at Hidcote Manor

Follow your nose through a clever series of small gardens that lead delightfully from one to the next. Among the best in England, Hidcote Gardens are at their fragrant peak from May through August.

Cost and Hours: £13; March-Sept daily 10:00-18:00, Oct until 17:00; Nov-Dec Sat-Sun 11:00-16:00, closed Mon-Fri; closed Jan-Feb; last entry one hour before closing, café, restaurant, tel. 01386/438-333, www.nationaltrust.org.uk/hidcote.

Getting There: If you're driving, it's four miles northeast of Chipping Campden—roughly toward Ilmington. The gardens are accessible by bus, then a 45-minute country walk uphill. Buses #1 and #2 take you to Mickleton (one stop past Chipping Campden), where a footpath begins next to the churchyard. Continuing more or less straight, the path leads through sheep pastures and ends at Hidcote's driveway.

Broad Campden, Blockley, and Bourton-on-the-Hill

This trio of pleasant villages, worth ▲, lines up along an off-the-beaten-path road between Chipping Campden and Moreton or Stow. **Broad Campden,** just on the outskirts of Chipping Campden, has some of the cutest thatched-roof houses I've seen. **Blockley,** nestled higher in the picturesque hills, is a popular setting for films. The same road continues on to **Bourton-on-the-Hill,** with fine views looking down into a valley.

All three of these towns are connected to Chipping Campden by bus #1 and #2, or you can walk (easy to Broad Campden, more challenging to the other two—see page 191).

STOW-ON-THE-WOLD

Located 10 miles south of Chipping Campden, Stow-on-the-Wold—with a name that means "meeting place on the uplands"—is the highest point of the Cotswolds. Despite its crowds, it retains its charm, and it merits ▲▲. Most of the tourists are day-trippers, so nights—even in the peak of summer—are peaceful. Stow has no real sights other than the town itself, some good pubs, antiques stores, and cute shops draped seductively around a big town square. Visit the church, with its evocative old door guarded by ancient yew trees and the tombs of wool tycoons. A visit to Stow is not complete until you've locked your partner in the stocks on the village green.

Orientation

Tourist Information: A small visitor information center staffed by volunteers is run out of the library in St. Edward's Hall on the main square (hours erratic, generally Mon-Sat 10:00-14:00, sometimes as late as 17:00, closed Sun, tel. 08452-305-420). Aside from the meager rack of brochures, don't expect much information—get your serious questions answered in Moreton-in-Marsh instead.

Parking: Park anywhere on Market Square free for two hours, and overnight between 18:00 and 9:00 (combining overnight plus daily 2-hour allowances means you can park free 16:00–11:00—they note your license, so you can't just move to another spot after your time is up; £50 tickets for offenders). You can also park for free on some streets farther from the center (such as Park Street and Well Lane) for an unlimited amount of time. A convenient pay-and-display lot is at the bottom of town (toward the Oddingtons), and there's a free lot at Tesco Supermarket—an easy five-minute walk north of town (follow the signs).

❂ Stow-on-the-Wold Walk

This four-stop self-guided walk covers about 500 yards and takes about 45 minutes.

Start at the **Stocks on the Market Square.** Imagine this village during the era when people were publicly ridiculed here as a punishment. Stow was born in pre-Roman times; it's where three trade routes crossed at a high point in the region

(altitude: 800 feet). This square was the site of an Iron Age fort, and then a Roman garrison town. Starting in 1107, Stow was the site of an international fair, and people came from as far away as Italy to shop for wool fleeces on this vast, grassy expanse. Picture it in the Middle Ages (minus all the parked cars, and before the buildings in the center were added): a public commons and grazing ground, paths worn through the grass, and no well. Until the late 1800s, Stow had no running water; women fetched water from the "Roman Well" a quarter-mile away.

With as many as 20,000 sheep sold in a single day, this square was a thriving scene. And Stow was filled with inns and pubs to keep everyone housed, fed, and watered. A thin skin of topsoil covers the Cotswold limestone, from which these buildings were made. The **Stow Lodge** (next to the church) lies a little lower than the church; the lodge sits on the spot where locals quarried stones for the church. That building, originally the rectory, is now a hotel. The church (where we'll end this little walk) is made of Cotswold stone, and marks the summit of the hill upon which the town was built.

Stow-on-the-Wold

The stocks on Market Square

The stocks are a great photo op (lock Dad up for a great family holiday card).

• *Walk past The White Hart Inn to the market, and cross to the other part of the square. Notice how locals stop to chat with each other to catch up on local news: This is a tight-knit little community. Enjoy the stone work and the crazy rooflines. Observe the cheap signage and think how shops have been coming and going for centuries in buildings that never change.*

For 500 years, the **Market Cross** stood in the market reminding all Christian merchants to "trade fairly under the sight of God." Notice the stubs of the iron fence in the concrete base—a reminder of how countless wrought-iron fences were cut down and given to the government to be melted down during World War II. (Recently, it's been disclosed that all that iron ended up in junk heaps—frantic patriotism just wasted.) One of the plaques on the cross honors the Lord of the Manor, who donated money back to his tenants, allowing the town to finally finance running water in 1878.

Scan the square for **The Kings Arms,** with its great gables and spindly chimney. It was once where travelers parked their horses before spending the night. In the 1600s, this was considered the premium "posting house" between London and Birmingham. Today, The Kings Arms cooks up pub grub and rents rooms upstairs.

During the English Civil War, which pitted Parliamentarians against royalists, Stow-on-the-Wold remained staunchly loyal to the king. (Charles I is said to have eaten at The Kings Arms before a great battle.) Because of its allegiance, the town has an abundance of pubs with royal names (King's This and Queen's That).

The stately building in the center of

Market Cross

St. Edward's Hall

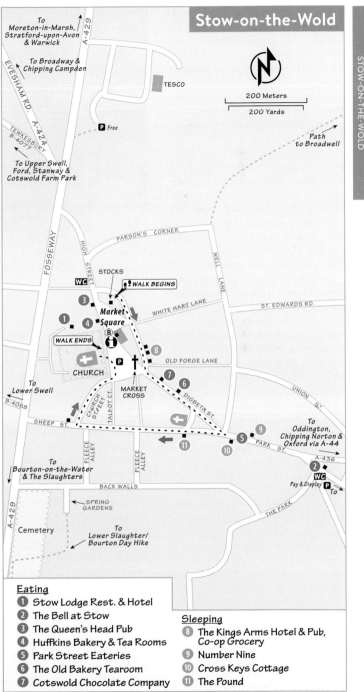

Stow-on-the-Wold

To Moreton-in-Marsh, Stratford-upon-Avon & Warwick

To Broadway & Chipping Campden

EVESHAM RD. A-424

TEWKESBURY B-4077

TESCO

P Free

To Upper Swell, Ford, Stanway & Cotswold Farm Park

Path to Broadwell

FOSSEWAY

HIGH STREET

PARSON'S CORNER

WELL LANE

STOCKS

WC

WALK BEGINS

Market Square

WHITE HART LANE

ST. EDWARDS RD.

WALK ENDS

CHURCH

To Lower Swell

B-4068

P

MARKET CROSS

OLD FORGE LANE

UNION ST.

CHURCH STREET

TALBOT CT.

DIGBETH ST.

SHEEP ST.

FLEECE ALLEY

FLEECE ALLEY

PARK ST.

To Oddington, Chipping Norton & Oxford via A-44

A-436

WC

Pay & Display

P To

To Bourton-on-the-Water & The Slaughters

A-429

BACK WALLS

SPRING GARDENS

THE PARK

Cemetery

To Lower Slaughter/ Bourton Day Hike

Eating
1 Stow Lodge Rest. & Hotel
2 The Bell at Stow
3 The Queen's Head Pub
4 Huffkins Bakery & Tea Rooms
5 Park Street Eateries
6 The Old Bakery Tearoom
7 Cotswold Chocolate Company

Sleeping
8 The Kings Arms Hotel & Pub, Co-op Grocery
9 Number Nine
10 Cross Keys Cottage
11 The Pound

the square with the wooden steeple is **St. Edward's Hall.** Back in the 1870s, a bank couldn't locate the owner of an account containing a small fortune, so it donated the funds to the town to build this civic center. It serves as a City Hall, library, TI, and meeting place. When it's open, you can wander around upstairs to see the largest collection of Civil War portrait paintings in England.

• *Walk past The Kings Arms down Digbeth Street. At the bottom of Digbeth you'll pass the traditional Lambournes butcher and a fragrant cheesemonger across the street. Digbeth ends at a little triangular park in front of the former Methodist Church and across from the Porch House Hotel (dating from 947; it claims—along with about 20 others—to be the oldest in England).*

Just beyond the small grassy triangle with benches was the place where locals gathered for bloody cockfights and bear-baiting (watching packs of hungry dogs tear at bears). Today this is where—twice a year, in May and October—the Stow Horse Fair attracts nomadic Roma (sometimes called Gypsies) and Irish Travellers from far and wide.

• *Hook right and hike up the wide street.*

As you head up **Sheep Street,** you'll pass a boutique-filled former brewery yard (on the left). Notice its fancy street-front office, with a striking flint facade. Sheep Street was originally not a street, but a staging place for medieval sheep markets. The sheep would be gathered here, then paraded into the Market Square down narrow alleys—just wide enough for a single file of sheep to walk down, making it easier to count them. You'll see several of these so-called "fleece alleys" as you walk up the street.

• *Walk a couple blocks until about 50 yards before the streetlight and the highway, then make a right onto Church Street, which leads to the church.*

Before entering the **church,** circle it. On the back side, a wooden door is flanked by two ancient yew trees. While

The door claimed by Tolkien fans as the portal to Middle Earth

many see the door and think of the Christian scripture, "Behold, I stand at the door and knock," J. R. R. Tolkien fans see something quite different. Tolkien hiked the Cotswolds, and had a passion for sketching evocative trees such as this. *Lord of the Rings* enthusiasts are convinced this must be the inspiration for the Doors of Durin, which lead into Moria.

While the church (usually open 9:00-18:00, except during services) dates from Saxon times, today's structure is from the 15th century. Its history is played up in leaflets and plaques just inside the door. The floor is paved with the tombs of big shots who made their money from wool and are still boastful in death. (Find the tombs crowned with the bales of wool.) Most of the windows are traditional Victorian (19th century) designs, but the two sets high up in the clerestory are from the dreamier Pre-Raphaelite school.

On the right wall as you approach the altar, a monument remembers the many boys from this small town who were lost in World War I (50 out of a population of 2,000). There were far fewer in World War II. The biscuit-shaped plaque remembers an admiral from Stow who lost four sons defending the realm. It's sliced from an ancient fluted column (which locals believe is from Ephesus, Turkey).

During the English Civil War in the mid-1600s, the church was ransacked, and more than 1,000 soldiers were imprisoned here. The tombstone in front of the altar remembers the royalist Captain Francis Keyt. His long hair, lace, and sash indicate he was a "cavalier," and true-blue to the king (Cromwellians were called "round heads"—named for their short hair). Study the crude provincial art—child-like skulls and (in the upper corners) symbols of his service to the king (armor, weapons).

Finally, don't miss the kneelers tucked in the pews. These are made by a committed band of women known as "the Kneeler Group." They meet most Tuesday mornings (except sometimes in summer) at 10:30 in the Church Room to needlepoint, sip coffee, and enjoy a good chat. (The vicar assured me that any tourist wanting to join them would be more than welcome. The help would be appreciated and the company would be excellent.) If you'd rather sing, the choir practices on the first and third Fridays of the month at 18:00, and visitors are encouraged to join in. And with Reverend Martin Short for the pastor, the services could be pretty lively.

Hiking

Stow is made to order for day hikes. The most popular is the downhill stroll to **Lower Slaughter** (3 miles), then on to **Bourton-on-the-Water** (about 1.5 miles more). It's a two-hour walk if you keep up a brisk pace and don't stop, but dawdlers should allow three to four hours. At the end, from Bourton-on-the-Water, a bus can bring you back to Stow. While those with keen eyes can follow this walk by spotting trail signs, it can't hurt to bring a map (ask to borrow one at your B&B). Note that these three towns are described in more detail starting on page 206.

To reach the trail, find the cemetery (from the main square, head down Church Street, turn left on Sheep Street, right into Fleece Alley, right onto Back Walls, and left onto Spring Gardens,

The old mill at Lower Slaughter

which has no street sign). Walk past the community's big pea patch, then duck right through the cemetery to the far end. Here, go through the gate and walk down the footpath that runs alongside the big A-429 road for about 200 yards, then cross the road and catch the well-marked trail (gravel road with green sign noting *Public Footpath/Gloucestershire Way*, next to Quarwood Cottage). Follow this trail for a delightful hour across farms, through romantic gates, across a fancy driveway, and past Gainsborough-painting vistas. You'll enjoy an intimate backyard look at local farm life. Although it seems like you might lose the trail, tiny easy-to-miss signs (yellow *Public Footpath* arrows— sometimes also marked *Gloucestershire Way* or *The Monarch's Way*—usually embedded in fence posts) keep you on target—watch for these very carefully to avoid getting lost. Finally, passing a cricket pitch, you reach **Lower Slaughter,** with its fine church and a creek leading up to its mill.

Hiking from Lower Slaughter up to **Upper Slaughter** is a worthwhile one-mile detour each way, if you have the time and energy.

From Lower Slaughter, it's a less-scenic 25-minute walk into the bigger town of **Bourton-on-the-Water.** Leave Lower Slaughter along its mill creek, then follow a bridle path back to A-429 and into Bourton. Walking through Bourton's burbs, you'll pass two different bus stops for the ride back to Stow; better yet, to enjoy some time in Bourton itself, continue all the way into town and—when ready—catch the bus from in front of the Edinburgh Woolen Mill (bus #801 departs roughly hourly, none on Sun except May-Aug when it runs about 2/day, 10-minute ride).

Eating

These places are all within a five-minute walk of each other, either on the main square or downhill on Queen and Park streets.

Restaurants and Pubs

$$ Stow Lodge is *the* choice of the town's proper ladies. There are two parts: The formal but friendly bar serves fine pub grub (daily 12:00-14:00 & 19:00-20:30); the restaurant serves a popular £30 three-course dinner (nightly, veggie options, good wines, just off main square, tel. 01451/830-485, Val). On a sunny day, the pub serves lunch in the well-manicured garden, where you'll feel quite aristocratic.

$$ The Bell at Stow, at the end of Park Street (on the edge of town), has a great scene and fun pub energy for a drink or for a full meal. They serve up classic English dishes with a lighter, sometimes Asian twist. Produce and fish are locally sourced (daily 12:00-21:00, reservations recommended, tel. 01451/870-916, www.thebellatstow.com). Enjoy live music on Sunday evenings.

$$ The Queen's Head faces the Market Square, near Stow Lodge. With a classic pub vibe, it's a great place to bring your dog and watch the eccentrics while you eat pub grub and drink the local Cotswold brew, Donnington Ale. They have a meat pie of the day, good fish-and-chips, and live music on Saturdays (beer garden out back, daily 12:00-14:30 & 18:30-21:00, tel. 01451/830-563, Johnny).

$$ Huffkins Bakery and Tea Rooms is a cute, old-school institution overlooking the center of the market square with to-go lunches and a well-worn tea room for bakery-fresh meals—soups, sandwiches, all-day breakfast, tea and scones, and gluten-free options (Mon-Sat 9:00-17:00, Sun 10:00-14:00, tel. 01451/832-870).

Cheaper Options and Ethnic Food

Head to the grassy triangle where Digbeth hits Sheep Street; there you'll find takeout fish-and-chips, Chinese, and Indian food.

Cheaper Options and Ethnic Food

$ Greedy's Fish and Chips, on Park Street, is the go-to place for takeout.

There's no seating, but they have benches out front (Mon-Sat 12:00-14:00 & 16:30-21:00, closed Sun, tel. 01451/870-821).

$ Jade Garden Chinese Take-Away is appreciated by locals who don't want to cook (Wed-Mon 17:00-23:00, closed Tue, 15 Park Street, tel. 01451/870-288).

$$ The Prince of India offers good Indian food to take out or eat in (nightly 18:00-23:30, 5 Park Street, tel. 01451/830-099).

$ The Old Bakery Tearoom is a local favorite hidden away in a tiny mall at the bottom of Digbeth Street with tradition cakes and light lunches (Mon-Wed & Fri-Sat 10:00-16:00, closed Thu and Sun, Digbeth Street, Alan and Jackie).

Rick's Tip: For **dessert,** *munch a locally-made chocolate treat under the trees on the square's benches and watch the sky darken, the lamps come on, and visitors having their photo fun in the stocks.*

The **Cotswold Chocolate Company** creates handmade chocolate bars, bon-bons, truffles, and more. Pop in to watch Tony working through a window in the back of the shop (his wife, Leidi, does the decorating after he's done). The friendly shopkeepers are happy to offer suggestions. If you're struggling to decide, try the fruit-and-chili bar, or the chocolate-covered...anything (daily 10:00-17:30, Digbeth Street, tel. 01451/798-082).

Groceries: Small grocery stores face the main square (the **Co-op** is open daily 7:00-22:00; next to The Kings Arms), and a big **Tesco** supermarket is 400 yards north of town.

Sleeping

$$$ Stow Lodge Hotel fills the historic church rectory with lots of old English charm. Facing the town square, with its own sprawling and peaceful garden, this lavish old place offers 21 large, thoughtfully appointed rooms with soft beds, stately public spaces, and a cushy-chair lounge (closed Jan, free parking, The Square, tel. 01451/830-485, www.stowlodge.co.uk, enquiries@stowlodge.co.uk, helpful Hartley family).

$$ The Kings Arms, with 10 rooms above a pub, manages to keep its historic Cotswold character while still feeling fresh and modern in all the right ways (steep stairs, three "cottages" out back, free parking, Market Square, tel. 01451/830-364, www.kingsarmsstow.co.uk, info@kingsarmsstow.co.uk, Lucinda and Felicity).

$$ Number Nine has three large, bright, refurbished, and tastefully decorated rooms. This 200-year-old home comes with watch-your-head beamed ceilings and beautiful old wooden doors (9 Park Street, tel. 01451/870-333, mobile 07779-006-539, www.number-nine.info, enquiries@number-nine.info, friendly James and Carol Brown and their dog Snoop).

$$ Cross Keys Cottage offers four smallish but smartly updated rooms—some bright and floral, others classy white—with modern bathrooms. Kindly Margaret and Roger Welton take care of their guests in this 17th-century beamed cottage (RS%, call ahead to confirm arrival time, Park Street, tel. 01451/831-128, www.crosskeyscottage.co.uk, rogxmag@hotmail.com).

$ The Pound is the quaint, centuries-old, slanty, cozy, and low-beamed home of Patricia Whitehead. She offers two bright, inviting rooms and a classic old fireplace lounge (cash only, downtown on Sheep Street next to the inn with the *Sheep* sign, tel. 01451/830-229, patwhitehead1@live.co.uk).

NEAR STOW-ON-THE-WOLD

These sights are all south of Stow: Some are within walking distance (the Slaughters and Bourton-on-the-Water), and one is 20 miles away (Cirencester). The Slaughters and Bourton are tied together by the countryside walk described on page 203.

Lower and Upper Slaughter

"Slaughter" has nothing to do with lamb chops. It likely derives from an Old English word, perhaps meaning sloe tree (the one used to make sloe gin). These villages are worth ▲ and a quick stop.

Lower Slaughter is a classic village, with ducks, a charming little church, a working water mill, and usually an artist busy at her easel somewhere. The Old Mill Museum is a folksy ensemble with a tiny museum, shop, and café complete with a delightful terrace overlooking the mill pond, enthusiastically run by Gerald and his daughter Laura, who just can't resist giving generous tastes of their homemade ice cream (£2.50 for museum, daily 10:00-18:00, Nov-Feb until dusk, tel. 01451/822-127, www.oldmill-lowerslaughter.com). Just behind the Old Mill, two kissing gates lead to the path that goes to nearby Upper Slaughter, a 15-minute walk or 2-minute drive away (leaving the Old Mill, take two lefts, then follow sign for Wardens Way). And if you follow the mill creek downstream, a bridle path leads to Bourton-on-the-Water (described next).

In **Upper Slaughter,** walk through the yew trees (sacred in pagan days) down a lane through the raised graveyard (a buildup of centuries of graves) to the peaceful church. In the back of the fine cemetery, the statue of a wistful woman looks over the tomb of an 18th-century rector (sculpted by his son). Notice the town is missing a war memorial—that's because every soldier who left Upper Slaughter for World War I and World War II survived the wars. As a so-called "Doubly Thankful Village" (one of only 13 in England and Wales), the town instead honors those who served in war with a simple wood plaque in the town hall.

Getting There: Though the stop is not listed on schedules, you should be able to reach these towns on bus #801 (from Moreton or Stow) by requesting the "Slaughter Pike" stop (along the main road, near the villages). Confirm with the driver before getting on. If driving, the small roads from Upper Slaughter to Ford and Kineton (and the Cotswold Farm Park, described later) are some of England's most scenic. Roll your window down and joyride slowly.

Bourton-on-the-Water

I can't figure out whether they call this "the Venice of the Cotswolds" because of its quaint canals or its miserable crowds. Either way, this town—four miles south of Stow and a mile from Lower Slaughter—is very pretty and worth ▲. But it can be mobbed with tour groups during the day: Sidewalks become jammed with disoriented tourists wearing nametags.

If you can avoid the crowds, it's worth a drive-through and maybe a short stop. It's pleasantly empty in the early evening and after dark.

The church at Upper Slaughter

Bourton-on-the-Water

Getting There: It's conveniently connected to Stow and Moreton by bus #801.

Parking: Finding a spot here can be tough. Even during the busy business day, rather than park in the pay-and-display parking lot a five-minute walk from the center, drive right into town and wait for a spot on High Street just past the village green (where the road swings left, turn right to go down High Street; there's a long row of free 1.5-hour spots starting in front of the Edinburgh Woolen Mills Shop, on the right).

Tourist Information: The TI is tucked across the stream a short block off the main drag, on Victoria Street, behind The Victoria Hall (Mon-Fri 9:30-17:00, Sat until 17:30, Sun 10:00-14:00 except closed Sun Oct-April, closes one hour earlier Nov-March, tel. 01451/820-211).

Bike Rental: Hartwells on High Street rents bikes by the hour or day and includes a helmet, map, and lock (£10/3 hours; £14/day, Mon-Sat 9:00-18:00, Sun from 10:00, tel. 01451/820-405, www. hartwells.supanet.com).

▲COTSWOLD MOTORING MUSEUM

Lovingly presented, this good, jumbled museum shows off a lifetime's accumulation of vintage cars, old lacquered signs, threadbare toys, prewar memorabilia, and sundry British pop culture knick-knacks. If you appreciate old cars, this is nirvana. Wander the car-and-driver displays, which range from the automobile's early days to slick 1970s models, including

period music to set the mood. Talk to an elderly Brit who's touring the place for some personal memories.

Cost and Hours: £5.75, daily 10:00-18:00, closed late Dec-mid-Feb, in the mill facing the town center, tel. 01451/821-255, www.cotswoldmotoringmuseum.co.uk.

Cotswold Farm Park

Here's a delight for young and old alike. This park, worth ▲, is the private venture of the Henson family, who are passionate about preserving rare and endangered breeds of native British animals. While it feels like a kids' zone (with all the family-friendly facilities you can imagine), it's actually a fascinating chance for anyone to get up close and (very) personal with piles of mostly cute animals, including the sheep that made this region famous—the big and woolly Cotswold Lion. The "listening posts" deliver audio information on each rare breed.

A busy schedule of demonstrations gives you a look at local farm life—check the events board as you enter for times for the milking, "farm safari," shearing, and well-done "sheep show." Join the included 20-minute tractor ride, with live narration.

Cost and Hours: £12, kids-£10.50, family ticket for 2 adults and 2 kids-£40, daily 10:30-17:00, Nov-Dec until 16:00, closed Jan, good guidebook (£6), decent cafeteria, tel. 01451/850-307, www. cotswoldfarmpark.co.uk.

Getting There: It's well-signposted about halfway between Stow and Stanway

Motor Museum

Cotswold Farm Park

(15 minutes from either), just off Tewkes-bury Road (B-4077, toward Ford from Stow). A visit here makes sense if you're traveling from Stow to Chipping Campden.

Northleach

One of the "untouched and untouristed" Cotswold villages, Northleach is worth a short stop. The town's impressive main square and church attest to its position as a major wool center in the Middle Ages. Park in the square called The Green or the adjoining Market Place. The town has no TI, but you may find a free town map and visitor guide at the Mechanical Music Museum, at the post office on the Market Place, or at other nearby shops. Information: www.northleach.gov.uk.

Getting There: Northleach is nine miles south of Stow, down the A-429. Bus #801 connects it to Stow and Moreton.

▲MECHANICAL MUSIC MUSEUM

This delightful little one-room place offers a unique opportunity to listen to 300 years of amazing self-playing musical instruments. It's run by people who are passionate about the restoration work they do on these musical marvels. The curators delight in demonstrating about 20 of the museum's machines with each hour-long tour. You'll hear Victorian music boxes and the earliest polyphones (record players) playing cylinders and then discs—all from an age when music was made mechanically, without the help of electricity. The admission fee includes an essential hour-long tour.

Cost and Hours: £8, daily 10:00-17:00, last entry at 16:00, tours go constantly—join one in progress, High Street, Northleach, tel. 01451/860-181, www.mechanicalmusic.co.uk.

Eating in Northleach: Tucked along unassuming Northleach's main drag is a foodies' favorite, **$$$$ The Wheatsheaf Inn.** With a pleasantly traditional dining room and a gorgeous sprawling garden, they offer an intriguing eclectic menu of modern English cuisine proudly served with a warm welcome, relaxed service, and a take-your-time approach to top-quality food. Reservations are smart (daily, on West End, tel. 01451/860-244, www.cotswoldswheatsheaf.com).

Bibury

Six miles northeast of Cirencester, this ▲ village is a favorite with British picnickers fond of strolling and fishing. Bibury (BYE-bree) offers some relaxing sights, including a row of very old weavers' cottages, a trout farm, a stream teeming with fat fish and proud ducks, and a church surrounded by rosebushes, each tended by a volunteer of the parish. A protected wetlands area on the far side of the stream hosts newts and water voles. Walk up the main street, then turn right along the old weavers' Arlington Row and back on the far side of the marsh, peeking into the rushes for wildlife.

For a closer look at the fish, cross the little bridge to the 15-acre **Trout Farm,** where you can feed them—or catch your own (£4.50 to walk the grounds, fish food-£0.60; daily 8:00-17:30, Oct and March until 17:00, Nov-Feb until 16:00; catch-your-own only on weekends March-Oct 10:00-17:00, no fishing in winter, call or email to confirm fishing schedule, tel. 01285/740-215, www.biburytroutfarm.co.uk).

Getting There: Take bus #801 from Moreton-in-Marsh or Stow, then change to #855 in Northleach or Bourton-on-the-Water (3/day, 1 hour total).

Cirencester

Almost 2,000 years ago, Cirencester (SIGH-ren-ses-ter) was the ancient Roman city of Corinium. Worth ▲, it's 20 miles from Stow down the A-429, which was called Fosse Way in Roman times. The TI, in the shop at the Corinium Museum, answers questions and sells a town map and a town walking-tour brochure (same hours as museum, tel. 01285/654-180).

Getting There: By bus, take #801 from Moreton-in-Marsh or Stow, then change

Bibury

Cirencester

to #855 in Northleach or Bourton-on-the-Water for Cirencester (3/day, 1.5 hours total). Drivers follow Town Centre signs and find parking right on the market square; if it's full, retreat to the Waterloo pay-and-display lot (a 5-minute walk away).

Visiting Cirencester: Stop by the impressive Corinium Museum to find out why they say, "If you scratch Gloucestershire, you'll find Rome." The museum chronologically displays well-explained artifacts from the town's rich history, with a focus on Roman times—when Corinium was the second-biggest city in the British Isles (after Londinium). You'll see column capitals and fine mosaics before moving on to the Anglo-Saxon and Middle Ages exhibits (£5.40, Mon-Sat 10:00-17:00, Sun from 14:00, Park Street, tel. 01285/655-611, www.coriniummuseum.org).

Cirencester's church is the largest of the Cotswold "wool" churches. The cutesy New Brewery Arts crafts center entertains visitors with traditional weaving and potting, workshops, an interesting gallery, and a good coffee shop (www.newbreweryarts.org.uk). Monday and Friday are general-market days, Friday features an antique market, and a crafts market is held every Saturday.

MORETON-IN-MARSH

This workaday town—worth ▲—is like Stow or Chipping Campden without the touristy sugar. Rather than gift and antique shops, you'll find streets lined with real shops: ironmongers selling cottage nameplates and carpet shops strewn with the remarkable patterns that decorate B&B floors. A traditional market of 100-plus stalls fills High Street each Tuesday, as it has for the last 400 years (8:00-15:30, handicrafts, farm produce, clothing, books, and people-watching; best if you go early). The Cotswolds has an economy aside from tourism, and you'll feel it here.

Orientation

Moreton has a tiny, sleepy train station two blocks from High Street, lots of bus connections, and the best TI in the region. Peruse the racks of fliers, confirm rail and bus schedules, and consider the £0.50 **Town Trail** self-guided walking tour leaflet (Mon 8:45-16:00, Tue-Thu until 17:15, Fri until 16:45, Sat 10:00-13:00—until 12:30 in winter, closed Sun, good public WC, tel. 01608/650-881).

Helpful Hints

Laundry: The handy launderette is a block in front of the train station on New Road (daily 7:00-19:00, last self-service wash at 18:00, drop-off service options available—call ahead to arrange, tel. 01608/650-888).

Parking: It's easy—anywhere on High Street is fine any time, as long as you want, for free (though there is a 2-hour parking limit for the small lot in the middle of the street). On Tuesdays, when the market makes parking tricky, try the **Budgens**

Moreton-in-Marsh

supermarket, where you can park for two hours.

Eating

A stroll up and down High Street lets you survey your options.

$$ The Marshmallow is relatively upscale but affordable, with a menu that includes traditional English dishes as well as lasagna and salads (afternoon tea, Mon 10:00-16:00, Tue-Sat until 20:00, Sun 10:30-18:00, closed for dinner in Jan, reservations smart, shady back garden for dining, tel. 01608/651-536, www. marshmallow-tea-restaurant.co.uk).

$$$ The Black Bear Inn offers traditional English food. Choose between the dining room on the left or the pub on the right (restaurant daily 12:00-14:00 & 18:30-21:00, pub daily 10:30-23:30, tel. 01608/652-992).

$$ Hassan Balti, with tasty Bangladeshi food, is a fine value for sit-down or takeout (daily 12:00-14:00 & 17:30-23:30, tel. 01608/650-798).

$$ Yellow Brick Café, run by Tom and Nicola, has a delightful outdoor patio, cozy indoor seating, and a tempting display of homemade cakes. It's good for a late breakfast, midday lunch, or early dinner after a full day of Cotswolds exploring (daily 9:00-17:00, 3 Old Market Way, tel. 01608/651-881).

$ Tilly's Tea House serves fresh soups, salads, sandwiches, and pastries for lunch in a cheerful spot on High Street across from the TI (good cream tea, Mon-Sat 9:00-17:00, Sun 10:00-16:00, tel. 01608/650-000).

$ Mermaid fish shop is popular for its takeout fish and tasty selection of traditional savory pies (Mon-Sat 11:30-14:00 & 17:00-22:00, closed Sun, tel. 01608/651-391).

Picnic: There's a small **Co-op** grocery on High Street (Mon-Sat 7:00-20:00, Sun 8:00-20:00), and a **Tesco Express** two doors down (Mon-Fri 6:00-23:00, Sat-Sun from 7:00). The big Budgens supermarket is indeed super (Mon-Sat 8:00-22:00, Sun 10:00-16:00, far end of High Street). You can picnic across the street in pleasant Victoria Park (with a playground).

Sleeping

$$$$ Manor House Hotel is Moreton's big old hotel, dating from 1545 but sporting such modern amenities as toilets and electricity. Its 35 classy-for-the-Cotswolds rooms and its garden invite relaxation (elevator, log fire in winter, attached restaurants, free parking, on far end of High Street away from train station, tel. 01608/650-501, www.cotswold-inns-hotels.co.uk, info@manorhousehotel.info).

$$ The Swan Inn is wonderfully perched on the main drag, with 10 en-suite rooms. Though the halls look a bit worn and you enter through a bar/restaurant that can be noisy on weekends, the renovated rooms themselves are classy and the bathrooms modern (free parking, restaurant gives guests 10 percent discount, High Street, tel. 01608/650-711, www.swanmoreton.co.uk, info@swanmoreton.co.uk, Sara and Terry

Moreton-in-Marsh

Eating
1. The Marshmallow
2. The Black Bear Inn
3. Hassan Balti
4. Yellow Brick Café
5. Tilly's Tea House & Mermaid Fish Shop
6. Co-op & Tesco Express
7. Budgens Supermarket

Sleeping
8. Manor House Hotel
9. The Swan Inn
10. Treetops B&B
11. Acacia B&B

Todd). Terry can pick up guests from the train station and may be able to drive guests to destinations within 20 miles if no public transport is available.

$$ **Treetops B&B** is plush, with seven spacious, attractive rooms, a sun lounge, and a three-quarter-acre backyard. Liz and Teddy (the family dog) will make you feel right at home (two-night minimum on weekends, two wheelchair-accessible ground-floor rooms have patios, set far back from the busy road, London Road, tel. 01608/651-036, www.treetopscotswolds.co.uk, treetops1@talk21.com, Liz and Brian Dean). It's an eight-minute walk from town and the train station (exit station, keep left, go left on bridge over train tracks, look for sign, then long driveway).

$ **Acacia B&B,** on the short road connecting the train station to the town center, is a convenient budget option. Dorothy has four small rooms: one is en suite, the other three share one bathroom. Rooms are bright and tidy, and most overlook a lovely garden (tel. 01608/650-130, 2 New Road, www.acaciainthecotswolds.co.uk, acacia.guesthouse@tiscali.co.uk).

TRANSPORTATION

Getting Around the Cotswolds

By Bus

The Cotswolds are so well-preserved, in part, because public transportation to and within this area has long been miserable. Fortunately, trains link the region to larger towns, and a few key buses connect the more interesting villages. Centrally located Moreton-in-Marsh is the region's transit hub—with the only train station and several bus lines.

To explore the towns, use the bus routes that hop through the Cotswolds about every 1.5 hours, lacing together main stops and ending at rail stations. In each case, the entire trip takes about an hour. Individual fares are around £4. If you plan on taking more than two rides in a day, consider the Cotswolds Discoverer pass, which offers unlimited travel on most buses including those listed below (£10/day, www.escapetothecotswolds.org.uk/discoverer).

The TI hands out easy-to-read bus schedules for the key lines described here (or check www.traveline.org.uk, or call the Traveline info line, tel. 0871-200-2233). Put together a one-way or return trip by public transportation, making for a fine Cotswold day. If you're traveling one-way between two train stations, remember that the Cotswold villages—generally pretty clueless when it comes to the needs of travelers without a car—have no official baggage-check services. You'll need to improvise; ask sweetly at the nearest TI or business.

Note that no single bus connects the three major towns described in this chapter (Chipping Campden, Stow, and Moreton); to get between Chipping Campden and Stow, you'll have to change buses in Moreton. Since buses can be unreliable and connections aren't timed, it may be better to call a driver or taxi to go between Chipping Campden and Stow.

The following bus lines are operated by Johnsons Coaches (tel. 01564/797-070, www.johnsonscoaches.co.uk): Buses **#1** and **#2** run from Moreton-in-Marsh to Batsford to Bourton-on-the-Hill to Blockley, then either to Broadway or Broad Campden on their way to Chipping Campden, and pass through Mickleton before ending at Stratford-upon-Avon.

The following buses are operated by Pulham & Sons Coaches (tel. 01451/820-369, www.pulhamscoaches.com): Bus **#801** goes nearly hourly in both directions from Moreton-in-Marsh to Stow-on-the-Wold to Bourton-on-the-Water; most continue on to Northleach and Cheltenham (limited service on Sun in summer). Bus **#855** goes from Moreton-in-Marsh and Stow to Northleach to Bibury to Cirencester.

Warning: Unfortunately, the buses described here aren't particularly reliable—it's not uncommon for them to show up late, early, or not at all. Leave yourself a sizeable cushion if using buses to make another connection (such as a train to London), and always have a backup plan (such as the phone number for a few taxis/drivers or for your hotel, who can try calling someone for you). Remember that bus service is essentially nonexistent on Sundays.

By Bike

Despite narrow roads, high hedgerows (blocking some views), and even higher hills, bikers enjoy the Cotswolds free from the constraints of bus schedules. For each area, TIs have fine route planners that indicate which peaceful, paved lanes are particularly scenic for biking. In summer, it's smart to book your rental bike a couple of days ahead. Note that only Chipping Campden and Bourton-on-the-Water have shops that rent out bikes.

In **Chipping Campden** your only choice is **Cycle Cotswolds,** at the Volunteer Inn pub (£12/day, daily 7:00-dusk, Lower High Street, mobile 07549-620-507, www.

cyclecotswolds.co.uk). If you make it to **Bourton-on-the-Water,** you can rent bicycles through **Hartwells** on High Street (£10/3 hours, £14/day, includes helmet, route map, and locks; Mon-Sat 9:00-18:00, Sun from 10:00; tel. 01451/820-405, www. hartwells.supanet.com).

If you're interested in a biking vacation, **Cotswold Country Cycles** offers self-led bike tours of the Cotswolds and surrounding areas (tours last 2-7 days and include accommodations and luggage transfer, see www.cotswoldcountrycycles.com).

By Foot

Consider venturing across the pretty hills and meadows of the Cotswolds. Walking guidebooks and leaflets abound, giving you a world of choices for each of my recommended stops (choose a book with clear maps). If you're doing any hiking whatsoever, get the excellent Ordnance Survey Explorer OL #45 map, which shows every road, trail, and ridgeline (£9 at local TIs). Nearly every hotel and B&B has a box or shelf of local walking guides and maps, including Ordnance Survey #45. Don't hesitate to ask for a loaner. For a quick **circular hike** from a particular

village, peruse the books and brochures offered by that village's TI, or search online for maps and route descriptions; one good website is www.nationaltrail. co.uk—select "Cotswold Way," then "Be Inspired," then "Circular Walks." Villages are generally no more than three miles apart, and most have pubs that would love to feed and water you.

Each of the home-base villages I recommend has several options. Stow-on-the-Wold, immersed in pleasant but not-too-hilly terrain, is within easy walking distance of several interesting spots and is probably the best starting point. Chipping Campden sits along a ridge, which means that hikes from there are extremely scenic, but also more strenuous. Moreton—true to its name—sits on a marsh, offering flatter and less picturesque hikes.

Here are two hikes to consider. I've selected these for their convenience to the home-base towns and because the start and/or end points are on bus lines, allowing you to hitch a ride back to where you started (or on to the next town) rather than backtracking by foot.

Stow, the Slaughters, and Bourton-on-the-Water: Walk from Stow to Upper and Lower Slaughter, then on to Bourton-on-the-Water (which has bus service back to Stow on #801). One big advantage of this walk is that it's mostly downhill (4 miles, about 2-3 hours one-way). For details, see page 203.

Chipping Campden, Broad Campden, Blockley, and Bourton-on-the-Hill: From Chipping Campden, it's an easy mile walk into charming Broad Campden, and from there, a more strenuous hike to Blockley and Bourton-on-the-Hill (which are both connected by buses #1 and #2 to Chipping Campden and Moreton). For more details, see page 193.

Or leave the planning to a company such as **Cotswold Walking Holidays,** which can help you design a walking vacation, provide route instructions and maps,

transfer your bags, and even arrange lodging. They also offer five- to six-night walking tours that come with a local guide. Walking through the towns allows you to slow down and enjoy the Cotswolds at their very best—experiencing open fields during the day and arriving into towns just as the day-trippers depart (www. cotswoldwalks.com).

By Car

Joyriding here truly is a joy. Winding country roads seem designed to spring bucolic village-and-countryside scenes on the driver at every turn. Distances are wonderfully short, and easily navigable with GPS. As a backup, you could invest in the Ordnance Survey map of the Cotswolds, sold locally at TIs and newsstands (the £9 Explorer OL #45 map is excellent but almost too detailed for drivers; a £5 tour map covers a wider area in less detail). Here are driving distances from Moreton: **Stow-on-the-Wold** (4 miles), **Chipping Campden** (8 miles), **Broadway** (10 miles), **Stratford-upon-Avon** (17 miles), **Warwick** (23 miles), **Blenheim Palace** (20 miles).

Car hiking is great. In this chapter, I cover the postcard-perfect (but discovered) villages. With a car and a good map (either GPS or the local Ordnance Survey), you can easily ramble about and find your own gems. The problem with having a car is that you are less likely to walk. Consider taking a taxi or bus somewhere, so that you can walk back to your car and enjoy the scenery.

Car Rental: The easiest option is to rent a car in Oxford then drive (30-45 minutes) into the Cotswolds. One place near Moreton-in-Marsh rents cars by the day, but you'll need to reserve in advance. **Robinson Goss Self Drive** is six miles north of town and won't bring the car to you in Moreton (£31-61/day plus extras like GPS and gas, Mon-Fri 8:30-17:00, Sat until 12:00, closed Sun, tel. 01608/663-322, www.robgos.co.uk).

By Taxi or Private Driver

Two or three town-to-town taxi trips can make more sense than renting a car. While taking a cab cross-country seems extravagant, the distances are short (Stow to Moreton is 4 miles, Stow to Chipping Campden is 10), and one-way walks are lovely. If you call a cab, confirm that the meter will start only when you are actually picked up. Consider hiring a private driver at the hourly "touring rate" (generally around £35), rather than the meter rate. For a few more bucks than taking a taxi, you can have a joyride peppered with commentary. Whether you book a taxi or a private driver, expect to pay about £25 between Chipping Campden and Stow and about £20 between Chipping Campden and Moreton.

Note that the drivers listed here are not typical city taxi services (with many drivers on call), but are mostly individuals—it's smart to call ahead if you're arriving in high season, since they can be booked in advance on weekends.

Moreton: Try Stuart and Stephen at **ETC,** "Everything Taken Care of" (tel. 01608/650-343 or toll-free 0800-955-8584, www.cotswoldtravel.co.uk); see also the taxi phone numbers posted outside the Moreton train station office.

Stow: Try **Tony Knight** (mobile 07887-714-047, anthonyknight205@btinternet.com).

Chipping Campden: Call James at **Cotswold Private Hire** (mobile 07980-857-833), or **Les Proctor,** who offers village tours and station pick-ups (mobile 07580-993-492, Les also co-runs Cornerways B&B—see page 192).

Tours: Tim Harrison at **Tour the Cotswolds** specializes in tours of the Cotswolds and its gardens, but will also do tours outside the area (mobile 07779-030-820, www.tourthecotswolds.co.uk).

By Tour

Departing from Bath: Lion Tours offers a Cotswold Discovery full-day tour, and can drop you and your luggage off in Stow (£5/person) or in Moreton-in-Marsh (£7.50/person; minimum two people for either). If you want to get back to London in time for a show, ask to be dropped off at Kemble Station; it's best to arrange drop-offs in advance (see page 152 of the Bath chapter).

Departing from Moreton-in-Marsh: Cotswold Tour offers a smartly arranged day of sightseeing for people with limited time and transportation. Reserve your spot online, then meet Becky at Moreton-in-Marsh's train station at 10:00. The tour follows a set route that includes a buffet lunch and cream tea served in her cottage and returns to the station by 16:30—good timing for day-trippers to return to London for the evening (£95/person, must reserve ahead online, tel. 01608/674-700, www.cotswoldtourismtours.co.uk).

Arriving and Departing
From Moreton-in-Marsh

Moreton, the only Cotswold town with a train station, is also the best base for exploring the region by bus.

Train Connections to: London's Paddington Station (every 1-2 hours, 2 hours), Bath (hourly, 3 hours, 1-2 transfers), Oxford (2/hour, 40 minutes), Stratford-upon-Avon (hourly, 3 hours, 2 transfers, slow and expensive, better by bus). Train info: Tel. 0345-748-4950, www.nationalrail.co.uk.

Bus Connections to: Stratford-upon-Avon (#1 and #2 go via Chipping Campden: Mon-Sat 8/day, none on Sun, 1-1.5 hours, Johnsons Coaches, tel. 01564/797-070, www.johnsonscoaches.co.uk).

From Chipping Campden

Bus Connections to: Stratford-upon-Avon (almost hourly, 40 minutes, www.johnsonscoaches.co.uk). If heading on to the Lake District, you can catch a bus or train from Stratford (see page 226).

BEST OF THE REST

Central England hosts a number of worthwhile sights. **Oxford** is one of England's great university towns. Historic **Blenheim Palace** is nearby; this marvelous Baroque building, with a sumptuous interior, also has beautiful gardens.

Stratford-upon-Avon is a must for Shakespeare fans; stay for a play. Near Stratford is **Warwick Castle**, a fine stop for families and knights and maidens of any age.

OXFORD

Oxford, founded in the seventh century and home to the oldest university in the English-speaking world, originated as a simple trade crossroads. Ever since the first homework was assigned in 1167, the University of Oxford's stellar graduates have influenced Western civilization; its alumni include 27 British prime ministers, more than 60 Nobel Prize winners, and even 11 saints. For Oxford's many tourists, this destination all about its historic colleges and literary connections.

Oxford is a convenient stop for people visiting the Cotswolds, Blenheim Palace, Stratford-upon-Avon, and Bath. Because of Oxford's proximity to other worthwhile destinations, and the relative economy of sleeping in a small-town B&B (such as the Cotswolds), a day-time visit to Oxford can be ideal.

Rick's Tip: *For a do-it-yourself tour, find the* **information panels** *around town that explain nearby sights. On the opposite side of each panel, a map will help you navigate the maze of streets.*

Orientation

While a typical American-style university has one campus, Oxford has colleges scattered throughout town. But the sightseers' Oxford is walkable and compact. Many of the streets in the center are pedestrian-only during the day.

Day Plan: If you follow my self-guided walk, visit a few colleges, and make a pass through the free Ashmolean Museum, you've covered the town. My top choice is the historically important Christ Church College. Leave time to sample a pint of

The spires of All Souls College, Oxford

local ale at one of the many pubs that dot the town.

To include Blenheim Palace on this day, arrive in Oxford in the morning, head to Blenheim first (by bus), then on your return, visit Oxford.

Getting There: Oxford is linked by **train** with London (Paddington Station, 2/hour direct, 1 hour), Bath (2/hour, 1.5 hours), and Moreton-in-Marsh (hourly, 40 minutes). Competing **bus** companies run frequently from London to Oxford's Gloucester Green bus station (about 2 hours, www.oxfordtube.com or www.oxfordbus.co.uk).

Arrival in Oxford: From the **train** station, the city center is a 10-minute walk (exit straight ahead and follow the signs); a taxi costs around £6. The **bus** station is a five-minute walk from the heart of Oxford and the TI. **Drivers** day-tripping into Oxford should use one of the outlying park-and-ride lots, which are about a 10-minute shuttle-bus ride from the town center. There are some pay parking lots closer to the center.

Tourist Information: The TI offers walking tours, a detailed town map, and *A Quick Guide to Oxford.* If you're headed to **Blenheim Palace,** buy your tickets here at a discount (daily, 15 Broad Street, tel. 01865/686-430, www.experienceoxfordshire.org).

Private Guide: William Underhill is a good Oxford-educated guide (mobile 07802-328-956, williamunderhill@gmail.com).

Tours: Blackwell's Walking Tours focus on literary and historic Oxford (mid-April-Oct Tue-Fri, 1.5 hours, 48 Broad Street, reserve ahead at oxford@blackwells.co.uk, www.blackwells.co.uk). Oxford Walking Tours are more casual and depart hourly from the Trinity College gates (daily, 1.5 hours, www.oxfordwalkingtours.com).

*Rick's Tip: For **great views** of Oxford's many spires and colleges, climb the 127 narrow, twisting stairs of the bell tower of the **University Church of St. Mary the Virgin** (£4, High Street) or the 99 steps of **Carfax Tower** (£2.70, intersection of High and Cornmarket streets).*

❷ Oxford Walk

This short stroll gives you the gist of the city and the university. Follow along using the map on page 220.
• *Start near the TI at the cross in the pavement in the middle of Broad Street.*

Broad Street
• *Turn your attention to the middle of the street.*

❶ The Cross in the Road marks the spot where the emphatically Catholic Queen Mary (a.k.a. "Bloody Mary") had three local bishops, known as "the Oxford Martyrs," burned at the stake for heresy in 1555. Their crime: Protestantism.
• *Ahead, on the left you'll see...*

Balliol College, one of the oldest (founded 1263), most charming (fine grounds, chapel, and dining hall), and cheapest (£3 admission) of the Oxford colleges.
• *Up the street on the left is...*

Blackwell's Bookstore, venerable and massive, a beloved Oxford institution that hides miles of shelves behind its unimpressive facade.
• *On your right, find the...*

❷ Museum of the History of Science
One of Europe's oldest museums, this place is free and worth ▲ (Tue-Sun 12:00-17:00). The concise and well-displayed exhibit fills three small floors with cases of scientific bric-a-brac that the scholars of Oxford used to change our world. You'll see a very early pendulum clock, a rare spherical astrolabe, equipment used

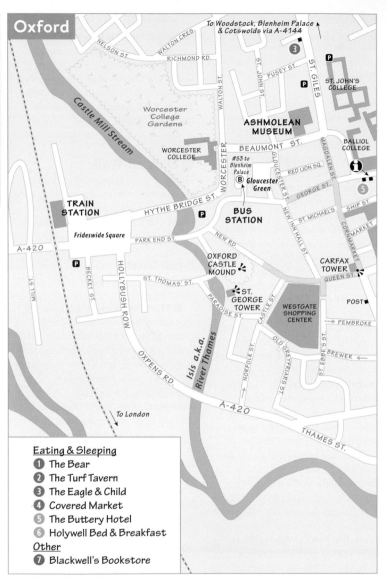

Oxford

To Woodstock, Blenheim Palace
& Cotswolds via A-4144

NELSON ST.
WALTON CRES.
RICHMOND RD.
WALTON ST.
ST. JOHN ST.
PUSEY ST.
ST. GILES
ST. JOHN'S COLLEGE

Castle Mill Stream

Worcester College Gardens

ASHMOLEAN MUSEUM

WORCESTER COLLEGE

BEAUMONT ST.

BALLIOL COLLEGE

MAGDALEN ST.
GLOUCESTER ST.
RED LION SQ.

#53 to Blenheim Palace
B Gloucester Green

GEORGE ST.
NEW INN HALL ST.
SHIP ST.
CORNMARKET ST.

TRAIN STATION

HYTHE BRIDGE ST.

BUS STATION

Frideswide Square

PARK END ST.

NEW RD.

ST. MICHAEL'S ST.

A-420

BECKET ST.

HOLLYBUSH ROW

ST. THOMAS' ST.

OXFORD CASTLE MOUND

PARADISE ST.

CASTLE ST.

ST. GEORGE TOWER

CARFAX TOWER

QUEEN ST.

WESTGATE SHOPPING CENTER

POST

PEMBROKE

MILL ST.

OXPENS RD.

Isis a.k.a. River Thames

NORFOLK ST.
OLD GREYFRIARS ST.
ST. EBBE'S ST.
BREWER ST.

To London

A-420

THAMES ST.

Eating & Sleeping
① The Bear
② The Turf Tavern
③ The Eagle & Child
④ Covered Market
⑤ The Buttery Hotel
⑥ Holywell Bed & Breakfast
Other
⑦ Blackwell's Bookstore

in developing penicillin, Lewis Carroll's photo-developing kit, and Einstein's chalkboard—still featuring his hand-scrawled equations from a lecture here.
• Next door, don't miss the...

❸ Sheldonian Theatre

The ceremonial hall of the university, the

▲ Sheldonian Theatre is where graduations and other important campus events take place (£3.50, usually daily 10:00-16:00). This was the second major building designed by Sir Christopher Wren, then an astronomy professor and budding architect who went on to rebuild much of London after the Great Fire. The interior

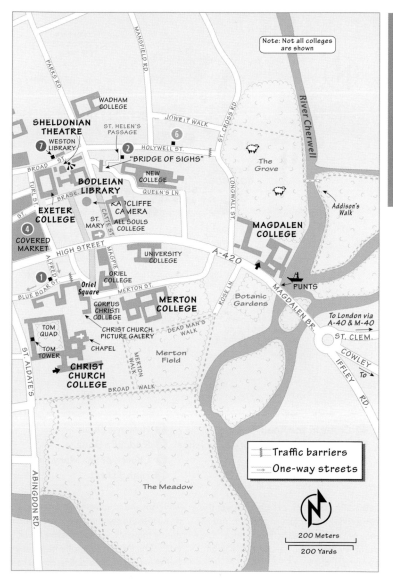

Note: Not all colleges are shown

is one main hall with a painted ceiling, wooden columns painted to look like marble, and an old pipe organ. You can climb 114 steps to a steamy, glassed-in cupola for a view over the colleges.

• *Across the street is the...*

Weston Library

A modern wing of the university's fabled Bodleian Library, the ▲ Weston welcomes visitors to its "Treasures" room (suggested £3 donation, Mon-Sat 10:00-17:00, Sun from 11:00). The gorgeously lit and displayed precious books, manuscripts, and letters are a literary treasure chest

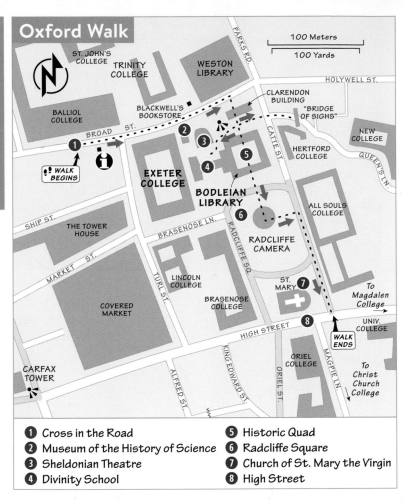

Oxford Walk

1 Cross in the Road
2 Museum of the History of Science
3 Sheldonian Theatre
4 Divinity School
5 Historic Quad
6 Radcliffe Square
7 Church of St. Mary the Virgin
8 High Street

celebrating the genius of Oxford over the centuries. Items rotate in and out: You may see a Shakespeare First Folio, a copy of the *Magna Carta*, handwritten scores by Handel, and more.

• *From the Weston Library, cross Broad Street. Walk through the stately four-columned facade of the Clarendon Building into a courtyard.*

▲▲Bodleian Library and the Heart of Oxford

This complex of buildings, dominated by the Bodleian Library, is where the university

was born and from where it is run today. If you want to see the inside of the library during this walk, you can make a quick visit to the Divinity School, which has a jaw-dropping vaulted ceiling, or you can take a Reading Room Tour that includes Duke Humfrey's Library (see below).

• *Stand in the middle of the courtyard, where the two stone walkways intersect. Begin by facing the big Neoclassical building you just walked through.*

The **Clarendon Building** was originally built to house the Oxford University Press. Among the books printed here was

Bodleian Library

version; check the schedule and buy your ticket at the kiosk; www.bodleian.ox.ac. uk/whatson).

• *Return to the center of the pebbled square and from there continue cutting through the buildings to the decorated...*

❺ Historic Quad

You're standing in the main courtyard of the Bodleian Library. Circling it are the original classrooms—each marked (clockwise from the tower) with the original curriculum: logic, astronomy, rhetoric, music, philosophy, medicine, morality, grammar, history, and physics. The tower comes with five architectural orders (Tuscan, Doric, Ionic, Corinthian, and combo Ionic/ Corinthian) and, at the top, King James I, who had this courtyard built in the 17th century.

• *Continue your walk through "the Bod" and emerge onto Radcliffe Square, which is dominated by the most distinctive university building of all.*

❻ Radcliffe Square

The round, columned structure is **Radcliffe Camera,** built as a medical library. It's now used as a reading room for a gigantic library complex that runs through tunnels underneath the square (not open to the public).

• *Grab the bars of the fancy college gate just left of Radcliffe Camera to peek into...*

All Souls College, named for the dead of the Hundred Years War that England fought with France in the 14th and 15th centuries. It is notorious for having the toughest entrance exam; famous alums include Lawrence of Arabia and Christopher Wren.

• *Just past Radcliffe Camera is the most important church in town.*

❼ Church of St. Mary the Virgin

Generally called the University Church, this is one Oxford landmark that predates the university. A thousand years ago, it marked the center of the original walled

the Lincoln Bible—used to inaugurate Presidents Lincoln and Obama.

The **Bodleian Library** is 90 degrees to the right. With some 11 million books and more than 100 miles of shelving in its underground stacks, "the Bod" is one of the world's largest and most famous libraries.

• *Angle right into a little courtyard between the library and the Sheldonian Theatre. From here you can visit the Divinity School (admission fee) and/or Duke Humfrey's Library (pay guided tour). Pause at the kiosk in the passage across the courtyard from the library entrance to buy your ticket.*

The ❹ **Divinity School**—rated ▲▲—is an impressive fan-vaulted hall (£1, Mon-Sat 9:00-17:00, Sun from 11:00). It was the university's first purpose-built classroom—constructed in the 15th century for teaching theology. It's well worth entering for its historic importance and its magnificent Gothic ceiling.

Duke Humfrey's Library, upstairs and only accessible on an escorted tour, is a world of musty, creaky old shelves of ancient-looking books, stacked neatly under a beautifully painted wooden ceiling (£6/30-minute tour, £8/one-hour

town. And when the university was just getting its start, this was the ceremonial and teaching center of the first Oxford schools (free, open Mon-Sat 9:30-17:00, Sun from 11:30). It comes with a climbable tower (for a fee and a view), a café in its garden, and a crypt.

• The church faces...

❽ High Street

The central axis of Oxford, High Street is lined with colleges to the left (east) and leads to the commercial core of the city to the right (west, beyond the church tower a couple of blocks away). Walking this city axis, it's easy to feel the town/gown dichotomy.

• Your walk is over.

Rick's Tip: The **entrance to each college** is easy to spot—just look for a doorway with crests and a flagpole on the top. Each entry has an office with a porter (live-in caretaker). Inquire there to find out if any plays, music, evensong services, or lectures are scheduled.

Colleges and Sights

▲CHRIST CHURCH COLLEGE

Christ Church College is Oxford's dominant college. It was founded by Henry VIII's chancellor, Cardinal Thomas Wolsey, in 1524 on the site of an abbey dissolved by the king. The buildings survived the tumult of the Reforma-

tion because the abbey and its cathedral served as part of the king's new Church of England. While all colleges boast of their esteemed alumni, none has a list as esteemed as Christ Church College: 13 of the 27 Oxford-educated prime ministers were Christ Church alums. William Penn (founder of Pennsylvania), John Wesley (influential Methodist leader), John Locke (English Enlightenment thinker), and Charles Dodgson (a.k.a. Lewis Carroll) also studied here.

When you buy your ticket, pick up the essential self-guided tour booklet with map. "Custodians" wearing bowler hats are posted around the college to answer questions. You'll be sent along a one-way route with these main stops: dining hall (familiar to Harry Potter fans), quadrangle, cathedral, and picture gallery.

Cost and Hours: £9, family ticket-£22, Mon-Sat 10:00-17:00, Sun from 14:00, last entry 45 minutes before closing, tel. 01865/276-492. Note that the dining hall is closed to outsiders when students are actually eating here. Call ahead or check the website (www.chch.ox.ac.uk, click on "Visitors")—and plan your visit accordingly.

Evensong: Most evenings in Christ Church Cathedral, an excellent choir service is open to anyone (free, Tue-Sun at 18:00, enter at Tom Tower, arrive 15-20 minutes early).

MAGDALEN COLLEGE

Sitting on the upper edge of town, this college (pronounced "maudlin")—where

Christ Church College

Christ Church dining hall

C. S. Lewis taught for 25 years—gets my vote for the prettiest in Oxford. Magdalen has the largest grounds of any of the Oxford colleges (big enough to include its own deer park, with actual deer browsing the grounds) and a peaceful café overlooking the sleepy river and lively punting scene.

Cost and Hours: £6, daily 10.00-19:00, Sept-June 13:00-18:00 or dusk—whichever is earlier, £10 guided tours offered mid-July-Aug, High Street next to Magdalen Bridge, tel. 01865/276-000.

Evensong: Evensong services in the exquisite chapel take place Tue-Sun at 18:00 (except July-Sept).

EXETER COLLEGE

A smaller college, 700-year-old Exeter is centrally located, free to visit, and worth a peek. The highlight is its jewel-like Neo-Gothic chapel—oh-so Victorian from the 1860s and inspired by Paris' Sainte-Chapelle. It features William Morris' Adoration of the Magi tapestry and a bust of J. R. R. Tolkien, who studied here.

Cost and Hours: Free, usually open daily 14:00-17:00, Turl Street, tel. 01865/279-600.

▲▲ASHMOLEAN MUSEUM OF ART AND ARCHAEOLOGY

In 1683, celebrated antiquary Elias Ashmole insisted his collection of curiosities deserved its own building. Half of his trove originated with an even-more-eccentric royal gardener, John Tradescant, who loved to seek out interesting items while traveling in search of plants. The vast collection features everything from antiquities to fine porcelain to paintings by some of the Old Masters.

Cost and Hours: Free but suggested £5 donation, Tue-Sun 10:00-18:00, closed Mon, basic café plus rooftop restaurant open until 22:00, Beaumont Street, tel. 01865/278-000, www.ashmolean.org.

PUNTING

Long, flat boats can be rented for punting (pushing with a long pole) along the River Cherwell. Chauffeurs are available, but the do-it-yourself crowd is having more fun...even if they are a little wet. Punting looks easier than it is; the guided ride includes a short lesson so you can actually learn how to do it right.

Cost and Hours: £22/hour per boat, £30 deposit, chauffeured punts-£30 per boat for 30 minutes and up to four people, rowboats and paddle boats available for the less adventurous, cash only, daily 9:30-dusk, closed Dec-Jan, Magdalen Bridge Boathouse, tel. 01865/202-643.

Eating and Sleeping

$$$ The Bear, close to the Christ Church Picture Gallery, is one of Oxford's most charming pubs (corner of Alfred and Blue Boar streets). The big and boisterous **$$$ Turf Tavern** is popular for its solid grub and outdoor beer garden (4 Bath Place). **$$ The Eagle and Child** was the gathering place for the likes of J. R. R. Tolkien and C. S. Lewis (49 St. Giles Street). The **$ Covered Market**—a farmers market maze of shops and stands—has fine selections for lunch or a picnic (between Market and High streets, near Carfax Tower).

If staying the night, **$$$ The Buttery Hotel** has good-value rooms (11 Broad Street, www.thebutteryhotel.co.uk), and the **$$$ Holywell Bed & Breakfast** is a real gem, hidden away in an ancient row house (14 Holywell Street, www.holywellbedandbreakfast.com).

The Bear pub

BLENHEIM PALACE

Just 30 minutes' drive from Oxford (and convenient to combine with a drive through the Cotswolds), Blenheim Palace is one of England's best—worth ▲▲▲. The 2,000-acre yard, designed by Lancelot "Capability" Brown, is as majestic to some as the palace itself.

Rick's Tip: *Americans who pronounce the place "blen-HEIM" are the butt of jokes.* **It's "BLEN-em."**

John Churchill, first duke of Marlborough, achieved a stunning victory over Louis XIV's armies at the Battle of Blenheim in 1704. A thankful Queen Anne rewarded Churchill by building him this nice home, perhaps the finest Baroque building in England. Eleven dukes of Marlborough later, the palace is as impressive as ever. In 1874, a later John Churchill's American daughter-in-law, Jennie Jerome, gave birth at Blenheim to another historic baby in that line...and named him Winston.

Orientation

Day Plan: Start with the included state rooms tour and Winston Churchill Exhibition (allow 90 minutes to see both). From there, head to the delightful gardens. If you're into all things palatial, add on the private apartment tour (requires a special ticket). Late in the afternoon, the palace is relaxed and quiet, even on the busiest of days.

Getting There: Blenheim Palace sits at the edge of the cute cobbled town of Woodstock. The train station nearest the palace (Hanborough, 1.5 miles away) has no taxi or bus service.

From **Oxford,** take bus #S3 (3/hour, 40 minutes, www.stagecoachbus.com) from Gloucester Green. It stops twice near Blenheim Palace: the "Blenheim Palace Gates" stop (about a half-mile walk to the palace itself) and the "Woodstock/Marl-borough Arms" stop (in the heart of the village of Woodstock). The Woodstock stop offers the most spectacular view of the palace and lake.

If you're coming from the **Cotswolds,** your easiest train connection is from Moreton-in-Marsh to Oxford, where you can catch the bus to Blenheim.

Drivers should head for Woodstock; the palace is well-signposted once in town. Buy your ticket at the gate, then park near the palace.

Cost and Hours: £24.90, park and gardens only-£14, family ticket available; open mid-Feb-Oct daily 10:30-17:30, Nov-mid-Dec generally closed Mon-Tue, park open but palace closed mid-Dec-mid-Feb. Doors to the palace close at 16:45, it's "everyone out" at 17:30, and the park closes at 18:00.

Rick's Tip: **Discount palace tickets** *are available at TIs in surrounding towns—including Oxford and Moreton-in-Marsh—or on the #S3 bus from Oxford.*

Information: Recorded info toll-free tel. 0800-849-6500, www.blenheimpalace.com.

Tours: Guided tours are available for the state rooms (included in admission, 2/hour, 40 minutes, daily except Sun), the private apartments (£5, 2/hour, about 40 minutes, most likely to run in summer, tickets are limited), and the gardens (included in admission).

Eating: The Water Terraces Café at the garden exit is appealing for a basic lunch and teatime treats. Just outside the palace gates, **$ Hampers Deli** is a good place to pick up provisions for a picnic (31 Oxford Street).

⊙ Self-Guided Tour

STATE ROOMS

Enter into the truly great Great Hall. While you can go "free flow" (reading info plaques and talking with docents in each room), you'll get much more out of your

Blenheim Palace

visit by taking the included guided tour.

These most sumptuous rooms in the palace are ornamented with fine porcelain, gilded ceilings, portraits of past dukes, photos of the present duke's family, and "chaperone" sofas designed to give courting couples just enough privacy...but not *too* much.

Enjoy the series of 10 Brussels tapestries that commemorate military victories of the First Duke of Marlborough, including the Battle of Blenheim. After winning that pivotal conflict, he scrawled a quick note on the back of a tavern bill notifying the queen of his victory (you'll see a replica). Finish with the remarkable "long library"—with its tiers of books and stuccoed ceilings.

WINSTON CHURCHILL EXHIBITION

This is a fascinating display of letters, paintings, and other artifacts of the great statesman who was born here. Along with lots of intimate artifacts from his life, you'll see the bed in which Sir Winston was born in 1874.

PRIVATE APARTMENTS

For a more extensive visit, book a spot as soon as you arrive for a 30-minute guided walk through the private apartments of the duke. Tours leave at the top and bottom of each hour—when His Grace is not in.

You'll see the chummy billiards room,

luxurious china, the servants quarters with 47 bells—one for each room to call the servants, private rooms, 18th-century Flemish tapestries, family photos, and so on.

CHURCHILLS' DESTINY

In the "stables block" is an exhibit that traces the military leadership of two great men who shared the name Churchill: John, who defeated Louis XIV at the Battle of Blenheim in the 18th century, and in whose honor this palace was built; and Winston, who was born in this palace, and who won the Battle of Britain and helped defeat Hitler in the 20th century. It's remarkable that arguably two of the most important military victories in the nation's history were overseen by distant cousins.

GARDENS

The palace's expansive gardens stretch nearly as far as the eye can see in every direction. From the main courtyard, you'll emerge into the Water Terraces; from there, you can loop around to the left, behind the palace, to see (but not enter) the Italian Garden. Or, head down to the lake to walk along the waterfront trail; going left takes you to the rose gardens and arboretum, while turning right brings you to the Grand Bridge. You can explore on your own (using the map and good signposting), or join a free tour.

STRATFORD-UPON-AVON

Stratford is Shakespeare's hometown. To see or not to see? It's a must for every big bus tour in England, and one of the most popular side-trips from London. Sure, it's touristy, and nonliterary types might find it's much ado about nothing. But the play's the thing to bring the Bard to life—and you'll see the Royal Shakespeare Company (the world's best Shakespeare ensemble) making the most of their state-of-the-art theater complex.

Just north of the Cotswolds, Stratford makes a convenient stop for Shakespeare fans either before, after, or even during a Cotswold stay.

Rick's Tip: *If coming by train or bus, be sure to request a ticket for "Stratford-upon-Avon," not just "Stratford" (to avoid a mix-up with Stratford Langthorne, near London). And don't get off at the Stratford Parkway train station—you want Stratford-upon-Avon.*

Orientation

Stratford, with around 30,000 people, has a compact old town, with the TI and theater along the riverbank, and Shakespeare's Birthplace a few blocks inland; you can easily walk to everything except Mary Arden's Farm and Anne Hathaway's Cottage.

Day Plan: It's worth a half-day—strolling the charming core and visiting your choice of Shakespeare sights. My favorites are Shakespeare's Birthplace, Mary Arden's Farm, and Anne Hathaway's Cottage. With limited time, visit only Shakespeare's Birthplace, which is the most central and offers the best historical introduction to the playwright.

If you can squeeze it in, stick around to see a play; in this case, you'll need to spend the night here or drive in from the Cotswolds (just 30 minutes away).

Getting There: Stratford is linked by **bus** with Cotswolds towns (bus #1 or #2, Mon-Sat 8/day, none on Sun, 35 minutes from Chipping Campden, 1.5 hours from Moreton-in-Marsh, www.johnsonscoaches.co.uk). Stratford is linked by **train** with London (3/day direct,

Stratford-upon-Avon is notable for its half-timbered architecture.

William Shakespeare (1564-1616)

To many, William Shakespeare is the greatest author, in any language, period. He helped define modern English—the unrefined tongue of everyday people—and granted it a beauty and legitimacy that put it on par with Latin.

Using borrowed plots, outrageous puns, and poetic language, Shakespeare wrote comedies (c. 1590—*Taming of the Shrew, As You Like It*), tragedies (c. 1600—*Hamlet, Othello, Macbeth, King Lear*), and fanciful combinations (c. 1610—*The Tempest*), exploring the full range of human emotions.

Think of his stock of great characters and great lines: Hamlet ("To be or not to be, that is the question"), Othello and his jealousy ("It is the green-eyed monster"), ambitious Mark Antony ("Friends, Romans, countrymen, lend me your ears"), rowdy Falstaff ("The better part of valor is discretion"), and the star-crossed lovers Romeo and Juliet ("But soft, what light through yonder window breaks").

With plots that entertained both the highest and the lowest minds, Shakespeare taught the play-going public about human nature. Even today, his characters strike a familiar chord. His friend and fellow poet, Ben Jonson, wrote in the preface to the First Folio, "He was not of an age, but for all time!"

2-2.5 hours, Marylebone Station), Oxford (every 2 hours, 1.5 hours), and Penrith/Lake District (4 hours, change in Birmingham). **Driving** is easy from Chipping Campden (12 miles) or Stow-on-the-Wold (22 miles).

Arrival in Stratford-upon Avon: If coming by train, get off at Stratford-upon-Avon (not Stratford Parkway); follow the main drag straight to the river.

For drivers, the Bridgefoot garage is big, easy, cheap, and central; the City Sightseeing bus stop and the TI are a block away. If overnighting, ask your hotelier about parking.

Tourist Information: The TI is in a small brick building on Bridgefoot, where the main street hits the river (tel. 01789/264-293, www.shakespeare-country.co.uk).

Combo-Tickets: The TI and the Shakespeare Birthplace Trust sights sell combo-tickets that cover the five trust sights (£22.50 if purchased at a covered sight, £22 at TI, £20.25 online), but only the TI offers a special "any-three" option covering your pick of three of the five (for £16.95). Booking online saves you 10 percent. Individual tickets are also sold at the sights.

Tours: Stratford Town Walks introduce you to the town and its famous playwright. Just show up at the Swan fountain (on the waterfront) in front of the Royal Shakespeare Theatre (£6, daily year-round at 11:00, Sat-Sun also at 14:00, www.stratfordtownwalk.co.uk).

City Sightseeing Bus Tours make the rounds, allowing visitors to hop on and hop off at all the Shakespeare sights.

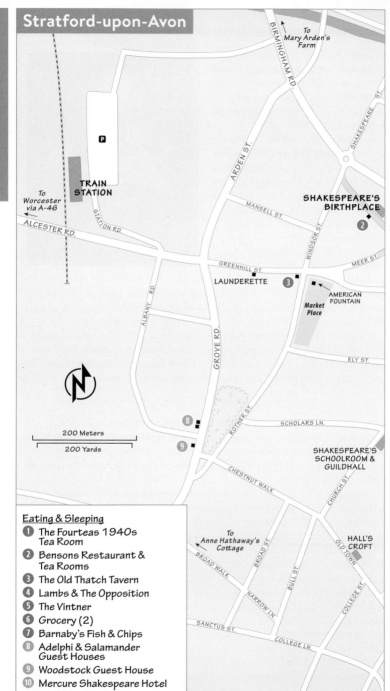

Stratford-upon-Avon

To Mary Arden's Farm

BIRMINGHAM RD.

SHAKESPEARE ST.

TRAIN STATION

To Worcester via A-46

ALCESTER RD.

STATION RD.

ARDEN ST.

MANSELL ST.

WINDSOR ST.

SHAKESPEARE'S BIRTHPLACE
2

MEER ST.

GREENHILL ST.

LAUNDERETTE 3

AMERICAN FOUNTAIN

Market Place

ALBANY RD.

GROVE RD.

ELY ST.

ROTHER ST.

SCHOLARS LN.

8
9

CHESTNUT WALK

SHAKESPEARE'S SCHOOLROOM & GUILDHALL

200 Meters
200 Yards

CHURCH ST.

To Anne Hathaway's Cottage

BROAD WALK

BROAD ST.

BULL ST.

NARROW LN.

SANCTUS ST.

COLLEGE LN.

COLLEGE ST.

OLD TOWN

HALL'S CROFT

Eating & Sleeping

1. The Fourteas 1940s Tea Room
2. Bensons Restaurant & Tea Rooms
3. The Old Thatch Tavern
4. Lambs & The Opposition
5. The Vintner
6. Grocery (2)
7. Barnaby's Fish & Chips
8. Adelphi & Salamander Guest Houses
9. Woodstock Guest House
10. Mercure Shakespeare Hotel

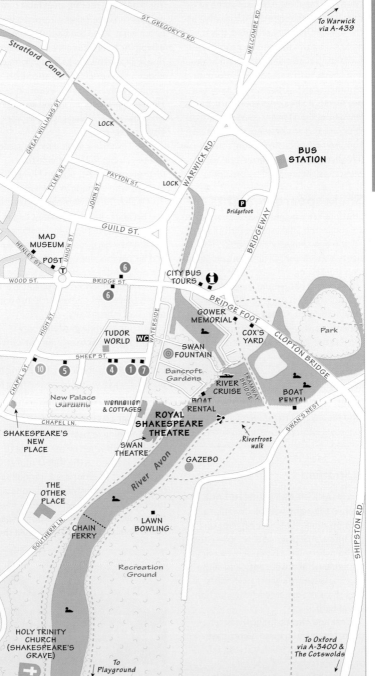

Given the far-flung nature of some of the Shakespeare sights, and the value of the fun commentary provided, this tour makes the town more manageable. The full 11-stop circuit takes about an hour and comes with a steady and informative commentary (£14, ticket valid 24 hours, buy tickets on bus or as you board; buses leave from the TI every 20 minutes 9:30-17:00 in high season, every 30 minutes and shorter hours off-season, some buses have live guides weekends April-Sept, www.citysightseeing-stratford.com).

Shakespearean Sights

Stratford's five biggest Shakespeare sights are run by the Shakespeare Birthplace Trust (www.shakespeare.org.uk). The sights are well-run, all different, and genuinely interesting.

Each sight has helpful, eager docents who love to tell a story; you'll have a far more informative visit if you listen to the docents' spiels or chat them up. They provide fun, gossipy insight into what life was like at the time.

Rick's Tip: *Expect crowds on the weekend nearest* **Shakespeare's birthday** *on April 23 (also the day he died); if overnighting, book your room and a play well in advance.*

In Stratford

▲▲SHAKESPEARE'S BIRTHPLACE

Touring this sight, you'll experience a modern exhibit before seeing Shakespeare's actual place of birth. While the birthplace itself is a bit underwhelming, the exhibit, helpful docents, and sense that Shakespeare's ghost still haunts these halls make it a good introduction to the Bard.

Cost and Hours: £17.50, daily 9:00-17:00, Nov-March 10:00-16:00, café, in town center on Henley Street, tel. 01789/204-016.

Visiting Shakespeare's Birthplace:

You'll begin by touring an **exhibit** that provides an entertaining introduction about what made the Bard so great. The exhibit includes a timeline of his plays, movie clips of his works, and information about his upbringing in Stratford, his family life, and his career in London. Historical artifacts, including an original 1623 First Folio of Shakespeare's work, are also on display.

You'll exit the exhibit into the garden, where you can follow signs to the **birthplace,** a half-timbered Elizabethan building where young William grew up. This is also the house where Shakespeare and his bride, Anne Hathaway, began their married life together. Upstairs are the rooms where young Will, his siblings, and his parents slept (along with their servants). After Shakespeare's father died and William inherited the building, the thrifty playwright converted it into a pub to make a little money.

Exit into the fine **garden** where Shakespearean **actors** often perform brief scenes (they may even take requests). Pull up a bench and listen, imagining the playwright as a young boy stretching his imagination in this very place.

SHAKESPEARE'S NEW PLACE

While nothing remains of the house the Bard built when he made it big (it was demolished in the 18th century), its atmospheric grounds are a tranquil spot to soak up some history. Modern sculptures and traditional gardens now adorn the grounds of the mansion Shakespeare called home for nearly 20 years. At the

Shakespeare's Birthplace

least, the sight has nostalgic value—especially for fans who can picture him writing *The Tempest* on this very spot. Next door, Nash's House (which belonged to Shakespeare's granddaughter and her husband) hosts exhibits, including a large-scale model of Shakespeare's house, domestic artifacts, and displays of period clothing.

Cost and Hours: £12.50, daily 9:00-17:00, Nov-March 10:00-16:00, 22 Chapel Street, tel. 01789/338-536.

HALL'S CROFT

This former home of Shakespeare's eldest daughter, Susanna, is in Stratford town center. A fine old Jacobean house, it's the fanciest of the group. Since she married a doctor, the exhibits are focused on 17th-century medicine. Ask the docent for the 15- to 20-minute introduction, or one of the large laminated self-guides, both of which help bring the plague—and some of the bizarre remedies of the time—to life.

Cost and Hours: £8.50, daily 10:00-17:00, Nov-March 11:00-16:00, on-site tearoom, between Church Street and the river on Old Town Street, tel. 01789/338-533.

Just Outside Stratford

To reach either of these sights, it's best to drive or take the hop-on, hop-off bus tour—unless you're staying at one of the Grove Road B&Bs, which are an easy 20-minute walk from Anne Hathaway's Cottage.

▲▲MARY ARDEN'S FARM

Along with Shakespeare's Birthplace, this is my favorite of the Shakespearean sights. Famous as the girlhood home of William's mom, it's built around two historic farmhouses (3 miles from Stratford). Today it's an open-air folk museum depicting 16th-century farm life...which happens to have ties to Shakespeare. The Bard is basically an afterthought here.

Cost and Hours: £15, daily 10:00-17:00, closed Nov-mid-March, on-site café and picnic tables, tel. 01789/338-535.

Visiting Mary Arden's Farm: The museum hosts many special **events,** including an enjoyable falconry show (daily, usually at 11:00, 12:30, 14:30, and 16:00). The day's events are listed on a chalkboard by the entry, or you can call ahead to find out what's on. There are always plenty of activities to engage kids: It's an active, hands-on place.

Pick up a map (and handful of organic animal feed) at the entrance and wander the grounds and buildings. Throughout the complex, you'll see period interpreters in Tudor costumes. They'll likely be going through the day's chores as people back then would have done—activities such as milking the sheep and cutting wood to do repairs on the house. Look out for typical farmyard animals including goats, woolly pigs, and friendly donkeys.

The first building, **Palmer's farm** (mistaken for Mary Arden's home for hundreds of years, and correctly identified in 2000), is furnished as it would have been in Shakespeare's day. Step into the kitchen to see food being prepared over an open fire—at 13:00 each day the "servants" (employees) sit down in the adjacent dining room for a traditional dinner.

Mary Arden actually lived in the neighboring **farmhouse,** covered in brick facade and seemingly less impressive. The house is filled with kid-oriented activities, including period dress-up clothes, board games from Shakespeare's day, and a Tudor alphabet so kids can write their names in fancy lettering.

▲ANNE HATHAWAY'S COTTAGE

Located 1.5 miles out of Stratford, this home is a 12-room farmhouse where the Bard's wife grew up. William courted Anne here—she was 26, he was only 18—and his tactics proved successful. (Maybe a little too much, as she was several months pregnant at their wedding.) Their 34-year marriage produced two more children, and lasted until his death in 1616 at age 52. The Hathaway family lived here for 400 years, until 1911, and much of the family's 92-acre farm remains part of the sight.

Cost and Hours: £12.50, daily 9:00-17:00, Nov-mid-March 10:00-16:00, on-site tearoom, tel. 01789/338-532.

Visiting Anne Hathaway's Cottage: After buying your ticket, turn right and head down through the garden to the thatch-roofed **cottage,** which looks cute enough to eat. The house offers an intimate peek at life in Shakespeare's day. In some ways, it feels even more authentic than his birthplace, and it's fun to imagine the writer of some of the world's greatest romances wooing his favorite girl right here during his formative years.

Maybe even more interesting than the cottage are the **gardens,** which have several parts (including a prizewinning "traditional cottage garden"). Follow the signs to the "Woodland Walk" (look for the music-note willow sculpture on your way), along with a fun sculpture garden littered with modern interpretations of Shakespearean characters. From April through June, the gardens are at their best, with birds chirping, bulbs in bloom, and a large sweet-pea display. You'll also find a music trail, a butterfly trail, and—likely—rotating exhibits, generally on a gardening theme.

The Royal Shakespeare Company

The Royal Shakespeare Company (RSC), undoubtedly the best Shakespeare company on earth, performs year-round in Stratford and in London. The RSC makes it easy to take in a play, thanks to their very user-friendly website, painless ticket-booking system, and chock-a-block schedule that fills the summer with mostly big-name Shakespeare plays. Except in January and February, there's almost always something playing. The smaller attached Swan Theatre hosts plays on a more intimate scale.

▲▲▲SEEING A PLAY

Performances take place most days (Mon-Sat generally at 19:15 at the Royal Shakespeare Theatre or 19:30 at the Swan, matinees around 13:15 at the RST or 13:30

at the Swan, sporadic Sun shows). Shows generally last three hours or more, with one intermission; for an evening show, don't count on getting back to your B&B much before 23:00. There's no strict dress code—and people dress casually (nice jeans and short-sleeve shirts are fine)—but shorts are discouraged.

Getting Tickets: Tickets range from £10 (standing) to £75, with most around £45. Saturday-evening shows—the most popular—are the most expensive. Tickets go on sale months in advance. You can book tickets as you like it: online (www.rsc.org.uk), by phone (tel. 01789/403-493), or in person at the box office (Mon-Sat 10:00-20:00, Sun until 17:00).

▲▲VISITING THE ROYAL SHAKESPEARE THEATRE

The RSC's main venue was updated head to toe in 2011, with both a respect for tradition and a sensitivity to the needs of contemporary theatergoers. You need to take a guided tour (explained later) to see the backstage areas, but you're welcome to wander the theater's public areas any time the building is open. Interesting tidbits of theater history and special exhibits make this one of Stratford's most fascinating sights. If you're seeing a play here, come early to poke around the building. Even if you're not, step inside and explore.

Cost and Hours: Free entry, Mon-Sat 10:00-23:00, Sun until 17:00.

Guided Tours: Well-informed RSC volunteers lead entertaining, one-hour building tours. Some cover the main theater while others take you into behind-the-scenes spaces, such as the space-age control room (try for a £8.50 behind-the-scenes tour, but if those aren't running, consider a £6.50 front-of-the-house tour—which skips the backstage areas; tour schedule varies by day, but there's often one at 9:15—call, check online, or go to box office to confirm schedule; best to book ahead, tel. 01789/403-493, www.rsc.org.uk/theatretours).

Background: The original Victorian-style

The Royal Shakespeare Theatre

theater was built in 1879 to honor the Bard, but it burned down in 1926. The big Art Deco-style building you see today was erected in 1932 and outfitted with a stodgy Edwardian "picture frame"-style stage. The recent renovation added an updated thrust-style stage. They've left the shell of the 1930s theater, but with the seats stacked at an extreme vertical pitch. There's not a bad seat in the house—no matter what, you're no more than 50 feet from the stage.

Visiting the Theater: From the main lobby and box office/gift shop area, there's plenty to see. First head left. In the circular **atrium** between the brick wall of the modern theater and fragments of the previous theater, notice the ratty old floorboards pried up from the 1932 stage and laid down here. Upstairs on level 2, find the **Paccar Room,** with exhibits assembled from the RSC's substantial collection of historic costumes, props, manuscripts, and other theater memorabilia. Continue upstairs to level 3 to the Rooftop Restaurant (described later). High on the partition that runs through the restaurant, facing the brick theater wall, notice the four **chairs** affixed to the wall. These are original seats from the earlier theater, situated where the back row used to be (90 feet from the stage)—illustrating how much more audience-friendly the new design is.

Tower View: For a God's-eye view of all of Shakespeare's houses, ride the elevator to the top of the RSC's **tower** (£2.50, buy ticket at box office, closes 30 minutes before the theater). The main attraction here is the 360-degree view over the theater building, the Avon, and the lanes of Stratford.

Eating: The theater has a casual **$ café** with a terrace overlooking the river (sandwiches, daily 10:00-21:00), as well as the fancier **$$ Rooftop Restaurant,** which counts the Queen as a patron (Mon-Sat 11:30 until late, Sun 10:30-18:15, dinner reservations smart, tel. 01789/403-449, http://www.rsc.org.uk/rooftop).

Eating and Sleeping

For lunch, try the retro-designed **$$ The Fourteas 1940s Tea Room** (24 Sheep Street) or friendly **$$ Bensons Restaurant and Tea Rooms** (across from Shakespeare's Birthplace). **$$ The Old Thatch Tavern** is the town's best pub (also open for dinner, Greenhill Street overlooking market square).

Rick's Tip: *For a* **cheap lunch out,** *get fish-and-chips from Barnaby's across from the riverfront park and have a picnic.*

For dinner, these pricey, trendy eateries on Sheep Street have good-value pre-theater menus before 19:00: the half-timbered **Lambs** (12 Sheep Street), the less formal **The Opposition** next door (closed Sun), and the popular **The Vintner** up the street (4 Sheep Street).

If staying overnight, consider the homey **$$ Adelphi Guest House** (RS%, 39 Grove Road, www.adelphi-guesthouse.com), the cheaper **$ Salamander Guest House** (40 Grove Road, www.salamanderguesthouse.co.uk), or the central, business-class **$$ Mercure Shakespeare Hotel** (Chapel Street, www.mercure.com).

WARWICK CASTLE

Just north of Stratford, you'll find England's single most spectacular castle: Warwick (rated ▲▲). This medieval masterpiece, which has been turned into a virtual theme park, is extremely touristy—but it's also historic and fun, and may well be Britain's most kid-friendly experience.

The town of Warwick, huddled protectively against the castle walls, is a half-timbered delight—enjoyable for a lunch or dinner, or even for an overnight.

Orientation

Warwick is small and manageable. The castle and old town center sit side by side, with the train station about a mile to the north. From the castle's main gate, a lane leads into the old town center a block away, where you'll find the TI and plenty of eateries.

Day Plan: Warwick Castle deserves at least three hours for a quick visit, but it can be an all-day outing for families. You can tour the sumptuous staterooms, climb the towers and ramparts for the views, stroll through themed exhibits populated by aristocratic wax figures, explore the sprawling grounds and gardens, and—best of all—interact with costumed docents who explain the place and perform fantastic demonstrations of medieval weapons and other skills.

Warwick Castle is a great family destination.

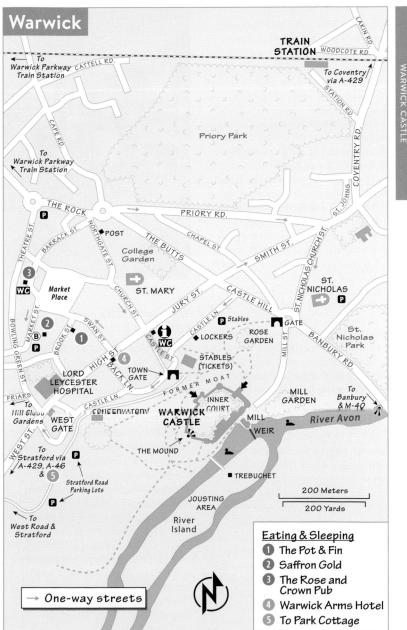

Warwick

TRAIN STATION

To Warwick Parkway Train Station

WOODCOTE RD.

To Coventry via A-429

LAKIN RD.

CATTELL RD.

CAPE RD.

To Warwick Parkway Train Station

Priory Park

STATION RD.

ST. JOHNS

COVENTRY RD.

THE ROCK

PRIORY RD.

THEATRE ST.

BARRACK ST.

NORTHGATE ST.

POST

THE BUTTS

CHAPEL ST.

College Garden

SMITH ST.

ST. NICHOLAS CHURCH ST.

ST. NICHOLAS

Market Place

WC

CHURCH ST.

ST. MARY

JURY ST.

CASTLE HILL

ST. NICHOLAS

St. Nicholas Park

BOWLING GREEN ST.

MARKET ST.

SWAN ST.

CASTLE ST.

CASTLE LN.

Stables

GATE

ROSE GARDEN

BANBURY RD.

B

P

BROOK ST.

HIGH ST.

WC

LOCKERS

MILL ST.

The Pot & Fin

BACK LN.

TOWN GATE

STABLES (TICKETS)

FORMER MOAT

To Banbury & M-40

LORD LEYCESTER HOSPITAL

CASTLE LN.

CONSERVATORY

INNER COURT

MILL GARDEN

FRIARS

To Hill Close Gardens

WEST GATE

WARWICK CASTLE

MILL

WEIR

River Avon

WEST ST.

To Stratford via A-429, A-46 &

THE MOUND

Stratford Road Parking Lots

TREBUCHET

200 Meters

200 Yards

To West Road & Stratford

JOUSTING AREA

River Island

Eating & Sleeping

1 The Pot & Fin

2 Saffron Gold

3 The Rose and Crown Pub

4 Warwick Arms Hotel

5 To Park Cottage

→ One-way streets

N

Rick's Tip: *Warwick's TI sells same-day* **Fast Track ticket vouchers** *to Warwick Castle for a reduced rate, about a £5 savings over buying them on-site (TI open daily in season but closed Sun Jan-Easter, The Court House, Jury Street, www.visitwarwick.co.uk).*

Getting There: Warwick has two **train** stations; you want the one called simply "Warwick" (Warwick Parkway Station is farther from the castle). To reach the castle or the town center, take a taxi (about £5) or walk (15 minutes, one mile).

Warwick is easy for **drivers**—the main Stratford-Coventry road cuts right through Warwick. Coming from Stratford (8 miles to the south), you'll hit the castle parking lots first (£6, buy token from machines at the castle entrance). You'll find plenty of other lots throughout Warwick.

Cost: Steep £28 entry fee (£24 for kids under age 12 and seniors) includes gardens and most castle attractions except for the gory (skippable) Castle Dungeon.

Hours: Daily July-Sept 10:00-18:00, Oct-June generally until 16:00 or 17:00.

Information: Recorded info tel. 0871-265-2000, www.warwick-castle.com.

Rick's Tip: *When you buy your castle ticket, be sure to* **pick up the daily events flier.** *Plan your day around these events, which can include jousting, archers, sword fights, jester acts, and falconry shows.*

⊙ Visiting the Castle

Buy your ticket and head through the turnstile into the moat area, where you'll get your first view of the dramatic castle—it's a 14th- and 15th-century fortified shell, holding an 18th- and 19th-century royal residence. From the moat, two entrance gateways lead to the castle's **inner courtyard.** The bulge of land at the far right end, called **The Mound,** is where the original Norman castle of 1068 stood. Under this "motte," the wooden stockade (the

A Warwick state room

"bailey") defined the courtyard in the way the castle walls do today.

GREAT HALL AND STATE ROOMS

The main attractions are in the largest buildings along the side of the courtyard: the Great Hall, five lavish staterooms, and the chapel. Progressing through these rooms, you'll see how the castle complex evolved over the centuries, from the militarized Middle Ages to civilized Victorian times, from a formidable defensive fortress to a genteel manor home.

Enter through the cavernous **Great Hall,** decorated with suits of equestrian armor. Adjoining the Great Hall is the state dining room, with portraits of English kings and princes. Then follow the one-way route through the **staterooms,** keeping ever more esteemed company as you go—the rooms closest to the center of the complex were the most exclusive, reserved only for those especially close to the Earl of Warwick.

You'll pass through a series of three drawing rooms: first, one decorated in a deep burgundy; then the cedar drawing room, with intricately carved wood

A young knight

up and down) to follow the whole route; claustrophobes should consider it carefully.

The **Princess Tower** offers children (ages 3-8) the chance to dress up as princesses and princes for a photo op. While it's included in the castle ticket, those interested must first sign up for a 15-minute time slot at the information tent in the middle of the courtyard, near the staterooms.

CASTLE GROUNDS

Surrounding everything is a lush, peacock-patrolled, picnic-perfect park, complete with a Victorian rose garden. The castle grounds are often enlivened by a knight in shining armor on a horse or a merry band of musical jesters. The grassy moat area is typically filled with costumed characters and demonstrations, including archery and falconry. Near the entrance to the complex is the **Pageant Playground,** with medieval-themed slides and climbing areas for kids, and the **Horrible Histories Maze,** which includes six "history zones" that cover the Vikings to World War I.

paneling, a Waterford crystal chandelier, and a Carrara marble fireplace; and finally the green drawing room, with a beautiful painted coffered ceiling and wax figures of Henry VIII and his six wives. The sumptuous Queen Anne Room was decorated in preparation for a planned 1704 visit by the monarch. Finally comes the blue boudoir, an oversized closet decorated in blue silk wallpaper. The portrait of King Henry VIII over the fireplace faces a clock once owned by Marie-Antoinette.

RAMPARTS AND TOWERS

You can climb up onto the **ramparts and tower**—a one-way, no-return route that leads you up and down the tallest tower (on very tight spiral stairs), leaving you at a fun perch from which to fire your imaginary longbow. The halls and stairs can be very crowded with young kids, and—as the signs warn—it takes 530 steep steps (both

Eating and Sleeping

Consider bringing a picnic to enjoy on the gorgeous grounds (otherwise you'll be left with the overpriced food stands). It's worth the 100-yard walk from the castle turnstiles to Warwick town's Market Place, with several lunch options on or near the square: **$ The Pot & Fin** (excellent fish-and-chips, closed Sun-Mon), **$$ Saffron Gold** (tasty Indian food, daily), or **$$$ The Rose and Crown** (pub classics, daily).

If you want to overnight in Warwick, try the charming **$$ Warwick Arms Hotel** (17 High Street, www.warwickarmshotel.com) or half-timbered **$$ Park Cottage** (113 West Street/A-429, www.parkcottagewarwick. co.uk).

The Lake District

William Wordsworth's poems still shiver in trees and ripple on ponds in the pristine playgrounds of the Lake District. Nature rules this land, and humanity keeps a wide-eyed but low profile. It's a place to relax, recharge, and renew your poetic license.

The Lake District, about 30 miles long and 30 miles wide, is nature's lush green playground, at a manageable scale (Scafell Pike, the tallest peak in England, is only 3,206 feet). You can explore the region by foot, bike, bus, or car.

There's a walking-stick charm about the way nature and the culture mix here. Cruising a lake, hiking along a windblown ridge, or climbing over a rock fence to look into the eyes of a ragamuffin sheep, even tenderfeet get a chance to feel very outdoorsy.

Expect rain mixed with brilliant "bright spells." Drizzly days can be followed by delightful evenings, so dress in layers. Pubs offer atmospheric shelter at every turn. Enjoy the long days. At this latitude it's light until 22:00 in midsummer.

Plan to spend the majority of your time in the unspoiled North Lake District. Make your home base in Keswick, near the lake called Derwentwater. The North Lake District works great by car or by bus (with easy train access via Penrith), delights nature lovers, and has good accommodations to boot. The South Lake District—slightly closer to London—is famous primarily for sights focused on Wordsworth and Beatrix Potter (of Peter Rabbit fame), and gets the promotion, the tour crowds, and the tackiness that comes with them. Buck the trend and focus on the north.

A visit here is only worthwhile if you make time to head up into the hills or out on the water at least once. And if great scenery is commonplace in your life, the Lake District can be more soothing (and rainy) than exciting.

THE LAKE DISTRICT IN 2 DAYS

Nearly all the activities on Day 1 can be enjoyed without a car.

Day 1: Spend the morning (3-4 hours) combining a Derwentwater lake cruise with a hike: Take the boat partway around the lake, get off at one of the stops to do either the Catbells high-ridge hike or the easier lakeside walk, then hop back on the boat at a later stop to finish the cruise.

For the afternoon, choose among hiking to Castlerigg Stone Circle (one-mile hike from Keswick, or three-mile drive), taking the Walla Crag hike (allow two hours), or visiting the Pencil Museum. Drivers could take the Latrigg Peak hike (trailhead is just outside Keswick).

On any evening: Enjoy a pub dinner and stroll through Keswick. Take a hike or evening cruise (or rent a rowboat), play pitch-and-putt golf, or see a play. Hike to the ancient stone circle—if you haven't yet—to toast the sunset (BYOT).

Day 2: Drivers have these options:

• Take the scenic loop drive from Keswick through the Newlands Valley, Buttermere, Honister Pass, and Borrowdale. Allow two hours for the drive; by adding stops for the Buttermere hike (an easy four miles) and the slate-mine tour at Honister Pass (last tour at 15:30), you'll have a full, fun day.

• Drive to Glenridding for a cruise and seven-mile hike along Ullswater (allow a day). For a shorter Ullswater experience, hike up to the Aira Force waterfall (1 hour) or up and around Lanty's Tarn (2-2.5 hours).

• You could day-trip into the South Lake District, though it only makes sense if you're interested in the Wordsworth and Beatrix Potter sights. Visiting the sights also works well en route if you're driving between Keswick and points south.

Nondrivers have these options:

• Take bus #77 or #77A, the Honister Rambler, which makes a lovely loop from Keswick around Derwentwater, over Honister Pass, through Buttermere, and down the Whinlatter Valley. You could get out at Buttermere to take the four-mile hike. Another good bus option is taking #78, the Borrowdale Rambler, which does another scenic loop from Keswick. For

The Lake District is arguably the most scenic district in all of England.

THE LAKE DISTRICT AT A GLANCE

North Lake District
In Keswick

▲▲**Theatre by the Lake** Top-notch theater a pleasant stroll from Keswick's main square. **Hours:** Shows generally at 19:30, also at 14:00 on Wed and Sat, winter times vary; box office open daily 9:30-20:00 on performance days, other days until 18:00. See page 257.

▲**Derwentwater** Lake immediately south of Keswick, with good boat service and trails. See page 247.

▲**Pencil Museum** Paean to graphite-filled wooden sticks. **Hours:** Daily 9:30-17:00. See page 252.

▲**Pitch-and-Putt Golf** Cheap, easygoing nine-hole course in Keswick's Hope Park. **Hours:** Daily from 10:00, last start at 18:00 but possibly later in summer, closed Nov-Feb. See page 257.

Near Keswick

▲▲▲**Scenic Circle Drive South of Keswick** Hour-long drive through the best of the Lake District's scenery, with plenty of fun stops (including the fascinating Honister Slate Mine) and short side-trip options. See page 254.

▲▲**Castlerigg Stone Circle** Evocative and extremely old (even by British standards) ring of Neolithic stones. See page 252.

▲▲**Catbells High Ridge Hike** Two-hour hike along dramatic ridge southwest of Keswick. See page 253.

▲▲**Buttermere Hike** Four-mile, low-impact lakeside loop in a gorgeous setting. See page 254.

▲**Honister Slate Mine Tour** A 1.5-hour guided hike through a 19th-century mine at the top of Honister Pass. **Hours:** Daily at 10:30, 12:30, and 15:30; also at 14:00 in summer; Dec-Jan 12:30 tour only. See page 255.

Ullswater Lake Area

▲▲**Ullswater Hike and Boat Ride** Long lake best enjoyed via steamer boat and seven-mile walk. **Hours:** Boats generally daily 9:45-16:55, 6-9/day April-Oct, fewer off-season. See page 260.

▲▲**Lanty's Tarn and Keldas Hill** Moderately challenging 2.5-mile loop hike from Glenridding with sweeping views of Ullswater.

▲**Aira Force Waterfall** Easy uphill hike to thundering waterfall. See page 261.

South Lake District

▲▲**Dove Cottage and Wordsworth Museum** The poet's humble home, with a museum that tells the story of his remarkable life. **Hours:** Daily 9:30-17:30, Nov-Feb 10:00-16:30 except closed Jan and for events in Dec and Feb (call ahead). See page 262.

▲**Rydal Mount** Wordsworth's later, more upscale home. **Hours:** Daily 9:30-17:00; Nov and Feb 11:00-16:00 and closed Mon-Tue; closed Dec-Jan. See page 264.

▲**Hill Top Farm** Beatrix Potter's painstakingly preserved cottage. **Hours:** June-Aug daily 10:00-17:30; mid-Feb-May and Sept-Oct until 16:30 and closed Fri; Nov-Dec until 15:30 and closed Mon-Thu; closed Jan-mid-Feb; often a long wait to visit—call ahead. See page 265.

▲**Beatrix Potter Gallery** Collection of artwork by and background on the creator of Peter Rabbit. **Hours:** Daily 10:30-16:00, closed Nov-mid-Feb. See page 266.

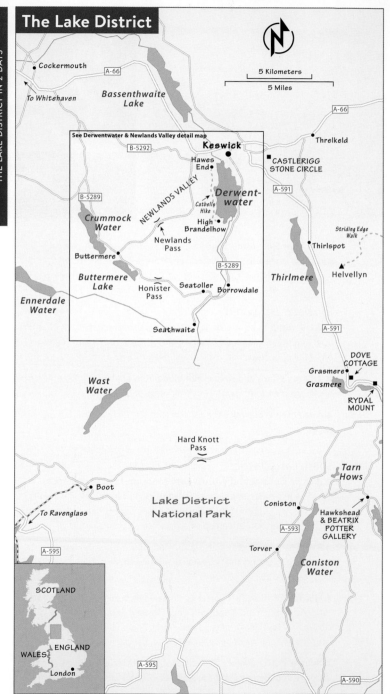

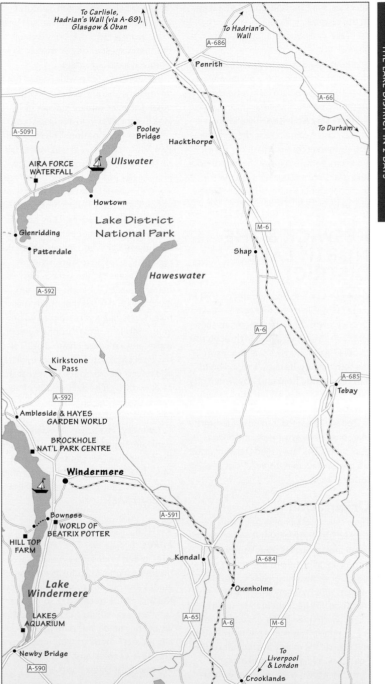

specifics, see "Transportation" at the end of this chapter.

• Take a minibus tour (see "Tours," later).

• Rent a bike in Keswick and make a three-hour loop along the old railway track (now a bike path) and return via the stone circle.

Rainy Day Activities: Take a hike anyway and wear rain gear; the weather could improve (or not). Visit the Pencil Museum, go swimming at the indoor pool, take a lake cruise (boats have a covered section), tour the slate mine, or relax at a pub or your B&B.

KESWICK & THE NORTH LAKE DISTRICT

Keswick (KEZ-ick, population 5,000) is far more enjoyable than other touristy Lake District towns. An important mining center for slate, copper, and lead through the Middle Ages, Keswick became a resort in the 19th century. Its fine Victorian buildings recall those Romantic days when city slickers first learned about "communing with nature."

Today, the compact town is lined with tearooms, pubs, gift shops, and hiking-gear shops. The lake called Derwentwater is a pleasant 10-minute walk from the town center.

Orientation

Keswick is an ideal home base, with plenty of good B&Bs, an easy bus connection to the nearest train station at Penrith, and a prime location near the best lake in the area, Derwentwater. In Keswick, everything is within a 10-minute walk of everything else: the pedestrian town square, the TI, recommended B&Bs, grocery stores, the wonderful municipal pitch-and-putt golf course, the main bus stop, a lakeside boat dock, and a central parking lot.

Keswick town is a delight for wandering. Its centerpiece, Moot Hall (meaning

"meeting hall"), was a 16th-century copper warehouse upstairs with an arcade below. The square is lively every day throughout the summer, especially on market days—Thursdays and Saturdays.

Keswick is popular with English holidaymakers who prefer to travel with their dogs. The town square in Keswick can look like the Westminster Dog Show.

Tourist Information: The National Park Visitors Centre/TI is in Moot Hall on the town square (daily 9:30-17:30, Nov-Easter until 16:30, tel. 017687/72645, www.lakedistrict.gov.uk and www.keswick.org). Staffers are pros at advising you about hiking routes. They can also help you figure out public transportation to outlying sights and tell you about the region's various adventure activities.

The TI sells theater tickets, Keswick Launch tickets, fishing licenses, and brochures and maps that outline nearby hikes (including a very simple and driver-friendly Lap Map featuring sights, walks, and a mileage chart). The TI also has books and maps for hikers, cyclists, and drivers (more books are sold at shops all over town). The daily weather forecast is posted just outside the front door (weather tel. 0844-846-2444).

Laundry: The town's launderette is on Bank Street, just up the side street from the post office (full- and self-service; Mon-Fri 8:00-19:00, Sat-Sun 9:00-18:00; coin-op soap dispenser, free Wi-Fi, tel. 017687/75448).

Tours

Hikes

KR Guided Walks offers private guided hikes of varying difficulty levels. The local guides also provide transportation from Keswick to the trailhead (£80/day, Easter-Oct, wear suitable clothing and footwear, bring lunch and water, must book in advance, tel. 017687/71302, mobile 0734-263-7813, keswickrambles.blogspot.co.uk, armstrongps1@gmx.com).

TIs throughout the region also offer

free walks led by "Voluntary Rangers" several times a month in summer (depart from Keswick TI; check schedule in the Events and Guided Walks guide, optional contribution welcome at end of walk).

Bus Tours

Bus tours are great for people with bucks who'd like to wring maximum experience out of their limited time and see the area without lots of hiking or messing with public transport. (For a cheaper alternative, take public buses.) **Mountain Goat Tours** is the region's dominant tour company. Unfortunately, they run their minibus tours out of Windermere, with pick-ups in Bowness, Ambleside, and sometimes in Grasmere. For those based in Keswick, add about an extra hour of driving or bus riding, round-trip, if you join their tours in Windermere, though they may be able to arrange tours from Keswick if you contact them in advance (tours run daily, £25/half-day, £44-50/day, year-round if there are sufficient sign-ups,

minimum 4 people to a maximum of 16 per hearty bus, book in advance by calling 015394/45161, www.mountain-goat.com, tours@mountain-goat.com).

Show Me Cumbria Private Tours, run by Andy, offers personalized tours all around the Lake District. They can pick up in Keswick and other locations (from £35/hour depending on group size, tel. 01768/864-825, mobile 0780-902-6357, based in Penrith, www.showmecumbria. co.uk, andy@showmecumbria.co.uk).

Sights

▲DERWENTWATER

One of Cumbria's most photographed and popular lakes, Derwentwater has four islands, good circular boat service, and plenty of trails. The pleasant town of Keswick is a short stroll from the shore, near the lake's north end. The roadside views aren't much, and while you can walk around the lake (fine trail, floods in heavy rains, 9 miles, 4 hours), much of the walk is boring. You're better off mixing a hike and

Derwentwater is just a 10-minute walk from the ideal home-base town of Keswick.

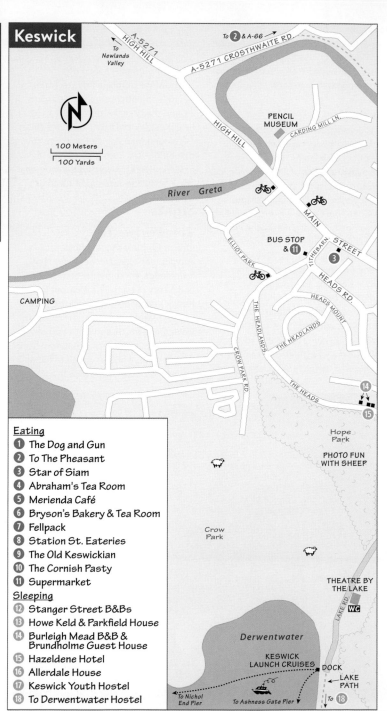

Keswick

To Newlands Valley

A-5271 HIGH HILL

To 2 & A-66

A-5271 CROSTHWAITE RD.

HIGH HILL

PENCIL MUSEUM

CARDING MILL LN.

River Greta

MAIN STREET

BUS STOP & 11

TITHEBARN STREET

3

ELLIOT PARK

HEADS RD.

HEADS MOUNT

CAMPING

THE HEADLANDS

THE HEADLANDS

CROW PARK RD.

THE HEADS

14

15

Hope Park

PHOTO FUN WITH SHEEP

Crow Park

THEATRE BY THE LAKE

LAKE RD.

WC

Derwentwater

KESWICK LAUNCH CRUISES

DOCK

LAKE PATH

To Nichol End Pier

To Ashness Gate Pier

To 18

100 Meters
100 Yards

Eating
1. The Dog and Gun
2. To The Pheasant
3. Star of Siam
4. Abraham's Tea Room
5. Merienda Café
6. Bryson's Bakery & Tea Room
7. Fellpack
8. Station St. Eateries
9. The Old Keswickian
10. The Cornish Pasty
11. Supermarket

Sleeping
12. Stanger Street B&Bs
13. Howe Keld & Parkfield House
14. Burleigh Mead B&B & Brundholme Guest House
15. Hazeldene Hotel
16. Allerdale House
17. Keswick Youth Hostel
18. To Derwentwater Hostel

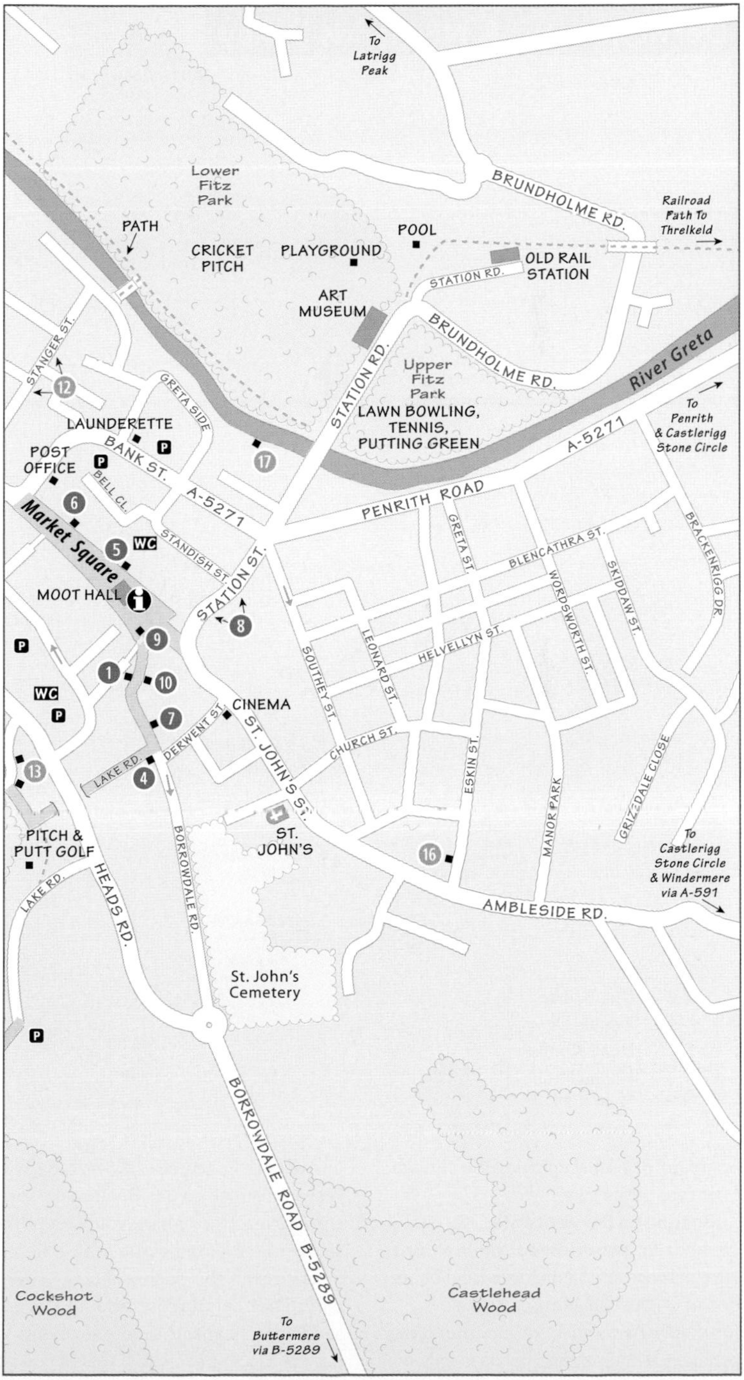

To
Latrigg
Peak

Lower
Fitz
Park

PATH

CRICKET
PITCH

PLAYGROUND

POOL

ART
MUSEUM

BRUNDHOLME RD.

Railroad
Path To
Threlkeld

STATION RD.

OLD RAIL
STATION

BRUNDHOLME RD.

River Greta

STANGER ST.

12

GRETA SIDE

Upper
Fitz
Park
LAWN BOWLING,
TENNIS,
PUTTING GREEN

To
Penrith
& Castlerigg
Stone Circle

LAUNDERETTE

P

BANK ST.

POST
OFFICE

6

BELL CL.

5 WC

STATION RD.

A-5271

STANDISH ST.

17

A-5271

PENRITH ROAD

GRETA ST.

BLENCATHRA ST.

SKIDDAW ST.

BRACKENRIGG DR.

Market Square

MOOT HALL

STATION ST.

8

WORDSWORTH ST.

9

1 10

SOUTHEY ST.

LEONARD ST.

HELVELLYN ST.

ESKIN ST.

WC

P

7

CINEMA

DERWENT ST.

ST. JOHN'S ST.

CHURCH ST.

MANOR PARK

GRIZEDALE CLOSE

13

4

LAKE RD.

BORROWDALE RD.

ST.
JOHN'S

16

To
Castlerigg
Stone Circle
& Windermere
via A-591

PITCH &
PUTT GOLF

LAKE RD.

HEADS RD.

AMBLESIDE RD.

St. John's
Cemetery

P

BORROWDALE ROAD B-5289

Cockshot
Wood

Castlehead
Wood

To
Buttermere
via B-5289

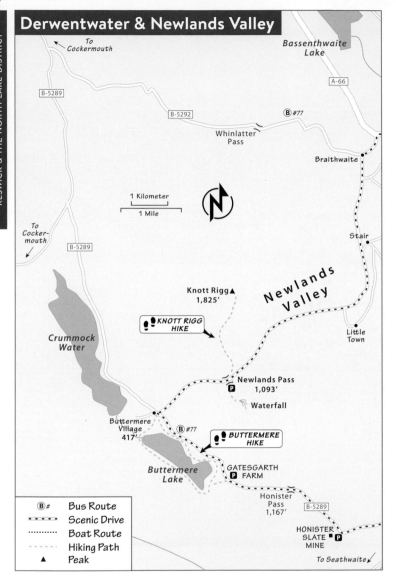

Derwentwater & Newlands Valley

Bassenthwaite Lake

To Cockermouth

B-5289

A-66

B-5292

Ⓑ #77

Whinlatter Pass

Braithwaite

1 Kilometer

1 Mile

To Cocker-mouth

B-5289

Stair

Knott Rigg ▲
1,825'

Newlands Valley

👣 KNOTT RIGG HIKE

Crummock Water

Little Town

Newlands Pass
Ⓟ 1,093'

☂ Waterfall

Buttermere Village
417'

Ⓑ #77

👣 BUTTERMERE HIKE

Buttermere Lake

GATESGARTH
Ⓟ FARM

Honister Pass
1,167'

B-5289

Ⓑ#	Bus Route
••••	Scenic Drive
••••••	Boat Route
-----	Hiking Path
▲	Peak

HONISTER
SLATE ■ Ⓟ
MINE

To Seathwaite ↙

boat ride, or simply enjoying the circular boat tour of the lake.

Boating on Derwentwater: Keswick Launch runs two **cruises** an hour, alternating clockwise and "anticlockwise" (boats depart on the half-hour, daily 10:00–16:30, July-Aug until 17:30, in winter 6/day generally weekends and holidays only, at

end of Lake Road, tel. 017687/72263, www. keswick-launch.co.uk). Boats make seven stops on each 50-minute round-trip (may skip some stops or not run at all if the water level is very high—such as after a heavy rain). The boat trip costs about £2.25 per segment (cheaper the more segments you buy) or £10.50 per circle (£1 less if you book

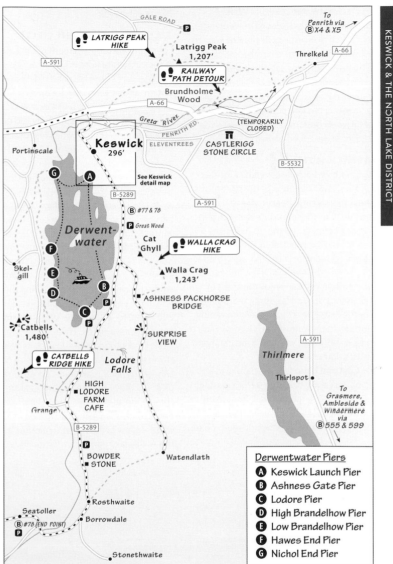

GALE ROAD

To Penrith via (B) X4 & X5

P

LATRIGG PEAK HIKE

Latrigg Peak 1,207'

Threlkeld

A-66

A-591

RAILWAY PATH DETOUR

Brundholme Wood

A-66

(TEMPORARILY CLOSED)

Greta River

PENRITH RD.

Keswick 296'

ELEVENTREES

CASTLERIGG STONE CIRCLE

Portinscale

See Keswick detail map

B-5532

B-5289

A-591

(B) #77 & 78

P Great Wood

Cat Ghyll

WALLA CRAG HIKE

Derwent-water

G

A

Walla Crag 1,243'

F

Skel-gill

E

B

ASHNESS PACKHORSE BRIDGE

D

P

C

P

Catbells 1,480'

SURPRISE VIEW

Thirlmere

A-591

Thirlspot

CATBELLS RIDGE HIKE

Lodore Falls

To Grasmere, Ambleside & Windermere via (B) 555 & 599

Grange

HIGH LODORE FARM CAFE

B-5289

Watendlath

P

BOWDER STONE

Seatoller

(B) #78 (END POINT)

P

Rosthwaite

Borrowdale

Stonethwaite

Derwentwater Piers

- **A** Keswick Launch Pier
- **B** Ashness Gate Pier
- **C** Lodore Pier
- **D** High Brandelhow Pier
- **E** Low Brandelhow Pier
- **F** Hawes End Pier
- **G** Nichol End Pier

through TI) with free stopovers; you can get on and off all you want, but tickets are collected on the boat's last leg to Keswick, marking the end of your ride. If you want to hop on a #77/#77A bus and also cruise Derwentwater, the £13 Derwentwater Bus & Boat all-day pass covers both. To be picked up at a certain stop, stand at the

end of the pier Gilligan-style, or the boat may not stop. See the map above for an overview of all the boat stops.

Keswick Launch also has a delightful **evening cruise** (see page 258) and rents **rowboats** for up to three people (open Easter-Oct, larger rowboats and motor boats available).

Derwentwater Lakeside Walk: A marked trail runs all along Derwentwater, but much of it (especially the Keswick-to-Hawes End stretch) is not that interesting. The best hour-long section is the 1.5-mile path between the docks at High Brandelhow and Hawes End, where you'll stroll a level trail through peaceful trees. This walk works best in conjunction with the lake boat described earlier.

▲PENCIL MUSEUM

Graphite was first discovered centuries ago in Keswick. A hunk of the stuff proved great for marking sheep in the 15th century. In 1832, the first crude Keswick pencil factory opened, and the rest is history (which is what you'll learn about here). While you can't tour the 150-year-old factory where the famous Derwent pencils were made, you can enjoy the smell of thousands of pencils getting sharpened for the first time. The adjacent charming and kid-friendly museum is a good way to pass a rainy hour; you may even catch an artist's demonstration.

Cost and Hours: £4.95, daily 9:30-17:00, last entry one hour before closing, humble café, 3-minute walk from town center, signposted off Main Street, tel. 017687/73626, www.pencilmuseum.co.uk.

Near Keswick

▲▲CASTLERIGG STONE CIRCLE

For some reason, 70 percent of England's stone circles are here in Cumbria. Castlerigg is one of the best and oldest in Britain, and an easy stop for drivers. The circle—90 feet across and 5,000 years old—has 38 stones mysteriously laid out on a line between the two tallest peaks on the horizon. They served as a celestial calendar for ritual celebrations. Imagine the ambience here, as ancient people filled this clearing in spring to celebrate fertility, in late summer to commemorate the harvest, and in the winter to celebrate the winter solstice and the coming renewal of light. Festival dates were dictated by how the sun rose and set in relation to the stones. The more that modern academics study this circle, the more meaning they find in the placement of the stones. The two front stones face due north, toward a cut in the mountains. The rare-for-stone-circles "sanctuary" lines up with its center stone to mark where the sun rises on May Day. (Party!) For maximum "goose pimples" (as they say here), show up at sunset (free, open all the time, 1-mile hike from town; by car it's a 3-mile drive east of Keswick—follow brown signs, 3 minutes off the A-66, easy parking).

Castlerigg Stone Circle

Experiences
Hikes and Drives

For an easy, flat stroll, consider the trail that runs alongside Derwentwater (see "Derwentwater Lakeside Walk," earlier). More involved options are described next. Be prepared on hikes; for a few tips, see page 268.

Rick's Tip: *Tiny* **biting insects called midges**—*similar to no-see-ums—might bug you in this region from late May through September, particularly at dawn and dusk.* **Insect repellant** *fends them off: Ask the locals what works if you'll be hiking.*

▲▲CATBELLS HIGH RIDGE HIKE

Catbells is probably the most dramatic family walk in the area. From Keswick, the lake, or your farmhouse B&B, you can see silhouetted figures hiking along this ridge. Wear sturdy shoes, bring a raincoat, and watch your footing. You'll be rewarded with a great "king of the mountain" feeling, 360-degree views, and a close-up look at the weather blowing over the ridge.

You'll hike above Derwentwater about two hours from Hawes End up along the ridge to Catbells (1,480 feet) and down to High Brandelhow. Because the mountaintop is basically treeless, you're treated to dramatic panoramas the entire way up. From High Brandelhow, you can catch the boat back to Keswick or take the easy path along the shore of Derwentwater to your Hawes End starting point. (Extending the hike farther around the lake to Lodore takes you to a waterfall, rock climbers, a fine café, and another boat dock for a convenient return to Keswick). Note: When the water level is very high (for example, after a heavy rain), boats can't stop at Hawes End—ask at the TI or boat dock before setting out.

Getting There: To reach the trailhead from Keswick, catch the "anticlockwise" boat (see "Boating on Derwentwater," earlier) and ride for 10 minutes to the second stop, Hawes End. (You can also ride to High Brandelhow and take this walk in the other direction, but I don't recommend it—two rocky scrambles along the way are easier and safer to navigate going uphill from Hawes End.) Note the schedule for your return boat ride. Drivers can park free at Hawes End, but parking is limited and the road can be hard to find—get very clear directions in town before heading out. (Hardcore hikers can walk to the foot of Catbells from Keswick via Portinscale, which takes about 40 minutes—ask your B&B or the TI for directions.) The Keswick TI sells a *Catbells* brochure about the hike.

The Route: The path is not signposted, but it's easy to follow, and you'll see plenty of other walkers. From Hawes End, walk away from the lake through a kissing gate to the turn just before the car park. Then turn left and go up, up, up. After about 20 minutes, you'll hit the first of two short scrambles (where the trail vanishes into a cluster of steep rocks), which leads to a bluff. From the first little summit (great for a picnic break), and then along the ridge, you'll enjoy sweeping views of the lake on one side and of Newlands Valley on the other. The bald peak in the distance is Catbells. Broken stones crunch under each step, wind buffets your ears, clouds prowl overhead, and the sheep baa comically. To anyone looking up from the distant farmhouse B&Bs, you are but a stick figure on the ridge. Just below the summit, the trail disintegrates

Catbells High Ridge

into another short, steep scramble. Your reward is just beyond: a magnificent hilltop perch.

After the Catbells summit, descend along the ridge to a saddle ahead. The ridge continues much higher, and while it may look like your only option, at its base a small, unmarked lane with comfortable steps leads left. Unless you're up for extending the hike, take this path down to the lake. To get to High Brandelhow Pier, take the first left fork you come across down through a forest to the lake. When you reach Abbot's Bay, go left through a swinging gate, following a lakeside trail around a gravelly bluff, to the idyllic High Brandelhow Pier, a peaceful place to wait for your boat back to Keswick. (You can pay your fare when you board.)

▲▲BUTTERMERE HIKE

Outside Keswick, this ideal little lake with a lovely circular four-mile stroll offers nonstop, no-sweat Lake District beauty. If you're not a hiker but wish you were, take this walk. If you're short on time, at least stop here and get your shoes dirty.

Buttermere is connected with Borrowdale and Derwentwater by a great road that runs over rugged Honister Pass. Buses #77/#77A make a 1.75-hour round-trip loop between Keswick and Buttermere that includes a trip over this pass. The two-pub hamlet of Buttermere has a pay-and-display parking lot and free parking along the roadside. There's also a pay parking lot at the Honister Pass end of the lake (at Gatesgarth Farm). The

Buttermere hike

Syke Farm in Buttermere is popular for its homemade ice cream.

▲▲▲SCENIC CIRCLE DRIVE SOUTH OF KESWICK

This hour-long drive, which includes Newlands Valley, Buttermere, Honister Pass, and Borrowdale, offers the North Lake District's best scenery. (To do a similar route without a car from Keswick, take loop bus #77/#77A.) Distances are short, roads are narrow and have turnouts, and views are rewarding. Get a good map and ask your B&B host for advice. (For an overview of the route, see map on page 250.)

From Keswick, leave town on Crosthwaite Road, then, at the roundabout, head west on Cockermouth Road (A-66, following *Cockermouth* and *Workington* signs). Don't take the first Newlands Valley exit, but do take the second one (through Braithwaite), and follow signs up the majestic Newlands Valley (also signed for *Buttermere*).

If the **Newlands Valley** had a lake, it would be packed with tourists. But it doesn't—and it isn't. The valley is dotted with 500-year-old family-owned farms. Shearing day is reason to rush home from school. Sons get school out of the way ASAP and follow their dads into the family business. Neighbor girls marry those sons and move in.

Grandparents retire to the cottage next door. With the price of wool depressed, most of the wives supplement the family income by running B&Bs (virtually every farm in the valley rents rooms). The road has one lane, with turnouts for passing. From the Newlands Pass summit, notice the glacial-shaped wilds, once forested, now not.

From the parking lot at **Newlands Pass,** at the top of Newlands Valley (unmarked, but you'll see a waterfall on the left), an easy 300-yard hike leads to a little waterfall. On the other side of the road, an easy one-mile hike climbs up to **Knott Rigg,** which probably offers more TPCB (thrills per calorie burned) than any walk in the region. If you don't have time for even a short hike, at least get out of the car and get a feel for the setting.

After Newlands Pass, descend to **Buttermere** (scenic lake, tiny hamlet with pubs and an ice-cream store—see "Buttermere Hike," earlier), turn left, drive the length of the lake, and climb over rugged **Honister Pass**—strewn with glacial debris, remnants from the old slate mines, and curious shaggy Swaledale sheep (looking more like goats with their curly horns). The U-shaped valleys you'll see are textbook examples of those carved out by glaciers. Look high on the hillsides for "hanging valleys"—small glacial-shaped scoops cut off by the huge flow of the biggest glacier, which swept down the main valley.

The **Honister Slate Mine,** England's last still-functioning slate mine (and worth ▲), stands at the summit of Honister Pass. The youth hostel next to it was originally built to house miners in the 1920s. The mine offers worthwhile tours (perfect for when it's pouring outside): You'll put on a hard hat, load onto a bus for a short climb, then hike into a shaft to learn about the region's slate industry.

It's a long, stooped hike into the mountain, made interesting by the guide and punctuated by the sound of your helmet scraping against low bits of the shaft. Even if you don't have time to take the tour, stop here for its slate-filled shop (£13.50, 1.5-hour tour; departs daily at 10:30, 12:30, and 15:30; additional tour at 14:00 in summer; Dec-Jan 12:30 tour only; call ahead to confirm times and to book a spot, helmets and lamps provided, wear good walking shoes and bring warm clothing even in summer, café and nice WCs, tel. 017687/77230, www.honister.com).

After stark and lonely Honister Pass, drop in to sweet and homey **Borrowdale,** with a few lonely hamlets and fine hikes from Seathwaite. Circling back to Keswick past Borrowdale, the B-5289 (a.k.a. the Borrowdale Valley Road) takes you past the following popular attractions.

A set of stairs leads to the top of the house-size **Bowder Stone** (signposted, a few minutes' walk off the main road). For a great lunch or snack, including tea and homemade quiche and cakes, drop in to the much-loved **High Lodore Farm Café** (daily 9:00-18:00, closed Nov-Easter, short drive uphill from the main road and over

You'll find scenic vistas everywhere you venture in the Lake District.

a tiny bridge, tel. 017687/77221). Farther along, **Lodore Falls** is a short walk from the road, behind Lodore Hotel (a nice place to stop for tea and beautiful views). **Shepherds Crag,** a cliff overlooking Lodore, was made famous by pioneer rock climbers. (Their descendants hang from little ridges on its face today.) This is serious climbing, with several fatalities a year.

A very hard right off the B-5289 (signposted *Ashness Bridge, Watendlath*) and a steep half-mile climb on a narrow lane takes you to the postcard-pretty **Ashness Packhorse Bridge,** a quintessential Lake District scene (parking lot just above on right). A half-mile farther up, park the car and hop out (parking lot on left, no sign). You'll be startled by the "surprise view" of Derwentwater—great for a lakes photo op. Continuing from here, the road gets extremely narrow en route to the hamlet of **Watendlath,** which has a tiny lake and lazy farm animals.

Return to the B-5289 and head back to Keswick. If you have yet to see it, cap your drive with a short detour from Keswick to the Castlerigg Stone Circle (described earlier).

LATRIGG PEAK

For the easiest mountain-climbing sensation around, take the short drive to the Latrigg Peak parking lot just north of Keswick, and hike 15 minutes to the top of the 1,200-foot-high hill, where you'll be rewarded with a commanding view of the town, lake, and valley, all the way to the next lake over (Bassenthwaite). At the traffic circle just outside Keswick, take the A-591 Carlisle exit, then an immediate right (direction: Ormathwaite/Underscar). Take the next right, a hard right, at the *Skiddaw* sign, where a long, steep, one-lane road leads to the Latrigg car park at the end of the lane. With more time, you can walk all the way from your Keswick B&B to Latrigg and back (it's a popular evening walk for locals).

RAILWAY PATH

The four-mile Railway Path from downtown Keswick follows an old train track and the river to the village of Threlkeld (with two pubs). However, parts of the path are indefinitely closed following a 2015 flood. Until the path is restored, walkers (but not cyclists) can take a detour through Brundholme Woods (just past Low Briery) to Brundholme Road and

Watendlath's little lake

into Threlkeld (expect some uphill segments; ask at TI for detour updates). You can either walk back along the same path, or loop back via the Castlerigg Stone Circle (described earlier, roughly eight miles total). The Railway Path starts behind the leisure center (as you face the center, head right and around back).

WALLA CRAG

From your Keswick B&B, a fine two-hour walk to Walla Crag offers great fell (mountain) walking and a ridge-walk experience without the necessity of a bus or car. Start by strolling along the lake to the Great Wood parking lot (or drive to this lot), and head up Cat Ghyl (where "fell runners"—trail-running enthusiasts—practice) to Walla Crag. You'll be treated to great panoramic views over Derwentwater and surrounding peaks—especially beautiful when the heather blossoms in the summer. You can do a shorter version of this walk from the parking lot at Ashness Packhorse Bridge.

▲Golf

A nine-hole pitch-and-putt golf course near the lush gardens in Hope Park separates the town from the lake and offers a classy, cheap, and convenient chance to golf near the birthplace of the sport. This is a great, fun, and inexpensive experience—just right after a day of touring and before dinner (£5 for pitch-and-putt, £3.25 for putting, £3.95 for 18 tame holes of "obstacle golf," daily from 10:00, last

round starts around 18:00, possibly later in summer, closed Nov-Feb, café, tel. 017687/73445, www.hopeleisure.com).

Swimming

While the leisure center lacks a serious adult pool, it does have an indoor pool kids love, with a huge waterslide and wave machine (swim times vary by day and by season—call or check website, no towels or suits for rent, lockers-£1 deposit, 10-minute walk from town center, follow Station Road past Fitz Park and veer left, tel. 017687/72760, www.better.org.uk—search for "Keswick").

Rick's Tip: Keswick Street Theatre, *a walk through the town and its history, takes place on Tuesday evenings in summer (£3, 1.5 hours, usually starts at 19:30, weekly late May-early July, details at TI).*

Nightlife

▲▲THEATRE BY THE LAKE

Keswickians brag that they enjoy "London theater quality at Keswick prices." Their theater offers events year-round and a wonderful rotation of six plays from late May through October (plays vary throughout the week, with music concerts on Sun in summer). There are two stages: The main one seats 400, and the smaller "studio" theater seats 100 (and features edgier plays that may involve rough language and/or nudity). Attending a play here is a fine opportunity to enjoy a classy night out.

Cost and Hours: £10-32, discounts for old and young; shows generally at 19:30, also at 14:00 on Wed and Sat, winter schedule varies; café, restaurant (pretheater dinners start at 17:30 and must be booked 24 hours ahead by calling 017687/81102), parking at the adjacent lot is free after 19:00. It's smart to buy tickets in advance—book at box office (daily 9:30-20:00 on performance days, other days until 18:00), by phone (tel. 017687/74411), at TI, or at www. theatrebythelake.com.

EVENING CRUISE

In Hope Park, Keswick Launch's **evening lake cruise** comes with a glass of wine and a midlake stop for a short commentary. You're welcome to bring a picnic dinner and munch scenically as you cruise (£10.75, £25 family ticket, 1 hour, daily mid-July-Aug at 18:30 and 19:30—weather permitting and if enough people show up).

Eating

Keswick has a variety of good, basic eateries, but nothing particularly outstanding. Most stop serving by 21:00.

$$ The Dog and Gun serves good pub food (I love their rump of lamb) with great pub ambience. Upon arrival, muscle up to the bar to order your beer and/or meal. Then snag a table as soon as one opens up. Mind your head and tread carefully: Low ceilings and wooden beams loom overhead, while paws poke out from under tables below, as Keswick's canines wait patiently for their masters to finish their beer (food served daily 12:00-21:00, famous goulash, dog treats, 2 Lake Road, tel. 017687/73463).

$$ The Pheasant is a walk outside town, but locals trek here regularly for fish pie, Cumbrian sausage, and guinea fowl as well as more inventive choices. There's a small restaurant section, but I much prefer eating in the bar (food served daily 12:00-14:00 & 18:00-21:00, bar open until 23:00, Crosthwaite Road, tel. 017687/72219). From the town square, walk past the Pencil Museum, hang a right onto Crosthwaite Road, and walk 10 minutes. For a more scenic route, cross the river into Fitz Park, go left along the riverside path until it ends at the gate to Crosthwaite Road, turn right, and walk five minutes.

$$ Star of Siam serves authentic Thai dishes in a tasteful dining room (daily 12:00-14:30 & 17:30-22:30, 89 Main Street, tel. 017687/71444).

$ Abraham's Tea Room, popular with townspeople, is a fine value for lunch. It's tucked away on the upper floor of the giant George Fisher outdoor store (gluten-free options; Mon-Sat 10:00-17:00, Sun 10:30-16:30, on the corner where Lake Road turns right, tel. 017687/71811).

$$ Merienda Café has a friendly staff and a small selection of tasty, reasonably priced fare along with wine and beer in a contemporary, inviting space (daily 9:00-21:00, 10 Main Street, tel. 017687/72024).

$$ Bryson's Bakery and Tea Room has an enticing ground-floor bakery, with sandwiches and light lunches. The upstairs is a popular tearoom. Order lunch to-go from the bakery, or for a few pence more, eat there, either sitting on stools or at a couple of sidewalk tables. Consider their two-person Cumberland Cream Tea made with local ingredients; it's a good deal for what most would consider "afternoon tea," with sandwiches, scones, and little cakes served on a three-tiered platter (daily 9:00-17:00, 42 Main Street, tel. 017687/72257).

$ Fellpack serves wraps, salads, and local dishes—all available to enjoy in their small café, or to-go for a picnic (daily 9:00-18:00, 19 Lake Road, tel. 017687/71177).

Eateries on Station Street: The street leading from the town square to the leisure center has several restaurants, including **$$ Casa Bella,** a popular and packed Italian place that's good for families—reserve ahead (daily 12:00-15:30 & 17:00-21:00, 24 Station Street, tel. 017687/75575). Across the street is **$$ Lakes Bar & Bistro,** with burgers, meat pies, and good fixed-price meal deals (daily 10:00-22:30, 25 Station Street, tel. 017687/74080).

Picnic Food: The fine **Booths supermarket** is right where all the buses arrive (Mon-Sat 8:00-21:00, Sun

9:30-16:00, Tithebarn Street). The recommended **Bryson's Bakery** does good sandwiches to go (described above). **$ The Old Keswickian,** on the town square, serves up old-fashioned fish-and-chips to go (daily 11:00-19:30, tel. 017687/73861). Just around the corner, **$ The Cornish Pasty** offers an enticing variety of fresh meat pies to go (daily 9:00-17:00 or until the pasties are all gone, across from The Dog and Gun on Borrowdale Road, tel. 017687/72205).

Rick's Tip: *Advertised throughout this area,* **Kendal mint cakes** *are a local candy—flat, mint-flavored sugar cubes worth a try.*

Sleeping

Reserve your room in advance in high season.

Many of my Keswick listings charge extra for a one-night stay and most won't book one-night stays on weekends (but if you show up and they have a bed free, it's yours). None have elevators and all have lots of stairs—ask about a ground-floor unit if steps are a problem. Most don't welcome young children; if you have trouble, try www.keswick.org to search for available rooms at a B&B that accepts small children.

Owners are enthusiastic about offering advice to get you on the right walking trail. Most accommodations have inviting lounges with libraries of books on the region and loaner maps.

On Stanger Street

This street, quiet but just a block from Keswick's town center, is lined with B&Bs situated in Victorian slate townhouses. Each of these places is small and family-run. They are all good, offering comfortably sized rooms, free parking, and a friendly welcome.

$$ Ellergill Guest House has four spic-and-span rooms with an airy, contemporary feel—several with views (2 percent

surcharge for credit cards, 2-night minimum, no children under age 10, 22 Stanger Street, tel. 017687/73347, www.ellergill. co.uk, stay@ellergill.co.uk, Clare and Robin Pinkney).

$$ Badgers Wood B&B, at the top of the street, has six modern, bright, unfrilly view rooms, each named after a different tree (3 percent surcharge for credit cards, 2-night minimum, no children under age 12, special diets accommodated, 30 Stanger Street, tel. 017687/72621, www. badgers-wood.co.uk, enquiries@badgers-wood.co.uk, chatty Scotsman Andrew and his charming wife Anne).

$$ Abacourt House, with a daisy-fresh breakfast room, has five pleasant doubles (3 percent surcharge for credit cards, 2-night minimum, no children, sack lunches available, 26 Stanger Street, tel. 017687/72967, www.abacourt.co.uk, abacourt.keswick@btinternet.com, John and Heather).

$ Dunsford Guest House rents four updated rooms at bargain prices. Stained glass and wooden pews give the blue-and-cream breakfast room a country-chapel vibe (RS%, cash only, 16 Stanger Street, tel. 017687/75059, www.dunsfordguesthouse. co.uk, info@dunsfordguesthouse.co.uk, Deb and Keith).

On The Heads

The classy area known as The Heads has B&Bs with bigger and grander Victorian architecture and great views overlooking the pitch-and-putt range and out into the hilly distance. A single yellow line on the curb means you're allowed to park there for free, but only overnight (16:00-10:00).

$$$ Howe Keld has the polished feel of a boutique hotel, but offers all the friendliness of a B&B. Its 12 contemporary-posh rooms are spacious and tastefully decked out in native woods and slate. It's warm, welcoming, and family-run, with an à la carte breakfast cooked to order by chef Jerome (cash and 2-night minimum preferred, sack lunches available, bike garage in basement, tel. 017687/72417 or toll-free 0800-783-0212, www.howekeld.co.uk, laura@howekeld.co.uk, run with care by Laura and Jerome Bujard).

$$ Parkfield House, thoughtfully run and decorated by John and Susan Berry, is a big Victorian house with a homey lounge. Its six rooms, some with fine views, are bright and classy (RS%, 2-night minimum, no children under age 16, free parking, tel. 017687/72328, www. parkfieldkeswick.co.uk, parkfieldkeswick@ hotmail.co.uk).

$$ Burleigh Mead B&B is a slate mansion from 1892 with wild carpeting. Gill (pronounced "Jill," short for Gillian) rents seven lovely rooms and offers a friendly welcome, as well as a lounge and peaceful front-yard sitting area that's perfect for enjoying the view (cash only, no children under age 8, tel. 017687/75935, www. burleighmead.co.uk, info@burleighmead. co.uk).

$$ Hazeldene Hotel, on the corner of The Heads, rents 10 spacious rooms, many with commanding views. There's even a "boot room" that doubles as a guest rec room with a ping-pong table. It's run with care by delightful Helen and Howard (one ground-floor unit available, free parking, tel. 017687/72106, www. hazeldene-hotel.co.uk, info@hazeldene-hotel.co.uk).

$$ Brundholme Guest House has four bright and comfy rooms, most with sweeping views at no extra charge—especially from the front side—and a friendly and welcoming atmosphere (minifridge, free parking, tel. 017687/73305, mobile 0773-943-5401, www.brundholme.co.uk, bazaly@hotmail.co.uk, Barry and Allison Thompson).

On Eskin Street

$$ Allerdale House, a classy, nicely decorated stone mansion, holds six rooms and is well-run by Barbara and Paul. It's within easy walking distance of downtown and the lake (RS%, 3 percent surcharge for

credit cards, free parking, 1 Eskin Street, tel. 017687/73891, www.allerdale-house. co.uk, reception@allerdale-house.co.uk).

Hostels

These inexpensive hostels are handy sources of information and social fun.

¢ Keswick Youth Hostel, with a big lounge and a great riverside balcony, fills a converted mill. Travelers of all ages feel at home here, but book ahead—family rooms book up July through September (breakfast extra, pay guest computer, café, bar, office open 7:00-23:00, center of town just off Station Road before river, tel. 017687/72484, www.yha.org.uk, keswick@yha.org.uk).

¢ Derwentwater Hostel, in a 220-year-old mansion on the shore of Derwent-water, is two miles south of Keswick (breakfast extra, family rooms, 23:00 curfew; follow the B-5289 from Keswick—entrance is 2 miles along the Borrowdale Valley Road about 150 yards after Ashness exit—look for cottage and bus stop at bottom of the drive; tel. 017687/77246, www.derwentwater.org, contact@ derwentwater.org).

ULLSWATER LAKE AREA

For advice on the Ullswater area, visit the **TI** at the pay parking lot in the heart of the lakefront village of Glenridding (daily 9:30-17:30, Nov-March until 15:30, tel. 017684/82414, www.visiteden.co.uk). This stop is easy for drivers. If busing from Keswick, you'd transfer in Penrith to bus #508 for Glenridding.

▲▲**ULLSWATER HIKE AND BOAT RIDE**
Long, narrow Ullswater, which some consider the loveliest lake in the area, offers eight miles of diverse and grand Lake District scenery. While you can drive it or cruise it, I'd ride the boat from the south tip halfway up (to Howtown—which is nothing more than a dock) and hike back. Or walk first, then enjoy an easy ride back.

An old-fashioned **"steamer" boat** (actually diesel-powered) leaves Glenridding regularly for Howtown (departs daily generally 9:45-16:55, 6-9/day April-Oct, fewer off-season, 40 minutes; £6.80 one-way, £10.80 round-trip, £14.20 round-the-lake ticket lets you hop on and off, covered by Ullswater Bus & Boat day pass, family rates, drivers can use safe pay-and-display parking lot, by public transit take bus #508 from Penrith, café at dock, £4 walking route map, tel. 017684/82229, www.ullswater-steamers.co.uk).

From Howtown, spend three to four hours hiking and dawdling along the well-marked path by the lake south to Patterdale, and then along the road back to Glenridding. This is a serious seven-mile walk with good views, varied terrain, and a few bridges and farms along the way. For a shorter hike from Howtown Pier, consider a three-mile loop around Hallin Fell. A rainy-day plan is to ride the covered boat up and down the lake to Howtown and Pooley Bridge at the northern tip of the lake (2 hours). Boats don't run in bad weather—call ahead if it looks iffy.

▲▲LANTY'S TARN AND KELDAS HILL

If you like the idea of an Ullswater-area hike, but aren't up for the long huff from Howtown, consider this shorter loop that leaves right from the TI's pay parking lot in Glenridding. It's 2.5 miles, moderately challenging, and plenty scenic; before embarking, buy the TI's well-described leaflet for this walk (allow 2 hours).

From the parking lot, head to the main road, turn right to cross the river, then turn right again immediately and follow the river up into the hills. After passing a row of cottages, turn left, cross the wooden bridge, and proceed up the hill through the swing gate. Just before the next swing gate, turn left (following *Grisedale* signs) and head to yet another gate. From here you can see the small lake called Lanty's Tarn.

While you'll eventually go through this gate and walk along the lake to finish the loop, first you can detour to the top of the adjacent hill, called Keldas, for sweeping views over the near side of Ullswater (to reach the summit, climb over the step gate and follow the faint path up the hill). Returning to—and passing through—the swing gate, you'll walk along Lanty's Tarn, then begin your slow, steep, and scenic descent into the Grisedale Valley. Reaching the valley floor (and passing a noisy dog breeder's farm), cross the stone bridge, then turn left and follow the road all the way back to the lakefront, where a left turn returns you to Glenridding.

▲AIRA FORCE WATERFALL

Wordsworth was inspired to write three poems at this powerful 60-foot-tall waterfall...and after taking this little walk, you'll know why.

Park at the pay-and-display lot, just where the Troutbeck road from the A-66 hits the lake, on the A-592 between Pooley Bridge and Glenridding. There's a delightful little park with parking, a ranger trailer, and easy trails leading half a mile uphill to the waterfall.

Ullswater steamer boat

Hike the Keldas Hill for a great view.

SOUTH LAKE DISTRICT

The South Lake District has a cheesiness that's similar to other popular English resort destinations. Here, piles of low-end vacationers suffer through terrible traffic, slurp ice cream, and get candy floss caught in their hair.

The area around Windermere is worth a drive-through if you're a fan of Wordsworth or Beatrix Potter, but you'll still want to spend the majority of your Lake District time (and book your accommodations) up north.

Without a car, I'd skip the South Lake District entirely. But Wordsworth fans could take bus #555 from Keswick to Windermere, then catch the hop-on, hop-off Lakeland Experience bus #599, which stops at the Wordsworth sights (3/hour Easter-late Sept, 2/hour late Sept-Oct, 50 minutes each way, £8 Central Lakes Dayrider all-day pass).

Sights
Wordsworth Sights

William Wordsworth was one of the first writers to reject fast-paced city life. During England's Industrial Age, hearts were muzzled and brains ruled. Science was in, machines were taming nature, and factory hours were taming humans. In reaction to these brainy ideals, a rare few—dubbed Romantics—began to embrace untamed nature and undomesticated emotions.

Back then, nobody climbed a mountain just because it was there—but Wordsworth did. He'd "wander lonely as a cloud" through the countryside, finding inspiration in "plain living and high thinking." He soon attracted a circle of like-minded creative friends.

The emotional highs the Romantics felt weren't all natural. Wordsworth and his poet friends Samuel Taylor Coleridge and Thomas de Quincey got stoned on opium and wrote poetry, combining their generation's standard painkiller drug with their tree-hugging passions (Coleridge's opium scale is on view in Dove Cottage). Today, opium is out of vogue, but the Romantic movement thrives as visitors continue to inundate the region.

▲▲DOVE COTTAGE AND WORDSWORTH MUSEUM

For poets, this two-part visit is the top sight of the Lake District. Take a short tour of William Wordsworth's humble cottage, and get inspired in its excellent museum, which displays original writings, sketches, personal items, and fine paintings.

The poet whose appreciation of nature and a back-to-basics lifestyle put this area on the map spent his most productive years (1799-1808) in this well-preserved stone cottage on the edge of Grasmere. After functioning as the Dove and Olive Bow pub for almost 200 years, it was bought by his family. This is where Wordsworth got married, had kids, and wrote much of his best poetry. Still owned by the Wordsworth family, the furniture was his, and the place comes with some amazing artifacts, including the poet's passport and suitcase (he packed light). Even during his lifetime, Wordsworth was famous, and Dove Cottage was turned into a museum in 1891—it's now protected by the Wordsworth Trust.

Cost and Hours: £8.95, daily 9:30-17:30, Nov-Feb 10:00-16:30 except closed Jan and for events in Dec and Feb (call

Dove Cottage

Wordsworth at Dove Cottage

Lake District homeboy William Wordsworth (1770-1850) was born in Cockermouth and schooled in Hawkshead. But the 30-year-old man who moved into Dove Cottage in 1799 was not the carefree lad who'd once roamed the district's lakes and fields.

At Cambridge University, he'd been a C student, graduating with no job skills and no interest in a career. Instead, he hiked through Europe, where he had an epiphany of the "sublime" atop Switzerland's Alps. He lived a year in France during its Revolution, which stirred his soul. He fell in love with a Frenchwoman who bore his daughter, Caroline. But lack of money forced him to return to England, and the outbreak of war with France kept them apart.

Pining away in London, William hung out in the pubs and coffeehouses with fellow radicals, where he met poet Samuel Taylor Coleridge. They inspired each other to write, edited each other's work, and jointly published a groundbreaking book of poetry.

In 1799, his head buzzing with words and ideas, William and his sister (and soul mate), Dorothy, moved into the former inn now known as Dove Cottage. He came into a small inheritance and dedicated himself to poetry full time. In 1802, with the war temporarily over, William returned to France to finally meet his daughter. (He wrote of the rich experience: "It is a beauteous evening, calm and free... / Dear child! Dear Girl! that walkest with me here, / If thou appear untouched by solemn thought, / Thy nature is not therefore less divine.")

Having achieved closure, Wordsworth returned home to marry a former kindergarten classmate, Mary. She moved into Dove Cottage, along with an initially jealous Dorothy. Three of their five children were born here, and the cottage was also home to Mary's sister, family dog Pepper (a gift from Sir Walter Scott), and frequent houseguests Scott, Coleridge, and Thomas de Quincey.

At Dove Cottage, Wordsworth penned his masterpieces. But after almost nine years, his family and social status had outgrown the humble cottage. They moved first to a house in Grasmere before settling down in Rydal Hall. After the Dove years, Wordsworth wrote less, settled into a regular job, drifted to the right politically, and was branded a sellout by some old friends. Still, his poetry—most of it written at Dove—became increasingly famous, and he died honored as England's Poet Laureate.

ahead), café, bus #555 from Keswick, bus #555 or #599 from Windermere, tel. 015394/35544, www.wordsworth.org.uk. Pay parking in the Dove Cottage lot off the main road (A-591), 50 yards from the site.

Visiting the Cottage and Museum: Even if you're not a fan, Wordsworth's appreciation of nature, his Romanticism, and the ways his friends unleashed their creative talents with such abandon are appealing. The 25-minute cottage tour (which departs regularly—you shouldn't have to wait more than 30 minutes) and adjoining museum, with lots of actual manuscripts handwritten by Wordsworth and his illustrious friends, are both excellent. In dry weather, the garden where the poet was much inspired is worth a wander. (Visit this after leaving the cottage tour

Wordsworth's Poetry

At Dove Cottage, Wordsworth was immersed in the beauty of nature. The following are select lines from two well-known poems from this fertile time.

Ode: Intimations of Immortality

There was a time when meadow, grove, and stream,
The earth, and every common sight, to me did seem
　Apparelled in celestial light,
　　The glory and the freshness of a dream.
It is not now as it hath been of yore;
　　Turn wheresoe'er I may,
　　By night or day,
The things which I have seen I now can see no more.

I Wandered Lonely as a Cloud (Daffodils)

I wandered lonely as a cloud
That floats on high o'er vales and hills,
When all at once I saw a crowd,
A host, of golden daffodils;
Beside the lake, beneath the trees,
Fluttering and dancing in the breeze.
. . . .

For oft, when on my couch I lie
　In vacant or in pensive mood,
They flash upon that inward eye
　Which is the bliss of solitude;
And then my heart with pleasure fills,
And dances with the daffodils.

and pick up the description at the back door. The garden is closed when wet.) Allow 1.5 hours for this visit.

At the Wordsworth Museum

▲RYDAL MOUNT

Located just down the road from Dove Cottage, this sight is worthwhile for Wordsworth fans. The poet's final, higher-class home, with a lovely garden and view, lacks the humble charm of Dove Cottage, but still evokes the time and creative spirit of the literary giant who lived here for 37 years. His family repurchased it in 1969 (after a 100-year gap), and his great-great-great-granddaughter still calls it home on occasion, as shown by recent family photos sprinkled throughout the house. After a short intro by the attendant, you'll be given an explanatory flier and are welcome to roam. Wander through the garden William himself designed, which has changed little since then. Surrounded by his nature, you can imagine the poet enjoying them with you. "O happy garden! Whose seclusion deep hath been so friendly to industrious hours; and to soft slumbers, that did gently steep our spirits, carrying with them dreams of flowers, and wild notes warbled among leafy bowers."

Cost and Hours: £7.50; daily 9:30-17:00, Nov and Feb 11:00-16:00 and closed Mon-Tue, closed all of Dec-Jan; occasionally closed for private functions—check website; tearoom, 1.5 miles north of Ambleside, well-signed, free and easy parking, bus #555 from Keswick, tel. 015394/33002, www.rydalmount.co.uk.

Beatrix Potter Sights

Beatrix Potter was a beloved author of children's books, of which the most well-known is *The Tale of Peter Rabbit*. Of the many commercial ventures in the Lake District that seek to capitalize on her popularity, there are two serious Beatrix Potter sights: her farm (Hill Top Farm) and her husband's former office, which is now the Beatrix Potter Gallery, filled with her sketches and paintings. The sights are two miles apart: Beatrix Potter Gallery is in Hawkshead, a cute but extremely touristy town that's a 20-minute drive south of Ambleside; Hill Top Farm is south of Hawkshead, in Near Sawrey village. The Hawkshead TI is inside the Ooh-La-La gift shop right across from the parking lot (tel. 015394/36946).

On busy summer days, the wait to get into Hill Top Farm can last several hours (only 8 people are allowed in every 5 minutes, and the timed-entry tickets must be purchased in person). If you like quaint towns engulfed in Potter tourism (Hawkshead), this extra waiting time can be a blessing. Otherwise, you'll wish you were in the woods somewhere with Wordsworth.

▲HILL TOP FARM

A hit with Beatrix Potter fans (and skippable for others), this dark and intimate cottage, swallowed up in the inspirational and rough nature around it, provides an enjoyable if quick experience. The six-room farm was left just as it was when she died in 1943. At her request, the house is set as if she had just stepped out—flowers on the tables, fire on, low lights. While there's no printed information here, guides in each room are eager to explain things. Fans of her classic *The Tale of Samuel Whiskers* will recognize the home's rooms, furniture, and views—the book and its illustrations were inspired by an invasion of rats when she bought this place.

Cost and Hours: Farmhouse-£10.90, tickets often sell out by 14:00 or even earlier during busy times; gardens-free; June-Aug daily 10:00-17:30; mid-Feb-May and Sept-Oct until 16:30 and closed Fri; Nov-Dec until 15:30 and closed Mon-Thu;

Rydal Mount

Hill Top Farm

Beatrix Potter (1866-1943)

As a girl growing up in London, Beatrix Potter vacationed in the Lake District, where she became inspired to write her popular children's books. Unable to get a publisher, she self-published the first two editions of *The Tale of Peter Rabbit* in 1901 and 1902. When she finally landed a publisher, sales of her books were phenomenal. With the money she made, she bought Hill Top Farm, a 17th-century cottage, and fixed it up, living there sporadically from 1905 until she married in 1913. Potter was more than a children's book writer; she was a fine artist, an avid gardener, and a successful farmer. She married a lawyer and put her knack for business to use, amassing a 4,000-acre estate. An early conservationist, she used the garden-cradled cottage as a place to study nature. She willed it—along with the rest of her vast estate—to the National Trust, which she enthusiastically supported.

closed Jan-mid-Feb; tel. 015394/36269, www.nationaltrust.org.uk/hill-top.

Buying Tickets: You must buy tickets in person. To beat the lines, get to the ticket office when it opens—15 minutes before Hill Top starts its first tour. If you can't make it early, call the farm for the current wait times (if no one answers, leave a message for the administrator; someone will call you back).

Getting There: Mountain Goat Tours runs a shuttle bus from across the Hawk-shead TI to the farm every 40 minutes (tel. 015394/45161). Drivers can take the B-5286 and B-5285 from Ambleside or the B-5285 from Coniston—be prepared for extremely narrow roads with no shoulders that are often lined with stone walls. Park and buy tickets 150 yards down the road, and walk back to tour the place.

▲BEATRIX POTTER GALLERY

Located in the cute but extremely touristy town of Hawkshead, this gallery fills Beatrix's husband's former law office with

Hill Top Farm, Beatrix Potter's home

Beatrix Potter Gallery

the wonderful and intimate drawings and watercolors that she did to illustrate her books. Each year the museum highlights a new theme and brings out a different set of her paintings, drawings, and other items. Unlike Hill Top, the gallery has plenty of explanation about her life and work, including touchscreen displays and information panels. Even non-Potter fans will find this museum rather charming and her art surprisingly interesting.

Cost and Hours: £6.50, daily 10:30-16:00, closed Nov-mid-Feb, Main Street, drivers use the nearby pay-and-display lot and walk 200 yards to the town center, tel. 015394/36355, www.nationaltrust.org.uk/beatrix-potter-gallery.

TRANSPORTATION

Getting Around the Lake District

By Car

Nothing is very far from Keswick and Derwentwater. Pick up a good map (any hotel can loan you one), get off the big roads, and leave the car, at least occasionally, for some walking. In summer, the Keswick-Ambleside-Windermere-Bowness corridor (A-591) suffers from congestion. Back lanes are far less trampled and lead you through forgotten villages, where sheep outnumber people and stone churchyards are filled with happily permanent residents.

To **rent a car** here, try Enterprise in Penrith. They'll pick you up in Keswick and drive you back to their office to get the car, and also drive you back to Keswick after you've dropped it off (Mon-Fri 8:00-18:00, Sat 9:00-12:00, closed Sun, requires drivers license and second ID, reserve a day in advance, located at the David Hayton Peugeot dealer, Haweswater Road, tel. 01768/893 840). Larger outfits are more likely to have a branch in Carlisle, which is a bit to the north but well-served by train (on the same Glasgow-Birmingham line as Penrith) and only a few minutes farther from the Keswick area.

Parking is tight throughout the region. It's easiest to park in the pay-and-display lots (generally about £3/2-3 hours, £5/4-5 hours, and £8/12 hours; have coins on hand; most machines don't make change or won't take credit cards without a chip). If you're parking for free on the roadside, don't block vital turnouts. Never park on double yellow lines.

By Bus

Those based in Keswick without a car manage fine. Because of the region's efforts to "green up" travel and cut down on car traffic, the bus service is quite efficient for hiking and sightseeing.

Keswick has no real bus station; buses stop at a turnout in front of the Booths supermarket. Local buses take you quickly and easily (if not always frequently) to all nearby points of interest. Check the schedule carefully to make sure you can catch the last bus home.

The *Lakes Connection* booklet explains the schedules (available at TIs or on any bus). On board, you can purchase an Explorer pass that lets you ride any Stagecoach bus throughout the area (£11/1 day, £25/3 days), or you can get one-day passes for certain routes; tickets can also be purchased with a credit card via the Stagecoach Bus app. The Derwentwater Bus & Boat all-day pass covers the #77/#77A bus and a boat cruise on Derwentwater. For bus and rail info, visit www.stagecoachbus.com and set your location for Keswick.

Buses **#X4** and **#X5** connect Penrith train station to Keswick (hourly, every 2 hours on Sun Nov-April, 45 minutes).

Bus **#77/#77A,** the Honister Rambler, makes the gorgeous circle from Keswick around Derwentwater, over Honister Pass, through Buttermere, and down the Whinlatter Valley (5-7/day clockwise, 4/day "anticlockwise," daily Easter-Oct, 1.75-hour loop). Bus **#78,** the Borrowdale Rambler, goes topless in the summer, affording a wonderful sightseeing experience in and of itself, heading from Keswick to Lodore Hotel, Grange, Rosthwaite, and Seatoller at the base of Honister Pass (hourly, daily Easter-Oct, 2/hour July-Sept, 30 minutes each way). Both of these routes are covered by the £8 Keswick and Honister Dayrider all-day pass.

Bus **#508,** the Kirkstone Rambler, runs between Penrith and Glenridding (near the bottom of Ullswater), stopping in Pooley Bridge (5/day, more frequent June-Aug with open-top buses, 50 minutes). Bus #508 also connects Glenridding and Windermere (1 hour). The £15 Ullswater Bus & Boat all-day pass covers bus #508 as well as steamers on Ullswater.

Bus **#505,** the Coniston Rambler, connects Windermere with Hawkshead (about hourly, daily Easter-Oct, 35 minutes).

Bus **#555** connects Keswick with the south (hourly, more frequent in summer, 1 hour to Windermere).

Bus #599, the open-top Lakeland Experience, runs along the main Windermere corridor, connecting the big tourist attractions in the south: Grasmere and Dove Cottage, Rydal Mount, Ambleside, Brockhole (National Park Visitors Centre), Windermere, and lake cruises from Bowness Pier (3/hour June-Sept, 2/hour May and Oct, 50 minutes each way, £8 Central Lakes Dayrider all-day pass).

By Boat

A circular boat service glides you around Derwentwater, with several hiker-aiding stops along the way (for a cruise/hike option, see "Derwentwater Lakeside Walk," earlier).

By Foot

Hiking information is available everywhere. Don't hike without a good, detailed map (wide selection at Keswick TI and at the many outdoor gear stores, or borrow one from your B&B). Helpful fliers at TIs and B&Bs describe the most popular routes. For an up-to-date weather report, ask at a TI or call 0844-846-2444. Wear suitable clothing and footwear (you can rent boots in town). Plan for rain. Watch your footing; injuries are common. Every year, several people die while hiking in the area (some from overexertion; others are blown off ridges).

By Bike

Keswick works well as a springboard for several fine days out on a bike; consider a three-hour loop trip up Newlands Valley. Ask about routes at the TI or your bike rental shop.

Several shops in Keswick rent road and mountain bikes (£20-25/day) and e-bikes (£30-50/day); rentals come with helmets and advice for good trips. Try **Whinlatter Bikes** (Mon-Sat 10:00-17:00, Sun until 16:00; free touring maps, 82 Main Street, tel. 017687/73940, www.whinlatterbikes.com); **e-venture** (daily 9:00-17:30, Elliot Park, tel. 0778/382 2722, www.e-venturebikes.co.uk); or **Keswick Bikes** (daily 9:00-17:30, 133 Main Street, tel. 017687/73355, www.keswickbikes.co.uk).

Arriving and Departing

The nearest train station to Keswick is in **Penrith** (no lockers). For train and bus info, check at a TI, visit www.traveline.org.uk, or call 0345-748-4950 (for train), or 0871-200-2233. Most routes run less frequently on Sundays.

By Train

From Penrith to: Stratford (4 hours, change in Birmingham), **Liverpool**

(hourly, 2.5 hours, change in Wigan or Preston), **Durham** (hourly, 3 hours, change in Carlisle and Newcastle), **York** (roughly 2/hour, 4 hours, 1-2 transfers), **London**'s Euston Station (hourly, 4 hours), **Edinburgh** (9/day direct, 2 hours).

By Bus
From Penrith to: Keswick (hourly, every 2 hours on Sun in Nov-April, 45 minutes, pay driver, Stagecoach bus #X4 or #X5),

Ullswater and **Glenridding** (5/day, more frequent June-Aug with open-top buses, 50 minutes, bus #508). The Penrith bus stop is just outside the train station (bus schedules posted inside and outside station).

By Car
The direct, easy way to Keswick is to leave the M-6 at Penrith and take the A-66 motorway for 16 miles to Keswick.

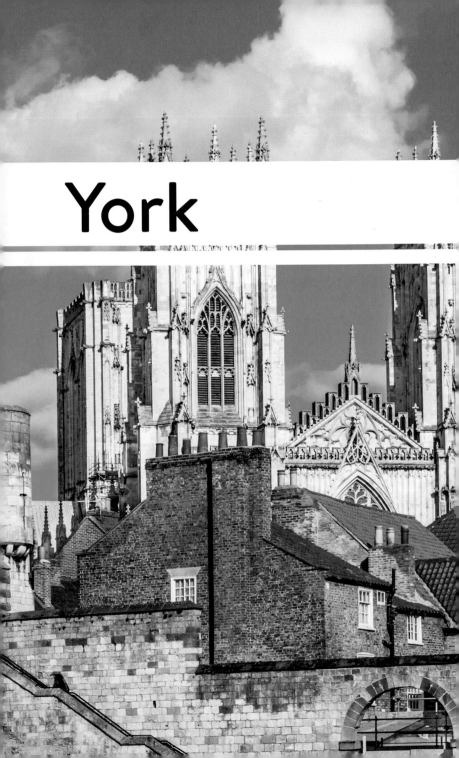

York

Historic York is loaded with world-class sights. Marvel at the York Minster, England's finest Gothic church. Ramble The Shambles, York's wonderfully preserved medieval quarter. Enjoy a walking tour led by an old Yorker. Hop a train at one of the world's greatest railway museums, travel to the 1800s in the York Castle Museum, head back 1,000 years to Viking times at the Jorvik Viking Centre, or dig into the city's buried past at the Yorkshire Museum.

York has a rich history. In A.D. 71 it was Eboracum, a Roman provincial capital—the northernmost city in the empire. Constantine was proclaimed emperor here in A.D. 306. In the fifth century, as Rome was toppling, the Roman emperor sent a letter telling England it was on its own, and York—now called Eoforwic—became the capital of the Anglo-Saxon kingdom of Northumbria.

The Vikings later took the town, and from the 9th through the 11th century, it was a Danish trading center called Jorvik. The invading and conquering Normans destroyed, and then rebuilt the city, fortifying it with a castle and the walls you see today.

Medieval York, with 9,000 inhabitants, grew rich on the wool trade and became England's second city. Henry VIII used the city's fine Minster as the northern capital of his Anglican Church.

In the Industrial Age, York was the railway hub of northern England. When it was built, York's train station was the world's largest. During World War II, Hitler chose to bomb York by picking the city out of a travel guidebook (not this one).

Today, York's leading industry is tourism. Everything that's great about Britain finds its best expression here. With its strollable cobbles and half-timbered buildings, grand cathedral, excellent museums, thriving restaurant scene, and welcoming locals, York entertains.

YORK AT A GLANCE

▲▲▲**York Minster** York's pride and joy, and one of England's finest churches, with stunning stained-glass windows, textbook Decorated Gothic design, and glorious evensong services. **Hours:** Mon-Sat 9:00-18:30, Sun 12:30-18:30; shorter hours for tower and undercroft; evensong services Tue-Sat and some Mon at 17:15, Sun at 16:00. See page 282.

▲▲▲**Walking Tours** Variety of guided town walks and evening ghost walks covering York's history. See page 275.

▲▲**Yorkshire Museum** Sophisticated archaeology and natural history museum with York's best Viking exhibit, plus Roman, Saxon, Norman, and Gothic artifacts. **Hours:** Daily 10:00-17:00. See page 287.

▲▲**Jorvik Viking Centre** Entertaining and informative Disney-style exhibit/ride exploring Viking lifestyles and artifacts. **Hours:** Daily 10:00-17:00, Nov-March until 16:00. See page 289.

▲▲**York Castle Museum** Far-ranging collection displaying everyday objects from Victorian times to the present. **Hours:** Daily 9:30-17:00. See page 289.

▲▲**National Railway Museum** Train buff's nirvana, tracing the history of all manner of rail-bound transport. **Hours:** Daily 10:00-18:00. See page 291.

▲**The Shambles** Atmospheric old butchers' quarter, with colorful, tipsy medieval buildings. See page 281.

▲**York Brewery** Honest, casual tour through an award-winning microbrewery with the guy who makes the beer. **Hours:** Mon-Sat at 12:30, 14:00, 15:30, and 17:00. See page 293.

▲**Fairfax House** Glimpse into an 18th-century Georgian family house, with enjoyably chatty docents. **Hours:** Tue-Sat 10:00-16:30, Sun 11:00-15:30, Mon by tour only at 11:00 and 14:00, closed Jan-mid-Feb. See page 289.

YORK IN 2 DAYS

Day 1: Take the free city walking tour on your first day. It's offered in the morning and afternoon (and in the summer, also in the evening).

After lunch, tour the Yorkshire Museum (or save it for tomorrow morning, before the self-guided walk). Visit the York Minster, and attend the evensong service (Tue-Sat at 17:15, Sun at 16:00).

On any evening: Splurge on dinner at one of the city's bistros (cheaper if you go before 19:00). Enjoy the ghost walk of your choice (or the free city walking tour in summer). Stroll or bike along the riverside path, or settle in at a pub.

Day 2: Take my self-guided York Walk, which starts from the Yorkshire Museum's garden. Explore the Shambles if it appeals.

In the afternoon, tour any of these fine museums: York Castle Museum, National Railway Museum, or the Fairfax House.

If you want to visit the popular Jorvik Viking Centre, you'll minimize your time in line if you go early, late, or pay a bit extra for a timed-entry ticket.

Have afternoon tea at an elegant tearoom (such as Bettys Café or Grays Court). Or go for a tasting at the York Brewery (afternoon tours Mon-Sat).

ORIENTATION

There are roughly 200,000 people in York and its surrounding area; about one in ten is a student. But despite the city's size, the sightseer's York is small. Virtually everything is within a few minutes' walk: sights, train station, TI, and B&Bs. The longest walk a visitor might take (from a B&B across the old town to the York Castle Museum) is about 25 minutes.

Bootham Bar, a gate in the medieval town wall, is the hub of your York visit. (In York, a "bar" is a gate and a "gate" is a street. Blame the Vikings.) At Bootham Bar and on Exhibition Square, you'll find the starting points for most walking tours

and bus tours, handy access to the medieval town wall, a public WC, and Bootham Street (which leads to my recommended B&Bs). To find your way around York, use the Minster's towers as a navigational landmark, or follow the strategically placed signposts, which point out all places of interest to tourists.

Tourist Information

York's TI is a block in front of the Minster (Mon-Sat 9:00-17:00, Sun 10:00-16:00, 1 Museum Street, tel. 01904/550-099, www. visityork.org).

Rick's Tip: *The TI sells a* **pricey sightseeing pass.** *You'd have to be a very busy sightseer to make this pass worth the cost (£38/1 day, multiday options available, www. yorkpass.com).*

Helpful Hints

Festivals: The **Viking Festival** features lur horn-blowing, warrior drills, and re-created battles in mid-February (www.jorvik-viking-centre.co.uk). The **Early Music Festival** (medieval minstrels, Renaissance dance, and so on) zings its strings in early July (www.ncem.co.uk/yemf.shtml). York fills up on horse-race weekends (once a month May-Oct, check schedules at www.yorkracecourse.co.uk). The **York Food and Drink Festival** takes a bite out of late September (www.yorkfoodfestival. com). And the St. Nicholas Fair Christmas market jingles its bells from mid-Novem-

Take a walking tour in York.

ber through Christmas. For a complete list of festivals, see YorkFestivals.com.

Laundry: Some B&Bs will do laundry for a reasonable charge. Otherwise the nearest place is **Haxby Road Launderette,** a long 15-minute walk north of the town center (or you can take a bus—ask your B&B for directions, 124 Haxby Road, call ahead for prices and hours—tel. 01904/623-379).

Tours
▲▲▲ *Walking Tours*
Free two-hour walks are offered by charming local volunteers who are energetic and entertaining. These tours often go long because the guides love to teach and tell stories. You're welcome to cut out early—but let them know, or they'll worry, thinking they've lost you (April-Oct daily at 10:15 and 14:15, June-Aug also at 18:15; Nov-March daily at 10:15 and 13:15; depart from Exhibition Square in front of the art gallery, tel. 01904/550-098, www.avgyork. co.uk).

Yorkwalk Tours are serious 1.5- to 2-hour walks with a history focus. They do four different walks—Essential York, Roman York, Secret York, and The Snickelways of York—as well as a variety of "special walks" on more specific topics. Tours go rain or shine, with as few as two participants (£6, daily at 10:30 and 14:15, no tours Dec-Jan, depart from Museum Gardens Gate, just show up, tel. 07970/848-709, www.yorkwalk.co.uk—check website, ask TI, or call to confirm schedule).

Rick's Tip: Hop-on, hop-off buses *circle York, taking tourists past secondary sights on the mundane perimeter of town. For most visitors,* **walking tours are a better choice.**

Ghost Walks
Each evening, the old center of York is crawling with creepy ghost walks. These

are generally 1.5 hours long, cost £5, and go rain or shine. There are no reservations (you simply show up) and no tickets (just pay at the start). At the advertised time and place, your black-clad guide appears, and you follow him or her to the first stop. Your guide gives a sample of the entertainment you have in store, humorously collects the "toll," and you're off.

Companies come and go, but I find there are three general styles of walks: historic, street theater, and storytelling (ask about RS%, limit two "victims").

The **Terror Trail Walk** is more historic, "all true," and a bit more intellectual (daily at 18:45, meet at The Golden Fleece at bottom of The Shambles, www. yorkterrortrail.co.uk).

The **Bloody Tour of York,** led by Mad Alice (an infamous figure in York lore), is an engaging walk with tales of history, violence, and mayhem (Thu-Sat at 18:00, also at 20:00 in April-Oct, no tours Sun-Wed, Dec-Jan by reservation only, meet outside St. Williams College behind the Minster on College Street, www.the-bloodytourofyork.co.uk).

The **Original Ghost Walk** was the first of its kind, dating back to the 1970s, and is more classic spooky storytelling rather than comedy (daily at 20:00, meet at The Kings Arms at Ouse Bridge, www. theoriginalghostwalkofyork.co.uk).

YORK WALK

Get a taste of Roman and medieval York on this easy, self-guided stroll, which begins just in front of the Yorkshire Museum, covers a stretch of the medieval city walls, and then cuts through the middle of the old town.

◑ Self-Guided Walk
Start at the ruins of...

St. Mary's Abbey: This abbey dates to the age of William the Conqueror—whose harsh policies (called the "Harrowing of the North") consisted of massacres and

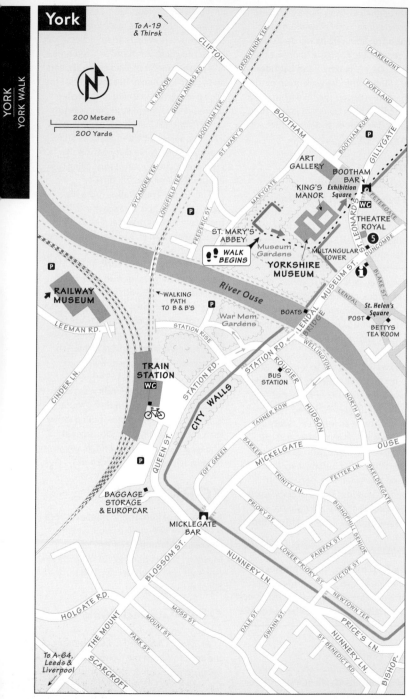

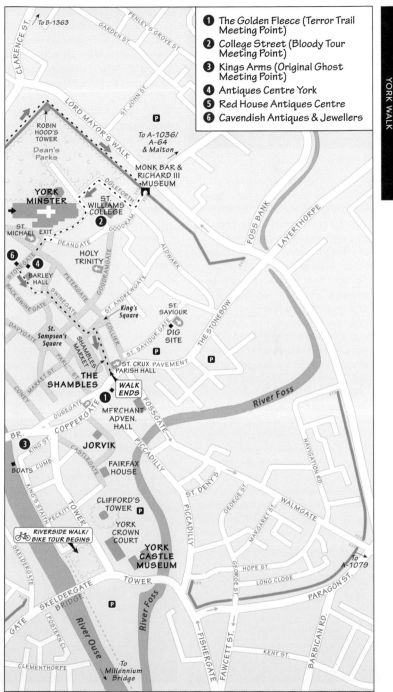

1 The Golden Fleece (Terror Trail Meeting Point)
2 College Street (Bloody Tour Meeting Point)
3 Kings Arms (Original Ghost Meeting Point)
4 Antiques Centre York
5 Red House Antiques Centre
6 Cavendish Antiques & Jewellers

St. Mary's Abbey

destruction, including the burning of York's main church. His son Rufus, who tried to improve relations in the 11th century, established a great church here. The church became an abbey that thrived from the 13th century until the dissolution of the monasteries in the 16th century. The dissolution, which accompanied the Protestant Reformation and break with Rome, was a power play by Henry VIII. The king wanted much more than just a divorce: He wanted the land and riches of the monasteries. Upset with the pope, he demanded that his subjects pay him taxes rather than give the Church tithes.

As you gaze at this ruin, imagine magnificent abbeys like this scattered throughout the realm. Henry VIII destroyed most of them, taking the lead from their roofs and leaving the stones to scavenging townsfolk. Scant as they are today, these ruins still evoke a time of immense monastic power. The one surviving wall was the west half of a very long, skinny nave. The tall arch marked the start of the transept. Stand on the nearby plaque that reads *Crossing beneath central tower,* and look up at the air that now fills the space where a huge tower once stood. (Fine carved stonework from the ruined abbey is on display in a basement room of the adjacent Yorkshire Museum.)

• *With your back to the abbey, see the fine Neoclassical building housing the Yorkshire Museum (well worth a visit and described later). Walk past this about 30 yards and turn left, following signs to the York Art Gallery. Ahead to the right is a corner of the city's Roman wall. A tiny lane on the right leads through the garden (past a yew tree) and under a small, gated arch (may be locked), giving a peek into the ruined tower.*

Multangular Tower: This 12-sided tower (c. A.D. 300) was likely a catapult station built to protect the town from enemy river traffic. The red ribbon of bricks was a Roman trademark—both structural and decorative. The lower stones are Roman, while the upper (and bigger) stones are medieval. After Rome fell, York suffered through two centuries of a dark age. Then, in the ninth century, the Vikings ruled. They built with wood, so almost nothing from that period remains. The Normans came in 1066 and built in stone, generally atop Roman structures (like this wall). The wall that defined the ancient Roman garrison town worked for the Norman town, too.

• *Now, return 10 steps down the lane and turn right, walking between the museum and the Roman wall. Continuing straight, the lane goes between the abbot's palace and the town wall. This is a "snickelway"—a small,*

Multangular Tower

Bootham Bar

characteristic York lane or footpath. The snickelway pops out on...

Exhibition Square: With Henry VIII's dissolution of the monasteries, the abbey was destroyed and the Abbot's Palace became the **King's Manor** (from the snickelway, make a U-turn to the left and through the gate). Enter the building under the coat of arms of Charles I, who stayed here during the English Civil War in the 1640s. Today, the building is part of the University of York. Because the northerners were slow to embrace the king's reforms, Henry VIII came here to enforce the dissolution. He stayed 17 days in this mansion and brought along 1,000 troops to make his determination clear.

Exhibition Square is the departure point for various walking and bus tours. You can see the towers of the Minster in the distance. Travelers in the Middle Ages could see the Minster from miles away as they approached the city. Across the street is a pay WC and **Bootham Bar**—one of the fourth-century Roman gates in York's wall—with access to the best part of the city walls (free, walls open 8:00-dusk).

• *Climb up the bar.*

Walk the Wall: Hike along the top of the wall behind the Minster to the first corner. Just because you see a padlock on an entry gate, don't think it's locked—give it a push, and you'll probably find it's open. York's 13th-century walls are three miles long. This stretch follows the original Roman wall. Norman kings built the walls to assert control over northern England. Notice the pivots in the crenellations (square notches at the top of a medieval wall), which once held wooden hatches to provide cover for archers. The wall was extensively renovated in the 19th century (Victorians added Romantic arrow slits).

At the corner with the benches—**Robin Hood's Tower**—you can lean out and see the moat outside. This was originally the Roman ditch that surrounded the fortified garrison town. Continue walking for a fine view of the Minster, with its truncated main tower and the pointy rooftop of its chapter house.

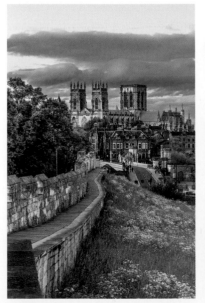

City walls

Monk Bar

Ⓐ *York's Old Town*

Ⓑ *Constantine statue*

Ⓒ *Snickelways*

Ⓓ *The Shambles*

Continue on to the next gate, **Monk Bar.** This fine medieval gatehouse is the home of the overly slick Richard III Museum.

• *Descend the wall at Monk Bar, and step past the portcullis behind you (last lowered in 1953 for the Queen's coronation) to emerge outside the city's protective wall. Take 10 paces and gaze up at the tower. Imagine 10 archers behind the arrow slits. Keep an eye on the 17th-century guards, with their stones raised and primed to protect the town.*

Return through the city wall. After a short block, turn right on Ogleforth.

York's Old Town: Walking down Ogle-forth, ogle (on your left) a charming little brick house from the 17th century called the **Dutch House.** It was designed by an apprentice architect who was trying to show off for his master, and was the first entirely brick house in town—a sign of opulence. Next, also of brick, is a former brewery, with a 19th-century industrial feel.

Ogleforth jogs left and becomes **Chapter House Street,** passing the Treasurer's House to the back side of the Minster. Circle around the left side of the church, past the stonemasons' lodge (where craftsmen are chiseling local lime-stone for the church, as has been done here since the 13th century), to the statue of Roman Emperor Constantine and an ancient Roman column.

Step up to lounging **Constantine.** Five emperors visited York when it was the Roman city of Eboracum. Constantine was here when his father died. The troops declared him the Roman emperor in A.D. 306 at this site, and six years later, he went to Rome to claim his throne. In A.D. 312, Constantine legalized Christianity, and in A.D. 314, York got its first bishop.

The **ancient column,** across the street from Constantine, is a reminder that the Minster sits upon the site of the Roman headquarters, or *principia.* The city placed this column here in 1971, just before cel-ebrating the 1,900th anniversary of the founding of Eboracum—a.k.a. York.

• *If you want to visit the York Minster now,*

find the entrance on its west side, ahead and around the corner. Otherwise, head into the town center. From opposite the Minster's south transept door (the door by Constantine), take a narrow pedestrian walkway—which becomes Stonegate—into the tangled commercial center of medieval York. Walk straight down Stonegate, a street lined with fun and inviting cafés, pubs, and restaurants. Just before the Ye Old Starre Inne banner hanging over the street, turn left down the snickelway called Coffee Yard. (It's marked by a red devil.) Enjoy strolling York's...

"Snickelways": This is a made-up York word combining "snicket" (a passageway between walls or fences), "ginnel" (a narrow passageway between buildings), and "alleyway" (any narrow passage)—snickelway. York—with its population packed densely inside its protective walls—has about 50 of these public passages. In general, when exploring the city, you should duck into these—both for the adventure and to take a shortcut. While some of York's history has been bulldozed by modernity, bits of it hide and survive in the snickelways.

Coffee Yard leads past Barley Hall, popping out at the corner of Grape Lane and Swinegate. Medieval towns named streets for the business done there. Swinegate, a lane of pig farmers, leads to the market. Grape Lane is a polite version of that street's original crude name, Gropec*nt Lane. If you were here a thousand years ago, you'd find it lined by brothels. Throughout England, streets for prostitutes were called by this graphic name. Today, if you see a street named Grape Lane, that's usually its heritage.

Skip Grape Lane and turn right down Swinegate to a market (which you can see in the distance). The recently upgraded **Shambles Market,** popular for cheap produce and clothing, was created in the 1960s with the demolition of a bunch of colorful medieval lanes.

• In the center of the market, tiny "Little Shambles" lane (on the left) dead-ends into the most famous lane in York.

The Shambles: This colorful old street (rated ▲) was once the "street of the butchers." The name was derived from "shammell"—a butcher's bench upon which he'd cut and display his meat. In the 16th century, this lane was dripping with red meat. Look for the hooks under the eaves; these were once used to hang rabbit, pheasant, beef, lamb, and pigs' heads. Fresh slabs were displayed on the fat sills, while people lived above the shops. All the garbage and sewage flushed down the street to a mucky pond at the end—a favorite hangout for the town's cats and dogs. Tourist shops now fill these fine, half-timbered Tudor buildings.

Turn right and slalom down The Shambles. Just past the tiny sandwich shop at #37, pop in to the snickelway and look for very old **woodwork.** Study the 16th-century carpentry: mortise-and-tenon joints with wooden plugs rather than nails.

Next door (on The Shambles) is the **shrine of St. Margaret Clitherow,** a 16th-century Catholic crushed by Protestants under her own door (as was the humiliating custom when a city wanted to teach someone a lesson). She was killed for hiding priests in her home. Step into the tiny shrine for a peaceful moment to ponder Margaret, who in 1970 was sainted for her faith.

At the bottom of The Shambles is the cute, tiny **St. Crux Parish Hall,** which charities use to raise funds by selling light meals. Take some time to chat with the volunteers.

With blood and guts from The Shambles' 20 butchers all draining down the lane, it's no wonder The Golden Fleece, just below, is considered the most haunted pub in town.

• Your town walk is finished. From here, you're just a few minutes from plenty of fun: street entertainment and lots of cheap eating options on King's Square, good restaurants on Fossgate, and the York Castle Museum (a few blocks farther downhill).

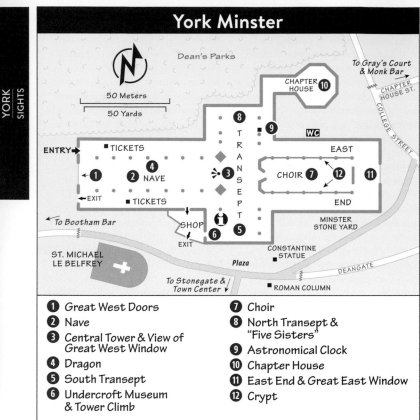

York Minster

- **1** Great West Doors
- **2** Nave
- **3** Central Tower & View of Great West Window
- **4** Dragon
- **5** South Transept
- **6** Undercroft Museum & Tower Climb
- **7** Choir
- **8** North Transept & "Five Sisters"
- **9** Astronomical Clock
- **10** Chapter House
- **11** East End & Great East Window
- **12** Crypt

SIGHTS

Inside York's Walls

▲▲▲YORK MINSTER

The pride of York, this largest Gothic church north of the Alps (540 feet long, 200 feet tall) brilliantly shows that the High Middle Ages were far from dark. The word "minster" means an important church chartered with a mission to evangelize. As it's the seat of a bishop, York Minster is also a cathedral. While Henry VIII destroyed England's great abbeys, this was not part of a monastery and was therefore left standing. It seats 2,000 comfortably; on Christmas and Easter, at least 4,000 worshippers pack the place. Today, more than 250 employees and 500 volunteers work to preserve its heritage and welcome 1.3 million visitors each year.

Cost: £10, includes guided tour, undercroft museum, and crypt; free for kids under age 16.

Hours: The cathedral is open for sightseeing Mon-Sat 9:00-18:30, Sun 12:30-18:30. It opens for worship daily at 7:30. Closing time flexes with activities, but last entry is generally at 17:00—call or look online to confirm. Sights within the Minster have shorter hours (listed later). The Minster may close for special events (check calendar on website).

Information: Tel. 01904/557-217 or 0844-393-0011, www.yorkminster.org.

Visitor Information: You'll get a free map with your ticket. For more information, pick up the inexpensive York Minster

Short Guide. Helpful Minster guides stationed throughout are happy to answer your questions.

Tower Climb: It costs £5 for 30 minutes of exercise (275 steps) and forgettable views. The tower opens at 10:00 (13:00 on Sun), with ascents every 45 minutes; the last ascent is generally at 17:30—later in peak season and earlier in winter (no children under 8, not good for acrophobes, closes in extreme weather). Be sure to get your ticket upon arrival, as only 50 visitors are allowed up at once; you'll be assigned an entry time.

Undercroft Museum: This museum focuses on the history of the site and its origins as a Roman fortress (Mon-Sat 10:00-17:00, Sun 13:00-16:00).

Tours: Free guided tours depart from the ticket desk every hour on the hour (Mon-Sat 10:00-15:00, can be more frequent during busy times, none on Sun, one hour, they go even with just one or two people). You can join a tour in progress, or if none is scheduled, request a departure.

Evensong: To experience the cathedral in musical and spiritual action, attend an evensong (Tue-Sat at 17:15, Sun at 16:00). On Mondays, visiting choirs fill in about half the time (otherwise it's a spoken service, also at 17:15). Visiting choirs also perform when the Minster's choir is on summer break (mid-July-Aug, confirm at church or TI). Arrive 15 minutes early and wait just outside the choir in the center of the church. You'll be ushered in and can sit in one of the big wooden stalls. As evensong is a worship service, attendees enter the church free of charge. For more on evensong, see page 104.

Church Bells: If you're a fan of church bells, you'll experience ding-dong ecstasy Sunday morning at about 10:00 and during the Tuesday practice session between 19:00 and 22:00. These performances are especially impressive, as the church holds a full carillon of 35 bells (it's the only English cathedral to have such a range). Stand in front of the church's west portal and imagine the gang pulling on a dozen ropes (halfway up the right tower—you can actually see the ropes through a little window) while one talented carillonneur plays 22 more bells with a keyboard and foot pedals.

○ SELF-GUIDED TOUR

Enter the great church through the west portal (under the twin towers). Upon entering, decide whether you're climbing the tower. If so, get a ticket (with an assigned time). Also consider visiting the undercroft museum (described later) if you want to get a comprehensive history and overview of the Minster before touring the church.

• *Entering the church, turn 180 degrees and look back at the...*

❶ **Great West Doors:** These are used only on special occasions. Flanking the doors is a list of archbishops (and other church officials) that goes unbroken back to the 600s. The statue of Peter with the key and Bible is a reminder that the church is dedicated to St. Peter, and the key to heaven is found through the word of God. While the Minster sits on

York Minster, south transept

The Church of England

The Anglican Church (a.k.a. the Church of England) came into existence in 1534 when Henry VIII declared that he, and not Pope Clement VII, was the head of England's Catholics. The pope had refused to allow Henry to divorce his wife to marry his mistress Anne Boleyn (which Henry did anyway, resulting in the birth of Elizabeth I). Still, Henry regarded himself as a faithful Catholic—just not a *Roman* Catholic—and made relatively few changes in how and what Anglicans worshipped.

Henry's son, Edward VI, later instituted many of the changes that Reformation Protestants were bringing about in continental Europe: an emphasis on preaching, people in the pews actually reading the Bible, clergy being allowed to marry, and a more "Protestant" liturgy in English from the revised Book of Common Prayer (1549). The next monarch, Edward's sister Mary I, returned England to the Roman Catholic Church (1553), earning the nickname "Bloody Mary" for her brutal suppression of Protestant elements. When Elizabeth I succeeded Mary (1558), she soon broke from Rome again. Today, many regard the Anglican Church as a compromise between the Catholic and Protestant traditions. In the US, Anglicans split off from the Church in England after the American Revolution, creating the Episcopal Church that still thrives today.

Ever since Henry VIII's time, the York Minster has held a special status within the Anglican hierarchy. After a long feud over which was the leading church, the archbishops of Canterbury and York agreed that York's bishop would have the title "Primate of England" and Canterbury's would be the "Primate of All England," directing Anglicans on the national level.

the remains of a Romanesque church (c. 1100), today's church was begun in 1220 and took 250 years to complete. Up above, look for the female, headless "semaphore saints," using semaphore flag code to spell out a message with golden discs: "Christ is here."

• *Grab a chair and enjoy the view down the...*

❷ **Nave:** Your first impression might be of its spaciousness and brightness. One of the widest Gothic naves in Europe, it was built between 1280 and 1360—the middle period of the Gothic style, called "Decorated Gothic." Rather than risk a stone roof, builders spanned the space with wood. Colorful shields on the arcades are the coats of arms of nobles who helped tall and formidable Edward I, known as "Longshanks," fight the Scots in the 13th century.

The coats of arms in the clerestory (upper-level) glass represent the nobles who helped his son, Edward II, in the same fight. There's more medieval glass in this building than in the rest of England combined. This precious glass survived World War II—hidden in stately homes throughout Yorkshire.

Walk to the very center of the church, under the ❸ **central tower.** Look up. An exhibit in the undercroft explains how gifts and skill saved this 197-foot tower from collapse. Use the neck-saving mirror to marvel at it.

Look back at the west end to marvel at the **Great West Window,** especially the stone tracery. While its nickname is the "Heart of Yorkshire," it represents the sacred heart of Christ, meant to remind people of his love for the world.

Choir screen with carvings of English monarchs

Find the ❹ **dragon** on the right of the nave (two-thirds of the way up the wall, affixed to the top of a pillar). While no one is sure of its purpose, it pivots and has a hole through its neck—so it was likely a mechanism designed to raise a lid on a baptismal font.

• *Facing the altar, turn right and head into the...*

❺ **South Transept:** Look up. The new "bosses" (carved medallions decorating the point where the ribs meet on the ceiling) are a reminder that the roof of this wing of the church was destroyed by fire in 1984, caused when lightning hit an electricity box. Some believe the lightning was God's angry response to a new bishop, David Jenkins, who questioned the literal truth of Jesus' miracles. (Jenkins had been interviewed at a nearby TV studio the night before, leading locals to joke that the lightning occurred "12 hours too late, and 17 miles off-target.")

Two other sights can be accessed through the south transept: the ❻ **Undercroft Museum** (explained later) and the **tower climb** (explained earlier). But for now, stick with this tour; we'll circle back to the south transept at the end, before exiting the church.

• *Head back into the middle of the nave and face the front of the church. You're looking at the...*

❼ **Choir:** Examine the choir screen—the ornate wall of carvings separating the nave from the choir. It's lined with all the English kings from William I (the Conqueror) to Henry VI (during whose reign it was carved, in 1461). Numbers indicate the years each reigned. It is indeed "slathered in gold leaf," which sounds impressive, but the gold is very thin...a nugget the size of a sugar cube is pounded into a sheet the size of a driveway.

Step into the choir, where a service is held daily. All the carving was redone after an 1829 fire, but its tradition of glorious evensong services (sung by choristers from the Minster School) goes all the way back to the eighth century.

• *To the left as you face the choir is the...*

❽ **North Transept:** In this transept, the grisaille windows—dubbed the **"Five Sisters"**—are dedicated to British servicewomen who died in wars. Made in 1260, before colored glass was produced in England, these contain more than 100,000 pieces of glass.

The 18th-century ❾ **astronomical**

clock is worth a look (the sign helps you make sense of it). It's dedicated to the heroic Allied aircrews from bases here in northern England who died in World War II (as Britain kept the Nazis from invading in its "darkest hour"). The Book of Remembrance below the clock contains 18,000 names.

• *A corridor leads to the Gothic, octagonal...*

❿ Chapter House: This was the traditional meeting place of the governing body (or chapter) of the Minster. On the pillar in the middle of the doorway, the Virgin holds Baby Jesus while standing on the devilish serpent. The Chapter House, without an interior support, is remarkable (almost frightening) for its breadth. The fanciful carvings decorating the canopies above the stalls date from 1280 (80 percent are originals) and are some of the Minster's finest. Stroll slowly around the entire room and imagine that the tiny sculpted heads are a 14th-century parade—a fun glimpse of medieval society. Grates still send hot air up robes of attendees on cold winter mornings. A

Chapter House

model of the wooden construction illustrates the impressive 1285 engineering.

The Chapter House was the site of an important moment in England's parliamentary history. Fighting the Scots in 1295, Edward I (the "Longshanks" we met earlier) convened the "Model Parliament" here, rather than down south in London. (The Model Parliament is the name for its early version, back before the legislature was split into the Houses of Commons and Lords.) The government met here through the 20-year reign of Edward II, before moving to London during Edward III's rule in the 14th century.

• *Go back out into the main part of the church, turn left, and continue all the way down the nave (behind the choir) to the...*

⓫ East End: This part of the church is square, lacking a semicircular apse, typical of England's Perpendicular Gothic style (15th century). Monuments (almost no graves) were once strewn throughout the church, but in the Victorian Age, they were gathered into the east end, where you see them today.

The **Great East Window,** the size of a tennis court, may still be under restoration when you visit. In the area beneath the window, the exhibit "Let There Be Light" gives an intimate look at Gothic stone and glasswork. Curators hope that this grand window will finally come out from its scaffolding within a year or two.

Because of the Great East Window's immense size, the east end has an extra layer of supportive stonework, parts of it wide enough to walk along. In fact, for special occasions, the choir has been known to actually sing from the walkway halfway up the window. But just as the window has deteriorated over time, so too has the stone. Nearly 3,500 stones need to be replaced or restored. On some days, you may even see masons in action in the stone yard behind the Minster.

• *Below the choir (on either side), steps lead down to the...*

⓬ Crypt: Here you can view the

boundary of the much smaller, but still huge, Norman church from 1100 that stood on this spot (look for the red dots, marking where the Norman church ended, and note how thick the wall was). You can also see some of the old columns and additional remains from the Roman fortress that once stood here, the tomb of St. William of York (actually a Roman sarcophagus that was reused), and the modern, concrete, save-the-church foundations (much of this church history is covered in the undercroft museum).

• You'll exit the church through the gift shop in the south transept. If you've yet to climb the tower, the entrance is in the south transept before the exit. Also before leaving, look for the entrance to the...

Undercroft Museum: Well-described exhibits follow the history of the site from its origins as a Roman fortress to the founding of an Anglo-Saxon/Viking church, the shift to a Norman place of worship, and finally the construction of the Gothic structure that stands today. Videos re-create how the fortress and Norman structure would have been laid out, and various artifacts and remains provide an insight into each period. The museum fills a space that was excavated following the near collapse of the central tower in 1967. Highlights include the actual remains of the Roman fort's basilica, which are viewable through a see-through floor. There are also patches of Roman frescoes, the Horn of Ulf (an intricately carved elephant's tusk presented to the Minster in 1030 by Ulf, a Viking nobleman), and the York Gospels manuscript (a thousand-year-old text containing the four gospels). Your last stop in the undercroft is a small and comfortable theater where you can enjoy three short videos (10 minutes total) showing the Minster in action. One is about Roman Emperor Constantine and the rise of Christianity, another covers a day in the life of the cathedral (skippable), and the final video explores hidden treasures of the Minster.

• This finishes your visit. Before leaving, take a moment to just be in this amazing building. Then, go in peace.

Nearby: As you leave through the south transept, notice the people-friendly plaza created here and how effectively it ties the church in with the city that stretches before you. To your left are the Roman column from the ancient headquarters, which stood where the Minster stands today (and from where Rome administered the northern reaches of Britannia 1,800 years ago); a statue of Emperor Constantine; and the covered York Minster Stone Yard, where masons are chiseling stone—as they have for centuries—to keep the religious pride and joy of York looking good.

▲▲YORKSHIRE MUSEUM

Located in a lush, picnic-perfect park next to the stately ruins of St. Mary's Abbey (described in my "York Walk," earlier), the Yorkshire Museum is the city's serious "archaeology of York" museum. You can't dig a hole in York without hitting some remnant of the city's long past, and most of what's found ends up here. While the hordes line up at Jorvik Viking Centre, this museum has no crowds and provides a broader historical context, with more real artifacts. The three main collections— Roman, medieval, and natural history— are well described, bright, and kid-friendly.

Cost and Hours: £7.50, kids under 16 free with paying adult, daily 10:00-17:00, within Museum Gardens, tel. 01904/687-687, www.yorkshiremuseum.org.uk.

Visiting the Museum: At the entrance, you're greeted by an original, early-fourth-century A.D. Roman statue of the god Mars. If he could talk, he'd say, "Hear me, mortals. There are three sections here: Roman (on this floor), medieval (downstairs), and natural history (a kid-friendly wing on this floor). Start first with the 10-minute video for a sweeping history of the city."

The **Roman** collection surrounds a large map of the Roman Empire, set on the floor. You'll see slice-of-life exhibits about Roman baths, a huge floor mosaic, and skulls accompanied by artists' renderings of how the people originally looked. (One man was apparently killed by a sword blow to the head—making it graphically clear that the struggle between Romans and barbarians was a violent one.) These artifacts are particularly interesting when you consider that you're standing in one of the farthest reaches of the Roman Empire.

The **medieval** collection is in the basement. During the Middle Ages, York was England's second city. One large room is dominated by ruins of the St. Mary's Abbey complex (one wall still stands just out front—be sure to see it before leaving). In the center of the ruins is the Vale of York Hoard, displaying a silver cup and the accompanying treasures it held— more than 600 silver coins as well as silver bars and jewelry. A father and son team discovered the hoard (thought to have been buried by Vikings in 927) while out for a day of metal detecting in 2007. You'll also see old weapons, glazed vessels, and a well-preserved 13th-century leather box.

The museum's prized pieces, a helmet and a pendant, are housed in this section (but may be on tour when you visit). The eighth-century Anglo-Saxon helmet (known as the York Helmet or the Coppergate Helmet) shows a bit of barbarian refinement. Examine the delicate carving on its brass trim. The exquisitely etched 15th-century pendant—called the Middleham Jewel—is considered the finest piece of Gothic jewelry in Britain. The noble lady who wore this on a necklace believed that it helped her worship and protected her from illness. The back of the pendant, which rested near her heart, shows the Nativity. The front shows the Holy Trinity crowned by a sapphire (which people believed put their prayers at the top of God's to-do list).

In addition to the Anglo-Saxon pieces, the Viking collection is one of the best in England. Looking over the artifacts, you'll find that the Vikings (who conquered most of the Anglo-Saxon lands) wore some pretty decent shoes and actually combed their hair. The Cawood Sword, nearly 1,000 years old, is one of the finest surviving swords from that era (also may be on tour during your visit).

The **natural history** exhibit (titled Extinct) is back upstairs, showing off skeletons of the extinct dodo and ostrich-like moa birds, as well as an ichthyosaurus.

Rick's Tip: *Lively* **King's Square,** *with its inviting benches, is great for people-watching—and prime real estate for buskers and street performers. Just beyond is the most characteristic street in old York: The Shambles.*

Yorkshire Museum

8th-century helmet

▲▲JORVIK VIKING CENTRE

Take the "Pirates of the Caribbean," sail them northeast and back in time 1,000 years, sprinkle in some real artifacts, and you get Jorvik (YOR-vik). Between 1976 and 1981, more than 40,000 artifacts were dug out of the peat bog right here in downtown York—the UK's largest archaeological dig of Viking-era artifacts. When the archaeologists were finished, the dig site was converted into this attraction, opened in 1984 and renovated following a flood in 2015.

Jorvik blends museum exhibits with a 16-minute ride on theme-park-esque "time capsules" that glide through the re-created Viking street of Coppergate as it looked circa the year 975. Animatronic characters and modern-day interpreters bring the scenes to life. Innovative when it first opened, the commercial success of Jorvik inspired copycat rides/museums all over England. Some love Jorvik, while others call it gimmicky and overpriced. If you think of it as Disneyland with a splash of history, Jorvik's fun. To me, Jorvik is a commercial venture designed for kids, with too much emphasis on its gift shop. But it's also undeniably entertaining, and—if you take the time to peruse its exhibits—it can be quite informative.

Cost and Hours: £10.25, various combo-tickets with Dig and/or Barley Hall, daily 10:00-17:00, Nov-March until 16:00, these are last-entry times, hours may vary for special events, tel. 01904/615-505, www.jorvik-viking-centre.co.uk.

Rick's Tip: *The popular* **Jorvik Viking Centre** *can come with* **long lines.** *At the busiest times (roughly 11:00-15:00), you may have to wait an hour or more—especially on school holidays. Come early or late in the day, when you'll more likely wait just 10-15 minutes. For £2 extra, you can* **book a slot in advance,** *either over the phone or on their website.*

Jorvik Viking Centre

▲FAIRFAX HOUSE

This well-furnished home, supposedly the "first Georgian townhouse in England," is perfectly Neoclassical inside. Each room is staffed by pleasant docents eager to talk with you. They'll explain how the circa-1760 home was built as the dowry for an aristocrat's daughter. The house is compact and bursting with stunning period furniture (the personal collection of a local chocolate magnate), gorgeously restored woodwork, and lavish stucco ceilings that offer clues as to each room's purpose. For example, stuccoed philosophers look down on the library, while the goddess of friendship presides over the drawing room. Taken together, this house provides fine insights into aristocratic life in 18th-century England.

Cost and Hours: £7.50, Tue-Sat 10:00-16:30, Sun 11:00-15:30, Mon by guided tour only at 11:00 and 14:00—the one-hour tours are worthwhile, closed Jan-mid-Feb, near Jorvik Viking Centre at 29 Castlegate, tel. 01904/655-543, www.fairfaxhouse.co.uk.

▲▲YORK CASTLE MUSEUM

This fascinating social-history museum is a Victorian home show, possibly the closest thing to a time-tunnel experience England has to offer. The one-way plan ensures that you'll see everything, including remakes of rooms from the 17th to 20th century, a re-creation of a Victorian street, a heartfelt WWI exhibit, and some eerie prison cells.

Reconstructed Victorian-era street at the Castle Museum

Cost and Hours: £10, kids under 16 free with paying adult, daily 9:30-17:00, roaming guides will happily answer your questions (no audioguide), cafeteria at entrance, tel. 01904/687-687, www.yorkcastlemuseum.org.uk. It's at the bottom of the hop-on, hop-off bus route. The museum can call you a taxi (worthwhile if you're hurrying to the National Railway Museum, across town).

Visiting the Museum: The exhibits are divided between two wings: the North Building (to the left as you enter) and the South Building (to the right).

Follow the one-way route through the complex, starting in the **North Building.** You'll first visit the Period Rooms, illuminating Yorkshire lifestyles during different time periods (1600s-1950s) and among various walks of life, and Toy Stories—an enchanting review of toys through the ages. Next is the Shaping the Body exhibit, detailing diet and fashion trends over the last 400 years. Check out the codpieces, bustles, and corsets that used to "enhance" the human form, and wonder over some of the odd diet fads that make today's paleo diet seem normal. For foodies and chefs, the exhibit showcasing fireplaces and kitchens from the 1600s to the 1980s is especially tasty.

Next, stroll down the museum's re-created Kirkgate, a street from the Victorian era, when Britain was at the peak of its power. It features old-time shops and storefronts, including a pharmacist, sweet shop, school, and grocer for the working class, along with roaming live guides in period dress. Around the back is a slum area depicting how the poor lived in those times.

Circle back to the entry and cross over to the **South Building.** In the WWI exhibit, erected to mark the war's centennial, you can follow the lives of five York citizens as they experience the horrors and triumphs of the war years. One room plunges you into the gruesome world of trench warfare, where the average life expectancy was six weeks (and if you fell asleep during sentry duty, you'd be shot). A display about the home front notes that York suffered from Zeppelin attacks in which six people died. At the end you're encouraged to share your thoughts in a room lined with chalkboards.

Exit outside and cross through the castle yard. A detour to the left leads to a flour mill (open sporadically). Otherwise, your tour continues through the door on the right, where you'll find another reconstructed historical street, this one capturing the spirit of the swinging

Period room

1960s—"a time when the cultural changes were massive but the cars and skirts were mini." Slathered with DayGlo colors, this street scene examines fashion, music, and television (including clips of beloved kids' shows and period news reports).

Finally, head into the York Castle Prison, which recounts the experiences of actual people who were thrown into the clink here. Videos, eerily projected onto the walls of individual cells, show actors telling tragic stories about the cells' one-time inhabitants.

Across the River

▲▲NATIONAL RAILWAY MUSEUM

If you like model railways, this is train-car heaven. The thunderous museum—displaying 200 illustrious years of British railroad history—is one of the biggest and best railroad museums anywhere.

Cost and Hours: Free but £5 suggested donation, daily 10:00-18:00, café, restaurant, tel. 0844-815-3139, www.nrm.org.uk.

Getting There: It's about a 15-minute walk from the Minster (southwest of town, up the hill behind the train station). From the train station itself, the fastest approach is to go all the way to the back of the station (using the overpass to cross the tracks), exit out the back door, and turn right up the hill. To skip the walk, a cute little "road train" shuttles you more quickly between the Minster and the Railway Museum (£3 one-way, runs daily Eas-

ter-Oct, leaves museum every 30 minutes 11:00-16:00 at :00 and :30 past each hour; leaves town—from Duncombe Place, 100 yards in front of the Minster—at :15 and :45 past each hour).

Visiting the Museum: Pick up the floor plan to locate the various exhibits, which sprawl through several gigantic buildings on both sides of the street. Throughout the complex, red-shirted "explainers" are eager to talk trains.

The museum's most impressive room is the **Great Hall** (head right from the entrance area and take the stairs to the underground passage). Fanning out from this grand roundhouse is an array of historic cars and engines, starting with the very first "stagecoaches on rails," with a crude steam engine from 1830. You'll trace the evolution of steam-powered transportation, from a replica of the Rocket (one of the first successful steam locomotives) to the era of the aerodynamic Mallard (famous as the first train to travel at a startling two miles per minute—a marvel back in 1938) and the striking Art Deco-style Duchess of Hamilton. The collection spans to the present day, with a replica of the Eurostar (Chunnel) train and the Shinkansen Japanese bullet train.

The Works is an actual workshop where engineers scurry about, fixing old trains. Live train switchboards show real-time rail traffic on the East Coast Main Line. Next to the diagrammed screens, you can look out to see the actual trains

National Railway Museum

York Brewery

moving up and down the line. The Warehouse is loaded with more than 10,000 items relating to train travel (including dinnerware, signage, and actual trains). Exhibits feature dining cars, post cars, sleeping cars, train posters, and info on the Flying Scotsman (the first London-Edinburgh express rail service, now running again).

Crossing back to the entrance side, continue to the **Station Hall,** with a collection of older trains, including ones that the royals have used to ride the rails (including Queen Victoria's lavish royal car and a WWII royal carriage reinforced with armor). Behind that are the South Yard and the Depot, with actual working trains in storage.

▲YORK BREWERY

This intimate, tactile, and informative 45-minute-long tour gives an enjoyable look at how this charming little microbrewery produces 5,700 pints per batch. Their award-winning Ghost Ale is strong, dark, and chocolaty. You can sample their beer throughout town, but to get it as fresh as possible, drink it where it's birthed, in their cozy Tap Room.

Cost and Hours: £8, includes four tasters of the best beer—ale not lager—

in town; tours Mon-Sat at 12:30, 14:00, 15:30, and 17:00—just show up, none on Sun; cross the river on Lendal Bridge and walk 5 minutes to Toft Green just below Micklegate, tel. 01904/621-162, www.york-brewery.co.uk.

EXPERIENCES

Shopping

With its medieval lanes lined with classy as well as tacky little shops, York is a hit with shoppers.

Antique malls are filled with stalls and cases owned by antique dealers from the countryside (all open daily). Each mall is a warren of rooms with cafés buried deep inside. These three are within a few blocks of one another: the **Antiques Centre York** (41 Stonegate, www.theantiquescentreyork.co.uk), the **Red House Antiques Centre** (a block from the Minster at Duncombe Place, www.redhouseyork.co.uk), and **Cavendish Antiques and Jewellers** (44 Stonegate, www.cavendishjewellers.co.uk).

Nightlife

York's atmospheric pubs make for convivial eating or drinking. Many serve inex-

Entertainment

Theatre Royal offers a full variety of dramas, comedies, and works by Shakespeare. The locals are proud of the high-tech main theater and little 100-seat theater-in-the-round (£10-22 tickets, shows usually Tue-Sun at 19:30, tickets easy to get, on St. Leonard's Place near Bootham Bar, booking tel. 01904/623-568, www. yorktheatreroyal.co.uk).

Riverside Walk or Bike Ride

The New Walk is a mile-long, tree-lined riverside lane created in the 1730s as a promenade for York's dandy class to stroll, see, and be seen—and is a fine place for today's visitors to walk or bike (Cycle Heaven rents bikes at the train station).

This hour-long walk is a delightful way to enjoy a dose of countryside away from York. It's paved, illuminated in the evening, and a popular jogging route any time of day.

Start from the riverside under Skeldergate Bridge (near the York Castle Museum), and walk south away from town about a mile to the striking, modern **Millennium Bridge.** Cross the bridge and head back towards York, passing **Rowntree Park** (you can enter the park through its fine old gate, stroll along the duck-filled pond near the Rowntree Park Café, and return to the riverside lane). Continue into York.

EATING

The York high-tech industry and university—along with the tourists—build a demand that sustains lots of creative and fun eateries. **Upscale Bistros**—trendy, pricey eateries—are a York forte. I've listed several of my favorites: Café No. 8, Café Concerto, The Star Inn the City, and Bistro Guy. These places are each romantic, laid-back, and popular with locals (so reservations are wise for dinner). They also have good-quality, creative vegetarian options. Most offer economical lunch

pensive lunches and/or early dinners, then focus on beer in the evening.

The York Brewery Tap Room is a private club, but you can be an honorary guest. It has five beloved varieties on tap (14 Toft Green, just below Micklegate, tel. 01904/621-162, www.york-brewery.co.uk).

The Maltings, just over Lendal Bridge, has classic pub ambience and serves good lunches. Local beer purists swear by this place (cross the bridge and look down and left to Tanners Moat, tel. 01904/655-387).

The Blue Bell, with an old-school York vibe and a time-warp Edwardian interior, is the smallest pub in York (east end of town at 53 Fossgate, tel. 01904/654-904).

The House of the Trembling Madness is cozily above a "bottle shop" that sells a stunning variety of beers to go (48 Stonegate).

Evil Eye Lounge is a funky space famous for its strong cocktails and edgy ambience (42 Stonegate, tel. 01904/640-002).

The Golden Fleece is considered the oldest and most haunted coaching inn in York. Its wooden frame has survived without foundations for 500 years and the tilty floors make you feel drunk even if you aren't (16 Pavement, across the street from the southern end of The Shambles, tel. 01904/625-171).

The Last Drop is a basic pub—no game machines, no children—owned by the York Brewery, with all their ales on tap (27 Colliergate facing King's Square, tel. 01904/621-951).

specials and early dinners. After 19:00 or so, main courses cost £16-26 and fixed-price meals (two or three courses) go for around £25. On Friday and Saturday evenings, many offer special, more expensive menus.

City Center
Cheap Eats Around King's Square

King's Square has several fine quick-and-cheap options for lunch and takeout. Picnic on the square to enjoy the street entertainers, or more peacefully in the Holy Trinity Church yard on Goodramgate (half a block to the right of York Roast Company).

$ York Roast Company is a local fixture, serving delicious and hearty pork sandwiches with applesauce, stuffing, and "crackling" (roasted bits of fat and skin). Other meats are also available. You can even oversee the stuffing of your own Yorkshire pudding. If Henry VIII wanted fast food, he'd eat here (corner of Low Petergate and Goodramgate, order at counter then dine upstairs or take away, daily 10:00-23:00, 74 Low Petergate, tel. 01904/629-197, second location at 4 Stonegate).

$ Drakes Fish & Chips across the street from York Roast Company, is a local favorite chippy (daily 11:00-22:30, 97 Low Petergate, tel. 01904/624-788).

$ The Cornish Bakery, facing King's Square, cooks up pasties to eat in or take away (30 Colliergate, tel. 01904/671-177).

$ Shambles Market has many food stalls and street food vendors offering fun and nutritious light meals (daily 7:00-17:00, until 16:00 in winter).

$ St. Crux Parish Hall is used by a medley of charities that sell tea, homemade cakes, and light meals (usually open Tue-Sat 10:00-16:00, closed Sun-Mon, at bottom of The Shambles at its intersection with Pavement, tel. 01904/621-756).

$ Harlequin Café is a charming place with good coffee and homemade cakes, as well as light meals. It's up a creaky staircase overlooking the square (Mon-Sat 10:00-16:00, Sun 11:00-15:00, 2 King's Square, tel. 01904/630-631).

On or near Stonegate

$$ The House of the Trembling Madness, considered the best pub in town, is easy to miss. Enter through The Bottle, a ground-floor shop selling an astonishing number of different takeaway beers. Climb the stairs to find a small but cozy pub beneath a high, airy, timbered ceiling. The food is more creative than standard pub grub (daily 10:30-24:00, 48 Stonegate, tel. 01904/640-009).

$$ Ask Restaurant is a cheap and cheery Italian chain. In York, it's inside the Neoclassical Grand Assembly Rooms, lined with Corinthian marble columns. The food may be pedestrian, but the atmosphere is 18th-century deluxe (daily 11:00-22:00, weekends until 23:00; Blake Street, tel. 01904/637-254).

Near Bootham Bar and Recommended B&Bs

$$$ Café Concerto, a casual and cozy bistro with wholesome food and a charming musical theme, has a loyal following. The fun menu features updated English favorites with some international options (vegetarian and gluten-free options; Tue-Sat 13:00-21:00, Sun-Mon until 17:00, smart to reserve for dinner—try for a window seat, also offers takeaway, facing the Minster at 21 High Petergate, tel. 01904/610-478, www.cafeconcerto.biz).

$$$ Café No. 8 is more romantic and modern. Grab one of the tables in front or in the sunroom, or enjoy a shaded little garden out back if the weather's good. Chef Chris Pragnell uses what's fresh in the market to shape his simple, elegant, and creative menu (daily 12:00-22:00, 8 Gillygate, tel. 01904/653-074, www.cafeno8.co.uk).

Lamb & Lion serves local ales alongside a classy **$$$ pub menu** in their wood-cozy bistro, back room snugs, and casual outdoor garden, or elegant **$$$$ dinners** in their country-cute parlor restaurant (Mon-Sat 12:00-21:00, restaurant open only for dinner from 17:00, closed Sun, 2 High Petersgate, tel. 01904/654-112, www.lambandlionyork.com).

$$$$ At **Bistro Guy,** chef Guy Whapples serves breakfast and lunch daily, and dinner—with a fancier modern English and international "bistro" tasting menu—three nights a week (daily 10:00-15:00, also open for dinner Thu-Sat 18:30-21:00—deposit required for dinner reservation, 40 Gillygate, tel. 01904/652-500, www.bistroguy.co.uk).

$$$$ The Star Inn the City is an offshoot of Chef Andrew Pern's Michelin-star-rated restaurant in the Yorkshire countryside—The Star Inn. Dine outside along the river or in the mod eatery that looks out over the Museum Gardens (daily 9:00-22:00, reservations smart, next to the river in Lendal Engine House, Museum Street, tel. 01904/619-208, www.starinnthecity.co.uk).

$$ The Exhibition Hotel pub has a classic pub interior, as well as a glassed-in conservatory and beer garden out back that's great for kids (food served daily 12:00-15:00 & 17:00-21:00, bar open late, facing Bootham Bar at 19 Bootham Street, tel. 01904/641-105).

$$ Mamma Mia is a popular choice for functional, affordable Italian. The casual eating area features a tempting gelato bar, and in nice weather the back patio is *molto bello* (daily 11:30-14:00 & 17:30-23:00, 20 Gillygate, tel. 01904/622-020).

Sainsbury's Local grocery store is handy and open late (long hours daily, 50 yards outside Bootham Bar, on Bootham).

At the East End of Town

This neighborhood is across town from my recommended B&Bs, but still central (and a short walk from the York Castle Museum). Reservations are smart.

$$$ Rustique French Bistro has one big room of tight tables and walls decorated with simple posters. The place has good prices and is straight French—right down to the welcome (daily 12:00-22:00, across from Fairfax House at 28 Castlegate, tel. 01904/612-744, www.rustiqueyork.co.uk).

$$$ Walmgate Ale House is a fun and casual place to eat. This homey, spacious, youthful restaurant (combining old timbers and mod tables) serves up elegantly simple traditional and international meals, all with a focus on local ingredients. The seating sprawls on several floors: ground-floor pub, upstairs bistro, and top-floor loft (Tue-Sun until 22:30, closed Mon, just past Fossgate at 25 Walmgate, tel. 01904/629-222).

$$ The Hop is a local favorite for its simple approach and winning combo: pizza and beer. The pub pulls real ales in the front, serves woodfire pies in an inviting space in the back, and offers live music Wed-Sun at 21:00 (daily 12:00-23:00, food served until 21:00—Sun until 20:00, 11 Fossgate, tel. 01904/541-466).

$$ At **The Hairy Fig,** try grabbing one of four tables in the quaint lunchtime café (simple soups, salads, toasties, and a £5 cream tea), or assemble a picnic out of freshly prepared pies, quiches, breads, and high-quality meat and cheese from their delicatessen (deli open Mon-Sat 9:00-17:30, café open 11:30-15:00, closed Sun, 39 Fossgate, tel. 01904/677-074).

$$ Mumbai Lounge is considered the best place in town for Indian food, so it's very popular. The space is big and high-energy, with a hardworking team of waiters in black T-shirts. I'd call to reserve a table on the ground floor—but avoid the basement (daily 12:00-14:00 & 17:30-23:30, 47 Fossgate, tel. 01904/654-155, www.mumbailoungeyork.co.uk).

Tearooms

York is famous for its elegant teahouses. These two places serve traditional afternoon tea as well as light meals in memorable settings. Travel partners on a budget

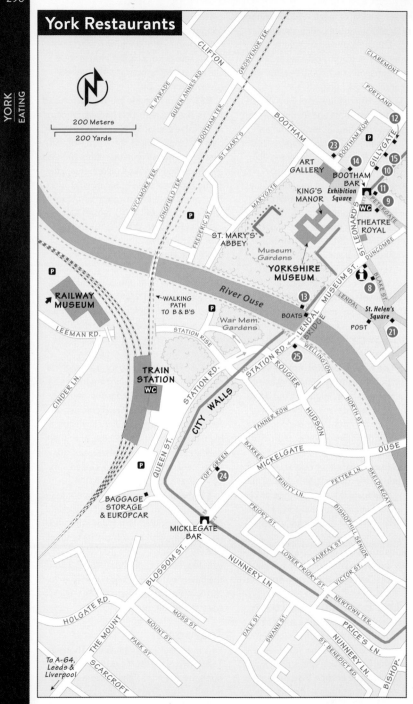

York Restaurants

N

200 Meters

200 Yards

CLIFTON

CLAREMONT

PORTLAND

12

GILLYGATE

BOOTHAM

23 BOOTHAM ROW

14

15

10

BOOTHAM BAR

11

9

PETERGATE

WC

ART GALLERY

KING'S MANOR

Exhibition Square

THEATRE ROYAL

MARYGATE

ST. LEONARD'S

Duncombe

ST. MARY'S ABBEY

Museum Gardens

YORKSHIRE MUSEUM

MUSEUM ST.

BLAKE ST.

8

River Ouse

13

LENDAL

St. Helen's Square

21

BOATS

LENDAL BRIDGE

POST

RAILWAY MUSEUM

WALKING PATH TO B & B'S

War Mem. Gardens

STATION RISE

25

WELLINGTON

LEEMAN RD.

CINDER LN.

TRAIN STATION

WC

STATION RD.

CITY WALLS

ROUGIER

NORTH ST.

OUSE

TANNER ROW

HUDSON

BARKER

MICKELGATE

TRINITY LN.

FETTER LN.

SKELDERGATE

24

TOFT GREEN

PRIORY ST.

BISHOPHILL SENIOR

BAGGAGE STORAGE & EUROPCAR

QUEEN ST.

MICKLEGATE BAR

FAIRFAX ST.

VICTOR ST.

LOWER PRIORY ST.

BLOSSOM ST.

NUNNERY LN.

NEWTON TER.

HOLGATE RD.

THE MOUNT

MOUNT ST.

MOSS ST.

DALE ST.

SWANN ST.

ST. BENEDICT RD.

PRICE'S LN.

NUNNERY LN.

BISHOP

PARK ST.

SCARCROFT

To A-64, Leeds & Liverpool

N. PARADE

QUEEN ANNES RD.

BOOTHAM TER.

GROSVENOR TER.

ST. MARY'S

SYCAMORE TER.

LONGFIELD TER.

FREDERIC ST.

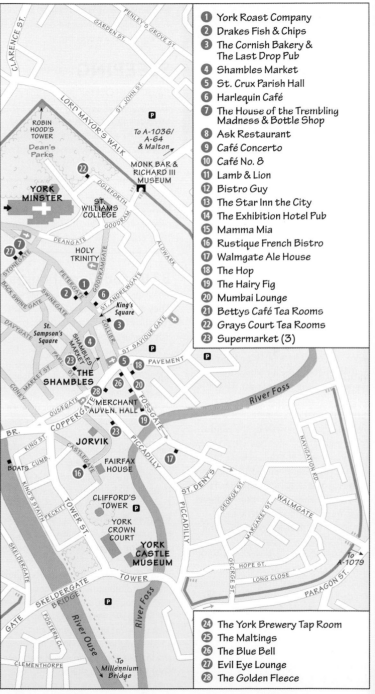

1. York Roast Company
2. Drakes Fish & Chips
3. The Cornish Bakery & The Last Drop Pub
4. Shambles Market
5. St. Crux Parish Hall
6. Harlequin Café
7. The House of the Trembling Madness & Bottle Shop
8. Ask Restaurant
9. Café Concerto
10. Café No. 8
11. Lamb & Lion
12. Bistro Guy
13. The Star Inn the City
14. The Exhibition Hotel Pub
15. Mamma Mia
16. Rustique French Bistro
17. Walmgate Ale House
18. The Hop
19. The Hairy Fig
20. Mumbai Lounge
21. Bettys Café Tea Rooms
22. Grays Court Tea Rooms
23. Supermarket (3)

24. The York Brewery Tap Room
25. The Maltings
26. The Blue Bell
27. Evil Eye Lounge
28. The Golden Fleece

can enjoy the experience for about half the price by having one person order "full tea" (with enough little sandwiches and sweets for two to share) and the other a simple cup of tea.

$$ Bettys Café Tea Rooms is a destination restaurant for many ladies. Choose between a Yorkshire Cream Tea (tea and scones with clotted Yorkshire cream and strawberry jam) or a full traditional English afternoon tea (tea, delicate sandwiches, scones, and sweets). Your table is so full of doily niceties that the food is served on a little three-tray tower. While you'll pay a little extra here (and the food's nothing special), the ambience and people-watching are hard to beat. They'll offer to seat you sooner in the bigger and less atmospheric basement, but wait for a place upstairs—ideally by the window (daily 9:00-21:00, "afternoon tea" served all day; on weekends the special £33 afternoon tea includes fresh-from-the-oven scones served 12:30-17:00 in upstairs room with pianist—must reserve ahead; piano music nightly 18:00-21:00 and Sun 10:00-13:00, St. Helen's Square tel. 01904/659-142, www.bettys.co.uk).

$$ Grays Court, tucked away behind the Minster, holds court over its own delightful garden just inside the town wall. For centuries, this was the residence of the Norman Treasurers of York Minster. Today it's home to a pleasant tearoom, small hotel, restaurant, and bar. Sit outside, at tables scattered in the pleasant garden, or inside, in their elegant dining room or Jacobean gallery (two-person "afternoon

tea" served 14:00-17:00, daily 11:00-21:00, Chapter House Street, tel. 01904/612-613, www.grayscourtyork.com).

SLEEPING

July through October are the busiest (and usually most expensive) months. B&Bs often charge more for weekends and sometimes turn away one-night bookings, particularly for peak-season Saturdays. (York is worth two nights anyway.)

Rick's Tip: Book a room well in advance during festival times *and on weekends any time of year. For a list of festivals, see www.yorkfestivals.com.*

B&Bs and Guesthouses

These places are all small and family-run. They come with plenty of steep stairs (and no elevators) but no traffic noise. Rooms can be tight; if maneuverability is important, say so when booking. For a good selection, contact them well in advance. Most have permits to lend for street parking.

The handiest B&B neighborhood is the quiet residential area just outside the old town wall's Bootham gate, along the road called Bootham. All of these are within a 10-minute walk of the Minster and TI, and a 5- to 15-minute walk from the station. If driving, head for the cathedral and follow the medieval wall to the gate called Bootham Bar. The street called Bootham leads away from Bootham Bar.

Getting There: Here's the most direct way to walk to this B&B area from the train station: Head to the north end of the station, to the area between platforms 2 and 4. Shoot through the gap between the men's WC and the York Tap pub, past some racks of bicycles, and into the short-stay parking lot. Walk to the end of the lot to a pedestrian ramp, and zigzag your way down. At the bottom, head left, following the sign for the riverside route. When you reach the river, cross over on the footbridge—you'll have to carry your bags up and down two-dozen steps. At the far end of the bridge, the Abbey Guest House is a few yards to your right, facing the river. To reach The Hazelwood (closer to the town wall), walk from the bridge along the river until just before the short ruined tower, then turn inland up onto Marygate. For other B&Bs, at the bottom of the footbridge, turn left immediately onto a path that skirts the big parking lot (parallel to the train tracks). At the end of the parking lot, you'll turn depending on your B&B: for the places on or near Bootham Terrace, turn left and go under the tracks; for B&Bs on St. Mary's Street, take the short stairway on your right.

On or near Bootham Terrace

$$ At St. Raphael Guesthouse has seven comfy rooms, each themed after a different York street, and each lovingly accented with a fresh rose (RS%, free drinks and ice in their guests' fridge, family rooms, 44 Queen Annes Road, tel. 01904/645-028, www.straphaelguesthouse.co.uk, info@straphaelguesthouse.co.uk).

$$ Alcuin Lodge, run by Darren and Mark, is a cozy place, with five rooms that feel personal yet up to date (one room with private WC in the hallway just outside; 15 Sycamore Place, tel. 01904/629-837, www.alcuinlodge.com, darren@alcuinlodge.com).

$$ Bronte Guesthouse is a modern B&B with five airy, bright rooms and a lovely back garden (family room available, 22 Grosvenor Terrace, tel. 01904/621-066, www.bronte-guesthouse.com, enquiries@bronte-guesthouse.com, Mick and Mandy).

$$ Arnot House, run by a hardworking daughter-and-mother team, is old-fashioned, homey, and lushly decorated with Victorian memorabilia (2-night minimum preferred, no children, huge DVD library, 17 Grosvenor Terrace, tel. 01904/641-

966, www.arnothouseyork.co.uk, kim.robbins@virgin.net).

$$ Bootham Guest House features creamy walls and contemporary furniture. Of the eight rooms, six are en suite, while two share a bath (RS%, 56 Bootham Crescent, tel. 01904/672-123, www.boothamguesthouse.co.uk, boothamguesthouse1@hotmail.com, Andrew).

$ Number 34, run by Amy and Jason, has five simple, light rooms at fair prices. It's clean and uncluttered, with modern decor (RS%, ground-floor room, 5-person apartment next door, 34 Bootham Crescent, tel. 01904/645-818, www.number34york.co.uk, enquiries@number34york.co.uk).

$ Queen Anne's Guest House has nine basic rooms in two adjacent houses. While it doesn't have the plushest beds or richest decor, it's clean and respectable (RS%, family room, lounge, 24 and 26 Queen Annes Road, tel. 01904/629-389, www.queen-annes-guesthouse.co.uk, info@queen-annes-guesthouse.co.uk).

On the River

$$ Abbey Guest House is a peaceful refuge overlooking the River Ouse, with five cheerful, contemporary-style rooms and a cute little garden. The riverview rooms will ramp up your romance with York (RS%, free parking, pay laundry service, 13 Earlsborough Terrace, tel. 01904/627-782, www.abbeyghyork.co.uk, info@abbeyghyork.co.uk).

On St. Mary's Street

$$ Number 23 St. Mary's B&B has nine extravagantly decorated and spaciously comfortable rooms, plus a classy lounge (discount for longer stays, family room, honesty box for drinks and snacks, lots of stairs, 23 St. Mary's, tel. 01904/622-738, www.23stmarys.co.uk, stmarys23@hotmail.com).

$ Crook Lodge B&B, with six tight but elegantly charming rooms, serves

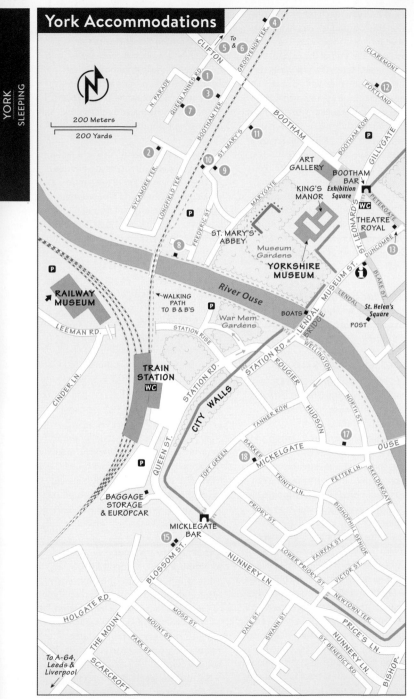

York Accommodations

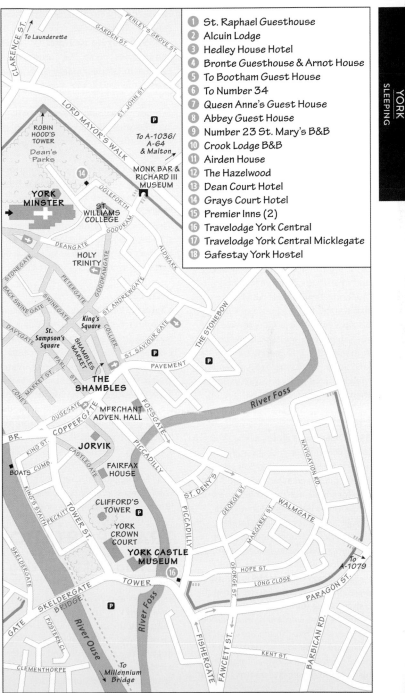

1. St. Raphael Guesthouse
2. Alcuin Lodge
3. Hedley House Hotel
4. Bronte Guesthouse & Arnot House
5. To Bootham Guest House
6. To Number 34
7. Queen Anne's Guest House
8. Abbey Guest House
9. Number 23 St. Mary's B&B
10. Crook Lodge B&B
11. Airden House
12. The Hazelwood
13. Dean Court Hotel
14. Grays Court Hotel
15. Premier Inns (2)
16. Travelodge York Central
17. Travelodge York Central Micklegate
18. Safestay York Hostel

breakfast in an old Victorian kitchen. The 21st-century style somehow fits this old house (one ground-floor room, free parking, quiet, 26 St. Mary's, tel. 01904/655-614, www.crooklodgeguesthouseyork. co.uk, crooklodge@hotmail.com).

$ Airden House rents 10 nice, mostly traditional rooms, though the two basement-level rooms are more mod (RS%, lounge, free parking, 1 St. Mary's, tel. 01904/638-915, www.airdenhouse.co.uk, info@airdenhouse.co.uk).

Closer to the Town Wall

$$ The Hazelwood, more formal than a B&B, rents 14 rooms sharing a garden patio and pleasant basement lounge complete with a guest fridge. The "standard" rooms have bright, cheery decor and small bathrooms, while the bigger "superior" rooms come with newer bathrooms (two-bedroom apartment also available, free laundry service for Rick Steves readers if you book directly with the hotel, free parking, 24 Portland Street, tel. 01904/626-548, www. thehazelwoodyork.com, reservations@ thehazelwoodyork.com).

Hotels

$$$$ Dean Court Hotel, a Best Western facing the Minster, is a big stately hotel with classy lounges and 37 comfortable rooms. It has a great location and friendly vibe for a business-class establishment. A few rooms have views for no extra charge—try requesting one (elevator, restaurant, Duncombe Place, tel. 01904/625-082, www.deancourt-york. co.uk, sales@deancourt-york.co.uk).

$$$$ Grays Court Hotel is a historic mansion—the home of dukes and archbishops since 1091—that now rents nine rooms and two suites to tourists. While its public spaces and gardens are lavish, its rooms are elegant yet modest. If it's too pricey for lodging, consider coming here for its recommended tearoom (Chapter House Street, tel. 01904/612-613, www. grayscourtyork.com).

$$$ Hedley House Hotel has 30 clean and spacious rooms. The outdoor hot tub/ sauna or in-house massage is a fine way to end your day (ask for a deal with stay of three or more nights, family rooms, good two-course evening meals, free parking, 3 Bootham Terrace, tel. 01904/637-404, www.hedleyhouse.com, greg@ hedleyhouse.com).

Budget Chain Hotels: If looking for something a little less spendy than the hotels listed above, consider several chains, with central locations in town. These include **Premier Inn** (two branches side-by-side) and **Travelodge** (one location near the York Castle Museum at 90 Piccadilly; second location on Micklegate).

Hostel

¢ Safestay York is a boutique hostel on a rowdy street (especially on Fridays and Saturdays). Located in a big old Georgian house, they rent 158 beds in 4- to 12-bed rooms, with great views, private prefab "pod" bathrooms, and reading lights for each bed. They also offer fancier, hotel-quality doubles (family rooms, breakfast extra, no elevator, air-con, Wi-Fi in public areas only, self-service laundry, TV lounge, game room, bar, lockers, no curfew, 5-minute walk from train station at 88 Micklegate, tel. 01904/627-720, www.safestay.com/ss-york-micklegate. html, bookings@safestay.com).

TRANSPORTATION

Arriving and Departing
By Train

The train station is a 10-minute walk from downtown. Day-trippers can pay to store baggage at the small hut next to the Europcar office just off Queen Street—as you exit the station, turn right and walk along a bridge to the first intersection, then turn right (cash only, daily until 20:00).

Recommended B&Bs are a 5- to 15-minute walk (depending on where you're staying). For specific walking directions to the B&Bs, see "Sleeping," earlier.

Taxis zip your to your B&B for £7-9. Queue up at the taxi stand, or call 01904/638-833 or 01904/659-659; cabbies don't start the meter until you get in.

To **walk downtown** from the station, exit straight, crossing the street through the bus stops, and turn left down Station Road, keeping the wall on your right. At the first intersection, turn right through the gap in the wall and then left across the river, and follow the crowd toward the Gothic towers of the Minster. After the bridge, a block before the Minster, you'll see the TI on your right.

Train Connections to: Durham (3-4/ hour, 45 minutes), **London**'s King's Cross Station (2/hour, 2 hours), **Bath** (hourly with change in Bristol, 5 hours, more with additional transfers), **Oxford** (1/hour direct, 3 hours), **Birmingham** (2/hour, 2.5 hours), **Keswick/Lake District** (train to Penrith: roughly 2/hour, 3.5 hours, 1-2 transfers; then bus, allow about 4.5 hours total), **Edinburgh** (2/hour, 2 hours). Train info: Tel. 0345-748-4950, www. nationalrail.co.uk.

Connections with London's Airports: Allow four hours minimum to reach York from either Heathrow or Gatwick. From **Heathrow,** take Heathrow Express train to London's Paddington Station, transfer by Tube to King's Cross, then take train to York. From **Gatwick South,** catch the First Capital Connect train to London's St. Pancras International Station; from there, walk to neighboring King's Cross Station, and catch train to York.

By Car

Driving and parking in York is maddening. Those day-tripping here should follow signs to one of several park-and-ride lots ringing the perimeter. At these lots, parking is free, and shuttle buses go every 10

minutes into the center.

If you're sleeping here, park your car where your B&B advises and walk. As you near York (and your B&B), you'll hit the A-1237 ring road. Follow this to the A-19/Thirsk roundabout (next to river on northwest side of town). From the roundabout, follow signs for *York,* traveling through Clifton into Bootham. All recommended B&Bs are four or five blocks before you hit the medieval city gate.

If you're approaching York from the south, take the M-1 until it becomes the A-1M, exit at junction 45 onto the A-64, and follow it for 10 miles until you reach York's ring road (A-1237), which allows you to avoid driving through the city center.

Rick's Tip: *If you're nearing the end of your trip,* **drop off your rental car upon arrival in York.** *The money saved by turning it in early just about pays for the train ticket that whisks you effortlessly to London.*

Car Rental: In York, you'll find these agencies: **Avis** (3 Layerthorpe, tel. 0844-544-6117); **Hertz** (at train station, tel. 0843 309 3082); **Budget** (near the National Railway Museum behind the train station at 75 Leeman Road, tel. 01904/644-919); and **Europcar** (off Queen Street near train station, tel. 0844-846-0872). Beware: Car-rental agencies close early on Saturday afternoons and all day Sunday. This is OK when dropping off, but picking up at these times is possible only by prior arrangement (and for an extra fee).

BEST OF THE REST

Once a grimy manufacturing city, **Liverpool** now sparkles with a revived waterfront and a buzzing cultural scene that pays homage to the city's musical past (Beatles, anyone?).

If you're looking for more ancient history in the north, go for a Roman ramble at **Hadrian's Wall,** a reminder that Britain was an important Roman colony 2,000 years ago. Marvel at England's greatest Norman church—**Durham's** cathedral—and enjoy an evensong service there. At the excellent Beamish Museum nearby, travel back in time to the 19th and early 20th centuries.

LIVERPOOL

The most iconic rock-and-roll band of all time was made up of four Liverpudlians who spent their formative years in Liverpool. The city has become a pilgrimage site for Beatlemaniacs, but even those with just a passing interest in the Fab Four are likely to find themselves humming their favorite tunes around town.

Orientation

Most general points of interest are concentrated in the pedestrian-friendly downtown and Albert Dock area. Beatles sights, however, are spread far and wide—it's much easier to connect them with a tour (listed later).

Day Plan: You can easily fill a day with Fab Four sights: Do the tour of John's and Paul's homes in the morning (reserve ahead), then return to the Albert Dock area to visit The Beatles Story and/or the British Music Experience. Take an afternoon bus tour from the Albert Dock to the other Beatles sights in town, winding up at the Cavern Quarter to enjoy a Beatles cover band in the reconstructed Cavern Club.

Getting There: Liverpool is linked by train with **Stratford** (2/hour, 3 hours),

the **Lake District** (via Penrith, hourly, 2.5 hours), **York** (at least hourly, 2.5 hours), **Edinburgh** (1-2/hour, 4.5 hours), and **London**'s Euston Station (at least hourly, 2.5 hours.

Arrival in Liverpool: Most **trains** use the main Lime Street train station. Regional trains also arrive in Liverpool at the much smaller Central Station, located just a few blocks south. Note that the greater Liverpool area transit system may still be under renovation when you visit; trains may use other stations in surrounding areas and connect you with the city center via bus service (check www.merseyrail.org).

From Lime Street Station to the Albert Dock is about a 20-minute walk or a quick trip by subway (from Lime Street Station to James Street Station, £2.30), or taxi (about £6).

Drivers approaching Liverpool first follow signs to City Centre and Waterfront, then brown signs to Albert Dock, where you'll find a huge pay parking lot at the dock.

Tourist Information: Liverpool's TI is at the **Albert Dock** (daily 9:00-16:30, just inland from The Beatles Story, www.visitliverpool.com).

Beatles Bus Tours: If you want to see as many Beatles-related sights as possible in a short time, these tours are the way to go. Each tour drives by the houses where the Fab Four grew up (exteriors only), places they performed, and spots made famous by the lyrics of their hits.

Your choices include the Magical Mystery Big Bus Tour (live commentary and Beatles tunes, £18, 5-8/day, fewer on Sun and in off-season, 2 hours, wise to book ahead at least a day, www.cavernclub.org); Phil Hughes Minibus Beatles and Liverpool Tours (£125 for private group tour with 1-5 people in 8-seat minibus, www.tourliverpool.co.uk); or Jackie Spen-

Albert Dock

cer Private Tours (up to 5 people in chauffeur-driven minivan-£240, 3 hours, www.beatleguides.com).

If you want to see inside the **childhood homes of Lennon and McCartney,** you'll need to prebook a minibus tour; for details, see under "Lennon and McCartney Homes," below.

Sights

▲THE BEATLES STORY

This exhibit—while overpriced and a bit small—is well done, the story's a fascinating one, and even an avid fan will pick up some new information. The Beatles Story has two parts: the original, main exhibit at the south end of the Albert Dock; and a much smaller branch in the Mersey Ferries terminal at Pier Head, just to the north. A free shuttle runs between the two locations every 30 minutes.

Cost and Hours: £16 covers both parts, tickets good for 48 hours, includes audioguide; daily 9:00-19:00, Nov-March 10:00-18:00, Pier Head exhibit has shorter hours, www.beatlesstory.com.

Visiting the Museum: Start in the **main exhibit** with a chronological stroll through the evolution of the Beatles, focusing on their Liverpool years. There are many actual artifacts (from George Harrison's first boyhood guitar to John Lennon's orange-tinted "Imagine" glasses), as well as large dioramas celebrating landmarks in Beatles lore (a reconstruction of the Cavern Club, a life-size re-creation of the *Sgt. Pepper* album cover, and a walk-through yellow submarine). The great audioguide captures the Beatles' charm and cheekiness in interviews with their families, friends, and collaborators.

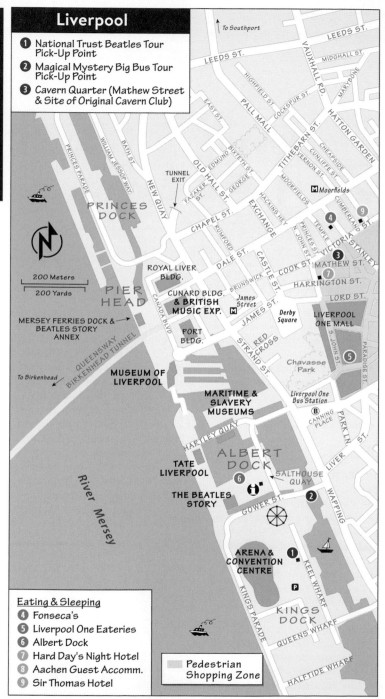

Liverpool

1 National Trust Beatles Tour Pick-Up Point
2 Magical Mystery Big Bus Tour Pick-Up Point
3 Cavern Quarter (Mathew Street & Site of Original Cavern Club)

Eating & Sleeping
4 Fonseca's
5 Liverpool One Eateries
6 Albert Dock
7 Hard Day's Night Hotel
8 Aachen Guest Accomm.
9 Sir Thomas Hotel

Pedestrian Shopping Zone

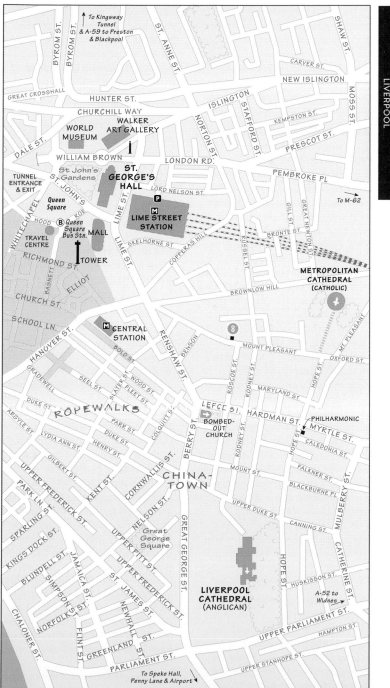

The **Pier Head exhibit** is less interesting, but it's included with the ticket. You'll find it upstairs in the Mersey Ferries terminal at Pier Head—a 10-minute walk north. The main attraction is a corny "Fab 4D Experience," an animated movie that strings together Beatles tunes into something resembling a plot.

▲▲BRITISH MUSIC EXPERIENCE

This museum, located in the Cunard Building at Pier Head, goes beyond Liverpool's Beatlemania, immersing visitors in the history of British music of all genres from 1945 until today. The multimedia exhibits include costumes, instruments, recordings, and memorabilia from artists and bands such as David Bowie, Queen, Amy Winehouse, Coldplay, and Adele, plus the chance to play professional-grade instruments in a sound studio. You could easily spend hours here, but plan for at least 90 minutes.

Cost and Hours: £16, includes multimedia guide, daily 9:00-19:00, Thu until 21:00, last entry 1.5 hours before closing; tel. 0344/335-0655, www. britishmusicexperience.com.

Visiting the Museum: Each section of the museum displays interesting facts about well-known artists, billboard art, costumes, instruments, and more. Your multimedia guide provides interviews, videos, and picture galleries. Timelines throughout place the music in historical context, describing its relation to the politics and culture of each decade.

In the back is a studio where you can exercise your own musical skills—take interactive instrument lessons, record your singing, or learn dance moves that have been popular over the decades.

BEATLES SIGHTS IN THE CAVERN QUARTER

The narrow, bar-lined Mathew Street, right in the heart of downtown, is ground zero for Beatles fans. The Beatles frequently performed in their early days together at the original Cavern Club,

deep in a cellar along this street. While that's long gone, a mock-up of the historic nightspot (built with many of the original bricks) lives on a few doors down. Still billed as "the **Cavern Club,**" dropping by in the afternoon for a live Beatles tribute act somehow just feels right (open daily 10:00-24:00; live music daily from mid-afternoon until late evening, free admission most of the time, small entry fee Thu-Sun evenings; www.cavernclub.org).

Across the street and run by the same owners, the **Cavern Pub** lacks its sibling's troglodyte aura, but makes up for it with walls lined with old photos and memorabilia from the Beatles and other bands who've performed here. The pub features frequent performances by Beatles cover bands and other acts (no cover, daily 11:00-24:00).

▲LENNON AND MCCARTNEY HOMES

John's and Paul's boyhood homes are now owned by the National Trust and have both been restored to how they looked during the lads' 1950s childhoods. While some Beatles bus tours stop here for photo ops, only the National Trust minibus tour gets you inside the homes. For die-hard Beatles fans who want to get a glimpse into the time and place that created these musical masterminds, the National Trust tour is worth ▲▲▲.

Cost: £23 for 2.5-hour tour.

Reservations: Advance booking is strongly advised, especially in summer and on weekends or holidays—at least two weeks ahead (tel. 0151/427-7231, www.nationaltrust.org.uk/beatles).

Tour Options: Tours run daily from the Albert Dock at 10:00, 11:00, and 14:15 (tours do not run Mon-Tue in mid-Feb-mid-March and Nov; no tours at all Dec-mid-Feb). They depart from the Jurys Inn (south across the bridge from The Beatles Story). An additional tour leaves at 15:00 from Speke Hall, eight miles southeast of Liverpool.

Visiting the Homes: A minibus takes you to the homes of John and Paul, with about 45 minutes inside each (no photos allowed inside either home). Each home has a caretaker who acts as your guide. These folks give an entertaining, insightful-to-fans talk that lasts about 30 minutes. You then have 10-15 minutes to wander through the house on your own.

Mendips (John Lennon's Home): Even though he sang about being a working-class hero, John grew up in the suburbs of Liverpool, surrounded by doctors, lawyers, and—beyond the back fence— Strawberry Field.

This was the home of John's Aunt Mimi, who raised him in this house from the time he was five years old and once told him, "A guitar's all right, John, but you'll never earn a living by it." John moved out at age 23. Yoko Ono bought the house in 2002 and gave it as a gift to the National Trust.

On the surface, it's just a 1930s house carefully restored to how it would have been in the past. But if you're a John Lennon fan, it's fun to picture him as a young boy drawing and imagining at his dining room table. His bedroom, with an Elvis poster and his favorite boyhood books, offers tantalizing hints at his later musical genius. Sing a song to yourself in the enclosed porch—John and Paul did this when they wanted an echo-chamber effect.

20 Forthlin Road (Paul McCartney's Home): In comparison to Aunt Mimi's house, the home where Paul grew up is simpler, much less "posh," and even a little ratty around the edges.

More than a hundred Beatles songs were written in this house (including "I Saw Her Standing There") during days Paul and John spent skipping school. Photos taken in the house help make the scene more interesting. Ask your guide how Paul would sneak into the house late at night without waking up his dad.

Rick's Tip: *If you find yourself with extra time in Liverpool, consider any of the city's* **fine free museums** *located at the Albert Dock and nearby: Museum of Liverpool, Merseyside Maritime Museum, and the International Slavery Museum (www. liverpoolmuseums.org.uk for all three), and the Tate Liverpool gallery (www.tate.org.uk).*

Eating and Sleeping

$$ Fonseca's is a casual bistro serving high-quality cuisine (closed Sun-Mon, 12 Stanley Street). The **Liverpool One** shopping center, right in the heart of town, has a row of popular chains, all with outdoor seating. The eateries at the **Albert Dock** aren't high cuisine, but they're handy to sightseeing—take your pick.

If you're overnighting in Liverpool, consider the tasteful **$$$ Hard Day's Night Hotel** (North John Street, www. harddaysnighthotel.com), the straightforward **$$ Aachen Guest Accommodations** (89 Mount Pleasant, www. aachenhotel.co.uk), or the comfortable **$$ Sir Thomas Hotel** (24 Sir Thomas Street, www.sirthomashotel.co.uk).

DURHAM

Without its cathedral, Durham would hardly be noticed. But this magnificently situated structure is hard to miss (even if you're zooming by on the train). Seemingly happy to go nowhere, Durham sits along the tight curve of its river, snug below its castle and famous church. Durham is home to England's third-oldest university, with a student vibe jostling against its lingering working-class mining-town feel.

Orientation

Day Plan: For the best quick visit to Durham, arrive by midafternoon, in time to tour the cathedral and enjoy the evensong service (Tue-Sat at 17:15, Sun at

15:30). If you're sleeping in Durham, you can visit Beamish the next morning before continuing on to your next destination.

Getting There: Frequent trains run from York (4/hour, 45 minutes) and Edinburgh (2/hour, 2 hours); from London, there's a direct train hourly (3 hours). Durham, near the A-1/M-1 motorway, is an easy stop for drivers.

Rick's Tip: If you don't feel like walking Durham's hills, hop on the convenient Cathedral Bus #40—it runs between the train station, Market Place, and the Palace Green (£1 all-day ticket, none on Sun).

Arrival in Durham: From the train station, the fastest and easiest way to reach the cathedral is to hop on the Cathedral Bus (see "Rick's Tip" for details). Drivers simply surrender to the wonderful 400-space Prince Bishops Shopping Centre parking lot (at the roundabout at the base of the old town, a short block from Market Place).

Tourist Information: Durham does not have a physical TI, but the town does maintain a call center and website (tel.

03000-262-626, www.thisisdurham.com). During the summer, volunteer Durham Pointers staff a tourist information cart in Market Place (late May-early Oct, www.durhampointers.co.uk).

Tours: Blue Badge guides offer 1.5-hour city walking tours on Saturdays at 14:00 in peak season (£4, meet at Durham World Heritage Site Visitor Centre, contact TI call center to confirm schedule, tel. 03000-262-626).

Private Guide: David Butler, the town historian, gives excellent private tours (www.dhent.co.uk).

Sights
In Durham
▲▲▲DURHAM'S CATHEDRAL

Built to house the much-venerated bones of St. Cuthbert, Durham's cathedral offers the best look at Norman architecture in England. ("Norman" is British for "Romanesque.") In addition to touring the cathedral, try to fit in an evensong service.

Cost: Free but £3 donation suggested; fee to climb the tower and to enter Open Treasure exhibit.

Hours: Mon-Sat 9:30-18:00, Sun 12:30-

Durham Cathedral

Cathedral nave

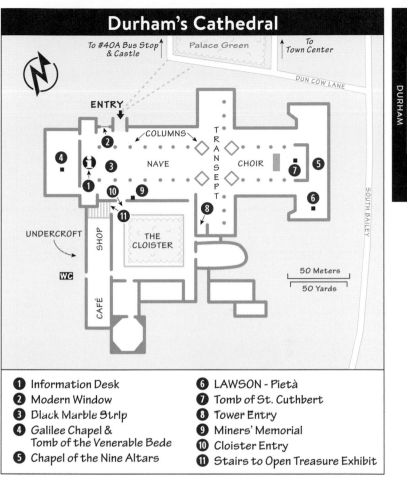

Durham's Cathedral

To #40A Bus Stop & Castle

Palace Green

To Town Center

DUN COW LANE

ENTRY

COLUMNS

T R A N S E P T

NAVE

CHOIR

SOUTH BAILEY

UNDERCROFT

SHOP

THE CLOISTER

WC

CAFÉ

50 Meters

50 Yards

❶ Information Desk
❷ Modern Window
❸ Black Marble Strip
❹ Galilee Chapel & Tomb of the Venerable Bede
❺ Chapel of the Nine Altars

❻ LAWSON - Pietà
❼ Tomb of St. Cuthbert
❽ Tower Entry
❾ Miners' Memorial
❿ Cloister Entry
⓫ Stairs to Open Treasure Exhibit

18:00, daily until 20:00 mid-July-Aug, opens daily at 7:15 for worship and prayer.

Information: Tel. 0191/386-4266, www.durhamcathedral.co.uk.

Evensong and Organ Recitals: To really experience the cathedral, attend an evensong service. Arrive early and ask to be seated in the choir. (Tue-Sat at 17:15, Sun at 15:30, 1 hour, sometimes sung on Mon). The organ plays most Wednesday evenings in July and August (£8, 19:30).

Tours: Regular tours run Monday through Saturday (£5; tours start at 10:30, 11:00, and 14:00; fewer in winter, call or check website to confirm schedule).

⮞ SELF-GUIDED TOUR

Begin your visit at the cathedral **door.** Check out the big, bronze, lion-faced knocker (a replica of the 12th-century original) used by criminals seeking sanctuary.

Inside, a handy ❶ **information desk** is at the back (right) end of the nave. Notice the ❷ **modern window** with the novel depiction of the Last Supper (above and to the left of the entry door).

Spanning the nave, the ❸ **black marble strip** on the floor was as close to the altar as women were allowed in the days when this was a Benedictine church (until 1540).

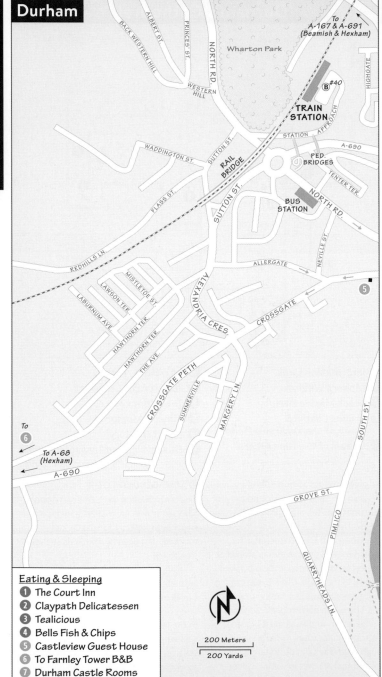

Durham

To
A-167 & A-691
(Beamish & Hexham)

ALBERT ST.
BACK WESTERN HILL
PRINCES ST.
NORTH RD.
WESTERN HILL
HIGHGATE

Wharton Park

B #40

TRAIN STATION

WADDINGTON ST.
SUTTON ST.
STATION APPROACH
A-690

RAIL BRIDGE
PED. BRIDGES
TENTER TER.

FLASS ST.
SUTTON ST.
BUS STATION
NORTH RD.

REDHILLS LN.
ALLERGATE
NEVILLE ST.

LABURNUM AVE.
LAWSON TER.
MISTLETOE ST.
HAWTHORN TER.
HAWTHORN TER.
THE AVE.
ALEXANDRIA CRES.
CROSSGATE
5

CROSSGATE PETH
SUMMERVILLE
MARGERY LN.

SOUTH ST.

To
6

To A-68
(Hexham)
A-690

GROVE ST.

PIMLICO
QUARRY HEADS LN.

Eating & Sleeping
1 The Court Inn
2 Claypath Delicatessen
3 Tealicious
4 Bells Fish & Chips
5 Castleview Guest House
6 To Farnley Tower B&B
7 Durham Castle Rooms

200 Meters
200 Yards

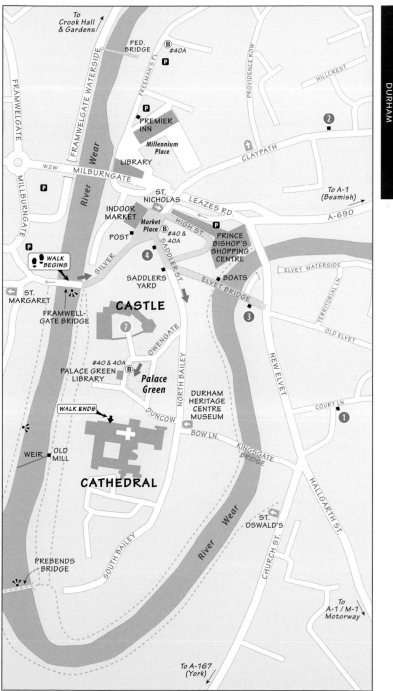

Take a seat and admire the fine proportions, rounded arches, and zigzag-carved decorations of England's best Norman nave. It is particularly harmonious because it was built in a mere 40 years (1093-1133) by well-traveled French masons and architects who knew the latest innovations from Europe. Its stone and ribbed roof, pointed arches, and flying buttresses were revolutionary in England.

At the back of the nave, enter the ❹ **Galilee Chapel** (late Norman, from 1175). The paintings of St. Cuthbert and St. Oswald (seventh-century king of Northumbria) on the side walls of the smaller altar are rare examples of Romanesque (Norman) paintings. On the right side of the chapel, the upraised tomb topped with a black slab contains the remains of the **Venerable Bede,** an eighth-century Christian scholar who wrote the first history of England.

Back in the main church, stroll down the nave to the center, under the highest **bell tower** in Europe (218 feet). Monks worshipped many times a day, and the choir in the center of the church provided a cozy place to gather. Mass has been said daily here in the heart of the cathedral for 900 years. The fancy wooden benches are from the 17th century. Behind the altar is the delicately carved Neville Screen from 1380 (made of Normandy stone in London, shipped to Newcastle by sea, then brought here by wagon). Until the Reformation, the niches contained statues of 107 saints.

Step down behind the high altar into the east end of the church, which contains the 13th-century ❺ **Chapel of the Nine Altars.** Built later than the rest of the church, this is Gothic—taller, lighter, and relatively more extravagant than the Norman nave. On the right, see the powerful modern ❻ **pietà** made of driftwood, with brass accents by local sculptor Fenwick Lawson.

Climb a few steps to the ❼ **tomb of St. Cuthbert.** An inspirational leader of the early Christian Church in north England, St. Cuthbert lived in the Lindisfarne monastery (100 miles north of Durham). When Vikings raided Lindisfarne in 875, the monks fled with his body (and the famous illuminated Lindisfarne Gospels, now in the British Library in London). In 995, after 120 years of roaming, the monks settled in Durham, and Cuthbert was reinterred—and this cathedral was built over his tomb.

In the **south transept** (to your left) is the ❽ **tower entry,** as well as an astronomical clock and the Chapel of the Durham Light Infantry, a regiment of the British Army. The old flags and banners hanging above were actually carried into battle.

Find your way toward the cloister (opposite the entry door). Along the wall by the door to the cloister, notice the ❾ **memorial honoring coal miners.** The last pit of the Durham coalfields closed in the 1980s, but the mining legacy here is still strong.

It's worth making a circuit of the Gothic ❿ **cloister** for a fine view back up to the church towers. From there, you can climb some stairs to enter the ⓫ **Open Treasure exhibit,** displaying cathedral treasures including a copy of the *Magna Carta* from 1216 and actual relics from St. Cuthbert's tomb.

DURHAM CASTLE

The castle still stands—as it has for a thousand years—on its motte (man-made mound) and now houses Durham University. Look into the old courtyard from the castle gate. It traces the very first and smallest bailey (protected area). As future bishops expanded the castle, they left their coats of arms as a way of "signing" the wing they built. Because the Norman kings appointed prince-bishops here to rule this part of their realm, Durham was the seat of power for much of northern England. The bishops had their own army and even minted their own coins. The castle is accessible with a 45-minute guided tour, which includes the courtyard, kitchens, great hall, and chapel.

Cost and Hours: £5, open most days when school is in session—but schedule varies so call ahead, buy tickets at Durham World Heritage Site Visitor Centre (near the cathedral) or Palace Green Library (on the green near the castle), tel. 0191/334-2932, www.dur.ac.uk/durham.castle.

Near Durham
▲▲▲ BEAMISH MUSEUM
This huge, 300-acre open-air museum, located 12 miles from Durham, re-creates life in northeast England during the 1820s, 1900s, and 1940s. It is England's best museum of its type. You'll want at least three hours to explore its four sections: Pit Village (a coal-mining settlement with an actual tourable mine), The Town (a 1913 street lined with actual shops), Pockerley Old Hall (a "gentleman farmer's" manor house), and Home Farm (a preserved farm and farmhouse). Attendants at each stop happily explain everything. In fact, the place is only really interesting if you talk to the attendants—who make it worth ▲▲▲.

A vintage building at the Beamish Museum

Cost and Hours: £19, children 5-16-£11, under 5-free; open Easter-Oct daily 10:00-17:00; off-season until 16:00, weekends only Dec-mid-Feb; check events schedule on chalkboard as you enter, last tickets sold at 15:00 year-round, tel. 0191/370-4000, www.beamish.org.uk.

Getting There: By car, the museum is five minutes off the A-1/M-1 motorway (one exit north of Durham at Chester-le-Street/Junction 63, well-signposted, 25-minute drive northwest of Durham).

Getting to Beamish from Durham by **bus** is a snap on peak-season Saturdays via direct bus #128 (8/day, 30 minutes, runs April-Oct only, stops at Durham train and bus stations). Otherwise, catch bus #21, #X21, or #50 from the Durham bus station (3-4/hour, 25 minutes) and transfer at Chester-le-Street to bus #8, #8A, or #28, which takes you right to the museum entrance (2/hour Mon-Sat, hourly Sun, 15 minutes, leaves from central bus kiosk a half-block away, tel. 0191/420-5050, www.simplygo.com). Show your bus ticket for a 25 percent museum discount.

Eating: Several eateries are scattered around Beamish, including a pub and tea-rooms (in The Town), a fish-and-chips stand (in the Pit Village), and various cafeterias and snack stands. Or bring a picnic.

❍ **Visiting the Museum:** From the entrance building, bear left along the road, then watch for the turnoff on the right to the Pit Village. This is a company town built around a coal mine, with a schoolhouse, a Methodist chapel, and a row of miners' homes with long, skinny pea-patch gardens out front. Poke into some of the homes to see their modest interiors.

Next, cross to the adjacent **Colliery** (coal mine), where you can take a fascinating—if claustrophobic—20-minute tour into the drift mine (check in at the "lamp camp"—tours depart when enough people gather, generally every 5-10 minutes). Nearby (across the tram tracks) is the fascinating **engine works,** where you can see the actual steam-powered winding engine used to operate the mine elevator.

A path leads through the woods to Georgian-era **Pockerley,** which has two parts. First you'll see the **Waggonway,** a big barn filled with steam engines, including the re-created, first-ever passenger train from 1825. (Occasionally this train takes modern-day visitors for a spin on 1825 tracks—a hit with railway buffs.)

Then, climb the hill to **Pockerley Old Hall,** the manor house of a gentleman farmer and his family. The house dates from the 1820s, and while not extremely wealthy, the farmer who lived here owned large tracts of land and could afford to hire help to farm it for him. This rustic home is no palace, but it was comfortable for the period. The small garden terrace out front provides beautiful views across the pastures.

From the manor house, hop on a vintage tram or bus or walk 10 minutes to the Edwardian-era **The Town** (c. 1913). In the Masonic Hall, ogle the grand high-ceilinged meeting room, and check out the fun, old metal signs inside the garage. The heavenly-smelling candy store sells old-timey sweets and has an actual workshop in back with trays of free samples. The newsagent sells stationery, cards, and old toys, while in the grocery, you can see old packaging and the scales used for weighing out products.

Finally, walk or ride a tram or bus to the **Home Farm** (skippable if you're running short on time) Here you'll get to experience a petting zoo and see a "horse gin" (a.k.a. "gin gan")—where a horse walking in a circle turned a crank on a gear to amplify its "horsepower," helping to replace human hand labor. Near the cafeteria, you can cross a busy road to the old farmhouse, still on its original site, where attendants sometimes bake goodies on a coal fire.

Eating and Sleeping

Durham is a university town with plenty of lively, inexpensive eateries. **$$ The Court Inn** offers an eclectic menu of pub grub and an open, lively atmosphere (daily, Court Lane). Creative **$ Claypath Delicatessen** is worth the five-minute uphill walk above Market Place for tasty sandwiches and salads (closed Sun-Mon; from Market Place, cross the bridge and walk up Claypath to #57). **$ Tealicious** serves homemade cakes and scones for their all-day tea (closed Mon, 88 Elvet Bridge). **$ Bells** is a standby for carryout fish-and-chips (daily, just off Market Place).

If you overnight in Durham, consider the restful **$$$ Castleview Guest House** (4 Crossgate, www.castle-view.co.uk); the decent **$$ Farnley Tower B&B** (The Avenue, www.farnley-tower.co.uk); or the student residence at **$$$ Durham Castle** (generally July-Sept only, Palace Green, www.dur.ac.uk/university.college).

HADRIAN'S WALL

In about A.D. 122, during the reign of Emperor Hadrian, the Romans constructed this great stone wall. Not just a wall, it was a military complex with forts, ditches, settlements, and roads. At every mile of the wall, a castle guarded a gate, and two turrets stood between each castle.

Once a towering 20-foot-tall fortification, these days the wall is only about three feet wide and three to six feet high. (The conveniently precut stones were carried away by peasants during the post-Rome Dark Ages for other structures.) In most places, what's left of the wall has been covered over by centuries of sod...making it effectively disappear into the landscape.

But for those intrigued by Roman history, Hadrian's Wall provides a fine excuse to take your imagination for a stroll. These are the most impressive Roman ruins in Britain. Three top sights

Hadrian's Wall is the finest Roman relic in Britain.

are worth visiting: Housesteads Roman Fort shows you where the Romans lived; Vindolanda's museum shows you how they lived; and the Roman Army Museum explains the empire-wide military organization that brought them here.

Orientation

This area, easiest for drivers, is located roughly between the midsize towns of Bardon Mill and Haltwhistle, along the busy A-69 highway. To get right up close to the wall, you'll need to head a couple of miles north to the adjacent villages of Once Brewed and Twice Brewed (along the B-6318 road).

Day Plan: If you have time for only one stop, choose Housesteads Roman Fort.

Drivers with time to do it all could follow this order: Roman Army Museum; Walltown Visitor Centre (pick up info on wall walks); Steel Rigg (hike partway along the wall to Sycamore Gap and return, or hike farther to Housesteads and bus back to your car); Vindolanda; and Housesteads Roman Fort.

Nondrivers can take a bus (runs only in

peak season), which stops at Housesteads, Vindolanda, and Walltown (Roman Army Museum and Visitor Centre).

Tourist Information: The **Walltown Visitor Centre** lies along the Hadrian's Wall bus #AD122 route and has information on the area (Easter-Oct daily, just off the B-6318 next to the Roman Army Museum, follow signs to *Walltown Quarry*, www.nnpa.org.uk).

A helpful **TI** is in Haltwhistle, a block from the train station inside the library (closed Sun, www.visitnorthumberland. com).

For an overview website, visit the Hadrian's Wall Country website at www. hadrianswallcountry.co.uk.

Getting Around Hadrian's Wall

Hadrian's Wall is anchored by the big cities of Newcastle to the east and Carlisle to the west. Driving is the most convenient way to see Hadrian's Wall. If you're coming by train, consider renting a car for the day at either Newcastle or Carlisle; otherwise, you'll need to rely on trains and a bus to connect the sights, hire taxis, or

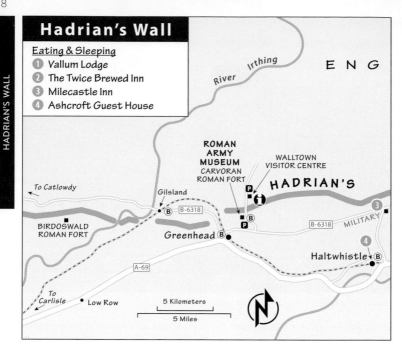

Hadrian's Wall

Eating & Sleeping
1. Vallum Lodge
2. The Twice Brewed Inn
3. Milecastle Inn
4. Ashcroft Guest House

River Irthing

E N G

To Catlowdy

ROMAN ARMY MUSEUM
CARVORAN ROMAN FORT

WALLTOWN VISITOR CENTRE

H A D R I A N ' S

Gilsland

B-6318

BIRDOSWALD ROMAN FORT

Greenhead

B-6318   MILITARY

Haltwhistle

A-69

To Carlisle

Low Row

5 Kilometers

5 Miles

N

book a private guide with a car.

By Car: Zip to this "best of Hadrian's Wall" zone on the speedy A-69; when you get close, head a few miles north and follow the B-6318, which parallels the wall. Official Hadrian's Wall parking lots have pay-and-display machines.

By Bus: Essential resources for navigating the wall by public transit include the *Hadrian's Wall Country Map,* the bus #AD122 schedule, and a local train timetable for Northern Line #4—all available at local visitors centers and train stations (also see www.hadrianswallcountry.co.uk). **Bus #AD122** (runs only in peak season) connects the Roman sights with train stations in **Haltwhistle** and **Hexham** (from £2/ride, £12.50 unlimited Day Rover ticket, buy tickets on board (tel. 01434/322-002). If you're planning to take this bus, it's smart to confirm whether it'll be running during your visit (tel. 01434/322-002, www. gonortheast.co.uk/ad122).

By Train: Northern Line's train route #4 runs parallel to and a few miles south of the

wall. While the train doesn't take you near the actual Roman sights, you can catch bus #AD122 at Hexham and Haltwhistle to get you there (no bus service off-season; train runs hourly, www.northernrail.org).

By Taxi: These Haltwhistle-based taxi companies can help you connect the dots: Sprouls (mobile 07712-321-064) or Diamond (mobile 07597/641-222). It costs about £14 one-way from Haltwhistle to Housesteads Roman Fort.

By Private Tour: Peter Carney, a former history teacher, offers tours with his car and also leads guided walks around Hadrian's Wall (£125/day for up to 5 people, £70/half-day, www.hadrianswall-walk.com).

Sights
▲▲HIKING THE WALL
For a good, craggy, three-mile, one-way, up-and-down walk along the wall, hike between Steel Rigg and Housesteads Roman Fort. For a shorter hike, begin at Steel Rigg (where there's a pay parking lot) and walk a mile to Sycamore Gap, then

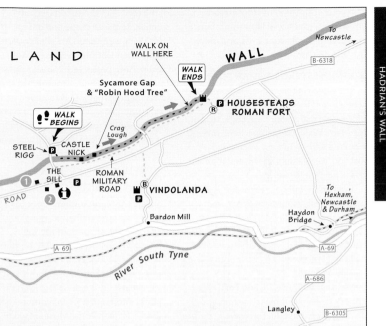

back again (the Still and Walltown visitors centers hand out a free sheet outlining this walk). These hikes are moderately strenuous and are best for those in good shape. You'll need sturdy shoes and a windbreaker to comfortably overcome the often blustery environment.

To reach the trailhead for the short hike from **Steel Rigg to Sycamore Gap,** take the little road off the B-6318 near the Twice Brewed Inn and park in the pay-and-display parking lot on the right at the crest of the hill. Walk through the gate to the shoulder-high stretch of wall, go to the left, and follow the wall running steeply down the valley below you. Walk down the steep slope into the valley, then back up the other side. Following the wall, you'll do a similar up-and-down routine three more times.

In the second gap is one of the best-preserved milecastles. Soon after, you'll reach the third gap, called Sycamore Gap for the large symmetrical tree in the middle. You can either hike back the way

you came or cut down toward the main road to find the less strenuous Roman Military Way path; this leads back to the base of the Steel Rigg hill, where you can huff back up to your car.

A hiker walking along Hadrian's Wall

If you continue on to Housesteads, you'll pass a traditional Northumbrian sheep farm, windswept lakes, and more ups and downs.

▲▲HOUSESTEADS ROMAN FORT

With its respectable museum, powerful scenery, and the best-preserved segment of the wall, this is your best single stop at Hadrian's Wall. It requires a steep hike up from the parking lot, but once there it's just you, the bleating sheep, and memories of ancient Rome.

Cost and Hours: £7.50 for site and museum; daily April-Sept 10:00-18:00, Oct until 17:00, Nov-March until 16:00; last entry 45 minutes before closing, pay parking, bus #AD122 stops here, info tel. 0370-333-1181, www.english-heritage.org. uk/housesteads.

Visiting the Museum and Fort: Hike about a half-mile uphill to the fort, and duck into the **museum** (on the left) before touring the site. Look for the giant Victory statue, which once adorned the fort's East Gate; her foot is stepping on a globe, serving as an intimidating reminder to outsiders of the Romans' success in battle.

Then head out to the sprawling ruins of the **fort.** All Roman forts were the same rectangular shape and design, containing a commander's headquarters, barracks, and latrines (Housesteads has the best-preserved Roman toilets found anywhere—look for them at the lower-right corner). This fort even had a hospital. The fort was built right up to the wall, which runs along its upper end. This is the one place along the wall where you're actually allowed to get up and walk on top of it for a photo op.

▲▲VINDOLANDA

This larger Roman fort (which actually predates the wall by 40 years) and museum are just south of the wall. Although Housesteads has better ruins and the wall, Vindolanda has the more impressive museum, packed with artifacts that reveal intimate details of Roman life.

Cost and Hours: £7, £11 combo-ticket includes Roman Army Museum, daily April-Sept 10:00-18:00, mid-Feb-March and Oct until 17:00, Nov-Dec until 16:00, closed Jan-mid-Feb, last entry one hour before closing, call first during bad weather, free parking with entry, bus #AD122 stops here, café.

The remains of Housesteads Roman Fort, part of Hadrian's Wall

Information: Tel. 01434/344-277, www. vindolanda.com.

Tours: Guided tours run twice daily on weekends only (typically at 10:45 and 14:00); in high season, archaeological talks and tours may be offered on weekdays as well. Both are included in your ticket.

Archaeological Dig: The Vindolanda site is an active dig—from Easter through September, you'll see the excavation work in progress (usually Mon-Fri, weather permitting).

Visiting the Site and Museum: Head out to the **site,** walking through 500 yards of grassy parkland decorated by the foundation stones of the Roman fort and a full-size replica chunk of the wall. Over the course of 400 years, at least nine forts were built on this spot. The Romans, by lazily sealing the foundations from each successive fort, left modern-day archaeologists with a 20-foot-deep treasure trove of remarkably well-preserved artifacts.

At the far side of the site, pass through the pleasant riverside garden area on the way to the museum. The well-presented **museum** pairs actual artifacts with insightful explanations—such as a collection of Roman shoes with a description about what each one tells us about its wearer. The weapons (including arrowheads and spearheads) and fragments of armor are a reminder that Vindolanda was an important outpost on Rome's northern boundary.

But the museum's main attraction is its collection of writing tablets. These letters bring Romans to life in a way that ruins alone can't. The most famous piece (described but not displayed here) is the first known example of a woman writing to a woman (an invitation to a birthday party).

Finally, you'll pass through an exhibit about the history of the excavations.

▲▲ROMAN ARMY MUSEUM

This museum, a few miles farther west at Greenhead (near the site of the Carvoran Roman fort), has cutting-edge, interactive exhibits illustrating the structure of the Roman Army that built and monitored this wall, with a focus on the everyday lifestyles of the Roman soldiers stationed here. Bombastic displays, life-size figures, and several different films—but few actual artifacts—make this entertaining museum a good complement to the archaeological emphasis of Vindolanda. If you're visiting all three Roman sights, this is a good one to start at, as it sets the stage for what you're about to see.

Cost and Hours: £5.75, £11 combo-ticket includes Vindolanda, April-Sept daily 10:00-18:00, mid-Feb-March and Oct daily until 17:00, Nov-Dec Sat-Sun only until 16:00, closed Jan-mid-Feb; free parking with entry, bus #AD122 stops here, tel. 01697/747-485, www. vindolanda.com.

Eating and Sleeping

Set your sights on the adjacent villages of Once Brewed and Twice Brewed, where you'll find the **$$ The Twice Brewed Inn,** with a friendly pub and basic rooms (Military Road, www.twicebrewedinn. co.uk), and the cushy **$$ Vallum Lodge** (Military Road, www.vallum-lodge.co.uk). The **$$ Milecastle Inn,** two miles to the west of the villages, offers the best dinner around—reserve ahead in summer (daily, North Road, tel. 01434/321-372). Near Haltwhistle, **$$ Ashcroft Guest House** has luxurious rooms (Lanty's Lonnen, www.ashcroftguesthouse.co.uk).

Edinburgh

Edinburgh (ED'n-burah—only tourists pronounce it like "Pittsburgh") is the historical, cultural, and political capital of Scotland. For nearly a thousand years, Scotland's kings, parliaments, writers, thinkers, and bankers have called Edinburgh home. Today, it remains Scotland's most sophisticated city.

Edinburgh feels like two cities in one. The Old Town stretches along the Royal Mile, from the grand castle on top to the palace on the bottom. Along this colorful labyrinth of cobbled streets and narrow lanes, medieval skyscrapers stand shoulder to shoulder, hiding peaceful courtyards.

A few hundred yards north of the Old Town lies the New Town. It's a magnificent planned neighborhood (from the 1700s). Here, you'll enjoy upscale shops, broad boulevards, straight streets, and Georgian mansions decked out in Greek-style columns and statues.

Since 1999, when Scotland regained a measure of self-rule, Edinburgh reassumed its place as home of the Scottish Parliament. The city hums with life. Students and professionals pack the pubs and art galleries. It's especially lively in August, when the Edinburgh Festival takes over the town. Historic, monumental, fun, and well-organized, Edinburgh is a delight.

EDINBURGH IN 2 DAYS

While the major sights can be seen in a day, I'd give Edinburgh two days and three nights.

Day 1: Tour the castle. Then, you could hop on the city bus tour (departing from a block below the castle at the Hub/Tolbooth Church). Or you could dive into my self-guided Royal Mile walk, stopping in at shops and museums that interest you (Gladstone's Land is tops but you can only visit it by booking a tour). At the bottom of the Mile, consider visiting the Scottish Parliament, the Palace of Holyroodhouse, or both. If the weather's good, you could hike back to your B&B along the Salisbury Crags.

On any evening: Options include various "haunted Edinburgh" walks, literary pub crawls, theater, or live music in pubs.

Day 2: Visit the National Museum of Scotland. After lunch, stroll through the Princes Street Gardens and the Scottish National Gallery. Then follow my self-guided walk through the New Town, visiting the Scottish National Portrait Gallery and the Georgian House—or squeeze in a quick tour of the good ship *Britannia* (check last entry time before you head out).

ORIENTATION

With 490,000 people (835,000 in the metro area), Edinburgh is Scotland's second-biggest city (after Glasgow). But the tourist's Edinburgh is compact: Old Town, New Town, and the B&B area south of the city center.

Edinburgh's **Old Town** stretches across a ridgeline slung between two bluffs. From west to east, this "Royal Mile" runs from the Castle Rock—which is visible from anywhere—to the base of the 822-foot extinct volcano called Arthur's Seat. For visitors, this east-west axis is the center of the action. Just south of the Royal Mile is the National Museum of Scotland; farther to the south is a handy B&B neighborhood that lines up along **Dalkeith Road.** North of the Royal Mile ridge is the **New Town,** a neighborhood of grid-planned streets and elegant Georgian buildings.

In the center of it all—in a drained lake bed between the Old and New Towns—sit the Princes Street Gardens park and Waverley Bridge, where you'll find the Waverley train station, TI, Waverley Mall, bus info office (starting point for most city bus tours), Scottish National Gallery, and a covered dance-and-music pavilion.

Tourist Information

The crowded TI is as central as can be, on the rooftop of the Waverley Mall and Waverley train station (Mon-Sat 9:00-17:00, Sun from 10:00, June daily until 18:00, July-Aug daily until 19:00; tel. 0131-473-3868, www.visitscotland.com).

For more information than what's included in the TI's free map, buy the excellent *Collins Discovering Edinburgh* map (which comes with opinionated commentary and locates almost every major sight). If you're interested in evening music, ask for the comprehensive entertainment listing, *The List.*

Tours
Royal Mile Walking Tours

Walking tours are an Edinburgh specialty; you'll see groups trailing entertaining guides all over town. Below I've listed good all-purpose walks; for literary pub crawls and ghost tours, see "Night Walks" on page 368.

Edinburgh Tour Guides offers a good historical walk (without all the ghosts and goblins). Their Royal Mile tour is a gentle two-hour downhill stroll from the castle to the palace (£16.50; daily at 9:30 and 19:00; meet outside Gladstone's Land, near the top of the Royal Mile, must reserve ahead, mobile 0785-888-0072, www.edinburghtourguides.com, info@edinburghtourguides.com).

Mercat Tours offers a 1.5-hour "Secrets of the Royal Mile" walk that's more entertaining than intellectual (£13; £30 includes optional, 45-minute guided Edinburgh Castle visit; daily at 10:00 and 13:00, leaves from Mercat Cross on the Royal Mile, tel. 0131/225-5445, www.mercattours.com). They also offer a variety of other tours (check their website).

Old Town

EDINBURGH AT A GLANCE

▲▲▲**Royal Mile** Historic road—good for walking—stretching from the castle down to the palace, lined with museums, pubs, and shops. **Hours:** Always open, but best during business hours, with walking tours daily. See page 331.

▲▲▲**Edinburgh Castle** Iconic hilltop fort and royal residence complete with crown jewels, Romanesque chapel, memorial, and fine military museum. **Hours:** Daily April-Sept 9:30-18:00, Oct-March until 17:00. See page 343.

▲▲▲**National Museum of Scotland** Intriguing, well-displayed artifacts from prehistoric times to the 20th century. **Hours**: Daily 10:00-17:00. See page 354.

▲▲**Gladstone's Land** Seventeenth-century Royal Mile merchant's residence. **Hours:** Daily 10:30-16:00 by tour only, closed Nov-March. See page 349.

▲▲**St. Giles' Cathedral** Preaching grounds of Scottish Reformer John Knox, with spectacular organ, Neo-Gothic chapel, and distinctive crown spire. **Hours:** May-Sept Mon-Fri 9:00-19:00, Sat 9:00-17:00; Oct-April Mon-Sat 9:00-17:00; Sun 13:00-17:00 year-round. See page 336.

▲▲**Scottish Parliament Building** Striking headquarters for parliament, which returned to Scotland in 1999. **Hours:** Mon-Sat 10:00-17:00, longer hours Tue-Thu when parliament is in session (Sept-June), closed Sun year-round. See page 338.

▲▲**Palace of Holyroodhouse** The Queen's splendid official residence in Scotland, with lavish rooms, 12th-century abbey, and gallery with rotating exhibits. **Hours:** Daily April-Oct 9:30-18:00, Nov-March until 16:30, closed during royal visits. See page 353.

▲▲**Scottish National Gallery** Choice sampling of European masters and Scotland's finest. **Hours:** Daily 10:00-17:00, Thu until 19:00; longer hours in Aug. See page 357.

▲▲**Scottish National Portrait Gallery** Beautifully displayed *Who's Who* of Scottish history. **Hours:** Daily 10:00-17:00. See page 360.

▲▲**Georgian House** Intimate peek at upper-crust life in the late 1700s. **Hours:** Daily April-Oct 10:00-17:00, March and Nov 11:00-16:00, closed Dec-Feb. See page 362.

▲▲**Royal Yacht** *Britannia* Ship for the royal family with a history of distinguished passengers, a 15-minute trip out of town. **Hours:** Daily 9:30-16:30, Oct until 16:00, Nov-March 10:00-15:30 (these are last entry times). See page 363.

▲**Scotch Whisky Experience** Gimmicky but fun and educational introduction to Scotland's most famous beverage. **Hours:** Generally daily 10:00-18:00. See page 349.

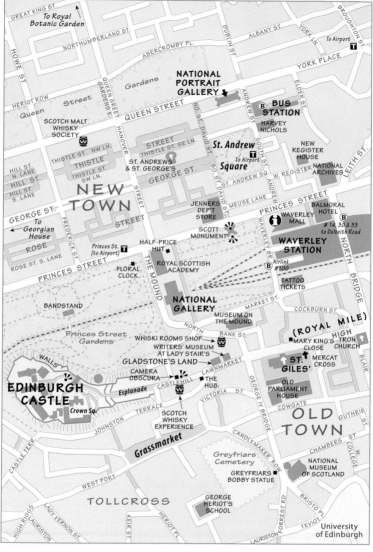

Rick's Tip: **Sunday is a good day to take a guided walking tour** *along the Royal Mile or a city bus tour (buses go faster in light traffic). Although many Royal Mile sights are closed on Sunday (except in Aug), other major sights and shops are open.*

Blue Badge Local Guides

The following guides charge similar prices and offer half-day and full-day tours: **Jean Blair** (a delightful teacher and guide, £190/day without car, £430/day with car, mobile 0798-957-0287, www. travelthroughscotland.com, scotguide7@ gmail.com) and **Ken Hanley** (who wears his kilt as if pants don't exist, £130/half-

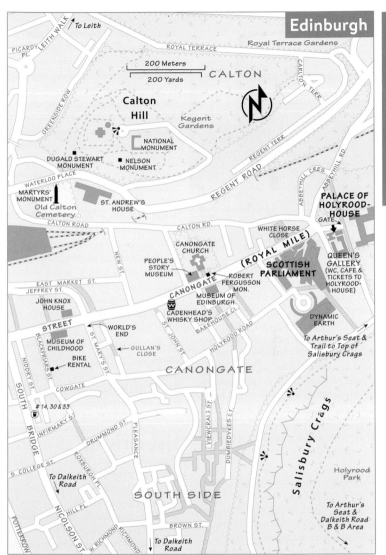

Edinburgh

day, £250/day, extra charge if he uses his car—seats up to six, tel. 0131/666-1944, mobile 0771-034-2044, www.small-world-tours.co.uk, kennethhanley@me.com).

Hop-On, Hop-Off Bus Tours

The following one-hour hop-on, hop-off bus tour routes, all run by the same company, circle the town center, stop-ping at the major sights. **Edinburgh Tour** (green buses) focuses on the city center, with live guides. **City Sightseeing** (red buses, focuses on Old Town) has recorded commentary, as does the **Majestic Tour** (blue-and-yellow buses, includes a stop at the *Britannia* and Royal Botanic Garden). You can pay for just one tour (£15/24 hours), but most people pay a few pounds more for a ticket covering all buses (£20; buses run April-Oct roughly 9:00-19:00, shorter hours off-season; every 10-15 minutes, buy tickets on board, tel. 0131/220-0770, www.edinburgh-tour.com). On sunny days the buses go topless, but come with increased traffic noise and exhaust fumes. For £52, the Royal Edinburgh Ticket covers two days of unlimited travel on all three buses, as well as admission (and line-skipping privileges) at Edinburgh Castle, the Palace of Holyroodhouse, and Britannia (www.royaledinburghticket.co.uk).

Day Trips from Edinburgh

Many companies run a variety of day trips to regional sights, as well as multiday and themed itineraries. (Several of the local guides listed earlier have cars, too.)

The most popular tour is the all-day **Highlands trip** (about £50, roughly 8:00-20:00). Itineraries vary but you'll generally visit/pass through the Trossachs, Rannoch Moor, Glencoe, Fort William, Fort Augustus on Loch Ness (some tours offer an optional boat ride), and Pitlochry. To save time, look for a tour that gives you a short glimpse of Loch Ness rather than driving its entire length or doing a boat trip. (Once you've seen a little of it, you've seen it all.)

Larger outfits, typically using bigger buses, include **Timberbush Highland Tours** (tel. 0131/226-6066, www.timberbushtours.com), **Gray Line** (tel. 0131/555-5558, www.graylinescotland.com), **Highland Experience** (tel. 0131/226-1414, www.highlandexperience.com), **Highland Explorer** (tel. 0131/558-3738, www.highlandexplorertours.com), and Scotline (tel. 0131/557-0162, www.scotlinetours.co.uk).

Other companies pride themselves on keeping group sizes small, with 16-seat minibuses; these include **Rabbie's** (tel. 0131/212-5005, www.rabbies.com) and **Heart of Scotland Tours: The Wee Red Bus** (10 percent Rick Steves discount on full-price day tours—mention when booking, does not apply to overnight tours or senior/student rates, occasionally canceled off-season if too few sign up—leave a contact number, tel. 0131/228-2888, www.heartofscotlandtours.co.uk, run by Nick Roche).

Rick's Tip: *If visiting in festival-filled* **August, book ahead** *for your must-see events, hotels, and fancy restaurant dinners. Expect hotel prices to jump.*

Helpful Hints

Baggage Storage: At the train station, you'll find pricey, high-security luggage storage near platform 2 (daily 7:00-23:00). There are also lockers at the bus station on St. Andrew Square, just two blocks north of the train station.

Laundry: The **Ace Cleaning Centre** launderette is located near my recommended B&Bs south of town. You can pay for full-service laundry (drop off in the morning for same-day service) or stay and do it yourself. For a small extra fee, they'll collect your laundry from your B&B and drop it off the next day (Mon-Fri 8:00-20:00, Sat 9:00-17:00, Sun 10:00-16:00, along bus route to city center at 13 South Clerk Street, opposite Queens Hall, tel. 0131/667-0549).

Bike Rental and Tours: The laid-back crew at **Cycle Scotland** happily recommends good bike routes with your rental (prices starting at £20/3 hours or £30/day, electric bikes available for extra fee, daily 10:00-18:00, may close for a couple of months in winter, just off Royal Mile at 29 Blackfriars Street, tel. 0131/556-5560, mobile 07796-886-899, www.cyclescotland.co.uk, Peter). They also run guided three-hour bike tours daily (£45/person, extra fee for e-bike, book ahead).

EDINBURGH WALKS

I've outlined two walks in Edinburgh: along the Royal Mile, and through the New Town. Many of the sights we'll pass on these walks are described in more detail later, under "Sights."

◆ The Royal Mile

The Royal Mile is one of Europe's most interesting historic walks—it's worth ▲▲▲. The following self-guided stroll is also available as a 🎧 downloadable Rick Steves audio tour; see page 29.

Overview

Start at Edinburgh Castle at the top and amble down to the Palace of Holyroodhouse. Along the way, the street changes names—Castlehill, Lawnmarket, High Street, and Canongate—but it's a straight, downhill shot totaling just over one mile. And nearly every step is packed with shops, cafés, and lanes leading to tiny squares.

As you walk, you'll be tracing the growth of the city—its birth atop Castle Hill, its Old Town heyday in the 1600s, its expansion in the 1700s into the Georgian New Town (leaving the old quarter an overcrowded, disease-ridden Victorian slum), and on to the 21st century at the modern Scottish parliament building (2004). Despite the drizzle, be sure to look up—spires, carvings, and towering Gothic "skyscrapers" give this city its unique urban identity.

This walk covers the Royal Mile's landmarks, but skips the many museums and indoor attractions along the way. Most of these sights are described in more detail under "Sights," later in this chapter. You can stay focused on the walk (which takes about 1.5 hours, without entering sights),

The Royal Mile

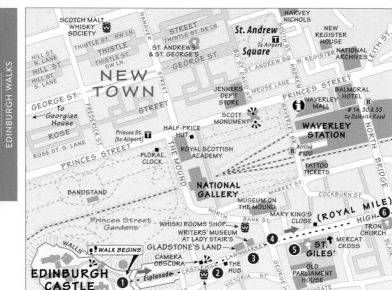

then return later to visit the various indoor attractions; or review the sight descriptions beforehand and pop into those that interest you as you pass them.

• *We'll start at the Castle Esplanade, the big parking lot at the entrance to…*

❶ EDINBURGH CASTLE

Edinburgh was born on the bluff—a big rock—where the castle now stands. Since before recorded history, people have lived on this strategic, easily defended perch.

The **castle** is an imposing symbol of Scottish independence. Flanking the entryway are statues of the fierce warriors who battled English invaders, William Wallace (on the right) and Robert the Bruce (left). Between them is the Scottish motto, *Nemo me impune lacessit*—roughly, "No one messes with me and gets away with it." (For a self-guided tour of Edinburgh Castle, see page 343.)

The esplanade—built as a military parade ground (1816)—is now the site of the annual Military Tattoo. This spectacular massing of regimental bands fills the square nightly for most of August. There are fine views in both directions from the esplanade. Facing north, you'll see the body of water called the Firth of Forth, and Fife beyond that. (The Firth of Forth is the estuary where the River Forth flows

Edinburgh Castle's Esplanade

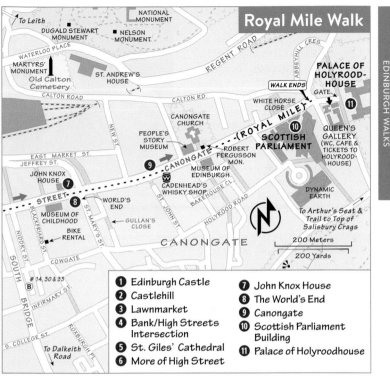

Royal Mile Walk

1 Edinburgh Castle
2 Castlehill
3 Lawnmarket
4 Bank/High Streets Intersection
5 St. Giles' Cathedral
6 More of High Street
7 John Knox House
8 The World's End
9 Canongate
10 Scottish Parliament Building
11 Palace of Holyroodhouse

into the North Sea.) Still facing north, find the lacy spire of the Scott Monument and two Neoclassical buildings housing art galleries. Beyond them, the stately buildings of Edinburgh's New Town rise. Panning to the right, find the Nelson Monument and some faux Greek ruins atop Calton Hill.

• *Start walking down the Royal Mile. The first block is a street called...*

❷ CASTLEHILL

You're immediately in the tourist hubbub. The big tank-like building on your left was the Old Town's **reservoir.** You'll see the wellheads it served all along this walk. While it once held 1.5 million gallons of water, today it's filled with the touristy Tartan Weaving Mill and Exhibition.

The black-and-white tower ahead on the left has entertained visitors since the 1850s with its **camera obscura,** a darkened room where a mirror and a series of lenses capture live images of the city surroundings outside. (Giggle at the funny mirrors as you walk fatly by.) Across the street, filling the old Castlehill Primary School, is a gimmicky-if-intoxicating whisky-sampling exhibit called the **Scotch Whisky Experience** (a.k.a. "Malt Disney"; described later).

• *Just ahead, in front of the church with the tall, lacy spire, is the old market square known as...*

❸ LAWNMARKET

During the Royal Mile's heyday, in the 1600s, this intersection was bigger and served as a market for fabric (especially "lawn," a linen-like cloth).

Towering above Lawnmarket, with the tallest spire in the city, is the former **Tolbooth Church.** This impressive Neo-

Gothic structure (1844) is now home to the Hub, Edinburgh's festival-ticket and information center. The world-famous Edinburgh Festival fills the month of August with cultural action. The various festivals feature classical music, traditional and fringe theater (especially comedy), art, books, and more. Drop inside the building to get festival info. This is a handy stop for its WC, café, and free Wi-Fi.

In the 1600s, this—along with the next stretch, called High Street—was the city's main street. At that time, Edinburgh was bursting with breweries, printing presses, and banks. Tens of thousands of citizens were squeezed into the narrow confines of the Old Town. Here on this ridge, they built **tenements** (multiple-unit residences) similar to the more recent ones you see today. These tenements, rising 10 stories and more, were some of the tallest domestic buildings in Europe.

• *Continue a half-block down the Mile.*

Gladstone's Land (at #477b, on the left), a surviving original tenement, was acquired by a wealthy merchant in 1617. Stand in front of the building and look up at this centuries-old skyscraper. This design was standard for its time: a shop or shops on the ground floor, with columns and an arcade, and residences on the floors above. Because window glass was expensive, the lower halves of window openings were made of cheaper wood, which swung out like shutters for ventilation—and were convenient for tossing out garbage. (Gladstone's Land can be seen by tour only and is closed Nov-March—consider dropping in and booking ahead for a spot. For details, see listing later.) Out front, you may also see trainers with live birds of prey. While this is mostly just a fun way to show off for tourists (and raise donations for the Just Falconry center), docents explain the connection: The building's owner was named Thomas Gledstanes—and *gled* is the Scots word for "hawk."

Branching off the spine of the Royal Mile are a number of narrow alleyways

that go by various local names. A "wynd" (rhymes with "kind") is a narrow, winding lane. A "pend" is an arched gateway. "Gate" is from an Old Norse word for street. And a "close" is a tiny alley between two buildings (originally with a door that "closed" at night). A "close" usually leads to a "court," or courtyard.

Opposite Gladstone's Land (at #322), a close leads to **Riddle's Court.** Wander through here and imagine Edinburgh in the 17th and 18th centuries, when tourists came here to marvel at its skyscrapers. Some 40,000 people were jammed into the few blocks between here and the World's End pub (which we'll reach soon). Visualize the labyrinthine maze of the old city, with people scurrying through these back alleyways, buying and selling, and popping into taverns.

No city in Europe was as densely populated—or perhaps as filthy. The dirt streets were soiled with sewage from bedpans that were emptied out windows. By the 1700s, the Old Town was rife with poverty and cholera outbreaks. The smoky home fires rising from tenements and the infamous smell (or "reek" in Scottish) that wafted across the city gave it a nickname that sticks today: "Auld Reekie."

• *Return to the Royal Mile and continue down it a few steps to take in some sights at the...*

❹ BANK/HIGH STREETS INTERSECTION

A number of sights cluster here, where Lawnmarket changes its name to High Street and intersects with Bank Street and George IV Bridge.

Begin with **Deacon Brodie's Tavern.** Read the "Doctor Jekyll and Mr. Hyde" story of this pub's notorious namesake on the wall facing Bank Street. Then, to see his spooky split personality, check out both sides of the hanging signpost. Brodie—a pillar of the community by day but a burglar by night—epitomizes the divided personality of 1700s Edinburgh. It was a rich, productive city—home to great philosophers and scientists, who actively contributed to the Enlightenment. Meanwhile, the Old Town was riddled with crime and squalor. (In the next century, in the late 1800s, novelist Robert Louis Stevenson would capture the dichotomy of Edinburgh's rich-poor society in his *Strange Case of Dr. Jekyll and Mr. Hyde.)*

In the late 1700s, Edinburgh's upper class moved out of the Old Town into a planned community called the New Town

(a quarter-mile north of here). Eventually, most tenements were torn down and replaced with newer **Victorian buildings.** You'll see some at this intersection.

Look left down Bank Street to the green-domed **Bank of Scotland.** This was the headquarters of the bank, which had practiced modern capitalist financing since 1695.

If you detour left down Bank Street toward the bank, you'll find the recommended Whiski Rooms Shop. If you head in the opposite direction, down George IV Bridge, you'll reach the excellent National Museum of Scotland, restaurant-lined Forrest Road, and photogenic Victoria Street, which leads to the pub-lined Grassmarket square (all described later in this chapter).

Otherwise, continue along the Royal Mile. As you walk, be careful crossing the streets along the Mile. Edinburgh drivers—especially cabbies—have a reputation for being impatient with jaywalking tourists. Notice and heed the pedestrian crossing signals, which don't always turn at the same time as the car signals.

Across the street from Deacon Brodie's Tavern is a seated green statue of hometown boy **David Hume** (1711-1776)—one of the most influential thinkers not only of Scotland, but in all of Western philosophy. The atheistic Hume was one of the towering figures of the Scottish Enlightenment of the mid-1700s.

Follow David Hume's gaze to the opposite corner, where a **brass H** in the pavement marks the site of the last public execution in Edinburgh in 1864. Deacon Brodie himself would have been hung about here (in 1788, on a gallows with a design he had helped to improve—smart guy).

• *From the brass H, continue down the Royal Mile, pausing just before the church square at a stone wellhead with the pyramid cap.*

All along the Royal Mile, **wellheads** like this (from 1835) provided townsfolk with water in the days before buildings had plumbing. This neighborhood well was served by the reservoir up at the castle.

• *Ahead of you (past the Victorian statue of some duke), embedded in the pavement near the street, is a big heart.*

The **Heart of Midlothian** marks the spot of the city's 15th-century municipal building and jail. In times past, in a nearby open space, criminals were hanged, traitors were decapitated, and witches were burned.

• *Make your way to the entrance of the church.*

❺ ST. GILES' CATHEDRAL

This is the flagship of the Church of Scotland (Scotland's largest denomination)—called the "Mother Church of Presbyterianism." The interior serves as a kind of Scottish Westminster Abbey, filled with monuments, statues, plaques, and stained-glass windows dedicated to great Scots and moments in history.

The reformer John Knox (1514-1572) was the preacher here. His fiery sermons helped turn once-Catholic Edinburgh into a bastion of Protestantism. During the Scottish Reformation, St. Giles' was transformed from a Catholic cathedral to a Presbyterian church. The spacious interior is well worth a visit (described later in "Sights").

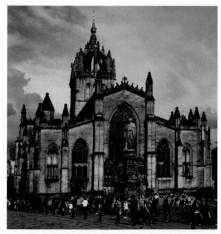
St. Giles' Cathedral

• *Facing the church entrance, curl around its right side, into a parking lot.*

SIGHTS AROUND ST. GILES'

The grand building across the parking lot from St. Giles' is the **Old Parliament House.** From the early 1600s until 1707, this building evolved to become the seat of a true parliament of elected officials. That came to an end in 1707, when Scotland signed an Act of Union, joining what's known today as the United Kingdom and giving up their right to self-rule. (More on that later in the walk.)

The great reformer **John Knox** is buried—with appropriate austerity—under parking lot spot #23. The statue among the cars shows King Charles II riding to a toga party back in 1685.

• *Continue on through the parking lot, around the back end of the church.*

Every Scottish burgh (town licensed by the king to trade) had three standard features: a "tolbooth" (basically a Town Hall, with a courthouse, meeting room, and jail); a "tron" (official weighing scale); and a "mercat" (or market) cross. The **mercat cross** standing just behind St. Giles' Cathedral has a slender column decorated with a unicorn holding a flag with the cross of St. Andrew. Royal proclamations have been read at this mercat cross since the 14th century. In 1952, a town crier heralded the news that Britain had a new queen—three days after the actual event (traditionally the time it took for a horse to speed here from London). Today, Mercat Cross is the meeting point for many of Edinburgh's walking tours—both historic and ghostly.

• *Circle around to the street side of the church.*

The statue to **Adam Smith** honors the Edinburgh author of the pioneering *Wealth of Nations* (1776), in which he laid out the economics of free market capitalism. Smith theorized that an "invisible hand" wisely guides the unregulated free market.

❻ MORE OF HIGH STREET

Continuing down this stretch of the Royal Mile, which is traffic-free most of the day (notice the bollards that raise and lower for permitted traffic), you'll see the Fringe Festival office (at #180), street musicians, and another wellhead (with horse "sippies," dating from 1675).

Notice those **three red boxes.** In the 20th century, people used these to make telephone calls to each other. (Imagine that!)

At the next intersection, on the left is **Cockburn Street** (pronounced "COE-burn"). This street has a reputation for its eclectic independent shops and string of trendy bars and eateries.

• When you reach the **Tron Church** (17th century, currently housing shops), you're at the intersection of **North and South Bridge streets.** These major streets lead left to Waverley Station and right to the Dalkeith Road B&Bs. Several handy bus lines run along here.

This is the halfway point of this walk. Stand on the corner diagonally across from the church. Look up to the top of the Royal Mile at the Hub and its 240-foot spire. Notwithstanding its turret and 16th-century charm, the **Radisson Blu Hotel** just across the street is entirely new construction (1990), built to fit in. The city is protecting its historic look.

In the next block downhill are three **characteristic pubs,** side by side, that offer free traditional Scottish and folk music in the evenings.

• Go down High Street another block, passing near the Museum of Childhood (on the right, at #42) and a fragrant fudge shop a few doors down, where you can sample various flavors (tempting you to buy a slab).

Directly across the street, just below another wellhead, is the...

❼ JOHN KNOX HOUSE

Remember that Knox was a towering figure in Edinburgh's history, converting Scotland to a Calvinist style of Protestantism. His religious bent was "Presbyterianism," in which parishes are governed by elected officials rather than appointed bishops. This more democratic brand of Christianity also spurred Scotland toward political democracy. Full disclosure: It's not certain that Knox ever actually lived here. Attached to the Knox House is the Scottish Storytelling Centre, where locals with the gift of gab perform regularly; check the posted schedule.

• A few steps farther down High Street, at the intersection with St. Mary's and Jeffrey streets, you'll reach...

❽ THE WORLD'S END

For centuries, a wall stood here, marking the end of the burgh of Edinburgh. For residents within the protective walls of the city, this must have felt like the "world's end," indeed. At the intersection, find the brass bricks in the street that trace the gate (demolished in 1764).

• Continue down the Royal Mile—leaving old Edinburgh—as High Street changes names to...

❾ CANONGATE

About 10 steps down Canongate, look left down Cranston Street (past the train tracks) to a good view of the Calton Cemetery up on **Calton Hill.** The obelisk, called Martyrs' Monument, remembers a group of 18th-century patriots exiled by London to Australia for their reform politics. The round building to

Calton Hill

the left is the grave of philosopher David Hume. And the big, turreted building to the right was the jail master's house. Today, the main reason to go up Calton Hill is for the fine views.

• *A couple of hundred yards farther along the Royal Mile (on the right at #172) you reach Cadenhead's, a serious place to learn about and buy whisky. About 30 yards farther along, you'll pass two free museums, the People's Story Museum (on the left, in the old tollhouse at #163) and Museum of Edinburgh (on the right, at #142). But our next stop is the church just across from the Museum of Edinburgh.*

The 1688 **Canongate Kirk** (Church)—located not far from the royal residence of Holyroodhouse—is where Queen Elizabeth II and her family worship whenever they're in town. (So don't sit in the front pew, marked with her crown.) The gilded emblem at the top of the roof, high above the door, has the antlers of a stag from the royal estate of Balmoral. The Queen's granddaughter married here in 2011.

The church is open only when volunteers have signed up to welcome visitors (and closed in winter). Chat them up and borrow the description of the place. Then step inside the lofty blue and red interior, renovated with royal money; the church is filled with light and the flags of various Scottish regiments. In the narthex, peruse the photos of royal family events here, and find the list of priests and ministers of this

parish—it goes back to 1143 (with a clear break with the Reformation in 1561).

• *After leaving the church, walk about 300 yards farther along the Royal Mile. In the distance you can see the Palace of Holyroodhouse (the end of this walk) and soon, on the right, you'll come to the modern Scottish parliament building.*

Just opposite the parliament building is **White Horse Close** (on the left, in the white arcade). Step into this 17th-century courtyard. It was from here that the Edinburgh stagecoach left for London. Eight days later, the horse-drawn carriage would pull into its destination: Scotland Yard. Note that bus #35 leaves in two directions from here—downhill for the Royal Yacht *Britannia,* and uphill along the Royal Mile (as far as South Bridge) and on to the National Museum of Scotland.

• *Now walk up around the corner to the flagpoles (flying the flags of Europe, Britain, and Scotland) in front of the...*

⓪ SCOTTISH PARLIAMENT BUILDING

Finally, after centuries of history, we reach the 21st century. And finally, after three centuries of London rule, Scotland has a parliament building...in Scotland. When Scotland united with England in 1707, its parliament was dissolved. But in 1999, the Scottish parliament was reestablished, and in 2004, it moved into this striking new home. Notice how the eco-friendly building, by the Catalan architect Enric Miralles, mixes wild angles, lots of light,

Canongate Kirk

White Horse Close

bold windows, oak, and native stone into a startling complex.

Since it celebrates Scottish democracy, the architecture is not a statement of authority. There are no statues of old heroes. There's not even a grand entry. You feel like you're entering an office park. Given its neighborhood, the media often calls the Scottish Parliament "Holyrood" for short (similar to calling the US Congress "Capitol Hill"). For details on touring the building and seeing parliament in action, see page 352.

• *Across the street is the Queen's Gallery, where she shares part of her amazing personal art collection in excellent revolving exhibits. Finally, walk to the end of the road (Abbey Strand), and step up to the impressive wrought-iron gate of the Queen's palace. Look up at the stag with its holy cross, or "holy rood," on its forehead, and peer into the palace grounds. (The ticket office and palace entryway, a fine café, and a handy WC are just through the arch on the right.)*

⓫ PALACE OF HOLYROODHOUSE

Since the 16th century, this palace has marked the end of the Royal Mile. Because Scotland's royalty preferred living at Holyroodhouse to the blustery castle on the rock, the palace grew over time. If the Queen's not visiting, the palace welcomes visitors.

• *Your walk—from the castle to the palace, with so much Scottish history packed in between—is complete. Enjoy the rest of Edinburgh.*

➲ Bonnie Wee New Town Walk

With some of the city's finest Georgian architecture (from its 18th-century boom period), the New Town has a completely different character than the Old Town. This self-guided walk—worth ▲▲—gives you a quick orientation in about one hour.

• *Begin on Waverley Bridge, spanning the gully between the Old and New towns; to get there from the Royal Mile, just head down*

the curved Cockburn Street near the Tron Church (or cut down any of the "close" lanes opposite St. Giles' Cathedral). Stand on the bridge overlooking the train tracks, facing the castle.

View from Waverley Bridge: From this vantage point, you can enjoy fine views of medieval Edinburgh, with its 10-story-plus "skyscrapers." It's easy to imagine how miserably crowded this area was, prompting the expansion of the city during the Georgian period. Pick out landmarks along the Royal Mile, most notably the open-work steeple of St. Giles'.

A big lake called the **Nor' Loch** once was to the north (nor') of the Old Town; now it's a valley between Edinburgh's two towns. The lake was drained around 1800 as part of the expansion. Before that, the lake was the town's water reservoir... and its sewer. Much has been written about the town's infamous stink (a.k.a. the "flowers of Edinburgh"). The town's nickname, "Auld Reekie," referred to both the smoke of its industry and the stench of its squalor.

The long-gone loch was also a handy place for drowning witches. With their thumbs tied to their ankles, they'd be lashed to dunking stools. Those who survived the ordeal were considered "aided by the devil" and burned as witches. If they died, they were innocent and given a good Christian burial. Edinburgh was Europe's witch-burning mecca—any perceived

View from Waverley Bridge

Bonnie Wee New Town Walk

200 Meters
200 Yards

❶ Princes Street Gardens
❷ Scott Monument
❸ Jenners Department Store
❹ St. Andrew Square
❺ George Street
❻ St. Andrew's & St. George's Church
❼ The Dome Restaurant
❽ King George IV Statue
❾ Thistle Street
❿ William Pitt Statue
⓫ Rose Street
⓬ Charlotte Square
⓭ Georgian House

"sign," including a small birthmark, could condemn you. Scotland burned more witches per capita than any other country—17,000 souls between 1479 and 1722.

Visually trace the train tracks as they disappear into a tunnel below the **Scottish National Gallery** (with lesser-known paintings by great European artists; you can visit it during this walk—see "Sights," later).

Turning 180 degrees (and facing the ramps down into the train station), notice the huge, turreted building with the clock tower. **The Balmoral** was one of the city's two grand hotels during its glory days (its opposite bookend, the **Waldorf Astoria Edinburgh,** sits at the far end of the former lakebed—near the end of this walk). Today The Balmoral is known mostly as the place where J. K. Rowling completed the final Harry Potter book.

• *Now walk across the bridge toward the New Town. Before the corner, enter the gated gardens on the left, and head toward the big, pointy monument. You're at the edge of...*

❶ Princes Street Gardens: This grassy park, filling the former lakebed, offers a wonderful escape from the bustle of the city. Once the private domain of the wealthy, it was opened to the public around 1870—not as a democratic gesture, but in hopes of increasing sales at the Princes Street department stores. Join the office workers for a picnic lunch break.

• *Take a seat on the bench indicated by the Livingstone (Dr. Livingstone, I presume?) statue. (The Victorian explorer is well equipped with a guidebook, but is hardly packing light—his lion skin doesn't even fit in his rucksack carry-on.)*

Look up at the towering...

❷ Scott Monument: Built in the early 1840s, this elaborate Neo-Gothic monument honors the great author Sir Walter Scott, one of Edinburgh's many illustrious sons. When Scott died in 1832, it was said that "Scotland never owed so much to one man." Scott almost singlehandedly created the Scotland we know. Just as the country was in danger of being assimilated into England, Scott celebrated traditional

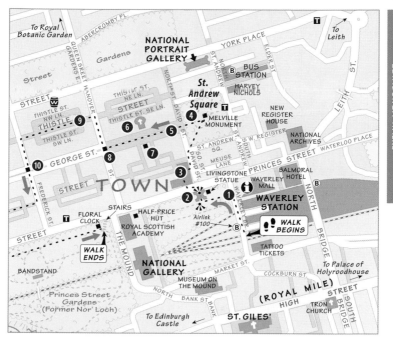

Scott Monument

songs, legends, myths, architecture, and kilts, thereby reviving the Highland culture and cementing a national identity. And, as the father of the Romantic historical novel, he contributed to Western literature in general. The 200-foot monument shelters a marble statue of Scott and his favorite pet, Maida, a deerhound who was one of 30 canines this dog lover owned during his lifetime. They're surrounded by busts of 16 great Scottish poets and 64 characters from his books. Climbing the tight, stony spiral staircase of 287 steps earns you a peek at a tiny museum midway, a fine city view at the top, and intimate encounters going up and down (£5, daily 10:00-19:00, Oct-March until 16:00, tel. 0131/529-4068).

• *Exit the gate near Livingstone and head across busy Princes Street to the venerable...*

❸ **Jenners Department Store:** As you wait for the light to change (and wait... and wait...), notice how statues of women support the building—just as real women support the business.

Jenners Department Store

St. Andrew Square

Step inside and head upstairs into the grand, skylit atrium. The central space—filled with a towering tree at Christmas—is classic Industrial Age architecture. The Queen's coat of arms high on the wall indicates she shops here.

• *From the atrium, turn right and exit onto South St. David Street. Turn left and follow this street uphill one block up to...*

❹ St. Andrew Square: This green space is dedicated to the patron saint of Scotland. In the early 19th century, there were no shops around here—just fine residences; this was a private garden for the fancy people living here. Now open to the public, the square is a popular lunch hangout for workers.

One block up from the top of the park is the excellent **Scottish National Portrait Gallery,** which introduces you to all of the biggest names in Scottish history (described later, under "Sights").

• *Follow the Melville Monument's gaze straight ahead out of the park. Cross the street and stand at the top of...*

❺ George Street: This is the main drag of Edinburgh's grid-planned New Town. Laid out in 1776, when King George III was busy putting down a revolution in a troublesome overseas colony, the New Town was a model of urban planning in its day. The architectural style is "Georgian"—British for "Neoclassical."

St. Andrew Square (patron saint of Scotland) and Charlotte Square (George III's queen) bookend the New Town, with its three main streets named for the royal family of the time (George, Queen, and Princes). Thistle and Rose streets—which we'll see near the end of this walk—are named for the national flowers of Scotland and England.

• *Halfway down the first block of George Street, on the right, is...*

❻ St. Andrew's and St. George's Church: Designed as part of the New Town plan in the 1780s, the church is a product of the Scottish Enlightenment. It has an elliptical plan (the first in Britain) so that all can focus on the pulpit. If it's open, step inside. A fine leaflet tells the story of the church, and a handy cafeteria downstairs serves cheap and cheery lunches.

Directly across the street from the church is another temple, this one devoted to money. This former bank building (now housing the recommended restaurant **❼ The Dome**) has a pediment filled with figures demonstrating various ways to make money, which they do with all the nobility of classical gods. Consider scurrying across the street and ducking inside to view the stunning domed atrium.

Continue down George Street to the intersection with a **❽** statue commemorating the visit by **King George IV.**

• *Turn right on Hanover Street; after just one (short) block, cross over and go down...*

❾ Thistle Street: This street seems sleepy, but holds characteristic boutiques

Charlotte Square

Scottish National Gallery

and good restaurants. Halfway down the street on the left, Howie Nicholsby's shop 21st Century Kilt updates traditional Scottish menswear.

You'll pop out at Frederick Street. Turning left, you'll see a ➓ statue of **William Pitt,** prime minister under King George III. (Pitt's father gave his name to the American city of Pittsburgh—which Scots pronounce as "Pitts-burrah"...I assume.)

• *For an interesting contrast, we'll continue down another side street. Pass the statue of Pitt (heading toward Edinburgh Castle), and turn right onto brash, boisterous...*

➓ **Rose Street:** This stretch of Rose Street feels commercialized, jammed with chain stores; the second block is packed with pubs and restaurants. As you walk, keep an eye out for the cobbled Tudor rose embedded in the brick sidewalk. When you cross the aptly named Castle Street, linger over the grand views to Edinburgh Castle. It's almost as if they planned it this way...just for the views.

• *Popping out at the far end of Rose Street, across the street and to your right is...*

➓ **Charlotte Square:** The building of the New Town started cheap with St. Andrew Square, but finished well with this stately space, designed by Scottish Robert Adam in 1791. Adam's design, which raised the standard of New Town architecture to "international class," created Edinburgh's finest Georgian square.

• *Along the right side of Charlotte Square, at*

#7 *(just left of the pointy pediment), you can visit the* ➓ ***Georgian House,*** *which gives you a great peek behind all of these harmonious Neoclassical facades (described later).*

Return Through Princes Street Gardens: From Charlotte Square, drop down to busy Princes Street (noticing the red building to the right—the grand Waldorf Astoria Hotel and twin sister of The Balmoral at the start of our walk). But rather than walking along the busy bus-and-tram-lined shopping drag, head into **Princes Street Gardens** (cross Princes Street and enter the gate on the left). With the castle looming overhead, you'll pass a playground, a fanciful Victorian fountain, more monuments to great Scots, war memorials, and a bandstand. Finally you'll reach a staircase up to the **Scottish National Gallery;** notice the oldest **floral clock** in the world on your left as you climb up.

• *Our walk is over. From here, you can tour the gallery; head up Bank Street just behind it to reach the Royal Mile; hop on a bus along Princes Street to your next stop (or B&B); or continue through another stretch of the Princes Street Gardens to the Scott Monument and our starting point.*

SIGHTS

▲▲▲EDINBURGH CASTLE

The fortified birthplace of the city 1,300 years ago, this imposing symbol of Edinburgh sits proudly on a rock high above you. The home of Scotland's kings and queens for centuries, the castle has witnessed royal births, medieval pageantry, and bloody sieges. Today it's a complex of various buildings, the oldest dating from the 12th century, linked by cobbled roads that survive from its more recent use as a military garrison. The castle—with expansive views, plenty of history, and the stunning crown jewels of Scotland—is a fascinating and multifaceted sight that deserves several hours of your time.

Cost and Hours: £17, daily 9:30-18:00, Oct-March until 17:00, last entry one hour before closing, tel. 0131/225-9846, www.edinburghcastle.gov.uk.

Rick's Tip: **To avoid the castle's ticket lines (worst in Aug), book online** *in advance. You can print your ticket at home, or pick it up at machines just inside the entrance or at the Visitor Information desk a few steps uphill on the right.*

Avoiding Lines: The castle is usually less crowded after 14:00 or so; if planning a morning visit, the earlier the better.

Getting There: Simply walk up the Royal Mile (if arriving by bus from the B&B area south of the city, get off at South Bridge and huff up the Mile for about 15 minutes). Taxis get you closer, dropping you a block below the esplanade at the Hub/Tolbooth Church.

Tours: Thirty-minute introductory **guided tours** are free with admission (2-4/hour, depart from Argyle Battery, see clock for next departure; fewer off-season). The informative audioguide provides four hours of descriptions, including the National War Museum Scotland (£3 if you purchase with your ticket; £3.50 if you rent it once inside, pick up inside Portcullis Gate).

Eating: You have two choices within the castle. The **$ Redcoat Café**—just past the Argyle Battery—is a big, bright, efficient cafeteria with great views. The **$ $ Tea Rooms** in Crown Square serves sit-down

meals and afternoon tea. A **Whisky Shop,** with tastings, is just through Foog's Gate.

> **SELF-GUIDED TOUR**

From the ❶ **entry gate,** start winding your way uphill toward the main sights—the crown jewels and the Royal Palace—located near the summit. Since the castle was protected on three sides by sheer cliffs, the main defense had to be here at the entrance. During the castle's heyday in the 1500s, a 100-foot tower loomed overhead, facing the city.

• *Passing through the portcullis gate, you reach the...*

❷ **Argyle (Six-Gun) Battery, with View:** These front-loading, cast-iron cannons are from the Napoleonic era (c. 1800), when the castle was still a force to be reckoned with.

From here, look north across the valley to the grid of the New Town. The valley sits where the Nor' Loch once was; this lake was drained and filled in when the New Town was built in the late 1700s, its swamps replaced with gardens. Later the

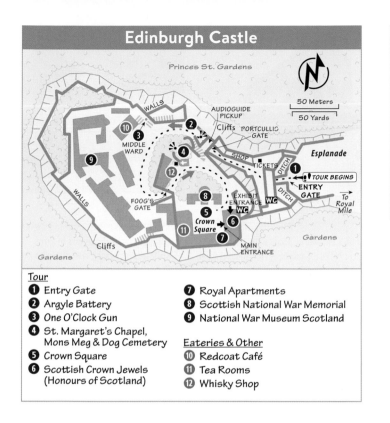

Edinburgh Castle

Tour
1. Entry Gate
2. Argyle Battery
3. One O'Clock Gun
4. St. Margaret's Chapel, Mons Meg & Dog Cemetery
5. Crown Square
6. Scottish Crown Jewels (Honours of Scotland)
7. Royal Apartments
8. Scottish National War Memorial
9. National War Museum Scotland

Eateries & Other
10. Redcoat Café
11. Tea Rooms
12. Whisky Shop

land provided sites for the Greek-temple-esque Scottish National Gallery and Waverley Station.

Now look down. The sheer north precipice looks impregnable. But on the night of March 14, 1314, 30 armed men silently scaled this rock face. They were loyal to Robert the Bruce and determined to recapture the castle, which had fallen into English hands. They caught the English by surprise, took the castle, and—three months later—Bruce defeated the English at the Battle of Bannockburn.

• A little farther along, near the café, is the...

❸ One O'Clock Gun: Crowds gather for the 13:00 gun blast, a tradition that gives ships in the bay something to set their navigational devices by. Before the gun, sailors set their clocks with help from the Nelson Monument—that's the tall pillar in the distance on Calton Hill. The

monument has a "time ball" affixed to the cross on top, which drops precisely at the top of the hour. But on foggy days, ships couldn't see the ball, so the cannon shot was instituted instead (1861). The tradition stuck, every day at 13:00. (Locals joke that the frugal Scots don't fire it at high noon, as that would cost 11 extra rounds a day.)

• Continue uphill, winding to the left and passing through Foog's Gate. At the very top of the hill, on your left, is...

❹ St. Margaret's Chapel: This tiny stone chapel is Edinburgh's oldest building (around 1120) and sits atop its highest point (440 feet). It represents the birth of the city.

In 1057, Malcolm III murdered King Macbeth (of Shakespeare fame) and assumed the Scottish throne. Later, he married Princess Margaret, and the family

St. Margaret's Chapel

Crown Square

settled atop this hill. Their marriage united Malcolm's Highland Scots with Margaret's Lowland Anglo-Saxons—the cultural mix that would define Edinburgh.

Step inside the tiny, unadorned church—a testament to Margaret's reputed piety. The style is Romanesque. The nave is wonderfully simple, with classic Norman zigzags decorating the round arch that separates the tiny nave from the sacristy. You'll see a facsimile of St. Margaret's 11th-century gospel book. The small (modern) stained-glass windows feature St. Margaret herself, St. Columba, and St. Ninian (who brought Christianity to Scotland in A.D. 397), St. Andrew (Scotland's patron saint), and William Wallace (the defender of Scotland). These days, the place is popular for weddings. (As it seats only 20, it's particularly popular with brides' parents.)

Margaret died at the castle in 1093, and her son King David I built this chapel in her honor (she was sainted in 1250). David expanded the castle and also founded Holyrood Abbey, across town. These two structures were soon linked by a Royal Mile of buildings, and Edinburgh was born.

Mons Meg, in front of the church, is a huge and once-upon-a-time frightening 15th-century siege cannon that fired 330-pound stones nearly two miles. Imagine.

Nearby, belly up to the banister and look down to find the **Dog Cemetery,** a tiny patch of grass with a sweet little line of doggie tombstones, marking the graves of soldiers' faithful canines in arms.

• *Continue on, curving downhill into...*

❺ **Crown Square:** This courtyard is the center of today's Royal Castle complex. Get oriented. You're surrounded by the crown jewels, the Royal Palace (with its Great Hall), and the Scottish National War Memorial.

• *We'll tour the buildings around Crown Square. First up: the crown jewels. Look for two entrances. The one on Crown Square, only open in peak season, deposits you straight into the room with the crown jewels but usually comes with a line. The other entry, around the side (near the WCs), takes you—often at a shuffle—through the interesting, Disney-esque "Honours of Scotland" exhibition, which tells the story of the crown jewels and how they survived the harrowing centuries, but lacks any actual artifacts.*

❻ **Scottish Crown Jewels (Honours of Scotland):** For centuries, Scotland's monarchs were crowned in elaborate rituals involving three wondrous objects: a jewel-studded crown, scepter, and sword. These objects—along with the ceremonial Stone of Scone (pronounced "skoon")—are known as the "Honours of Scotland." Scotland's crown jewels may not be as impressive as England's, but they're treasured by locals as a symbol of Scottish nationalism. They're also older than England's; while Oliver Cromwell

Diorama in the Honours of Scotland *exhibit*

destroyed England's jewels, the Scots managed to hide theirs.

History of the Jewels: The Honours of Scotland exhibit that leads up to the Crown Room traces the evolution of the jewels, the ceremony, and the often turbulent journey of this precious regalia. Here's the SparkNotes version:

In 1306, Robert the Bruce was crowned with a "circlet of gold" in a ceremony at Scone—a town 40 miles north of Edinburgh, which Scotland's earliest kings had claimed as their capital. Around 1500, King James IV added two new items to the coronation ceremony—a scepter (a gift from the pope) and a huge sword (a gift from another pope). In 1540, James V had the original crown augmented by an Edinburgh goldsmith, giving it the imperial-crown shape it has today.

These Honours were used to crown every monarch: nine-month-old Mary, Queen of Scots (she cried); her one-year-old son James VI (future king of England); and Charles I and II. But the days of divine-right rulers were numbered.

In 1649, the parliament had Charles I (king of both England and Scotland) beheaded. Soon Cromwell's rabid English antiroyalists were marching on Edinburgh.

When the monarchy was restored, the regalia were used to crown Scotland's last king, Charles II (1660). Then, in 1707, the Treaty of Union with England ended Scotland's independence. The Honours came out for a ceremony to bless the treaty.

The crown's most recent official appearance was in 1999, when it was taken across town to the grand opening of the reinstated parliament, marking a new chapter in the Scottish nation. As it represents the monarchy, the crown is present whenever a new session of parliament opens. (And if Scotland ever secedes, you can be sure that crown will be in the front row.)

The Honours: Finally, you enter the Crown Room to see the regalia itself. The four-foot steel **sword** was made in Italy under orders of Pope Julius II (the man who also commissioned Michelangelo's Sistine Chapel and St. Peter's Basilica). The **scepter** is made of silver, covered with gold, and topped with a rock crystal and a pearl. The gem- and pearl-encrusted **crown** has an imperial arch topped with a cross. Legend says the band of gold in the center is the original crown that once adorned the head of Robert the Bruce.

The **Stone of Scone** (a.k.a. the "Stone of Destiny") sits plain and strong next to the jewels. It's a rough-hewn gray slab of sandstone, about 26 by 17 by 10 inches. As far back as the ninth century, Scotland's kings were crowned atop this stone, when it stood at the medieval capital of Scone. But in 1296, the invading army of Edward I of England carried the stone off to Westminster Abbey. For the next seven centuries, English (and subsequently British) kings and queens were crowned sitting on a coronation chair with the Stone of Scone tucked in a compartment underneath.

In 1996, in recognition of increased Scottish autonomy, Queen Elizabeth II agreed to let the stone go home, on one condition: that it be returned to Westminster Abbey for all British coronations. One day, the next monarch of the United Kingdom—Prince Charles is first in line—will sit atop it, re-enacting a coronation ritual that dates back a thousand years.

• *Exit the crown jewel display, heading down the stairs. But just before exiting into the courtyard, turn left through a door that leads into the...*

❼ **Royal Apartments:** Scottish royalty lived in the Royal Palace only when safety or protocol required it (they preferred the Palace of Holyroodhouse at the bottom of the Royal Mile). Here you can see several historic but unimpressive rooms. The first one, labeled **Queen Mary's Chamber,** is where Mary, Queen of Scots (1542-1587), gave birth to James VI of Scotland, who later became King James I of England. Nearby **Laich Hall** (Lower Hall) was the dining room of the royal family.

The **Great Hall** (through a separate entrance on Crown Square) was built by James IV to host the castle's official banquets and meetings. It's still used for such purposes today. Most of the interior—its fireplace, carved walls, pikes, and armor—is Victorian. But the well-constructed wood ceiling is original. This hammer-beam roof (constructed like the hull of a ship) is self-supporting.

• *Across the Crown Square courtyard is the...*

❽ **Scottish National War Memorial:** This commemorates the 149,000 Scottish soldiers lost in World War I, the 58,000 who died in World War II, and the nearly 800 (and counting) lost in British battles since. This is a somber spot (no photos). To appreciate how important this place is, consider that Scottish soldiers died at twice the rate of other British soldiers in World War I.

• *Our final stop is worth the five-minute walk to get there. Backtrack to the café (and One O'Clock Gun), then head downhill to the War Museum.*

❾ **National War Museum Scotland:** This thoughtful museum covers four

Laich Hall

Great Hall

centuries of Scottish military history. Instead of the usual musty, dusty displays of endless armor, there's a compelling mix of videos, uniforms, weapons, medals, mementos, and eloquent excerpts from soldiers' letters.

Here you'll learn the story of how the fierce and courageous Scottish warrior changed from being a symbol of resistance against Britain to being a champion of that same empire.

This museum shows the human side of war as well as the cleverness of government-sponsored ad campaigns that kept the lads enlisting. Two centuries of recruiting posters make the same pitch that still works today: a hefty signing bonus, steady pay, and job security with the promise of a manly and adventurous life—all spiked with a mix of pride and patriotism.

Stepping outside the museum, you're surrounded by cannons that no longer fire, dramatic views of this grand city, and the clatter of tourists (rather than soldiers) on cobbles. Consider for a moment all the bloody history and valiant struggles, along with British power and Scottish pride, that have shaped the city over which you are perched.

Sights on and near the Royal Mile

▲THE SCOTCH WHISKY EXPERIENCE

This attraction seems designed to distill money out of your pocket. The 50-minute experience consists of a "Malt Disney" whisky-barrel ride through the production process followed by an explanation and movie about Scotland's five main whisky regions. Though gimmicky, it does succeed in providing an entertaining yet informative orientation to the creation of Scottish firewater (things get pretty psychedelic when you hit the yeast stage). Your ticket also includes sampling a wee dram and the chance to stand amid the world's largest Scotch whisky collection (almost 3,500 bottles). At the end, you'll find yourself in the bar, with a fascinating

wall of unusually shaped whisky bottles. Serious connoisseurs should stick with the more substantial shops in town, but this place can be worthwhile for beginners.

Cost and Hours: £15 "silver tour" includes one sample, £26 "gold tour" includes samples from each main region, generally daily 10:00–18:00, tel. 0131/220-0441, www.scotchwhiskyexperience.co.uk.

▲▲GLADSTONE'S LAND

This is a typical 16th- to 17th-century merchant's "land," or tenement building. These multistory structures—in which merchants ran their shops on the ground floor and lived upstairs—were typical of the time (the word "tenement" didn't have the slum connotation then that it has today). At six stories, this one was still just half the height of the tallest "skyscrapers."

Gladstone's Land, which you'll visit via one-hour guided tour, comes complete with an almost-lived-in, furnished interior and 400-year-old Renaissance painted ceiling. The downstairs cloth shop and upstairs kitchen and living quarters are brought to life by your guide.

Gladstone's Land

Stained-glass window in St. Giles' Cathedral

Cost and Hours: £7, tours run daily 10:30-16:00, 3-8 tours/day, must book ahead by phone or in person; closed Nov-March, tel. 0131/226-5856, www.nts.org.uk/Visit/Gladstones-Land.

▲▲ST. GILES' CATHEDRAL

This is Scotland's most important church. Its ornate spire—the Scottish crown steeple from 1495—is a proud part of Edinburgh's skyline. The fascinating interior contains nearly 200 memorials honoring distinguished Scots through the ages.

Cost and Hours: Free but £3 donation encouraged; May-Sept Mon-Fri 9:00-19:00, Sat 9:00-17:00; Oct-April Mon-Sat 9:00-17:00; Sun 13:00-17:00 year-round; info sheet-£1, guidebook-£6, tel. 0131/225-9442, www.stgilescathedral.org.uk.

Concerts: St. Giles' busy concert schedule includes free organ recitals and visiting choirs (frequent events at 12:15 and concerts Sun at 18:00, also sometimes Wed, Thu, or Fri at 20:00, see schedule or ask for *Music at St. Giles* pamphlet at welcome desk or gift shop).

◗ Self-Guided Tour: Today's facade is 19th-century Neo-Gothic, but most of what you'll see inside is from the 14th and

15th centuries. Engage the cathedral guides in conversation; you'll be glad you did.

Just inside the entrance, turn around to see the modern stained-glass Robert Burns window, which celebrates Scotland's favorite poet. The top is a rosy red sunburst of creativity, reminding Scots of Burns' famous line, "My love is like a red, red rose"—part of a song near and dear to every Scottish heart.

To the right of the Burns window is a fine **Pre-Raphaelite window.** Like most in the church, it's a memorial to an important patron (in this case, John Marshall). From here stretches a great swath of war memorials.

As you walk along the north wall, find **John Knox's statue** (standing like a six-foot-tall bronze chess piece). Knox, the great religious reformer and founder of austere Scottish Presbyterianism, first preached here in 1559. His insistence that every person should be able to personally read the word of God—notice that he's pointing to a book—gave Scotland an educational system 300 years ahead of the rest of Europe.

Knox preached Calvinism. Consider that the Dutch and the Scots both embraced

Scotland's Literary Greats

Edinburgh was home to Scotland's three greatest literary figures, pictured above: Robert Burns (left), Robert Louis Stevenson (center), and Sir Walter Scott (right).

Robert Burns (1759-1796), known as "Rabbie" in Scotland and quite possibly the most famous and beloved Scot of all time, moved to Edinburgh after achieving overnight celebrity with his first volume of poetry (staying in a house on the spot where Deacon Brodie's Tavern now stands). Even though he wrote in the rough Scots dialect and dared to attack social rank, he was a favorite of Edinburgh's high society.

One hundred years later, **Robert Louis Stevenson** (1850-1894) also stirred the Scottish soul with his pen. Traveling through Scotland, Europe, and around the world, he distilled his adventures into Romantic classics, including *Kidnapped* and *Treasure Island* (as well as *The Strange Case of Dr. Jekyll and Mr. Hyde*).

Sir Walter Scott (1771-1832) wrote the *Waverley* novels, including *Ivanhoe* and *Rob Roy*. He's considered the father of the Romantic historical novel. Through his writing, he generated a worldwide interest in Scotland, and reawakened his fellow countrymen's pride in their heritage.

The best way to learn about and experience these literary greats is to take Edinburgh's Literary Pub Tour (see page 368).

Consider also the other great writers with Edinburgh connections: J. K. Rowling (who captures the "Gothic" spirit of Edinburgh with her Harry Potter series); current resident Ian Rankin (with his "tartan noir" novels); J. M. Barrie (who attended University of Edinburgh and later created Peter Pan); Sir Arthur Conan Doyle (who was born in Edinburgh and is best known for inventing Sherlock Holmes); and James Boswell (who lived in Edinburgh and is revered for his biography of Samuel Johnson).

this creed of hard work, frugality, and strict ethics. This helps explain why the Scots are so different from the English (and why the Dutch and the Scots—both famous for their thriftiness and industriousness—are so much alike).

The oldest parts of the cathedral—the **four massive central pillars**—are Norman and date from the 12th century.

Cross over to the **organ** (1992, Austrian-built, one of Europe's finest) and take in its sheer might. (To light it up, find the button behind the organ to the right of the glass.)

Immediately to the right of the organ (as you're facing it) is a tiny chapel for silence and prayer. The dramatic **stained-glass window** above shows the commotion that surrounded Knox when he preached. The bearded, fiery-eyed Knox had a huge impact on this community. Notice how there were no pews back then.

Head toward the east (back) end of the church, and turn right to see the Neo-Gothic **Thistle Chapel** (£3 donation requested, volunteer guide is a wealth of information). The interior is filled with intricate wood carving. Built in two years (1910-1911), entirely with Scottish materials and labor, it is the private chapel of the Order of the Thistle, the only Scottish chivalric order. Are there bagpipes in heaven? Find the tooting stone angel at the top of a window to the left of the altar, and the

wooden one to the right of the doorway you came in.

Downstairs you'll find handy public WCs and an inviting **$ café**—a good place for paupers to munch prayerfully (simple, light lunches, coffee and cakes; Mon-Sat 9:00-17:00, Sun from 11:00, in basement on back side of church, tel. 0131/225-5147).

▲▲SCOTTISH PARLIAMENT BUILDING

Scotland's parliament originated in 1293 and was dissolved when Scotland united with England in 1707. But after the Scottish electorate and the British parliament gave their consent, in 1997 it was decided that there should again be "a Scottish parliament guided by justice, wisdom, integrity, and compassion." Formally reconvened by Queen Elizabeth II in 1999, the Scottish parliament now enjoys self-rule in many areas (except for matters of defense, foreign policy, immigration, and taxation). The current government, run by the Scottish Nationalist Party (SNP), is pushing for even more independence.

The innovative building, opened in 2004, brought together all the functions of the fledgling parliament in one complex. It's a people-oriented structure, conceived by Catalan architect Enric Miralles. Signs are written in both English and Gaelic (the Scots' Celtic tongue).

For a peek at the building and a lesson in how the Scottish parliament works, drop in, pass through security, and find the

Scottish Parliament exterior

Scottish Parliament interior

visitors' desk. You're welcome in the public parts of the building, including a small ground-floor exhibit on the parliament's history and function and, up several flights of stairs, a viewing gallery overlooking the impressive Debating Chambers.

Cost and Hours: Free; Mon-Sat 10:00-17:00, Tue-Thu 9.00-18.30 when parliament is in session (Sept-June), closed Sun year-round. For a complete list of recess dates or to book tickets for debates, check their website or call their visitor services line, tel. 0131/348-5200, www.parliament.scot.

Tours: Free worthwhile hour-long tours covering history, architecture, parliamentary processes, and other topics are offered by proud locals. Tours generally run throughout the day Mon and Fri-Sat in session (Sept-June) and Mon-Sat in recess (July-Aug). While you can try dropping in, these tours can book up—it's best to book ahead online or over the phone.

Seeing Parliament in Session: The public can witness the Scottish parliament's hugely popular debates (usually Tue-Thu 14:00-18:00; book ahead online, over the phone, or at the info desk).

On Thursdays from 11:40 to 12:45 the First Minister is on the hot seat and has to field questions from members across all parties (reserve ahead for this popular session over the phone a week in advance; spots book up quickly—call at 9:00 sharp on Thu for the following week).

▲▲PALACE OF HOLYROODHOUSE

Built on the site of the abbey/monastery founded in 1128 by King David I, this palace was the true home, birthplace, and coronation spot of Scotland's Stuart kings in their heyday (James IV; Mary, Queen of Scots; and Charles I). It's particularly memorable as the site of some dramatic moments from the short reign of Mary, Queen of Scots—including the murder of her personal secretary, David Rizzio, by agents of her jealous husband. Today, it's one of Queen Elizabeth II's official residences. She usually manages her Scottish affairs here during Holyrood Week, from late June to early July (and generally stays at Balmoral in August). Holyrood is open to the public outside of the Queen's visits. The one-way audioguide route leads you through the fine apartments and tells

Palace of Holyroodhouse

some of the notable stories that played out here.

Cost: £12.50, includes quality one-hour audioguide; £17.50 combo-ticket includes the Queen's Gallery; £21.50 combo-ticket adds guided tour of palace gardens (April-Oct only); tickets sold in Queen's Gallery to the right of the castle entrance (see next listing).

Hours: Daily 9:30-18:00, Nov-March until 16:30, last entry 1.5 hours before closing, tel. 0131/556-5100, www.royalcollection.org.uk. It's still a working palace, so it's closed when the Queen or other VIPs are in residence.

Visiting the Palace: The building, rich in history and decor, is filled with elegantly furnished Victorian rooms and a few darker, older rooms with glass cases of historic bits and Scottish pieces that locals find fascinating. Bring the palace to life with the audioguide. The tour route leads you into the grassy inner courtyard, then up to the royal apartments: dining rooms, *Downton Abbey*-style drawing rooms, and royal bedchambers, including the private chambers of Mary, Queen of Scots, where conspirators stormed in and stabbed her secretary 56 times.

After exiting the palace, you're free to stroll through the evocative **ruined abbey** (destroyed by the English during the time of Mary, Queen of Scots, in the 16th century) and the **palace gardens** (closed Nov-March except some weekends).

Nearby: Hikers, note that the wonderful trail up Arthur's Seat starts just across the street from the gardens (see "Urban Hikes," later for details).

QUEEN'S GALLERY

This small museum features rotating exhibits of artwork from the royal collection. Though the gallery occupies just a few rooms, its displays can be exquisite. The entry fee includes an excellent audioguide, written and read by the curator.

Cost and Hours: £7, £17.50 combo-ticket includes Palace of Holyroodhouse, daily 9:30-18:00, Nov-March until 16:30, last entry one hour before closing, café, on the palace grounds, to the right of the palace entrance, www.royalcollection.org.uk. Buses #35 and #36 stop outside, saving you a walk to or from Princes Street/North Bridge.

South of the Royal Mile
▲▲▲ NATIONAL MUSEUM OF SCOTLAND

This huge museum has amassed more historic artifacts than every other place I've seen in Scotland combined. It's all wonderfully displayed, with fine descriptions offering a best-anywhere hike through the history of Scotland.

Cost and Hours: Free, daily 10:00-17:00; two long blocks south of St. Giles' Cathedral and the Royal Mile, on Chambers Street off George IV Bridge, tel. 0131/247-4422, www.nms.ac.uk.

Ruined abbey

Queen's Gallery

Tours: Free one-hour general tours are offered daily at 11:00 and 13:00; themed tours at 15:00 (confirm tour schedule at info desk or on TV screens). The National Museum of Scotland Highlights app provides thin coverage of select items but is free and downloadable using their free Wi-Fi.

Eating: A $$ brasserie is on the ground floor near the information desks, and a $ café with coffee, tea, cakes, and snacks is on the level 3 balcony overlooking the Grand Gallery. On the museum's fifth floor, the dressy and upscale $$$ **Tower restaurant** serves good food with a castle view (lunch/early bird special, afternoon tea, three-course dinner specials; daily 10:00-22:00—use Tower entry if eating after museum closes, reservations recommended, tel. 0131/225-3003, www.tower-restaurant.com). A number of good eating options are within a couple of blocks of the museum (see "Eating," later).

Overview: The place gives you two museums in one. One wing houses the Natural World galleries (T. Rex skeletons and other animals), the Science and Technology galleries, and more. But we'll focus on the other wing, which sweeps you through Scottish history covering Roman and Viking times, Edinburgh's witch-burning craze and clan massacres, the struggle for Scottish independence, the Industrial Revolution, and right up to Scotland in the 21st century.

⊙ **Self-Guided Tour:** Get oriented on level 1, in the impressive glass-roofed Grand Gallery right above the entrance hall. Just outside the Grand Gallery is the millennium clock, a 30-foot high clock with figures that move to a Bach concerto on the hour from 11:00 to 16:00. The clock has four parts (crypt, nave, belfry, and spire) and represents the turmoil of the 20th century, with a pietà at the top.

• *To reach the Scottish history wing, exit the Grand Gallery at the far right end, under the clock and past the statue of James Watt.*

On the way, you'll pass through the science and technology wing. While walking through, look for Dolly the sheep—the world's first cloned mammal—born in Edinburgh and now stuffed and on display. Continue into Hawthornden Court (level 1), where our tour begins. (It's possible to detour downstairs from here to level -1 for Scotland's prehistoric origins—geologic formation, Celts, Romans, Vikings.)

• *Enter the door marked...*

Kingdom of the Scots (c. 1300-1700): From its very start, Scotland was determined to be free. You're greeted with proud quotes from what's been called the Scottish Declaration of Independence—the Declaration of Arbroath, a defiant letter written to the pope in 1320. As early as the ninth century, Scotland's patron saint, Andrew (see the small statue in the next room), had—according to legend—miraculously intervened to help the Picts

National Museum of Scotland

Replica tomb of Mary, Queen of Scots

and Scots of Scotland remain free by defeating the Angles of England. Andrew's X-shaped cross still decorates the Scottish flag today.

Enter the first room on your right, with imposing swords and other objects related to Scotland's most famous patriots—William Wallace and Robert the Bruce. Bruce's descendants, the Stuarts, went on to rule Scotland for the next 300 years. Eventually, James VI of Scotland (see his baby cradle) came to rule England as well (as King James I of England).

In the next room, a big guillotine recalls the harsh justice meted out to criminals, witches, and "Covenanters" (17th-century political activists who opposed interference of the Stuart kings in affairs of the Presbyterian Church of Scotland). Nearby, also check out the tomb (a copy) of Mary, Queen of Scots, the 16th-century Stuart monarch who opposed the Presbyterian Church of Scotland. Educated and raised in Renaissance France, Mary brought refinement to the Scottish throne. After she was imprisoned and then executed by Elizabeth I of England in 1587, her supporters rallied each other by invoking her memory. Pendants and coins with her portrait stoked the irrepressible Scottish spirit (see display case near tomb).

Browse the rest of level 1 to see everyday objects from that age: carved panels, cookware, and clothes.
• *Backtrack to Hawthornden Court and head up to level 3.*

Scotland Transformed (1700s): You'll see artifacts related to Bonnie Prince Charlie and the Jacobite rebellions as well as the ornate Treaty of Union document, signed in 1707 by the Scottish parliament. This act voluntarily united Scotland with England under the single parliament of the United Kingdom. For some Scots, this move was an inevitable step in connecting to the wider world, but for others it symbolized the end of Scotland's existence.

Union with England brought stability and investment to Scotland. In this same era, the advances of the Industrial Revolution were making a big impact on Scottish life. Mechanized textile looms (on display) replaced hand craftsmanship. The huge Newcomen steam-engine water pump helped the mining industry to develop sites with tricky drainage. Nearby is a model of a coal mine (or "colliery"); coal-rich Scotland exploited this natural resource to fuel its textile factories.
• *Journey up to level 5.*

Industry and Empire (1800s): Turn right and do a counterclockwise spin around this floor to survey Scottish life in the 19th century. Industry had transformed the country. Highland farmers left their land to find work in Lowland factories and foundries. Modern inventions—the phonograph, the steam-powered train, the kitchen range—revolutionized everyday life. In Glasgow near the turn of the century, architect Charles Rennie Mackintosh helped to define Scottish Art Nouveau. Scotland was at the forefront of literature (Robert Burns, Sir Walter Scott, Robert Louis Stevenson), science (Lord Kelvin, James Watt, Alexander Graham Bell...he

Newcomen steam-engine water pump

was born here, anyway!), world exploration (John Kirk in Africa, Sir Alexander Mackenzie in Canada), and whisky production.

• *Climb the stairs to level 6.*

Scotland: A Changing Nation (1900s): Turn left and do a clockwise spin through this floor to bring the story to the present day. The two world wars decimated the population of this already wee nation. In addition, hundreds of thousands emigrated, especially to Canada (where one in eight Canadians has Scottish origins). Other exhibits include Scots in the world of entertainment (from early boy-band Bay City Rollers to actor-comedian Billy Connolly); a look at the recent trend of devolution from the United Kingdom (1999 opening of Scotland's own parliament and the landmark 2014 referendum on Scottish independence); and a sports Hall of Fame (from golfer Tom Morris to auto racers Jackie Stewart and Jim Clark).

• *Finish your visit on level 7, the rooftop.*

Garden Terrace: The well-described roof garden features grasses and heathers from every corner of Scotland and spectacular views of the city.

Museums in the New Town

These sights are linked by the "Bonnie Wee New Town Walk" on page 339.

▲▲SCOTTISH NATIONAL GALLERY

This delightful, small museum has Scotland's best collection of paintings. In a short visit, you can admire well-described works by Old Masters (Raphael, Rembrandt, Rubens), Impressionists (Monet, Degas, Gauguin), and a few underrated Scottish painters. (Scottish art is better at the National Portrait Gallery, described next.) Although there are no iconic masterpieces, it's a surprisingly enjoyable collection that's truly world-class.

Cost and Hours: Free; daily 10:00-17:00, Thu until 19:00, longer hours in Aug; café downstairs, The Mound (between Princes and Market streets), tel. 0131/624-6200, www.nationalgalleries.org.

Expect Changes: The museum is undergoing major renovation to increase the space of its Scottish collection and build a grand main entrance from Princes Street Gardens.

Visiting the Museum: Start at the

Scottish National Gallery

Van der Goes, The Trinity Panels

gallery entrance (at the north end of the building). Climb the stairs to the upper level (north end), and take a left. You'll run right into...

Van der Goes, *The Trinity Panels,* c. 1473-1479: For more than five centuries, these two double-sided panels have remained here—first in a church, then (when the church was leveled to build Waverley train station) in this museum. The panels likely were the wings of a triptych, flanking a central scene of the Virgin Mary that was destroyed by Protestant vandals during the Reformation.

In one panel is the Trinity: God the Father, in a rich red robe, cradles a spindly, just-crucified Christ, while the dove of the Holy Spirit hovers between them. (This is what would have been seen when the triptych was closed.) The flip side of the Christ panel depicts Scotland's king and queen, who are best known to history as the parents of the boy kneeling alongside them. He grew up to become James IV, the Renaissance king who made Edinburgh a cultural capital. On the other panel, the church's director (the man who commissioned the painting from the well-known Flemish painter) kneels and looks on while an angel plays a hymn on the church organ. On the opposite side is Margaret of Denmark, Queen of Scots, being presented by a saint.

In a typical medieval fashion, the details are meticulous—expressive faces, intricate folds in the robes, Christ's pallid skin, observant angels. The donor's face is a remarkable portrait, with realistic skin tone and a five-o'clock shadow. But the painting lacks true 3-D realism—God's gold throne is overly exaggerated, and Christ's cardboard-cutout body hovers weightlessly.

• *Go back across the top of the skylight, to a room where the next two paintings hang.*

Botticelli, *The Virgin Adoring the Sleeping Christ Child,* c. 1485: Mary looks down at her baby, peacefully sleeping in a flower-filled garden. It's easy to appreciate Botticelli's masterful style: the precisely drawn outlines, the Virgin's pristine skin, the translucent glow. Botticelli creates a serene world in which no shadows are cast. The scene is painted on canvas—unusual at a time when wood panels were the norm. For the Virgin's rich cloak, Botticelli used ground-up lapis lazuli (a very pricey semiprecious stone), and her hem is decorated with gold leaf.

Raphael, *Holy Family with a Palm Tree,* 1506-1507: Mary, Joseph, and the Christ Child fit snugly within a round frame (a tondo), their pose symbolizing geometric perfection and the perfect family unit. Joseph kneels to offer Jesus flowers. Mary curves toward him. Baby Jesus dangles in between, linking the family together. Raphael also connects the figures through eye contact: Mary eyes Joseph, who locks onto Jesus, who gazes precociously back. Like in a cameo, we see the faces incised in profile, while their bodies bulge out toward us.

• *Back downstairs at ground level is the main gallery space. Circle around the collection chronologically, watching for works by Bellini, Titian, Velázquez, and El Greco. In Room 7, look for the next two paintings.*

Rubens, *Feast of Herod,* c. 1635-1638: All eyes turn to watch the dramatic culmination of the story of John the Baptist. Salome (standing in center) presents John's severed head on a platter to a horrified King Herod, who clutches the tablecloth and buries his hand in his beard to stifle a gag. Meanwhile, Herod's wife—who cooked up the nasty plot—pokes spitefully at John's head with a fork. A dog tugs at Herod's foot like a nasty conscience. The canvas—big, colorful, full of motion and drama—is totally Baroque.

Rembrandt, *Self-Portrait, Aged 51,* c. 1657: It's 1657, and 51-year-old Rembrandt has just declared bankruptcy. Besides financial hardship and the auctioning-off of his personal belongings, he's also facing social stigma and behind-his-back ridicule. Once Holland's most renowned painter, he's begun a slow decline into poverty and obscurity. His face says it all.

• *In Room 11, find…*

Gainsborough, *The Honorable Mrs. Graham,* 1775-1777: The slender, elegant, lavishly dressed woman was the teenage bride of a wealthy Scottish landowner. She leans on a column, ostrich feather in hand, staring off to the side (Thoughtfully? Determinedly? Haughtily?). Her faultless face and smooth neck stand out from the elaborately ruffled dress and background foliage. This 18th-century woman wears a silvery dress that echoes 17th-century style—Gainsborough's way of showing how, though she was young, she was classy. Thomas ("Blue Boy") Gainsborough—the product of a clothes-making father and a flower-painting mother—

uses aspects of both in this lush portrait. The ruby brooch on her bodice marks the center of this harmonious composition.

• *Climb the stairs to the upper level (south end, opposite from where you entered) and turn right for the Impressionists and Post-Impressionists.*

Impressionist Collection: The gallery has a smattering of (mostly smaller-scale) works from all the main artists of the Impressionist and Post-Impressionist eras. You'll see Degas' ballet scenes, Renoir's pastel-colored family scenes, Van Gogh's peasants, and Seurat's pointillism.

• *Keep an eye out for these three paintings.*

Monet's *Poplars on the River Epte* (1891) was part of the artist's famous "series" paintings. He set up several canvases in a floating studio near his home in Giverny. He'd start on one canvas in the morning (to catch the morning light), then move to the next as the light changed. This particular canvas captures a perfect summer day, showing both the poplars on the riverbank and their mirror image in the still water. The subject matter begins to dissolve into a pure pattern of color, anticipating abstract art.

Gainsborough, The Honorable Mrs. Graham

Gauguin's *Vision of the Sermon* (1888) shows French peasant women imagining the miraculous event they've just heard preached about in church—when Jacob wrestles with an angel. The painting is a watershed in art history, as Gauguin throws out the rules of "realism" that had reigned since the Renaissance. The colors are surreal, there are no shadows, the figures are arranged almost randomly, and there's no attempt to make the wrestlers appear distant. The diagonal tree branch is the only thing separating the everyday world from the miraculous. Later, when Gauguin moved to Tahiti (see his *Three Tahitians* nearby), he painted a similar world, where the everyday and magical coexist, with symbolic power.

Sargent's *Lady Agnew of Lochnaw* (1892) is the work that launched the career of this American-born portrait artist. Lady Agnew—the young wife of a wealthy old Scotsman—lounges back languidly and gazes out self-assuredly. The Impressionistic smudges of paint on her dress and the chair contrast with her clear skin and luminous eyeballs. Her relaxed pose (one arm hanging down the side)

Sargent's Lady Agnew of Lochnaw

contrasts with her intensity: head tilted slightly down while she gazes up, a corner of her mouth askew, and an eyebrow cocked seductively.

▲▲SCOTTISH NATIONAL PORTRAIT GALLERY

Put a face on Scotland's history by enjoying these portraits of famous Scots from the earliest times until today. From its Neo-Gothic facade to a grand entry hall featuring a *Who's Who* of Scotland, to galleries highlighting the great Scots of each age, this impressive museum will fascinate anyone interested in Scottish culture. The gallery also hosts temporary exhibits highlighting the work of more contemporary Scots. Because of its purely Scottish focus, many travelers prefer this to the (pan-European) main branch of the National Gallery.

Cost and Hours: Free, daily 10:00-17:00, good $ cafeteria serving healthy meals, 1 Queen Street, tel. 0131/624-6490, www.nationalgalleries.org.

Visiting the Gallery: In the stirring **entrance hall** you'll find busts of great Scots and a full-body statue of Robbie "Rabbie" Burns, as well as (up above) a glorious frieze showing a parade of historical figures and murals depicting important events in Scottish history. (These are better viewed from the first floor and its mezzanine—described later.) We'll start on the **second floor,** right into the thick of the struggle between Scotland and England over who should rule this land.

Reformation to Revolution (gallery 1): The collection starts with a portrait of Mary, Queen of Scots (1542-1587), her cross and rosary prominent. This controversial ruler set off two centuries of strife. Mary was born with both Stuart blood (the ruling family of Scotland) and the Tudor blood of England's monarchs (Queen Elizabeth I was her cousin). Catholic and French-educated, Mary felt alienated from her own increasingly Protestant homeland. Her tense conversations with the reformer John Knox must have been epic. Then came a series of scandals: She married unpopular Lord Darnley, then (possibly) cheated on him, causing Darnley to (possibly) murder her lover, causing Mary to (possibly) murder Darnley, then (possibly) run off with another man, and (possibly) plot against Queen Elizabeth.

Amid all that drama, Mary was forced by her own people to relinquish her throne to her infant son, James VI. Find his portraits as a child and as a grown-up. James grew up to rule Scotland, and when Queen Elizabeth (the "virgin queen") died without an heir, he also became king of England (James I). But James' son, Charles I, after a bitter civil war, was arrested and executed in 1649: See the large Execution of Charles I painting high on the far wall, his blood-dripping head displayed to the crowd; nearby is a portrait of Charles in happier times, as a 12-year-old boy. His son, Charles II, restored the Stuarts to power. He was then succeeded by his Catholic brother James VII of Scotland (II of England), who was sent

Mary, Queen of Scots

into exile in France. There the Stuarts stewed, planning a return to power, waiting for someone to lead them in what would come to be known as the Jacobite rebellions.

The Jacobite Cause (gallery 4): One of the biggest paintings in the room is *The Baptism of Prince Charles Edward Stuart.* Born in 1720, this Stuart heir to the thrones of Great Britain and Ireland is better known to history as "Bonnie Prince Charlie." (See his bonnie features in various portraits nearby, as a child, young man, and grown man.) Charismatic Charles convinced France to invade Scotland and put him back on the throne there. In 1745, he entered Edinburgh in triumph. But he was defeated at the tide-turning Battle of Culloden (1746). The Stuart cause died forever, and Bonnie Prince Charlie went into exile, eventually dying drunk and wasted in Rome, far from the land he nearly ruled.

• *The next few rooms (galleries 5-6) contain special exhibits that swap out every year or two—they're worth a browse.*

The Age of Improvement (gallery 7): The faces portrayed here belonged to a new society that used hard work and public spirit to achieve progress with a Scottish accent. Social equality and the Industrial Revolution "transformed" Scotland—you'll see portraits of the great poet Robert Burns, the son of a farmer (Burns was heralded as a "heaven-taught ploughman" when his poems were first published), and the man who perfected the steam engine, James Watt.

• *Check out the remaining galleries, with more special exhibits, then head back down to the first floor for a good look at the...*

Central Atrium (first floor): Great Scots! The atrium is decorated in a parade of late 19th-century Romantic Historicism. The **frieze** (working counterclockwise) is a visual encyclopedia, from an ax-wielding Stone Age man and a druid, to the early legendary monarchs (Macbeth), to warriors William Wallace and Robert the

Central atrium of Scottish National Portrait Gallery

Bruce, to many kings (James I, II, III, and so on), to great thinkers, inventors, and artists (Allan Ramsay, Flora MacDonald, David Hume, Adam Smith, James Boswell, James Watt), the three greatest Scottish writers (Robert Burns, Sir Walter Scott, Robert Louis Stevenson), and culminating with the historian Thomas Carlyle, who was the driving spirit (powered by the fortune of a local newspaper baron) behind creating this portrait gallery.

Around the first-floor mezzanine are large-scale **murals** depicting great events in Scottish history, including the landing of St. Margaret at Queensferry in 1068, the Battle of Stirling Bridge in 1297, the Battle of Bannockburn in 1314, and the marriage procession of James IV and Margaret Tudor through the streets of Edinburgh in 1503.

• *Also on this floor you'll find the...*

Modern Portrait Gallery: This space is dedicated to rotating art and photographs highlighting Scots who are making an impact in the world today, such as Annie Lennox, Alan Cumming, and physicist Peter Higgs (theorizer of the Higgs boson, the so-called God particle).

▲▲GEORGIAN HOUSE

This refurbished Neoclassical house, set on Charlotte Square, is a trip back to 1796. It recounts the era when a newly gentrified and well-educated Edinburgh was nicknamed the "Athens of the North." Begin on the second floor, where you'll watch an interesting 16-minute video dramatizing the upstairs/downstairs lifestyles of the aristocrats and servants who lived here. Try on some Georgian outfits, then head downstairs to tour period rooms and even peek into the fully stocked medicine cabinet. Info sheets are available in each room, along with volunteer guides who share stories and trivia, such as why Georgian bigwigs had to sit behind a screen while enjoying a fire. A walk down George Street after your visit here can be fun for the imagination.

Cost and Hours: £7.50, daily April-Oct 10:00-17:00, March and Nov 11:00-16:00, closed Dec-Feb, last entry 45 minutes before closing; 7 Charlotte Square, tel. 0131/226-3318, www.nts.org.uk.

Near Edinburgh

▲▲ROYAL YACHT *BRITANNIA*

This much-revered vessel, which transported Britain's royal family for more than 40 years on 900 voyages (an average of once around the world per year) before being retired in 1997, is permanently moored in Edinburgh's port of Leith. Queen Elizabeth II said of the ship, "This is the only place I can truly relax." Today it's open to the curious public, who have access to its many decks—from engine rooms to drawing rooms—and offers a fascinating time-warp look into the late-20th-century lifestyles of the rich and royal. It's worth the 20-minute bus or taxi ride from the center; figure on spending about 2.5 hours total on the outing.

Cost and Hours: £15.50, includes 1.5-hour audioguide, daily 9:30-16:30, Oct until 16:00, Nov-March 10:00-15:30, these are last entry times, tearoom; at the Ocean Terminal Shopping Mall, on Ocean Drive in Leith; tel. 0131/555-5566, www.royalyachtbritannia.co.uk.

Getting There: From central Edinburgh, catch Lothian bus #11 or #22 from Princes Street (just above Waverley Station), or #35 from the bottom of the Royal Mile (alongside the parliament building) to Ocean Terminal (last stop). From the B&B neighborhood, you can either bus to the city center and transfer to one of the buses above, or take bus #14 from Dalkeith Road to Mill Lane, then walk about 10 minutes. The Majestic Tour hop-on, hop-off bus stops here as well. Drivers can park free in the blue parking garage. Take the shopping center elevator to level E, then follow the signs.

Visiting the Ship: First, explore the museum, filled with engrossing royal-family-afloat history. You'll see lots of family photos that evoke the fine times the Windsors enjoyed on the *Britannia*, as well as some nautical equipment and uniforms. Then, armed with your audioguide, you're welcome aboard.

This was the last in a line of royal yachts that stretches back to 1660. With all its royal functions, the ship required a crew of more than 200. Begin in the captain's bridge, which feels like it's been preserved from the day it was launched in 1953. Then head down a deck to see the officers' quarters, then the garage, where a Rolls Royce was hoisted aboard to use in places where the local transportation wasn't up to royal standards. The Veranda Deck at the back of the ship was the favorite place for outdoor entertainment. Ronald Reagan, Boris Yeltsin, Bill Clinton, and Nelson Mandela all sipped champagne here. The Sun Lounge, just off the back Veranda Deck, was the Queen's favorite, with Burmese teak and the same phone system she was used to in Buckingham Palace. When she wasn't entertaining, the Queen liked it quiet. The crew wore sneakers, communicated in hand signals, and (at least near the Queen's quarters) had to be finished with all their work by 8:00 in the morning.

Royal Yacht Britannia

Take a peek into the adjoining his-and-hers bedrooms of the Queen and the Duke of Edinburgh (check out the spartan twin beds), and the honeymoon suite where Prince Charles and Lady Di began their wedded bliss.

Heading down another deck, walk through the officers' lounge (and learn about the rowdy games they played) and past the galleys (including custom cabinetry for the fine china and silver) on your way to the biggest room on the yacht, the state dining room. Now decorated with gifts given by the ship's many noteworthy guests, this space enabled the Queen to entertain a good-size crowd. The drawing room, while rather simple (the Queen specifically requested "country house comfort"), was perfect for casual relaxing among royals. Princess Diana played the piano, which is bolted to the deck. Note the contrast to the decidedly less plush crew's quarters, mail room, sick bay, laundry, and engine room.

EXPERIENCES

Urban Hikes
▲▲HOLYROOD PARK

Rising up from the heart of Edinburgh, Holyrood Park is a lush green mountain squeezed between the parliament/Holyroodhouse (at the bottom of the Royal Mile) and my recommended B&B neighborhood. For an exhilarating hike, connect these two zones with a moderately strenuous 30-minute walk along the **Salisbury Crags**—reddish cliffs with sweeping views over the city. Or, for a more serious climb, make the ascent to the summit of **Arthur's Seat**, the 822-foot-tall remains of an extinct volcano. You can run up like they did in *Chariots of Fire*, or just stroll—at the summit, you'll be rewarded with commanding views of the town and surroundings. On May Day, be on the summit at dawn and wash your face in the morning dew to commemorate the Celtic holiday of Beltane, the celebration of spring. (Morning dew is supposedly very good for your complexion.)

You can do this hike either from the bottom of the Royal Mile, or from the B&B neighborhood.

From the Royal Mile: Begin in the parking lot below the Palace of Holyroodhouse. Facing the cliff, you'll see two trailheads. For the easier hike along the base of the Salisbury Crags, take the trail to the right. At the far end, you can descend into the Dalkeith Road area or—if you're up for more hiking—continue steeply up the switchbacked trail to the Arthur's Seat summit. If you know you'll want to ascend Arthur's Seat from the start, take the wider path on the left from the Holyroodhouse parking lot (easier grade, through the abbey ruins and "Hunter's Bog").

From the B&B Neighborhood: If you're staying in this area, enjoy a pre-breakfast or late-evening hike start-

Mountain skyline of Holyrood Park

Hiking along the Salisbury Crags

ing from the other side (in June, the sun comes up early, and it stays light until nearly midnight). From the Commonwealth Pool, take Holyrood Park Road, bear left at the first roundabout, then turn right at the second roundabout (onto Queen's Drive). Soon you'll see the trailhead, and make your choice: Bear right up the steeper "Piper's Walk" to Arthur's Seat (about a 20-minute hike from here, up a steeply switchbacked trail). Or bear left for an easier ascent up the "Radial Road" to the Salisbury Crags, which you can follow—with great views over town—all the way to Holyroodhouse Palace.

By Car: If you have a car, you can drive up most of the way to Arthur's Seat from behind (follow the one-way street from the palace, park safely and for free by the little lake, and hike up).

▲CALTON HILL

For an easy walk for fine views over all of Edinburgh, head up to Calton Hill—the monument-studded bluff that rises up from the eastern end of the New Town. From the Waverley Station area, simply head east on Princes Street (which becomes Waterloo Place).

About five minutes after passing North Bridge, watch on the right for the gated entrance to the **Old Calton Cemetery**— worth a quick walk-through for its stirring monuments to great Scots.

The views from the cemetery are good, but for even better ones, head back out to the main road and continue a few more minutes on Waterloo Place. Across the street, steps lead up into **Calton Hill.** Explore. Informational plaques identify the key landmarks. At the summit of the hill is the giant, unfinished replica of the Parthenon, honoring those lost in the Napoleonic Wars. Donations to finish it never materialized, leaving it with the nickname "Edinburgh's Disgrace." Nearby, the old observatory is filled with an avant-garde art gallery, and the back of the hillside boasts sweeping views over the Firth of Forth and Edinburgh's sprawl. Back toward the Old Town, the tallest tower celebrates Admiral Horatio Nelson—the same honoree of the giant pillar on London's Trafalgar Square. The best views are around the smaller, circular Dugald Stewart Monument, with postcard panoramas overlooking the spires of the Old Town and the New Town.

Whisky and Gin Tasting
Whisky Tasting

One of the most accessible places to learn about whisky is at the **Scotch Whisky Experience** on the Royal Mile, an expensive but informative overview to whisky, including a tasting (listed in "Sights," earlier).

To get more into sampling whisky, try one of the early-evening tastings at the **Cadenhead's Whisky Shop** on the Royal Mile. They're a hit with aficionados (£25, Mon-Fri at 17:45, best to book ahead in peak season; shop open Mon-Sat 10:30-17:30, closed Sun, 172 Canongate, tel. 0131/556-5864, www.wmcadenhead.com).

At **Whiski Rooms Shop,** just off the Royal Mile, you can order a flight in the bar (includes written info on the whiskies) or opt for a guided tasting, which you can book in advance (flights and tours start around £25, daily 10:00-18:00, bar until 24:00, both open later in Aug, 4 North Bank Street, tel. 0131/225-1532, www. whiskirooms.com).

Calton Hill

Gin Distillery Tours

The residents of Edinburgh drink more gin per person than any other city in the United Kingdom, and the city is largely responsible for the recent renaissance of this drink, so it's only appropriate that you visit a gin distillery while in town. Two distilleries right in the heart of Edinburgh offer hourlong tours with colorful guides who discuss the history of gin, show you the stills involved in the production process, and ply you with libations. Both tours are popular and fill up; book ahead on their websites.

Pickering's is located in a former vet school and animal hospital at Summerhall, halfway between the Royal Mile and the B&B neighborhood—you'll still see cages lining the walls (£10, 3/day Thu-Sun, meet at the Royal Dick Bar in the central courtyard at 1 Summerhall, tel. 0131/290-2901, www.pickeringsgin.com).

Edinburgh Gin is in the New Town, next to the Waldorf Astoria Hotel. Besides the basic tour, there's a connoisseur tour with more tastings and a gin-making tour (basic tour £10, 3/day daily, 1A Rutland Place, tel. 0131/656-2810, www.edinburgh-gin.com). If you can't get on to one of their tours, visit their Heads & Tales bar to taste their gins (daily 17:00-24:00).

Edinburgh's Festivals

Every summer, Edinburgh's annual festivals turn the city into a carnival of the arts. The season begins in June with the international film festival (www.edfilmfest.org.uk); then the jazz and blues festival in July (www.edinburghjazzfestival.com).

In August a riot of overlapping festivals known collectively as the **Edinburgh Festival** rages simultaneously—international, fringe, book, and art, as well as the Military Tattoo. There are enough music, dance, drama, and multicultural events to make even the most jaded traveler giddy with excitement. Every day is jammed with formal and spontaneous fun. Many city sights run on extended hours. It's a glorious time to be in Edinburgh...if you have (and can afford) a room.

If you'll be in town in August, book your room and tickets for major events (especially the Tattoo) as far ahead as you can lock in dates. Plan carefully to ensure you'll have time for festival activities as well as sightseeing. Check online to confirm dates; the best overall website is www.edinburghfestivals.co.uk. Several publications—including the festival's official schedule, the *Edinburgh Festivals Guide Daily, The List, Fringe Program, and Daily Diary*—list and evaluate festival events.

The official, more formal **Edinburgh International Festival** is the original. Major events sell out well in advance (ticket office at the Hub, in the former Tolbooth Church near the top of the Royal Mile, tel. 0131/473-2000, www.hubtickets.co.uk or www.eif.co.uk).

The less formal **Fringe Festival,** featuring edgy comedy and theater, is huge—with 2,000 shows—and has eclipsed the original festival in popularity (ticket/info office just below St. Giles' Cathedral on the Royal Mile, 180 High Street, bookings tel. 0131/226-0000, www.edfringe.com). Tickets may be available at the door, and half-price tickets for some events are sold on the day of the show at the Half-Price Hut, located at The Mound, near the Scottish National Gallery.

The **Military Tattoo** is a massing of bands, drums, and bagpipes, with groups

from all over the former British Empire and beyond. Displaying military finesse with a stirring lone-piper finale, this grand spectacle fills the Castle Esplanade (nightly during most of Aug except Sun, performances Mon-Fri at 21:00, Sat at 19:30 and 22:30, £25-63, booking starts in Dec, Fri-Sat shows sell out first, all seats generally sold out by early summer, some scattered same-day tickets may be available; office open Mon-Fri 10:00-16:30, closed Sat-Sun, during Tattoo open until show time and closed Sun; 32 Market Street, behind Waverley Station, tel. 0131/225-1188, www.edintattoo.co.uk).

Shopping

Shops are usually open around 10:00-18:00 (later on Thu, shorter hours or closed on Sun). Tourist shops are open longer hours.

Rick's Tip: *If you want to be sure you're buying local merchandise,* **check if the labels read: "Made in Scotland."** *"Designed in Scotland" actually means "Made in China."*

Shopping Streets and Neighborhoods

Near the Royal Mile: The Royal Mile is intensely touristy, mostly lined with interchangeable shops selling made-in-China souvenirs.

In general, the area near **Grassmarket,** an easy stroll from the top of the Royal Mile, offers more originality. **Victoria Street,** which climbs steeply downhill from the Royal Mile (near the Hub/Tolbooth Church) to Grassmarket, has a fine concentration of local chain shops, including I.J. Mellis Cheesemonger and Walker Slater for designer tweed (both described later), plus Calzeat (scarves, throws, and other textiles), a Harry Potter store, and more clothing and accessory shops. **Candlemaker Row,** exiting Grassmarket opposite Victoria Street, is a little more artisan, with boutiques selling hats (everything from dapper men's caps to outrageous fascinators), jewelry, art, design items, and even fossils. The street winds a couple of blocks up toward the National Museum.

If it's **whisky** you want, try the shops I

Victoria Street, lined with shops

recommend for tasting (see page 369); they're on or near the Royal Mile.

In New Town: For mass-market shopping, you'll find plenty of big chain stores along **Princes Street.** In addition to Marks & Spencer, H&M, Zara, Primark, and a glitzy Apple Store, you'll also see the granddaddy of Scottish department stores, Jenners (generally daily 9:30-18:30, open later on Thu, shorter hours on Sun). Parallel to Princes Street, **George Street** has higher-end chain stores (including many from London, such as L.K. Bennett, Molton Brown, and Karen Millen). Just off St. Andrew Square is a branch of the high-end London department store Harvey Nichols.

For more local, artisan shopping, check out **Thistle Street,** lined with some fun eateries and a good collection of shops. You'll see some fun boutiques selling jewelry, shoes, and clothing. This is also the home of Howie Nicolsby's 21st Century Kilts, which attempts to bring traditional Scottish menswear into the present day.

Night Walks

▲▲LITERARY PUB TOUR

This two-hour walk is interesting even if you think Sir Walter Scott won an Oscar for playing General Patton. You'll follow the witty dialogue of two actors as they debate whether the great literature of Scotland was high art or the creative re-creation of fun-loving louts fueled by a passion for whisky. You'll wander from the Grassmarket over the Old Town and New Town, with stops in three pubs, as your guides share their takes on Scotland's literary greats. The tour meets at the Beehive Inn on Grassmarket (£14, book online and save £2, May-Sept nightly at 19:30, April and Oct Thu-Sun, Jan-March Fri and Sun, Nov-Dec Fri only, tel. 0800-169-7410, www.edinburghliterarypubtour.co.uk).

▲GHOST WALKS

A variety of companies lead spooky walks around town, providing an entertaining and affordable night out (offered nightly, most around 19:00 and 21:00, easy socializing for solo travelers). These two options are the most established.

The theatrical and creatively staged **The Cadies & Witchery Tours,** the most established outfit, offers two different 1.25-hour walks: "Ghosts and Gore" (April-Aug only, in daylight and following a flatter route) and "Murder and Mystery" (year-round, after dark, hillier, more surprises and scares). The cost for either tour is the same (£10, includes book of stories, leaves from top of Royal Mile, outside the Witchery Restaurant, near Castle Esplanade, reservations required, tel. 0131/225-6745, www.witcherytours.com).

Auld Reekie Tours offers a scary array of walks daily and nightly (£12-16, 60-90 minutes, leaves from front steps of the Tron Church building on Cockburn Street, tel. 0131/557-4700, www.auldreekietours.com). Auld Reekie focuses on the paranormal, witch covens, and pagan temples, taking groups into the "haunted vaults" under the old bridges (complete with screaming Gothic "jumpers").

Theater

Even outside festival time, Edinburgh is a fine place for lively and affordable theater. Pick up *The List* for a complete rundown of what's on (free at TI; also online at www.list.co.uk).

▲▲LIVE MUSIC IN PUBS

While traditional music venues have been eclipsed by beer-focused student bars, Edinburgh still has a few good pubs that can deliver a traditional folk-music fix. The monthly Gig Guide (free at TI, accommodations, and various pubs, www.gigguide.co.uk) lists several places each night that have live music, divided by genre (pop, rock, world, and folk).

South of the Royal Mile: Sandy Bell's is a tight little pub with live folk music nightly from 21:30 (near National Museum of Scotland at 25 Forrest Road, tel. 0131/225-

2751). Food is very simple (toasted sandwiches and pies), drinks are cheap, tables are small, and the vibe is local. They also have a few sessions earlier in the day (Sat at 14:00, Sun at 16:00, Mon at 17:30).

Captain's Bar is a cozy, music-focused pub with live sessions of folk and traditional music nightly around 21:00—see website for lineup (4 South College Street, http://captainsedinburgh.webs.com).

The Royal Oak is another good—if small—place for a dose of folk and blues (just off South Bridge opposite Chambers Road at 1 Infirmary Street, tel. 0131/557-2976).

The **Grassmarket** neighborhood (below the castle) bustles with live music and rowdy people spilling out of the pubs. Thanks to the music and crowds, you'll know where to go...and where not to. Have a beer and follow your ear to places like **Biddy Mulligans** or **White Hart Inn** (both on Grassmarket). **Finnegans Wake,** on Victoria Street (which leads down to Grassmarket), also has live music in a variety of genres each night.

On the Royal Mile: Three characteristic pubs within a few steps of each other on High Street (opposite Radisson Hotel) offer a fun setting, classic pub architecture and ambience, and live music for the cost of a beer: **Whiski Bar** (mostly trad and folk; nightly at 22:00), **Royal Mile** (variety of genres; nightly at 22:00), and **Mitre Bar** (acoustic pop/rock with some trad; Fri-Sun at 21:30).

In the New Town: Head for Rose Street, packed with pubs offering live music.

EATING

Reservations for restaurants are essential in August and on weekends, and a good idea anytime. Children aren't allowed in many of the pubs.

Either seek out—or avoid—Scotland's specialty, haggis (meaty stuffed intestines).

The Old Town

Pricey places abound on the Royal Mile (listed later). While those are tempting, I prefer the two areas described first, each within a few minutes' walk of the Mile—just far enough to offer better value and a bit less touristy crush.

On Victoria Street, Near Grassmarket

$$$$ Grainstore Restaurant, a sedate and dressy world of wood, stone, and candles tucked away above busy Victoria Street, has served Scottish produce with a French twist for more than two decades. While they have inexpensive £14 two-course lunch specials, dinner is à la carte. Reservations are recommended (daily 12:00-14:30 & 18:00-21:30, 30 Victoria Street, tel. 0131/225-7635, www.grainstore-restaurant.co.uk).

$$$ Maison Bleue Restaurant is popular for their à la carte French/Scottish/North African menu and dinner special before 18:30 (18:00 on Fri-Sat; open daily 12:00-22:00, 36 Victoria Street, tel. 0131/226-1900).

$ Oink carves from a freshly roasted pig each afternoon for sandwiches that come in "oink" or "grunter" sizes. Watch the pig shrink in the front window throughout the day (daily 11:00-18:00 or whenever they run out of meat, cash only, 34 Victoria Street, tel. 01890/761-355). Another location is at the bottom end of the Royal Mile, near the parliament building (at 82 Canongate).

Near the National Museum

These restaurants are happily removed from the Royal Mile melee and skew to a youthful clientele with few tourists. After passing the Greyfriars Bobby statue and the National Museum, fork left onto Forrest Road.

$ Union of Genius is a creative soup kitchen that also serves good salads and fresh-baked breads. The "flight" comes

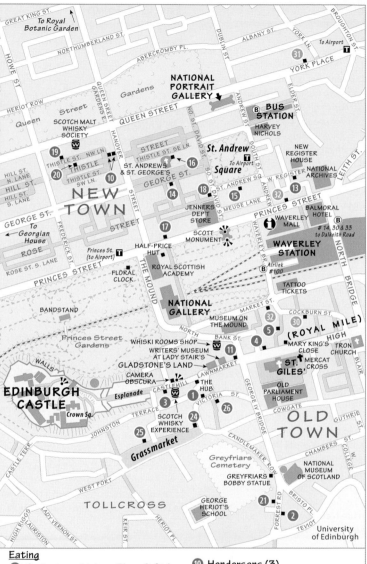

Eating

1. Grainstore, Maison Bleue & Oink
2. Union of Genius & Mums
3. The Witchery by the Castle
4. Angels with Bagpipes
5. Devil's Advocate
6. Wedgwood Restaurant
7. Edinburgh Larder
8. Mimi's Bakehouse Picnic Parlour
9. Clarinda's Tea Room
10. Hendersons (3)
11. Deacon Brodie's Tavern
12. The World's End Pub
13. Café Royal
14. The Dome Restaurant
15. Dishoom
16. St. Andrew's & St. George's Church Undercroft Café
17. Marks & Spencer Food Hall
18. Sainsbury's

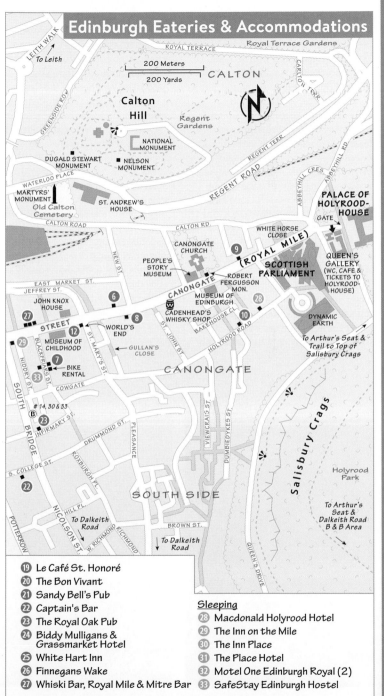

Edinburgh Eateries & Accommodations

19 Le Café St. Honoré
20 The Bon Vivant
21 Sandy Bell's Pub
22 Captain's Bar
23 The Royal Oak Pub
24 Biddy Mulligans & Grassmarket Hotel
25 White Hart Inn
26 Finnegans Wake
27 Whiski Bar, Royal Mile & Mitre Bar

Sleeping
28 Macdonald Holyrood Hotel
29 The Inn on the Mile
30 The Inn Place
31 The Place Hotel
32 Motel One Edinburgh Royal (2)
33 SafeStay Edinburgh Hostel

with three small cups of soup and three types of bread. Line up at the counter, then either take your soup to go or sit in the cramped interior, with a couple of tables and counter seating (Mon-Fri 10:00-16:00, Sat from 12:00, closed Sun, 8 Forrest Road, tel. 0131/226-4436).

$$ Mums is a kitschy diner serving up comfort food just like mum used to make. The menu runs to huge portions of heavy, greasy Scottish/British standards—bangers (sausages), meat pies, burgers, and artery-clogging breakfasts (served until 12:00)—all done with a foodie spin, including vegetarian options (Mon-Sat 9:00-22:00, Sun from 10:00, 4A Forrest Road, tel. 0131/260-9806).

Along the Royal Mile

Though the eateries along this most-crowded stretch of the city are invariably touristy, the scene is fun. Sprinkled in this list are some places a block or two off the main drag offering better values and maybe fewer tourists.

SIT-DOWN RESTAURANTS
These are listed roughly in downhill order, starting at the castle. You'll have more success getting into any of these with a reservation, especially on weekends.

$$$$ The Witchery by the Castle is set in a lushly decorated 16th-century building just below the castle on the Royal Mile, with wood paneling, antique candlesticks, tapestries, and opulent red leather upholstery. Frequented by celebrities, tourists, and locals out for a splurge, the restaurant's emphasis is on pricey Scottish meats and seafood. Their Secret Garden dining room, in a separate building farther back, is also a special setting—down some steps and in a fanciful room with French doors opening on to a terrace. Reserve ahead for either space, dress smartly, and bear in mind you're paying a premium for the ambience (two-course lunch specials—also available before 17:30 and after 22:30, three-course dinner menu, daily 12:00-23:30, tel. 0131/225-5613, www.thewitchery.com).

Haggis — an acquired taste

The Witchery by the Castle

$$$$ **Angels with Bagpipes,** conveniently located across from St. Giles' Cathedral, serves sophisticated Scottish staples in its dark, serious, plush interior (two- and three-course lunches, tasting menus at dinner, daily 12:00-21:30, 343 High Street, tel. 0131/220-1111, www. angelswithbagpipes.co.uk).

$$$ **Devil's Advocate** is a popular gastropub that hides down the narrow lane called Advocates Close, directly across the Royal Mile from St. Giles'. With an old cellar setting—exposed stone and heavy beams—done up in modern style, it feels like a mix of old and new Edinburgh. Creative whisky cocktails kick off a menu that dares to be adventurous, but with a respect for Scottish tradition (daily 12:00-22:00, later for drinks, 8 Advocates Close, tel. 0131/225-4465).

$$$$ **Wedgwood Restaurant** is romantic, contemporary, chic, and as gourmet as possible with no pretense. Paul Wedgwood cooks while his wife Lisa serves with appetizing charm. The cuisine: creative, modern Scottish with an international twist and a whiff of Asia. The pigeon and haggis starter is scrumptious. Paul and Lisa believe in making the meal the event of the evening—don't come here to eat and run. I like the ground level with the Royal Mile view, but the busy kitchen ambience in the basement is also fine (fine wine by the glass, daily 12:00-15:00 & 18:00-22:00, reservations advised, 267 Canongate on Royal Mile, tel. 0131/558-8737, www.wedgwoodtherestaurant.co.uk).

QUICK, EASY, AND CHEAP LUNCH OPTIONS

$ **Edinburgh Larder** promises "a taste of the country" in the center of the city. They focus on high-quality, homestyle breakfast and lunches made from seasonal, local ingredients. The café, with table service, is a convivial space with rustic tables filled by local families. The takeaway shop next door has counter service and a few dine-in tables (Mon-Fri 8:00-16:00, Sat-Sun from 9:00, 15 Blackfriars Street, tel. 0131/556-6922).

$ **Mimi's Bakehouse Picnic Parlour,** a handy Royal Mile outpost of a prizewinning bakery, serves up baked goods—try the scones—and sandwiches in their cute and modern shop (daily 9:00-18:00, 250 Canongate, tel. 0131/556-6632).

$ **Clarinda's Tea Room,** near the bottom of the Royal Mile, is a charming and girlish time warp—a fine and tasty place to relax after touring the Mile or the Palace of Holyroodhouse. Stop in for a quiche, salad, or soup lunch. It's also great for sandwiches and tea and cake anytime (Mon-Sat 9:00-16:30, Sun from 10:00, 69 Canongate, tel. 0131/557-1888).

$$ **Hendersons** is a bright and casual local chain with good vegetarian dishes to go or eat in (daily 9:00-17:00, 67 Holyrood Road—three minutes off Royal Mile near Scottish Parliament end, tel. 0131/557-1606; for more details, see the Hendersons listing later, under "The New Town").

HISTORIC PUBS ALONG THE MILE

To drink a pint or grab some forgettable pub grub in historic surroundings, consider one of the landmark pubs described on my self-guided walk: $$ **Deacon Brodie's Tavern,** at a dead-center location on the Royal Mile (a sloppy pub on the ground floor with a sloppy restaurant upstairs) or $$ **The World's End Pub,** farther down the Mile at Canongate (a colorful old place dishing up hearty meals from a creative menu in a fun, dark, and noisy space, live music Thu-Sat 21:00, 4 High Street). Both serve pub meals and are open long hours daily.

The New Town

In the Georgian part of town, you'll find a bustling world of office workers, students, and pensioners doing their thing. All of these eateries are within a few minutes' walk of the TI and Waverley Station.

Elegant Spaces near Princes Street

These places provide a staid glimpse at grand old Edinburgh. The ambience is generally better than the food.

Café Royal is a movie producer's dream pub—the perfect fin de siècle setting for a coffee, beer, or light meal. (In fact, parts of *Chariots of Fire* were filmed here.) Drop in, if only to admire the 1880 tiles featuring famous inventors (daily 12:00-14:30 & 17:00-21:30, bar food available all day, two blocks from Waverley Mall on 19 West Register Street, tel. 0131/556-1884, www.caferoyaledinburgh.co.uk). There are two eateries here: the noisy **$$ pub** and the dressier **$$$ restaurant,** specializing in oysters, fish, and game (reserve for dinner—it's quite small and understandably popular).

$$$$ The Dome Restaurant, in what was a fancy bank, serves modern international cuisine around a classy bar and under the elegant 19th-century skylight dome. With soft jazz and chic, white-tablecloth ambience, it feels a world apart. Come here not for the food, but for the opulent atmosphere (daily 12:00-23:00, food served until 21:30, reserve for dinner, open for a drink any time under the dome; the adjacent, more intimate Club Room serves food Mon-Thu 10:00-16:00, Fri-Sat until 21:30, closed Sun; 14 George Street, tel. 0131/624-8624, www.thedomeedinburgh.com).

Casual and Cheap near St. Andrew Square

$$ Dishoom, in the New Town, is the first non-London outpost of this popular Bombay café. You'll enjoy upscale Indian cuisine in a bustling, dark, 1920s dining room on the second floor overlooking St. Andrew Square. You can also order from the same menu in the basement bar at night (daily 9:00-23:00, 3A St. Andrew Square, tel. 0131/202-6406).

$ St. Andrew's and St. George's Church Undercroft Café, in the basement of a fine old church, is the cheapest place in town for lunch (Mon-Fri lunch only, closed Sat-Sun, at 13 George Street, just off St. Andrew Square, tel. 0131/225-3847).

Supermarkets: Marks & Spencer Food Hall is just a block from the Scott Monument and the picnic-perfect Princes Street Gardens (Mon-Sat 8:00-19:00, Thu until 20:00, Sun 11:00-18:00, Princes Street 54—separate stairway next to main M&S entrance leads directly to food hall, tel. 0131/225-2301). **Sainsbury's** supermarket, a block off Princes Street, also offers grab-and-go items (daily 7:00-22:00, on corner of Rose Street on St. Andrew Square, across the street from Jenners).

Hip Eateries on and near Thistle Street

$$$ Le Café St. Honoré, tucked away like a secret bit of old Paris, is a charming place with friendly service and walls lined by wine bottles. It serves French-Scottish cuisine in tight, Old World, cut-glass elegance to a dressy crowd (three-course lunch and dinner specials, daily 12:00-14:00 & 17:30-22:00, reservations smart—ask to sit upstairs, down Thistle Street from Hanover Street, 34 Northwest Thistle Street Lane, tel. 0131/226-2211, www.cafesthonore.com).

$$$ The Bon Vivant is woody, youthful, and candlelit, with a rotating menu of French/Scottish dishes, a good cocktail list, and a companion wine shop next door. They have fun tapas plates and heartier dishes, served either in the bar up front or in the restaurant in back (daily 12:00-22:00, 55 Thistle Street, tel. 0131/225-3275, www.bonvivantedinburgh.co.uk).

$$ Hendersons has fed a generation of New Town vegetarians hearty cuisine and salads. Even carnivores love this place for its delectable salads, desserts, and smoothies. Henderson's has two separate eateries: Their main restaurant, facing Hanover Street, is self-service by day but has table service after 17:00. Each evening after 19:00, they have pleasant live music—generally guitar or jazz (Mon-Sat 9:00-22:00, Sun 10:30-16:00, between Queen and George streets at 94 Hanover

Street, tel. 0131/225-2131). Just around the corner on Thistle Street, **Henderson's Vegan** has a strictly vegan menu and feels a bit more casual (daily 12:00-21:30, tel. 0131/225-2605).

In the B&B Neighborhood
Pub Grub
$$ **The Salisbury Arms Pub,** with a nice garden terrace and separate restaurant area, serves upscale, pleasing traditional classics with yuppie flair in a space that exudes more Martha Stewart and Pottery Barn than traditional public house (book ahead for restaurant, food served daily 12:00-22:00, across from the pool at 58 Dalkeith Road, tel. 0131/667-4518, www. thesalisburyarmsedinburgh.co.uk).

$$ **The Old Bell Inn,** with an old-time sports-bar ambience—fishing, golf, horses, televisions—serves pub meals. This is a classic "snug pub"—all dark woods and brass beer taps, littered with evocative knickknacks. It comes with sidewalk seating and a mixed-age crowd (bar tables can be reserved, food served daily until 21:15, 233 Causewayside, tel. 0131/668-1573, http://oldbelledinburgh.co.uk).

Other Eateries
$$$$ **Aizle** is a delicious night out. They serve a set £45 five-course tasting menu based on what's in season—ingredients are listed on the chalkboard (with notice, they can accommodate dietary restrictions). The restaurant is intimate but unpretentious, and they only serve 36 people a night to keep the experience special and unrushed (dinner only Wed-Sun, this is not a walk-in type of place—book ahead at least a week, 107 St. Leonard's Street—five minutes past the Royal Commonwealth Pool, tel. 0131/662-9349, www.aizle.co.uk).

$$ **Southpour** is a nice place for a local beer, craft cocktail, or a reliable meal from a menu of salads, sandwiches, meat dishes, and other comfort foods.

The brick walls, wood beams, and giant windows give it a warm and open vibe (daily 10:00-22:00, 1 Newington Road, tel. 0131/650-1100).

$$ **Ristorante Isola** is a calm and casual place with 15 tables surrounding a bright yellow bar. They serve pizzas, pastas, and meat or seafood *secondi* with an emphasis on Sardinian specialties (Mon-Tue 17:00-22:30, Wed-Sun 12:00-22:30, 85 Newington Road, tel. 0131/662-9977).

$$ **Voujon Restaurant** serves a fusion menu of Bengali and Indian cuisines. Vegetarians appreciate the expansive yet inexpensive offerings (daily 17:00-23:00, 107 Newington Road, tel. 0131/667-5046).

Groceries: Several grocery stores are on the main streets near the restaurants, including Sainsbury's Local and Co-op on South Clerk Road, and Tesco Express and another Sainsbury's Local one block over on Causewayside (all open late—until at least 22:00).

SLEEPING

To stay in the city center, you'll likely have to stay in a larger hotel or more impersonal guesthouse. For the classic B&B experience, look to the area south of town, along Dalkeith Road. From the B&Bs, it's a long walk to the city center (about 25 minutes) or a quick bus or taxi/Uber ride.

While many of my B&B listings are not cheap (generally around £90-130), most come with friendly hosts and great cooked breakfasts. And they're generally cheaper than staying at a city-center hotel.

Note that during the Festival in August, prices skyrocket and most places do not accept bookings for one- or even two-night stays. If coming in August, book far in advance.

Conventions, rugby matches, school holidays, and weekends can make finding a room tough at other times of year, too. In winter, when demand is light, some B&Bs close, and prices at all accommodations get soft.

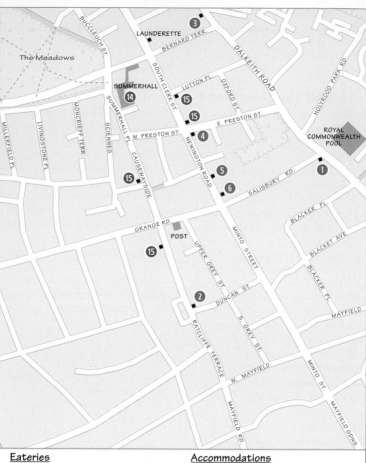

Eateries
1. The Salisbury Arms Pub
2. The Old Bell Inn
3. Aizle
4. Southpour
5. Ristorante Isola
6. Voujon

Accommodations
7. Gil Dun Guest House
8. Gifford House
9. AmarAgua Guest House
10. Hotel Ceilidh-Donia
11. Ard-Na-Said B&B
12. Dunedin Guest House
13. Airdenair Guest House

B&Bs South of the City Center

At these not-quite-interchangeable places, character is provided by the personality quirks of the hosts and sometimes the decor. In general, cash is preferred and can lead to discounted rates. Book direct—you will pay a much higher rate through a booking service.

Near the B&Bs, you'll find plenty of fine eateries (see "Eating in Edinburgh," earlier). A few places have their own private parking; others offer access to easy, free street parking (ask when booking—or better yet, don't rent a car for your time in Edinburgh). The nearest launderette is

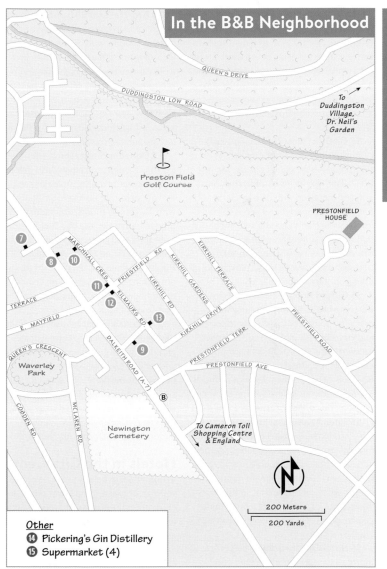

In the B&B Neighborhood

QUEEN'S DRIVE

DUDDINGSTON LOW ROAD

To Duddingston Village, Dr. Neil's Garden

Preston Field Golf Course

PRESTONFIELD HOUSE

MARCHHALL CRES

PRIESTFIELD RD

KIRKHILL TERRACE

KIRKHILL GARDENS

KIRKHILL RD

KIRKHILL DRIVE

TERRACE

E. MAYFIELD

KILMAURS RD

PRIESTFIELD ROAD

QUEEN'S CRESCENT

Waverley Park

DALKEITH ROAD (A-7)

PRESTONFIELD TERR.

PRESTONFIELD AVE.

COBDEN RD

MCLAREN RD

Newington Cemetery

To Cameron Toll Shopping Centre & England

200 Meters

200 Yards

Other
- 14 Pickering's Gin Distillery
- 15 Supermarket (4)

Ace Cleaning Centre (which picks up and drops off; see page 330).

Taxi or Uber fare between the city center and the B&Bs is about £7. If taking the bus from the B&Bs into the city, hop off at the South Bridge stop for the Royal Mile (£1.60 single ride, £4 day ticket, use exact change; see below for more bus specifics). Most of

my B&Bs near Dalkeith Road are located south of the Royal Commonwealth Pool. This comfortable, safe neighborhood is a ten-minute bus ride from the Royal Mile.

To get here from the train station, catch the bus around the corner on North Bridge: Exit the station onto Princes Street, turn right, cross the street, and walk up the bridge to the bus stop in front of the Marks & Spencer department store (#14, #30, or #33). About 10 minutes into the ride, after following South Clerk Street for a while, the bus makes a left turn, then a right. Depending on where you're staying, you'll get off at the first or second stop after the turn (confirm specifics with your B&B).

$$ Gil Dun Guest House, with eight rooms—some contemporary, others more traditional—is on a quiet cul-de-sac just off Dalkeith Road. It's comfortable, pleasant, and managed with care by Gerry and Bill; Maggie helps out and keeps things immaculate (family rooms, two-night minimum in summer preferred, limited off-street parking, 9 Spence Street, tel. 0131/667-1368, www.gildun.co.uk, gildun.edin@btinternet.com).

$$ Gifford House, on busy Dalkeith Road, is a bright, flowery retreat with six peaceful rooms (some with ornate cornices and views of Arthur's Seat) and compact, modern bathrooms (RS%, family rooms, cash preferred, street parking, 103 Dalkeith Road, tel. 0131/667-4688, www.giffordhouseedinburgh.com, giffordhouse@btinternet.com, David and Margaret).

$$ AmarAgua Guest House is an inviting Victorian home away from home, with five welcoming rooms, a Japanese garden, and eager hosts (one double has private bath down the hall, 2-night minimum, no kids under 12, street parking, 10 Kilmaurs Terrace, tel. 0131/667-6775, www.amaragua.co.uk, reservations@amaragua.co.uk, Lucia and Kuan).

$$ Hotel Ceilidh-Donia is bigger (17 rooms) and more hotel-like than other nearby B&Bs, with a bar and a small reception area, but managers Kevin and Susan and their staff provide a guesthouse warmth. The back deck is a pleasant place to sit on a warm day (family room, two-night minimum on peak-season weekends, 14 Marchhall Crescent, tel. 0131/667-2743, www.hotelceilidh-donia.co.uk, reservations@hotelceilidh-donia.co.uk).

$$ Ard-Na-Said B&B, in an elegant 1875 Victorian house, has seven bright, spacious rooms with modern bathrooms, including one ground-floor room with a pleasant patio (two-night minimum preferred in summer, off-street parking, 5 Priestfield Road, tel. 0131/283-6524, mobile 07476-606-202, www.ardnasaid.co.uk, info@ardnasaid.co.uk, Audrey Ballantine and her son Steven).

$$ Dunedin Guest House (dun-EE-din) is bright and plush, with seven well-decorated rooms, an angelic atrium, and a spacious breakfast room/lounge with TV (family rooms, one room with private bath down the hall, includes continental breakfast, extra charge for cooked breakfast, limited off-street parking, 8 Priestfield Road, tel. 0131/468-3339, www.dunedinguesthouse.co.uk, reservations@dunedinguesthouse.co.uk, Mary and Tony).

$ Airdenair Guest House is a hands-off guesthouse, with no formal host greeting (you'll get an access code to let yourself in) and a self-serve breakfast buffet. But the price is nice and the five simple rooms are well-maintained (29 Kilmaurs Road, tel. 0131/468-0173, http://airdenair-edinburgh.co.uk/, contact@airdenair-edinburgh.co.uk, Duncan).

Hotels in the City Center

While a B&B generally provides more warmth, character, and lower prices, a city-center hotel gives you more walkability and access to sights and Edinburgh's excellent restaurant and pub scene. Prices are very high in peak season and drop substantially in off-season (a good time to shop around). In each case, I'd skip the institutional breakfast and eat out. You'll generally pay about £10 a day to park near these hotels.

$$$$ Macdonald Holyrood Hotel is a four-star splurge, with 157 rooms up the street from the parliament building and Holyroodhouse Palace. With its classy marble-and-wood decor, fitness center, spa, and pool, it's hard to leave. On a gray winter day in Edinburgh, this could be worth it (pricey breakfast, elevator, pay valet parking, near bottom of Royal Mile, across from Dynamic Earth, 81 Holyrood Road, tel. 0131/528-8000, www.macdonaldhotels. co.uk, newres@macdonald-hotels.co.uk).

$$$$ The Inn on the Mile is your trendy, central option, filling a renovated old bank building right in the heart of the Royal Mile (at North Bridge/South Bridge). The nine bright and stylish rooms are an afterthought to the busy upmarket pub, which is where you'll check in. If you don't mind some noise (from the pub and the busy street) and climbing lots of stairs, it's a handy home base (breakfast extra, complimentary drink, 82 High Street, tel. 0131/556-9940, www.theinnonthemile. co.uk, info@theinnonthemile.co.uk).

$$$$ The Inn Place, part of a small chain, fills the former headquarters of *The Scotsman* newspaper—a few steep steps below the Royal Mile—with 41 characterless, minimalist rooms ("bunk rooms" for 6-8 people, best deals on weekdays, breakfast extra, elevator, 20 Cockburn Street, tel. 0131/526-3780, www.theinnplaceedinburgh.co.uk, reception@theinnplaceedinburgh.co.uk).

$$$ Grassmarket Hotel's 42 rooms are quirky and fun, from the Dandy comic-book wallpaper to the giant wall map of Edinburgh equipped with planning-your-visit magnets. The hotel is in a great location right on Grassmarket overlooking the Covenanters Memorial and above Biddy Mulligans Bar (family rooms, two-night minimum on weekends, elevator only serves half the rooms, 94 Grassmarket, tel. 0131/220-2299, www.grassmarkethotel. co.uk).

$$$ The Place Hotel, sister of the Inn Place listed above, has a fine New Town location 10 minutes north of the train station. It occupies three grand Georgian townhouses, with no elevator and long flights of stairs leading up to the 47 contemporary, no-frills rooms. Their outdoor terrace with retractable roof and heaters is a popular place to unwind (save money with a smaller city double, 34 York Place, tel. 0131/556-7575, www.yorkplace-edinburgh.co.uk, frontdesk@yorkplace-edinburgh.co.uk).

$$ Motel One Edinburgh Royal, part of a stylish German budget hotel chain, is between the train station and the Royal Mile; it feels upscale and trendy for its price range (208 rooms, pay more for a park view or less for a windowless "budget" room with skylight, breakfast extra, elevator, 18 Market Street, tel. 0131/220-0730, www. motel-one.com, edinburgh-royal@motel-one.com; second location in the New Town/shopping zone at 134 Princes Street).

Chain Hotels in the Center: Besides my recommendations above, you'll find a number of cookie-cutter chain hotels close to the Royal Mile, including **Jurys Inn** (43 Jeffrey Street), **Ibis Hotel** (two convenient branches: near the Tron Church and another around the corner along the busy South Bridge), **Holiday Inn Express** (two locations: just off the Royal Mile at 300 Cowgate and one in the New Town), and **Travelodge Central** (just below the Royal Mile at 33 St. Mary's Street; additional locations in the New Town).

Hostel

¢ SafeStay Edinburgh, just off the Royal Mile, rents 272 bunks in pleasing purple-accented rooms. Dorm rooms have 4 to 12 beds, and there are also a few private singles and twin rooms (all rooms have private bathrooms). Bar 50 in the basement has an inviting lounge. Half of the rooms function as a university dorm during the school year, becoming available just in time for the tourists (breakfast extra, kitchen, laundry, free daily walking tour, 50 Blackfriars Street, tel. 0131/524-1989, www.safestay.com, reservations-edi@safestay.com).

Waverley Station

TRANSPORTATION

Getting Around Edinburgh

Many of Edinburgh's sights are within walking distance of one another, but **buses** come in handy—especially if you're staying at a B&B south of the city center. Double-decker buses come with fine views upstairs. It's easy once you get the hang of it: Buses come by frequently (screens at bus stops show wait times) and have free, fast Wi-Fi on board. The only hassle is that you must pay with exact change (£1.60/ride, £4/all-day pass). As you board, tell your driver where you're going (or just say "single ticket") and drop your change into the box. Ping the bell as you near your stop. You can pick up a route map at the TI or at the transit office at Old Town end of Waverley Bridge (tel. 0131/555-6363, www.lothianbuses.com). Edinburgh's single **tram** line (also £1.60/ride) is designed more for locals than tourists; it's most useful for reaching the airport.

The 1,300 **taxis** cruising Edinburgh's streets are easy to flag down (ride between downtown and the B&B neighborhood costs about £7; rates go up after 18:00 and on weekends). They can turn on a dime, so hail them in either direction. Uber also works well here.

Arriving and Departing
By Plane

Edinburgh Airport is located eight miles northwest of the center (airport code: EDI, tel. 0844-481-8989, www.edinburghairport.com).

Taxis or **Uber rides** between the airport and city center are about £20-25 (25 minutes to downtown or Dalkeith Road).

The airport is also well connected to central Edinburgh by tram and bus. Just follow signs outside; the tram tracks are straight ahead, and the bus stop is to the right, along the main road in front of the terminal. **Trams** make several stops in town, including along Princes Street and at St. Andrew Square (£5.50, buy ticket from machine, runs every 10 minutes from early morning until 23:30, 35 minutes, www.edinburghtrams.com).

The Lothian **Airlink bus #100** drops you

at Waverley Bridge (£4.50, £7.50 round-trip, runs every 10 minutes, 30 minutes, tel. 0131/555-6363, http://lothianbuses.co.uk).

Whether you take the tram or bus to the center, to continue on to my recommended B&Bs south of the city center, you can either take a taxi (about £7) or hop on a city bus (for directions, see "Sleeping in Edinburgh," earlier). To get from the B&Bs to the Airlink or tram stops downtown, you can take a taxi...or ride a city bus to North Bridge, turn left at the grand Balmoral Hotel, and walk a short distance down Princes Street. Turn right up St. Andrew Street to catch the tram at St. Andrew Square, or continue up to the next bridge, Waverley, for the Airlink bus.

By Train

Arriving by train at Waverley Station puts you in the city center and below the TI. Taxis line up outside, on Market Street or Waverley Bridge. For the TI or bus stop, follow signs for Princes Street and ride up several escalators. From here, the TI is to your left, and the city bus stop is two blocks to your right.

TRAIN CONNECTIONS
From Edinburgh to: Glasgow (10/hour, 50 minutes), **Inverness** (6/day direct, 3.5 hours, more with transfer), **York** (3/hour, 2.5 hours), **London** (2/hour, 4.5 hours), **Durham** (hourly direct, 2 hours, less frequent in winter), **Newcastle** (3/hour, 1.5 hours), **Keswick/Lake District** (8/day to Penrith—more via Carlisle, 2 hours, then 45-minute bus ride to Keswick), **Birmingham** (hourly, 5 hours, less with transfer),

Bristol, near Bath (hourly, 6.5 hours). Train info: Tel. 0345-748-4950, www.nationalrail.co.uk.

By Bus

Edinburgh's bus station (with luggage lockers) is in the New Town, just off St. Andrew Square, two blocks north of the train station. For long-distance bus info, stop by the station or check Scottish Citylink (tel. 0871-266-3333, www.citylink.co.uk), National Express (www.national-express.com), or Megabus (www.megabus.com).

Rick's Tip: *If you plan to* **rent a car, pick it up on your way out of Edinburgh**—*you won't need it in town.*

By Car

If you're driving in on the A-68 from the south, first follow signs for *Edinburgh South & West* (A-720), then exit at *A-7(N)/Edinburgh* and follow the directions above.

Car Rental: These places have offices both in the town center and at the airport—**Avis** (24 East London Street, tel. 0844-544-6059, airport tel. 0844-544-6004), **Europcar** (Waverley Station, near platform 2, tel. 0871-384-3453, airport tel. 0871-384-3406), **Hertz** (10 Picardy Place, tel. 0843-309-3026, airport tel. 0843-309-3025), and **Budget** (24 East London Street, tel. 0844-544-9064, airport tel. 0844-544-4605).

England: Past & Present

Origins
(2000 B.C.-A.D. 500)

When Julius Caesar landed on the misty and mysterious isle of Britain in 55 B.C., England entered the history books. He was met by primitive Celtic tribes whose druid priests made human sacrifices and worshipped trees. (Those Celts were themselves immigrants, who had earlier conquered the even more mysterious people who built Stonehenge.) The Romans eventually settled in England (A.D. 43) and set about building towns and roads and establishing their capital at Londinium (today's London).

But the Celtic natives—consisting of Gaels, Picts, and Scots—were not easily subdued. Around A.D. 60, Boadicea, a queen of the Isle's indigenous people, defied the Romans and burned Londinium before the revolt was squelched. Some decades later, the Romans built Hadrian's Wall near the Scottish border as protection against their troublesome northern neighbors.

Dark Ages
(500-1000)

As Rome fell, so fell Roman Britain—a victim of invaders and internal troubles. Barbarian tribes from Germany, Denmark, and northern Holland, called Angles, Saxons, and Jutes, swept through the southern part of the island, establishing Angle-land. These were the days of the real King Arthur, possibly a Christianized Roman general who fought valiantly—but in vain—against invading barbarians.

In 793, England was hit with the first of two centuries of savage invasions by barbarians from Norway, called the Vikings or Norsemen. King Alfred the Great (849-899) liberated London from Danish Vikings, reunited England, reestablished Christianity, and fostered learning. Nevertheless, for most of this 500-year period, the island was plunged into a dark age.

Norman Britain and the Middle Ages
(1000-1500)

In 1066, William the Conqueror and his Norman troops crossed the English Chan-

Royal Families: Past & Present

802-1066:	Saxon and Danish kings
1066-1154:	Norman invasion (William the Conqueror), Norman kings
1154-1399:	Plantagenet (kings with French roots)
1399-1461:	Lancaster
1462-1485:	York
1485-1603:	Tudor (Henry VIII, Elizabeth I)
1603-1649:	Stuart (civil war and beheading of Charles I)
1649-1653:	Commonwealth, no royal head of state
1653-1659:	Protectorate, with Cromwell as Lord Protector
1660-1714:	Restoration of Stuart dynasty
1714-1901:	Hanover (four Georges, William IV, Victoria)
1901-1910:	Saxe-Coburg (Edward VII)
1910-now:	Windsor (George V, Edward VIII, George VI, Elizabeth II)

nel from France. William crowned himself king in Westminster Abbey (where all subsequent coronations would take place). He began building the Tower of London, as well as Windsor Castle, which would become the residence of many monarchs to come.

Over the succeeding centuries, French-speaking kings would rule England, and English-speaking kings invaded France as the two budding nations defined their modern borders. Richard the Lionheart (1157-1199) ruled as a French-speaking king who spent most of his energy on distant Crusades. In 1215, King John (Richard's brother), under pressure from England's barons, was forced to sign the *Magna Carta,* establishing the principle that even kings must follow the rule of law.

London asserted itself as England's trade center. London Bridge—the famous stone version, topped with houses—was built (1209), and Old St. Paul's Cathedral was finished (1314).

Then followed two centuries of wars, chiefly the Hundred Years' War with France (1337-1443). In 1348, the Black Death (bubonic plague) killed half of London's population.

In the 1400s, the noble York and Lancaster families duked it out for the crown in a series of dynastic civil wars.

The Tudor Renaissance
(1500s)
England was finally united by the "third-party" Tudor family. Henry VIII, a Tudor, was England's Renaissance king. He went through six wives in 40 years, divorcing, imprisoning, or executing them when they no longer suited his needs. When the Pope refused to grant Henry a divorce so he could marry Anne Boleyn, Henry "divorced" England from the Catholic Church. He established the Protestant Church of England (the Anglican Church), thus setting in motion a century of bitter Protestant/Catholic squabbles. Henry's own daughter, "Bloody" Mary, was a staunch Catholic who presided over the burning of hundreds of prominent Protestants.

After Mary came another of Henry's daughters (by Anne Boleyn)—Queen Elizabeth I. She reigned for 45 years, making England a great trading and naval power (defeating the Spanish Armada) and treading diplomatically over the Protestant/Catholic divide. Elizabeth presided

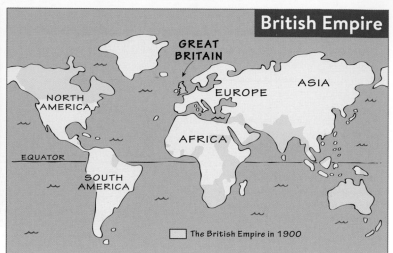

British Empire

GREAT BRITAIN

NORTH AMERICA

EUROPE

ASIA

AFRICA

EQUATOR

SOUTH AMERICA

The British Empire in 1900

over a cultural renaissance known as the "Elizabethan Age." Playwright William Shakespeare moved from Stratford-up-on-Avon to London, beginning a remarkable career as the earth's greatest playwright. Sir Francis Drake circumnavigated the globe. Sir Walter Raleigh explored the Americas, and Sir Francis Bacon pioneered the scientific method.

But Elizabeth—the "Virgin Queen"—never married or produced an heir. So the English Parliament invited Scotland's King James (Elizabeth's first cousin twice removed) to inherit the English throne.

Kings vs. Parliament
(1600s)

The enduring quarrel between England's kings and Parliament's nobles finally erupted into the 1642 Civil War. The war pitted the Protestant Puritan Parliament against the Catholic aristocracy. Parliament forces under Oliver Cromwell defeated—and beheaded—King Charles I. After Cromwell died, Parliament invited Charles' son to take the throne—the "restoration of the monarchy."

This turbulent era was followed by back-to-back disasters—the Great Plague of 1665 (which killed 100,000) and the

Great Fire of 1666 (which incinerated London). London was completely rebuilt in stone, centered on the new St. Paul's Cathedral, built by Christopher Wren.

In the war between kings and Parliament, Parliament finally got the last word when it deposed Catholic James II and imported the Dutch monarchs William and Mary in 1688, guaranteeing a Protestant succession.

Colonial Expansion
(1700s)

Britain grew as a naval superpower, colonizing and trading with all parts of the globe. Eventually, Britannia ruled the waves, exploiting the wealth of India, Africa, Australia, and America...at least until those ungrateful Yanks revolted in 1776. Throughout the century, the country was ruled by the German Hanover family, including four kings named George.

The "Georgian Era" was one of great wealth. London's population was now a half-million, and one in seven Brits lived in London. The nation's first daily newspapers hit the streets. The cultural scene was refined: painters (like William Hogarth, Joshua Reynolds, and Thomas Gainsborough), theater (with actors like David

The British Accent

In the olden days, a British person's accent indicated his or her social standing. Eliza Doolittle had the right idea—elocution could make or break you. Wealthier families would send their kids to fancy private schools to learn proper pronunciation. But these days, in a sort of reverse snobbery that has gripped the nation, accents are back. Politicians, newscasters, and movie stars are favoring deep accents over the Queen's English. While it's hard for American ears to pick out the variations, most Brits can determine where a person is from based on their accent... not just the region, but often the village, and even the part of town.

power, with a colonial empire that covered one-fifth of the world.

Meanwhile, there was another side to Britain's era of superiority and industrial might. A generation of Romantic poets (William Wordsworth, John Keats, Percy Shelley, and Lord Byron) longed for the innocence of nature. Jane Austen and the Brontë sisters wrote romantic tales about the landed gentry. Painters like J. M. W. Turner and John Constable immersed themselves in nature to paint moody landscapes.

The gritty modern world was emerging. Popular novelist Charles Dickens brought literature to the masses, educating them about Britain's harsh social and economic realities. Rudyard Kipling critiqued the colonial system. Charles Darwin questioned the very nature of humanity when he articulated the principles of natural selection and evolution.

Garrick), music (Handel's *Messiah*), and literature (Samuel Johnson's dictionary). Scientist James Watt's steam engines laid the groundwork for a coming Industrial Revolution.

In 1789, the French Revolution erupted, sparking decades of war between France and Britain. Britain finally prevailed in the early 1800s, when Admiral Horatio Nelson defeated Napoleon's fleet at the Battle of Trafalgar and the Duke of Wellington stomped Napoleon at Waterloo. By war's end, Britain had emerged as Europe's top power.

Victorian Britain
(1800s)

Britain reigned supreme, steaming into the Industrial Age with her mills, factories, coal mines, gas lights, and trains.

Eighteen-year-old Victoria became queen in 1837. She ruled for 64 years, presiding over an era of unprecedented wealth, peace, and middle-class ("Victorian") values. Britain was at its zenith of

World Wars and Recovery
(20TH CENTURY)

The 20th century was not kind to Britain. Two world wars and economic struggles whittled Britain down from a world empire to an island chain struggling to compete in a global economy.

In World War I, Britain joined France and other allies to battle Germany in trench warfare. A million British men died.

In the 1920s, London was home to a flourishing literary scene, including T. S. Eliot, Virginia Woolf, and E. M. Forster. In 1936, the country was rocked and scandalized when King Edward VIII abdicated to marry a divorced American commoner, Wallis Simpson.

In World War II, the Nazi Blitz reduced much of London to rubble, sending residents into Tube stations for shelter and the government into a fortified bunker (now the Churchill War Rooms). Britain was rallied through its darkest hour by two leaders: Prime Minister Winston Churchill, a remarkable orator, and King George VI. Amid the chaos of war, the colonial empire began to dwindle to almost nothing, and Britain emerged from the war as a shell of its former superpower self.

Culturally, Britain remained world-class. Oxford professor J. R. R. Tolkien wrote *The Lord of the Rings* and his friend C. S. Lewis wrote *The Chronicles of Narnia*. In the 1960s, "Swinging London" became a center for rock music, film, theater, youth culture, and Austin Powers-style joie de vivre. America was conquered by a "British Invasion" of rock bands.

The 1970s brought massive unemployment, labor strikes, and recession. A conservative reaction followed in the 1980s and '90s, led by Prime Minister Margaret Thatcher—the "Iron Lady." As proponents of traditional, Victorian values—community, family, hard work, thrift, and trickle-down economics—the Conservatives took a Reaganesque approach to Britain's serious social and economic problems. They cut government subsidies to old-fashioned industries (closing many factories, earning working-class ire) as they tried to nudge Britain toward a more modern economy.

In 1981, the world was captivated by the spectacle of Prince Charles marrying Lady Diana in St. Paul's Cathedral. Their children, Princes William and Harry, grew up in the media spotlight, and when Diana died in a car crash (1997), the nation—and the world—mourned.

The 1990s saw Britain finally emerging from decades of economic stagnation and social turmoil. An energized nation prepared for the new millennium.

England Today

After two decades of Conservative politics, Britain entered the new millennium ruled by a Labour (left-of-center) government under Prime Minister Tony Blair. Labour began shoring up a social-service system (health care, education, minimum wage) undercut by years of Conservative rule. But Blair's popularity was undermined when he joined the US invasion of Iraq.

Get It Right

Americans tend to use "England," "Britain," and "United Kingdom" (or "UK") interchangeably, but they're not quite the same.

England is the country occupying the center and southeast part of the island.

Britain is the name of the island.

Great Britain is the political union of the island's three countries: England, Scotland, and Wales.

The United Kingdom (UK) adds a fourth country, Northern Ireland.

The British Isles (not a political entity) also includes the independent Republic of Ireland.

The British Commonwealth is a loose association of possessions and former colonies (including Canada, Australia, and India) that profess at least symbolic loyalty to the Crown.

On the morning of July 7 ("7/7") in 2005, London's commuters were rocked by four terrorist bombs that killed dozens across the city. In subsequent years, Britain has had numerous terrorist plots that either caused destruction or were foiled by police.

The question remains how to balance security with privacy concerns. The British have surveillance cameras everywhere—you'll frequently see signs warning you that you're being recorded.

The terrorist threats have highlighted issues relating to Britain's large immigrant population (nearly 4 million). Brits are stunned that many terrorists (like the notorious "Jihadi John" of ISIS) speak the king's English and are born and raised in Britain. And some radical Islamic clerics seem to be preaching jihad in the mosque down the street. It raises the bigger question: How well is the nation assimilating its many immigrants? On the other hand, consider that in 2016, Londoners elected a second-generation Muslim—human-rights lawyer Sadiq Khan—as their mayor.

The large Muslim population is just one thread in the tapestry of today's Britain. While 9 out of 10 Brits are white, the country has large minority groups, mainly from Britain's former colonies: India, Pakistan, Bangladesh, Africa, the Caribbean, and many other places. Despite the tension between some groups, for the most part Britain is relatively integrated, with minorities represented in most (if not all) walks of life.

Then there's the eternal question of the royals. Is having a monarch (who's politically irrelevant) and a royal family (who fill the tabloids with their scandals and foibles) worth it? In decades past, many Brits wanted to toss the whole lot of them. But the recent marriage of the popular William and Kate and the birth of their cute kids have boosted royal esteem. According to pollsters, four out of five Brits want to keep their Queen and let the tradition live on.

But the single biggest issue facing Britain today is dealing with the repercussions of "Brexit"—the 2016 referendum in which 52 percent of Brits voted to leave the European Union. The Brexit vote stunned Britain, throwing it into uncharted territory with no clear path forward. It also raises questions about Britain's role in the wider, global culture.

The Brexit vote demands a split with the European Union, but it remains to be seen exactly what that will mean. No country has ever left the EU, and the process could take years.

Practicalities

TOURIST INFORMATION

Before your trip, start with the Visit Britain website, which contains a wealth of knowledge on destinations, activities, accommodations, and transport in Great Britain. Families will especially appreciate the "Britain for Kids & Families" travel suggestions. Maps, airport transfers, sightseeing tours, and theater tickets can be purchased online (www.visitbritain.com, www.visitbritainshop.com/usa for purchases).

In England, a good first stop is generally the tourist information office (abbreviated **TI** in this book and locally as **TIC,** for "tourist information centre"). In London, the **City of London Information Centre,** near St. Paul's Cathedral, is helpful. Some TIs have information on the entire country or at least the region, so try to pick up maps and printed information for destinations you'll be visiting later in your trip.

TRAVEL TIPS

Time Zones: Britain, which is one hour earlier than most of continental Europe, is five/eight hours ahead of the East/West Coasts of the US. The exceptions are the beginning and end of Daylight Saving Time: Britain and Europe "spring forward" the last Sunday in March (two weeks after most of North America), and "fall back" the last Sunday in October (one week before North America). For a handy online time converter, see www.timeanddate.com/worldclock.

Business Hours: Most stores are open Monday through Saturday (roughly 9:00 or 10:00 to 17:00 or 18:00). In cities, some stores stay open later on Wednesday or Thursday (until 19:00 or 20:00). Some big-city department stores are open later throughout the week (Mon-Sat until about 21:00).

Watt's Up? Britain's electrical system is 220 volts, instead of North America's 110 volts. Most newer electronics convert automatically, so you won't need a converter, but you will need an adapter plug with three square prongs, sold inexpensively at travel stores in the US.

Discounts: Discounts (called "concessions" or "concs" in Britain) for sights are generally not listed in this book. However, many sights, buses, and trains offer discounts to youths (up to age 18), students (with proper identification cards, www.isic.org), families, seniors (loosely defined as retirees or those willing to call themselves seniors), and groups of 10 or more. Always ask. Some discounts are available only for British citizens.

HELP!
Emergency and Medical Help
Dial 999 or 112 for police help or a medical emergency. If you get sick, do as the locals do and go to a pharmacy and see a "chemist" (pharmacist) for advice. Or ask at your hotel for help—they'll know of the nearest medical and emergency services.

Theft or Loss
To replace a passport, you'll need to go in person to a US embassy. If your credit and debit cards disappear, cancel and replace them. If your things are lost or stolen, file a police report, either on the spot or within a day or two; you'll need it to submit an insurance claim for rail passes or travel gear, and it can help with replacing your passport or credit and debit cards. For more information, see www.ricksteves.com/help.

Avoiding Theft

Pickpockets are common in crowded, touristy places, but fortunately, violent crime is rare. Thieves don't want to hurt you; they just want your money and gadgets.

My recommendations: Stay alert and wear a money belt (tucked under your clothes) to keep your cash, debit card, credit card, and passport secure; carry only the money you need for the day in your front pocket.

Treat any disturbance (e.g., a stranger bumping into you, spilling something on you, or trying to get your attention for an odd reason) as a smoke screen for theft. Be on guard waiting in line at sights, at train stations, and while boarding and leaving crowded buses and subways. Thieves target tourists overloaded with bags or distracted by phones.

When paying for something, be aware of how much cash you're handing over (state the denomination of the bill when paying a cabbie) and count your change.

There's no need to stress; just be smart and prepared.

Embassies and Consulates
US Consulate and Embassy in London: Tel. 020/7499-9000 (all services), 24 Grosvenor Square, Tube: Bond Street, https://uk.usembassy.gov/

High Commission of Canada in London: Tel. 020/7004-6000, Canada House, Trafalgar Square, Tube: Charing Cross, www.unitedkingdom.gc.ca

MONEY
Here's my basic strategy for using money in Europe:
- Upon arrival, head for a cash machine (ATM) at the airport and load up on

Exchange Rate

1 British pound (£1) = about $1.40
Britain uses the pound sterling. The British pound (£), also called a "quid," is broken into 100 pence (p). Pence means "cents." You'll find coins ranging from 1p to £2 and bills from £5 to £50.

To convert prices from pounds to dollars, add about 40 percent: £20=about $28, £50=about $70. (Check Oanda.com for the latest exchange rates.)

local currency, using a debit card with low international transaction fees.
• Withdraw large amounts at each transaction (to limit fees) and keep your cash safe in a money belt.
• Pay for most items with cash.
• Pay for larger purchases with a credit card with low (or no) international fees.

What to Bring

I pack the following and keep it all safe in my money belt.

Debit Card: Use at ATMs to withdraw local cash.

Credit Card: Use to pay for larger items (at hotels, larger shops and restaurants, travel agencies, car-rental agencies, and so on).

Backup Card: Some travelers carry a third card (debit or credit; ideally from a different bank), in case one gets lost, demagnetized, eaten by a temperamental machine, or simply doesn't work.

US Dollars: I carry $100-200 US dollars as a backup. While you won't use it for day-to-day purchases, American cash in your money belt comes in handy for emergencies, such as if your ATM card stops working.

What NOT to Bring: Resist the urge to buy pounds before your trip or you'll pay the price in bad stateside exchange rates. Wait until you arrive to withdraw money.

Before You Go

Report your travel dates. Let your bank know that you'll be using your debit and credit cards in Europe, and when and where you're headed.

Know your PIN. Make sure you know the numeric, four-digit PIN for each of your cards, both debit and credit. Request it if you don't have one and allow time to receive the information by mail.

Adjust your ATM withdrawal limit. Find out how much you can take out daily and ask for a higher daily withdrawal limit if you want to get more cash at once. Note that European ATMs will withdraw funds only from checking accounts; you're unlikely to have access to your savings account.

Ask about fees. For any purchase or withdrawal made with a card, you may be charged a currency conversion fee (1-3 percent), a Visa or MasterCard international transaction fee (1 percent), and—for debit cards—a $2-5 transaction fee each time you use a foreign ATM.

In Europe

Using Cash Machines: European cash machines work just like they do at home—except they spit out local currency instead of dollars, calculated at the day's standard bank-to-bank rate.

In most places, ATMs are easy to locate—in Britain ask for a "cashpoint." When possible, withdraw cash from a bank-run ATM located just outside that bank.

If your debit card doesn't work, try a lower amount—your request may have exceeded your withdrawal limit or the ATM's limit. If you still have a problem, try a different ATM or come back later—your bank's network may be temporarily down.

Avoid "independent" ATMs, such as Travelex, Euronet, Moneybox, Cardpoint, and Cashzone. These have high fees, can be less secure than a bank ATM, and may try to trick users with "dynamic currency conversion" (see below).

Exchanging Cash: Avoid exchanging money in Europe; it's a big rip-off. In a pinch you can always find exchange desks at major train stations or airports—convenient but with crummy rates. Banks in some countries may not exchange money unless you have an account with them.

Using Credit Cards: US cards no longer require a signature for verification, but don't be surprised if a European card reader generates a receipt for you to sign. Some card readers will accept your card as is; others may prompt you to enter your PIN (so it's important to know the code for each of your cards). If a cashier is present, you should have no problems.

At self-service payment machines (transit-ticket kiosks, parking, etc.), results are mixed, as US cards may not work in unattended transactions. If your card is rejected, look for a cashier who can process your card manually—or pay in cash.

Drivers Beware: Be aware of potential problems using a credit card to fill up at an unattended gas station, enter a parking garage, or exit a toll road. Carry cash and be prepared to move on to the next gas station if necessary. When approaching a toll plaza, use the "cash" lane.

Dynamic Currency Conversion: Some European merchants and hoteliers cheerfully charge you for converting your purchase price into dollars. If it's offered, refuse this "service" (called dynamic currency conversion, or DCC). You'll pay extra for the expensive convenience of seeing your charge in dollars.

Tipping

Tipping in Britain isn't as automatic and generous as it is in the US. For special service, tips are appreciated, but not expected. As in the US, the proper amount depends on your resources, tipping philosophy, and the circumstances, but some general guidelines apply.

Restaurants: It's not necessary to tip if a service charge is included in the bill (common in London—usually 12.5 percent). Otherwise, it's appropriate to tip about 10-12 percent for good service.

Taxis: For a typical ride, round up your fare a bit, but not more than 10 percent (for instance, if the fare is £7.40, pay £8). If the cabbie hauls your bags and zips you to the airport to help you catch your flight, you might want to toss in a little more. But if you feel like you're being driven in circles or otherwise ripped off, skip the tip.

Services: In general, if someone in the tourism or service industry does a super job for you, a small tip of a pound or two is appropriate...but not required. If you're not sure whether (or how much) to tip, ask a local for advice.

Getting a VAT Refund

Wrapped into the purchase price of your British souvenirs is a Value-Added Tax (VAT) of about 20 percent. You're entitled to get most of that tax back if you purchase more than £30 (about $40) worth of goods at a store that participates in the VAT-refund scheme (although individual stores can require that you spend more—Harrods, for example, won't process a refund unless you spend £50). Typically, you must ring up the minimum at a single retailer—you can't add up your purchases from various shops to reach the required amount. (If the store ships the goods to your US home, VAT is not assessed on your purchase.)

Getting your refund is straightforward... and worthwhile if you spend a significant amount on souvenirs.

Get the paperwork. Have the merchant completely fill out the necessary refund document (either an official VAT customs form, or the shop or refund company's own version of it). You'll have to present your passport at the store. Get the paperwork done before you leave the shop to ensure you'll have everything you need (including your original sales receipt).

Get your stamp at the border or airport. Process your VAT document at your last stop in the European Union (such as at the airport) with the customs agent who deals with VAT refunds. Arrive an additional hour early before you need to check in to allow time to find the customs office—and to stand in line.

Collect your refund. Many merchants work with a service that has offices at major airports, ports, or border crossings. These services, which extract their own fee (usually around 4 percent), can refund your money immediately in cash or credit your card (within two billing cycles).

Customs for American Shoppers

You can take home $800 worth of items per person duty-free, once every 31 days. As for alcohol, you can bring in one liter duty-free (it can be packed securely in your checked luggage).

To bring alcohol (or liquid-packed foods) in your carry-on bag on your flight home, buy it at a duty-free shop at the airport. You'll increase your odds of getting it onto a connecting flight if it's packaged in a "STEB"—a secure, tamper-evident bag. But stay away from liquids in opaque, ceramic, or metallic containers, which usually cannot be successfully screened (STEB or no STEB).

For details on allowable goods, customs rules, and duty rates, visit http://help.cbp.gov.

SIGHTSEEING

Sightseeing can be hard work. Use these tips to make your visits to England's finest sights meaningful, fun, efficient, and painless.

Plan Ahead

Set up an itinerary that allows you to fit in all your must-see sights. For a one-stop look at opening hours, see the "At a Glance" sidebars for major destinations in this book. Most sights keep stable hours, but you can easily confirm the latest by checking with the TI or visiting museum websites.

Many museums are closed or have reduced hours at least a few days a year, especially on holidays such as Christmas, New Year's, and Bank Holiday Mondays in May and August. A list of holidays is on page 417; check online for possible museum closures during your trip. Off-season, many museums have shorter hours.

This book offers tips on the best times to see specific sights. Try visiting popular sights very early or very late. Evening visits (when possible) are usually peaceful, with fewer crowds.

At Sights

Here's what you can typically expect:

Entering: Be warned that you may not be allowed to enter if you arrive less than 30 to 60 minutes before closing time. And guards start ushering people out well before the actual closing time, so don't save the best for last.

Many sights have a security check, where you must open your bag or send it through a metal detector. Some sights require you to check daypacks and coats. (If you'd rather not check your daypack, try carrying it tucked under your arm like a purse as you enter.)

Photography: If the museum's photo policy isn't clearly posted, ask a guard. Generally, taking photos without a flash or tripod is allowed. Some sights ban selfie sticks; others ban photos altogether.

Expect Changes: Artwork can be on tour, on loan, out sick, or shifted at the whim of the curator. Pick up a floor plan as you enter, and ask museum staff if you can't find a particular item.

Audioguides and Apps: Many sights rent audioguides, which generally offer excellent recorded descriptions. If you bring your own earbuds, you can enjoy better sound. Museums and sights often offer free apps that you can download to your mobile device (check their websites).

Sightseeing Passes

Many sights in England are managed by either English Heritage or the National Trust. Each organization has a combo-deal that can save some money for busy sightseers.

Membership in **English Heritage** includes free entry to more than 400 sights in England and discounted or free admission to about 100 more sights in Scotland and Wales. For most travelers, the **Overseas Visitor Pass** is a better choice than the pricier one-year membership (Visitor Pass: £31/9 days, £37/16 days, discounts for couples and families, www.english-heritage.org.uk/ovp).

Membership in the **National Trust** is best suited for garden-and-estate enthusiasts, ideally those traveling by car. It covers more than 350 historic houses, manors, and gardens throughout Great Britain, including 100 properties in Scotland. From the US, it's easy to join online through the Royal Oak Foundation, the National

Trust's American affiliate (one-year membership: $65 for one person, $95 for two, family and student memberships, www.royal-oak.org). For more on National Trust properties, see www.nationaltrust.org.uk.

Restaurant Code

Eateries in this book are categorized according to the average cost of a typical main course. Drinks, desserts, and splurge items (steak and seafood) can raise the price considerably.

$$$$ **Splurge:** Most courses over £20
  $$$ **Pricier:** £15-20
   $$ **Moderate:** £10-15
    $ **Budget:** Under £10

In Great Britain, carryout fish-and-chips and other takeout food is $; a basic pub or sit-down eatery is $$; a gastropub or casual but more upscale restaurant is $$$; and a swanky splurge is $$$$.

EATING

These days, the stereotype of "bad food in Britain" is woefully dated. Britain has caught up with the foodie revolution, and I find it's easy to eat very well here.

Tipping: At pubs and places where you order at the counter, you don't have to tip. At restaurants and fancy pubs with waitstaff, it's not necessary to tip if a service charge is already included in the bill (common in London—usually 12.5 percent). Otherwise, it's appropriate to tip about 10-12 percent; you can add a bit more for finer dining or extra good service. Tip only what you think the service warrants (if it isn't already added to your bill), and be careful not to tip double.

Restaurant Pricing

I've categorized my recommended eateries based on price, indicated with a dollar-sign rating (see sidebar). The price ranges suggest the average price of a typical main course—but not necessarily a complete meal. The dollar-sign categories also indicate the overall personality and "feel" of a place.

Breakfast (Fry-Up)

The traditional fry-up or full English breakfast—generally included in the cost of your room—is famous as a hearty way to start the day. Also known as a "heart attack on a plate," your standard fry-up comes with your choice of eggs, Canadian-style bacon and/or sausage, a grilled tomato, sautéed mushrooms, baked beans, and sometimes potatoes, kippers (herring), or fried bread (sizzled in a greasy skillet). Toast comes in a rack (to cool quickly and crisply) with butter and marmalade. The meal typically comes with your choice of tea or coffee. Many B&B owners offer alternative, creative variations on the traditional breakfast.

Much as the full breakfast fry-up is a traditional way to start the morning, these days most places serve a healthier continental breakfast as well—with a buffet of yogurt, cereal, fruit, and pastries.

Lunch and Dinner on a Budget

Even in pricey cities, plenty of inexpensive choices are available.

I've found that portions are huge, and **sharing plates** is generally just fine. Ordering two drinks, a soup or side salad, and splitting a £10 meat pie can make a good, filling meal. If you're on a limited budget, share a main course in a more expensive place for a nicer eating experience.

Pub grub is the most atmospheric budget option. You'll usually get hearty lunches and dinners priced reasonably at £8-15 under ancient timbers (see "Pubs," later).

Classier restaurants have some affordable deals. Lunch is usually cheaper than dinner; a top-end, £30-for-dinner-type restaurant often serves the same quality two-course lunch deals for about half the price.

Many restaurants have **early-bird** or **pre-theater specials** of two or three courses, often for a significant savings. They are usually available only before 18:30 or 19:00 (and sometimes on weekdays only).

Ethnic restaurants add spice to Britain's cuisine scene. Eating Indian, Bangladeshi, Chinese, or Thai is cheap (even cheaper if you do takeout).

Fish-and-chips are a heavy, greasy, but tasty British classic. Every town has at least one "chippy" selling takeaway fish-and-chips in a cardboard box or (more traditionally) wrapped in paper for about £5-7.

Picnicking saves time and money. Fine park benches and polite pigeons abound in most towns and city neighborhoods.

Pubs

Pubs are a fundamental part of the British social scene, and whether you're a teetotaler or a beer guzzler, they should be a part of your travel here. Smart travelers use pubs to eat, drink, get out of the rain, watch sporting events, and make new friends.

Though hours vary, pubs generally serve beer daily from 11:00 to 23:00, though many are open later, particularly on Friday and Saturday. (Children

are served food and soft drinks in pubs, but you must be 18 to order a beer.) As it nears closing time, you'll hear shouts of "Last orders." Then comes the 10-minute warning bell. Finally, they'll call "Time!" to pick up your glass, finished or not, when the pub closes.

A cup of darts is free for the asking. People go to a public house to be social. They want to talk. Get vocal with a local. The pub is the next best thing to having relatives in town. Cheers!

Pub Grub: For £8-15, you'll get a basic budget hot lunch or dinner in friendly surroundings. In high-priced London, this is your best indoor eating value. (For something more refined, try a **gastropub**, which serves higher-quality meals for £12-20.) The Good Pub Guide is an excellent resource (www.thegoodpubguide.co.uk).

Pubs generally serve traditional dishes, such as fish-and-chips, roast beef with Yorkshire pudding (batter-baked in the oven), and assorted meat pies, such as steak-and-kidney pie or shepherd's pie (stewed lamb topped with mashed potatoes) with cooked vegetables. Side dishes include salads, vegetables, and— invariably—"chips" (French fries). "Crisps" are potato chips. A "jacket potato"

(baked potato stuffed with fillings of your choice) can almost be a meal in itself. A "ploughman's lunch" is a traditional British meal of bread, cheese, and sweet pickles. These days, you'll likely find more pasta, curried dishes, and quiche on the menu than traditional fare.

Meals are usually served from 12:00 to 14:00 and again from 18:00 to 20:00— with a break in the middle (rather than serving straight through the day). There's generally no table service. Order at the bar, then take a seat. Either they'll bring the food when it's ready or you'll pick it up at the bar. Pay at the bar (sometimes when you order, sometimes after you eat). It's not necessary to tip unless it's a place with full table service. For details on ordering beer and other drinks, see the "Beverages" section, later.

Good Chain Restaurants

I know—you're going to Britain to enjoy characteristic little hole-in-the-wall pubs, so mass-produced food is the furthest thing from your mind. But several excellent chains with branches across the UK offer long hours, reasonable prices, reliable quality, and a nice break from pub grub. My favorites are Pret (a.k.a. Pret à Manger),

Wasabi, and Eat; other dependable chains include Le Pain Quotidien, Wagamama Noodle Bar, Loch Fyne Fish Restaurant, Busaba Eathai, and Thai Square. Expect to see these familiar names wherever you go.

Carry-Out Chains: Major supermarket chains have smaller, offshoot branches that specialize in prepared foods to go. The most prevalent—and best—is **M&S Simply Food** (there's one in every major train station). **Sainsbury's Local** grocery stores also offer decent prepared food; **Tesco Express** and **Tesco Metro** run a distant third.

Indian Cuisine

Eating Indian food is "going local" in cosmopolitan, multiethnic Britain. You'll find Indian restaurants in most cities, and even in small towns. Take the opportunity to sample food from Britain's former colony. Indian cuisine is as varied as the country itself. In general, it uses more exotic spices than British or American cuisine—some hot, some sweet. Indian food is very vegetarian-friendly, offering many meatless dishes. An easy way to taste a variety of dishes is to order a *thali*—a sampler plate, generally served on a metal tray, with small servings of various specialties.

Afternoon Tea

Once the sole province of genteel ladies in fancy hats, afternoon tea has become more democratic in the 21st century. These days, people of leisure punctuate their day with an afternoon tea at a tearoom. Tearooms, which often serve appealing light meals, are usually open for lunch and close at about 17:00, just before dinner.

The cheapest "tea" on the menu is generally a "cream tea"; the most expensive is the "champagne tea." **Cream tea** is simply a pot of tea and a homemade scone or two with jam and thick clotted cream. **Afternoon tea**—what many Americans would call "high tea"—is a pot of tea, small finger foods (such as sandwiches with the crusts cut off), scones, an assortment of small pastries, jam, and thick clotted

cream. **Champagne tea** includes all of the goodies, plus a glass of bubbly. **High tea** to the English generally means a more substantial late afternoon or early evening meal, often served with meat or eggs.

Desserts (Sweets)

To the British, the traditional word for dessert is "pudding," although it's also referred to as "sweets" these days.

Trifle is the best-known British concoction, consisting of sponge cake soaked in brandy or sherry (or orange juice for children), then covered with jam and/or fruit and custard cream. Whipped cream can sometimes put the final touch on this "light" treat.

The British version of **custard** is a smooth, yellow liquid. Cream tops most everything that custard does not. There's single cream for coffee. Double cream is really thick. Whipped cream is familiar, and clotted cream is the consistency of whipped butter.

Fool is a dessert with sweetened pureed fruit (such as rhubarb, gooseberries, or black currants) mixed with cream or custard and chilled.

Flapjacks here aren't pancakes, but are dense, sweet oatmeal cakes (a little like a cross between a granola bar and a brownie). They come with toppings such as toffee and chocolate.

Beverages

Beer: The British take great pride in their beer. Many locals think that drinking beer cold and carbonated, as Americans do, ruins the taste. Most pubs will have **lagers** (cold, refreshing, American-style beer), **ales** (amber-colored, cellar-temperature beer), **bitters** (hop-flavored ale, perhaps the most typical British beer), and **stouts** (dark and somewhat bitter, like Guinness).

At pubs, long-handled pulls (or taps) are used to draw the traditional, rich-flavored "real ales" up from the cellar. Served straight from the brewer's cask at cellar temperature, real ales finish fermenting naturally and are not pasteurized or filtered, so they must be consumed within two or three days after the cask is tapped. Naturally carbonated, real ales vary from sweet to bitter, often with a hoppy or nutty flavor.

Short-handled pulls mean colder, fizzier, mass-produced, and less interesting keg beers. Mild beers are sweeter, with a creamy malt flavoring. Irish cream ale is a smooth, sweet experience. Try the draft cider (sweet or dry)...carefully.

Order your beer at the bar and pay as you go, with no need to tip. An average beer costs about £4. Part of the experience is standing before a line of hand pulls, and wondering which beer to choose.

As dictated by British law, draft beer and cider are served by the pint (20-ounce imperial size) or the half-pint (9.6 ounces). In 2011, the government sanctioned an in-between serving size—the schooner, or two-thirds pint (it's become a popular size for higher alcohol-content craft beers). Proper English ladies like a shandy (half beer and half 7-Up).

Other Alcoholic Drinks: Many pubs also have a good selection of wines by the glass and a fully stocked bar for the gentleman's "G and T" (gin and tonic). **Pimm's** is a refreshing and fruity summer liqueur, traditionally popular during Wimbledon.

Nonalcoholic Drinks: Teetotalers can order from a wide variety of soft drinks—both the predictable American sodas and other more interesting bottled drinks,

such as ginger beer (similar to ginger ale but with more bite), root beers, or other flavors (Fentimans brews some unusual options that are stocked in many pubs). Note that in Britain, "lemonade" is lemon-lime soda (like 7-Up).

SLEEPING

I favor hotels and restaurants that are handy to your sightseeing activities. In Britain, small bed-and-breakfast places (B&Bs) generally provide the best value, though I also include some bigger hotels.

Book your accommodations as soon as your itinerary is set, especially if you want to stay at one of my top listings or if you'll be traveling during busy times. See page 417 for a list of major holidays and festivals; for tips on making reservations, see page 399.

Sleep Code

Hotels in this book are categorized according to the average price of a typical en suite double room with breakfast in high season.

$$$$	**Splurge:**	Most rooms over £160
$$$	**Pricier:**	£120-160
$$	**Midrange:**	£80-120
$	**Budget:**	£40-80
¢	**Backpacker:**	Under £40
RS%	Rick Steves discount	

Unless otherwise noted, credit cards are accepted and free Wi-Fi is available. Comparison-shop by checking prices at several hotels (on each hotel's own website, on a booking site, or by email). For the best deal, always book directly with the hotel. Ask for a discount if paying in cash; if the listing includes RS%, request a Rick Steves discount.

Rates and Deals

I've categorized my recommended accommodations based on price, indicated with a dollar-sign rating (see sidebar). The price ranges suggest an estimated cost for a one-night stay in a typical en suite double room with a private toilet and shower in high season, and assume you're booking directly with the hotel.

While B&B prices tend to be fairly predictable, room rates are especially volatile at larger hotels that use "dynamic pricing" to set rates. Once your dates are set, check the specific price for your preferred stay at several hotels by comparing prices on Hotels.com or Booking.com, or by checking the hotels' own websites.

Staying in B&Bs and small hotels can save money over sleeping in big hotels. Chain hotels can be even cheaper, but they don't include breakfast. When comparing prices between chain hotels and B&Bs, remember you're getting two breakfasts (about a £25 value) for each double room at a B&B.

Types of Accommodations
Hotels

In cities, you'll find big, Old-World elegant hotels with modern amenities, as well as familiar-feeling business-class and boutique hotels no different from what you might experience at home. But you'll also find hotels that are more uniquely European.

An "en suite" room has a bathroom (toilet and shower/tub) attached to the room; a room with a "private bathroom" can mean that the bathroom is all yours, but it's across the hall. If you want your own bathroom inside the room, request "en suite." If money's tight, ask about a room with a shared bathroom. You'll almost always have a sink in your room, and as more rooms go en suite, the hallway bathroom is shared with fewer guests.

Note that to be called a "hotel," a place technically must have certain amenities, including a 24-hour reception (though this rule is loosely applied).

Modern Hotel Chains: Chain hotels—common in bigger cities all over Great Britain—can be a great value (£60-100, depending on location and season; more expensive in London). These hotels are about as cozy as a Motel 6, but they come with private showers/WCs, elevators, good security, and often an attached restaurant. Branches are often located near the train station, on major highways, or outside the city center.

This option is especially worth considering for families, as kids often stay for free. While most of these hotels have 24-hour reception and elevators, breakfast and Wi-Fi generally cost extra, and the service lacks a personal touch (at some, you'll check in at a self-service kiosk).

Room rates change from day to day with volume and vary depending on how far ahead you book. The best deals generally must be prepaid a few weeks ahead and may not be refundable—read the fine print carefully.

The biggest chains are **Premier Inn** (www.premierinn.com) and **Travelodge** (www.travelodge.co.uk). Both have attractive deals for prepaid or advance bookings. Other chains operating in Britain include the Irish **Jurys Inn** (www.jurysinns.com) and the French-owned **Ibis** (www.ibishotel.com). Couples can consider **Holiday Inn Express,** which generally allow only two people per room (make sure Express is part of the name or you'll be paying more for a regular Holiday Inn, www.hiexpress.co.uk).

Making Hotel Reservations

Requesting a Reservation: For family-run hotels, it's generally cheaper to book your room direct via email or a phone call. For business-class hotels, or if you'd rather book online, reserve directly through the hotel's official website (not a booking agency's site). For complicated requests, send an email.

Here's what the hotelier wants to know:
- type(s) of rooms and size of your party
- number of nights you'll stay
- your arrival and departure dates, written European-style as day/month/year
- special requests (such as en suite bathroom vs. down the hall, cheapest room, twin beds vs. double bed, quiet room)
- applicable discounts (such as a Rick Steves reader discount, cash discount, or promotional rate)

Confirming a Reservation: Most places will request a credit-card number to hold your room. If you're using an online reservation form, look for the https or a lock icon at the top of your browser. If you book direct, you can email, call, or fax this information.

Canceling a Reservation: If you must cancel, it's courteous—and smart—to do so with as much notice as possible, especially for smaller family-run places (which describes many of the hotels I list). Cancellation policies can be strict; read the fine print or ask about these before you book. Many discount deals require pre-payment, with no cancellation refunds.

Reconfirming a Reservation: Always call or email to reconfirm your room reservation a few days in advance. For B&Bs or very small hotels, I call again on my day of arrival to tell my host what time to expect me (especially important if arriving late—after 17:00).

Phoning: For tips on calling hotels overseas, see page 404.

Arrival and Check-In: Many of my recommended hotels have three or more floors of rooms and steep stairs. Older properties often do not have elevators. If stairs are an issue, ask for a ground-floor room or choose a hotel with a lift (elevator). Air-conditioning isn't a given (I've noted which of my listings have it), but most places have fans. On hot summer nights, you'll want your window open—and in a big city, street noise is a fact of life. Bring earplugs or request a room on the back side. If you suspect night noise will be a problem (if, for instance, your room is over a noisy pub), ask for a quieter room on an upper floor.

In Your Room: Note that all of Britain's accommodations are nonsmoking. Electrical outlets may have switches that turn the current on or off; if your appliance isn't working, flip the switch at the outlet.

To guard against theft in your room, keep valuables out of sight. Some rooms come with a safe, and other hotels have safes at the front desk. I've never bothered using one and in a lifetime of travel, I've never had anything stolen from my room.

Breakfast: Your room cost usually

includes a traditional full cooked breakfast (fry-up) or a lighter, healthier continental breakfast.

Checking Out: While it's customary to pay for your room upon departure, it can be a good idea to settle your bill the day before, when you're not in a hurry and while the manager is there. That way you'll have time to discuss and address any points of contention.

Hotelier Help: Hoteliers can be a good source of advice. Most know their city well, and can assist you with everything from public transit and airport connections to finding a good restaurant, the nearest launderette, or a late-night pharmacy.

Hotel Hassles: Even at the best places, mechanical breakdowns occur. Report your concerns clearly and calmly at the front desk. For more complicated problems, don't expect instant results. Above all, keep a positive attitude. Remember, you're on vacation. If your hotel is a disappointment, spend more time out enjoying the place you came to see.

B&Bs and Small Hotels

B&Bs and small hotels are generally family-run places with fewer amenities but more character than a conventional hotel. They range from large inns with 15-20 rooms to small homes renting out a spare bedroom. Places named "guesthouse" or

"B&B" typically have eight or fewer rooms. The philosophy of the management determines the character of a place more than its size and amenities.

B&B proprietors are selective about the guests they invite in for the night. Many do not welcome children. If you'll be staying for more than one night, you are a "desirable." In popular weekend-getaway spots, you're unlikely to find a place to take you for Saturday night only. If my listings are full, ask for guidance. Mentioning this book can help. Owners usually work together and can call up an ally to land you a bed. Many B&B owners are also pet owners. If you're allergic, ask about resident pets when you reserve.

Rules and Etiquette: B&Bs and small hotels come with their own etiquette and quirks. Keep in mind that owners are at the whim of their guests—if you're getting up early, so are they; if you check in late, they'll wait up for you. Most B&Bs have set check-in times (usually in the late afternoon). If arriving outside that time, they will want to know when to expect you (call or email ahead). Most will let you check in earlier if the room is available (or they'll at least let you drop off your bag).

Most B&Bs and guesthouses serve a hearty cooked breakfast of eggs and much more (for details on breakfast, see the Eating section, earlier). Because the owner is often also the cook, breakfast hours are usually abbreviated. It's an unwritten rule that guests shouldn't show up at the very end of the breakfast period and expect a full cooked breakfast.

B&Bs and small hotels often come with thin walls and doors, and sometimes creaky floorboards, which can make for a noisy night. If you're a light sleeper, bring earplugs. And please be quiet in the halls and in your rooms at night...those of us getting up early will thank you for it.

In the Room: Every B&B offers "tea service" in the room—an electric kettle, cups, tea bags, coffee packets, and a pack of biscuits.

The Good and Bad of Online Reviews

User-generated review sites and apps such as Yelp, Booking.com, and TripAdvisor can give you a consensus of opinions about everything from hotels and restaurants to sights and nightlife. If you scan reviews of a hotel and see several complaints about noise or a rotten location, it tells you something important that you'd never learn from the hotel's own website.

But as a guidebook writer, my sense is that there is a big difference between the uncurated information on a review site and a guidebook. A user-generated review is based on the experience of one person, who likely stayed at one hotel in a given city and ate at a few restaurants there (and who doesn't have much of a basis for comparison). A guidebook is the work of a trained researcher who, year after year, visits many alternatives to assess their relative value. I recently checked out some top-rated user-reviewed hotel and restaurant listings in various towns; when stacked up against their competitors, some were gems, while just as many were duds.

Both types of information have their place, and in many ways, they're complementary. If something is well-reviewed in a guidebook, and also gets good ratings on one of these sites, it's likely a winner.

Your bedroom probably won't include a phone, but nearly every B&B has free Wi-Fi. However, the signal may not reach all rooms; you may need to sit in the lounge to access it.

You're likely to encounter unusual bathroom fixtures. The "pump toilet" has a flushing handle or button that doesn't kick in unless you push it just right: too hard or too soft, and it won't go. (Be decisive but not ruthless.) Most B&B baths have an instant water heater. This looks like an electronic box under the showerhead with dials and buttons: One control adjusts the heat, while another turns the flow off and on (let the water run for a bit to moderate the temperature before you hop in). If the hot water doesn't work, you may need to flip a red switch (often located just outside the bathroom). If the shower looks mysterious, ask your B&B host for help... *before* you take off your clothes.

Paying: Many B&Bs take credit cards, but may add the card service fee to your bill (about 3 percent). If you do need to pay cash for your room, plan ahead to have enough on hand when you check out.

Short-Term Rentals

A short-term rental—whether an apartment (or "flat"), house, or room in a local's home—is an increasingly popular alternative, especially if you plan to settle in one location for several nights. For stays longer than a few days, you can usually find a rental that's comparable to—and even cheaper than—a hotel room with similar amenities. Many places require a minimum night stay, and compared to hotels, rentals usually have less flexible cancellation policies.

Finding Accommodations: Aggregator websites such as Airbnb, FlipKey, Booking.com, and the HomeAway family of sites (HomeAway, VRBO, and VacationRentals) let you browse properties and correspond directly with European property owners or managers. If you prefer to work from a curated list of accommodations, consider using a rental agency such as InterhomeUSA.com or RentaVilla.com. Agency-represented apartments typically cost more, but this method often offers more help and safeguards than booking direct.

Confirming and Paying: Many places require you to pay the entire balance before your trip. It's easiest and safest to pay through the site where you found the listing. Be wary of owners who want to take your transaction offline to avoid fees; this gives you no recourse if things go awry. Never agree to wire money (a key indicator of a fraudulent transaction).

Hostels

A hostel provides cheap beds in dorms where you sleep alongside strangers for about £20-30 per night. Travelers of any age are welcome if they don't mind dorm-style accommodations and meeting other travelers. Most hostels offer kitchen facilities, guest computers, Wi-Fi, and a self-service laundry. Hostels almost always provide bedding, but not towels (though you can usually rent one for a small fee). Family and private rooms are often available.

Independent hostels tend to be easygoing, colorful, and informal (no membership required; www.hostelworld.com). You may pay slightly less by booking direct with the hostel.

Official hostels are part of Hostelling International (HI) and share an online booking site (www.hihostels.com). In Britain, these official hostels are run by the Youth Hostel Association (YHA, www.yha.org.uk). HI hostels typically require that you be a member or pay extra per night.

STAYING CONNECTED

One of the most common questions I hear from travelers is, "How can I stay connected in Europe?" The short answer is: more easily and cheaply than you might think.

The simplest solution is to bring your own device—mobile phone, tablet, or laptop—and use it just as you would at home (following the tips below, such as connecting to free Wi-Fi whenever possible). Another option is to buy a European SIM card for your mobile phone—either your US phone or one you buy in Europe. Or, you can use European landlines and computers to connect. Each of these options is described later, and more details are at www.ricksteves.com/phoning. For a very practical one-hour talk covering tech issues for travelers, see www.ricksteves.com/mobile-travel-skills.

Using a Mobile Phone in Europe

Here are some budget tips and options.

Sign up for an international plan. Using your cellular network in Europe on a pay-as-you-go basis can add up. To stay connected at a lower cost, sign up for an international service plan through your carrier. Most providers offer a simple bundle that includes calling, messaging, and data. Your normal plan may already include international coverage (T-Mobile's does).

Before your trip, call your provider or check online to confirm that your phone will work in Europe, and research your provider's international rates. Activate the plan a day or two before you leave, then remember to cancel it when your trip's over.

Use free Wi-Fi whenever possible. Unless you have an unlimited-data plan, you're best off saving most of your online tasks for Wi-Fi. You can access the Internet, send texts, and even make voice calls over Wi-Fi.

Most accommodations in Europe offer free Wi-Fi, but some—especially expensive hotels—charge a fee. Many cafés (including Starbucks and McDonald's) have free hotspots for customers; look for signs offering it and ask for the Wi-Fi password when you buy something. You'll also often find Wi-Fi at TIs, city squares, major museums, public-transit hubs, airports, and aboard trains and buses.

Minimize the use of your cellular network. Even with an international data plan, wait until you're on Wi-Fi to Skype, download apps, stream videos, or do other megabyte-greedy tasks. Using a navigation app such as Google Maps over a cellular network can take lots of data, so do this sparingly or use it offline.

Tips on Internet Security

Make sure that your device is running the latest versions of its operating system, security software, and apps. Next, ensure that your device and key programs (like email) are password- or passcode-protected. On the road, use only secure, password-protected Wi-Fi hotspots. Ask the hotel or café staff for the specific name of their Wi-Fi network, and make sure you log on to that exact one.

If you must access your financial info online, use a banking app rather than accessing your account via a browser. A cellular connection is more secure than Wi-Fi. Avoid logging onto personal finance sites on a public computer.

Never share your credit-card number (or any other sensitive information) online unless you know that the site is secure. A secure site displays a little padlock icon, and the URL begins with *https* (instead of the usual *http*).

Limit automatic updates. By default, your device constantly checks for a data connection and updates apps. It's smart to disable these features so your apps will only update when you're on Wi-Fi.

Use Wi-Fi calling and messaging apps. Skype, Viber, FaceTime, and Google+ Hangouts are great for making free or low-cost voice and video calls over Wi-Fi. With an app installed on your phone, tablet, or laptop, you can log on to a Wi-Fi network and contact friends or family members who use the same service. If you buy credit in advance, with some of these services you can call any mobile phone or landline worldwide for just pennies per minute.

Many of these apps also allow you to send messages over Wi-Fi to any other person using that app.

Using a European SIM Card

With a European SIM card, you get a European mobile number and access to cheaper rates than you'll get through your US carrier. This option works well for those who want to make a lot of voice calls or needing faster connection speeds than their US carrier provides. Fit the SIM card into a cheap phone you buy in Europe, or swap out the SIM card in an "unlocked" US phone.

SIM cards are sold at mobile-phone shops, department-store electronics counters, some newsstands, and vending machines. Costing about $5-10, they usually include prepaid calling/messaging credit, with no contract and no commitment. Expect to pay $20-40 more for a SIM card with a gigabyte of data. If you travel with this card to other countries in the European Union, there may be extra roaming fees.

Public Phones and Computers

Most **hotels** charge a fee for placing calls—ask for rates before you dial. You can use a prepaid international phone card (available at post offices, newsstands,

How to Dial

International Calls

Whether phoning from a US landline or mobile phone, or from a number in another European country, here's how to make an international call. I've used one of my recommended London hotels as an example (tel. 020/7730-8191).

Initial Zero: Drop the initial zero from international phone numbers—except when calling Italy.

Mobile Tip: If using a mobile phone, the "+" sign can replace the international access code (for a "+" sign, press and hold "0").

US/Canada to Europe

Dial 011 (US/Canada international access code), country code (44 for Britain), and phone number.

▶ To call the London hotel from home, dial 011-44-20/7730-8191.

Country to Country Within Europe

Dial 00 (Europe international access code), country code, and phone number.

▶ To call the London hotel from Spain, dial 00-44-20/7730-8191.

Europe to the US/Canada

Dial 00, country code (1 for US/Canada), and phone number.

▶ To call from Europe to my office in Edmonds, Washington, dial 00-1-425-771-8303.

Domestic Calls

To call within Britain (from one British landline or mobile phone to another), simply dial the phone number, including the initial 0 if there is one.

▶ To call the London hotel from Edinburgh, dial 020/7730-8191.

More Dialing Tips

British Phone Numbers: Numbers beginning with 071 through 079 are mobile numbers, which are more expensive to call than a landline.

street kiosks, tobacco shops, and train stations) to call out from your hotel.

Public pay phones are hard to find in Britain, and they're expensive. To use one, you'll pay with a major credit card (minimum charge–£1.20) or coins (minimum charge–£0.60).

Most hotels have **public computers** in their lobbies for guests to use; otherwise you may find them at Internet cafés or public libraries.

Mail

You can mail one package per day to yourself worth up to $200 duty-free from Europe to the US (mark it "personal purchases"). If you're sending a gift to someone, mark it "unsolicited gift." For details,

Toll and Toll-Free Calls: Numbers starting with 0800 and 0808 are toll-free. Those beginning with 084, 087, and 03 are generally inexpensive toll numbers (£0.15/minute from a landline, £0.20-.40/minute from a mobile). Numbers beginning with 09 are pricey toll lines. If you have questions about a prefix, call 100 for free help. International rates apply to US toll-free numbers dialed from Britain—they're not free.

More Phoning Help: See www.howtocallabroad.com.

European Country Codes		Ireland & N. Ireland	353 / 44
Austria	43	Italy	39
Belgium	32	Latvia	371
Bosnia-Herzegovina	387	Montenegro	382
Croatia	385	Morocco	212
Czech Republic	420	Netherlands	31
Denmark	45	Norway	47
Estonia	372	Poland	48
Finland	358	Portugal	351
France	33	Russia	7
Germany	49	Slovakia	421
Gibraltar	350	Slovenia	386
Great Britain	44	Spain	34
Greece	30	Sweden	46
Hungary	36	Switzerland	41
Iceland	354	Turkey	90

visit www.cbp.gov, select "Travel," and search for "Know Before You Go."

The British postal service works fine, but for quick transatlantic delivery (in either direction), consider services such as DHL (www.dhl.com). For postcards, get stamps at the neighborhood post office, newsstands within fancy hotels, and some mini-marts and card shops.

TRANSPORTATION

In England, I connect big cities by train and explore rural areas (Cornwall, Dartmoor, the Cotswolds, the Lake District) footloose and fancy-free by rental car. The mix works quite efficiently (e.g., London, Bath, and York by train, with a rental car for the rest).

Rail Passes

A **BritRail Pass** lets you travel by train in Scotland, England, and Wales for three to eight days within a one-month period, 15 days within two months, or for continuous periods of up to one month. In addition, BritRail sells England-only and other regional passes. Discounted rates are offered for children, youths, seniors, or for three or more people traveling together.

BritRail passes are best purchased outside Europe (through travel agents or Rick Steves' Europe). For more on the ins and outs of rail passes, including prices, download my **free guide to Eurail Passes** (www.ricksteves.com/rail-guide) or go to www.ricksteves.com/rail.

If you're taking just a couple of train rides, individual **point-to-point train tickets** may save you money over a pass. Use this map to add up approximate pay-as-you-go fares for your itinerary, and compare that to the price of a rail pass. Keep in mind that significant discounts on point-to-point tickets may be available with advance purchase.

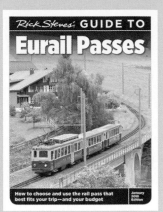

Map shows approximate costs, in US$, for one-way, second-class tickets at off-peak rates.

Trains

Regular tickets on Britain's great train system (15,000 departures from 2,400 stations daily) are the most expensive per mile in all of Europe. For the greatest savings, book online in advance and leave after rush hour (after 9:30 weekdays).

Since Britain's railways have been privatized, a single train route can be operated by multiple companies. However, one website covers all train lines (www.nationalrail.co.uk), and another covers all bus and train routes (www.traveline.org.uk for information, not ticket sales). Another good resource, which also has schedules for trains throughout Europe, is German Rail's timetable (www.bahn.com).

While generally not required, reservations are free and can normally be made well in advance. They are an especially good idea for long journeys or for travel on Sundays or holidays. Make reservations at any train station, by phone, or online when you buy your ticket. With a point-to-point ticket, you can reserve as late as two hours before train time, but rail-pass holders should book seats at least 24 hours in advance.

Rail Passes: Since Britain's pay-as-you-go train tickets are some of the most expensive in Europe, BritRail passes can pay for themselves quickly, especially if you ride a long-distance train (for example, between London and Scotland). A rail pass offers hop-on flexibility and no need to lock in reservations, except for overnight sleeper cars.

BritRail passes cannot be purchased locally; buy your pass through an agent before leaving the US. Make sleeper reservations in advance; you can also make optional, free seat reservations (recommended for busy weekends) at staffed train stations.

For more detailed advice on figuring out the smartest rail-pass options for your train trip, visit www.ricksteves.com/rail.

Buying Train Tickets in Advance: The best fares go to those who book their trips well in advance of their journey. To book ahead, go in person to any station, book online at www.nationalrail.co.uk, or call 0345-748-4950 (from the US, dial 011-44-20-7278-5240, phone answered 24 hours) to find out the schedule and best fare for your journey; you'll then be referred to the appropriate vendor—depending on the particular rail company—to book your ticket. You'll pick up your ticket at the station, or you may be able to print it at home.

Buying Train Tickets as You Travel: If you'd rather have the flexibility of booking tickets as you go, you can save a few pounds by buying a round-trip ticket, called a "return ticket" (a same-day round-trip, called a "day return," is particularly cheap); buying before 18:00 the day before you depart; traveling after the morning rush hour (this usually means after 9:30 Mon-Fri); and going standard class instead of first class. Preview your

Public Transportation Routes in Great Britain

Legend:
- Rail
- Eurostar
- Bus
- (8H) Ferry with crossing time

Orkney Islands

Scrabster · Gill · John o' Groats
Thurso

Lewis

Elgin

Skye
Portree · Inverness · Culloden
Kyle · Loch Ness · Aviemore · Aberdeen
Mallaig ·
Fort William
SCOTLAND
Pitlochry
Mull · Dundee
Iona · Oban · Perth · Leuchars
Stirling · St. Andrews
Edinburgh
Glasgow · Berwick
Holy Island

Larne · (2H) · Cairnryan · Hexham
(2.3H) · Stranraer · Carlisle · Newcastle · To Amsterdam (15H)
Belfast · Keswick · Penrith · Durham
NORTHERN IRELAND · Windermere · Danby · Whitby · North Sea
(8H) · Isle of Man · North York Moors · Scarborough
Irish Sea · Blackpool · **ENGLAND** · York · Hull
Dublin · (7H) · Preston · Leeds · To Zeebrugge (10H)
Holyhead · Conwy · Liverpool · Manchester · Grimsby
(2-3H) · Bangor · Chester · Lincoln
Caernarfon · Betws-y-Coed · Stoke · Peter-borough · King's Lynn
REPUBLIC · Bed. · Blaenau · Derby · Norwich
OF · Pwllheli · Ffest. · Telford · Wolv. · Birmingham · Ely
IRELAND · Harlech · Ironbridge Gorge · Coventry · Cambridge
Aberystwyth · Stratford · Warwick · Harwich
Rosslare · (3.5H) · **WALES** · Cheltenham · Moreton · To Hoek van Holland (6H)
Fishguard · Carmarthen · Stow · Oxford · Ebbs-fleet
Newport · Reading · London · Canterbury
Swansea · STONEHENGE · Woking · Dover (7.5H)
Cardiff · **Bath** · Ashford
Bristol · Wells · West-bury · Salisbury · Brighton · Calais
Glastonbury · Newhaven · EUROSTAR (2.5H)
Atlantic Ocean · Exeter · Southampton · To Dieppe (4H) · To Paris & Brussels
Dartmoor · Portsmouth
Truro · **English Channel** · To Ouistreham (6H)
St. Ives · Plymouth
Penzance · Falmouth · To St-Malo (11H)
To Roscoff (6H) · **FRANCE**

50 Kilometers
50 Miles

options at www.nationalrail.co.uk.

Senior, Youth, Partner, and Family Deals: To get a third off the price of most point-to-point rail tickets, seniors can buy a Senior Railcard (ages 60 and up), younger travelers can buy a 16-25 Railcard (ages 16-25, or full-time students 26 and older), and two people traveling together can buy a Two Together Railcard (ages 16 and over). A Family and Friends Railcard gives adults about 33 percent off for most trips and 60 percent off for their kids ages 5 to 15 (maximum 4 adults and 4 kids). Each Railcard costs £30; see www.railcard.co.uk.

Buses

Most domestic buses are operated by **National Express** (www.nationalexpress.com); their international departures are called **Eurolines** (www.eurolines.co.uk). A smaller company called **Megabus** undersells National Express with deeply discounted promotional fares—the further ahead you buy, the less you pay (www.megabus.com).

Try to avoid bus travel on Friday and Sunday evenings, when weekend travelers are more likely to make buses sell out. To ensure getting a ticket—and to save money with special promotions—book your ticket in advance online or over the phone. The cheapest prepurchased tickets can usually be changed (for a £5 fee), but not refunded. Check if the ticket is only "amendable" or also "refundable" when you buy. If you have a mobile phone, you can order online and have a "text ticket" sent right to your phone for a small fee.

Renting a Car

Rental companies in Britain require you to be at least 21 years old and to have held your license for one year. Drivers under the age of 25 may incur a young-driver surcharge, and some rental companies will not rent to anyone 75 or older.

Most of the major US rental agencies (including Avis, Budget, Enterprise, Hertz, and Thrifty) have offices throughout Europe. Also consider the two major Europe-based agencies, Europcar and Sixt. It can be cheaper to use a consolidator, such as Auto Europe/Kemwel (www.autoeurope.com—or the often cheaper www.autoeurope.eu).

Always read the fine print or query the agent carefully for add-on charges—such as one-way drop-off fees, airport surcharges, or mandatory insurance policies—that aren't included in the "total price."

For the best deal, rent by the week with unlimited mileage. I normally rent the smallest, least expensive model with a stick shift (generally cheaper than automatic). Almost all rentals are manual by default, so if you need an automatic, request one in advance. An automatic makes sense for most American drivers: With a manual transmission in Britain, you'll be sitting on the right side of the car, and shifting with your left hand...while driving on the left side of the road. When selecting a car, chose a smaller model; they're more maneuverable on narrow, winding roads.

Figure on paying roughly $250 for a one-week rental. Allow extra for supplemental insurance, fuel, tolls, and parking.

Picking Up Your Car: Big companies have offices in most cities, but small local rental companies can be cheaper. If you pick up your car in a smaller city or at an airport (rather than downtown), you'll more likely survive your first day on the road. Be aware that Brits call it "hiring a car," and directional signs at airports and train stations will read *Car Hire*.

Compare pickup costs (downtown can be less expensive than the airport) and explore drop-off options. Always check the hours of the location you choose: Many rental offices close from midday Saturday until Monday morning and, in smaller towns, at lunchtime.

When you pick up the rental car, check it thoroughly and make sure any damage is noted on your rental agreement. Rental agencies in Europe tend to charge for even minor damage, so be sure to mark everything. Before driving off, find out how your car's lights, turn signals, wipers, radio, and fuel cap function, and know what kind of fuel the car takes (diesel vs. unleaded). When you return the car, make sure the agent verifies its condition with you. Some drivers take pictures of the returned vehicle as proof of its condition.

The AA: The services of Britain's Automobile Association are included with most rentals (www.theaa.com), but check for this when booking to be sure you understand its towing and emergency road-service benefits.

Car Insurance Options

When you rent a car, you are liable for a very high deductible, sometimes equal to the entire value of the car. Limit your financial risk with one of these three options: Buy Collision Damage Waiver (CDW) coverage with a low or zero deductible from the car-rental company, get coverage through your credit card (free, if your card automatically includes zero-deductible coverage), or get collision insurance as part of a larger travel-insurance policy.

Basic **CDW** includes a very high deductible (typically $1,000-1,500), costs $15-30 a day (figure roughly 30-40 percent extra) and reduces your liability, but does not eliminate it. When you reserve or pick up the car, you'll be offered the chance to "buy down" the basic deductible to zero (for an additional $10-30/day; this is sometimes called "super CDW" or "zero-deductible coverage").

If you opt for **credit-card coverage,** you'll technically have to decline all coverage offered by the car-rental company, which means they can place a hold on your card (which can be up to the full value of the car). In case of damage, it can be time-consuming to resolve the charges with your credit-card company. Before you decide on this option, quiz your credit-card company about how it works.

For more on car-rental insurance, see www.ricksteves.com/cdw.

Navigation Options

If you'll be navigating using your phone or a GPS unit from home, remember to bring a car charger and device mount.

Mobile Device: The mapping app on your mobile phone works fine for navigation in Europe, but for real-time turn-by-turn directions and traffic updates, you'll generally need Internet access. And driving all day while online can be very expensive. Helpful exceptions are Google Maps, Here WeGo, and Navmii, which provide turn-by-turn voice directions and recalibrate even when they're offline.

Download your map before you head out—it's smart to select a large region. Then turn off your cellular connection so you're not charged for data roaming. Call up the map, enter your destination, and you're on your way. View maps in standard view (not satellite view) to limit data demands.

GPS Devices: If you prefer the convenience of a dedicated GPS unit, known as a "satnav" in Britain, consider renting one with your car ($10-30/day). These units offer real-time turn-by-turn directions and traffic without the data requirements of an app. Note that the unit may only come loaded with maps for its home country; if you need additional maps, ask.

A less-expensive option is to bring a GPS device from home. Be aware that you'll need to buy and download European maps before your trip.

Maps and Atlases: Even when navigating primarily with a mobile app or GPS, I always make it a point to have a paper map. It's invaluable for getting the big picture, understanding alternate routes, and filling in when my phone runs out of juice. Several good road atlases cover all of Britain. Ordnance Survey, Collins, AA, and Bartholomew

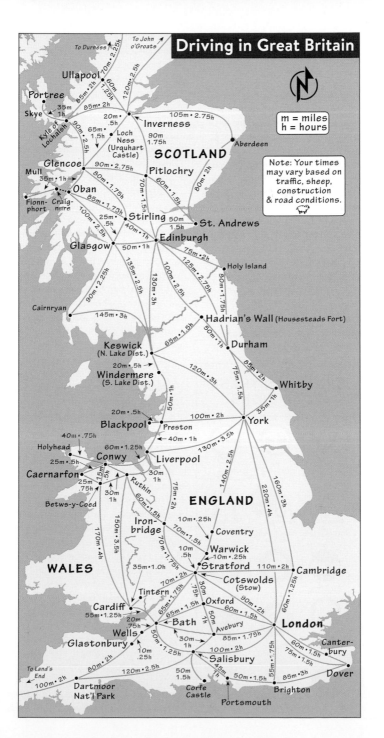

Driving in Great Britain

m = miles
h = hours

Note: Your times
may vary based on
traffic, sheep,
construction
& road conditions.

editions are all available at tourist information offices, gas stations, and bookstores.

Driving in England

Driving here is basically wonderful—once you remember to stay on the left and after you've mastered the roundabouts. Every year, however, I get a few notes from traveling readers advising me that, for them, trying to drive in Britain was a nerve-racking and regrettable mistake. Many Yankee drivers find the hardest part isn't driving on the left, but steering from the right. Your instinct is to put yourself on the left side of your lane, which means you may spend your first day or two drifting into the left shoulder or curb. It helps to remember that the driver always stays close to the centerline.

Road Rules: Be aware of Britain's rules of the road. Seat belts are mandatory for all, and kids under age 12 (or less than about 4.5 feet tall) must ride in an appropriate child-safety seat. It's illegal to use a mobile phone while driving. In Britain, you're not allowed to turn left on a red light unless a sign or signal specifically authorizes it. For more information about driving in Britain, ask your car-rental company, read the Department for Transport's *Highway Code* (www.direct.gov.uk—click on "Driving and transport" and look for "The Highway Code" link), or check the US State Department website (www.travel.state.gov, click on "International Travel," then specify your country of choice and click "Traffic Safety and Road Conditions").

Speed Limits: Speed limits are in miles per hour: 30 mph in town, 70 mph on the motorways, and 60 or 70 mph elsewhere. The national sign for the maximum speed is a white circle with a black slash. Motorways have electronic speed limit signs; posted speeds can change depending on traffic or the weather.

Note that road-surveillance cameras strictly enforce speed limits. Any driver (including foreigners renting cars) photographed speeding will get a nasty bill in the mail. Signs (an image of an old-fashioned camera) alert you when you're entering a zone that may be monitored by these "camera cops." Heed them.

Roundabouts: Don't let a roundabout spook you. After all, you routinely merge into much faster traffic on American highways back home. Traffic flows clockwise, and cars already in the roundabout have the right-of-way; entering traffic yields (look to your right as you merge). You'll probably encounter "double-roundabouts"—figure-eights where you'll slingshot from one roundabout directly into another. Just go with the flow and track signs carefully. When approaching an especially complex roundabout, you'll first pass a diagram showing the layout and the various exits. And in many cases, the pavement is painted to indicate the lane you should be in for a particular road or town.

Freeways (Motorways): The shortest

AND LEARN THESE ROAD SIGNS

50 Speed Limit (mph)	Yield	No Passing	**End** of No Passing Zone
One Way	Intersection	Roundabout Ahead	Expressway
Danger	No Entry	Cars Prohibited	All Vehicles Prohibited
No Through Road	**End** Restrictions No Longer Apply	Yield to Oncoming Traffic	No Stopping
Parking	No Parking	Road Narrows	Peace

How to Navigate a Roundabout

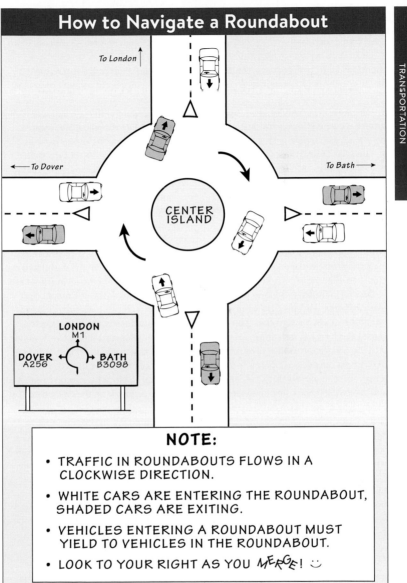

NOTE:

- TRAFFIC IN ROUNDABOUTS FLOWS IN A CLOCKWISE DIRECTION.
- WHITE CARS ARE ENTERING THE ROUNDABOUT, SHADED CARS ARE EXITING.
- VEHICLES ENTERING A ROUNDABOUT MUST YIELD TO VEHICLES IN THE ROUNDABOUT.
- LOOK TO YOUR RIGHT AS YOU MERGE! ☺

distance between any two points is usually the motorway (what we'd call a "freeway"). In Britain, the smaller the number, the bigger the road. For example, the M-4 is a freeway, while the B-4494 is a country road.

Motorway road signs can be confusing, too few, and too late. Miss a motorway

exit and you can lose 30 minutes. Study your map before taking off. Know the cities you'll be lacing together, since road numbers are inconsistent. British road signs are rarely marked with compass directions (e.g., A-4 West); instead, you need to know what major town or city you're heading for (A-4 Bath). The driving directions in this book are intended to be used with a good map.

Unless you're passing, always drive in the "slow" lane on motorways (the lane farthest to the left). Remember to pass on the right, not the left.

Rest areas are called "services" and often have amenities, such as restaurants, cafeterias, gas stations, shops, and motels.

Fuel: Gas (petrol) costs about $5.50 per gallon and is self-serve. Pump first and then pay. Diesel costs about the same. Diesel rental cars are common; make sure you know what kind of fuel your car takes before you fill up. Unleaded pumps are usually green. Note that self-service gas pumps, automated tollbooths, and parking garages often accept only cash or a chip-and-PIN credit card (see page 391).

Driving in Cities: Whenever possible, avoid driving in cities. Be warned that London assesses a congestion charge. Most cities have modern ring roads to skirt the congestion. Follow signs to the parking lots outside the city core—most are a 5- to 10-minute walk to the center—and avoid what can be an unpleasant grid of one-way streets (as in Bath) or roads that are restricted to public transportation during the day (as in Oxford).

Driving in Rural Areas: Outside the big cities and except for the motorways, British roads tend to be narrow. Adjust your perceptions of personal space: It's not "my side of the road" or "your side of the road," it's just "the road"—and it's shared as a cooperative adventure. If the road's wide enough, traffic in both directions can pass parked cars simultaneously, but frequently you'll have to take turns—follow the locals' lead and drive defensively.

Narrow country lanes are often lined with stone walls or woody hedges—and no shoulders. Some are barely wide enough for one car. Go slowly, and if you encounter an oncoming car, look for the nearest pullout (or "passing place")—the driver who's closest to one is expected to

use it, even if it means backing up to reach it. If another car pulls over and blinks its headlights, that means, "Go ahead; I'll wait to let you pass."

Parking: Pay attention to pavement markings to figure out where to park. One yellow line marked on the pavement means no parking Monday through Saturday during work hours. Double yellow lines mean no parking at any time. Broken yellow lines mean short stops are OK, but you should always look for explicit signs or ask a passerby. White lines mean you're free to park.

In towns, rather than look for street parking, I generally just pull into the most central and handy pay-and-display parking lot I can find. To pay and display, feed change into a machine, receive a timed ticket, and display it on the dashboard or stick it to the driver's-side window. Most machines in larger towns accept credit cards with a chip, but it's smart to keep coins handy for machines that don't.

In some municipalities, drivers will see signs for "disc zone" parking. This is free, time-limited parking. But to use it, you must obtain a clock parking disc from a shop and display it on the dashboard (set the clock to show your time of arrival). Return within the signed time limit to avoid being ticketed.

Some parking garages (a.k.a. car parks) are totally automated and record your license plate with a camera when you enter. The Brits call a license plate a "number plate" or just "vehicle registration." The payment machine will use these terms when you pay before exiting.

Flights

The best comparison search engine for both international and intra-European flights is Kayak.com. An alternative is Google Flights, which has an easy-to-use system to track prices. For inexpensive flights within Europe, try Skyscanner.com.

Flying to Europe: Start looking for international flights about four to six months before your trip, especially for

It's cheaper to fly to England in winter, and London makes the season fun.

peak-season travel. Off-season tickets can usually be purchased a month or so in advance. Depending on your itinerary, it can be efficient to fly into one city and out of another.

Flying Within Europe: Several cheap, no-frills airlines affordably connect Britain with other destinations in the British Isles and throughout Europe. If you're considering a train ride that's more than five hours long, a flight may save you both time and money. When comparing your options, factor in the time it takes to get to the airport and how early you'll need to arrive to check in.

Well-known cheapo airline **Easy-Jet** flies from London (Gatwick, Luton, Stansted, and Southend) and Liverpool.

Ryanair also flies from London (mostly from Stansted, as well as Gatwick and Luton) and Liverpool. Other airlines to consider include **CityJet** (based at London City Airport), **TUI, Flybe,** and **Brussels Airlines.**

But be aware of the potential drawbacks of flying with a discount airline: nonrefundable and nonchangeable tickets, minimal or nonexistent customer service, pricey and time-consuming treks to secondary airports, and stingy baggage allowances with steep overage fees. To avoid unpleasant surprises, read the small print before you book. These days you can also fly within Europe on major airlines affordably—and without all the aggressive restrictions—for around $100 a flight.

Resources from Rick Steves

Begin Your Trip at www.RickSteves.com

My mobile-friendly **website** is *the* place to explore Europe. You'll find thousands of fun articles, videos, photos, and radio interviews; a wealth of money-saving tips for planning your dream trip; my travel talks and blog; and guidebook updates (www.ricksteves.com/update).

Our **Travel Forum** is an immense collection of message boards, where our travel-savvy community answers questions and shares personal travel experiences—and our well-traveled staff chimes in when they can help.

Our **online Travel Store** offers bags and accessories designed to help you travel smarter and lighter. These include my popular bags (which I live out of four months a year), money belts, totes, toiletries kits, adapters, guidebooks, planning maps, and more.

Choosing the right **rail pass** for your trip can drive you nutty. Our website will help you find the perfect fit for your itinerary and your budget: We offer easy, one-stop shopping for rail passes, seat reservations, and point-to-point tickets.

Guidebooks, TV Shows, Audio Europe, and Tours

Books: *Rick Steves Best of England* is just one of many books in my series on European travel, which includes country and city guidebooks, Snapshot guides (excerpted chapters from my country guides), Pocket Guides (full-color little books on big cities, including London), and my budget-travel skills handbook, *Rick Steves Europe Through the Back Door*. My phrase books are practical and budget-oriented. A more complete list of my titles appears near the end of this book.

TV Shows: My public television series, *Rick Steves' Europe,* covers Europe from top to bottom with over 100 half-hour episodes. To watch full episodes online for free, see www.ricksteves.com/tv. Or to raise your travel I.Q. with video versions of our popular classes (including my talks on travel skills, packing smart, most European countries, and European art), see www.ricksteves.com/travel-talks.

Audio: My weekly public radio show, *Travel with Rick Steves,* features interviews with travel experts from around the world. A complete archive is available at www.soundcloud.com/rick-steves, and much of this audio content is available, along with my audio tours of Europe's (and Spain's) top sights, through my free **Rick Steves Audio Europe** app (see page 29).

Small-Group Tours: Want to travel with greater efficiency and less stress? We offer **tours** with more than 40 itineraries reaching the best destinations in this book...and beyond. You'll find European adventures to fit every vacation length, and you'll enjoy great guides and a fun but small group of travel partners. For all the details, and to get our tour catalog, visit www.ricksteves.com or call us at 425/608-4217.

HOLIDAYS AND FESTIVALS

This list includes selected festivals in England plus national holidays observed throughout Britain. Many sights and banks close on national holidays—keep this in mind when planning your itinerary. Before planning a trip around a festival, verify the dates with the festival website, the Visit Britain website (www.visitbritain.com), or my "Upcoming Holidays and Festivals in England" web page (www.ricksteves.com/europe/england/festivals).

Mid-Feb	London Fashion Week (www.londonfashionweek.co.uk)
Mid-Feb	Jorvik Viking Festival, York (www.jorvik-viking-festival.co.uk)
Late Feb-early March	Literature Festival, Bath (www.bathlitfest.org.uk)
Early May	Early May Bank Holiday (first Mon)
Early-mid-May	Jazz Festival, Keswick (www.keswickjazzfestival.co.uk)
Late May	Spring Bank Holiday (last Mon)
Late May	Chelsea Flower Show, London (www.rhs.org.uk/chelsea)
Late May-early June	International Music Festival, Bath (www.bathmusicfest.org.uk)
Late May-early June	Fringe Festival, Bath (www.bathfringe.co.uk)
Early June	Beer Festival, Keswick (www.keswickbeerfestival.co.uk)
Early-mid-June	Trooping the Colour, London (Queen's birthday parade; http://qbp.army.mod.uk)
Late June	Royal Ascot Horse Race, Ascot (www.ascot.co.uk)
Late June-early July	Wimbledon Tennis Championship, London (www.wimbledon.org)
Mid-July	Early Music Festival, York (www.ncem.co.uk)
Late Aug	Notting Hill Carnival, London (www.thenottinghillcarnival.com)
Late Aug	Late Summer Bank Holiday (last Mon)
Mid-Sept	London Fashion Week (www.londonfashionweek.co.uk)
Late Sept	Jane Austen Festival, Bath (www.janeausten.co.uk)
Late Sept	York Food and Drink Festival (www.yorkfoodfestival.com)
Nov 5	Bonfire Night (bonfires, fireworks, effigy burning of 1605 traitor Guy Fawkes)
Dec 24-26	Christmas holidays

CONVERSIONS AND CLIMATE

Numbers and Stumblers

- Some British people write a few of their numbers differently than we do: 1 = 𝟣 , 4 = 𝟦 , 7 = 𝟩.
- In Europe, dates appear as day/month/year, so Christmas 2019 is 25/12/19.
- What Americans call the second floor of a building is the first floor in Britain.
- On escalators and moving sidewalks, Brits keep the left "lane" open for passing. Keep to the right.
- To avoid the British version of giving someone "the finger," don't hold up the first two fingers of your hand with your palm facing you. (It looks like a reversed victory sign.)
- And please...don't call your waist pack a "fanny" pack.

Weights and Measures

Britain uses the metric system for nearly everything. Weight and volume are typically calculated in metric: A kilogram is 2.2 pounds, and one liter is about a quart (almost four to a gallon). Temperatures are given in Celsius. Driving distances and speed limits are measured in miles. Beer is sold as pints, and a person's weight is measured in stone.

> 1 stone = 14 pounds
> 1 British pint = 1.2 US pints
> 1 imperial gallon = 1.2 US gallons or about 4.5 liters

Clothing Sizes

When shopping for clothing, use these US-to-UK comparisons as general guidelines.

Women: For pants an dresses, add 4 (US 10 = UK 14). For blouses and sweaters, add 2. For shoes, subtract 2½ (US size 8 = UK size 5½)

Men: For clothing, US and UK sizes are the same. For shoes, subtract about ½ (US size 9 = UK size 8½)

England's Climate

First line, average daily high; second line, average low; third line, average days without rain. For more weather statistics for destinations in this book (and elsewhere), check www.wunderground.com.

London

J	F	M	A	M	J	J	A	S	O	N	D
43°	44°	50°	56°	62°	69°	71°	71°	65°	58°	50°	45°
36°	36°	38°	42°	47°	53°	56°	56°	52°	46°	42°	38°
16	15	20	18	19	19	19	20	17	18	15	16

York

J	F	M	A	M	J	J	A	S	O	N	D
43°	44°	49°	55°	61°	67°	70°	69°	64°	57°	49°	45°
33°	34°	36°	40°	44°	50°	54°	53°	50°	44°	39°	36°
14	13	18	17	18	16	16	17	16	16	13	14

Packing Checklist

Clothing

- [ ] 5 shirts: long- & short-sleeve
- [ ] 2 pairs pants or skirt
- [ ] 1 pair shorts or capris
- [ ] 5 pairs underwear & socks
- [ ] 1 pair walking shoes
- [ ] Sweater or fleece top
- [ ] Rainproof jacket with hood
- [ ] Tie or scarf
- [ ] Swimsuit
- [ ] Sleepwear

Money

- [ ] Debit card
- [ ] Credit card(s)
- [ ] Hard cash ($20 bills)
- [ ] Money belt or neck wallet

Documents & Travel Info

- [ ] Passport
- [ ] Airline reservations
- [ ] Rail pass/train reservations
- [ ] Car-rental voucher
- [ ] Driver's license
- [ ] Student ID, hostel card, etc.
- [ ] Photocopies of all the above
- [ ] Hotel confirmations
- [ ] Insurance details
- [ ] Guidebooks & maps
- [ ] Notepad & pen
- [ ] Journal

Toiletries Kit

- [ ] Toiletries
- [ ] Medicines & vitamins
- [ ] First-aid kit
- [ ] Glasses/contacts/sunglasses (with prescriptions)
- [ ] Earplugs
- [ ] Packet of tissues (for WC)

Miscellaneous

- [ ] Daypack
- [ ] Sealable plastic baggies
- [ ] Laundry soap
- [ ] Clothesline
- [ ] Sewing kit
- [ ] Travel alarm/watch

Electronics

- [ ] Smartphone or mobile phone
- [ ] Camera & related gear
- [ ] Tablet/ereader/media player
- [ ] Laptop & flash drive
- [ ] Earbuds or headphones
- [ ] Chargers
- [ ] Plug adapters

Optional Extras

- [ ] Flipflops or slippers
- [ ] Mini-umbrella or poncho
- [ ] Travel hairdryer
- [ ] Belt
- [ ] Hat (for sun or cold)
- [ ] Picnic supplies
- [ ] Water bottle
- [ ] Fold-up tote bag
- [ ] Small flashlight
- [ ] Small binoculars
- [ ] Small towel or washcloth
- [ ] Inflatable pillow
- [ ] Tiny lock
- [ ] Address list (to mail postcards)
- [ ] Postcards/photos from home
- [ ] Extra passport photos
- [ ] Good book

INDEX

MAP INDEX

Start your trip at

Our website enhances this book and turns

Explore Europe

At ricksteves.com you can browse through thousands of articles, videos, photos and radio interviews, plus find a wealth of money-saving travel tips for planning your dream trip. And with our mobile-friendly website, you can easily access all this great travel information anywhere you go.

TV Shows

Preview the places you'll visit by watching entire half-hour episodes of Rick Steves' Europe (choose from all 100 shows) on-demand. for free.

ricksteves.com

your travel dreams into affordable reality

Radio Interviews

Enjoy ready access to Rick's vast library of radio interviews covering travel tips and cultural insights that relate specifically to your Europe travel plans.

Travel Forums

Learn, ask, share! Our online community of savvy travelers is a great resource

for first-time travelers to Europe, as well as seasoned pros. You'll find forums on each country, plus travel tips and restaurant/hotel reviews. You can even ask one of our well-traveled staff to chime in with an opinion.

Travel News

Subscribe to our free Travel News e-newsletter, and get monthly updates from Rick on what's happening in Europe.

Audio Europe™

Rick's Free Travel App

Get your FREE Rick Steves Audio Europe™ app to enjoy…

- Dozens of self-guided tours of Europe's top museums, sights and historic walks
- Hundreds of tracks filled with cultural insights and sightseeing tips from Rick's radio interviews
- All organized into handy geographic playlists
- For Apple and Android

With Rick whispering in your ear, Europe gets even better.

Pack Light and Right

Gear up for your next adventure at ricksteves.com

Light Luggage

Pack light and right with Rick Steves' affordable, custom-designed rolling carry-on bags, backpacks, day packs and shoulder bags.

Accessories

From packing cubes to moneybelts and beyond, Rick has personally selected the travel goodies that will help your trip go smoother.

Rick Steves has

Experience maximum Europe

Save time and energy

This guidebook is your independent-travel toolkit. But for all it delivers, it's still up to you to devote the time and energy it takes to manage the preparation and logistics that are essential for a happy trip. If that's a hassle, there's a solution.

Rick Steves Tours

A Rick Steves tour takes you to Europe's most

great tours, too!

with minimum stress

interesting places with great guides and small groups of 28 or less. We follow Rick's favorite itineraries, ride in comfy buses, stay in family-run hotels, and bring you intimately close to the Europe you've traveled so far to see. Most importantly, we take away the logistical headaches so you can focus on the fun.

travelers—nearly half of them repeat customers—along with us on four dozen different itineraries, from Ireland to Italy to Athens.

Is a Rick Steves tour the right fit for your travel dreams? Find out at ricksteves.com, where you can also request Rick's latest tour catalog.

Europe is best experienced with happy travel partners. We hope you can join us.

Join the fun

This year we'll take thousands of free-spirited

See our itineraries at ricksteves.com

A Guide for Every Trip

BEST OF GUIDES

Full-color easy-to-scan format, focusing on Europe's most popular destinations and sights.

Best of England
Best of Europe
Best of France
Best of Germany
Best of Ireland
Best of Italy
Best of Spain

COMPREHENSIVE GUIDES

City, country, and regional guides with detailed coverage for a multi-week trip exploring the most iconic sights and venturing off the beaten track.

Amsterdam & the Netherlands
Barcelona
Belgium: Bruges, Brussels, Antwerp & Ghent
Berlin
Budapest
Croatia & Slovenia
Eastern Europe
England
Florence & Tuscany
France
Germany
Great Britain
Greece: Athens & the Peloponnese
Iceland
Ireland
Istanbul
Italy
London
Paris
Portugal
Prague & the Czech Republic
Provence & the French Riviera
Rome
Scandinavia
Scotland
Spain
Switzerland
Venice
Vienna, Salzburg & Tirol

HE BEST OF ROME

e, Italy's capital, is studded with
an remnants and floodlit-fountain
es. From the Vatican to the Colos-
with crazy traffic in between, Rome
derful, huge, and exhausting. The
, the heat, and the weighty history

of the Eternal City where Caesars walked
can make tourists wilt. Recharge by taking siestas, gelato breaks, and after-dark
walks, strolling from one atmospheric
square to another in the refreshing evening air.

Pantheon—which
e dome until the
2,000 years old
over 1,500).

Athens in the Vat-
es the humanistic

diators fought
her, entertaining

tome ristorante.
at St. Peter's

Rick Steves guidebooks are published by Avalon Travel, an imprint of Perseus Books, a Hachette Book Group company.

POCKET GUIDES

Compact, full-color city guides with the essentials for shorter trips.

Amsterdam	Munich & Salzburg
Athens	Paris
Barcelona	Prague
Florence	Rome
Italy's Cinque Terre	Venice
London	Vienna

SNAPSHOT GUIDES

Focused single-destination coverage.

Basque Country: Spain & France
Copenhagen & the Best of Denmark
Dublin
Dubrovnik
Edinburgh
Hill Towns of Central Italy
Krakow, Warsaw & Gdansk
Lisbon
Loire Valley
Madrid & Toledo
Milan & the Italian Lakes District
Naples & the Amalfi Coast
Normandy
Northern Ireland
Norway
Reykjavik
Sevilla, Granada & Southern Spain
St. Petersburg, Helsinki & Tallinn
Stockholm

Rick Steves books are available
from your favorite bookseller.
Many guides are available as ebooks.

CRUISE PORTS GUIDES

Reference for cruise ports of call.

Mediterranean Cruise Ports
Scandinavian & Northern European
Cruise Ports

Complete your library with...

TRAVEL SKILLS & CULTURE

*Study up on travel skills before visiting
"Europe through the back door" or gain
insight on European history and culture.*

Europe 101
European Christmas
European Easter
European Festivals
Europe Through the Back Door
Postcards from Europe
Travel as a Political Act

PHRASE BOOKS & DICTIONARIES

French
French, Italian & German
German
Italian
Portuguese
Spanish

PLANNING MAPS

Britain, Ireland & London
Europe
France & Paris
Germany, Austria & Switzerland
Ireland
Italy
Spain & Portugal

PHOTO CREDITS

Avalon Travel
Hachette Book Group
1700 Fourth Street
Berkeley, CA 94710

Printed in China by RR Donnelley
First printing September 2018

ISBN 978-1-63121-802-6

For the latest on Rick's talks, guidebooks, tours, public television series, and public radio show, contact Rick Steves' Europe, 130 Fourth Avenue North, Edmonds, WA 98020, 425/771-8303, www.ricksteves.com, rick@ricksteves.com.

RICK STEVES' EUROPE
Special Publications Manager: Risa Laib
Managing Editor: Jennifer Madison Davis
Project Editor: Suzanne Kotz
Editorial & Production Assistant: Jessica Shaw
Graphic Content Director: Sandra Hundacker
Maps & Graphics: David C. Hoerlein, Lauren Mills, Mary Rostad

AVALON TRAVEL
Senior Editor and Series Manager: Madhu Prasher
Editor: Jamie Andrade
Editor: Sierra Machado
Copy Editor: Kelly Lydick
Proofreader: Patrick Collins
Indexer: Stephen Callahan
Cover Design: Kimberly Glyder Design
Interior Design: McGuire Barber Design
Interior Layout: Tabitha Lahr
Maps & Graphics: Kat Bennett, Mike Morgenfeld

Let's Keep on Travelin'

Your trip doesn't need to end.

Follow Rick on social media!

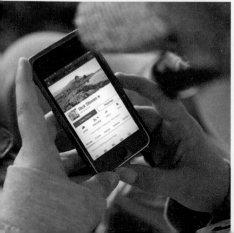